With Our Backs to the Wall

DAVID STEVENSON

With Our Backs to the Wall
Victory and Defeat in 1918

The Belknap Press of
Harvard University Press
Cambridge, Massachusetts
2011

First published in 2011 in the United Kingdom by the Penguin Group.

Library of Congress Cataloging-in-Publication Data

Stevenson, D. (David), 1954–
With our backs to the wall : victory and defeat in 1918 / David Stevenson.
p. cm.
Includes bibliographical references and index.
ISBN 978-0-674-06226-9 (cloth : alk. paper)
1. World War, 1914–1918—Campaigns—Western Front.   I. Title.
D531.S73 2011
940.4´34—dc22   2011011916

Contents

List of Illustrations

Pictures 18, 20, 21 and 27–32 courtesy of Susan Yates, from *1914–1918 Us and Them: A Pictorial History of the War on the Western Front* (ISBN 978–0–956–01930–1), copyright © Susan Yates

List of Maps

List of Tables

Abbreviations

AC	Austen Chamberlain papers, Birmingham University Library
ACS	Archivio centrale di stato, Rome
ADM	Admiralty papers, TNA
AEF	American Expeditionary Force
AFGG	*Les Armées françaises dans la Grande Guerre* (French official history)
AFL	American Federation of Labor
AIF	Australian Imperial Force
AIR	Air Ministry papers, TNA
AMAE	Archives du Ministère des Affaires étrangères, Paris
AMTC	Allied Maritime Transport Council
AMTE	Allied Maritime Transport Executive
AN	Archives nationales, Paris
ANC	Allied Naval Council
AOK	Armee Oberkommando (Austro-Hungarian high command)
ASE	Amalgamated Society of Engineers
ASL	Auxiliary Service Law
BA-MA	Bundesarchiv-Militärarchiv, Freiburg im Breisgau
BDF	Bund der Frauen
BDFA	*British Documents on Foreign Affairs*
BEF	British Expeditionary Force
BEV	Beveridge papers, British Library of Political and Economic Science
BHStA	Bayerische Hauptstaatsarchiv, Munich
BL	Manuscripts Department, British Library
BTY	Beatty papers, National Maritime Museum, Greenwich
CAB	Cabinet papers, TNA
CAS	Chief of the Admiralty Staff (Germany)
CCAC	Churchill College Archive Centre, Cambridge

CGS	Chief of the General Staff
CGT	Confédération générale du travail (French trade union centre)
CID	Committee of Imperial Defence
CIGS	Chief of the Imperial General Staff
CND	Council of National Defense (US)
CNS	Chief of the Naval Staff
CPI	Committee on Public Information
CRB	Commission for the Relief of Belgium
CS	Comando supremo (Italian high command)
CUP	Committee of Union and Progress (Young Turk party)
DCG	Deputy Commanding General (Germany)
DDP	Deutsche Demokratische Partei
DORA	Defence of the Realm Act
EEF	Egyptian Expeditionary Force
EFC	Emergency Fleet Corporation
EMA	Etat-major de l'armée (French general staff)
FO	Foreign Office papers, TNA
FOCP	Foreign Office Confidential Print
GAR	Groupe d'Armées de Réserve
GDP	gross domestic product
GGS	Great General Staff (*Grosser Generalstab* – Germany)
GHQ	General Headquarters
GK	Generalkommission (German trade union centre)
GNP	gross national product
GQG	Grand Quartier-général (French high command)
HHStA	Haus-, Hof-, und Staatsarchiv, Vienna
HMM	*History of the Ministry of Munitions*
HO	Home Office papers, TNA
HNKY	Hankey papers, Churchill College Archive Centre, Cambridge
HSF	High Seas Fleet
IACWPF	Inter-Allied Council on War Purchases and Finance
IF	Independent Force
ISB	International Socialist Bureau
IWC	Imperial War Cabinet
IWM	Imperial War Museum
IWW	International Workers of the World

JO	*Journal officiel de la République française. Débats parlementaires: Chambre des députés*
KAM	Bayerische Hauptstaatsarchiv, Munich, Abteilung IV, Kriegsarchiv
KAW	Kriegsarchiv, Vienna
KRA	Kriegsrohstoffabteilung
KÜA	Kriegsüberwachungsamt
LAB	Ministry of Labour papers, TNA
LC	Liddle Collection, Leeds University Library
LDB	'La Dame Blanche' papers, IWM
LG	Lloyd George papers, Parliamentary Archives
LHCMA	Liddell Hart Centre for Military Archives, King's College London
LOC	Manuscripts Division, Library of Congress
MAF	Records of Agriculture, Fisheries, and Food Departments, TNA
MFGB	Miners' Federation of Great Britain
MLN	Milner papers, Bodleian Library, Oxford
MOFB	*Military Operations: France and Belgium* (British official history)
MT	Transport ministries papers, TNA
MUN	Ministry of Munitions papers, TNA
NAA	Northern Arab Army
NAC	National Archives of Canada
NARA	National Archives and Records Administration, College Park, Maryland
NLS	National Library of Scotland
NNP	net national product
NOT	Netherlands Overseas Trust
NWAC	National War Aims Committee
OHL	Oberste Heeresleitung (German army high command)
OPDA	Ottoman Public Debt Administration
ÖULK	E. Glaise von Horstenau and R. Kiszling, eds., *Österreich-Ungarns Letzter Krieg* (Austro-Hungarian official history)
PSI	Partito Socialista Italiano
PMR	Permanent Military Representatives (of SWC)
PWW	A. S. Link et al., eds., *The Papers of Woodrow Wilson*

RFC	Royal Flying Corps
RMA	Reichsmarineamt (German Imperial Navy Office)
RNAS	Royal Naval Air Service
SBR	Small Box Respirator
SFIO	Section française de l'Internationale ouvrière (French socialist party)
SHA	Service historique de l'armée de terre, Vincennes
SKL	Seekriegsleitung
SPA	Socialist Party of America
SPD	Sozialdemokratische Partei Deutschlands (German Social Democratic Party)
SWC	Supreme War Council
T	Treasury papers, TNA
TF	Territorial Force
TNA	The National Archives, Kew
TUC	Trades Union Congress
UDC	Union of Democratic Control
UDZ	W. Schücking et al., eds., *Die Ursachen des deutschen Zusammenbruchs im Jahre 1918*
UGACPE	Union des grandes associations contre la propagande ennemie
USAWW	*The United States Army in the World War* (American official history)
USFA	United States Food Administration
USPD	Unabhängige Sozialdemokratische Partei Deutschlands (German Independent Social Democratic Party)
USRA	United States Railroad Administration
USSB	United States Shipping Board
WIB	War Industries Board
WK	Reichsarchiv, *Der Weltkrieg* (German official history)
WMYS	Wemyss Papers, Churchill College Archive Centre, Cambridge
WO	War Office Papers, TNA
WUMBA	Waffen und Munitions Beschaffungsamt
WWS	'Women, War, and Society 1914–1918', IWM

Note on Military and Naval Terminology

In 1914 a full-strength *infantry division* in the German army comprised 17,500 officers and men, 72 artillery pieces, and 24 machine guns; in the French army 15,000 officers and men, 36 artillery pieces, and 24 machine guns; in the British army 18,073 officers and men, 76 artillery pieces, and 24 machine guns. These figures were regulation strengths, and combat strengths after fighting began were almost invariably lower. During the war most armies reduced regulation strengths while increasing firepower. However, American divisions were much larger than the European norm: c. 28,000 officers and men each.

An *army corps* normally comprised two infantry divisions, and an *army* two or more army corps. An *army group* (to be found in the French and German armies) comprised a number of armies, totalling from 500,000 to over 1 million men. Conversely, the normal components of infantry divisions were *brigades* (4,000–5,000 men), *regiments* (2,000–3,000), *battalions* (600–1,000), *companies* (100–200), *platoons* (30–50), and *squads* or *sections* (8–11).

Artillery pieces (usually referred to in the text as 'guns') were divided into *cannon* (possessing a long barrel with a flat/horizontal trajectory for the projectile) and *howitzers* or *mortars* (possessing a short barrel and curved/plunging trajectory). They were also categorized by their calibre (the diameter of the barrel bore), although many British guns were named after the weight of their ammunition. Thus the standard light cannon ('field gun') was the 75 mm in the French army, the 77 mm in the German army, and the 18-pounder in the British army. Medium field howitzers included the German 120 mm and 150 mm, the French 155 mm, and the British 6-inch. Heavier field cannon were generally over 170 mm in calibre; heavier howitzers ranged from 200 to 400 mm.

The German *Minenwerfer* ('mine throwers') were short, muzzle-loading mortars in light, medium, and heavy sizes.

Machine guns were divided into heavy and light models. Heavy machine guns weighed at least 40–60 kilograms and required a crew of three to six men. Light (9–14 kilograms) machine guns were developed during the war, and could be carried by one man or mounted in an aircraft.

The British Royal Flying Corps (merged into the Royal Air Force from April 1918) was divided into *brigades, wings, squadrons,* and *flights.* In 1914 an RFC squadron comprised twelve aircraft. The basic unit of the French air force was the *escadrille.* German fighter aircraft were divided into *Jagdgruppen, Jagdgeschwader,* and *Jagdstaffeln.*

The most powerfully armed warships of the period are referred to collectively as 'capital ships'. They comprised *battleships* and *battle-cruisers.* Battlecruisers carried comparable artillery to battleships, but were faster because more lightly armoured. The most modern capital ships were known as 'dreadnought' battleships or battlecruisers (c. 17,000 tons or more in displacement) if they had speed and firepower comparable to or greater than those of the British HMS *Dreadnought* (1906). *Cruisers* were divided into heavy (or 'armoured') cruisers (over 10,000 tons), which were intended to fight as scouting vessels in fleet actions alongside capital ships, and light cruisers (2,000–14,000 tons), which were less heavily protected and intended to guard trade routes or colonial outposts. *Destroyers* (500–800 tons in 1914) were normally deployed in flotillas and armed with torpedoes as well as light guns.

Preface

The victor . . . is the one who can believe for a quarter of an hour longer than the enemy that he is not beaten.

The French Premier, Georges Clemenceau,
citing a samurai proverb[1]

This book grew out of a simple question: why did the First World War end at the time and in the manner that it did? In the defeated countries after 1918 the search for explanation became obsessive. The German Reichstag established an inquiry commission into 'The Causes of the German Collapse' that laboured for a decade and whose testimony ran into twelve volumes.[2] Characteristically – in the charged atmosphere of the Weimar Republic – its proceedings were marred by partisanship and its agreed conclusions few.[3] Yet at the same time in the victor countries public interest centred not on the war's termination but on its origins and on the tribulations of those who served in it. Only later, as the prospect of a second anti-German struggle loomed, did suspicions multiply about whether the Allies' victory had really been one after all.

Explaining how the Great War ended yields insights applicable to other conflicts. It elucidates not only the events that followed but also the war itself. To view the struggle from this vantage point is to reverse the telescope, so that no longer the idealistic energy of 1914 looms largest but instead a weary world, its human and material wellsprings nearing exhaustion. In large measure, as Clemenceau's observation highlights, victory depended on endurance and the victors endured longer. Yet to understand why they endured and triumphed we must investigate *how* they did so, by mobilizing men and resources, transporting them across the oceans, and wresting the advantage in fighting effectiveness.

Winning required not only courage and willpower but also organization. In an Atlantic civilization where the modern corporation had only recently been born,[4] military officials and public servants brought in professional civilian managers and became managers themselves, counting and recording as they did so. The American commander, Pershing, described his country's war effort as 'a great business enterprise'.[5] For all the suffering that accompanied it, victory rested on a prodigious administrative achievement.

As we near the First World War's centenary, nearly all the veterans of the conflict have passed away, and our links to it have grown attenuated. Yet its power to haunt the imagination lingers. The story of the 11 November armistice possesses an inherent drama,[6] and many surveys cover the final year of fighting, albeit mostly from a British or American viewpoint.[7] But the decisions that ended the war need setting in a broader context and to be recounted on both sides – the reasons why the victors granted a ceasefire being more complex and elusive than those why Germany and the other Central Powers sought one. Niall Ferguson's *The Pity of War* remains a provocative starting point. Tim Travers's *How the War was Won*, written primarily from a British Empire perspective, offers crucial insights, as on the opposing side does David Zabecki's *The German 1918 Offensives*. François Cailletau's *Gagner la Grande Guerre* adds more, particularly on manpower questions.[8] The fullest survey of all the belligerents is Jörg Duppler's and Gerhard Groß's *Kriegsende 1918*, which contains contributions of high quality. Yet whereas comprehensive investigations now exist into the outcomes of other modern conflicts, the First World War still lacks one.[9]

The interpretations offered up for other wars have clarified the range of approaches. At one extreme are those viewing defeat and victory as largely determined by disparities in resources;[10] at the other those focusing on less quantifiable factors such as morale and patriotism.[11] Between them fall approaches emphasizing the ability to convert resources into battlefield effectiveness and the role of leadership.[12] The high commands form a vital part of the picture, not least for their capacity to make grievous errors. Yet finally warfare incorporates an element of hazard and unpredictability that resists all efforts to reduce it to a formula, and reconstructing the narrative of events remains central.

In contrast to the Second World War, in which Axis expansion was followed by a sustained Allied resurgence and after 1942–3 the outcome was predictable, in the First the advantage shuttled between one side and the other. The First Battle of the Marne in September 1914 has strong claims to be a turning point, but the Central Powers largely held the campaigning initiative between May 1915 and June 1916, and again between October 1917 and July 1918. In 1917 American intervention was offset by the Russian Revolution, and the final eighteen months were dominated by a race between the repercussions set in motion by these two events, one favouring the Allies but the other favouring their enemies. Although Allied victory was now the most probable outcome, exactly when and on what scale remained imponderable, as did the question of how and at what cost it could be accomplished against what remained a formidable antagonist. In the event it came earlier and more completely than hardly anyone had foreseen, even if less emphatically than in the American Civil and Franco-Prussian Wars, or in 1945. At the end of 1917 the endgame to an extent remained open, and German as well as Allied decisions determined its course. The ensuing reversal of fortunes bore out the wisdom of Clausewitz's seemingly paradoxical precept that 'the defensive form of warfare is intrinsically stronger than the offensive'.[13] Once the Germans in spring 1918 took the offensive in the main war theatre they lost much of their advantage, whereas while the Allies had been on the attack they had worn themselves down. To this extent the Germans defeated themselves, and by the autumn they had no alternative but to attempt a desperate exercise in damage limitation, which largely failed them.

What follows is therefore a study in historical interconnectedness. It balances narrative – and the play of chronology and contingency – against analysis. The prologue outlines the pre-1918 obstacles to resolving an impasse that every day for over four years claimed thousands of lives. Chapters 1 and 2 focus on strategy and tactics, examining respectively the Central Powers' offensives between March and July of the final year and the Allied counteroffensives between July and November. Chapters 3–7 then turn to intelligence, technology, and logistics; to manpower and morale; to seapower; to the war economies; and to the politics of the home fronts; before Chapter 8 concludes with the making of the ceasefires. The military, naval, political, and economic stories are interwoven, not least because economic factors in particular have been misunderstood and neglected. The first great surge of modern globalization had crested before 1914 and the Allies stood to benefit most from it, whereas the Germans tried to organize the resources of a continent. The treatment is both international and comparative, examining both sides and all the war theatres, although the Western and Italian Fronts receive closest attention. None the less, the focus is on the topic in hand, rather than retelling the conflict's history in its entirety. The account refers to Macedonia, Palestine, and Mesopotamia, but touches only in passing on East Africa, where after the Battle of Mahiwa in October 1917 the German forces were too weak to fight another major action and the survivors retreated to Portuguese East Africa, where they supplied themselves by raiding isolated Portuguese and British garrisons. Both sides in the East African theatre were winding down their efforts,[14] and although the campaigning there had terrible consequences for the local inhabitants it contributed little to the Central Powers' overall defeat.

In attempting so wide-ranging a study I have been enormously indebted to the works of other historians, and to the proliferation of research in recent decades. But in addition the inter-war official histories are mines of information, as are the volumes in the Carnegie series on the conflict's economic and social aspects. To read this material is to gain a profound respect for its authors. Nevertheless, archival sources illuminate as do no others the commanders' and statesmen's unavowed concerns. They pinpoint the tensions between the victors that bulked large in their decision to terminate hostilities. In addition, if much attention in what follows is given to logistics, this reflects its salience in the documents. Among other things, the war was a contest between lorries and horses and ships and trains.

I have incurred many debts and obligations, which it is a pleasure to acknowledge. The Leverhulme Trust awarded me a Research Fellowship that made possible a sabbatical year and most of the archival visits. The London School of Economics provided a second sabbatical, and financial support from its Staff Research Fund. Among my colleagues in the International History Department I have to thank particularly Dr Steve Casey, who provided me with photocopies of the papers of Peyton C. March; Dr Heather Jones, who allowed me to cite her forthcoming monograph on violence against prisoners of war and who read Chapter 4; and Professor MacGregor Knox, for comments on the argument in the conclusion. Two of my doctoral students, Marvin Fried and

Charles Sorrie, copied documentation from the Austrian and French archives. Chapter drafts have been tried out in seminars in the International History Department, the German Historical Institute, the University of Ulster/Queen's University Belfast, and the University of Nottingham. Dr Jim Beach of Salford University provided advice on intelligence matters and kindly allowed me to cite his Ph.D. thesis. Dr John Salavrakos provided useful bibliographical pointers. Kevin Matthews and Andrea Heatley provided hospitality in Washington. Among the archives and libraries in which I have gathered material, I wish to thank the British Library, the British Library of Political and Economic Science, the German Historical Institute London, the Institute of Historical Research, the National Archives, the Imperial War Museum, the Liddell Hart Centre for Military Archives, the National Maritime Museum, the Bodleian Library, the Parliamentary Archives, Churchill College Archive Centre, Birmingham University Library, the Liddle Collection in the University of Leeds Library, the National Archives and Records Administration and the Library of Congress Manuscript Division in Washington DC, the Library and Archives Canada in Ottawa, the Archives nationales in Paris, the Service historique de l'armée de terre at Vincennes, the Archivio centrale di stato in Rome, the Bundesarchiv-Militärarchiv at Freiburg im Breisgau, the Bayerische Hauptstaatsarchiv Abt. IV (Kriegsarchiv) and Abt. I in Munich, the Hauptstaatsarchiv Stuttgart, and the Haus-, Hof- und Staatsarchiv and the Kriegsarchiv in Vienna. Extracts from the Hankey and Wemyss papers have been reproduced with permission of the Master and Fellows of Churchill College, Cambridge. I am indebted to the Trustees of the Imperial War Museum and the copyright holders for allowing access to the papers of Second Lieutenant A. R. Armfield, Lieutenant Howard Francis Bowser, Joseph Sheard Bramley, R. Cude, R. von Dechend, Lieutenant R. G. Dixon, Major Charles Dudley Ward, Gunner P. Fraser, Captain L. Gameson, Major L. B. Garretson, Lieutenant George Harvard Thomas, Captain T. F. Grady, Captain Martin Hardie, Captain C. J. Lodge Patch, and A. E. Wrench. Every effort has been made to trace copyright holders, and the author and the Imperial War Museum would be grateful for any information which might help to trace those whose identities or addresses are not currently known.

I would also like to thank my literary agent, Andrew Wylie, James Pullen in his London office, and my exceptionally enthusiastic and forbearing editor at Penguin Books, Simon Winder, as well as Caroline Elliker, Jenny Fry, Richard Duguid, Mark Handsley (for his scrupulous copy-editing), Christopher Phipps (for his excellent index), and the rest of the Penguin team.

Completing this work has meant neglect of home and family. I am grateful to my friends and relatives and indebted above all to my long-suffering wife, Sue Taylor, for her exemplary encouragement and patience. Responsibility for any errors and shortcomings in the book remains my own.

David Stevenson
July 2010

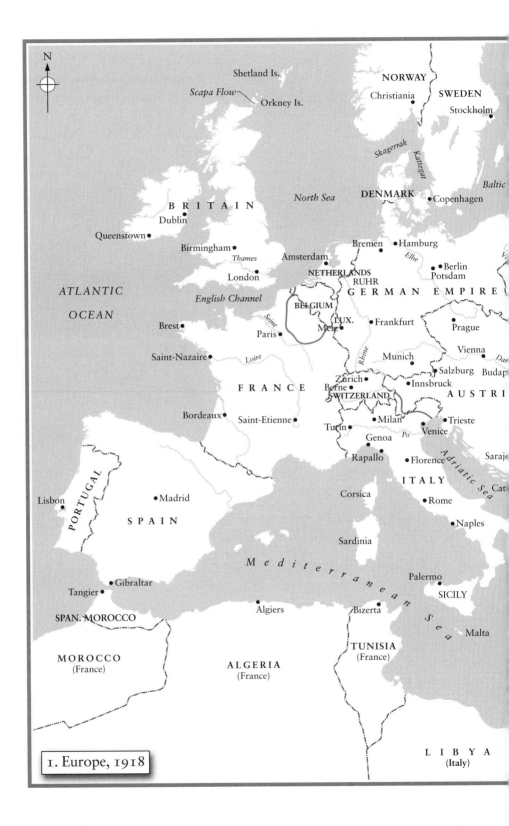

1. Europe, 1918

FINLAND
L. Ladoga
Helsingfors • • Petrograd
of Finland Kronstadt

ESTONIA

LIVONIA
LATVIA
• Riga

• Moscow

THUANIA
ST
SSIA
nenberg
• Minsk

Niemen

R U S S I A

Don

Volga

Ural Mts

Volga

• Brest-Litovsk
• Cholm
rsaw
LAND

Kiev • Kharkov •
Dnieper   Donets

GALICIA

UKRAINE

Caspian Sea

arpathian Mts
Jassy •

BESSARABIA

• Odessa

CRIMEA

Baku •

UNGARY
• Focșani

ROMANIA
Bucharest •
Belgrade
ERBIA

DOBRUDJA

Sebastopol •

Black Sea

Batum •
Ardahan •

Caucasus Mts

GEORGIA

AZERBAIJAN

Kars •
ARMENIA

BULGARIA
• Sofia

• Constantinople

PERSIA

Salonika •

GREECE

Aegean Sea

O T T O M A N
E M P I R E

Tigris

• Athens

Euphrates

CRETE

CYPRUS
(Britain)

PALESTINE

A R A B I A

Alexandria •

Cairo •

0   100   200   300 miles
0   200   400 km

E G Y P T

Maximum advance of the
Central Powers, 1918

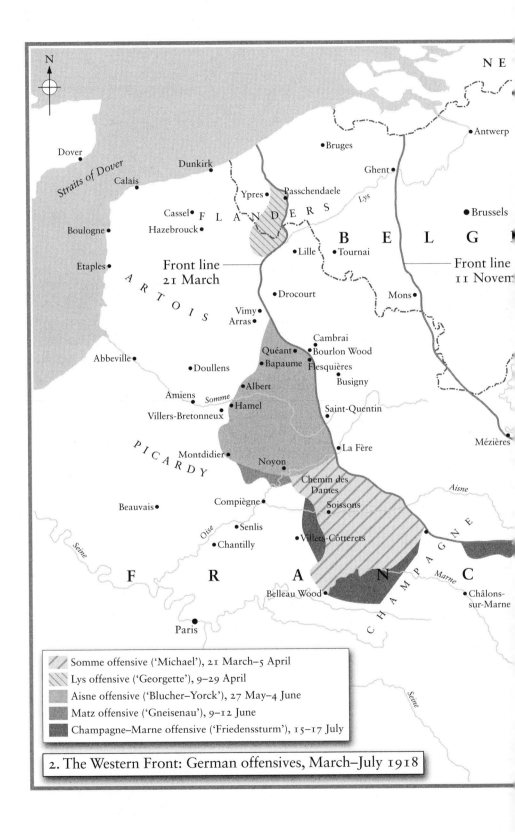

N

NE

Dover

Straits of Dover

Calais

Dunkirk

Bruges

Antwerp

Ghent

Boulogne

Cassel F L A N D E R S

Hazebrouck

Ypres Passchendaele

Lys

Brussels

Etaples

Front line
21 March

Lille Tournai

B E L G I

Front line
11 Novem

A R T O I S

Drocourt

Mons

Vimy
Arras

Cambrai
Quéant Bourlon Wood
Bapaume Flesquières

Busigny

Abbeville

Doullens

Albert

Saint-Quentin

Amiens Somme Hamel

Villers-Bretonneux

P I C A R D Y

Montdidier

Noyon

La Fère

Mézières

Chemin des
Dames

Aisne

Beauvais

Compiègne

Soissons

Senlis

Chantilly

Villers-Côtterets

C H A M P A G N E

F R A N

C

Seine

Oise

Belleau Wood

Marne

Châlons-
sur-Marne

Paris

Seine

Somme offensive ('Michael'), 21 March–5 April

Lys offensive ('Georgette'), 9–29 April

Aisne offensive ('Blucher–Yorck'), 27 May–4 June

Matz offensive ('Gneisenau'), 9–12 June

Champagne–Marne offensive ('Friedenssturm'), 15–17 July

2. The Western Front: German offensives, March–July 1918

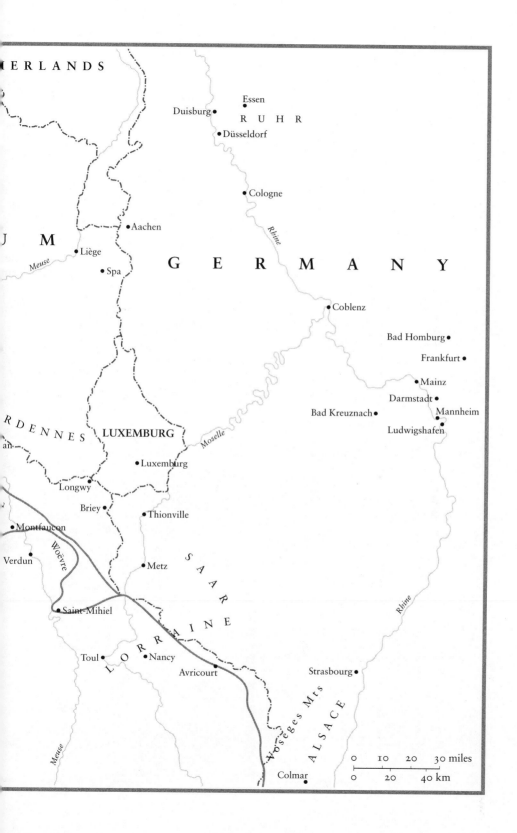

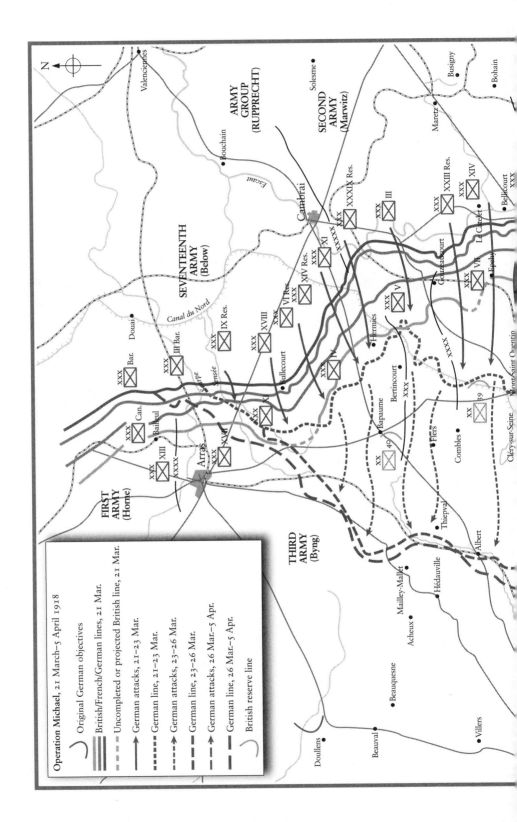

Operation Michael, 21 March–5 April 1918

Original German objectives

British/French/German lines, 21 Mar.

Uncompleted or projected British line, 21 Mar.

German attacks, 21–23 Mar.

German line, 21–23 Mar.

German attacks, 23–26 Mar.

German line, 23–26 Mar.

German attacks, 26 Mar–5 Apr.

German line, 26 Mar–5 Apr.

British reserve line

N

ARMY GROUP (RUPPRECHT)

SEVENTEENTH ARMY (Below)

SECOND ARMY (Marwitz)

FIRST ARMY (Horne)

THIRD ARMY (Byng)

Valenciennes

Bouchain

Solesme

Busigny

Bohain

Maretz

Bellicourt

Cambrai

XXXIX Res.

XXIII Res.

XIV

XXX

XXX

XXX

III

XXXXX

XI

XIV Res.

XXX

VI Res.

XXX

XVIII

IV

V

XXX

Gouzeaucourt

Le Catelet

Épehy

VII

XXX

Escaut

Canal du Nord

Douai

Bar.

III Bar.

IX Res.

Hermies

XXX

XXXX

XXX

Sensée

Scarpe

Bullecourt

Bapaume

Bertincourt

XXX

Cléry-sur-Seine

Mont-Saint-Quentin

Can.

Bailleul

XXX

XIII

XXX

Arras

XVII

39

XX

40

XX

XX

Flers

Combles

Thiepval

Albert

Hédauville

Mailley-Maillet

Acheux

Beauquesne

Villers

Beauval

Doullens

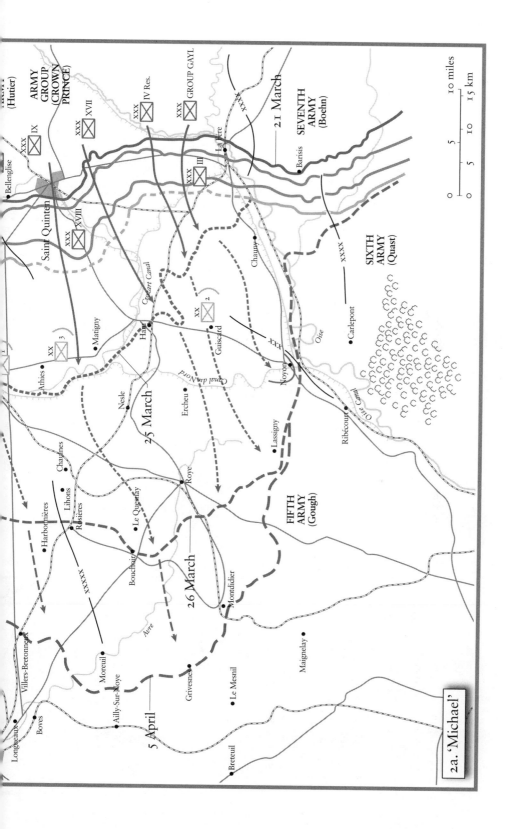

2a. 'Michael'

ARMY GROUP (CROWN PRINCE)

(Hutier)

XXX IX

XXX XVII

XXX IV Res.

XXX GROUP GAYL

GROUP GAYL

21 March

SEVENTH ARMY (Boehn)

Barisis

Bellenglise

Saint Quinten

XXX XVIII

XXX III

La Fère

XXX XVIII

SIXTH ARMY (Quast)

Chaumy

xxxx

Cartepont

XX 2

Matigny

Croizat Canal

Ham

XX 3

Athies

Guiscard

Oise

xxxx

Canal du Nord

Noyon

Oise Canal

Ribécourt

Nesle

25 March

Ercheu

Lassigny

Chaulnes

Roye

Lihons

Rosières

Le Quesnay

26 March

Montdidier

FIFTH ARMY (Gough)

Harbonnières

xxxxx

Bouchoir

Avre

Maignelay

Villers-Bretonneux

Moreuil

Grivesnes

Le Mesnil

Longueaux

Boves

Ailly-Sur-Noye

5 April

Breteuil

10 miles

15 km

0   5   10

0   5   10   15

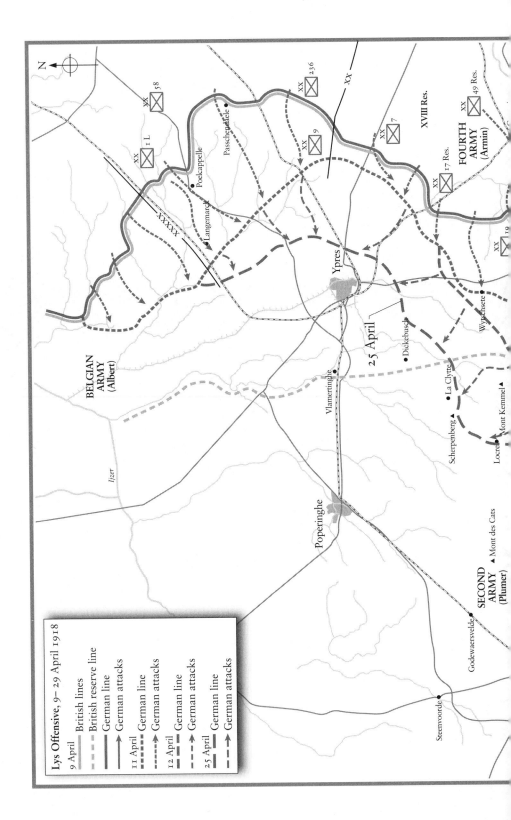

Lys Offensive, 9–29 April 1918

9 April
━━━ British lines
┄┄┄ British reserve line
━━━ German line
→ German attacks

11 April
━━━ German line
⟶ German attacks

12 April
━━━ German line
⟶ German attacks

25 April
━ ━ German line
⟶ German attacks

N

BELGIAN ARMY (Albert)

FOURTH ARMY (Armin)

XVIII Res.

SECOND ARMY (Plumer)

Poelcappelle
Passchendaele
Langemarck
Ypres
Poperinghe
Vlamertinghe
Dickebusch
La Clytte
Scherpenberg ▲
▲ Mont Kemmel
Locre
Wytschaete
Godewaersvelde
▲ Mont des Cats
Steenvoorde

Ijzer

25 April

XXXXX

XX 58
XX 1 L
XX 236
XX 9
XX 7
XX 17 Res.
XX 49 Res.
XX 19

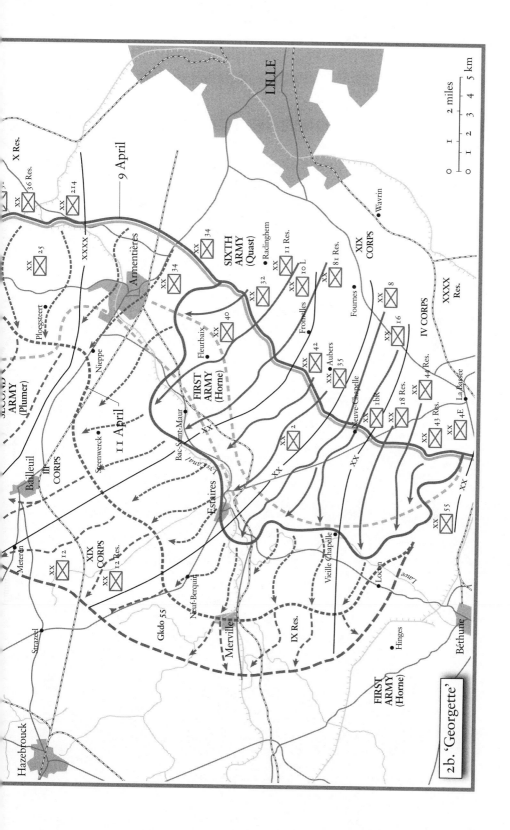

2b. 'Georgette'

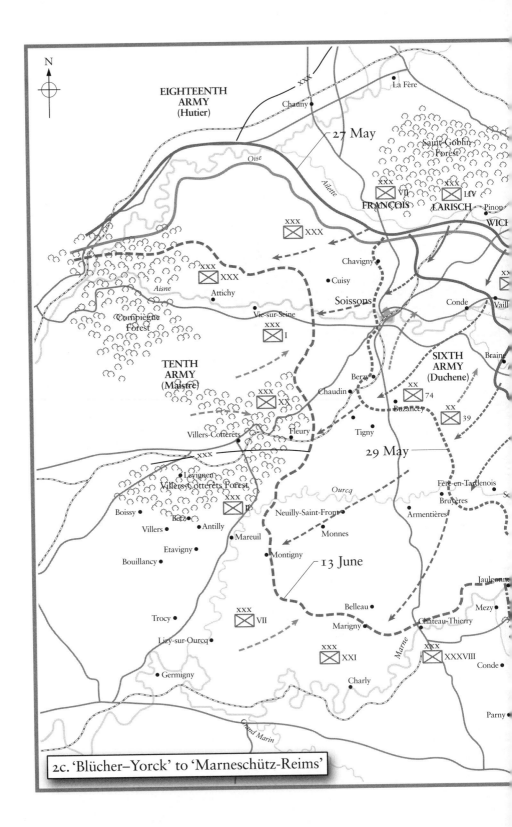

N

EIGHTEENTH
ARMY
(Hutier)

La Fère

Chauny

27 May

Saint-Gobain
Forest

Oise

Aillette

XXX VII
FRANÇOIS

XXX LIV
LARISCH

Pinon

WICH

XXX XXX

Chavigny

Cuisy

Soissons

Condé

Vaill

XX

Aisne

XXX XXX

Attichy

Vic-sur-Seine

Compiègne
Forest

XXX I

Berzy

Braine

SIXTH
ARMY
(Duchene)

TENTH
ARMY
(Maistre)

XXX XX

Chaudin

XX 74

Buzancy

XX 39

Villers-Cotterêts

Fleury

Tigny

29 May

XXX

Levignen

Villers-Cotterêts Forest

Ourcq

Fère-en-Tardenois

Bruyères

Se

Boissy

Berzy

Antilly

XXX IX

Neuilly-Saint-Front

Armentières

Villers

Monnes

Etavigny

Mareuil

Bouillancy

Montigny

13 June

Belleau

Mezy

Jaulgonne

Trocy

XXX VII

Marigny

Château-Thierry

Lizy-sur-Ourcq

Conde

XXX XXI

XXX XXXVIII

Germigny

Charly

Marne

Parny

Grand Marin

2c. 'Blücher–Yorck' to 'Marneschütz-Reims'

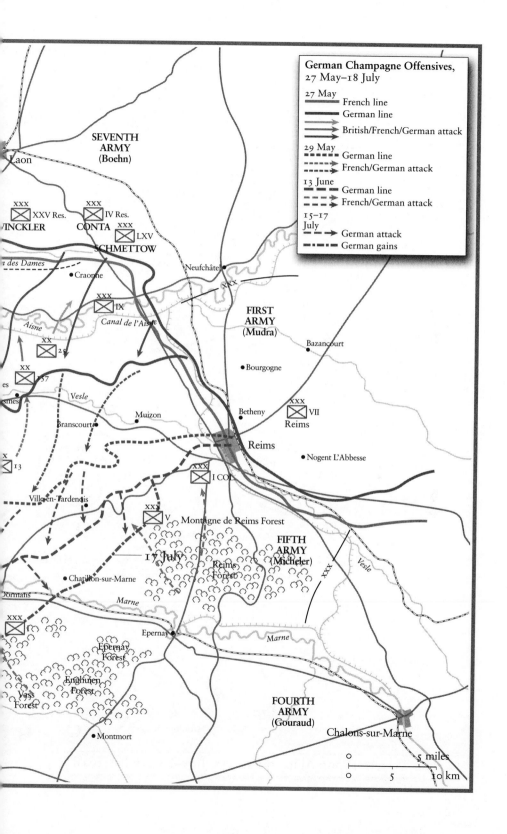

**German Champagne Offensives,
27 May–18 July**

27 May
— French line
— German line
⟹ British/French/German attack

29 May
▪▪▪ German line
▪▪▪▶ French/German attack

13 June
━ ━ German line
╍ ╍▶ French/German attack

15–17
July
━ ━▶ German attack
━ ▪ ━ German gains

SEVENTH
ARMY
(Boehn)

Laon

xxx
XXV Res.
VINCKLER

xxx
IV Res.
CONTA

xxx
LXV
SCHMETTOW

_ des Dames

• Craonne

Neufchâtel

xxx

FIRST
ARMY
(Mudra)

xxx
IX

Canal de l'Aisne

Aisne

xx
25

xx
157

Vesle

Muizon

Branscourt

Bethany

x
13

Bazancourt

• Bourgogne

xxx
VII
Reims

Reims

• Nogent L'Abbesse

xxx
I COL

Villc-en-Tardenois

xxx
V

Montagne de Reims Forest

17 July

Reims
Forest

FIFTH
ARMY
(Micheler)

Vesle

xxx

• Chatillon-sur-Marne

Marne

Dormans

xxx

Epernay •

Marne

Epernay
Forest

Enghien
Forest

Vass
Forest

FOURTH
ARMY
(Gouraud)

• Montmort

Chalons-sur-Marne

0   5 miles

0   5   10 km

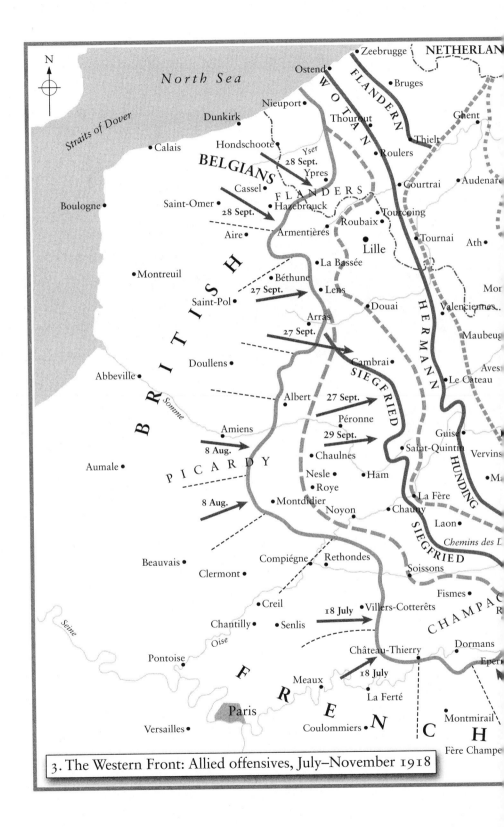

3. The Western Front: Allied offensives, July–November 1918

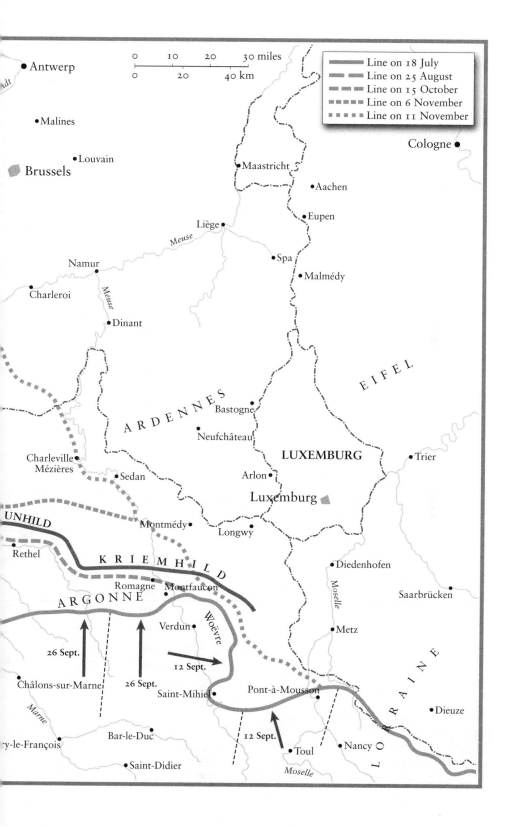

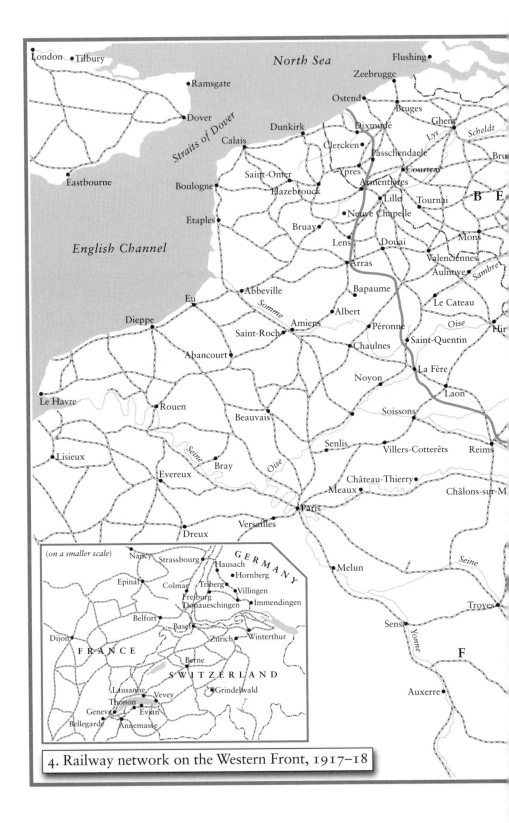

4. Railway network on the Western Front, 1917–18

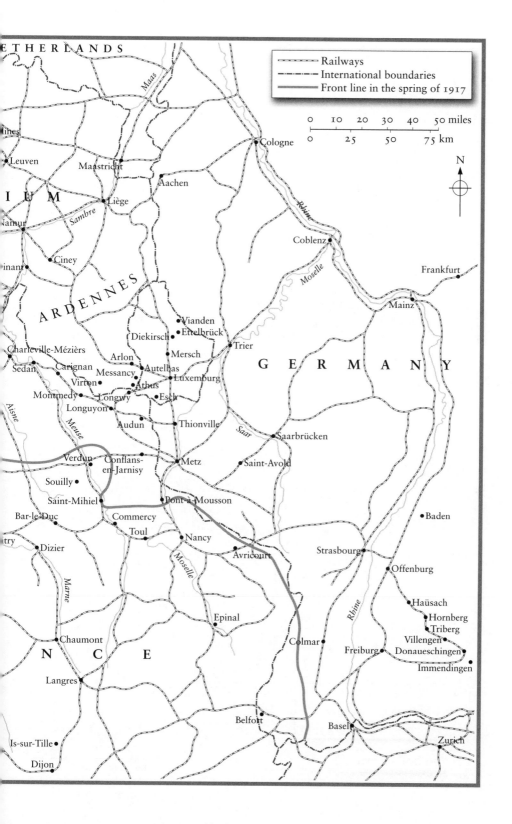

5. The Italian Front

Line in May 1916
Line in January 1918
Line on 4 November 1918

SWITZERLAND

TYROL

Brenner Pass

4 November 1918

Tonale Pass

TRENTINO

Trent

Monte Gra
Asiago
Bassano

LOMBARDY

Milan

Lake Garda

ITALY

Verona

Vicenza

Pa

Adige

Po

Po

0   10   20   30 m
0   10   20   30   40 km

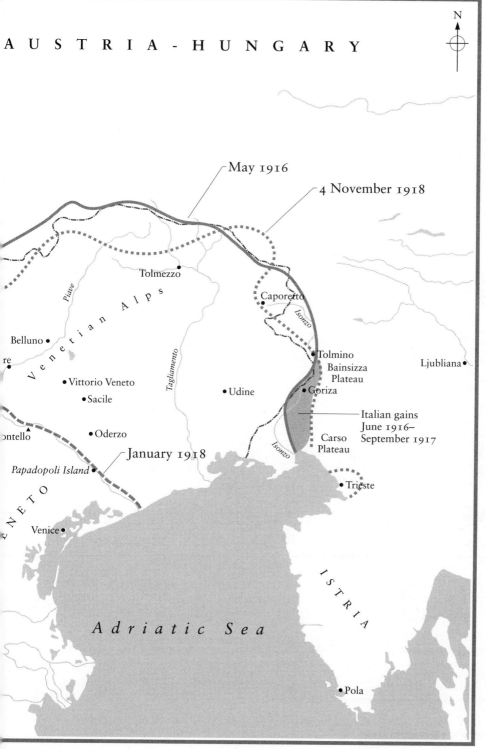

N

AUSTRIA - HUNGARY

May 1916

4 November 1918

Tolmezzo

Caporetto

Isonzo

Piave

V e n e t i a n   A l p s

Belluno •

re •

Tagliamento

• Tolmino
Bainsizza
Plateau

Ljubliana •

• Vittorio Veneto

• Goriza

• Sacile

• Udine

Italian gains
June 1916–
September 1917

• Oderzo

ntello ▲

Carso
Plateau

Isonzo

January 1918

Papadopoli Island •

• Trieste

V E N E T O

Venice •

I S T R I A

A d r i a t i c   S e a

• Pola

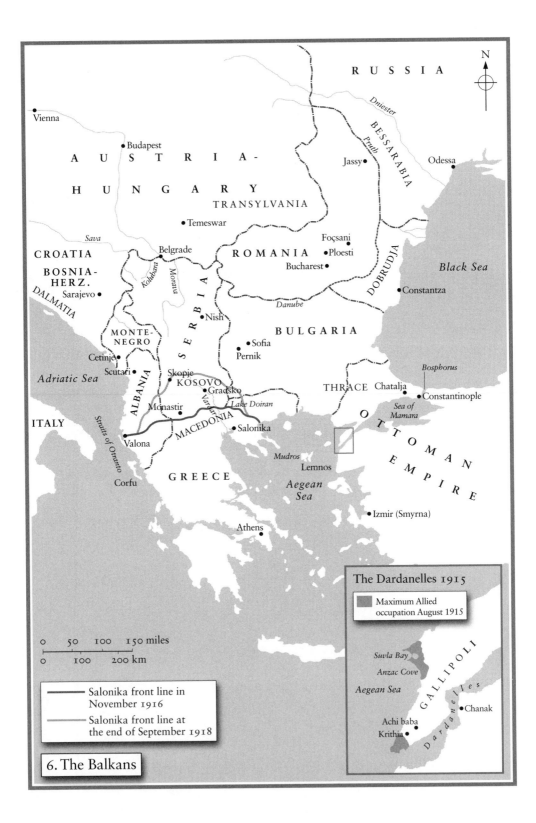

N

RUSSIA

Dniester

Vienna

• Budapest

A U S T R I A -

H U N G A R Y

TRANSYLVANIA

Sava

CROATIA

BOSNIA-
HERZ.

DALMATIA

Sarajevo •

Belgrade •

Kolubara

Morava

S E R B I A

Nish •

MONTE-
NEGRO

Cetinje •

Scutari •

Adriatic Sea

ALBANIA

Skopje •

KOSOVO

• Gradsko

Vardar

Lake Doiran

Monastir •

ITALY

Straits of Otranto

Valona •

MACEDONIA

Salonika •

GREECE

Corfu •

Athens •

• Temeswar

Foçsani •
• Ploesti

R O M A N I A

Bucharest •

Danube

B U L G A R I A

• Sofia

Pernik •

THRACE

Jassy •

BESSARABIA

Pruth

Odessa •

Black Sea

DOBRUDJA

Constantza •

Bosphorus

Chatalja •

Constantinople •

*Sea of
Mamara*

O T T O M A N

E M P I R E

Izmir (Smyrna) •

Mudros
Lemnos

*Aegean
Sea*

0 50 100 150 miles

0 100 200 km

Salonika front line in
November 1916

Salonika front line at
the end of September 1918

6. The Balkans

The Dardanelles 1915

Maximum Allied
occupation August 1915

Suvla Bay

Anzac Cove

Aegean Sea

GALLIPOLI

Dardanelles

Chanak •

Achi baba •

Krithia •

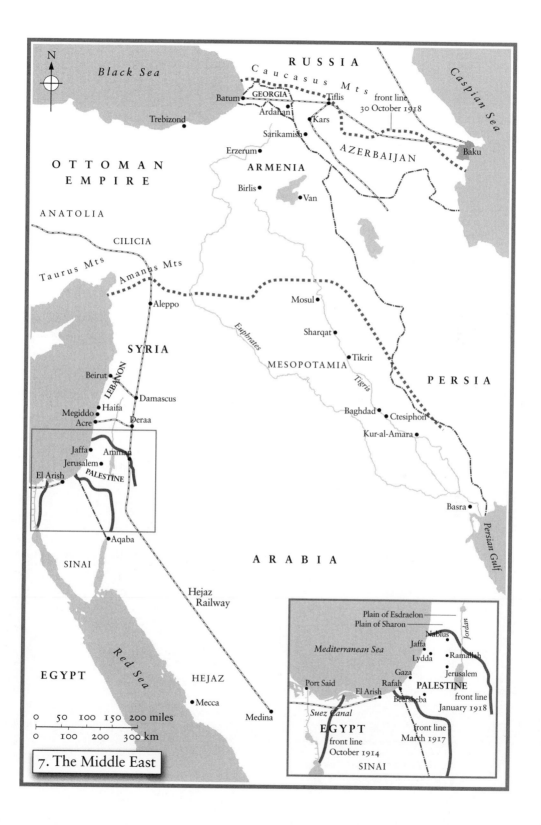

N

Black Sea

RUSSIA

C a u c a s u s   M t s

Caspian Sea

Trebizond

Batum • •GEORGIA Tiflis•
Ardahan• front line
30 October 1918
•Kars
Sarikamish•
Erzerum• Baku•

**OTTOMAN
EMPIRE**

AZERBAIJAN

ANATOLIA

ARMENIA

Birlis •
•Van

CILICIA

T a u r u s   M t s

A m a n u s   M t s

•Aleppo

Mosul•

SYRIA

Euphrates

Sharqat•

Tikrit•

MESOPOTAMIA

Tigris

PERSIA

Beirut•

LEBANON

•Damascus

Megiddo• Haifa•
Acre• •Deraa

Baghdad• •Ctesiphon
Kur-al-Amara•

Jaffa• •Amman
Jerusalem•
El Arish• PALESTINE

ARABIA

Basra•

•Aqaba

SINAI

Hejaz
Railway

Persian Gulf

Red Sea

EGYPT

HEJAZ

•Mecca

0   50   100   150   200 miles
0   100   200   300 km

Medina•

7. The Middle East

Plain of Esdraelon
Plain of Sharon

Jordan

Mediterranean Sea

Nablus•
Jaffa•
Lydda• •Ramallah
Jerusalem•
Gaza•
Port Said• Rafah• **PALESTINE**
El Arish• Beersheba• front line
January 1918
Suez Canal
EGYPT
front line
October 1914
SINAI
front line
March 1917

SAXONY

SILESIA

GERMAN
EMPIRE

SUDETENLAND

•Eger •Prague
BOHEMIA
•Plzen

CZECHS

BAVARIA

Danube

Linz

Vienna•
Baden•

Bratis

Munich•

•Innsbruck

SWITZERLAND

Graz•

CARINTHIA
Klagenfurt•

TRENTINO
Trent•

SLOVENIA
SLOVENES

Trieste•

Zagreb•
CROATS
SLAVONIA

•Fiume

CROATIA

SER
AN
CRO

BOSNIA-
HERZEGOVIN

ITALY

Adriatic Sea

•Spalato

8. Austria-Hungary

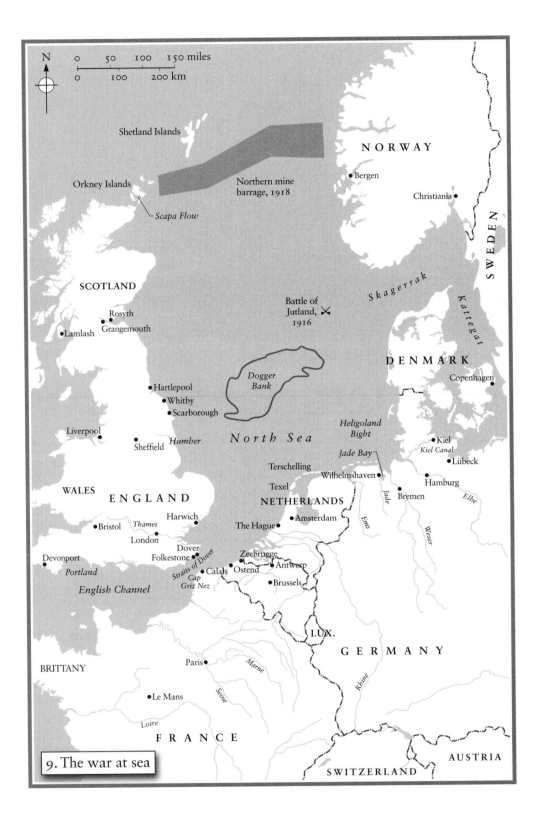

N

0   50   100   150 miles
0   100   200 km

Shetland Islands

Orkney Islands

Scapa Flow

NORWAY

•Bergen

Christiania•

Northern mine
barrage, 1918

SWEDEN

SCOTLAND

Rosyth
•Lamlash •Grangemouth

Battle of
Jutland, ✕
1916

Skagerrak

Kattegat

DENMARK

Copenhagen•

•Hartlepool
•Whitby
•Scarborough

*Dogger
Bank*

Liverpool•

Sheffield• *Humber*

North Sea

*Heligoland
Bight*

•Kiel
Kiel Canal

•Lübeck

WALES

ENGLAND

Thames
Harwich•

•Bristol
London•

Devonport•
Portland

Dover
Folkestone•

Straits of Dover
*Cap
Griz Nez*

BRITTANY

English Channel

Terschelling

Texel

NETHERLANDS

The Hague• •Amsterdam

Zeebrugge•
•Calais Ostend• •Antwerp
•Brussels

Jade Bay
Wilhelmshaven•

Jade

Ems

Bremen•

Hamburg•

Weser

Elbe

LUX.

GERMANY

Paris• *Marne*

•Le Mans

Seine

Loire

FRANCE

Rhine

SWITZERLAND

AUSTRIA

9. The war at sea

Prologue: Deadlock, 1914–1917

Thus at eleven o'clock this morning came to an end the cruellest and most terrible war that has ever scourged mankind. I hope we may say that thus, this fateful morning, came to an end all wars.

David Lloyd George in the House of Commons,
11 November 1918[1]

Since the day when I had stood at my mother's grave, I had not wept ... But now I could not help it. And so it had all been in vain ... Did all this happen only so that a gang of wretched criminals could lay hands on the fatherland? In these nights hatred grew in me, hatred for those responsible for this deed. In the days that followed, my own fate became known to me ... I, for my part, decided to go into politics.

Adolf Hitler, *Mein Kampf*[2]

The eleventh hour of the eleventh day of the eleventh month of 1918 was an exceptional juncture. It remains imprinted in the Western calendar. As our distance from it lengthens, it has grown more emblematic of war in general, and it has become impossible to view the armistice without irony, as a forlorn expression of the hope that such a catastrophe could never happen again. Even on the day itself Clemenceau's daughter pleaded with him: 'Tell me Papa that you are happy.' He responded that 'I cannot say it because I am not. *It will all be useless.*'[3]

The ceasefire aroused a gamut of emotions, but reconciliation was not one of them. The road that led there had been too painful and the former belligerents were too profoundly antagonized. To understand that road and that antagonism we must dig back decades into the roots of the conflict. The 1914–18 catastrophe grew from fissures at the heart of nineteenth-century Europe, which became chasms after fighting broke out. Until the outcome on the battlefield had been decided, attempts to bridge them by diplomacy proved fruitless.

The Great War was so destructive because it involved the strongest powers of the day. By its closing phases it had drawn in all of them. In 1918 one coalition (the Central Powers), based on the interior of Central Europe and Asia Minor, faced another (the Allies and the United States), which drove inland towards the heart of the Eurasian landmass. The Allies and Americans could do so because the Victorian revolution in communications epitomized in the railway, the telegraph, and the steamship gave them mastery of worldwide resources, and because they marshalled those resources in new ways. During the pre-war decades, agricultural and manufacturing growth and the cross-border expansion of trade, investment, and migration had knitted the Atlantic world together.[4] They had also spread democratization, as the traditional rulers of the European countries, through a mixture of fear, idealism, and calculation, had extended voting rights and civil liberties to increasingly urban and articulate middle and working classes. These developments made it likely that any new great war would be fought quite differently from in the past, but – contrary to the predictions of more idealistic commentators – they did not make such a war unthinkable. On the contrary, European politics remained rooted in the untrammelled sovereignty of the great powers, which were now more formidably armed than ever. Nor did the growth of trade unions and socialist parties consolidate peace, for the spread of popular patriotism offset their influence and to a large extent they shared in it.

Among the most visceral antagonisms leading to war was that between Germany and France. According to the German foreign minister, by 1917 an 'ocean of hate' separated the two countries.[5] German unification under Otto von Bismarck had realigned the European power balance even before the Franco-Prussian War of 1870–71 inflicted on the French both humiliating defeat and the loss of their provinces of Alsace and northern Lorraine. After 1871 French governments recognized that a war of revenge was impracticable, but periodic détentes between Paris and Berlin never became an alliance, and the two powers' armies continued to be ranged against each other. Alongside this first line of tension a second stemmed from rivalry in the Balkans between Tsarist Russia under its Romanov dynasty and the Dual Monarchy of Austria-Hungary under the Habsburgs. During the 1870s and 1880s Bismarck linked both Russia and Austria-Hungary with Germany (ruled by the Hohenzollerns) in an alignment of conservative monarchies, but after the Emperor Wilhelm II came to the German throne and Bismarck fell from office this balancing act broke down. In 1891–4 Russia concluded an alliance with the French Third Republic. Even if ideologically Paris and St Petersburg were worlds apart, they were united in suspicion of the Germans, who correspondingly grew more dependent on their 1879 alliance with Austria-Hungary. From now on the Continental powers were divided into opposing blocs, consolidated by secret alliances and military conventions, and this division would persist until 1918.

For a while the confrontation remained manageable, not least because between the 1880s and 1905 European diplomacy centred on imperialist rivalries in Africa and Asia, where France, Germany, and Russia all clashed with Britain. Only gradually did a further line of tension emerge in the North Sea following Germany's decision – as a personal policy of Wilhelm, though implemented by his Navy Secretary, Alfred von Tirpitz – to create a High Seas Fleet of modern capital ships that challenged the Royal Navy's predominance. The British responded with new building, above all when in 1906 they commissioned HMS *Dreadnought*, which ratcheted up the naval race into a costlier phase of competition in more powerful vessels. But they also responded diplomatically, and the years 1904–7 proved a watershed. On the one hand Russia was defeated in the Russo-Japanese War and revolutionary unrest threatened Tsar Nicholas II's authority. On the other, the Germans exploited the situation by challenging France's efforts to control Morocco and by bidding to realign Europe through the creation of a German–French–Russian bloc. But France and Britain had settled their extra-European disagreements in the 1904 agreement known as the 'Entente Cordiale', and in the Moroccan crisis of 1905–6 the new Liberal government in London both gave the French diplomatic encouragement and initiated secret conversations on military and naval co-operation. In 1907 a further agreement demarcated British and Russian spheres of influence in Central Asia, and the Foreign Secretary, Sir Edward Grey, explicitly intended this arrangement to help contain Germany in Europe.

Germany was now estranged from three great powers. Moreover Italy, which had formed the Triple Alliance with Germany and Austria-Hungary in 1882, reached a secret understanding with the French in 1902. Although it remained a Triple Alliance member, after 1904 it launched a land and naval arms race against Austria-Hungary. Hostility between Rome and Vienna had its origins in Austria's nineteenth-century opposition to Italian unification, but now centred on the issue of the Italian-speakers living in the Trentino and round Trieste, who remained under Habsburg rule. Austria-Hungary was Germany's one dependable great-power ally, but it had enemies not only in Russia and Italy but also in the Balkans, where its influence over Serbia crumbled after a coup d'état in 1903 brought a more nationalist dynasty to the throne in Belgrade. Both of the 'Central Powers' now faced what the German Chancellor characterized as 'encirclement'. They would react to their predicament by going to war.

Germany's and Austria-Hungary's internal structures were essential to this story. Both states were hybrids between autocracy and constitutionalism. The German Empire was a federation, although one dominated by Prussia, whose king was also German Emperor and whose Minister President was German Chancellor. Although the navy was an imperial service, there was no imperial army. The larger German states retained their own land forces, but the Prussian General Staff became the sole strategic planning agency. The Chief of the General Staff (CGS) reported to the Emperor, and not to the civilian government headed by the Chancellor (between 1909 and 1917 Theobald von Bethmann Hollweg), but the Chancellor too was appointed and dismissed by Wilhelm and did not need a majority in the lower house of the imperial parliament, the Reichstag. (The upper house, the Bundesrat, represented the state governments.) On the other hand, a Reichstag majority was necessary to pass legislation, including bills for tax increases, conscription, and armaments, and the lower house was chosen on an adult-male franchise by an electorate that was free to organize in political parties and pressure groups. By 1914 most of the one third of German voters who were Catholic were voting for the Centre Party, whose loyalty the Protestant Prussian establishment viewed as suspect. The Social Democratic Party (SPD), which wanted more democratization, had become the largest in parliament, while support for the conservative parties that traditionally had buttressed the regime was waning. Class, confessional, and regional conflicts divided the empire, although its non-German minorities – Poles in the east, Danes in the north, and Alsatians and Lorrainers in the west – were small.

In contrast, Austria-Hungary contained twelve major ethnic groups, and the two most influential – the Germans and Magyars – together numbered less than half its population. Since 1867 it had been divided into Austrian and Hungarian components (also known as Cisleithania and Transleithania), and Franz Joseph I was technically Austrian Emperor but King of Hungary. The two halves had separate parliaments, governments, budgets, and even armies, the latter serving alongside the common army. Their finance ministers held the purse strings for the common army, navy, and foreign ministry. The Hungarian government held a veto over major foreign policy decisions, and it rested on a severely restricted franchise, the non-Magyars accounting for 47 per cent of the population of the Hungarian half but only 14 per cent of the parliamentary seats.[6] In the Austrian half, in contrast, the lower chamber (Reichsrat) was elected after 1907 by manhood suffrage and its nationalities could organize more freely. But by the eve of war political life had so fragmented that the Austrian government could not form a stable parliamentary majority, and it used Article 14 of the constitution to rule by decree.

These difficulties must be placed in context. Despite the SPD's revolutionary talk, it was law-abiding and orderly. Hardly any of the nationalist politicians in Austria-Hungary demanded secession. The external rather than the internal situation mesmerized the Berlin and Vienna leaders. In a first development, after 1905 a succession of diplomatic crises over Morocco and the Balkans polarized the two alliance blocs. The crises came in ever quicker succession, each was more acute than its predecessor, and in each the armed forces were placed on higher stages of alert, the most dangerous accompanying the Balkan Wars of 1912–13. In the First Balkan War a coalition of Serbia, Montenegro, Greece, and Bulgaria, formed with Russian assistance, defeated Ottoman Turkey and annexed most of its European territories. In the Second War, Serbia, Montenegro, and Greece defeated Bulgaria, and Austria-Hungary's and Germany's traditional ally Romania joined them, unsettling the Balkan balance of power to Austria-Hungary's detriment. A second development was the transformation of the arms race. After 1912 Britain and Germany eased off their naval spending and Britain remained ahead, but a contest in land armaments took off between the Austro-German and Franco-Russian blocs and both sides' general staffs adopted more aggressive war plans. Third, the diplomatic crises and the armaments rivalry crystallized public opinion into pro- and anti-preparedness camps, and a vociferous new nationalism encapsulated the pre-war mood.

By 1914 most members of the Austro-Hungarian leadership believed that only force could answer the menace to their empire's integrity from South Slav nationalism supported by Serbia. They saw the assassination at Sarajevo on 28 June of the Archduke Franz Ferdinand, the heir to the throne, as the opportunity to act. The German government supported them, welcoming a Balkan war between Austria-Hungary and Serbia and deliberately risking a Continental European one, believing that at present it held the advantage in the land arms race but that by 1917 France and Russia would have caught up. When Russia supported Serbia and mobilized its armed forces, Germany sent ultimata to Russia to desist and to France to pledge its neutrality, and when neither complied it declared war on them. As Germany's war plan, conventionally known as the Schlieffen–Moltke Plan after the two General Staff chiefs who had devised it, entailed first sending the bulk of its army against France and outflanking the French border fortresses by traversing neutral Belgium, the outbreak of hostilities immediately caused a crisis with Britain. The British government had no obligation to aid the French, but its leading members believed that Britain would be endangered if it stood by while France was overwhelmed. Germany's invasion of Belgium, a small neutral state that under the 1839 Treaty of London the European powers had placed under guarantee, raised an issue of principle that convinced most of the Liberal Cabinet to support a war that on national security grounds the Unionist opposition was willing to back.[7]

The circumstances in which the conflict broke out help explain why it became so intractable. The German authorities maintained they had responded to Russian aggression, as well as to French revanchism and a British-inspired web of encirclement. The French insisted they had been the victims of an unprovoked attack, and they seemed vindicated by disclosures in 1918 that if Paris had pledged neutrality Germany would have demanded the surrender of France's border fortresses.[8] But the Austro-Hungarian government – and even the Russian one – also benefited at first from an unwonted unity among its citizens. Modern research has demolished the myth of widespread enthusiasm for hostilities, but the socialist-led protests in the early phases of the July 1914 crisis quickly deflated and gave way to acceptance.[9] Similarly, we now know that many military chiefs expected a war of up to two years, but among politicians and the general public the hope that this, like other recent conflicts, would be a matter of months was prevalent.[10] Developments would speedily disabuse them.

The opening offensives led to nearly unremitting failure. In the east, Austria-Hungary's invasion of Russian Poland was repelled, as was its invasion of Serbia. Although Russia overran the Austrian province of Galicia, at the battles of Tannenberg and the Masurian Lakes much smaller German forces drove back the tsarist advance into East Prussia. In the west, French offensives into Lorraine and the Ardennes were similarly halted, the great wheeling manoeuvre by the German army across Belgium and northern France was checked east of Paris at the First Battle of the Marne, and when the First Battle of Ypres concluded in November the opposing lines of trenches that would become notorious as the Western Front were forming from Switzerland to the North Sea. For a generation the European powers had been spared high casualty bills, but already losses far exceeded those in 1870 and hostilities were only just beginning. The weekly numbers killed and wounded in the opening phase – among troops rarely yet protected by digging in – were some of the highest of the war. By the end of 1914 French casualties numbered 528,000, German 800,000, and British 90,000.[11] Mobile campaigning also meant devastation, occupation, and atrocities against civilians,[12] which were not mere fictions of Allied propagandists. Yet in no theatre did the fighting produce a decision, and if suspicion and xenophobia had divided the blocs before July now the obstacles to reconciliation were vastly greater. Germany held most of Belgium and France's northern provinces, including great cities such as Antwerp and Lille, as well as strategic coastline, industries, and coal and iron ore. Negotiating while it remained there would place the Allies at a fundamental disadvantage, but nor could the Berlin government justify to its people abandoning conquests that had cost so much, unless the compensation were commensurate. In the east, where Austria-Hungary and Russia had also both lost territory and suffered enormous casualties, similar considerations applied. The pre-1914 'Triple Entente' became the Allies after France, Britain, and Russia signed the Pact of London in

September 1914, undertaking not to make peace separately. As Japan declared war on Germany in August and Ottoman Turkey joined the Central Powers in November, not only were the fault lines deepening within Europe but the conflict was spreading outside.

Over the ensuing months and years of deadlock, the barriers to peace rose higher. One reason why the story of the 1918 armistice is so compelling is that previous efforts to end the bloodshed had proved so fruitless. The essential problem was an interlocking triple stalemate in the conflict's military, domestic political, and diplomatic aspects, which not only barred all exits from the impasse but also drove the belligerents to intensified levels of violence.

The first element in the stalemate – and the one that ever since has seared the Western imagination – was military. Nothing in previous history was comparable to the 475 miles of earthworks that made up the Western Front. During 1915 trench stalemates also became established on the Gallipoli peninsula, where the Allies were attempting to reach Constantinople; along the Isonzo river, after Italy entered the war against Austria-Hungary; in Macedonia, after Allied forces landed at Salonika; and by the end of the year between Germany, Austria-Hungary, and Russia in Poland. On every front military technology disadvantaged the attacker. The introduction of the breech-loading rifle since the 1840s, the heavy machine gun since the 1880s, and the quick-firing recoilless field gun since the 1890s had revolutionized defensive firepower. Infantry ensconced in trenches and in dugouts, shielded by barbed wire, and fed by rail with reinforcements and munitions, were too strong for attacking forces to overcome without casualty rates that, sooner or later, halted them. Neither poison gas (first used on the Western Front in 1915) nor tanks (introduced in 1916) much altered the position. The core of the eventual solution was the intensive and intelligent use of far greater concentrations of artillery, but heavy guns and shells needed years to be manufactured in the requisite numbers, and tens of thousands of gunners had to learn the exacting art of operating their weapons. While the attackers refined their tactics, so did the defenders, whose positions in the most vulnerable sectors evolved from rudimentary ditches in 1914 into multiple lines stretching back for miles and incorporating thirty-foot-deep dugouts on the Somme in 1916 or hundreds of concrete pillboxes a year later at Ypres. It would be wrong, however, simply to equate the two sides. The French and the British Expeditionary Force (BEF) had to recapture occupied territory, and it was they who were usually on the offensive, normally with numerical superiority but inferior equipment and driving uphill without the benefit of surprise. The Italians – who had not lost territory but entered the war in order to gain it – were placed similarly, as, later, was the Allied Macedonian expedition.

The military stalemate was not just technological. It also reflected the distribution of forces between the different theatres, and the two sides' strategies. During 1915 Allied efforts were poorly co-ordinated, Britain's biggest operation being directed against Turkey at Gallipoli while the French suffered nearly half a million further casualties in offensives in Champagne and Artois. Early in the year Austria-Hungary was in desperate straits, but by the time Italy intervened in May the Germans had sent reinforcements to the Eastern Front and relieved the pressure on their partner by forcing the Russians back. For the rest of the year Germany's efforts remained concentrated in the east, where the Central Powers drove Russia out of Poland and Lithuania before overrunning Serbia and its ally Montenegro with help from Bulgaria (which joined the Central Powers in September), whereas the Allied forces that landed at Salonika in October failed to give Serbia much assistance. A pattern was emerging whereby the Russians almost invariably defeated the Austrians, but the Germans almost invariably defeated the Russians, yet were obliged to maintain a third of their army in Eastern Europe while being unable to compel the tsar to make peace. None the less, Russia appeared sufficiently weakened for the German CGS, Erich von Falkenhayn, to turn in February 1916 to the Western Front and to Verdun, where he launched a battle initially intended to commit only limited numbers of German infantry but to inflict such losses with his artillery that the French army would break.[13] The fighting proved much more evenly matched than he expected, and it was now the Central Powers' co-ordination that faltered, for Falkenhayn had not consulted the Austrians about Verdun and in May they launched an offensive of their own against the Italians in the Trentino. Not only did the Italians halt this attack, but to undertake it the Austrians had transferred their best forces from the Eastern Front, where in June the Russians unleashed against them the 'Brusilov offensive', named after the general who directed it. Half the Austro-Hungarian army on the Eastern Front became casualties (400,000 of them prisoners), and once again the Germans had to rush troops to the rescue.

After their 1915 setbacks the Allies too had reviewed their strategy, and at the Chantilly conference that December they agreed on synchronized attacks for summer 1916. The Brusilov offensive, brought forward to help the Italians, was the first, but was soon followed by the opening in July of an Anglo-French offensive on the Somme, in August by Romania joining the Allies and invading Hungary, and by attacks on the Isonzo and in Macedonia. For the first time in a year the Allies regained the strategic initiative, and they subjected the Central Powers to the severest pressure yet. Like Verdun, the Brusilov offensive – which lasted until October – and the Somme – which lasted until November – were the prototypes for a new kind of battle, measured not in days but in months, and claiming casualties in the hundreds of thousands. In the longer term, they helped cause both the Russian Revolution and American intervention, the events that would reshape the conflict. But, in the short term, neither offensive achieved what the Allies had hoped from them and until autumn 1918 the Allies mounted no comparably sustained effort.

This Allied failure resulted partly from a change of leadership in Berlin. In August 1916 the direction of the German army high command (OHL, or Oberste Heeresleitung) passed from Falkenhayn to Paul von Hindenburg as CGS and Erich Ludendorff as First Quartermaster-General. The new team shut down operations at Verdun, adopted more flexible defensive tactics, took command powers over the Austro-Hungarian army, and marshalled forces to defeat and overrun much of Romania. Early in 1917 they withdrew to a new and shorter set of defences in the west, the central portion of which received the characteristically Wagnerian appellation of the 'Siegfried Position' (although dubbed by the Allies the Hindenburg Line). On the Somme the German army was sorely tested, but its commanders remained confident it could handle the situation.[14] Undeterred, at a second Chantilly conference in November 1916 the Allied generals planned to renew their co-ordinated offensives as early in the new year as the weather permitted, but instead in spring 1917 they suffered a succession of disasters and the squeeze relaxed its grip.

First among these disasters was revolution in Russia, where Nicholas II was overthrown in March. His successor, the Russian Provisional

Government, delayed until June before delivering its offensive, which the Central Powers quickly halted before counter-attacking. In the west the Allies still went ahead in April. The British preliminary assault at the Battle of Arras displayed undeniable tactical improvements, but after a spectacular start it ground to a halt: and the main French attack against the Chemin des Dames ridge, usually known as the Nivelle offensive after the new French commander, Robert Nivelle, was a debacle from its opening morning. This was one disappointment too many, and in summer 1917 not only the Russian but also the French army was paralysed by mutiny. Moreover, for the duration of the spring campaign the Allied governments had placed the British commander on the Western Front, Sir Douglas Haig, under Nivelle's authority, and this first experiment with a supreme command now terminated. For the rest of the year the Allies reverted to the 1915 pattern of going their separate ways.

One element in the stalemate of the central period of the war was therefore that neither side could win a decisive military success. A second was that both could draw on enormous quantities of manpower and equipment. Although the Allies exceeded the Central Powers in population and in industrial potential, the German army's superior effectiveness (and that of the Austrian army over the Italians) for long cancelled out this advantage. One reason why the military position altered in summer 1916 was that by then the Allies had completed a long-term build-up, during which the British and Italian armies grew rapidly and the Russian army was re-equipped. But, though impressive, the achievement was insufficient, and the strain on the Allies' home economies contributed to their ensuing setbacks.

Even in 1914 the European armies were several times bigger than in nineteenth-century wars. By 1916 they were bigger still and much better provided with the basic panoply of rifles, machine guns, field guns, and shells, as well as with more sophisticated devices such as gas, heavy guns, and aircraft. Borrowing largely paid for this accomplishment. No belligerent covered more than a fraction of the cost of war by taxation; and most of the borrowing came in the form of short- and long-term bonds bought by the home population, although additionally the Central Powers imported on credit from the European neutrals and the Allies from the US. In response to the 'shell shortages' from which all the belligerents suffered in 1914–15, war ministries used the proceeds from the bonds to enlarge the capacity of the state arsenals and to convert the civilian engineering and chemical industries to weapons production. Extra workers were recruited among women and juveniles, soldiers were released from the armies, and every country registered extraordinary output increases. Almost equally impressive was the continuing supply of military manpower, achieved by conscripting able-bodied young men who before the war had been exempted; by calling up eighteen-year-olds as they came of age; and by sending up to three quarters of the wounded back to the front. Training, for both officers and men, was more perfunctory than in peacetime, and if the 1916 armies were bigger than those of 1914 the officers in charge of them judged their quality to be lower. Moreover, the armed forces' require-ments had to be balanced against those of the war industries and against civilian production, especially of food. The longer the war went on, the harder it became to square the circle, and the consequences of neglect-ing agriculture graver. None the less, the Allies' underlying advantages were becoming more manifest. While their navies sealed off the Central Powers, Britain and France recruited additional manpower from their empires and commodities from across the globe for as long as they could muster foreign exchange and shipping to purchase and transport them. By October 1916 Allied trade with the United States had quadru-pled since war began, and 40 per cent of the British government's purchases for its war effort were made in North America.[15] On the Somme the German army for the first time faced better-armed oppo-nents, and another of Hindenburg and Ludendorff's innovations was the 'Hindenburg Programme' for a crash acceleration in weapons pro-duction, which in the bitter winter of 1916–17 proved too ambitious for the German economy to deliver. Yet simultaneously the Allies were nearing the limits of their capacity to finance dollar purchases, while Nicholas II's armaments drive set off a disastrous spiral of inflation and overtaxed Russia's railways. The consequent shortfall in urban food deliveries triggered the strikes and demonstrations which, when the Petrograd garrison went over to the protestors, brought down the tsar-ist regime.

Even so, from today's perspective – in a world incomparably less tolerant of casualties – it remains astonishing how weak were protest movements in the belligerents, and how united were both politicians and public opinion in supporting the war effort. This unity was a fur-ther powerful factor perpetuating the carnage. It helped that for the first half of the war civilian living standards held up reasonably well. After initial dislocation, full employment returned to the towns, farmers enjoyed rising prices for their produce, and families with absent bread-winners received subsistence allowances. In addition, repression played a role: in Austria and for much of the time in Russia parliament was suspended, and everywhere elections ceased, the press was censored, and governments took decree powers. But Britain, France, and Germany, at least, were free enough for it to be as clear as possible (in the absence of opinion polls) that the national cause had widespread backing. The war effort could not have functioned without the willingness of millions of citizens to assist it, by working in farms and factories and running charitable organizations; while in the United Kingdom 2.4 million young men had volunteered for military service by 1916.[16]

Many factors that had encouraged the initial pro-war consensus continued to operate. French soil remained invaded, the British still highlighted Belgium in their propaganda, and the German government still argued, with diminishing persuasiveness, that it was fighting defensively. Nor did civilians yet resign themselves to a prolonged conflict: on the contrary, much evidence suggests that even after 1914 they still looked to an outcome within a matter of months.[17] Fundamental too was that both sides still had reason to believe in victory, the Central Powers because most of the campaigning went in their favour, and the Allies because of their greater resources. New developments strengthened the evidence that the enemy were barbarians: U-boat warfare, Zeppelin raids on London and Paris, and Germany's use of poison gas; but also the tightening of the Allied blockade, which targeted civilians by denying food and medical supplies. Germany's ally, Ottoman Turkey, went even further, with the attempted genocide of its Armenian population in summer 1915.[18] On both sides, churchmen and intellectuals disseminated ideological justifications for carrying on: Germany was championing heroic spiritual values against decadent liberalism and materialism, while the Allies were upholding law and justice against brutish militarism.[19] As the casualty lists lengthened and few families remained unscathed, it became harder still for governments to call a halt until they could demonstrate that the sacrifice had been worthwhile. For all these reasons, the political truces established between the political parties held firm, and until 1917 the likelihood of any country being forced to stop by revolution or by domestic unrest remained small. Cabinet reshuffles in France and Italy broadened the bases of their governments, and the new coalition ministry formed in London in December 1916 under David Lloyd George was determined to rule more decisively and mobilize the home economy more drastically while rejecting talk of compromise.

If the war could not be ended by military breakthrough or by revolution, nor could it be ended by negotiation. On the contrary, its ripples spread as wider circles of belligerents entered, and the incompatibility between the two sides' objectives deepened. Austria-Hungary's war aims, as defined in early 1916, included dominating the Western Balkans by partitioning Serbia, but in order to avoid absorbing still larger disaffected minorities the Dual Monarchy envisaged only limited annexations. Similarly, the Germans wanted only small territorial acquisitions within Europe but to secure their territory by means of buffer states on their western and eastern borders. Luxemburg would be annexed, as would the Longwy–Briey iron ore basin lying across the French frontier, and the transport hub of Liège. But Germany would control the rest of Belgium indirectly, by stationing garrisons in the country's cities, running its railways, forming a customs union, establishing naval bases on the Flanders coast, and encouraging Flemish separatism. In the east, Poland held an analogous position: the Austrians hoped to bring it under Habsburg sovereignty, but in November 1916 they agreed that the formally Russian-controlled part of Poland (now under Austro-German occupation) would become nominally independent. In reality Germany would control its foreign policy and railways, and annex 'frontier strips' on its northern and western borders, which Germans would resettle. The Germans developed similar plans for indirect control of Lithuania and Courland, and by 1917 they also hoped to separate the Ukraine from Russia and convert it into a German satellite. In addition they wanted a Central European customs union, an enormous (and mineral-rich) colony stretching from coast to coast in Central Africa, and a worldwide system of naval bases, although these overseas goals' prerequisite was a crushing victory over Britain that never seemed probable and even the Continental plans for buffer states within Europe caused much disagreement. Chancellor Bethmann Hollweg was willing to compromise in order to split the enemy by reaching a separate peace with one or other of the Allies. But the Hindenburg–Ludendorff duo opposed concessions that they feared would compromise the core objective of safeguarding Germany's future, and Wilhelm was sufficiently afraid of his commanders to jettison both Bethmann and other officials whom the OHL deemed too soft. A negotiated peace therefore had little prospect while Hindenburg and Ludendorff believed victory was possible; and the other Central Powers' war aims depended on German success.[20]

A second obstacle to negotiation was that the Allies had no intention of being split and soon acquired war aims of their own. The Russians were first off the mark, their key objective within Europe being to unite the Polish-inhabited areas under German, Austro-Hungarian, and Russian rule into a single kingdom under the Romanov sceptre. In December 1914 the French government publicly vowed not to end the war until it had regained Alsace-Lorraine, and early in 1917 it secretly decided to demand not only the lost provinces but also the adjoining Saar coalfield, agreeing with Nicholas II to detach the west bank of the Rhine from Germany and reorganize the region as a system of buffer states.[21] The French withheld these objectives from the British, whose own deliberations proceeded more slowly. The British were committed to restoring Belgium's independence and integrity; in addition, ministers assumed that Germany would lose most of its navy and colonies, and by the end of 1916 Allied forces had overrun the latter, except for part of German East Africa. But during the war the British Cabinet never established a position on Germany's European frontiers, and although Lloyd George and others believed a democratic Germany would be less aggressive they never made one an unconditional goal.[22]

The barriers to compromise were formidable. Britain and Germany were polarized over Belgium and the German colonies; France and Germany over Alsace-Lorraine and the Rhineland; and Russia and the Central Powers over Poland. The territorial issues mattered for economic and strategic reasons but also because of the prestige invested in them, in a struggle costing millions of lives. But in the first half of the war peace feelers were hardly very sustained anyway. The most important public exchanges took place in December 1916, when the Central Powers declared their willingness to negotiate and the American President, Woodrow Wilson, called on both sides to state their war aims, but the Allies were confident about their prospects in spring 1917 and they rejected the enemy proposal, which they rightly suspected had primarily a public relations purpose. Even from the misleading war aims statements that the two sides sent to Washington, it was clear that they stood far apart.

In addition, both coalitions had expanded and further claimants had joined them. A series of parallel wars flared up, as new participants sought to profit from the conflict. The first extension was into East Asia, where Japan declared war on Germany on 23 August 1914. Although the Japanese had been allied to Britain since 1902 and were responding to a British request for naval assistance, their interest was in overrunning Germany's island colonies in the North Pacific and its leased territory of Qingdao in China, and by the end of the year they had done so. From then on they helped their partners little.

The second extension was into the Middle East, after the Ottoman Empire joined the Central Powers in November 1914. Fighting spread to the Caucasus, to Mesopotamia (present-day Iraq), to Egypt and Palestine, to the Dardanelles, and to the Arabian peninsula. Although the Constantinople government was headed by a Grand Vizier appointed by the Sultan, it had been controlled since 1913 by the leaders of the Young Turk party, organized in the Committee of Union and Progress, or CUP, who favoured modernizing, authoritarian, and, increasingly, Turkish nationalist policies to arrest the empire's centuries-old decay. Their primary fear was of their traditional enemy, Russia, and they saw allying with Germany as their best chance of safety. But in addition they hoped to recapture territory lost to Russia in the Caucasus and to challenge British control of the Suez Canal.[23]

In practice the Turks had to fight mainly defensively, though at first with considerable success, as in 1915 they repelled the Allies' efforts to capture Constantinople by landing on the Gallipoli peninsula, and at Kut-al-Amara in 1916 they surrounded and captured a British expedition sent against Baghdad. Their entry diverted Russian and British forces towards the Middle East and prompted a major expansion of Allied war aims. While the Germans bound themselves in 1916 to fight as long as necessary to preserve the Ottoman Empire's integrity, the Russian government in spring 1915 extracted from Britain and France a secret promise that it could annex Constantinople and the shores of the Bosphorus and the Dardanelles, and this 'Straits agreement' led on to a series of partition arrangements. Most notorious was the Anglo-French Sykes–Picot Agreement of 1916, which envisaged British control of much of Mesopotamia, French control of Syria and the Lebanon, and most of Palestine coming under an international regime. It was difficult to reconcile this with the British undertakings in the 'McMahon–Hussein correspondence' to Sharif Hussein of Mecca, who in June 1916 launched the Arab Revolt in return for sweeping but ambiguous promises of independence for the Arab lands under Turkish rule. None the less, the Allies were now agreed on breaking up the Ottoman Empire in Asia, whereas the Germans hoped at least to preserve that dominion and the Turks themselves hoped for aggrandisement.

The third extension was into Mediterranean Europe, where Italy declared war on Austria-Hungary in May 1915 (and on Germany in 1916) following its secret Treaty of London with the Allies in April. The treaty promised the Italians not only the Italian-speaking areas under Habsburg rule, but also the German-speaking South Tyrol (which would provide a strategic frontier on the Brenner Pass), and Slovene- and Croatian-speaking lands in Istria and Dalmatia (which would enable Italy to dominate both shores of the Adriatic). The Italian government therefore wanted more than could be justified by self-determination and was patently attacking an opponent that had no interest in Italian territory, wanted to avoid war, and tried to buy it off. In good measure for these reasons, public support for the war in Italy was weak. The government hoped for a quick victory while the Austrians were under pressure in Eastern Europe, but it botched its timing. A new stalemated fighting front was formed, from Lake Garda to the river Isonzo, and between June 1915 and September 1917 eleven Battles of the Isonzo cost the Italians hundreds of thousands of casualties for an advance of barely twenty miles.

Finally, through stages, the campaigning in the Balkans also widened. In September 1915 Bulgaria, the loser in the 1913 Balkan War, accepted Austro-German promises of Serbian territory. It joined the Central Powers and took part in the joint campaign that overran Serbia and Montenegro. The Allies countered by landing at Salonika, at the invitation of a Greek government headed by Eleutherios Venizelos that was almost immediately replaced by another committed to staying neutral, a commitment shared by Greece's King Constantine. But the Salonika troops remained (and increasingly the Allies intervened in Greek domestic politics), and another stalemate opened up in Macedonia, where French, British, Italian, and Russian units (accompanied by the Serbian remnants) faced mainly Bulgarian forces, backed up by Germans and

Austrians. Although the Allies attacked in summer 1916 and spring 1917, they made little headway. Moreover, when Romania joined them in August 1916 (having been promised the Romanian-speaking area in Transylvania from Austria-Hungary), it too was overwhelmed by a German, Austrian, Bulgarian, and Turkish invasion. Only the north of the country remained unoccupied, and the Romanian front became an appendage to the Russian one. In June 1917 Greece joined the Allies after Constantine abdicated and Venizelos returned to office, but militarily the Balkans now quietened down.

The Allies had distributed undertakings to Japan, Italy, Serbia, Romania, and the Arabs; the Central Powers to Bulgaria and Turkey. These pledges further magnified the difficulty of restoring peace. Their implications were dwarfed, however, in April 1917 by those of American intervention, which along with the Russian Revolution in March marked the most important turning point since the Western Front had bogged down. The timing of American entry was determined by developments at sea, where each side was trying to debar the other from access to supplies. In March 1915 the Allies had declared a total blockade, applying to imports not just of military goods but also of food and medicine, and their fleets could clear the Central Powers' shipping from most of the world's sea lanes. However, Germany still imported Swedish iron ore and Dutch and Danish foodstuffs, and down to 1916 the blockade was in practice far from hermetic, although conversely the Austro-Hungarian and German navies presented little challenge to Allied command of the oceans. Partly this was for technological reasons: since the late nineteenth century mines, submarines, and torpedoes had become increasingly dangerous to warships that if sunk might take years to replace. Wilhelm II had built Germany's High Seas Fleet as much to apply political leverage to Britain as actually to destroy the Royal Navy, and he intended to preserve it for that purpose at the peace conference. The decryption unit in Room 40 of the London Admiralty building could read enemy wireless messages and warn when the Germans put to sea, but Sir John Jellicoe, the commander of the British Grand Fleet, had little incentive to risk his vessels when the status quo already favoured him. Hence during the entire war the British and German main battle fleets came within firing range only for a few minutes during the Battle of Jutland on 31 May 1916. And even though the Germans' marksmanship at Jutland inflicted losses on the British almost twice as heavy as their own, the High Seas Fleet commander, Reinhard Scheer, judged that he had had a narrow escape, and that submarine warfare offered better prospects of breaking Allied dominance.

Jutland was therefore one reason for the German leaders' resolution at the Pless Conference on 9 January 1917 to inaugurate from 1 February an unrestricted submarine warfare campaign. In a 'prohibited region' around the British Isles and Western France anything afloat – belligerent or neutral, warship, freighter, or passenger liner – was liable to be torpedoed without warning. The Germans had already experimented with an unrestricted campaign in 1915, but until now two factors had held them back. First, they had too few U-boats (and only a third were likely to be patrolling at any one time), carrying as few as four torpedoes each. Second, after the torpedoing in May 1915 of the British passenger liner the *Lusitania* – with 1,198 dead, 128 of them American – President Wilson had reacted far more rigorously than he did against the Allied blockade. During months of confrontation Wilson demanded that the U-boats should stick to 'cruiser rules' – i.e. first surfacing and giving warning to their victims, even though doing so made the submarines more vulnerable – and eventually threatened to break off diplomatic relations. Bethmann Hollweg, who feared war with America, bowed to Wilson's demands, but after Jutland the navy lobbied for unrestricted warfare to resume. By now it had built more U-boats and professed that it could force the British to surrender within five months; US intervention was expected but the submarines would sink any American troop transports and British surrender would make America irrelevant. The admirals enjoyed backing from a majority of the Reichstag and from Hindenburg and Ludendorff, who wanted to sever American supplies before the spring 1917 Allied offensives. Wilhelm II also tilted towards the hawks, and Bethmann, isolated, acquiesced. Yet if the Germans had been in less of a hurry, and had continued operating under cruiser rules with an expanded submarine fleet, they could still have inflicted heavy losses and it is reasonable to assume that the Russian Revolution and the 1917 French army mutinies would have happened anyway. And although for four months the results matched the navy's predictions, the U-boats were unable to sustain an all-out effort for longer, and after May the British introduced the convoy system and sinkings declined. The supreme crisis in the naval war came a year earlier than on land, and by the end of 1917 Lloyd George believed the greatest danger from the U-boats had passed.[24] Following Germany's calamitous error in starting the war in the first place, the Pless decision deprived it of its greatest opportunity to extricate itself on favourable terms.

Wilson saw no alternative but to follow through and break off relations, which he did in February 1917. As American merchantmen went down, he further felt obliged to arm them and to crew them with navy personnel, which implied a shooting war with Germany on the high seas. Yet he hesitated to recommend to Congress a declaration of hostilities, and could not contemplate doing so until the British intercepted, decrypted, and disclosed to him the 'Zimmermann Telegram' to the Mexican President from the German foreign minister, which proposed an anti-American alliance of Germany, Mexico, and Japan. The firestorm after Wilson authorized the telegram's publication meant that for the first time he could go to Congress in the expectation that it would vote for war. He decided to do so, however, not only because he believed the public would support him but also because he believed the Allies were nearing victory, and he and his advisers hoped that in return for sending a modest expeditionary force to Europe and for extending naval and financial assistance the US could attend the peace conference as an equal. Wilson believed it was in America's interest to combat German militarism – and he hoped for German democratization, though like Lloyd George he never made it an unconditional demand – but he also diagnosed the war as emanating from a balance-of-power system whose secret diplomacy and arms races appalled him. Already during the neutrality period he had decided that international politics must be restructured and had declared his backing for a League of Nations, which he hoped America would join. The precondition for its success was not only to defeat the Germans but also to restrain the Allies, whose demands, he feared, would simply breed another conflict. Hence, on entering, the United States styled itself as an 'Associated Power', neither signing the 1914 Pact of London nor undertaking to make no separate peace, and Washington distanced itself from the inter-Allied war aims agreements.

Without American intervention it is difficult to see the Allies managing better than an unfavourable draw. But it also threatened to obstruct them in the event of victory, the more so because it followed the revolution in Russia. The formation of the Provisional Government in

Petrograd, composed of liberals and moderate socialists, enabled the Allies to portray the war as a crusade of democracies against autocracies. But the revolution also broke the back of their intended spring 1917 offensive, and the Provisional Government was in rivalry with the Petrograd Soviet, or Council of Soldiers' and Workers' Deputies, whose call for 'a peace without annexations or indemnities' had wide resonance. The revolution inspired the Left across Europe, and radicalized the socialist parties and trade union leaderships who had supported the war effort. As it also coincided with accelerated inflation and pressure on living standards, the spring and summer saw the biggest strikes and protests since the war had begun. In France a growing 'minority' tendency within the Socialist Party (Section française de l'Internationale ouvrière, or SFIO) opposed participation in government. In Germany the SPD expelled its 'minority', which formed an independent party (the USPD) and demanded a compromise peace.

Much of the revival of domestic controversy revolved around war aims, and two episodes highlighted them. One was the 'Peace Resolution' passed on 19 July by a new majority in the Reichstag comprising the SPD, the Centre, and the two liberal parties. Although its wording was ambiguous, it appeared to repudiate annexations and indemnities. Hindenburg and Ludendorff were incensed and insisted on Bethmann Hollweg's removal, and Bethmann's successor, Georg Michaelis, was an OHL nominee who accepted the resolution only 'as I understand it'.[25] The second episode was an invitation to all socialist parties to send representatives to a conference at Stockholm, which the German and Austro-Hungarian governments were willing to let their socialists attend. The Russian government supported the initiative, but the Allied governments blocked it by refusing passports. Because of the controversy the SFIO withdrew from participation in the French government, and the Labour Party chairman, Arthur Henderson, left Lloyd George's Cabinet in Britain, although another Labour representative replaced him.

By summer 1917 public opinion had become more war-weary and the Allies' strategy of co-ordinated offensives had been jettisoned, while the U-boats had failed to starve Britain out. The auspices seemed favourable for what became the most sustained peace feelers of the war, but uniformly the contacts proved abortive. Soundings began with the new Austrian Emperor, Karl, who succeeded Franz Joseph in November

1916. He used his brother-in-law, Prince Sixte de Bourbon, to contact the French, without telling the Germans what he was doing, and on 24 March 1917 he rashly sent a letter supporting France's 'just claims' to Alsace-Lorraine.[26] Karl disliked the Germans and found them overbearing, whereas he had no direct quarrel with France and Britain, who were not yet committed to breaking Austria-Hungary up. They did hope, however, to lure it into a separate peace, and felt bound by the pledges to transfer Austrian territory that they had made to Italy. As Karl felt too weak to make a separate peace, and ruled out cessions to the Italians, the exchanges led nowhere. Simultaneous Russian feelers to Germany encountered similar barriers: the Provisional Government refused to detach itself from its partners, and as the Germans wanted it to abandon Poland and the Baltic littoral it had little incentive to do so.

In the autumn, in contrast, the Germans themselves approached France and Britain. The impetus came from Michaelis's new foreign minister, Richard von Kühlmann. Kühlmann proceeded with a feeler that had started before he took over, extended via Belgian intermediaries to the ex-French Premier, Aristide Briand. Briand was willing to meet in Switzerland with a German official, the Baron Oscar von der Lancken-Wakenitz, and supposed Alsace-Lorraine was on offer, but in fact the Germans were willing to cede at most a few frontier villages. The French government divined that the real purpose was to part France from its allies and vetoed a meeting. But Kühlmann placed most hope in London, whence he received encouragement after Pope Benedict XV on 1 August appealed to all sides to return to the pre-1914 status quo. The British response to Benedict invited Germany to clarify its intentions over Belgium, and in a conference at Schloss Bellevue on 11 September the German leaders temporarily waived their demands for Flanders naval bases, although Hindenburg and Ludendorff still wanted to subordinate the country in other respects. A message sent via a Spanish diplomat, the Marquis de Villalobar, indicated that Kühlmann was willing to talk, and the Cabinet hesitated. Lloyd George was willing to acquiesce in German expansion in Russia but his colleagues were not, and the British consulted their partners, who opposed further contact.

Although both sides were willing to moderate their objectives, their differences remained unbridgeable. Germany would relinquish neither Belgium nor Alsace-Lorraine; Italy upheld its demands on Austria. Each coalition was trying to split its opponents rather then seek a general settlement. Despite the shift in public opinion, governments were emollient or evasive in their declarations about war aims rather than diluting their substance. Nor had either side abandoned hope of winning. Russia's upheavals would allow the Central Powers to transfer forces from the east, while France and Britain could look to victory with American aid. The latter calculation was explicit in Paris and in London, and it assumed both that American intervention gave them the long-term advantage and that they could still achieve their war aims, despite Wilson's refusal to endorse them. Moreover, the President and his advisers believed it was against America's interest to halt the fighting while the Germans had the upper hand, and he both refused Stockholm passports for the American socialists and rebuffed the Pope's peace note, thus setting his sails against compromise. He did so believing that continuing the war would make the European Allies more dependent on him, and augment his leverage over both camps. It was therefore very much as a gamble in imponderable circumstances that the French and British governments rejected Kühlmann's blandishments and carried on. But their decision was confirmed when the French government of Paul Painlevé resigned in November and President Raymond Poincaré picked as his successor not Joseph Caillaux, who was suspected of favouring negotiations, but Georges Clemenceau, who was committed to pursuing the war.

Although the Allies rejected peace approaches, it remained unclear how they were ever going to prevail. Three shocks underlined the point: at Caporetto, in Petrograd, and at Cambrai. During summer 1917 the Italians launched the tenth and eleventh battles of the Isonzo, and the latter, during which the attackers overran the Bainsizza plateau, pressed the Austrians harder than ever. Karl requested – and belatedly received – German assistance, seven divisions being transported and a special Fourteenth Army formed under General Otto von Below, composed equally of German and Austrian units: in the early hours of 24 October it fell upon the Italian Second Army in the Caporetto sector of the middle Isonzo valley. The Italian high command (Comando supremo – CS) had suspended its attacks and its infantry supposed the campaigning season was over; the CS knew about the German reinforcements and received several days' warning, but did remarkably little to prepare. When the blow fell its impact was overwhelming. The bombardment, using poison gas against which Italian masks were useless, killed thousands before the German infantry infiltrated along the valley floors, isolating and surrounding the garrisons on the heights: some 40,000 Italians were killed and wounded but 265,000 surrendered while 400,000 'disbanded' soldiers (*sbandati*) abandoned their units and streamed to the rear. The Second Army's implosion forced the adjoining Third and Fourth Armies to retreat as well, and territory that had taken two and a half years to conquer was lost in as many days, the attackers advancing up to fifty miles and crossing the Isonzo and Tagliamento before halting in early November on the Piave. Along this river the CS had been preparing defences since earlier in the year, and although the attackers forded it, they were driven back. As important as Italian resistance, however, were the victors' limitations. The OHL had intended this to be a restricted operation, and had transferred fewer than half the divisions that the Austrians wanted. The breakthrough opened up a war of movement for which the Central Powers were ill equipped, and in the absence of an agreed plan of advance or command structure they jostled for space, lacking enough lorries and horses to maintain progress.

All the same, the blow to the Italians and their partners was severe.[27] British ministers noted morosely that yet another ally had been rendered hors de combat, and a hastily summoned conference at Rapallo agreed to send reinforcements that soon totalled five British and six French divisions. The Allies insisted on the Italian commander, Luigi Cadorna, being sacked, and the new ministry of Vittorio Orlando was eager to do so anyway, replacing Cadorna by Armando Diaz with Pietro Badoglio as his deputy.[28] The Premier told Diaz that the Piave line must be held 'at all costs', and in fact during the rest of the year the Italian army rallied, and the Central Powers failed to break through in the Asiago and Monte Grappa sectors on its northern flank.[29] While the British and French deployed in Lombardy, the Italian army halted the enemy unaided, fighting at extraordinary altitudes in temperatures that at night plunged far below zero. Yet, although the Italians regained their ability to fight defensively, Germany had taken the pressure off the Austrians and no further big Italian offensive took place until the war's final month.[30]

The second shock came in the east. During 1917 Hindenburg and Ludendorff waited for the Russian army to disintegrate, using propaganda and fraternization to accelerate the process. Their counter-attack after the Russian summer offensive cleared Austrian territory, and subsequently they focused on the Baltic coast, where on 1 September they captured Riga. Like Caporetto, the Battle of Riga was notable – and remarked upon by Allied staffs – for innovative artillery and infantry tactics that in 1918 would be adopted on a grander scale. It struck at a neuralgic point on the approaches to Petrograd, and it contributed, as intended, to Russia's political radicalization. The Provisional Government had neither improved economic conditions nor ended the war, and an opportunity had opened for Lenin and the Bolsheviks as the one major Russian grouping that demanded an immediate peace. Although the Germans subsidized Lenin's party and had organized his return from exile in Zurich, he advocated seizing power on the grounds that conditions in Germany were auspicious for revolution to spread there. But neither did he hold allegiance to the Allies, and positioning the Bolsheviks as the one party willing to break with them both benefited him politically and conformed with his analysis of the war as an imperialist enterprise in which the proletariat had no stake. In September the Bolsheviks gained a majority in the Petrograd Soviet, and under the banner of demanding all power to the soviets they could now justify overthrowing the Provisional Government before it abandoned the capital. Once the government started preparations against them, they took over Petrograd with the support of its garrison on 7–8 November. On 15 December a ceasefire with the Central Powers duly ensued. While what remained of the Russian army drifted home, Romania, now isolated, also signed an armistice.

The Bolshevik Revolution was fundamental to the 1918 political and military landscape. From November 1917 the OHL was moving divisions westwards, at the same time as negotiations with the Russians began at Brest-Litovsk. Germany and Austria-Hungary deepened the rift between Lenin and the Allies by joining the Bolsheviks in paying lip-service to the principle of national self-determination, while the Russians embarrassed their former partners by publishing the secret treaties concluded with Nicholas II to carve up the Middle East, cede Austrian territory to Italy, and consign the Rhineland to French domination. Yet it soon became clear that the Central Powers planned to use the slogan of self-determination as a cover for expansion by depriving Russia of Poland, its southern Baltic provinces, and the Ukraine, and converting them into satellite states. In his Fourteen Points address on 8 January Woodrow Wilson appealed to the Russians and to the European Left by unilaterally proclaiming a more moderate and progressive programme of Allied and American war aims, and in the weeks that followed anti-war strikes rocked Vienna and Berlin. It was in vain. Hindenburg and Ludendorff had lost patience and at the Bad Homburg Crown Council on 13 February they insisted on imposing peace by renewing the advance on Petrograd. The Russians were incapable of resistance, and Lenin carried the Bolshevik Central Committee in favour of an arrangement – the Brest-Litovsk peace treaty – that he intended to honour no longer than he had to but which kept his regime in power and took Russia out of the war. The treaty also hardened the OHL's resolve to take the offensive in the west: the final fateful error that made possible an Allied victory far earlier than had seemed plausible in the winter of 1917–18.

For down to that winter the stasis on the Western Front had continued, despite indications that the advantage enjoyed by the defensive was slipping. Although the French army was now recuperating from the mutinies, Nivelle's successor, Philippe Pétain, had renounced all-out assaults and sought to reaccustom his forces to attacking by deploying colossal firepower to gain limited objectives. At La Malmaison on 23–25 October the French advanced six kilometres and captured the heights of the Chemin des Dames, where they had failed in April, but at a formidable cost in materiel.[31] Over thirty-two days before the attack 266 trains moved up 80,000 tons of munitions, the weight of shell per kilometre exceeding by six or seven times that in the September 1915 French offensive and costing over 500 million francs – twice the total for all French tank construction during the war.[32] A similar siege-warfare operation was conducted by the British Second Army under Sir Herbert Plumer in the Battle of Messines Ridge between 7 and 12 June, the attackers exploding nineteen enormous mines that their sappers had been digging since 1915 and firing twice as many shells as before the first day on the Somme. Although they captured the ridge and for once suffered fewer casualties than the defenders, this operation too entailed an expenditure of resources quite disproportionate to the territory gained.

The problem of how the Allies could win was posed still more emphatically by the Third Battle of Ypres between 31 July and 10 November 1917, another attrition struggle (approved by Lloyd George's Cabinet with the greatest reluctance) in which the BEF advanced six miles into an angular salient that Haig acknowledged was scarcely defensible.[33]

Haig had argued that an attack here, in conjunction with a seaborne landing, could capture the main enemy lateral railway and clear the Belgian coast: in the event the Germans held him, as they had envisaged, on 'Flandern I', the third of their five defensive lines.[34] By now the British were both better equipped and tactically more proficient than on the Somme, and they fired six times more weight of ordnance than did the defenders,[35] but the latter too had changed their methods. The Germans' artillery bombarded the BEF from concealed positions on the Gheluvelt plateau, using newly developed mustard gas shells, and they held the bulk of their infantry well behind the front line, repeatedly retaking lost ground by prompt counter-attacks. During September the British paused for three weeks before trying again, Plumer and his staff taking over from the much criticized Fifth Army command under Sir Hubert Gough, and launching three more carefully planned assaults in drier weather. This time the Germans found it harder to cope and the OHL was rattled, garrisoning the forward lines more strongly in the Battle of Broodseinde on 4 October and losing thousands of men. But now the weather deteriorated, while Plumer left a shorter interval between his attacks and planned them less thoroughly, with the result that they again lost momentum. In the final phase predominantly Canadian forces under Sir Arthur Currie captured the Passchendaele ridge at the cost of 16,000 casualties, progressing methodically across a water-logged wilderness, but any chance of achieving the initial objectives had long since gone. Although both sides found the conditions intensely depressing and difficult, BEF morale suffered more, and the British took heavier casualties than the Germans with a smaller army.[36]

Nor did the final Western Front battle of 1917, at Cambrai between 20 November and 5 December, bring much encouragement. Six British divisions with 476 tanks (216 in the front line) achieved almost complete surprise when they attacked in a quiet sector supported by a bombardment from 1,000 guns without prior ranging shots: on the opening morning they opened a gap five miles wide. But more than half the tanks were hit or broke down on the first day, German reinforcements arrived rapidly, and the battle settled down into the usual pattern of repeated infantry attacks before the Germans in turn achieved surprise with a massive counterstroke that infiltrated the improvised British defences and recaptured most of the conquered territory. There was little confirmation here that enemy resistance was being worn down; or that even radically innovative tactics could win more than transient success, while the Germans were already pioneering new assault methods (which Haig's GHQ failed to recognize). Something had gone badly wrong, and the Cabinet sensed that the military had misled it.[37] After Cambrai, in Winston Churchill's words, 'A sudden sinister impression was sustained by the General Staff. The cry for a fresh offensive died away. The mood swung round to pure defence – and against heavy odds.'[38]

On 7 October Lloyd George had told the Cabinet Secretary, Maurice Hankey, that he feared another Flanders-style offensive in 1918. The British army must rest as the French one had done, to win as a part of a concerted effort in 1919, or else America rather than Britain would deliver the decisive blow.[39] Yet only in the following month did the first units of the American Expeditionary Force (AEF) enter the front line in Lorraine, and American strategy, as agreed between the AEF commander, John J. Pershing, and the War Department in Washington, envisaged a gradual build-up and a decisive advance north-eastwards in 1919. Pétain intended his principal 1918 effort for Alsace, to capture land desired by France in peace negotiations, in contrast to the more ambitious strategies co-ordinated with his allies in previous years, and Poincaré noted that French ministers agreed that 'one third of the Deputies ... desire peace, without daring to admit it'.[40] But Lloyd George too and many of his Cabinet, as well as the Chief of the Imperial General Staff, Sir William Robertson, now doubted whether a decisive victory over Germany was possible, at any rate at an acceptable cost or in the foreseeable future.[41] In spring 1917 they had determined to win control over Mesopotamia and Palestine, and reinforced British expeditions took Baghdad in March and Jerusalem in December. In parallel, in a gesture that undermined the international status for Palestine envisaged in the Sykes–Picot Agreement, the British in November issued the 'Balfour Declaration', an open letter by the Foreign Secretary supporting the establishment there of a Jewish 'national home'. For the new year, although Haig wanted to renew the attack in Flanders, the Cabinet favoured a further drive beyond Jerusalem: the Turkish war effort had passed its peak and the temptation was to concentrate on the Levant. In the key European battlegrounds, in contrast, no trend towards Allied superiority was evident, and little consensus about the appropriate strategy.

After Dunkirk in 1940 Churchill reminded the House of Commons that 'During the first four years of the last war the Allies experienced nothing but disaster and disappointment ... we repeatedly asked ourselves the question: How are we going to win?'[42] At the close of 1917 the Allies confronted a dilemma: further fighting on the Third Ypres model promised to cripple the British army as surely as it had crippled the French and Italian ones; yet progress such as at Messines and at La Malmaison, though preferable in the short term, on a larger scale would also be prohibitive. Diaz, in contrast, was preoccupied with how to repel another enemy offensive, and soon the Western Front commanders were obliged to follow him. Among the governments, the British was the most pessimistic, but French hopes rested largely on the Americans, and the Americans' hopes on a still untested confidence in their soldiers' combat superiority. Although merchant shipping losses were diminishing, they exceeded new building and the tonnage available to the Allies was still shrinking and appeared inadequate to the projected demands on it. Even the Allied war economies, on paper so superior, were experiencing one supply crisis after another, while during 1917 British, French, and Italian public opinion had all plumbed depths of despondency. The sustainability of the Allies' war effort in the longer term remained imponderable, whereas a short-run military victory appeared to face insuperable obstacles.[43] In sum, their immediate prospects were more difficult than at any time since spring 1916 and their exhausted troops now faced a terrifying onslaught. As it turned out, that onslaught would be the means of their salvation.

I

On the Defensive, March–July 1918

There are strategic attacks that have led directly to peace, but these are the minority. Most of them only lead up to the point where their remaining strength is just enough to maintain a defence and wait for peace. Beyond that point the scale turns and the reaction follows with a force that is usually much stronger than that of the original attack.

Carl von Clausewitz, *On War*, 528

For the Allies during 1917 almost every aspect of the fighting had gone badly. At the end of the year their leaders were unsure what sort of victory, if any, was obtainable, and were preparing for a long haul. Their forebodings proved unjustified because the Germans attacked. Between March and July 1918 the OHL launched five major Western Front offensives: the first (codenamed 'Michael'), from 21 March to 5 April; the Battle of the Lys ('Georgette') from 9 to 29 April; the Battle of the Chemin des Dames ('Blücher–Yorck') from 27 May to 4 June; the Battle of the Matz ('Gneisenau') from 9 to 14 June; and an assault east and west of Reims ('Marneschütz-Reims' or the 'Friedenssturm') from 15 to 17 July. Between 15 and 24 June the Austrians were on the attack in Italy (the Battle of the Piave), while in the east the Central Powers drove deep into former Russian territory. For much of the spring and summer the Allied leaders were anxious and even despondent, unable to retaliate against a rain of blows. Yet in the longer perspective the Central Powers failed. They neither captured vital territory nor broke their opponents' will, and so damaged themselves that once the Allies finally counterattacked they did so against beaten armies. The months before rather than after July 1918 determined the war's outcome.[1] The Allies' success on the defensive was the precondition for their success on the offensive, and would enable them to end the fighting on their terms.

Germany's assault in the west was therefore crucial. On other fronts the Central Powers were already on the offensive, but achieved more and at lower cost. In addition to the unrestricted submarine campaign, they had captured Riga and broken through at Caporetto. Yet Germany's previous bids for victory in the west – on the Marne and at Verdun – had been frustrated. Ludendorff acknowledged the intractability of the task and that despite the Allies' superior resources they had also failed in it. Although he had long envisaged a culminating Western Front offensive, as of September 1917 he still envisaged staying on the defensive in the spring, but in the following weeks he changed his mind and planning began.[2]

PREPARATIONS

German strategy for 1918 emerged from consultations between the OHL and the headquarters of the army groups and armies on the Western Front. Germany's allies had little involvement in the process; as too Wilhelm II and Chancellor Georg Hertling, although they approved the end-product. Yet Crown Prince Rupprecht of Bavaria, commanding the northern army group, and Crown Prince Wilhelm of Prussia, commanding the central one, were both unconvinced about an offensive, and their staff officers shared their scepticism. Ludendorff himself was the primary driver of the 'Michael' operation, and few others shared his viewpoint. He also provided the impetus in the central OHL relationship.

Paul von Beneckendorff und von Hindenburg had been born in 1847 as the son of an army lieutenant. Raised on a modest estate near Posen (now Poznán) in West Prussia, he went to cadet school at eleven and served with distinction in the Austro-Prussian and Franco-Prussian wars. He became a staff officer, married a general's daughter, and ended as a corps commander who reputedly angered Wilhelm II by besting him in annual manoeuvres. In 1911 he retired from a successful if far from high-flying career, only to return to duty three years later, first as the commander of the Eighth Army at Tannenberg, then as commander on the Eastern Front (in both cases with Ludendorff as his Chief of Staff), and finally as Chief of the Prussian General Staff and de facto commander-in-chief, with Ludendorff as his First Quartermaster-General. An ethic of service and of maintaining iron composure served him well during the vicissitudes of the war and in his dealings with Ludendorff, a man also from Posen but a generation younger, born to a poorer and non-aristocratic family in 1865. Erich Friedrich Wilhelm Ludendorff had likewise attended cadet school, but his subsequent professional progress was faster. Before the war he headed the second section in the General Staff but made so many enemies that in 1913 he was demoted to a provincial command. Wilhelm II disliked him, regarding him as uncouth and consumed by ambition, and until the war salvaged his reputation Ludendorff was under a cloud. Cold, tense, and humourless, he was given to nerves and rages, but was also a tireless organizer and relentless bureaucratic infighter.[3]

Once the duo took over the OHL, Hindenburg, who looked to his place in history, became the front man (though never merely that) while Ludendorff and his subordinates supplied ideas and energy and liaised with politicians, businessmen, and commanders. A stream of initiatives emanated from the new team, who – always on the justification of what was necessary for victory – extended their purview to the economy, public opinion management, and high politics. Because of Hindenburg's prestige as the victor of Tannenberg and the architect of Germany's triumphs in the east, who was brought to the OHL to save the situation in 1916, Wilhelm feared to confront him. Instead the Emperor succumbed to the duumvirate's resignation threats by jettisoning officials of whom they disapproved, Bethmann Hollweg among them.[4] Yet Ludendorff refused suggestions that he become Chancellor himself, and the OHL vetoed policies it disliked rather than taking over the government. This was a recipe for impasse and confusion, epitomized in an exchange of letters between Hindenburg and Chancellor Hertling in January 1918. Hertling insisted that the Chancellor alone was responsible for the current peace negotiations with the Bolsheviks: the OHL could advise on military aspects but in case of disagreement Wilhelm's decision was final. Hindenburg replied that 'military interests' could embrace not only relations with other states but also domestic politics, and he and Ludendorff were responsible to the German nation, to history, and to their own consciences for the shape of the peace. Even after Wilhelm endorsed a further memorandum from Hertling objecting to Hindenburg and Ludendorff's use of resignation threats, they continued to invoke them.[5]

In deciding for an offensive, Ludendorff was motivated not only by military considerations, but also by political ones. He dreaded revolution but opposed attempting to forestall it by democratization. In his view, not to win the war would be to lose it, not least because of the domestic blowback if there were nothing to show for measureless sacrifice. He told Rupprecht that Germany 'must either triumph or go under'.[6] Opting for an offensive meant rejecting a negotiated peace, although events suggested that a deal was anyway not on offer. After the failure of the Villalobar feeler to the British in September 1917, Hindenburg had withdrawn his willingness for concessions,[7] and the German civilians, too, hardened their line, Kühlmann declaring in the Reichstag that Germany could 'never' return Alsace-Lorraine.[8] When Woodrow Wilson set out an ostentatiously moderate peace programme in his Fourteen Points address the SPD was prepared to accept it as a basis for a settlement, but Hertling told a parliamentary committee that Wilson had shown little willingness for peace and that Germany's military position had never been more favourable. Similarly Wilhelm II wrote that the possibility of peace with London 'no longer exists! One must go under! And that is England', and he agreed to an offensive in order to impose German demands: 'First victory in the west with the collapse of the Entente, then we will make conditions that they must accept! And which will be tailored purely accordingly to our interest.'[9] By late January both Wilhelm and the government had approved the principle of an attack, with none of the agonizing or interrogation of the military that had preceded France's Nivelle offensive and Britain's Third Ypres campaign.[10]

The OHL had never felt much eagerness for a compromise, Prince Rupprecht recording Ludendorff's dread 'that the English would come forward with a peace offer that for domestic political reasons we would not be able to refuse'.[11] Instead, the OHL looked to safeguard Germany externally by territorial gains, to position it advantageously for the successor war that the military chiefs expected.[12] Ludendorff's Chief of Military Operations, Georg Wetzell, advised that rivalry with Britain, France, Russia, and America would continue, and 'we cannot come out of the peace strong enough'. Germany must hold the Ostend–Metz–Strasbourg line as a jumping-off ground 'for the probability of a decisive confrontation in the west', and control the Belgian railways so that it could invade France quickly and head off British reinforcements.[13] Hindenburg wanted years of military occupation of Belgium and permanent control of Liège to protect the Ruhr.[14] Revealing was Ludendorff's rejection of a memorandum from the liberal deputy Friedrich Naumann, who proposed a public commitment to restoring Belgium's independence, in order to undermine support in Britain for Lloyd George, to unify the German population and reduce the threat of revolution, and to prevent the war from stretching into 1919. Ludendorff responded that 'We do not have the choice between peace and war, as long as we strive for a secure and economically strong Fatherland': they must act. Belgium's future was indeed a touchstone, the German leaders objecting to relinquishing it or ceding territory to France, being determined to retain their eastern gains, and fearing an Allied economic boycott after the war.[15] On 7 January Hertling wrote to Hindenburg that if the offensive 'leads to the hoped for successful breakthroughs, we will thereby be in a position to pose those conditions for a peace with the Western Powers that will be needed to secure our frontiers, our economic interests, and our international position after the war'.[16] The Chancellor told the Reichstag that although Germany would not annex Belgium, it must have guarantees against the country becoming an enemy base: 'Our war aim from the start has been the defence of the Fatherland, the preservation of our territorial integrity and the freedom to develop economically in every direction. *Our grand strategy, even where it must proceed aggressively, is defensive in purpose.*'[17] In summary, Hindenburg told Wilhelm: 'to assure us the political and economic position that we need, we must strike the Western Powers'.[18] Possessing a wasting asset of military superiority, rather than negotiate it away Germany would use it.

By attacking, the OHL would abandon the 1917 strategy of remaining passive in the west and awaiting results from the U-boats. Although the navy promised important results in 1918, its submarines had neither halted American troop shipments nor forced Britain to surrender. According to Ludendorff's section chief, Max Bauer, if the Germans could advance along the Channel to Le Havre the U-boat campaign might yield definitive results by autumn 1918 or spring 1919.[19] But Ludendorff had reason to distrust the Admiralty's forecasts, and he assumed that time was against him: 'Only action brings success ... Therefore we will and must not wait until the Entente with American help feels strong enough to attack us ... The attack has always been the German manner of fighting. The German army ... looks forward to the prospect of escaping from trench warfare.'[20] And if at sea the prospects were uncertain, for Germany's allies they were poor indeed. Turkey, Ludendorff commented in retrospect, was loyal but exhausted; Bulgaria was inclined to a separate peace; and although Austria-Hungary could hold out against Italy, once its army was no longer willing to fight the Dual Monarchy would not carry on. Only hope of German victory held the Central Powers together.[21] Similarly, Hindenburg reflected afterwards that although he had considered fighting defensively in 1918, doing so would not have ended the war, and even if Germany could have carried on for longer, could its partners? The defensive spelled 'a gradual death by exhaustion': and he did not regret the gamble, as Germany's 'heroism' would aid its moral recovery from defeat. Moreover, although attacking in other theatres had its advocates (Rupprecht favoured another blow against Italy), the OHL never considered this alternative seriously. Bauer commented afterwards that driving the Allies from Salonika might merely have enabled Bulgaria to make its exit, while forcing Italy to surrender would have taken too long.[22]

The time factor mattered above all because of the Americans. The OHL considered them brave but poorly trained; yet it feared their numbers. Even though it failed to predict the massive US troop shipments in summer 1918, it foresaw that American deployments would tilt the balance back against the Central Powers.[23] In addition, although the defence had long enjoyed the advantage on the Western Front, that advantage was diminishing. The German army commanders and many of their troops were wearying of defensive fighting, and it was questionable whether Germany's defensive successes could continue: the battles of Broodseinde and La Malmaison had shaken the OHL, and that at Cambrai had taken it by surprise, even though it had retrieved the situation.[24] Conversely, returning to the offensive might now deliver results. Hindenburg started from his fundamental confidence in his army's superior effectiveness, which its recent victories served to bolster. In any case the offensive *had* to be attempted, as the alternative was surrender.[25]

However, firmer grounds existed for Hindenburg's confidence, including reinforcements from the east and a revolution in tactics. Hindenburg and Ludendorff knew that in the medium term they faced an insoluble manpower crisis,[26] but in the short term the numerical balance was favourable. In 1914 Germany had invaded Western Europe with fewer fighting troops than its opponents; in 1916 Falkenhayn had started the Verdun attack with just nine divisions; but on 21 March 1918 Ludendorff had eight times that number. Whereas on 1 November 1917 the German army on the Western Front numbered 3.25 million men, by 1 April 1918 it numbered over 4 million. In the interim the Germans had withdrawn from Italy, and the Ostheer (Eastern army) in Russia, the Balkans, and Turkey fell from about 2 million to 1.5 million.[27] In autumn 1917 the Ostheer had been at its strongest ever, but by March 1918 the divisions in the east had fallen from eighty-five to forty-seven while those in the west had risen from 147 to 191.[28] Most of the troops who would jump the parapet did *not* come from the east, but redeploying the transferred troops into quieter sectors enabled the OHL to amass its veterans into an immense strategic reserve that for Allied planners was the stuff of nightmares. As of 21 March the Allies had only 175 Western Front divisions, and although (because German divisions tended to be smaller) the two sides' total numbers were similar, the OHL would repeatedly amass big local superiorities at the attack points.[29]

The Germans benefited less from raw numerical superiority than from greater fighting efficiency. Even in equipment they lacked a clear advantage, although by autumn 1917 the Hindenburg Programme was finally achieving its targets and fulfilling their needs in the basic categories of rifles, machine guns, field artillery, mortars, and shells.[30] Heavy guns were slow and difficult to manufacture and had begun to run short during 1917, constituting a serious restriction. Aircraft were essential for artillery observation and the OHL planned to use them for ground attack, but although the German air force routinely inflicted much heavier losses than it suffered and could establish a local advantage, along the Western Front as a whole it was heavily outnumbered. Finally – and critically – the German army lacked mobility. It had two dozen tanks (the best being captured British models); in lorries it was outnumbered ten to one (and those it possessed were short of fuel and had iron instead of rubber tyres); finally, it was almost cripplingly short of horses, divisions by the end of March being typically 200–300 below strength.[31] The Germans had an impressive and intensively exploited railway system for strategic transfers such as those from Russia, but their weakness came in movement beyond the railhead. They were equipped to smash through Allied defences rather than manoeuvre in the open country beyond.

Ludendorff paid close attention to artillery and infantry tactics, which were vital to his hopes of success.[32] Of the two, the new artillery procedures were the more important and innovative. They were associated particularly with Colonel Georg Bruchmüller, an artillery officer with an unspectacular pre-war career who was on the retired list in 1914, but made his way up on the Eastern Front from local operations in 1915 to directing the artillery in the Battle of Riga. His methods aimed at regaining surprise by opening fire without prior 'registration' (ranging shots). Their objective was less to destroy the enemy positions (which repeated experience had shown was extraordinarily difficult, and that even the attempt so shattered the ground as to impede any advance) than to 'neutralize' them by suppressing resistance. Bruchmüller's system required centralized control and a uniform fire plan, the barrage being concentrated into a few hours and directed first to silencing the enemy's artillery by counter-battery fire (especially with gas shells, whose contents would sink into the gun pits) and to long-range heavy howitzer bombardments of the command posts, before turning to the forward positions, breaking up their protecting wire and stupefying the survivors. Finally, a creeping barrage (*Feuerwalze*) would, in theory, move ahead of the infantry through successive enemy positions, forcing the defenders to keep their heads down until the assailants were upon them. In November 1917 Bruchmüller and his staff moved to the Western Front, and the OHL insisted on the whole of the army adopting their methods, although the Western Front commanders objected to several (the guns being stationed as far forward as possible, non-persistent gases used in close support of the infantry, and medium and heavy as well as light artillery being employed for the creeping barrage). They also objected to the Pulkowsky Method, named after Captain Erich Pulkowsky, which entailed painstakingly calibrating the idiosyncrasies of a gun's firing trajectory by trials away from the line, so that when used in action it could target a map co-ordinate accurately without registration. As the OHL did not insist on the method's universal adoption, some units dispensed with it before 21 March and it became general only later.[33]

The new artillery practice formed part of the broader doctrine of offensive tactics embodied in the memorandum on 'The Attack in Position Warfare' issued by the OHL on 1 January 1918. This was the gospel of the German 'infiltration tactics', which have attracted much attention – arguably more than they deserve. They were not applied consistently in 1918, and the Allies' new defensive system based on forward strongpoints was easier to penetrate than were continuous lines: their later counter-tactics of defence in depth proved an adequate answer to the German methods. None the less, the German doctrines distilled experience gleaned from operations since Verdun, including Caporetto and the Cambrai counter-attack. The aim was a rapid breakthrough and restoration of a war of movement by 'eating through the enemy positional system'. The advance should 'in no circumstances come to a halt'. Protected by the creeping barrage and supported by aircraft, the forward infantry must by-pass strongpoints such as woods and villages and leave them for those following on. The lead units, carrying iron rations and portable weapons (the light machine gun was critical), were to progress as rapidly as possible without relief: by implication the best troops would keep going until annihilated.[34]

If a transient numerical advantage and new tactical procedures gave the OHL reason to hope for a breakthrough, it needed to determine where that breakthrough should occur and how it would fit into a larger scheme. Decisions on these matters emerged from weeks of discussion between October 1917 and March 1918. Although during this period Germany's strategic situation was improving rapidly, Ludendorff eventually launched an offensive he had conceived of in the previous autumn, albeit with over seventy divisions instead of thirty-five; and his scheme enjoyed little confidence among either his headquarters staff or his front commanders. That he prevailed none the less was due not only to his strength of will and to habits of deference, but also to the lack of any widely accepted alternative. As Ludendorff was impatient to start before the Americans arrived in strength (in fact underestimating the time remaining to him), the imperative was to choose a sector permitting rapid tactical success. Initially discussion was of a counterstroke if Haig renewed his Flanders drive. Whereas Rupprecht's northern army group envisaged attacking the BEF, however, Friedrich von der Schulenberg, the Chief of Staff to Crown Prince Wilhelm, saw the French as the target, and Wetzell agreed. Both men favoured a pincer attack against Verdun, succeeding where Falkenhayn had failed in 1916, and inflicting a psychological wound that would make the French abandon the war. Ludendorff allowed planning for a Verdun operation to run on, but was unconvinced by it, partly because the hills there favoured the defender, but fundamentally because he saw the British as more vulnerable, with a smaller and clumsier army and a less determined government.[35] The French army's morale remained adequate for defensive purposes, and it had both a larger strategic reserve than the BEF and fresh American troops behind it, whereas success against the British would more quickly bring control of militarily significant territory. The Mons conference on 11 November 1917 – held between Ludendorff and the army group chiefs of staff, with no civilians in attendance – reviewed the options without reaching a decision. But Ludendorff summed up that 'We must strike the English'; and he confirmed to Kuhl that the BEF would be the quarry.[36]

Although Rupprecht's army group would deliver the main blow, its preference for an offensive across the Lys valley towards the railway junctions at Hazebrouck and Bailleul was unacceptable to Ludendorff, as the marshy terrain would delay a start until late spring. Ludendorff authorized preparations for it, but rejected it as the principal operation and envisaged it as a second stroke if his favoured conception failed. He told the Mons conference that he envisaged attacking in Picardy, around Saint-Quentin and towards the Somme, the drier ground there facilitating a breakthrough early in the season followed by a drive north-westwards with the river protecting the army's left flank as it 'rolled up' the British. Support for the idea came from General Krafft von Delmensingen, one of the architects of the Caporetto victory, who had returned from Italy to become the Seventeenth Army's Chief of Staff;[37] Wetzell, Rupprecht, and Kuhl still considered it second-best to the Lys. After a second conference with Kuhl and Schulenberg, held at Kreuznach on 27 December, the OHL ordered plans by 10 March not only for Saint-Quentin ('Michael') but also for the Lys ('St Georg') and an assault north and south of Arras ('Mars'), as well as attacks further east. But after visiting Rupprecht's front Ludendorff told a further conference at Avesnes on 21 January that the decision was for 'Michael'. 'St Georg' was too vulnerable to delay by the weather, and 'Mars' entailed assaulting very strong positions. Wilhelm approved the OHL proposals, and on 10 March Hindenburg issued the attack order.[38]

Throughout this process Ludendorff stressed tactical considerations. Both sides' Western Front offensives had underestimated the difficulty of piercing enemy defences, without which returning to a war of manoeuvre was impossible.[39] He refused to set territorial objectives and reserved the right to respond opportunistically to circumstances after the offensive began. He indeed selected a more suitable sector than the other contenders: flatter than Verdun, drier than the Lys, less heavily defended than Arras, and not previously fought over. Also, it lay at the junction between the French and British armies, which proved a big advantage. The aim envisaged in the 10 March order was to cut off the shallow British Flesquières salient – remaining from the Cambrai battle – and advance towards the Arras–Albert line. If things went well, the Germans would widen the attack sector northwards, until the entire British front was destabilized.[40] To an extent this was a mirror image of the Allies' 1916 plan for the British and French to attack shoulder to shoulder on both sides of the Somme, prior to driving north-eastwards. That plan had stumbled at the first, tactical hurdle. Ludendorff's did not, but once his troops had overwhelmed the defences their problems would be just beginning.

Even tactically the point selected was not especially suitable. Once the Germans got beyond the British lines they would traverse the area they themselves had devastated when retreating in 1917, followed by the still more desolate 1916 Somme battlefield. Moreover, because Saint-Quentin was a quiet sector, it would be harder to conceal the preparations, although all agreed that lack of surprise had been a key Allied failing. Ludendorff's guidance, none the less, was 'Surprise not at the expense of precision'.[41] Part of the reason why the British defences here were weaker was precisely that they were more distant than those further north from vital communications and stores, coalfields, and the coast. Even if the Germans did break through they would strike into a void. This was the more serious because their transport weaknesses ruled out such lightning movements as would occur in 1940. It reflected the shortcomings of Ludendorff's army that he selected the sector where it was easiest to break through quickly rather than that closest to strategic objectives, and notwithstanding his subordinates' pleas he left those objectives unspecified.

The German order of battle reflected this uncertainty. Three armies would take part: from north to south the Seventeenth, Second, and Eighteenth. The Seventeenth was a new creation, placed under General Otto von Below, who had led the German forces at Caporetto, with Krafft von Delmensingen as his Chief of Staff. He was abrasive and got on poorly with Rupprecht. A further cause of friction was Ludendorff's transfer of the Eighteenth Army (another new creation, placed under Oskar von Hutier, the victor at Riga) from Rupprecht's to Wilhelm's army group.[42] His objective seems to have been to exert more control than if he acted through a single army group command. But the move strengthened the Eighteenth Army's ability to lobby for a larger mission than just a supporting role, and in a last-minute telephone conversation Ludendorff agreed that if circumstances permitted it could drive beyond the Somme to split the French and British, thus attacking both Allies instead of concentrating on the BEF. That the three armies were allocated approximately equal reserves displayed a similar open-mindedness: indeed, the Eighteenth had the largest, although assigned the easiest task.[43]

Ludendorff also hedged his bets in a more fundamental respect. Subsequently he insisted that 'Michael' was intended in its own right to achieve decisive results: 'Obviously a decision was desired. I hoped for a breakthrough success.'[44] At the beginning of the planning process he had said that Germany had strength for only one main blow, and at the Mons conference he considered a Verdun followed by a Flanders attack but immediately rejected the idea in favour of just the 'Michael' operation. In February, to Kuhl's disquiet, he ruled out preliminary diversionary strikes, even though far larger numbers of divisions were now available. Yet it was becoming evident that if 'Michael' failed Ludendorff would try again. He rejected the Allied model of repeated attritional hammering on the same spot, not least because he could not afford the casualties. But he admitted to Kuhl that 'Michael' might just create a salient:[45] even if it succeeded, he would follow up with attacks to the north and south, and if it failed he would execute the Lys operation. This approach resembled Wetzell's concept of destabilizing the British front by successive hammer blows; and Ludendorff admitted to Wilhelm and to Hertling that this would be a much more difficult task than Caporetto and was likely to require repeated assaults. He warned the Emperor that 'The struggle in the West is the weightiest military task that was ever presented to an army.' All the German military chiefs regarded the offensive as a high-stakes gamble, Hindenburg admitting in retrospect that he knew it might not bring decisive results: 'Then it would remain open only to continue the decision-seeking battle at another location, until the enemy weakened.' Meanwhile Schulenberg and Rupprecht foresaw an initial but indecisive success that might worsen Germany's position, but believed that now the decision had been taken they must make the best of it.[46]

Churchill, who witnessed the preliminary bombardment, described 'Michael' as 'the greatest onslaught in the history of the world'.[47] Until May 1940 its scale would not be exceeded,[48] and its organization was a masterpiece of staff work. An elaborate deception effort convinced the French that it was merely the preliminary to a larger attack in Champagne. By 21 March seventy-six divisions had gathered in the assault sector with 6,608 guns – nearly half the German army's total – and 3,354 *Minenwerfer* ('mine throwers'). They outnumbered their opponents by 2.6:1 in men and 2.5:1 in guns, and even though on the Western Front as a whole Germany was outnumbered 3:1 in the air, over the 'Michael' battlefield it accumulated 1,070 aircraft to the Allies' 579.[49] In the three months beforehand, field railway, road, and telephone networks were constructed, alongside airfields and assembly areas. Twenty-five thousand tons of supplies were moved up each day, the Eighteenth Army alone requiring 650 troop and 500 supply trains.[50] For secrecy, the men detrained well back, moving by night to concealed positions, and extra air activity was avoided. In a measure that Ludendorff regretted, but equipment shortages necessitated, the army was divided into 'positional' and 'attack' divisions, the latter made up of men aged twenty-five to thirty-five who were rotated out of the line during the winter for three weeks of training in assault tactics and mobile warfare, as well as being better fed and better provided with horses and light machine guns. Older troops with lower priority for equipment remained in the east or in quieter parts of the line. Germany was gathering its best men and resources to strike with all the strength it could muster.[51]

The Germans benefited, more than they appreciated, from their opponents' errors, although the Allies did enough to withstand the impact. The three outstanding points were the Americans' absence, the mutual aid between the British and French, and the preparations by the British themselves. Although fear of the American build-up impelled Ludendorff to strike early, the Americans' tardiness had desperately disappointed the Allies, and only after – and in good measure due to – his offensive were shipments accelerated. To this extent the Germans committed suicide for fear of death, and by attacking they brought closer the very threat they feared while weakening their capacity to confront it. Between November 1917 and March 1918 American numbers in France rose from 78,000 to 220,000, of whom 139,000 were combatants. The American First Division entered the line in January, and three more by March, but a single regiment participated in the 'Michael' battle.[52] Certainly the Americans started from a lower level of preparedness and a much greater distance than had Britain, but the delay did not simply reflect the time required to recruit and train a citizen army and transport it to the combat zone. The obstacle was also one of policy; and it tested the alliance.

For the French and British, both of whom faced grave manpower shortages, the imperative was to incorporate more American infantry into their armies and under their command, at least during training and acclimatization. Yet proposals for 'amalgamation' were anathema to Pershing and ran contrary to his instructions to preserve the US forces' distinct identity. Pershing's view, as telegraphed to War Secretary Newton D. Baker, was that 'our entrance saved the Allies from defeat. Hence our position in this war very strong and should enable us largely to dictate policy to Allies in future.' Moreover, 'When the war ends, our position will be stronger if our army acting as such shall have played a distinct and definite part.'[53] The American army must safeguard its integrity in part to buttress American political influence, and Pershing's priority was to create an independent force (for which he needed not only his own commanders and staffs but also supply and logistic services – hence a high proportion of non-combatants) with a distinctive ethic and a war-winning strategic purpose. Not only did he want to train his men for fast-moving 'open' campaigning: he also envisaged staging a war-winning offensive in 1919. From its concentration zone in Lorraine the AEF could threaten the Saar coalfield, the Longwy–Briey steel mills and iron ore basin, the German fortification complex round Metz, and the eastern end of the great trunk railway that ran behind the German front and linked it to the homeland.[54]

This vision entailed the risk of America's allies collapsing before the decisive blow could be delivered, and in the ominous winter of 1917–18 it seemed more and more dangerous. In the French government's War Committee on Boxing Day 1917, Clemenceau reported that 'the deployment of the American troops was suffering an exasperating delay', and Pétain insisted that 'at the present moment, amalgamation is the only possible form of American collaboration, because it provides personnel and at present American assistance can only take the form of men'.[55] The French and British stepped up the pressure for American troops to serve at least temporarily under Allied command, and the War Department authorized Pershing to agree to it if necessary to meet an emergency. But for Pershing even a temporary amalgamation would threaten his troops' identity and training, and he suspected the British of not wanting an independent American force at all.[56] Although he accepted in January that six American divisions could be transported in British ships and trained with the British for ten weeks, he refused any more general arrangement.[57] Heated dispute resulted, Haig's GHQ complaining that 'The American situation is quite unsatisfactory ... It will be well on in 1919 and more probably 1920 before they have an Army in the sense in which the French or English Armies may be considered today.'[58] Underlying the technical issues were political questions about whether the AEF would be an instrument of American policy and a focus for American nationalism, which was partly why, although Pershing's masters in Washington expressed themselves more temperately, they were unwilling to overrule him. Wilson and War Secretary Baker believed Lincoln had interfered too much with his generals during the American Civil War, and in good measure they gave Pershing a free hand.

Although Pershing was a Republican, until the last weeks of the war he was in general sympathy with the administration's foreign policy (or at least he did not question it) and he had the determination to resist the Allies through the winter, which he characterized in retrospect as his most difficult time.[59] Born in 1860 in rural Missouri, he was a career officer who had graduated from West Point to serve in the cavalry against the Sioux and the Apache, fought in the Spanish–American War of 1898 and the subsequent guerrilla campaign in the Philippines, and witnessed the Russo-Japanese War as an observer. He had visited France and had some knowledge of French. Most recently, in 1916 he had led the expedition into Mexico that pursued Pancho Villa's revolutionary forces after they had raided across the US border. If not the most senior general on the American service list, he was the most experienced, and the obvious choice to command. In 1915 tragedy had befallen him when his wife and daughters had perished in a fire: the loss had further hardened him into a determined and imposing figure, commanding respect rather than affection.

Meanwhile France and Britain would have to parry Ludendorff. Italy could give little front-line assistance, the small Belgian army in Flanders remained inactive until September, and in April the unfortunate Portuguese detachment to the Western Front collapsed when the Germans assailed it. The Franco-British partnership was a strange one, reconstructed since 1904 after centuries of rivalry. If together its armies remained comparable in numbers to the Germans, the lack of a unified command fundamentally handicapped them, and before March none of the expedients adopted to address this problem amounted to much. For the first half of the war the French army had far outnumbered the BEF, and French initiatives had dominated Western Front strategy. In 1917 Lloyd George had subordinated Haig to Nivelle for the duration of the disastrous spring offensive. Nivelle's successor, Philippe Pétain, and Haig then proceeded independently, Haig fighting Third Ypres in the north while Pétain conducted smaller operations in the east. For 1918 the two men envisaged attacking at opposite ends of the line, Haig in Flanders and Pétain in Alsace, the latter as a political strategy aimed at territory that France wanted in the peace treaty.[60]

Haig's and Pétain's headquarters (GHQ and GQG) remained the centres of strategy formulation despite the Allied governments' efforts to co-ordinate them through the Supreme War Council (SWC). Established by the Rapallo conference in November 1917, after the Caporetto disaster, the SWC consisted of monthly meetings of Allied political leaders (normally prime ministers) and a council of Permanent Military Representatives (the PMR) at Versailles, which acted as a secretariat and source of recommendations. The Americans were represented on the PMR (by General Tasker H. Bliss), but only by an observer at the monthly meetings. Although the SWC accomplished some useful work, it depended on the national governments and military authorities for information and to implement its decisions. The idea for it originated with Sir Henry Wilson, and was taken up by Lloyd George, who wanted an alternative source of advice to Haig and to Sir William Robertson, the Chief of the Imperial General Staff in London, but did not feel that British public opinion would yet support an Allied generalissimo (who was likely to be French), and told the House of Commons one was not needed.[61] The French government, in contrast, supported the SWC precisely because it hoped it would lead to a generalissimo. At the start of 1918 the Council did serve as the forum for discussing a common strategy. The Allies agreed to concentrate their resources (as the French and Americans wished) on the Western and Italian Fronts. Operations against the Ottoman Empire, as desired by Lloyd George, were authorized only if no resources were diverted from the main theatre.[62] Events soon overtook this resolution as the danger from Germany mounted, ruling out any offensives in the lesser theatres anyway.

The limits to the SWC's authority showed up most clearly in the controversy over an Inter-Allied General Reserve. This was a proposal to earmark up to thirty divisions that would remain provisionally assigned to their armies but could be redeployed at the discretion of the PMR (for this purpose renamed the Executive War Board) under the chairmanship of Ferdinand Foch. This scheme too originated with Sir Henry Wilson:[63] the London and Paris governments initially supporting it and the SWC endorsing it, yet it proved stillborn, neither Haig nor Pétain designating the units in question. Haig, who took the lead and expressed himself most bluntly, had a central BEF reserve of only eight divisions. Rather than place it under a committee in which Britain had only one voice, he was ready to resign.[64] Lloyd George hesitated to press him when the Cabinet was already confronting the military by attempting to replace Robertson by Wilson as CIGS. Robertson rejected the alternative of moving to the Executive War Board, and having been appointed in 1915 with the exceptional prerogative of being designated the government's sole source of professional strategic advice, he also rejected the option of continuing as CIGS with reduced authority. But the Cabinet insisted on regaining its freedom to take advice elsewhere, and after days of tension Robertson was demoted to a home command while Wilson moved from Versailles to replace him.[65] Although Robertson had supported Haig (over his own better judgement) at the time of the Third Ypres offensive, Haig did not reciprocate, advising Robertson to comply with the Cabinet's wishes.[66] But in turn Lloyd George did not insist on the General Reserve plan – over which he was being criticized in parliament – when Haig condemned it as impractical. And once the British government had turned, so did the French one, Clemenceau having considered all along (or so he told the Chamber of Deputies Army Commission) that the scheme would not work.[67] When Foch remonstrated in the SWC the Premier silenced him. In the absence of an overriding authority, all would depend on bilateral co-operation between the British and French commands.[68]

Haig and Pétain were contrasting personalities, though both would become intensely controversial: Haig reviled as the butcher of the British soldiery, Pétain as the saviour of his nation in the First World War who betrayed it in the Second. Haig was born in Edinburgh in 1861, into a prosperous middle-class background as the son of a whisky distiller. As was quite customary at the period, he studied at Oxford University without taking his degree, proceeding to Sandhurst to train as a cavalry officer. He passed out first, and although initially failing to gain admittance to staff college, he later excelled there. In the South African War he served as a staff officer and commanded a mobile column. He became Director of Staff Duties and Director of Military Training at the War Office in 1906–9 and Chief of Staff in India in 1909–11 before returning to Whitehall. In 1914 he commanded the BEF First Corps and then the BEF First Army before in December 1915 he became Commander-in-Chief at the age of fifty-four. In 1905 he had married Doris, a maid of honour to Queen Alexandra who was barely half his age, but they established a contented partnership that produced four children. Haig was well connected but he also had wide experience and considerable intellect, as well as physical courage. He was interested in modern technology and enthusiastic about applying it. His judgement was firm, though not always consistent, and he had strong likes and dislikes, many of the latter confined to his diary (which he intended to publish). Among the dislikes were the French – with whom none the less he generally co-operated loyally and whose language he spoke adequately – and politicians, against whom he sniped but towards whom he could be surprisingly deferential. During his tenure the BEF suffered hundreds of thousands of casualties, and yet a big majority elected him the first President of the British Legion after the war. He believed the struggle could not be won by staying on the defensive, or by operations in secondary theatres, and that an extended period of attrition would be needed before victory became attainable – a victory that none the less through 1916 and 1917 he had supposed to be closer than it was. He seems never to have questioned that victory's necessity, although the peace terms he envisaged were moderate.[69]

Pétain's origins were more modest. He was born in 1856 to a northern French peasant family; his mother died when he was two, and he went to Jesuit College before proceeding to Saint-Cyr to become a career officer. In contrast to Haig's Presbyterian religiosity and familial decorum, he was a sceptic in matters of faith and a libertine with a string of conquests. Also in contrast to Haig, his career progression was slow, in part because of his unorthodox stress on the importance of firepower in infantry tactics. He was not afraid to express his views, and he did not suffer fools gladly. He taught at the Ecole supérieure de guerre and reached the rank of colonel, but as of 1914 had no prospect of a generalship and had bought a pair of secateurs for his retirement. Like Hindenburg he revived his career through active service, by commanding attacks in Artois in 1915 and above all by directing the defence of Verdun. Made Commander-in-Chief in May 1917 in the aftermath of Nivelle's Chemin des Dames attack (which he had opposed), he responded to the French army mutinies with exemplary punishments but also by suspending great offensives, promising and delivering improvements in his soldiers' welfare, and preparing for a smaller, better-equipped force that would return to the attack with greater firepower and American assistance. He shared with Haig a dry, laconic style and a tendency to the caustic; unlike Haig he was a realist to the point where he appeared more pessimistic and occasionally defeatist than he actually was.[70]

Haig and Pétain made two agreements: to extend the British line and for mutual reinforcement. The British sector was shorter than the French one and garrisoned more densely: in May 1917 the BEF held 158 kilometres with sixty-five divisions; the French 580 with 109.[71] Proximity to the coast and to strategic railways and coalfields gave the British less room for retreat. Moreover, most of their line was 'active', the scene of constant bombardments and skirmishes, whereas the French front east of Verdun was quieter and much of it too forested and hilly for major operations. Essential to Pétain's plans for reviving his weary troops, however, was releasing the older men and giving the others more leave; essential to his plans for repelling the Germans was a big mobile reserve. Hence he had to shorten his line, and Clemenceau pressed the British hard. Lloyd George and the Cabinet were sympathetic, but they left the commanders to settle the details. Haig had opposed an extension, on the grounds that his army too was tired; and indeed the second half of 1917 had tried it more sorely than the French and its leave was less generous. The SWC PMR recommended extending the British line to Berry-au-Bac, but Haig and Pétain compromised on taking it to the river Oise near Barisis. This still meant a lengthening from some ninety-three to 125 miles, with no extra troops arriving from Britain, and the new positions were sketchy and neglected. Haig was justified in pleading extenuating circumstances when on this sector two months later the Germans made their deepest breakthrough.[72]

None the less, Pétain did establish a bigger reserve than Haig, comprising thirty-nine divisions, some of which could help the BEF. The GHQ–GQG mutual support agreements that were finalized on 7 March envisaged six French divisions transferring to British command and being concentrated behind the British line.[73] They would go into action as a unit: in other words the situation was expected to develop gradually. In the event, after 21 March the British crumbled faster than anticipated and received much more French aid, Pétain going beyond both the letter of the agreement and the provisions of the general reserve plan. For all the friction between the two partners, French assistance would prove indispensable.

Haig did not lack supplies and equipment, and his army's enormous 1918 losses would be quickly replaced from stores, but he was short of men. Between January and November 1917 the BEF had suffered 790,000 casualties, and after Passchendaele its morale was at a low ebb. Between January 1917 and January 1918 its total strength had risen, but the number of combatant troops had fallen from 1.07 million to 969,000, and during the 1917–18 winter the BEF shrank from sixty-two to fifty-eight infantry divisions and from five to three cavalry divisions.[74] Haig warned London that without reinforcements he would face a very serious manpower crisis even in the absence of the heavy fighting that everyone expected. A GHQ note on 28 January envisaged 'normal casualties' of 41,000 per month, plus at least 500,000 battle losses, and the BEF shrinking by November to thirty-five divisions.[75] None the less, the War Cabinet approved a recommendation by its Man Power committee to reinforce the BEF in 1918 by only 100,000 'A'-grade men, disregarding GHQ's request for 650,000 and overriding objections by the military members of the Army Council in the War Office.[76] The reasons stemmed back to the dismal record of 1917 and the Cabinet's conviction that Britain must be able to continue until at least 1919, so that staying power was vital. Hence manpower was needed for shipbuilding and the navy, for the air force (to defend London), and for agriculture and tree felling (to reduce imports): all of them higher priorities than the army. But even allowing for these exigencies, more men could have been provided, and in the emergency that followed March they were, many by reducing the forces retained for home defence. It seems likely that the government feared that if it did supply more troops it could not stop Haig squandering them in fresh offensives; and although Churchill, as Minister of Munitions, urged that the front must be reinforced and the Cabinet if necessary restrain GHQ, his opinion was disregarded.[77]

Instead, as recommended by the Man Power committee, the Cabinet restructured Haig's fifty-six non-Dominion divisions from twelve to nine battalions each. The task was carried out between 29 January and 4 March, and although intended to increase the proportion of guns per thousand infantry it was radically disruptive. The battalions – comprising in principle 1,000 men but normally fewer – were the 'home' of the British infantry, to which men felt great loyalty, but now with little warning 115 were disbanded and thirty-eight amalgamated. As each division kept the same length of front, three battalions would have to do the work of four, meaning that the infantry would be more thinly distributed or face longer periods in the line.[78]

Haig had been forced to extend his sector without receiving reinforcements, and to restructure his army on the eve of an attack. His predicament in spring 1918 was therefore partly due to government policy, but was also of his own making. GHQ was slow to realize how fundamentally the Bolshevik Revolution had altered the military balance, and into 1918 Haig still assumed he could renew his Flanders attack. Even after accepting he must stand on the defensive, he remained sanguine. He told the War Cabinet that 'A long-continued offensive by the Germans would use up all our present reserves, and our losses would continue to be heavy; but, after consultation with his Army Commanders, he was satisfied the conditions and <u>moral</u> [sic] of the British Army were such as to give him every confidence that the British Army would hold its own . . .', although it must be kept up to strength. Evidently he envisaged a slow-burning operation like the Somme and Third Ypres, which was precisely what the OHL intended to avoid.[79] By the time he met his commanders on 2 March he was more robust: 'I was only afraid that the Enemy would find our front so very strong that he will hesitate to commit his army to the attack with the almost certainty of losing very heavily.' On the eve of the offensive he approved special leave for 88,000 men, and reassured the General Staff in London that he could hold an attack for at least eighteen days, with the result that they kept back the 'mobile reserve' at home.

The BEF's preparedness did little to justify such confidence. Since 1914 it had had little experience in defensive warfare. GHQ now envisaged a version of the defence in depth used by its enemies, which meant committing its soldiers to a massive construction programme during the winter. In 1917 the Germans had divided their positions into three zones and stationed the bulk of their troops and guns in the middle one, beyond the range of the enemy artillery. Strongpoints had replaced a continuous forward line, and once an attack lost impetus in a labyrinth of machine-gun nests local commanders held delegated authority to launch prompt counterstrokes.[80] GHQ envisaged similarly that a ('red') Forward Zone would guard against surprise and break up the enemy assault; the central ('blue') Battle Zone 2,500 yards back would be organized for an active defence in depth over a belt of 2,000–3,000 yards; and a similarly constituted ('green') Rear Zone would lie two to four miles behind.[81] When Churchill in February 1918 visited the future attack sector, he found conditions very different from during his front command in 1915–16. Instead of a continuous and strongly manned front line, a fringe of outposts faced the enemy, behind which mutually supporting machine guns stretched over 2,000 yards to the main battle zone. Communication trenches allowed relief at night, and the barbed wire broke at intervals to draw the enemy into fields of fire; while the main zone too comprised a series of redoubts, with heavy and medium guns further back still.[82] Regrettably, the model sector he visited was not representative. As of 12 February GHQ understood that north of the river Scarpe (the mid-point of the British sector) the new defences were coming on well, but south of it they were in 'a backward state', and the troops and guns more thinly distributed. On the eve of the attack, the Third Army held the north of the 'Michael' sector and the Fifth Army the south. Both armies' Forward Zones were in a good state and their Battle Zones 'fair' but incomplete (the Fifth Army's lacked dugouts), but whereas the Third Army had done a good deal with the Rear Zone the Fifth Army had little more than marked it out. The former, moreover, had held most of its front for a year or more, whereas the latter had only very recently occupied the southernmost part of its line.[83]

Haig told the Cabinet that 'The whole difficulty presented to him was one of labour.'[84] He needed to rest and train his troops as well as build defences, and he lacked auxiliary workers. Between 2 February and 15 March the labour force available to the Fifth Army rose from 24,217 to 48,154, but most of it was for road, railway, and depot construction so that the numbers available to build defences rose from a mere four in the week ending 12 January to 8,830 in the week ending 10 March, therefore arriving at the last minute. Not only was the physical infrastructure incomplete but also the soldiers were unfamiliar and uncomfortable with the new dispositions. Many preferred the solidarity of a continuous line to isolated 'bird cages',[85] while their officers lacked clear instructions about when to deliver counter-attacks and were unused to using their initiative: a central refrain in retrospective accounts was the confusion caused by lack of orders.[86] Without prompt counter-attacks, the garrisons in the Forward Zone (generally lacking deep dugouts or pillboxes) had little incentive to fight on in the hope of being relieved. Moreover, GHQ left a good deal of the implementation to army commanders, and both Sir Julian Byng of the Third Army and Gough of the Fifth stationed men and guns further forward than the Germans had done. On 21 March, it has been estimated, 84 per cent of the British battalions in the battle sector were within 3,000 yards of the front line (compared with a maximum of 50 per cent in the German system), which meant that they were speedily overwhelmed and few remained for counterstrokes.[87] If subjected to a surprise bombardment and to infiltration tactics the system might prove a house of cards.

If the Fifth Army could not help itself, little assistance would be close by. As the official historian put it, 'The smallness of the general reserve was very disappointing, for only by throwing in fresh divisions can a commander influence a battle.'[88] Much of GHQ's central reserve lay behind the north and centre of the British line, as Haig had placed two divisions behind each of his four armies – running southwards, the Second, First, Third, and Fifth. Moreover, only four of the French reserve divisions were near the British left flank. Although each army also had its own reserve divisions, the Fifth, with one division to 18,000 yards of front, was the most overstretched. Not only did it hold the junction with the French, but also its fortifications were unfinished and its manpower thin, whereas the Eighteenth Army facing it was the strongest German contingent.[89]

It was reasonable for Haig to spread his reserves before he knew where the blow would fall and whether it would be the first of many; although he did not change that distribution when warned it would come in the south and was imminent. But he planned for flexibility and devoted much of his labour force to preparing two north–south railway lines to shuttle units laterally.[90] As the Fifth Army sector was the furthest from the coast, ground there could be yielded most safely and Haig expected that it would be. On 1 February, Gough pointed out to GHQ the incompleteness of his defences: Herbert Lawrence, Haig's Chief of Staff, replied that 'it may well be desirable to fall back to the rearward defences of Péronne and the Somme while linking up with the Third Army on the north, and preparing for counter-attack'. Indeed, GHQ's assessment was that rail communications would better support a Péronne–Somme concentration than one further east.[91] Gough understood GHQ was prepared for him to retreat, which weakened his incentive to invest in his defences. He also anticipated that Hutier would use 'Riga' tactics, about which a paper was circulating in GHQ, but Haig foresaw a more gradual advance that would give him time to bring up reinforcements while the enemy pressed into a non-vital area. Indeed, on the first day there seems to have been confidence at GHQ that the Germans were driving into a trap that had been snared for them. In reality the combination of flawed defensive tactics with the Fifth Army's strategic dispositions resulted in a much faster German advance and British retreat than expected. Although much slack remained within the system – American reinforcements were available to rush across the Atlantic and British ones to cross the Channel, while a unitary command could enhance co-operation – releasing it required an emergency.

'MICHAEL'

On Thursday, 21 March, the German artillery opened up at 4.40 a.m. On the first day the Germans fired 3.2 million rounds, one third of them chemical.[92] British observers were startled by the suddenness with which a tremendous roar and sheet of flame penetrated the darkness. The Flesquières salient – which the Germans planned to encircle rather than assault directly – was drenched in mustard gas. To the north and south of it the bombardment concentrated for the first two hours on the British rear, hitting targets over thirty kilometres away that included the artillery, command posts, and telephone exchanges; then on the Forward and Battle Zones; and finally on the front line.[93] Although the largest bombardment yet seen on the Western Front, it was spread along some fifty miles, and could not and did not seek to annihilate the enemy positions. None the less, it smashed the field telephones (severing communications between the front-line units and their battalion commanders), cut much of the wire, and temporarily silenced most of the BEF artillery, whose absence was much remarked on by participants and caused the British infantry to feel abandoned. On the other hand, the barrage heartened and exhilarated the assailants, who, often standing in safety above their trenches, observed the pyrotechnics ahead of them. Meanwhile the defenders, cold and without breakfast, often made sick – or worse – by inhaling gas, saw their comrades blown to pieces or buried alive. Even if most survived – their casualties have been estimated at 2,500 killed and 5,000–6,000 wounded in a force of 100,000 – many were benumbed by the pounding, absorbed with their own predicament, and scarcely able to think or act.[94]

At 9.45 the German infantry went in, no fewer than thirty divisions in the first wave. By late morning the fog had lifted and the British witnessed an awesome sight: instead of the usual desolate appearance of the Western Front, whose fire-swept area seemed devoid of human existence, the battleground swarmed with horses and men. The assaulting forces – carrying rifles and 'potato masher' stick grenades, and wearing packs, steel helmets, and overcoats – at first encountered little opposition. Even where a continuous defending line existed – mainly in the north – the artillery had levelled much of it, and the occupants were dead or wounded, had gone to the rear, or were ready to surrender. Few machine guns were still firing, which was fortunate for the attackers as their barrage progressed faster than the infantry, the mist preventing the gunners from seeing enough to regulate the pace. The British and German official histories disagree about the fog, the latter judging it a hindrance but the former stating that it immensely aided the advance.[95] Despite impeding the artillery and aircraft, it facilitated surprise by shielding the infantry, who time and again materialized right in front of (or even behind) the British. Some 30 per cent of Gough's Fifth Army infantry may have been lost to their commander in the first ninety minutes, surrendering in isolated outposts.

The attack zone was a monotonous, open, arable plateau with few natural features and previously little fought over, so the ground, though wet, provided relatively easy going until the Germans reached the redoubts in the centre of the British Forward Zone, a dozen running from the Flesquières salient to the Oise. Here the British troops benefited from better visibility and more senior officers, although they knew they had almost no prospect of assistance, as the German lead infantry pushed on and follow-up units brought up light artillery and mortars. The redoubts had been planned to hold for up to two days, but by the evening of the first all had fallen. Within hours the Germans overran the Forward Zone along virtually the entire sector – an achievement without precedent in three years of trench warfare – and in most places they were well beyond it. Even so, after the first euphoria the resistance was fiercer than expected and once the mist cleared the infantry (often not dispersed but in massed ranks) presented easy targets for snipers and machine gunners, whereas it took longer than expected to bring the artillery forward. By evening the Germans had advanced on average 4–5 kilometres but only at two points were they through the British Battle Zone and these lay in the south, whereas the OHL had hoped to take all of it on Day One and viewed the north as crucial. Although 138 British guns were captured, the great majority were not, and the Flesquières salient had not been pinched out. In short, 21 March did not achieve what the OHL had hoped for it, and Haig's diary betrayed no sense of panic.[96]

None the less, for the Allies the ensuing week was one of crisis. The casualties on 21 March have been estimated as follows:

Table 1.1. German and British casualties, 21 March 1918[97]

	Killed	Wounded	Prisoners	Total
Germany	10,851	28,778	300	39,929
Britain	7,512	10,000	21,000	38,512

These were the heaviest losses in one day's fighting in the entire war (although more were actually killed on 1 July 1916); and at first sight appear comparable on the two sides; but whereas many of the German wounded would fight again the British prisoners would not, and the Germans had done disproportionate damage to a smaller army. Moreover, the manner in which the Forward Zone was lost endangered the defence of the Battle Zone. Whereas the Third Army and the northern part of the Fifth Army had held on reasonably well, the southern part of the Fifth Army, spread out in newly occupied positions where the fog was thickest, fell back faster, and when a unit withdrew it forced its neighbours to do likewise. Although much of this resulted from decisions by the men on the spot, Gough approved a retreat in his sector, and received Haig's endorsement. The decision blighted Gough's career, but it prevented even larger numbers of his men from falling into enemy hands, for whereas Byng had divisions in the rear to reinforce his army (and was feeding them in on the first afternoon), Gough had placed his own reserves too far forward and could count on help from neither the French nor GHQ. The French units set in motion on the 21st could not intervene in strength until the 23rd or 24th, and although GHQ prepared two reinforcement divisions it could promise no more for at least three days. But Lawrence told Gough he did not expect the Germans to keep on coming, which indicated that GHQ still envisaged a slowly unfolding danger.[98]

In fact, on 22 March the Germans pressed on, again protected by thick fog. In the evening the British counter-attacked with twenty-five tanks, but lost sixteen and were beaten back.[99] Ludendorff reinforced his Eighteenth Army, which had made the most progress, while ordering his Seventeenth to move artillery northwards in preparation for the 'Mars' battle. By the evening of the 23rd the Germans had taken 400 guns – about one in six – and 40,000 prisoners and were everywhere through the Battle Zone. In the north they were on the verge of breaking into open country and Byng reluctantly evacuated the Flesquières salient, most of its garrison narrowly escaping encirclement. In the south the attackers were twenty kilometres beyond the Battle Zone, and crossing the Crozat Canal and the Somme. Although it had taken three days to achieve the first-day objectives, many Allied offensives had never reached comparable objectives at all.[100]

The Germans' advance soon undermined their opponents' complacency. By the 23rd (or so Haig added to his diary retrospectively) he was surprised at the speed of the retreat, the lack of resistance, and the tiredness of the men. The next day he warned Henry Wilson that 'The situation is serious', and according to Churchill, who had now returned from France and was conferring with Lloyd George, 'I never remember in the whole course of the war a more anxious evening.' Clemenceau warned his ministers that they might have to evacuate Paris,[101] and the Germans added to the tension by beginning their bombardment with the 'Paris Gun'. Planned and crewed by the German navy, this weapon was a 380 mm railway gun converted by the Krupp firm so that it could fire its shells into the stratosphere, where wind resistance was lower. It commanded unprecedented range, though it lacked accuracy. Fired seventy-five miles from the forest of Saint-Gobain, its shells each weighed twenty stone, and between 23 and 25 March seventy-three hit the French capital.[102] Nerves in both Paris and London were on edge when a conflict between the high commands threatened to break the Allies apart.

Down to 24 March co-operation had worked well. On the afternoon of 21 March Pétain began preparing troop and aircraft movements even before Haig asked him. On the 22nd Haig asked for the French Third Army of six infantry divisions to intervene on the British Fifth Army's right, and Pétain issued the orders. Early on the 23rd, Haig went well beyond the co-operation agreement by asking the French to take over the British line up to Péronne, or more than half the sector under attack, which Pétain none the less approved without hesitation, it being understood that the British Fifth Army and the French Third and First Armies would be incorporated into a new Groupe d'Armées de Réserve (GAR) under General Marie-Emile Fayolle. By the evening of the 23rd French troops had reached the battle zone and staged a counter-attack, although their supplies and equipment had yet to join them and the Germans repelled it. None the less, French assistance helped Haig take forces from his own northern armies and form a new reserve of four to five divisions. Moreover, both allies were determined to remain in contact as a top priority.[103] By the evening of the 23rd Pétain had sent nine infantry and five cavalry divisions to Haig and had set in motion twenty-one of his forty reserve divisions, and even though many were rushed into action by lorry the railways could carry no more.[104]

Yet Pétain's staff remained uncertain about whether Ludendorff had delivered his main attack. As of 21 March French intelligence (GQG's 2ème Bureau) could not locate twenty-four German divisions and believed another fifteen were in transit from the east: this meant thirty-nine remained available, comparable in size to Pétain's entire strategic reserve. In all, Germany was believed to have fifty-five reserve divisions (all fresh) ready to strike elsewhere, packing almost as big a punch as

'Michael' itself.[105] French intelligence had numerous indications of a threat in Champagne, where the Germans were bombarding every night, German prisoners suggested an attack was set for 26 March, and Pétain's commanders clamoured for reinforcements.[106] In fact the French were taken in by German deception, and although the British agreed that large enemy forces remained uncommitted, they believed Pétain's disposition of his reserve divisions already took account of the threat.[107] As Haig's appeals became more pressing, Pétain had to balance them against the possibility that 'Michael' was simply the preliminary to a drive on Paris. When he met Haig at Dury at 4 p.m. on the 23rd, he said that the two armies must not be driven apart, but when Haig made a new suggestion for concentrating twenty divisions round Amiens, Pétain (as Haig recorded retrospectively) resisted moving yet further units.[108] On the following day the Germans forced back Byng's Third Army as well as Gough's Fifth, crossing the Somme and progressing northwards; while French troops intervening were again thrown back. While Haig alerted his reserves north of the Somme, and sent no more south of the river, Pétain decided to reinforce Champagne, and indicated his priorities in instructions to his commanders that evening: '*above all maintain the cohesion of the body of the French armies*; in particular do not let the GAR [Fayolle's reserve army group] be cut off from the rest of our force. *Then, if possible, conserve liaison with the British forces.*' If the BEF continued to fall back, his priority was to hold his army together.[109]

British troops had now begun the 'March retreat': an orderly but forced withdrawal that made command and communication increasingly difficult.[110] Haig warned Henry Wilson that 'the junction with French army can only be re-established by vigorous offensive action of French while I do the best I can from the north in combination with them'.[111] At a difficult second meeting at Dury at 11 p.m. he again proposed a French concentration round Amiens, and Pétain reiterated that he saw 'definite signs' of imminent attack in Champagne. But the French divisions arriving round Montdidier had instructions to retreat (if necessary) south-westwards – away from the British – and Pétain showed Haig his memorandum stating that French army unity was his top priority.[112] Although Haig later doctored his diary to strengthen the impression that Pétain and his government were more concerned to cover Paris than keep contact with the BEF, he had genuine reason for anxiety; even though Pétain did order two more divisions to the Somme that evening and the Frenchman's habitual pessimism may have caused misunderstanding.[113] On the 25th Haig predicted that a split between the armies was 'only . . . a question of time'; and he reiterated his demand for at least twenty French divisions to counter-attack against the German flank while the BEF 'must fight its way slowly back covering the Channel ports'.[114] Both commanders were now looking to their lines of retreat, anticipating the Franco-British divide of 1940.

In reality the outlook was less menacing, and the Allies quickly remedied the crisis in command, while the measures already adopted took effect and German weaknesses were exposed. The most important of those weaknesses were inherent in 'Michael' from its conception: as the German official history acknowledged, the enterprise was beyond the army's strength.[115] But in addition Ludendorff failed to conduct the offensive to best advantage. His demeanour during 'Michael' – veering between euphoria and exasperation – mortified his subordinates. When his crucial Seventeenth Army failed to achieve what he had set for it, he railed against its leaders. He by-passed the command chain by cutting out the Rupprecht army group and going direct to the armies, and his telephone manner was abrupt and impatient.[116] Yet he also displayed exaggerated optimism, commenting on 23 March that 'It is going excellently', and telling Kuhl and Schulenberg that fifty British divisions had been beaten and a relieving French attack was no longer likely, the aim being now to split the enemy by thrusting along both banks of the Somme. Instead of rolling up the British north-westwards, the German armies should splay out, the Seventeenth following the original track but the Second advancing westwards and the Eighteenth south-westwards across the Oise, which meant a drive against the French as well as the British.[117] Moreover, Ludendorff was now strengthening the Eighteenth Army and following on success rather than reinforcing the sector he had originally deemed decisive: six more divisions went to Hutier on the evening of 21 March, and three days later Ludendorff ordered Hutier's left to be reinforced again. In a reappraisal on 26 March, still believing 'that the breakthrough is succeeding', he instructed the Second Army too to go south of the Somme, towards Amiens, and the Eighteenth to cross the Avre and move westwards, while the Seventeenth would continue advancing, also now westwards, against the BEF.[118]

By this time the advance in the north, always the most difficult, had almost stalled, and Ludendorff intended to revive it by staging his 'Mars' attack east and north of Arras. With this new blow, he believed, the entire British front could be shaken loose.[119] The operation's complete and costly failure within hours on 28 March was therefore a very serious setback, Ludendorff describing it as 'one of the most unfortunate events and heaviest with consequences of the entire war'.[120] By abandoning 'Mars', Ludendorff effectively cancelled his original plan, substituting a new scheme ('Georgette') to attack in Flanders in early April. In the meantime the OHL pinned its hopes on the Eighteenth Army, whose southern advance was bringing it within striking distance of the trunk railway junction at Amiens. But still Ludendorff did not fully apply the principle of concentration, as he was already moving forces northwards for 'Georgette' (and may have lacked the rail capacity to reinforce the Eighteenth Army further). On 30 March a new attack, launched on a 55-kilometre front from the Somme to the Oise with twenty-two divisions in the forward line, was another failure, dispelling the OHL's confidence that a rapid breakthrough against the French might still be possible. Ludendorff now agreed with his commanders that a pause to rebuild ammunition stocks was needed, even though it would also give the Allies time to recover. He still ordered one more try south of the Somme, with fourteen divisions, on 4 April. When this too failed, the OHL suspended all further attacks in the 'Michael' sector. Ludendorff had been determined not to fight a battle of attrition and now he cut his losses. Hoping first to defeat the British army, then to separate it from the French and defeat both, and finally at least to reach Amiens, he attained none of these objectives.

This outcome was not simply due to the OHL's vacillations. The new tactics burned out the leading divisions, which were expected to press on relentlessly, reinforcements being fed in not to relieve them but to keep up the momentum. Sleeping rough in the bitter March nights and carrying only two days' rations, they pillaged Allied depots but became exhausted. The OHL noted their declining spirit and that they were harder to replace than expected, but decided to withdraw them only exceptionally and then just for a few days. Of thirty-seven divisions in the front line on 26 March, eight were already there for the second time.[121] Troop morale had been extremely high, but partly for the dangerous reason that this battle was expected to end the war. When resistance stiffened and progress slowed, enthusiasm faltered, prisoners complaining to the Allies that they were given neither food nor definite targets and left to go on until they dropped.[122] And even if men could be fed on the move, horses could not: their needs were much greater and the retreating British burned their fodder stocks. The Germans lost 29,000 more horses during 'Michael', thus storing up worse mobility problems for the future. The OHL had known all along that horses were critical and neither lorries nor field railways an adequate substitute, and anyway building road and rail links across the battle zone took longer than expected. One road supplied seven Second Army divisions, and although shells and water received priority (at first even over food), as early as 25 March some units had to halve munitions consumption. By the 26th the Eighteenth Army was fifty-six kilometres ahead of its nearest normal-gauge railhead, and eventually sixty-nine kilometres: these distances approached those before the 1914 Battle of the Marne.[123] To begin with the ground was unusually dry, but the lorries' iron tyres chewed up the roads and in the later stages it rained; while from 24 March the Germans were crossing the old Somme battlefield, a trackless and disorientating maze of shell holes that not only slowed the advance but made it even harder to supply the troops who ventured beyond. The 30 March offensive south of the Somme followed a bombardment of only thirty minutes, and for that of 4 April, even after several days' pause, munitions were again inadequate. 'The supply situation' was the reason OHL cited for suspending 'Michael', and although some commanders questioned its severity, it seems to have been real enough.[124]

Yet logistical difficulties were not the only reason momentum was lost. The circumstances permitting the 21–23 March breakthrough were exceptional and hard to replicate, as the 'Mars' debacle on 28 March demonstrated. 'Mars' had been long prepared, and after another Bruchmüller-style bombardment twenty-nine German divisions attacked only sixteen Allied ones. But the barrage was hasty with fewer guns and shells than planned, and fog was absent. The British held their forward positions lightly, and most of their machine guns and artillery survived. The Germans attacked uphill against more strongly garrisoned and long established defences than Gough's on 21 March, and the British field guns fired record numbers of shells – up to 750 each in one day. The German infantry, advancing in bunches, were halted on the edge of the battle zone.[125] Both 'Mars' and the offensives south of the Somme showed the attackers were becoming less formidable, as they grew weary and artillery support more meagre, while after the first two days the Allies regained air superiority and used it to harry their enemies.

'Michael' also lost momentum because the Allies recovered, most visibly by attending to the problem of command. The Doullens conference of 26 March 1918 was one of the great symbolic moments of the war, although its practical import was greater for the future of the 1918 campaign than for the battle in progress. At Doullens the French and British governments charged Foch with 'co-ordinating the action of the Allied armies on the Western Front'. At the Beauvais conference on 3 April the British, French, and Americans gave him the power of command and elevated his mission to 'the strategic direction of military operations', although Haig, Pétain, and Pershing retained full control over the 'tactical conduct' of their forces and if they judged that an instruction from Foch endangered them they could appeal to their governments. In effect Foch became commander-in-chief or generalissimo – the Italians accepting his co-ordinating role though not command power – but he was not so described, the governments preferring the title of 'General-in-Chief of the Allied armies'.[126]

Foch had long desired such a position, and by the Doullens conference he was the only plausible contender for it. Born in Pau in 1851, he trained as an artillery officer and was a pre-war corps commander but owed his reputation to his books and lectures on the theory of the offensive. A devout and practising Catholic all his life, he none the less avoided anti-Republican involvement.[127] In 1914 he commanded the French Ninth Army at the Battle of the Marne and co-ordinated the inter-Allied forces during the First Battle of Ypres. Subsequently he commanded the French Northern Army Group, earning a reputation for ruthlessness, and after the Battle of the Somme he was under a cloud until appointed CGS in 1917. Foch lacked the diplomatic skills of Dwight D. Eisenhower, the Allied supreme commander in the Second World War: he had suffered head injuries in a car crash, which intensified his penchant for extravagant language and disconcerting abruptness. None the less, perhaps through having known adversity, he became more flexible and open-minded. He remained in favour of offensives, but not pursued indefinitely at the same point in the manner of the Somme and of Third Ypres – which latter he considered 'abominable'.[128] In fact his ideas had something in common with Wetzell's, and later in

1918 he would have the opportunity to apply them. In a memorandum of 1 January to the Versailles PMR he had argued that the Allies must prepare to meet a German attack, but also be ready to seize every chance to take the offensive, the 'only method leading to victory', either by counter-attacking on the same ground or through relieving blows elsewhere. One reason why Haig and Pétain had opposed the Inter-Allied General Reserve plan was that they saw it as an instrument of Foch's counter-attack conception, which at that stage they rightly deemed too adventurous.[129]

When 'Michael' began Pétain rather than Foch was the leading influence on French strategy, but on 24 March Foch took the initiative. He urged on Clemenceau that 'a French mass held in reserve' should be organized north-east of Amiens 'to meet all unexpected contingencies and if necessary to counter-attack against the German offensive', and he proposed 'a directing organ of the war'.[130] He was therefore waiting in the wings with an idea of what was needed, and the crisis created his opportunity. It removed Haig's opposition to a generalissimo if creating one would lever out French reinforcements, and it raised Foch's stock with Clemenceau while lowering Pétain's. Haig claimed retrospectively that after his gloomy meeting with Pétain on the night of the 24th he appealed for London to send a representative, but in fact the news from France had already persuaded the British government to do so, and the mission proved the catalyst. Lloyd George sent Alfred Lord Milner (the War Cabinet member who liased with the PMR), accompanied by Henry Wilson. They found a grim situation, GHQ saying the Fifth Army had been 'shattered'. But whereas Pétain said that sending further divisions would endanger Champagne, Foch said more must be done, and holding Amiens was so important that risks must be taken. Both Clemenceau and the French President, Raymond Poincaré, foresaw that the British and French armies might be split and the latter forced backwards, endangering Paris; both agreed that holding them together was an absolute priority, and Pétain decided to override his staff and reconsider. As Milner and Wilson were already converted to the idea of a supreme command, the preconditions for agreement existed even before the meetings on the morning of Tuesday, 26 March at Doullens town hall.

On the way up, Wilson proposed and Milner agreed that Foch should be entrusted with supreme direction of Allied strategy, in order to get the maximum French reserves committed as soon as possible. At Doullens Haig conferred with his army commanders, arguing it was 'vitally important' to cover Amiens but the British First and Third Armies must stay together and if the town fell they should retreat northwards. Haig then saw Milner, who warned that precisely what the French feared was a British retreat towards the ports that left Amiens exposed. Haig believed he could avoid this if he got enough French assistance, and he welcomed working with Foch. At the Anglo-French meeting that followed, all agreed that 'Amiens must be secured at all costs' and Pétain said he was doing everything he could, having committed nine divisions already and started moving another fifteen, but still he gave Milner an impression of calculation, 'like a man playing for safety', whereas Foch interjected that no more ground should be yielded and implied that things could and must be done faster. Hence Milner and Clemenceau agreed to charge Foch with co-ordinating operations in front of Amiens, which at Haig's suggestion was broadened to cover the Western Front as a whole. Haig accepted the outcome with relief and Pétain, as was his wont, more guardedly. At this juncture, the British were actually more enthusiastic than Clemenceau, who caustically remarked that Foch now had the situation he so coveted: Foch rejoining that he had received the poisoned chalice of a battle lost.[131]

Yet the battle was not lost, and by 26 March the tide was turning. Foch took over at an opportune moment, and his appointment seemed to cause the Allies' deliverance when in fact it coincided with it. Beginning with a tiny staff, he depended on the national commanders for intelligence and information. His position was of an orchestral conductor: he could advise and urge but not instruct. Thus on his first afternoon he unceremoniously admonished Gough to retreat no further, but the withdrawal continued and Foch controlled no reserves that could have encouraged Gough to stand firm. Similarly, although Pershing (who was not at Doullens) promised to place the American forces at Foch's disposal, this was largely a token gesture while he upheld his opposition to amalgamation, which was what America's partners really wanted.[132] Nor did Foch's appointment lead immediately to help for the British, and whereas Haig had wanted twenty French divisions astride the Somme, in early April they still numbered only eight.[133] Foch spent much of his time exhorting and cajoling, and found his Doullens mandate inadequate even for a defensive battle, let alone the offensive that he hoped would follow it: hence he lobbied for the command power that, with Clemenceau's support, he received under the Beauvais agreement. All the same, an immediate consequence of Doullens was that Pétain revoked his order of 24 March and told Fayolle that the priority was to cover both Amiens and Paris and to maintain liaison with Haig. Similarly, on the 30th Foch's first general directive stipulated that Amiens must be held, there must be no further retreat, and the British and French armies must stay together, even to the jeopardy of the rest of the French front, although he also wanted to build up reserves for a counterstroke. As this missive suggested, to some extent Foch owed his appointment to his refusal to choose, and his priorities differed less from Pétain's than it seemed. He was fortunate that the choice between Paris and the Channel had not to be confronted after all.[134]

More crucial than Doullens was that on 25 March the 2ème Bureau had told Pétain that the Germans were becoming less active in Champagne and lacked the divisions there to launch a second major offensive. As a result Pétain decided that evening, i.e. *before* Doullens, that he could move more divisions westwards (although the knowledge of Clemenceau's attitude may also have contributed to his reappraisal). He was assisted by his government's decision to recall two divisions from Italy, as well as by American willingness to move more units into quiet sections of the line. On the 26th Pétain committed thirteen extra French divisions to the battle, and when Foch took over Pétain had moved or alerted over forty. Foch's appointment did not accelerate the movement of French divisions to help the British, because they were already moving as fast as they could go.[135]

Bit by bit the reinforcements delivered results. This was soonest true of aviation. Once the morning mists had cleared, from 21 to 23 March German aircraft strafed the Allies' infantry columns and artillery and bombed their railways, downing sixty-one Allied aircraft for thirty German ones. But by the 24th reinforcements had restored equality and Allied squadrons of up to sixty planes hounded the German infantry; by 28 March, French aircraft were in action day and night.[136] On the ground, the tide was slower to turn, but, in the words of the British official history, repeatedly 'the arrival in the field of even the infantry of one fresh division ... stemmed, at any rate for a time, the German onrush'.[137] French troops at first arrived in dribs and drabs, without artillery support. It took days to set up logistics, a chain of command, gun batteries, and hospitals, and the early French counter-attacks failed. On the 27th Pétain appealed to his men: 'France's destiny is at stake.' But troops were now arriving in sufficient numbers to place reserves behind the line, and the counter-attacks began to achieve results as artillery and tanks deployed in support of them. After repulsing the Germans on the 30th, the French commanders sensed that the crisis was nearing its end: the Germans could prevent the Allies from reconquering lost territory, but could advance no further.[138] Although in retrospect Haig churlishly minimized the French contribution ('Between 21st March and 15th April the French did practically nothing and took little part in the fighting'), at the time he was desperate for their help, and it is unlikely that the BEF could have held 'Michael' unaided. Hindenburg, in contrast, in his memoirs highlighted the French threat to his advance's southern flank and the importance of the French artillery and infantry in protecting Amiens.[139]

That being said, the British took the entire weight of the attack in the first few days, and were solely responsible for halting it north of the Somme. To quote their official history again, 'It was the incomparable British soldier who averted defeat.'[140] Although south of the Somme French assistance was essential, north of the river the German Seventeenth and Second Armies throughout progressed more slowly, partly because the relief was more challenging, with more high ground and waterways.[141] Once the attackers had overrun the three prepared defence lines, the 1917 devastated area and the 1916 Somme battlefield detained them. By 27 March twenty-nine British divisions had been in the line since the fighting began but had received nine reinforcing divisions, all but one of them north of the Somme: not only did Haig provide what he could, but the War Cabinet shipped more men over the water. It agreed to send all available reinforcements from the British Isles at once, to lower the minimum age for overseas service abroad from nineteen to eighteen and a half, and to call up thousands of munitions workers: between 17 and 23 March 12,471 men crossed the Channel, but between 24 and 27 March 39,384 did so, and in the first week of April 73,618; over the whole period from 21 March to 31 August the figure was 544,005. Not only were men rushed over; equipment losses were made up from stores, and the stores replenished from Britain, so that by the end of March equipment reserves were as high as when the battle began. Unlike the Germans, and despite the more mobile campaigning, the

British forces continued to be regularly fed and supplied (apart from occasional water shortages) and even to receive their post.[142]

After 26 March the Germans made little further headway north of the Somme, and the 'Mars' disaster failed to restore their momentum. The danger point lay south of the river, where the Allies' lines were thinner, and they feared a drive on Amiens. The issue was partly symbolic, Foch viewing Amiens as a *ne plus ultra* like Ypres and Verdun,[143] but was also eminently practical, as the double-tracked trunk line from Paris to the Channel ports ran through it. The BEF's supplies via Calais, Boulogne, and Dunkirk came mostly via Hazebrouck; those from Dieppe, Rouen, and Le Havre via Amiens, and 80 per cent of the north–south rail traffic along the BEF front went through the town. If it were lost all that remained available would be an inferior line via Beauvais and Abbeville, which for part of its length was single-tracked. The Germans penetrated to sixteen kilometres from Amiens and from the high ground near Villers-Bretonneux they could bombard it, impeding the use of the trunk railway but not making it impossible. If Ludendorff had from the start identified Amiens as his key objective and concentrated on it single-mindedly, he would have had an excellent chance of capturing it, thereby not paralysing the British war effort but at least severely constraining it. Instead, he focused on the town too late.[144]

All the same, at the time the British Cabinet saw 21 March as a major defeat. When Haig defended Gough, Milner lost patience: 'The *general* causes of the disaster are well known. But when all is said and done, it was much greater than, even given the general conditions, it need have been.' By implication, British generalship was responsible.[145] Haig had expected to lose ground and men, but not on such a scale. The Germans had completely overrun the British defence lines along a fifty-mile sector, occupying 1,200 square miles of territory and capturing 90,000 prisoners (75,000 of them British) and 1,300 guns. This dwarfed the Allies' accomplishments at Third Ypres, where the attackers' numerical superiority had been bigger.[146] Ludendorff summed up that the first blow had achieved 'a great success', and 'the English army is at present not operational'. The Bavarian General Staff concluded more soberly: 'A great tactical victory has been accomplished, the strategic exploitation must follow': an understated way of saying that the Germans had acquired masses of strategically unimportant territory.[147] Although they had broken an Amiens–Arras transverse line at Albert, they had not taken Amiens itself or divided the British and French armies, still less reached the Channel, and now they held a lengthened front that required extra forces to garrison and which Ludendorff was reluctant to order them to fortify.[148] On the other hand, the Germans' losses in 'Michael' were 239,800; the Allies' 254,739 (British 177,739 and French 77,000).[149] These were not much smaller than the Third Ypres casualties, and suffered in a much shorter period of time, which underlined the price paid for more mobile campaigning. None the less, the Germans had broken another rule – that attackers suffered more than defenders – and in the short term they had widened the imbalance between themselves and their enemies. But in the longer term they were less well placed than were the Allies, with their impending American reinforcements, to plug the gaps, and they now risked exposure in untenable positions if the balance turned against them. As Ludendorff had feared, 'Michael' had not proved enough, but the OHL's very logic in launching the battle left it no alternative but to go on.

'GEORGETTE'

The second great German attack began on 9 April. Its codeword was 'Georgette': the French official history dubbing it the Third Battle of Flanders and the British the Battle of the Lys, although identifying half a dozen subsidiary battles within it.[150] The fighting ran along a narrower front than 'Michael', but expanded from Givenchy and Festubert in the south to the Ypres salient. According to Ludendorff it became a 'principal operation' and not aimed simply at limited objectives. Among the British, it caused even greater anxiety than the first attack, Churchill describing 12 April as 'probably, after the Marne, the climax of the war'. Yet 'Georgette' too was halted without attaining any critical objectives, in part because of difficulties that bedevilled it from its outset.[151]

A southern Flanders offensive had been high on the Germans' menu. Planning for it centred on the Rupprecht army group, its Chief of Staff, Kuhl, and the Sixth and Fourth Armies (commanded respectively by Ferdinand von Quast and Friedrich Sixt von Armin). Initially codenamed 'GEORG I', the project was conceived on a grand scale, with thirty to forty divisions sweeping across the Lys, taking the Hazebrouck railway junction, protecting Germany's coastal U-boat bases against any renewed British offensive, and driving towards Dunkirk and Calais, while 'GEORG II' attacks overran Ypres. On 10 February Ludendorff informed the army group that 'Georg' would go in second if 'Michael' stalled, and he expected 'a breakthrough success'. In the euphoria after 21 March when it seemed that 'Michael' was succeeding, the OHL suspended planning, but then authorized its continuation on a smaller scale, with 'Georgette' as the appropriately diminutive sobriquet. Wetzell would have liked to launch it instead of 'Mars', but Ludendorff with his usual impatience disagreed, as the latter could start sooner.[152] But in early April the scheme was expanded again and now prepared with breakneck speed. Ludendorff was in a hurry to strike while the BEF's reserves were further south and to achieve surprise. The local commanders advised that the ground was firm enough and the OHL knew that part of the British line was held by Portuguese troops, whom it expected to offer little resistance.[153] According to the OHL, after dealing the BEF an 'annihilating blow' the attackers would drive southwestwards – but once again the strategic objectives were vague.[154]

Bruchmüller and his staff moved to the Sixth Army, which would deliver the principal assault in the form of an arrowhead directed towards Hazebrouck, but whereas they had had seven weeks to prepare the 'Michael' bombardment, this time they had only nine days. Shells and artillery also had to go north, via overstretched railways or along the roads in drenching rain with too few horses.[155] The heavy-artillery shortage necessitated a two-stage opening, the Sixth Army attacking on 9 April and the 'battering train' then being relocated so the Fourth Army could follow on the 10th. All the same, the firepower was impressive: fewer artillery pieces than for 'Michael' but on a front of less than half the length, the Sixth Army deploying 1,686 guns against 511 British ones and the Fourth Army 571. In all, the two armies disposed of twenty-nine divisions and 492 aircraft. But as the highest-grade divisions had all been used in Picardy, the OHL deployed not only less well-equipped and well-trained and lower-strength units, but even 'positional divisions' with so few horses that they moved their field guns with great difficulty and for infantry munitions had no animals at all. Even the best divisions had lost many of their finest officers and were fatigued by the march north; moreover, they had been promised that 'Michael' would win the war, and its failure to do so meant that morale, though apparently good enough, was brittle.[156]

The new battle zone was bounded by the La Bassée canal on the south and to the north by a chain of low hills extending southwards from Passchendaele to the Messines ridge and then westwards through Mount Kemmel and the Scherpenberg to the Mont des Cats. The Lys itself was an appreciable obstacle: navigable and up to fifteen metres wide. It flowed past market towns such as Estaires and Bailleul and the manufacturing centre of Armentières, through a countryside of arable farms, criss-crossed by thorn hedges and irrigation ditches, with clay soil and a water table only one foot down, so that wheeled vehicles could travel only along the roads. The sector had been quiet since 1915, and seemed to be one where British commanders could run risks. It favoured the defenders more than did Picardy and the BEF had had time to prepare its defences, which were in the normal three-zone pattern but mostly breastworks and machine-gun pillboxes rather than trenches.[157] The principal weakness was the Portuguese, whom the Germans deliberately struck at most heavily. Portugal had entered the war in 1916, hoping to win Allied sympathy for its empire's survival; but an anti-war ministry had come to power that neglected the country's expeditionary force. The officers cared little for the troops, who unlike their superiors were entitled to no home leave and found themselves isolated in an alien landscape for a cause that meant little to them. Sir Henry Horne, the commander of the British First Army, had warned that the Portuguese were unfit to meet an attack, but Haig had advised that the Germans could capture only part of the Portuguese sector. In any case, it was difficult to replace them. In fact the 1st Portuguese Division was pulled out and the men of the 2nd were due for relief on the night of 9/10 April, but until then they held an even more extended line.[158] Although plans existed to help them, Horne's First Army was the most thinly spread after the ill-fated Fifth, and like Sir Herbert Plumer's Second Army to the north it had sent its reserves and many line divisions to the battle in Picardy, the replacement units having lost 70–80 per cent of their infantry and being made up with nineteen-year-olds straight from Britain, 45-year-olds, or men just back from convalescence, often serving under inexperienced officers. Five of the six British divisions on the attack front on 9 April had fought in 'Michael', whereas none of the fourteen first-wave German divisions had done so, and thirteen of them came from rest.[159]

A final British disadvantage was surprise. Although it is conventional to divide the German offensive into the 'Michael' and the 'Georgette' phases, for the Allies March and April were months of continuous crisis. Foch fully expected more thrusts south of the Somme, where from 6 to 9 April another German attack took 2,000 French prisoners. British military intelligence estimated that of 199 German divisions on the Western Front, thirty-one were fresh and in reserve and sixteen of these units faced them. Both GHQ and the General Staff in London, however, thought the most likely target was south – not north – of the Lys, between the La Bassée canal and Arras.[160] Haig believed he could not weaken this sector, where dumps, hospitals, and aerodromes were clustered behind the battlefront, and as of 7 April GHQ still expected the next attack to come there. Such was the Germans' haste, however, that unlike before 'Michael' they carried out movements in daylight, ground and air observers detected their preparations opposite the Portuguese, and on 8 April Horne told Haig that he expected to be attacked the next day. Even so, at first the Cabinet was informed that 'Georgette' was probably just a diversion.[161]

Once more Haig had few reserves to spare, and Foch withheld the help on which he counted, so that Anglo-French relations again grew acrimonious. Foch remained preoccupied with the threat at Amiens and wanted to gather forces there to drive the Germans back; he too feared an attack round Arras. Haig wanted the French to take over more of the British line, which Foch refused to authorize, although he did tell Pétain to move up four divisions west of Amiens, where they were better positioned to intervene but also encumbered British communications.[162] On 8 April Haig lamented: 'How difficult these "Latins" are to deal with. They mean to bleed the British to the utmost', but he had lost much of his meagre remaining credit in London and the government was unwilling to support him in a confrontation with Foch. Hence when the Lys began Haig had less assurance than before 'Michael' that he could count on French aid.[163]

On 9 April (it was Ludendorff's birthday) the Germans once again benefited from dense fog. The barrage began at 4.15 a.m. and followed the usual pattern, gas shells silencing the Allied batteries, but the *Feuerwalze*, reflecting the lessons of 21 March, was slower. The infantry attacked with overwhelming superiority against the Portuguese, two thirds of whom fled to the rear (some seizing the bicycles of a British cyclist battalion sent up to assist) and failed to blow up the bridges behind them. To the north the 40th Division was outflanked and had to fall back too, and the Germans achieved the fastest single-day advance since the advent of trench warfare. By the evening they had established a pocket ten miles wide and five and a half deep and a bridgehead across the Lys.[164] Hence the opening was spectacular, and the Fourth Army's follow-up attack on 10 April succeeded against not Portuguese but British forces, the Ninth Corps of Plumer's Second Army, comprising three divisions that during 'Michael' had all lost more than half their strength. The Fourth Army was also assisted by mist: it overran Ploegsteert wood and higher ground towards Messines, repelling counter-attacks, while the Sixth Army continued to progress and captured Estaires. Armentières was now threatened on both sides and the British evacuated it, and by the second evening the Germans had taken 11,000 prisoners and 146 guns.[165] Yet from now on the Germans felt disappointment with their progress even as the British sense of crisis reached its zenith.

The sources of this crisis were partly logistic. To the south of the battlefield lay the Bruay–Béthune coalfield, which the Germans could now shell. On 12 April Clemenceau told Haig that 70 per cent of the coal for France's armaments came from Bruay and the country had only five days' worth in reserve.[166] The British retaliated with counter-battery fire, but the coal shortage did hamper French steel and armaments production, forcing the British to ship more coal to France even when their own output was falling because they were recalling miners to military service. Meanwhile German shelling of the Amiens goods yards forced the Allies to divert troop movements to the less efficient coastal route. If Hazebrouck fell too the transport bottlenecks would be even greater, and by the evening of 12 April the Germans were within six miles of it.[167] Henry Wilson noted that the news was 'very disquieting . . . This is the devil' and that if Hazebrouck fell Dunkirk would follow, which the Admiralty feared meant losing the Channel itself.[168] Sir George MacDonagh, the Director of Military Intelligence, predicted that without more Allied aid Britain faced 'a decisive defeat', and according to Lloyd George 'the second German offensive made an almost deeper impression on the public mind in our country than even the first. The Germans at Amiens would be hard enough, but the Germans in possession of territory in view of our own shore was an infinitely more alarming prospect.'[169] In these circumstances on Thursday the 11th Haig issued a 'Special Order of the Day':

> Three weeks ago to-day the enemy began his terrific attacks against us on a fifty-mile front. His objects are to separate us from the French, to take the Channel Ports, and destroy the British Army . . .
>
> Many amongst us are now tired. To those I would say that Victory will belong to the side which holds out the longest. The French Army is moving rapidly and in great force to our support.
>
> There is no course open to us but to fight it out. Every position must be held to the last man: there must be no retirement. With our backs to the wall and believing in the justice of our cause each one of us must fight on to the end. The safety of our homes and the Freedom of mankind alike depend upon the conduct of each one of us at this critical moment.

Vera Brittain, nursing behind the front at Etaples, wrote in retrospect that 'Although since that date, the publication of official "revelations" has stripped from the Haig myth much of its glory, I have never been able to visualise Lord Haig as the colossal blunderer, the self-deceived optimist of the Somme massacre in 1916. I can think of him only as the author of that Special Order, for after I had read it I knew that I should go on, whether I could or not. There was a braver spirit in the hospital that afternoon . . .'[170] Haig's peroration has passed into the language. Yet its idiom was uncharacteristic for him, and his otherwise voluminous diary failed to record it. His real target may have been Foch, for in reality the French army was coming neither in the numbers nor at the speed that Haig wanted. His impact on the fighting troops is also hard to demonstrate: the BEF continued to resist determinedly but not to the last man, and the German advance edged further forward.[171]

Foch was willing to move French troops to Flanders, the first units arriving from 12 April onwards, but he categorically refused to put them in the front line while fighting was in progress (especially as he understood that Germany still had fresh divisions for a new assault elsewhere), while Pétain protested that extra help to the British would endanger his own position. As in March, Foch forbade the British to retreat but did not reinforce them.[172] Both Lloyd George and the British official history accepted in retrospect that he had been vindicated, even though his firmness cost British lives: and for a while the BEF managed to contain the situation.[173] After the opening days its retreat was more gradual and controlled than during 'Michael', partly owing to a better communication system with deeper-buried cables. In the south of the pocket the 55th Division of Lancashire territorials, occupying a more traditional trench line with machine guns, held the higher ground round Givenchy against repeated attacks. In the centre the German drive was more formidable, but once reinforcements arrived (notably the 1st Australian Division), two defence lines were organized. According to the British official history, a stand by a weary brigade of Grenadier Guards against four German regiments covered the Australians while they detrained and 'saved Hazebrouck'.[174] The British were also fortunate in their Second Army commander, Sir Herbert Plumer. Originating from the Yorkshire squirearchy, he had been an officer in the Indian army and seen action in African colonial wars. He ran an efficient headquarters and presided over the capture of Messines ridge in 1917 and the later stages of Third Ypres. A commander who believed in being visible, he regularly visited divisional and brigade HQs. Haig interfered little with Plumer's conduct of the battle, and gave him responsibility for most of the British front.[175] On 14 April, Plumer reluctantly decided to evacuate the gains made in the previous autumn, thereby pre-empting a German plan to pinch off the tip of the Ypres salient and releasing British forces to strengthen resistance further south. But no senior commander could determine what happened day after day on the firing line. GHQ's information was that spirits were excellent: the letters home read by the field censor suggested that the German offensive had stopped the previous 'grumbling' and 'it can safely be said that it [morale] has never been higher'. Supply again worked well, and the troops received food and enough ammunition, which they used in prodigious quantities. None the less, Plumer doubted that his men could hold for very much longer. While he and Haig discussed retreats to successive lines in the rear, Henry Wilson urged opening the sluice gates to inundate the area parallel to the coast.[176] 16 April was a particularly bad day, when both Wytschaete and Meteren were lost.

At this stage Foch finally moved up the French troops that he had gathered behind the battlefront. While the Belgians extended their sector north of Ypres, from 17 April the six French divisions organized as a 'Northern Army Detachment' moved into a seven-mile stretch south of the Flemish hills. These steps enabled Plumer to pull seven and a half

British divisions out of the line. Foch made up his mind after visiting Plumer's headquarters and acted despite his own previous reservations and protests from Pétain that too much help was going to 'the English battle'.[177] French reserves were indeed now down to a very low level, and, after his initial caution on the Lys Foch eventually ran considerable risks, but he shared the British concern to hold the Channel ports and he ordered that the Flanders hills must be held. Haig was greatly relieved, and accepted in return a proposal for *roulement* – that tired British divisions would help the French by taking over quiet sections of their line.[178] Bit by bit, the two armies were becoming more and more interconnected, although the process entailed a loss of independence and fuelled resentment on both sides.

By the time French troops were committed the pressure was easing anyway. Whereas Haig's headquarters by 11–12 April was more alarmed than at any other time in the war, the Germans were again falling short of their targets and Ludendorff paraded his impatience.[179] According to the Nineteenth Army Corps's post-battle appraisal, the biggest single obstacle was in preparing usable supply routes. The roads were few and mostly lay athwart the line of advance, and on the first day almost all the corps labour was needed to make just one usable. The second- and third-wave infantry also had to help in the work, which exhausted them. The British concealed swarms of machine guns behind bushes and hedges, which the infantry baulked from attacking unaided and which German gunners could not locate because of the failure to reach over-looking ground further west. Both sides increasingly used artillery, in which the Germans lost their initial superiority.[180] Not only was it difficult to bring up guns and shells, but the overcast skies also impeded aerial observation – though the Allies quickly restored their air superiority anyway. The infantry toiled forward, once again suffering terrible casualties in mass attacks, and from early on were easily distracted by Allied stores and by looting opportunities in captured towns. Many in the second wave had already fought in 'Michael', and as the battle bogged down their discipline cracked, the Sixth Army reporting that 'the troops do not attack, despite being ordered'. On 18 April Kuhl noted that 'The troops appear to be finished [*zu Ende*].'[181] Ludendorff accepted the Fourth Army's call for a mid-April halt, but when the attacks were renewed they made even less progress than before, and after 19 April a longer suspension followed, the Germans bringing up artillery and supplies while the French moved into line. Rupprecht's army group warned that 'The combats are becoming a battle of materiel', and once more Ludendorff faced an attrition contest that his resources ruled out.[182]

As during 'Michael', while the battle proceeded the OHL shifted its strategic emphasis. If initially the target was Hazebrouck, after 13 April it became Bailleul, and in the final phase the Flanders hills and especially Mount Kemmel.[183] The latter rose 300–350 feet above the Flanders plain, commanding distant observation to north and south, and it could give the Germans a commanding position that might force the evacuation of the Ypres salient. Ludendorff therefore prepared for a major assault on Kemmel and its French garrison, but he had also decided to renew his efforts in front of Amiens, where the Eighteenth Army languished in improvised positions under French bombardment.[184] In the final week of April the Germans therefore assaulted both ends of the fighting line. The southern attack was meant to ease the situation in the salient south of the Somme and gain high ground for a long-distance bombardment of Amiens, by capturing the area round Villers-Bretonneux. It would be a sizeable operation with ten divisions on a fifteen-kilometre-wide sector, supported by 1,208 guns, 710 aircraft, and thirteen tanks, but it did not seek a breakthrough, which was just as well, as the units concerned had not had their March casualties replaced, and many were sick and demoralized. None the less the infantry attack on 24 April did at first make headway in thick fog against seven French and British divisions, capturing the town and the terrain to the south, even though this time the Allies had had warning. The Allied trenches were shallow and incomplete, with few dugouts, and as the defenders had no anti-tank weapons they gave way, until British tanks intervened and in the first ever tank versus tank battle were able to halt their enemies. A prompt counter-attack by the Australians that night then pushed the Germans most of the way back to their starting line.[185]

In contrast the Mount Kemmel battle began with a stunning German tactical success, but in the longer term was a failed opportunity. As at Villers-Bretonneux, the Allies knew an attack was coming, and fresh French forces had just taken over established British positions. But on 25 April a bombardment of exceptional intensity silenced the French artillery, before a dawn assault by six German divisions (against three defending ones) captured the summit within three hours while the surviving French infantry fell back in disorder. But the attackers paused before the next hill in the chain, the Scherpenberg, as their orders for once had not told them to advance as fast as possible and they waited for their artillery to catch up. Hence the Allies had time to organize a scratch defence, strengthened when on 26–27 April the British gave up most of the rest of the Ypres salient, and retreated almost to the walls of the city. A final assault on the 29th failed against Allied machine guns and artillery arranged in depth, and from now on the Flanders fighting subsided.[186]

The Lys ended up as a major operation. Ludendorff committed fifty-five German divisions; thirty-two Allied infantry divisions and three cavalry divisions participated. German casualties numbered 86,000, British 82,000, and French 30,000. The battle distorted the Allies' defensive deployment: after losing Mount Kemmel, Foch accepted the French would have to stay in Flanders, whither he eventually sent nine French infantry and three cavalry divisions.[187] As of 1 May twenty-nine French reserve infantry divisions were north of the river Oise while only sixteen covered Paris and the east between the Oise and Switzerland, which was the more serious as GQG estimated Germany's reserve divisions still numbered sixty-four, of which forty-nine could not be located.[188] The Allies remained at a disadvantage and could not tell where Ludendorff would strike next. Since 21 March the total Allied line had extended by fifty-five kilometres to 750 kilometres, but the French share of it by ninety-seven to 580, and the Belgian by three to thirty-five, whereas the British share had fallen by forty-five to 135 kilometres. But the BEF had been much weakened: it had been driven to within sixty kilometres of Calais, fifty-five of its divisions had been involved in the fighting – twenty-nine of them twice and six three times – and ten of them were reduced to cadre formations.[189] On the other hand, the Germans also had to hold a longer and more improvised line with fewer troops, and they had captured neither Hazebrouck railway junction nor the remaining Flanders hills. Allied rail communications were hampered but not severed, and although the Germans had done more damage than they had suffered, time remained against them, especially as their own initiative had accelerated American troop shipments. Although Ludendorff had intended to avoid a battle of attrition, the fighting had been even more intensive than on the Somme and at

Third Ypres. Between 21 March and 29 April nearly 700,000 men became combat casualties: 326,000 Germans, 107,000 French, and 260,000 British.[190] In a microcosm of the war as a whole, the OHL had started an enterprise so costly that it could hardly stop while a chance remained of ending it successfully; whereas the Allied leaders and home fronts were committed to fighting to a finish. For the time being, however, the initiative remained with Germany; and the OHL saw no cause yet to relinquish it.

'BLÜCHER–YORCK'

The Germans' next blow was technically still more formidable, and yet its very success would prove their undoing. 'Michael' and 'Georgette' had been aimed against the British, menacing Allied communications in the congested confines between the front and the sea. The attack on 27 May, however, came in the French interior, directed towards the Paris eastern approaches, and it created a further salient that the final two attacks on 9 June and 15 July were meant – but failed – to disengage. It is difficult not to see here a fundamental misjudgement, which squandered resources while the hourglass sand ran out. The German army, for all its virtuosity, was let down by a failure of generalship.

The new operation began in reaction to French assistance to the BEF. By the end of April the OHL had decided it could make no further progress against what Wetzell described as now an 'Entente Front' rather than a British one. Instead he envisaged a surprise attack and 'a far-reaching success' against the French, which would draw off their reserves from the north and achieve 'profound political consequences'. As the most promising location he identified the Chemin des Dames ridge.[191] Ludendorff was sympathetic to the project as a means of drawing off reserves, though from the beginning the Germans disagreed (as they had in 1916 about Verdun) over whether this was a limited operation or a win-the-war thrust. At this stage the OHL remained confident. Albrecht von Thaer, on being transferred there from a front posting, found Hindenburg and Ludendorff unresponsive to his reports of troop despondency at the prospect of endless fighting. On the contrary, they believed morale was good, envisaged attacking repeatedly into the autumn, and still expected eventual victory. Wetzell told the German official history about the OHL's unanimity that the new operation would bring 'a military and political breakthrough success'. Ludendorff knew manpower was dwindling, but he was not short of shells ('Men are scarce. Munitions are there').[192] In a conference at Tournai on 4 May Ludendorff said that by the end of the month the army would be strong enough: the BEF would not recover quickly and the Americans remained few, while the French army had launched no major offensive since April 1917 and remained in crisis. In contrast General Hutier's conclusion from the conference was: 'Everything failed. Future plans changing. How the homeland will be disappointed', and unless the Chemin des Dames attack achieved a 'real breakthrough success . . . we are definitively stalled'. None the less, on 8 May the attack date was set.[193]

Whereas Rupprecht's army group had taken the lead in March and April, this time Crown Prince Wilhelm's would do so, and as saints' names had proved unpropitious the OHL invoked the Prussian military pantheon, codenaming the new scheme 'Blücher' after the commander who had relieved Wellington at Waterloo, with a westward extension named after Blücher's contemporary, Yorck. According to Ludendorff's memoirs the aim was to keep the initiative, use up Allied forces, and rest the Rupprecht army group for a new Flanders attack, once 'the present unity front of the Entente' was broken.[194] Thus he built in an intermediate stage before his final objective, which now began receding from him like the Cheshire cat's smile. From early May planning proceeded for both 'Blücher' and the Flanders drive, the latter bestowed with the dubious Wagnerian appellation of 'Hagen'. First planned for north of Ypres, 'Hagen' was reformulated as another offensive south of the city, directed towards the Flanders hills and Hazebrouck, and postponed until July for maximum preparedness.[195]

The inadequacy of Germany's artillery siege train still limited it to one major operation at a time. The heavy guns had taken twelve days to move from Picardy to the Lys, and 'Blücher' was both more challenging and further away. But generally the OHL concluded that 'Georgette' had vindicated the new attack procedures: in particular the opening barrages had silenced the enemy batteries. The creeping barrage had advanced too fast, the troops had bunched too much, and they should use machine guns more and take additional artillery with them – but these failings could be rectified. Infantry companies now received five light machine guns instead of four, and more rifle grenades, while marching columns and baggage trains were given machine-gun protection against air attack.[196] Unlike before the Lys, the attackers had almost a month to prepare, and the infrastructure favoured them, three double-tracked lines and one single-tracked line running into the designated sector, whereas the French had only two single-track railways. This was as well, as the Chemin des Dames presented formidable obstacles. Named after the 'ladies' way' travelled by Louis XV's daughters, the ridge had been the stage for Nivelle's disastrous offensive, but after the Malmaison battle the Germans had vacated it. Running sixteen miles from west to east, it was narrow, bare, and pocked by shells. Its northern slope rose 400 feet above the river Ailette, itself some sixty feet wide. Yet perhaps because of the sector's natural strength, the Germans knew it was one of the most thinly garrisoned of the French line: and recuperating British divisions held part of it, offering a similar weak point to that presented by the Portuguese.[197] None the less, the attackers left little to chance. Even more artillery than usual was needed, much of it hidden barely a kilometre from the front line. The divisions in the attack zone were more than quadrupled from eight to thirty-six, the men and their equipment (which included river bridges) remaining concealed by day and all movement proceeding in darkness, with well-greased axles and wheel rims covered by rugs. Troops spotted by aircraft had instructions to reverse direction and march away from the line, and a night chorus of frogs in the Ailette provided further assistance.[198]

Allied weaknesses assisted the attackers' skill and daring. During May the Allied high commands foresaw another German attack, but had no idea where. Perhaps a sign of the times was the proclamation by the American government of 30 May as 'a day of public humiliation, prayer, and fasting ... beseeching [God] that he will give victory to our armies'.[199] Although Pétain ordered day and night overflights of German lines and offered bonuses for prisoner captures, during May his intelligence could not locate the enemy reserves, and he knew their lateral railways could quickly move them south of the Oise. Yet almost until the eve of the attack GQG accepted that an attack north of the river was most likely, and the French army's distribution changed little, despite Pétain's protests that it was skewed. Foch insisted that the north was the most likely target and the bulk of the reserves must stay there. Between the Oise and the North Sea the Allies in early May had one division in line for every 4–5 kilometres of front and one in reserve for every six; between the Oise and Switzerland the figures were one for every twelve and thirty-three.[200] This distribution reflected not only apprehensions about where the Germans might strike next, but also Foch's continuing vision of a counteroffensive. On 20 May, with remarkable overconfidence, he instructed Haig and Fayolle to prepare attacks to push the Germans back from the Amiens–Paris railway and the Bruay coalfield. Meanwhile Pétain arranged for rapid reinforcement if the Germans struck in Champagne or Lorraine, and stationed his reserves along the railways, although these precautions merely mitigated the danger.[201]

The shortcomings of the French Sixth Army commander, General Denis Duchêne, compounded the unpreparedness. Clemenceau told the French Chamber Army Commission that Duchêne was of 'bad character', and at GQG he had the reputation of a martinet. He was irascible and difficult, and his staff dreaded working for him, so that the disaster that befell his army caused little surprise. However, he was well connected: his brother-in-law, General François Anthoine, had a senior position at Pétain's headquarters, and he himself was a Foch protégé.[202] This mattered because Duchêne took Foch's side in the bitter dispute among the French leaders about defence in depth. Pétain's Directive No. 4 of December 1917 had advocated concentrating the bulk of the defending forces in the second line, out of range of the enemy bombardment, the first line having the sacrificial function of slowing down the advance before the main force counter-attacked. The principle – which meant copying German doctrine and giving up French territory – was controversial, and it had forced the soldiers to spend the winter preparing a second position, which nevertheless remained incomplete. Duchêne believed it would be dangerous to yield ground on the Paris approaches, and demoralizing to abandon soil for which so many men had died. He expected Foch would back him in resisting Pétain's doctrine, and decided to defend his sector on the first position, in striking contrast with Plumer's reluctant realism in abandoning Passchendaele. Pétain and the army group commander, General Louis Franchet d'Espèrey, both disagreed with Duchêne, but Pétain acquiesced in his defiance and Duchêne instructed his corps commanders to hold the first line.[203]

Pétain commented in retrospect that he hesitated to relieve a commander when an attack might be imminent, and whereas Duchêne had a strong first position on the Chemin des Dames the second was incomplete and his men too few to hold both. Indeed, Duchêne had only one battalion for each 750 metres of front, and he had weakened his units by releasing men for leave and retraining. Moreover, at the eastern end of the ridge were the exhausted British divisions whom the Germans had detected, transferred under the *roulement* arrangement agreed in April to release intact French divisions for Foch's planned counter-attacks.[204] The British units had suffered very badly indeed, and been made up with poorly trained new recruits. They found themselves in beautiful and ominously tranquil countryside and occupying defences that were shallow, insanitary, and dilapidated. Their commander believed their sector was too wide for their numbers and protested to Duchêne, only to be rebuffed.[205] Meanwhile warnings by Captain Hubbard, of AEF intelligence, that the Germans were concentrating were disregarded, Duchêne's command reporting that everything was quiet. Although from mid-May evidence reached the French (via prisoners, deserters, and escapees) that an attack on the ridge was impending, only on the 26th did German captives disclose that it would come that night or the night after.[206] Both Duchêne and Pétain started preparations, but before the bombardment opened they had only a matter of hours. Not only were the defenders surprised, but their forces were too far forward and few reserves were in position to intervene.

The Germans aimed to redistribute the Allied reserves and to take at least the Chemin des Dames and if possible the heights south of the river Vesle.[207] Given these limited objectives, it turned out that they had massively overprepared. Once again they began with local air superiority, achieved by 500 aircraft, and they also used captured tanks. But their primary assault weapon remained the artillery, in which they achieved the largest superiority (3.7:1 in gun tubes) that they ever enjoyed on the Western Front, made up of 5,263 guns and 1,233 trench mortars. This was a bigger deployment than for 'Georgette' and not far short of that for 'Michael', on a much shorter front than for the latter. The density of guns per kilometre was 96, compared with 88 for earlier attacks, and on the most challenging sector it reached 110. Bruchmüller and his staff again had entire responsibility for organizing the bombardment, and enjoyed five weeks to do so. Gas would be followed by gas plus high explosive, so that the defenders had to keep their masks on, and all the guns used the Pulkowsky Method, the bombardment being conducted entirely in darkness. Three million rounds were fired on the first day, 50 per cent of them gas shells, and an asphyxiating cloud enveloped the ridge, muzzling the Allies' artillery, swamping their trenches, and breaking communications with the rear.[208] When the infantry stormed forward at 4.40 a.m., the men were buoyed up. The pause during May had allowed divisions to be rested and retrained (as before 21 March), and re-equipped to enhance their mobile firepower. The German Seventh Army attacked with thirty-six divisions (all but eight of which had been involved in 'Michael' and 'Georgette'); Duchêne's Sixth Army had eleven divisions in line (three British) and five (one British) behind. Even before the bombardment the German density of infantry per kilometre outnumbered that of the defenders by up to five times.[209]

By 9 a.m. the Germans held the crest of the ridge and were descending the southern slope, while their pontoons spanned the Ailette. Duchêne was blinded to the gravity of the situation, and continued to move up units, so thinning out his next position as to make it too untenable. By mid-morning the Germans had reached the river Aisne, where they captured some eighty bridges, not one being blown up. Duchêne had indeed prepared to do so, but he feared cutting off supplies to the forward troops and underestimated the speed of the collapse: hence the setting of the charges came too late, as did the order to detonate them.[210] The Germans overran the food, wine, and weaponry stored behind the front, and their bombardment was so accurate that it destroyed the tracks behind the French railway guns, several of which they captured. During the afternoon the attackers overran the French second position, between the Aisne and Vesle; that evening they crossed the latter, while lorries brought up reinforcement divisions and artillery moved forward. In one day the advance carved out a salient twenty-five miles wide at the base and up to twelve miles deep. Although the Germans had not achieved all their objectives on their flanks, in the centre they had advanced almost as fast as in a day on the march, wildly exceeding expectations. On the following morning some twenty German divisions resumed against the equivalent of seven and a half broken-up French and British ones.[211] Only a thin screen remained in front of them, although the British supply line remained open and an organized resistance remained in being, though only just, the Allies being bundled backwards rather than retreating at their own pace.

The Germans had scored a smashing victory over the army they considered their most formidable opponent. Startled by the speed of the collapse, Ludendorff resolved to widen the gap to left and right and weaken the French as much as possible: he could not therefore order his troops to halt, and he admitted in retrospect to a contradiction between the aims of the operation and its development. The Germans already controlled the initial OHL objective of the heights south of the Vesle when at 2.36 p.m. on the 28th the high command set a new line from Soissons via Fère-en-Tardenois to Reims, and after that a further one from Compiègne to Dormans and Epernay, expanding the objectives both southwards and to west and east. On the 29th the stakes were raised again: not only must Reims be taken, but the Marne was the new target destination, while a drive south-westwards would threaten Paris. Once again Ludendorff was succumbing to mission creep, exploiting success while losing sight of his larger goals, and this time irretrievably.[212]

During the next week the Germans drove deeper into a sack. By the end of Day Two they had taken 20,000 prisoners and advanced up to five miles more. They again used infiltration, avoiding frontal attacks and forcing their opponents to retreat by threatening their flanks, before deploying machine guns and trench mortars against pockets of resistance. They found so much food and drink in the captured depots that they could concentrate on bringing up ammunition, and resistance was so slight that less ammunition than usual was needed.[213] For several days the Allies seemed to have no answer. On the first day they lost most of their prepared positions, and when Pétain ordered a stand on the Vesle the river had already fallen. Reinforcements were fed in piecemeal, and were used up in their turn. None the less, Pétain at first showed commendable coolness, despite his reserves being up to two days' journey away. GQG started the pre-planned road and rail movements on the evening of 26 May, alerted further divisions on the 27th, and on the 28th committed still more. Having failed to hold the Germans in the centre, Pétain sought to contain the breach by forming 'moles of resistance' on its flanks, but this endeavour too was challenged when the advance broadened out to the west, the railway centre of Soissons – in contrast to Amiens – falling on 29 May. He then prepared a counteroffensive against both sides of the salient, but as launched on 31 May it hit the west only and with weaker forces than envisaged: German machine guns and counter-attacks halted it.[214] When Clemenceau visited the front to rally Duchêne and the other generals, he found a battle out of control and a far from orderly retreat. The danger now loomed that the entire eastern section of the French front would be cut off, and on 30 May Pétain secretly instructed his commander there, Curières de Castelnau, to prepare an evacuation.[215] On the following day, he told Clemenceau that the government should evacuate Paris, the Premier responding that if the city fell France must continue fighting. With the Germans now on the Marne and thirty-nine miles from the capital, Pétain warned Foch that his troops could not hold and 'the situation is therefore very serious'. That evening he told Franchet d'Espèrey that the Fifth Army west of Reims must stay in place: 'Do not hesitate to employ violence if necessary.'[216]

As Pétain committed more and more of his reserves he was obliged to have recourse to Foch, who understood that moving forces from the north would play along with Ludendorff's game. Foch at first believed that the attack was so peripheral that it must be a feint, but as it developed he accepted be must respond to it. He agreed to Pétain's reinforcement measures, which meant that by the 28th almost all available French forces – at least twenty infantry divisions – were moving towards the battle zone. When Pétain also asked for the French forces that had gone to Flanders, Foch agreed only to move them close to railway embarkation points, although he sent five US divisions that were under training in the British zone to take over quiet French sectors.[217]

Alarm was spreading to the alliance as a whole. When Pershing dined with Foch and his staff, he found 'It would be difficult to imagine a more depressed group of officers.' He informed Washington that the situation was 'very grave' and the time had come for the US to bear the brunt of the war. Similarly Haig found Foch more anxious than he had ever seen him, and Henry Wilson told the Cabinet that the French troops had shown poor morale and Soissons and Reims were likely to fall, creating a base line for operations against Paris.[218] Wilson ordered detailed preparations to evacuate the BEF, and contingency plans were readied to abandon the Channel ports and from everywhere north of the Somme.[219] Throughout the summer anxiety remained high in London, where work proceeded on the 'Z' scheme for evacuating over 1.75 million troops and civilians from the area north of the Somme, it being accepted that the BEF would have to jettison nearly all of its equipment. Finally between 1 and 3 June a bad-tempered meeting of the Supreme War Council convened at Versailles: Foch condemned the British for their tardiness in reconstituting their cadre divisions; the Europeans did not hide their exasperation with Pershing. Haig (in contrast to the French in March and April) said he could help little because so many Germans still faced him. He reluctantly accepted the transfer of the American divisions training with the British, but when Foch ordered that British reserve divisions should also be prepared for movement, and authorized French forces to be moved from Flanders there was another command crisis. Haig appealed to London and Milner was sent over, to find Haig once more fearing that he would be forced back on the Channel. Fortunately it was clarified that Foch was asking for British reserve divisions only to be made ready, and they turned out not to be needed.[220]

While these shock waves rolled round the alliance the danger was beginning to ease. Despite the failure of Pétain's counter-attacks, the French leaders detected that enemy momentum was subsiding. Although the Germans brought up fresh troops each morning, their lead divisions again had instructions to advance as far and fast as they could. The captured food and drink were a mixed blessing, officers losing control as their men ransacked cellars filled with *pinard*, and the *Feldpolizei* struggled to move them on. By 30 May the Allies were regaining air superiority while the Germans found their munitions running low. Ludendorff was anxious to take Reims, through which he could supply the emerging salient from the north-east, but this objective eluded him, in part precisely due to shell shortages that halted attacks against French positions on the heights south of the city.[221] As in earlier offensives, in fact, the Germans' objectives widened as their progress decelerated. Once they reached the Marne the critical sector became the south-west of the salient, between the Marne and Aisne. Here the French were ensconced in wooded hills round Villers-Cotterêts, and the OHL acquiesced in the Wilhelm army group's wish to focus its efforts against them rather than towards Reims. Ludendorff may have viewed threatening Paris as a means of drawing off Allied reserves from the north, but Wetzell, the army group, and the German Seventh Army seem now to have viewed the French capital as itself the target, a Seventh Army directive referring to 'the further march forward in the direction of Paris'. But by now the attackers once more faced stiffening resistance and mounting casualties. The French artillery became strong enough to lay down a protective barrage while aircraft strafed the attackers' infantry and guns. Pétain feared the Germans might bypass Villers-Cotterêts by the south, but as reinforcements were fed in more methodically the troops dug in and organized first and second defence lines, as well as maintaining better communications with their headquarters. On 4 June Foch warned Pétain he could make no more reductions in the northern forces, but on the same day Ludendorff accepted the Seventh Army's advice to minimize losses by halting major operations in favour of smaller attacks.[222] The acutest danger was over.

In the final phase American forces for the first time played a significant role. On 31 May the AEF Third Division helped to halt the German advance along the Marne at Château-Thierry and on 6 June its Second Division attacked Belleau Wood, eventually clearing it and repelling counter-attacks at the cost of nearly 10,000 casualties.[223] The tonic effect should not be underestimated: Jean de Pierrefeu, the communiqué writer at GQG, likened it to a blood transfusion for the French veterans, who cheered the Americans as they moved up. Pétain predicted that 'The junction [la soudure] will take place, it is imminent, and we will have no more to fear': if they could hang on to July, victory would be assured. Clemenceau commented similarly: 'I told you on my first day, I am gambling the war on American intervention which will bring us such resources that we cannot fail to finish the Germans off.' None the less, he justly attributed prime responsibility for halting Ludendorff to the French infantry, fighting for days and nights without sleep against odds of over two to one.[224] Once again the Germans' 105,370 killed, wounded, captured, and missing were exceeded by the Allies' 127,337.[225] By 1 June, according to Pétain, thirty-seven French divisions had been engaged and seventeen 'completely used up'. The OHL was pleased to have delivered such a blow to its most dangerous antagonist, and Italian and British observers felt a certain Schadenfreude in seeing the French humiliated as they had been at Caporetto and by 'Michael'.[226] More concretely, the Germans had interrupted the Paris–Nancy trunk railway, which was both a lateral line running parallel to the front and a link between the French-held Lorraine steel mills and the Paris armament plants, intensifying the economic disruption caused by their menace to Amiens and the Bruay coalfield.

None the less, in its larger goals the battle had failed. Ludendorff had hoped for a political crisis in France and, according to Pershing, there was 'something akin to a panic' in Paris, which a million inhabitants had abandoned since the spring, while Clemenceau's Council of Ministers and the Chamber of Deputies rounded on the generals.[227] Despite this, Clemenceau defended his government and his commanders relatively easily. And if Foch eventually moved French and American divisions from the north, Ludendorff diverted an extra thirteen 'attack' divisions from Rupprecht's army group in pursuit of his enlarged goals for the operation. Although the Germans now presented a standing threat to Paris, they had created yet another exposed salient with a long perimeter, improvised defences, and fragile communications. By failing to take Reims, they had also failed to take the Reims–Soissons trunk railway, while the north–south Laon–Soissons line leading into the salient was both dangerously close to the front and blocked by a tunnel at Vauxaillon that the Germans themselves had blown up in 1917.[228] 'Blücher' might have been a tactical tour de force but it was an operational disaster, postponing any further attack in Flanders and trapping the Germans in an exposed position that they could neither enlarge nor evacuate. This dilemma would preoccupy them until the pendulum moved back in favour of their enemies.

'GNEISENAU'

The German army was never so dangerous again, and from now on even its tactical effectiveness diminished, while the Allies perfected methods that checkmated its assault procedures. The changing balance became evident during the fourth of Ludendorff's offensives: operation 'Gneisenau', or the Battle of the Matz, between 9 and 14 June. Starting only five days after 'Blücher' was suspended, the operation had been conceived in early May as a supplement to it. The Eighteenth Army (which had spearheaded the drive on Amiens) attacked between the 'Michael' and 'Blücher' salients. If successful it would improve German lateral communications by taking the Montdidier–Compiègne road, as well as drawing off additional enemy reserves, but this was the weakest of the five attacks. It was never envisaged as a war-winning effort, and the OHL and the Wilhelm army group scaled it down. Like 'Georgette' it was handicapped by the shortage of heavy artillery, the need to reposition the siege train after 'Blücher' delaying operations until the latter had been suspended and therefore assisting the French to recover.[229]

Furthermore, this time the French were not surprised. Overflights reported railway movements and preparations in the sector, and on 3 June the French decrypted a radio communication that detailed an attack for 7 June, while a sudden increase in deserters was a sure sign that an operation was impending, and this time they disclosed the exact date and hour.[230] Forewarning enabled the French to place an aerial screen above their positions, while Pétain and Fayolle, the army group commander, readied sixteen divisions for intervention and Fayolle envisaged holding them for a counterstroke.[231] Once again, however, confusion over defensive tactics impaired these dispositions. General Humbert, who commanded the Third Army on the threatened sector, opposed Pétain's system of defence in depth, and as the French had held the position only since March his field fortifications were sketchy. His first line was more or less complete but the second only roughed out, according to Humbert because of a lack of labour but perhaps also because he was organizing the sector as a jumping-off point for an offensive. Fayolle instructed the infantry to be moved out of range of the German mine-launchers, but Humbert placed them in an intermediate position, given that the second line was incomplete. Although the infantry were not as far forward as on 27 May, when the Germans attacked about half of them were within two miles of the front line. Churchill, who visited on the evening before, found them 'very calm and gallant'. But this time most of the French artillery was placed further back, and during the night it put up harassing fire. Conversely, the Germans had assembled 2,276 guns against 1,058 French ones, so their superiority was less crushing than on 27 May and their preparation less thorough, Bruchmüller being again in charge but ailing.[232]

The attack proceeded on a west–east front some thirty-three kilometres long. Eleven divisions were in the first wave and seven behind: fewer than expected by the French, who had seven divisions, with others ready to intervene. To the east the battle zone lay among wooded hills, but in the west lay an open plateau that better favoured the attacker. Again the Germans' progress on Day One was swift: they advanced up to nine kilometres, took 5,000 prisoners, and reached the second line. Yet French casualties were lower and the retreat more orderly than in May, while the Germans' creeping barrage was too light, the artillery came forward too slowly, and telephone cable and munitions ran short.[233] On the second day French reinforcement divisions arrived, counter-attacks slowed progress, and when the Germans reached the Oise, its bridges had been blown up. Hence the French felt able to launch a counterstroke, which Fayolle had envisaged beforehand but was improvised with extraordinary speed, being planned and put together in barely twenty-four hours and assigned to Charles Mangin, one of the most aggressive French generals, who had been discredited by his part in the Nivelle offensive but was now returning to favour. The troops moved up by night and the attack achieved surprise at 11 a.m. on 11 June after a half-hour bombardment, four infantry divisions supported by aircraft and 163 tanks going in behind a rolling barrage against the Germans' west flank. This attack also bore marks of haste: the French artillery failed to silence the German guns, the mist had cleared, the Germans were initially surprised but speedily recovered, and sixty-three tanks received hits. The French advanced three kilometres and took 1,000 prisoners but by the evening the attack had halted and when renewed the next day it was halted again.[234] None the less, it prevented any further German advance.

As Mangin proclaimed in his orders, after two months on the receiving end the French army was regaining the initiative. 'Gneisenau' was stopped in its tracks, barring the routes to Compiègne and Paris. The Eighteenth Army's post-battle review recognized that the French had been forewarned and that – given the brevity of the summer nights – the preliminary period had been too short. The French guns had been deployed in depth and had reduced the effect of German gas by last-minute changes of location; and although the Pulkowsky Method had worked well it needed impeccable preparation. The barrage had advanced too fast and had silenced neither all the French machine guns, nor sharpshooters in trees, while the French tanks had made a considerable impression on the German infantry and aerial harassment had been 'very vexing'. Ludendorff was 'disappointed' with the outcome, and well he might have been, as for the first time the Germans had not made even tactically significant gains.[235]

Ludendorff had even greater cause for disappointment with operation 'Hammer Blow', delivered on 12 June in the area south of Soissons that had seen the final 'Blücher' attacks early in June and meant as a follow-up to 'Gneisenau'. Once again the effort to orchestrate assaults in quick succession was overambitious: the French detected the preparations and drew back their artillery, which stopped the advance by the first afternoon. In total during the Matz fighting German casualties numbered about 25,000 and French ones 40,000 so the balance still operated in the Germans' favour, but the OHL knew its men's efficiency was fading.[236] The French detected both 'Gneisenau' and 'Hammer Blow' several days beforehand and carried out tactical withdrawals before attacks whose edge was blunted by hurried positioning of the guns and by shortages of shells and infantry. The German army was now being assailed by the first of the three waves of the 1918–19 influenza pandemic, which reached it some three weeks earlier than it did the Allied troops. Starting in May, the disease affected 139,000 men during June and peaked in early July. It was much less lethal than the second wave in the autumn, but it lasted for four to six days on average and even after men got over the symptoms it left them debilitated.[237] The outbreak was one more reason why the German attack formula that had seemed all-conquering was losing its potency, while the French and British were finding answers to it. The reversal of fortunes would be demonstrated spectacularly by what, in mid-July, would be the turning point not only of the 1918 campaign but also of the war.

RUSSIA AND THE NEAR EAST

Before coming to the climax of the defensive phase, it is necessary to range more widely. Events in other theatres profoundly influenced those in France and Belgium, not least because up to a fifth of the German army remained in former Russian territory. In the Ottoman Empire the German presence was small: 4,500 in summer 1917. After Caporetto the Germans withdrew from Italy, and their expeditionary force in Macedonia, which in summer 1917 was still some 70,000 men strong, fell to 33,000 by the end of August 1918, four infantry battalions being moved in the spring and six more after the peace treaty signed at Bucharest in May with Romania. Some went to Palestine, but most returned to the Western Front, despite the protestations of the Bulgarian army commander.[238] But Germany's continuing presence on the Eastern Front dwarfed its other commitments, and after March 1918 transfers from Russia to the west slowed down, two divisions being moved in May but no more until the autumn. The forty-three eastern divisions on 21 March fell to thirty-four by early November, and troop numbers on the Eastern Front from just over a million to about half that figure. All the same, the force remained substantial, and alongside it Austria-Hungary maintained a further ten divisions and a quarter of a million men: in September the two empires together still had some 600,000 troops in the Ukraine.[239] It was true that the eastern divisions sacrificed mobility by giving up horses and lost their men aged under thirty-five. None the less, like the divisions that returned before March they could have garrisoned quieter Western Front sectors and released younger men for the assault waves, in a similar role to that performed by the Americans. They still constituted an under-utilized reserve when man-power was desperately needed.

The eastern commitment was the more remarkable as the Central Powers and Soviet Russia were supposedly at peace. Ludendorff's bête noire, the foreign minister, Kühlmann, had tried to limit the involve-ment. At the Bad Homburg conference in February he had favoured acquiescing in a walk-out by the Soviets from the Brest-Litovsk peace negotiations, rather than driving deeper into Russia to impose German terms. But he lacked support from Chancellor Hertling, and Wilhelm II sympathized with Hindenburg's and Ludendorff's determination to achieve 'clear conditions' in the east.[240] The Germans renewed their advance and a peace treaty was signed. Henceforth Kühlmann avoided further confrontations with the OHL, and his ministry's misgivings were sidelined while Ludendorff himself, despite his crushing responsi-bilities elsewhere, signed an impressive number of key statements on eastern policy.

For Ludendorff it made little sense to draw further troops from Russia to strengthen his hand in France, for much of the purpose of the western campaign was to maintain Germany's Brest-Litovsk gains. And in the absence of a protecting garrison, the eastern *Imperium* would crumble. At the Spa conference of 2–3 July 1918, Germany's civilian and military authorities agreed that the formerly Russian portion of Poland, occupied since 1915 even if promised nominal independence, must remain under German economic, military, and political domina-tion, as a source of raw materials, an outlet for agricultural settlement, and a security buffer zone.[241] In addition, the Germans had overrun the Baltic provinces of Lithuania and Courland (the latter today in Latvia), which were administered by their Eastern army headquarters, *Oberost*. In conjunction with the German settlers there a quasi-colonial reorganization had begun, including plans for economic exploitation and resettlement.[242] Although under the March 1918 peace treaty Germany did not annex these regions, Russian sovereignty over them ended. It also ended in the Ukraine, where the Central Powers signed a separate treaty with the Kiev government.

Germany therefore had a major stake in a region where it had lost hundreds of thousands of soldiers. After March its Eastern European ambitions expanded, and the Allies could do little to frustrate them. The process centred on two drives towards Scandinavia and the Black Sea. In the north 13,000 German soldiers landed in Finland in April, to assist the anti-Bolshevik forces in the Finnish Civil War. They took Helsingfors (Helsinki) and defeated the Reds within weeks. The Germans wanted a friendly government in Finland, but they also wanted raw materials such as nickel, while the navy hoped for bases on the Baltic and the Barents Sea.[243] During the summer Wilhelm and the OHL were tempted by an even larger undertaking in the shape of Operation 'Keystone', a plan to occupy Kronstadt and Petrograd before advancing against the Allied forces that had landed at Murmansk, and replacing the Bolsheviks by a reactionary Russian regime. They objected ideologically to dealing with Lenin, whereas the foreign ministry feared that Germany would overextend itself and argued that the Bolsheviks were anyway serving the Central Powers by keeping Russia weak and divided. The ministry got its way in the supplementary agreements to the Brest-Litovsk peace treaty signed on 27 August, which left the Soviet regime in place but obliged the Russians to abandon sovereignty over Livonia and Estonia and brought the frontier of German influence even closer to Petrograd. Only in September, however, did defeat in the west finally force 'Keystone' to be dropped.[244]

The Black Sea drive ranged even wider. In April, German forces occupied the Crimea, Ludendorff describing the operation as a military, political, and economic necessity, to control the ports, seize supplies, and protect the German settlers there: during the summer he discussed plans to make the peninsula a German colony.[245] In the Caucasus, the German leaders felt threatened by their own ally, the Ottoman Empire, which like them did not rest content with the Brest-Litovsk treaty and expanded northwards at the expense of the newly independent state of Transcaucasia, which in May broke up into its components of Azerbaijan, Armenia, and Georgia. While the foreign ministry wanted to limit Turkish influence, the OHL saw Transcaucasia as a long-term partner like Finland. The economics and war ministries coveted the manganese of the region, which was needed to make special steels for armaments.[246] Agreements concluded in May gave Germany rights to use the Georgian railways, which its troops occupied. The OHL also hoped to distract the Turks further eastwards, so that the two countries could jointly dominate the Caspian Sea as a basis for co-operating with Afghanistan, attacking British interests in Persia, and threatening India. As Ludendorff put it, sending troops to the Caucasus would still be a move against Britain: 'We are thus fighting there not a new but an old enemy ... whether the troops fight there or elsewhere does not matter.'[247]

Relatively few troops went to the Crimea and the Caucasus. It was the Ukraine that swallowed soldiers and as the springboard for further operations was central to the Black Sea undertaking. In the Ukraine the OHL took on a commitment comparable to the post-2003 American occupation of Iraq, in an area larger than Germany itself, while simultaneously fighting a life and death struggle in the west. After the Bolshevik Revolution the government of the Rada (or parliament) in Kiev had declared independence, but early in 1918 the Ukrainian Bolsheviks, with Russian support, ousted it. In response to a Rada appeal the Central Powers invaded in February and occupied the cities and railways. But the Rada was disagreeable to them as an egalitarian regime committed to upholding peasant land seizures at the landlords' expense. In April, with German connivance, Pavel Skoropadsky overthrew it and declared himself Hetman ('Leader').[248] As the Germans resisted the creation of a Ukrainian army, they were now drawn into Ukrainian politics to uphold a dictatorship that effectively they had created.

Ludendorff told Kühlmann that the Ukraine was essential for Germany's survival and raw materials supply, and that German troops must stay there. Georgia too was necessary for its raw materials and must be protected as a Christian state against the Turks; while Finland was needed as an ally.[249] The emergent eastern empire could weaken the Allied blockade and sustain Germany in the next war, underpinning its world power status. The Germans wanted not only food and minerals but also to forestall any revival of Russian power and to reduce the threat from Bolshevism. As the summer went by, however, peasant resistance to requisitioning grew, and under Skoropadsky food deliveries remained well short of what was hoped for and what the Ukrainian authorities had promised to provide.[250] Grain, eggs, and horses arrived in useful quantities, but the occupation helped principally by keeping the occupation army fed. However, it also kept open the possibility of access to the oilfields at Baku, which before 1914 had been among the most productive in the world and during 1918 were occupied by a British expedition from Persia in August and then by Turkish forces in September. No Baku oil ever reached Germany, but Ludendorff believed obtaining it was 'urgently necessary' and essential for continuing the war into 1919. Wilhelm Groener, the Chief of Staff to the Ukrainian expeditionary force until he became Ludendorff's successor, commented as late as September that 'we must prepare for war *ad aeturnum*' and that lubricating oil was vital for the Ukrainian railways, as was fuel for Germany's U-boats, lorries, and ships. It must occupy not just the Caspian but as far as Turkestan.[251]

The Allies also denuded the other theatres of war in order to concentrate on the central struggle. During the defensive phase on the Western Front, they had to batten down the hatches. For the Americans this order of priority was anyway never in question. Wilson never declared war on Bulgaria or Turkey; and did so on Austria-Hungary only as a morale booster for the Italians after Caporetto. The US sent only one regiment (the 132nd Ohio) to the Italian theatre; it arrived as a propaganda gesture in July and remained for almost all its stay in the rear.[252] The War Department and Pershing's GHQ believed from the beginning that America's land military effort should be concentrated on the Western Front, and although Wilson queried whether alternatives existed he accepted their advice. In the First as in the Second World War the Americans favoured the direct approach of exerting maximum force in what they deemed the decisive theatre.[253] To a large extent the same applied to the Italians, who after Caporetto withdrew many of their forces from Macedonia, although they sent 60,000 labourers to the Western Front in return for Allied assistance, and supplied the French with two divisions, which took part in the Champagne fighting in mid-July.[254] As for the French, despite their territorial ambitions in the Middle East, their troop presence there was minimal, their detachment in Palestine being mostly Armenians. Of the six divisions that they sent to Italy after Caporetto, in March they withdrew three. Salonika remained by far their most important foreign commitment, but even here the numbers were whittled down from 232,000 to 209,000 between June and October 1918.[255]

Much the most widely distributed of the Allied land forces was the British, and they too applied the principle of concentration, even though at the beginning of the year the Supreme War Council endorsed Middle East offensives if they entailed no large diversion of resources away from the Western Front. As Henry Wilson put it, 'Every man we have in the world is going to France.'[256] Their dilemma was that the consequences of Russia's collapse simultaneously threatened them in Western Europe and jeopardized their imperial presence in Asia. Most of the members of Lloyd George's Cabinet feared a compromise peace (or worse) that would leave Germany invulnerable to blockade and positioned to replace Russia as a menace to India.[257] Little could be done to restore an Eastern Front, and British hopes in the first half of 1918 rested on the chimera of a Japanese advance from Vladivostok, where, however, the Japanese politicians refused to land unless the Americans participated. A commitment from Washington was lacking until the Czech Legion, composed of some 40,000 Czech prisoners from Austria-Hungary who had formed a separate unit in the Tsarist army, rebelled against the Bolsheviks in May, and Wilson reluctantly agreed to intervention in order to rescue them. Even then, however, the American–Japanese expeditionary force did not venture into the interior. The government of India believed it faced a threat from German agents and collaborators at a time when much of the Indian army was overseas and the white troops who since the 1857 Mutiny had formed a third of it had fallen from a peacetime 77,000 to – at one stage – only 15,000.[258] The Commander-in-Chief in India signalled 'a notable change, to our disadvantage, in the east': he needed at least three more divisions, and although he did not expect Germans to attack him, Indians under German leadership might. In this matter, however, Henry Wilson, whose judgement was often questionable, correctly advised that no imminent attack was feasible. The Germans were preoccupied in France, and they or the Turks could only invade via Afghanistan, an enterprise slow enough for India to be reinforced against it if need be.[259]

India was therefore not reinforced, although each Indian unit in Mesopotamia released officers and a company of men as nuclei for new battalions recruited in the subcontinent.[260] Indeed, Mesopotamia became the key loser. After Britain's humiliation at Kut in 1916 the theatre had been reinforced, and as late as March 1918 British Empire troops were advancing further up the Euphrates. But in the winter of 1917–18 the army there was ordered to release two divisions to Palestine, and from each remaining brigade one Indian battalion was to be transferred to Macedonia, while much transport capacity was diverted to supporting intervention in Persia and at Baku. During the baking summer months the British stayed quiet.[261] Yet although Palestine gained at Mesopotamia's expense the army there (the Egyptian Expeditionary Force, or EEF, under Sir Edmund Allenby) was also stinted. It too had been reinforced in 1917, for the purpose of capturing Jerusalem. Once it had done so, the War Cabinet wanted Allenby in 1918 to advance another 400 miles to Aleppo, but he judged he could not progress without additional men. After the 'Michael' offensive he had to send many of his troops to France, being left eventually with only one all-white division. His other six infantry divisions each lost nine of their twelve battalions, which were replaced by Indians, many of them raw recruits and others Moslem, so that Allenby doubted their reliability.[262] In all he sent to France over 60,000 officers and men,[263] and in these circumstances his main concern became to maintain contact with the irregulars of the Arab Revolt who were besieging the Turks in Medina and threatening the Hejaz railway, the main Turkish line of communication running down to the east of the British.[264] In the meantime, as he summed up, 'my role is to be the active Defensive'.[265] This role included sending two large raids into Transjordan in March–April and April–May to try to break the Turkish communication lines along the railway, but both failed because of insufficient men, transport, and weaponry.[266] During the hot season Allenby settled down to training his new recruits and preparing an advance in the autumn.

In Macedonia, too, the defensive phase was for the Allies a time of troop redistribution. Since landing at Salonika in October 1915, Allied troops had stayed in part because of French domestic politics. Their commander, Maurice Sarrail, had a following among the left and centre in the Chamber of Deputies and recalling him risked endangering consensus in a country where civil–military relations had long been divisive. The other Allied governments distrusted Sarrail as an incompetent political general and the British military detested the Macedonia commitment and would have liked to withdraw, but British politicians hesitated to damage inter-Allied relations.[267] What was salvaged of the Serb army held part of the Allied front, as did the Italians, who had ambitions in the Balkans and were fighting a parallel war against the Austrians in Albania. By 1917 over 680,000 Allied troops were in the Balkan theatre, and whereas many of them could have been transferred elsewhere their opponents were mostly Bulgarians, whom their government refused to move. Hence the net balance greatly favoured the Germans, who labelled Macedonia their 'largest internment camp',[268] Clemenceau disparaging the men there as 'the gardeners of Salonika'.[269] After the revolution in Russia, South Slav prisoners of war released from there reinforced the Serb contingents, and once Greece entered the war it too supplied forces. But even though the Greeks received Allied finance and supplies, their build-up was disappointingly slow, although their morale improved after, on 30 May, they captured a hill known as the Skra de Legen. The remaining Russians were disarmed, and the Italian and French troops were scaled down. Two British divisions had gone in 1917 to Palestine, and the four remaining were now reduced from twelve to nine battalions each, yielding twelve battalions for the Western Front. Indian troops were scheduled to replace them, but only later.[270] After May, therefore, Salonika followed the other smaller fronts into somnolence. Clemenceau, who governed without support from the French Left, replaced Sarrail by the experienced and energetic General Marie Guillaumat in December 1917, but the new commander's strategy centred on a contingency plan against Germany repeating in Macedonia what it had achieved at Caporetto, and he insisted on defence in depth and on constructing a second line. His focus was on supply and troop morale and on rebuilding relations with the British commander, General George Milne.

PIAVE

If the Germans slowly ran down their garrison in the former Russian territories, the Allies could be more thoroughgoing in denuding the outlying fronts, in large measure because they had Greeks and Indians to draw on. In Italy, however, three each of the French and British divisions sent out in 1917 remained after March, and this front did not wind down for the summer: on the contrary, the battle fought between 15 and 24 June was the biggest yet to take place there, and it wreaked similar havoc on the Austro-Hungarian army to that wreaked by the Ludendorff offensives on the German. And whereas the Austrians deliberately imitated the Germans' new tactics, the Italians countered them with similar methods to those of the French. The battle has been little studied in English-language writing, but it deserves to be better known.

Whereas the Bulgarians refrained from attacking in 1918, and the Turks diverted their attention to the Caucasus, the Austrians like the Germans launched an all-out offensive on their principal front. The origins of the Battle of the Piave were connected with the 'Czernin incident', a dramatic development in Austro-German political relations. Ottokar Czernin, the Austro-Hungarian foreign minister, wanted to improve relations with Berlin, which Karl's peace soundings had damaged. On 2 April he tried to smoke out the peace lobbyists in the Emperor's circle by delivering a bellicose speech in Vienna city hall, in which he asserted that France had made approaches before 'Michael' and Austria-Hungary had rejected them. The account was factually in error, but Clemenceau perceived a challenge to his government's credibility and to French morale and retaliated by publishing the letter – unknown to Czernin – of March 1917 in which Karl had supported France's claims in Alsace-Lorraine. Although Karl said he was the victim of lies, his credibility was shattered, not only with Czernin (whom he replaced by Stephan Burián), but also with the army high command and with the Germans. In May he met Wilhelm at Spa and accepted a long-term alliance, economic agreements, and a military convention that would establish a common high command and standardize uniforms and weapons.[271] The Germans were well placed to insist on an Austro-Hungarian contribution to their offensive drive and pressed for an early Austrian offensive in Italy while they attacked in France, although in fact the Austrian offensive was delayed until after the Chemin des Dames and Matz operations.[272]

The Germans were pushing on an open door, for the Austrian high command (AOK – Armee Oberkommando) was also willing. Field Marshal Svetozar Boroević, who had commanded the Austrians on the Isonzo and now did so on the Piave front, doubted the value of a new offensive, but his was a minority view.[273] Karl, who approved the venture, needed to placate the Germans but also hoped a victory would enable him to reassert his independence.[274] Under Karl, Franz Conrad von Hötzendorff, the CGS from 1906 to 1917, had been demoted to the command of the Tyrol group of armies, and his place taken by General Arthur Arz von Straussenberg, with General Johann von Waldstätten as his Chief of Operations. All three men wanted an offensive, but their approaches to the problem differed. While the Italians had pushed north-eastwards towards Trieste, they had left themselves vulnerable in the north, where they held a shallow rim on the edge of the mountains. Conrad had masterminded Austria-Hungary's unsuccessful attempt in 1916 to descend from the Trentino into the North Italian plain, and he wanted to strike out into the lowlands again. He dreamt of reaching Venice and knocking Italy out of the war. Arz believed Conrad's plan was too ambitious, and foresaw logistical problems in moving up artillery shells. Instead he favoured two attacks, not only in the mountains but also on the Veneto plain across the middle section of the Piave. He envisaged the thrusts as mutually supporting, and Karl embraced the concept.[275] During March, Conrad and Boroević were asked to draw up plans,[276] Boroević considering that if there must be an offensive, its principal weight should be on the middle Piave, attacking towards Treviso. Here the supply difficulties would be fewer, although the swollen river would be an obstacle and the Italian defences could be deeper. But the outcome was a compromise that conformed with Arz's and Karl's conception while suiting neither front commander: a pincer attack with approximately equal forces in each arm, neither being reinforced to the extent that Conrad and Boroević thought necessary.

Arz privately believed the offensive could gain useful but limited objectives, but to the Germans he predicted an Italian 'collapse' and he found his army confident when he visited it.[277] Although the Germans had now left, the defeat of Serbia, Russia, and Romania enabled the Austrians to concentrate their energies on Italy and to attack with larger numbers than at Caporetto. Like Germany, Austria-Hungary was moving divisions from the Eastern Front: four in February, nine in March/April, seven in May, and one in June, totalling twenty-one. By the end of June it had also received back 517,000 prisoners of war from Russian captivity.[278] The latter proved to be a mixed blessing and took part in a series of mutinies, but on paper they brought the depleted divisions back up to strength. In other ways, too, the army had been consolidated. Arz had presided over a reorganization that had standardized the composition of divisions and boosted the number of technical troops, artillery batteries, and aviation squadrons. Although the Austrians had no tanks, the usefulness of these devices was limited in the precipitous heights and marshy lowlands that made up much of the Italian theatre, whereas the density of the Austrian artillery in June 1918 was up to twice that in the previous October. During the winter Arz had insisted on intensive training and had sent his officers to observe the Germans' tactics, which he would now attempt to emulate: after an intense bombardment the infantry would infiltrate as far and fast as possible behind a creeping barrage.[279] Over 6 million shells, 7,500 guns of all calibres, and 623 aircraft were assembled. Of the sixty divisions in the reorganized army, fifty were in the two attack sectors (twenty-seven in the mountains and twenty-three on the Piave), but Arz kept a reserve of four under his control that was only near enough to reinforce Boroević, thus advantaging him over Conrad.[280] On the other hand, the Austrians also shared some German weaknesses. They were short of horses, the numbers available in June 1918 being less than half the 1 million at the end of 1916. Nor might the soldiers have the stamina to exploit a breakthrough, after the exhausting work of preparation (especially in the mountains), carried out on meagre rations. Some attacking troops received only eight ounces of inedible bread plus three ounces of meat per day.[281] In addition to organizing a propaganda campaign against 'our hereditary enemy', the AOK held out the prospect of capturing enemy supplies – and of peace – if the operation succeeded. But Austrian war production was in steep decline, and the civilian economy in even worse condition: although weaponry was accumulated for the initial stage, it would be difficult to maintain supply in the follow-up and the railway system was so congested that much equipment was still en route when the battle began.[282]

The Austrians were attacking an enemy who since the previous autumn had rallied. Recovery flowed partly from change at the top. Luigi Cadorna has earned opprobrium as one of the most callous and incompetent of First World War commanders, and his successor, Armando Diaz, proved a welcome contrast. Diaz's family came from Naples (though originally Spain); he was trained as an artillery and engineering officer before proceeding to Staff College; in 1912 he held a field command during the Libyan war against Turkey and was wounded severely. In the First World War he took divisional and corps commands but was relatively unknown before being promoted to Commander-in-Chief.[283] Yet his appointment, along with those of Pétain, Guillaumat, and Allenby, was one of several that brought competent managers to senior Allied commands. He had a more consultative style than Cadorna, working well with and meeting regularly the King and his ministers, as well as being courteous towards Italy's allies.

Although Foch gained a nominal co-ordinating power over the Italian front, it did not amount to much, and Diaz spent much of 1918 resisting Allied pressure to attack, concentrating like Pétain in 1917 on morale and re-equipment. By February the post-Caporetto reorganization was completed; and the *sbandati* had been reconstituted into units. Diaz halted pointless limited attacks and abandoned exposed positions that could be held only with constant losses. He rebuilt fighting spirit and cohesion as well as attending to practical grievances such as leave and food. He also, in collaboration with the government, made good equipment losses with new and better replacements, giving airpower particular priority. In fact the army's re-equipment was rapid, and most of it completed by Italian industry, although the losses were not completely made good until August.[284] With more men and more equipment Diaz could press his commanders to adopt defence in depth: he insisted on the construction of a second position and infantry not being massed in the forward line. He told his commanders that in France the Germans had advanced further than they need have done because of the Allies' failure to apply defence in depth, and Italy should not repeat this mistake; but nor would he commit his reserves until the situation demanded it. Under pressure from Foch during the 'Michael' and Lys crises Diaz agreed to a relieving attack on the Asiago plateau, where the British and French would fight alongside the Italians, but the operation was to last only one day and even so was cancelled at the end of May when it became clear that the enemy onslaught was imminent.[285]

In the coming battle Diaz would not be surprised. The Allies regained air superiority early in 1918, in good measure through the British, who between January and March destroyed some eighty-one enemy aircraft for the loss of fifteen of their own. The Italians received very precise information from overflights as well as from listening in on enemy field telephone conversations – the Austrians used field telephones a lot, without the benefit of a new British device that prevented eavesdropping.[286] As on the Western Front the best evidence of all came from deserters, who as the offensive approached became more numerous, especially Czechs – although the Allies also stepped up prisoner-gathering raids. By the end Diaz knew in minute detail the timing and configuration of the enemy bombardment, as well as when (and mostly where) the infantry attacks would follow. Moreover, he had actually approximately equal forces to the attackers: fifty-six divisions, 676 aircraft, and over 7,000 guns (with eight to ten days' supplies of shells), and although the Austrians had more light field guns, their opponents had many more heavy ones. But whereas Arz had a central reserve of only four divisions, Diaz deployed thirty-seven divisions in the threatened sectors and kept nineteen in reserve.[287] In contrast to the situation on the Western Front, where the Germans benefited from interior lines of communication, the Italians were on the inside of a circle and could exploit the Po basin road and rail networks. Lorry transport had helped to save the situation in 1916 and Diaz intended to use it again. He assembled a park of 1,800 automobiles between Vicenza and Padua, and he could move two divisions in a day to any threatened sector. But he correctly judged that the most serious problem would come on the Piave, and he placed the weight of his reserves towards the east.[288]

The dispositions at the outset of the battle therefore shaped its course. The Italians dubbed it the Battle of the Piave or the Battle of the Solstice; the Austrians referred to operation 'Radetzky' in the mountains and operation 'Albrecht' on the river. It began with an attack on the Tonale Pass sector on the far west of the front on 13 June: the Italians were forewarned and their artillery and machine guns stopped the Austrians from getting much beyond their starting points. The main attack was postponed from 11 to 15 June because the river was high, and on the day itself it remained so, but further delay would make it difficult to keep the assembled men fed. On the 15th the main bombardment and attack therefore proceeded, on both the mountain and the Piave sectors. In the former the Austrians had mixed fortunes but generally it was clear by the end of the first day that they had failed. On the Asiago plateau, where Allied forces occupied undulating and thickly forested ground with a steep downward slope only three miles behind them, the French stopped the attack with fire alone. The British (their intelligence for once being deficient) had expected just a bombardment, which their troops found unexpectedly intense, though not comparable to the Western Front. The Austrian infantry broke through the front line in places but by midday were halted, while the British divisional officers had been trained in elastic defence and regained all the captured ground by the following morning.[289] In the Italian sectors the Italian artillery staged a counter-bombardment before the Austrian one began, and although the Austrians made more progress where they deployed elite divisions, by the end of the first day they had come to a standstill. Their gas shells were less devastating than at Caporetto, because the Italians had been equipped with 3 million British masks, and when opposed the attackers paused rather than keeping going. The British on the Asiago noted that the Austrians did not push their advantage and could have done with larger numbers. To an extent this bears out Conrad's view that his plan was sabotaged by lack of troops, but it also suggests that reinforcements would have made little difference.[290]

The Austrian defeat in the mountains freed Diaz to send his reserves to the Piave, where his enemies made more progress and fought on longer. Here too the Austrian barrage was neither a surprise nor particularly formidable, many of the shells proving defective and bursting their own guns. Though modelled on the German bombardment of 21 March, it used one gun every sixteen metres instead of one every nine. Nor could the Austrians locate the Italian batteries, partly because they lacked air superiority. None the less, under cover of mist the Austrians (who had been training for the purpose) crossed the wide but shallow river and established two bridgeheads, a smaller one on the eastern end of the heights of the Montello and a larger one further south between Oderzo and Treviso. Fourteen divisions got across and advanced up to three kilometres. They found Italian morale still unsteady and the infantry surrendered to them in thousands, but the Italian artillery and machine guns, concealed in vineyards and in fields with the grain high, were difficult to knock out. Nor could the Austrians get heavy weaponry across, because of pouring rain and the river being in spate, but also because Allied aircraft strafed their pontoons, which drifting timber repeatedly damaged. By the 19th Diaz had sent in enough reserve divisions to allow a counter-attack. Like its French counterpart on the Matz it was quickly halted, but the Austrians made no further progress and Karl and his generals now debated whether to call the operation off, as little heavy equipment or supplies could cross the river, and nor could the wounded be evacuated. On the night of 22/23 June the Austrians abandoned their bridgeheads, the Italians not attempting to obstruct them, and on the 24th Diaz reported that the battle had ended in success.[291]

Diaz believed Cadorna's greatest error had been to persist with the Bainsizza plateau offensive in summer 1917. He did not press his counter-attack, nor – to the chagrin of the British commander, Lord Cavan – did he try to cross the Piave, and his government supported his caution.[292] Losses on both sides were comparable to those in Western Front battles: the Austrians had lost 70,000 killed and captured and the Allies 84,000.[293] The Italian army had failed to prevent the Austrians from either crossing the Piave or re-crossing it in good order. Yet the Austrians never attacked again, and Diaz correctly judged the outcome as a major strategic reverse for them and that their army would now dissolve without his assistance. He showed a commitment to avoiding unnecessary losses that other Allied commanders, including Haig and Foch, would later emulate. In contrast, although the Austrian high command had been well aware of its army's weaknesses, it had engaged all its available resources with plausible hopes of a substantial success, only to be defeated within days. As the public had expected another Caporetto, a firestorm of criticism followed in the press and parliament, the Vienna Reichsrat holding a secret session to inquire into the causes of the debacle. Poor generalship was widely blamed, and Conrad, who was dismissed, became the principal scapegoat; Arz, whose strategic concept had been followed and actually bore more responsibility, offered to resign but Karl insisted on his staying.[294] Austria-Hungary also lost standing with the OHL, which on 19 June called on its ally to suspend the offensive and send divisions to the Western Front. Having previously resisted, the Austrians now sent four divisions.[295] None the less, Ludendorff considered the Piave a very serious setback for the Central Powers.[296] At a moment when the Allies still feared disaster, the Piave like the Matz was a heartening demonstration that their opponents' methods could be answered. On the Western Front itself this was now to be demonstrated again, and in the most conclusive fashion.

'FRIEDENSSTURM'

The fifth of Ludendorff's western onslaughts, cumbersomely codenamed 'Marneschütz-Reims' (though also, more optimistically, as the 'peace storm' – 'Friedenssturm'), was the most ambitious since 21 March. It was envisaged as a pincer movement west and east of Reims, and was intended to capture the city and the heights to the south. It committed three armies, with 900 aircraft and 6,353 guns, on a frontage of 119 kilometres.[297] Yet in spite of the resources engaged and the long preparation time, it became evident on the opening morning that the attack had failed, and its gains were insignificant. The Allies finally had the measure of their enemies.

The Matz and 'Hammer Blow' had been followed by another pause. Ludendorff knew that time was running out, but in ever less promising circumstances he still refused to throw in his hand. The OHL officially adjudged 'Blücher' a great success,[298] and although 'Gneisenau' had been much less so, it had been smaller and more hasty. The issue of principle was raised on 24 June, when Kühlmann (whom Hindenburg and Ludendorff had long distrusted) told the Reichstag that the war could not be won by military means alone, which, even if the foreign minister believed it, Ludendorff considered, he should not have said. Once again Ludendorff and Hindenburg removed a minister they disliked, by insisting that they would resign unless Kühlmann did so, and Hertling made no effort to defend him.[299] Kühlmann was replaced by Paul von Hintze, whom the OHL found it easier to deal with, and at the Spa conference on 2–3 July the military and civilian authorities reaffirmed their commitment to expansionist war aims.[300] The strategic corollary was that Ludendorff again rejected the defensive, advising his commanders on 25 June that the war could be won only by more big attacks. As before, his hopes rested on 'Hagen', which he asserted must 'bring the decision', and in a post-war interview he confirmed that 'I always kept in mind the renewal of the Flanders operation.'[301] But to implement it required conditions that 'Blücher' and 'Gneisenau' had not delivered: on 7 June the OHL advised the army groups that fewer Allied reserves had moved from Flanders than had been expected. Wetzell believed that now was a favourable time for 'Hagen', as the French could no longer help the British, but first another attack was needed in the south, which he recommended should be on the Marne.[302]

The operation was needed not just to draw off forces from Flanders but also because of the vulnerability of the new salient. Its periphery was over 100 kilometres long, and its defences were rudimentary. Although the Laon–Soissons railway was unblocked at the Vauxaillon tunnel on 7 July, it was only single-tracked. The Germans had either to abandon the salient (which Ludendorff ruled out) or to expand it: in which case Reims was the crucial objective.[303] Planning for an attack there began in early June, initially via a drive just from the west, but a conference between Ludendorff and the commanders of the Seventh, First, and Third Armies at Rethel on 18 June enlarged the scope of the operation. The final scheme was to strike both on the Marne (west) and in Champagne (east) of Reims, and to overrun the Montagne de Reims south of the city. A further advance to the Marne, down to a line with Epernay, would then extend the German frontage on the river. If successful, this plan would actually drive the Germans further south-eastwards into the French interior and away from Paris, while creating a still larger periphery to garrison. On the other hand, it would ameliorate their logistics, and Reims was not just a communications centre but also a symbolic prize, a hero city whose bombarded cathedral had become an emblem of French Christian civilization. Ludendorff still hoped a big enough success could make France sue for peace, and he viewed the sector east of Reims as another weak point, comparable to those he had punctured previously.[304]

This time, the German commanders believed, surprise would matter more than ever. Yet widening the operation meant lengthier preparations and more chance that the Allies would detect it. And delay meant knock-on delay to 'Hagen', for, as Ludendorff emphasized, the course of operations needed to be viewed as a whole. After the infantry had stormed forward, the siege artillery and aircraft would move north, and the transfer, which would greatly tax the railways, would need two weeks, to enable 'Hagen' to begin on 1 August. Although Ludendorff wanted the Flanders attack to be decisive, it would be smaller than 'Marneschütz-Reims', involving thirty-nine divisions (twenty in the first line) and 3,269 guns. The OHL was already planning for further operations into the autumn, with 'Hagen' to be followed by 'Kurfürst', south of the Aisne towards Amiens and Paris. As Hindenburg put it, Germany would fall under the hammer unless it kept it in its hand.[305] The concept was for a left hook against Reims followed by a right hook in Flanders and one or more blows in the middle.

In general the Germans planned to repeat the 'Blücher' tactics: surprise and a rapid advance, without the pauses of 'Georgette'. But their forces were past their prime. Hindenburg knew morale and discipline were cracking, and intensive use was wearing out the heavy guns more quickly than the workshops could replace them.[306] The artillery crews were tired and although the operation again came under Bruchmüller his planning this time was less masterly, and post-war commentaries criticized it. Artillery superiority was less than 2:1, the lowest for any of the five offensives, and air support was also weaker. Yet despite his subordinates' doubts, and the mounting tension as the date approached, Ludendorff predicted that France would soon collapse and he continued to radiate confidence.[307]

During June the Allies were again in an intelligence fog, and uncertainty exacerbated their disagreements. Foch agreed with Haig that the British were the likeliest next target. The biggest argument therefore divided Foch from Pétain, who opposed restoring to the BEF the remnants of its British divisions that had fought on the Chemin des Dames or sending more French artillery to Flanders.[308] Whereas most of the French reserves had been committed against 'Blücher', French military intelligence estimated that the Germans still had ominously large reserves available – fifty-six divisions on 13 June and seventy-five by the 30th – and Pétain insisted that he must be strong enough to resist a new drive against Paris.[309] Clemenceau intervened in the dispute, his government agreeing that 'General Foch has too much oriented himself towards to the north', though also ruling that Pétain must obey Foch's instructions without appealing against them.[310] But although Pétain was subordinated, he won some of the substance of the debate, and the Paris approaches received more attention. All the same, the Allies remained apprehensive. Clemenceau's War Committee discussed the evacuation of the capital;[311] in London the Admiralty briefed the War Office on the mass embarkation of British troops 'in certain eventualities . . .'[312]

In its retrospective analysis of the Reims battle, the OHL agreed the loss of surprise was crucial. It had suspected a similar loss before 'Gneisenau' and 'Hammer Blow', but this time the Germans deluded themselves that security had not been compromised. Certainly the usual precautions were taken, but concealment was harder in the short and bright summer nights, and in early July it was betrayed. The approach of an offensive multiplied the numbers of captives and deserters, and escaped French prisoners provided further information. On the other hand, preparations were also evident opposite the British, between Arras and Ypres, and only on 10–11 July did Pétain convince Foch that the blow in the south would come first and would be heavy. Initially the evidence pointed to a German attempt to cross the Marne, but new disclosures, along with aerial reconnaissance, suggested preparations for an offensive on both sides of Reims. Finally a raid on the 14th took prisoners who revealed the bombardment would start soon after midnight. On the same day, air observers saw so much movement that the German lines resembled an ants' nest.[313]

Prior notification enabled the French to ready reinforcements and adopt appropriate defensive tactics. Their divisions between the Marne and the Argonne rose from seventeen in line and nine in reserve on 1 July to twenty and fifteen respectively by the 15th, while others were alerted. On the 13th Foch asked Haig to send four divisions to the French front at once and prepare four more, but this demand caused another Anglo-French crisis.[314] Haig questioned the evidence that German divisions would attack east of Reims, and opposed sending British troops to Champagne. On 14 July he still saw no definite evidence of what was impending, and the British remained mesmerized by the enemy preparations in Flanders.[315] Henry Wilson had frightened the War Cabinet with the possibility that eighty-five German divisions were available on the British front while the French 'for political reasons' were prioritizing Paris: he was authorized to write in similar vein to Foch, and Lloyd George warned Clemenceau that Foch's position would be endangered if a disaster occurred on the British front, while the Cabinet invited Haig to use his right of appeal against the generalissimo under the Beauvais agreement.[316] By the time Haig met Foch on the afternoon of 15 July, however, the Germans had struck and the French had contained them, dashing Haig's forebodings and making the British look foolish. Haig had meanwhile agreed to send two British divisions and after meeting Foch he sent two more.[317] During these weeks Foch came under fire from both the French and British governments, but in the event he both insured against 'Hagen' and adequately reinforced Pétain, largely with French units.

Arguably more important in French preparations was the application of defence in depth. For the first time Pétain's doctrine was fully implemented, though only east of Reims, where he prevailed upon Henri Gouraud, the Fourth Army commander, who had previously been a Foch disciple and had a reputation as an aggressive leader. Gouraud agreed to a 'red' or 'observation' line furthest forward, a 'yellow' or principal defence line at least 2,000 metres from the enemy front where two thirds of his infantry and a quarter of his artillery were concentrated, and a 'green' line in the rear. West of Reims Pétain had less success with Henri Berthelot and Jean Degoutte, the commanders of the Fifth and Sixth Armies, even though they held weaker lines on the east of the new German salient. Admittedly Degoutte could argue that his front was the Marne, which was eighty metres wide and without bridges, densely wooded on both banks, and both a plausible barrier and a line of symbolic significance. None the less, the French divisions under Degoutte and the French and Italian ones under Berthelot were again placed too far forward.[318]

The final element in French planning was for not just a defensive but also for a counterstroke, resembling that on the Matz but bigger. Foch and Pétain disputed the authorship of the idea, but the idea of attacking the enemy positions round Château-Thierry dated back to 14 June and was developed into a counterstroke notion once it became clear that Ludendorff would strike in Champagne.[319] The force delivering it would again come under Mangin, and again it would hit the Germans' west flank after their initial onslaught.

Hence there were many vulnerabilities in the German position, and many strengths in the French one. As before the Matz, the French put down a pre-emptive counter-bombardment against the massing German troops at 12.30 a.m. The German bombardment, with 6,400 guns and 2,200 mine launchers, began forty minutes later, along the usual Bruchmüller lines though using fewer gas shells and more smoke before the infantry went forward at 4.50 a.m. – twelve divisions west of Reims and fifteen east of it, supported by tanks. In all the Germans had amassed some forty-eight divisions; the Allies had some thirty-six in the battle sector (including three American and two Italian ones), but also a reserve behind them and the counterstroke force (mainly French but including American divisions) assembling in the west.[320] East of Reims, where the Germans followed a creeping barrage across open, chalky, shell-holed ground, and were easy to observe, the outcome was decided quickly. After first meeting little resistance they found themselves by 11 a.m. confronting the largely undamaged French main defence line and realized their bombardment had mostly been wasted: their artillery was still moving up and days would be needed to set up a new barrage. Many French batteries had been undetected, and further attacks had no success. West of Reims, in contrast, and north of the Marne, the Germans did break thorough the main resistance lines but ran into strong and intact positions further back. Most progress was made along the river, which the attackers crossed with rafts and rowing boats and pontoons, before being held up in the woods beyond. By the evening it was clear to the Germans that the French had deliberately staged a tactical withdrawal, accepting loss of territory but preserving their infantry and artillery.[321] Kuhl recorded that Ludendorff was 'very sad about the paltry outcome'.[322] The OHL authorized continued attacks west of Reims on the following day, but they made slight progress. In the absence of surprise, there was little prospect of further advance without lengthy new preparations, and the OHL, once again, shunned a long attrition struggle, both the Matz and 'Marneschütz-Reims' therefore being liquidated much faster than the two spring battles. On the evening of the 16th it decided to suspend the offensive but on the following day French gunfire damaged the Marne pontoon bridges, and lack of horses to bring up munitions meant the Germans could not keep the French artillery at bay. That evening preparations were ordered to abandon the bridgehead. Before the Allied counterstroke went in early on the 18th the offensive had already halted and its gains were about to be abandoned. From now on, Germany would be on the defensive.

The attackers' casualties in the three days' fighting were over 50,000 (more than 20,000 of them prisoners); the defenders' casualties 59,000. A smaller Allied force had defeated a larger German one.[323] Once more Ludendorff had suffered from divided objectives: if he had not kept forces in the north he would have had a better chance of at least taking Reims, and would then have been better placed to resume the drive toward Paris. But irrespective of the numbers, success turned on the viability of the new tactics, and with these thwarted the OHL had run out of expedients. The German fighting methods that had seemed so formidable had evolved surprisingly little in the light of experience, were being applied less skilfully, and being halted faster and faster. Having once more failed to broaden out the southern salient, Ludendorff was thrashing in a trap of his own making, while his army's casualties since the spring numbered nearly a million. Even if the OHL refused to recognize the game was up, that truth was more and more evident to its men. In the Second Battle of the Marne that had now opened, the reserve of fresh divisions that in June still so perturbed the Allies began rapidly to run down, leaving the Germans with the only option of submitting to their enemies' assaults until they could endure no more.

2

On the Attack: July–November 1918

the general advance now in progress along the whole front of more than 200 miles between the Meuse and the sea is a strategical operation on a scale which has never been attempted since the commencement of trench warfare.

'A' Branch, War Office, Daily Intelligence Summary,
8/9 October 1918[1]

During 1918 the Central Powers tried first to break out of their fortress and then were driven back into it. In the first half of the year the Allies withstood a succession of all-out assaults. Well into the summer, the outcome seemed to many observers to hang in the balance. Yet during these same months the German and Austrian armies lost much of their edge, and once the Allies returned to the offensive they found their task far easier than in 1916 or 1917. Experience had so traumatized them, however, that most in authority continued to anticipate a final victory in 1919 or even 1920. As late as 12 September the British Ambassador in Washington cabled that the 'general view among military chiefs in France is that with great effort the war might be ended in 1919'.[2] Only when the Allied armies suddenly delivered a series of spectacular successes on all fronts did it become conceivable that the war might end that autumn; and hardly had it done so than the enemies who had seemed so formidable were suing for peace. The tide turned first in the west, where from mid-July to mid-September the Allies regained the territory lost since March. They then broke through the strongest German positions. In late September the Allied armies in the Balkans knocked out Bulgaria and those in Palestine annihilated the Turkish forces opposite them. A month later the Italians broke the main Austro-Hungarian army, while the Allies in the west herded their enemy towards the German border. By early November not only had the Habsburg forces disintegrated but the German army was in full retreat, and in both empires revolution had overthrown the ruling dynasties. Military breakthrough triggered internal collapse.

SECOND MARNE

In July 1918 the initiative on the Western Front changed sides. All the major battles since March had begun with German attacks. Foch and the Allied commanders had made contingency plans for counterstrokes, and at the Battle of the Matz had implemented one. But down to mid-July they supposed that the Germans had amassed reserve divisions in Flanders, there to drive once more against the British. So nervous were the latter that on the eve of Ludendorff's 'Friedenssturm' offensive they appealed to Foch to allow American divisions to stay with the BEF, Lloyd George telling Clemenceau that the situation caused 'the gravest anxiety in the minds of all the members of the Imperial War Cabinet'.[3] Ludendorff indeed began moving his artillery immediately after 15 July, and intended to strike in Flanders within days. But instead it was the Allies who were on the attack for the next four months, the OHL being reduced to regulating the pace of retreat.

The turning point was the halting of the 'Friedenssturm' on 15–16 July, followed by the Allied counterstroke against the Soissons–Reims salient on the 18th. From late May until early August, Champagne was the storm centre, as the Germans drove in the French front and widened the resulting salient on its western and its eastern flank, before being forced back to their starting line. The new counterstroke was modelled on that on the Matz in June, but delivered on a larger scale and with bigger consequences, for it in turn provided a model for later triumphs.

The counterstroke's origins dated back for over a month. The western fringe of the Champagne salient pointed towards Paris but was also the channel for the German main communication lines, running east of the forests and hills that lay south-west of the Soissons railway knot. The Germans had tried and failed to broaden this position with the Matz offensive, and Foch perceived an opportunity. He asked Pétain to devise an operation that would capture the heights west of Soissons, from which to bombard the Germans' supply lines if they attacked again.[4] After 5 July, as it became clear that the Germans indeed planned to attack, Pétain, in collaboration with Foch, developed a grander scheme for a defensive battle against the Germans that would be linked to a blow against their flank.[5] Mangin, whose Tenth Army would lead the latter operation, was positioning artillery from June, and his soldiers' raids had indicated that the Germans opposite were poorly placed to resist. On the morning of the 15th, when the Germans were crossing the Marne, Pétain wanted to move forces from the west of the salient to deal with the threat on its south, but Foch countermanded the order and insisted on the prearranged plan.[6] Three days later, with the Germans now deeply committed, Mangin's troops jumped off.

Not for the last time, the Germans were wholly surprised. Part of the reason was overconfidence: Crown Prince Wilhelm had thought the Allies too weak both to defend Reims and to counter-attack.[7] In addition, Mangin took elaborate precautions. Although the counteroffensive was delivered along a front of 105 kilometres and by four armies – the Fifth in the east, Ninth in the south, and Sixth and Tenth in the west – the latter two would constitute the spearhead, intended to cut off the base of the German salient and encircle its defenders, while (as at the first Marne battle in 1914) other forces struck it head-on. As all agreed that surprise was of the essence, the pre-attack concentration was carried out over just four days, all movements proceeding in darkness, and the tanks and infantry being hidden in the Villers-Cotterêts forest. For the Americans serving under Mangin this meant a night march through woodland in a heavy storm: they had to run the final section and reached open country just in time. The 2,100 Tenth and Sixth Army guns opened fire with gas and high explosive simultaneously with the infantry advance, which was launched at 4.35 a.m. by eighteen divisions, supported by almost 500 tanks and over 1,000 aircraft.[8]

The attacking forces enjoyed a tremendous initial superiority. To lead them, Mangin used his Twentieth Corps, comprising the American 1st and 2nd Divisions and between them the 1st Moroccan Division. The ferocity of the latter (actually mostly Senegalese) startled the Americans, who themselves were among the fittest and most experienced AEF units, including many regulars. The tanks were mainly newly delivered light Renault models, armed with machine guns and able to move at up to

8 mph. They burst out of a thick mist against denuded and unsuspecting defenders, who offered little resistance. According to the Germans' post-battle analysis, their positions were poorly developed, their machine guns encircled and too slow to retreat, and their artillery too far forward.[9] After 9 a.m. the mist cleared and Allied aircraft provided more support, but the advancing troops ran into greater opposition, from defenders hidden in cornfields, villages, and ravines and after the second day reinforced by new arrivals rushed in by lorry. The pace slowed down. The American 1st Division took twice as many casualties on Day Two and by the time it was pulled out on the 21st it had lost 7,317 men; the 2nd Division by the end of Day Two had lost 4,000. Some 270,000 Americans saw action in the Champagne salient between 18 July and 4 August, almost twice the 140,000 who had fought against the five German offensives from 21 March to 15 July.[10] None the less, the Second Battle of the Marne was predominantly a French effort, Pétain following up the 18 July attack by an offensive on the 20th against the south and east sides of the salient. Eventually he committed fifty French divisions to the fighting and had no fresh reserve divisions left.[11]

By the time the situation stabilized in early August, the Allies had driven the Germans out of most of their gains since 27 May and liberated Château-Thierry and Soissons, distancing the invaders from the capital and the symbolic Marne barrier and clearing the Paris–Avricourt trunk line. But progress was slow, and it took three times longer to clear the salient than it had for the Germans to create it. After 20 July the Allies were advancing through unfortified but wooded, rolling country, criss-crossed with machine-gun nests. They were beyond their artillery range, most of their tanks were out of action, and surprise was lost. Foch tried repeatedly to use cavalry, and repeatedly had to abandon the attempt.[12] Part of the problem was French tactical caution, but in addition arguments continued between Foch and Pétain, as the generalissimo moved forces westwards to parry a possible counter-counter-attack and reinforced the British. The Germans strengthened the two shoulders of the salient while pulling back and salvaged most of their men and equipment.[13] On 27 July Ludendorff decided to withdraw to the river Vesle, running across the salient's northern baseline, but before doing so the Germans made a stand between Fère-en-Tardenois and Ville-en-Tardenois, which Pétain overcame by launching an attack with American troops that drew off German reserves. Once the new line was reached Ludendorff hoped to rest his divisions while Pétain decided against assaulting well-prepared defences on high ground. Foch was also willing for a halt, as he had promised forces for a new combined attack with the British east of Amiens. For both sides, Champagne now had a lower priority than being able to move troops elsewhere.[14]

Although the OHL could not understand how it had been so completely surprised, it felt relief that the army had been extricated. And although the Germans lost 30,000 prisoners, over 600 artillery pieces, and 3,000 machine guns, their total casualties of 110,000 were again lower than the Allies' 160,000.[15] None the less, the Germans (by British estimates) had engaged no fewer than seventy-three infantry divisions in the battle, and had transferred down thirteen from Rupprecht's army group in the north. Between 18 July and 6 August their total of reserve divisions dwindled from forty-one to twenty-nine.[16] Moreover, whereas on 18 July Ludendorff still planned to launch 'Hagen' imminently, on the 19th he suspended any attacks against the BEF so that he could use all available forces on the Marne front, Foch at once divining that the Flanders attack would now be delayed.[17] Friedrich von Lossberg, the Chief of Staff of the Fourth Army (which would have carried out 'Hagen'), wanted to evacuate all the ground gained since March, in order to shorten the German line and rest the troops before the offensive. But Ludendorff ruled out this option (despite acknowledging its military merits) on political grounds – by which he meant 'Consideration of the impressions on the enemy, on our army, and on the homeland!',[18] thus setting his course for the step-by-step defence over the next six weeks. During the crisis Ludendorff was nervous, angry, and depressed: he blamed Wetzell for the setbacks and quarrelled violently with Hindenburg,[19] rejecting the latter's suggestion for a counter-counter-attack. Instead Ludendorff used troops from Flanders to buttress the west side of the Champagne salient. When the line settled down his nerves recovered, and the OHL authorized more offensives to be planned. It wrote off 18 July as an aberration, believed no further big Allied attacks were likely, and judged that it could stop them if they came.[20] The Second Marne therefore ended Ludendorff's offensives but did not paralyse his willingness to keep trying. It was a very big battle, whose significance has been understated,[21] but no single Western Front engagement was decisive. Rather, a succession of assaults completed the demoralization of the German infantry and wore their commanders down.

AMIENS

Even before the Second Marne had finished, Foch (in a striking use of his co-ordinating position) convened a meeting with Pétain, Pershing, and Haig on 24 July, at his headquarters in a Louis XIII chateau at Bombon. Following an enormous lunch (which was wasted on the frugal Haig), he presented a position paper by his adjutant (and the ill-starred French commander in 1940), Maxime Weygand. It declared that the Allies had reached the 'turning point in the road' and must keep the regained initiative. Although Foch had long advocated an offensive strategy, this time he had plausible grounds for saying events had caught up with his preferences, not only because of the progress in Champagne but also because the Allies had gained numerical parity (and superiority in tanks, aircraft, and guns), whereas the Germans were suffering from a 'crisis of effectives'. He therefore envisaged a succession of surprise attacks at rapid intervals, to prevent the enemy from regrouping or amassing reserves and to establish a base for later operations by securing transport links and raw materials, clearing the trunk lines running east and north from Paris, pinching out the Saint-Mihiel salient, and driving the Germans back from the Channel ports and the French northern coal mines, while menacing their iron ore in Lorraine. Although acknowledging a consensus view that decisive operations would not be feasible until next year, the memorandum envisaged, if all went well, 'an important offensive' in the late summer or autumn.[22]

Foch was a man in a hurry, for he envisaged a maximum effort by all the Allies next year: he had so advised Clemenceau and urged him to call up the 1920 conscript cohort in October 'in view of the major interest France will have at the start of 1919 in weighing the most heavily on the discussions of the war and its consequences ...'[23] In other words, France's political leverage would be greatest if it threw its strength into a decisive battle in the spring, for which it should lay the groundwork now. Yet Foch found the commanders surprised by the memorandum's ambition, and Pétain the most reserved about it. Although Pétain accepted the plan, he thought that operations against the Saint-Mihiel and Lys salients would be the most that was feasible that year, the French army playing a supportive role in British- and American-led attacks. For now it should let its allies make the running and husband its strength. He warned that twenty-seven of his thirty-five reserve divisions had been in action and he had just one fresh division left: 'The troops at the front or leaving the battle have certainly an excellent morale, but the fatigue is extreme. We are at the limits of effort.' Pétain also knew his army was running down its 75 mm and 105 mm shell stocks, and in his view munitions expenditure had been extravagant, wearing out the gun barrels and making the infantry unnecessarily dependent on artillery protection. He had therefore rationed the quantities made available and counselled 'a wise economy' from now on.[24] As the OHL correctly assessed, the French army was too exhausted to keep up a sustained hammering.

In contrast, Haig and Pershing agreed more willingly to the Bombon scheme.[25] As usual with successful operations, many have claimed paternity of what on 8 August became the Battle of Amiens-Montdidier,[26] and Haig and Foch had discussed the idea in May. But the immediate origins lay with General Sir Henry Rawlinson's BEF Fourth Army, which had replaced Gough's hapless Fifth Army and held the sector east of Amiens. Australian raids revealed that the Germans' defences were sketchy and their resistance lacking in vigour, and the Battle of Hamel on 4 July confirmed this impression.[27] Hamel was a dawn attack against a ridge by two brigades of mainly Australian troops and some Americans, with no prior bombardment but supported by sixty tanks and a creeping barrage. It achieved complete surprise and attained all its objectives in ninety minutes. The OHL had ordered the defences in the sector to be strengthened, but little had been done: an indication of fraying German discipline, although the army group concerned had had difficulty in transporting building materials and had deliberately minimized fortification work in order to suggest that it might resume the offensive.[28] After Hamel, Rawlinson was impatient to profit from the situation before the enemy took remedial action, writing to Henry Wilson that the Germans were 'dog tired and full of flu' and with three more divisions he could get a 'good knock' at them. He broached the idea with Haig, to whom on 17 July he submitted a proposal for an assault on opposing trenches that had little wire and whose occupiers were demoralized. The open, dry, and uncratered country was excellent for tanks, of which he wanted as many as possible, reinforced by five extra infantry divisions (four of them Canadian).[29] Rawlinson had commanded most of the British attack front on the disastrous first day of the Battle of the Somme, and although he had always been one of the more open-minded British generals the immeasurable superiority of the planning for 8 August 1918 over that for 1 July 1916 testified to the distance the BEF had travelled in the interim.[30] Hence Haig arrived at Bombon with a plan that fitted precisely into Foch's scheme of protecting the Paris–Amiens railway, and the meeting approved it, although Foch insisted on the French First Army participating on Rawlinson's southern (right) flank, and temporarily placed it under Haig's orders.

Unlike the Somme, 8 August was always intended as a limited operation: a larger version of Hamel that imitated the model the latter provided, as well as the Battle of Cambrai and the 18 July counterstroke. None the less, GHQ tried to expand the plan's scope. In 1916 Haig had insisted on Rawlinson preparing for a breakthrough attack, with the result that the Somme bombardment was dispersed over too great a depth of the enemy front. Now he required him to set a further target twenty-seven rather than seven miles distant from the starting point, but only if the first day went well, and this time the goal was a hypothetical one that did not alter the practical dispositions. Also as in 1916, the parallel French advance widened the attack front – from 19,000 to 30,000 yards – but it little modified the conception.[31] The aim was to push the Germans away from Amiens and the railway, but in addition Fourth Army intended to deliver a stunning blow to German morale.

Fundamental once again were surprise and secrecy, which were built in from the earliest stages.[32] All movements forward would be by night, and the RAF would fend off hostile aircraft. The roads were covered with straw, and wheels wrapped round with rope. The tanks too – and Haig placed at Rawlinson's disposal almost the entire BEF fleet, including the most modern and reliable Mk V models – would move in concealment, aircraft overflying the German trenches to obscure the engine noise. The artillery was lavishly supplied with more shells than it needed, and no more shots were fired during the run-up than in preceding days, again to avoid raising the alert. There would be no prior bombardment, and the aim was not to destroy the opposing trench lines but to keep down the enemy infantry by a creeping barrage from the field guns. Meanwhile two thirds of the heavy artillery would be directed against the opposing batteries. By 1918 the British were adept at locating enemy artillery by aerial photography and other methods, and 95 per cent of the German guns in the sector were identified. They would be silenced not only by high explosive but also by gas shells, though less gas was used than at Hamel as this time it was intended to drive beyond the enemy artillery line.[33]

All of these measures were meant to lessen casualties. The Allies had only a small numerical advantage, the operation being launched on a narrower front than on 18 July and with ten infantry divisions. Although the number of divisions was similar to that on 1 July 1916, the number of men would be 50,000 instead of 100,000, so much had the average size of a British unit diminished, although its average firepower had more than doubled. Whereas a 1916 battalion had four Lewis light machine guns and two light trench mortars, its 1918 equivalent had thirty Lewis guns, eight light trench mortars and sixteen rifle grenadiers, as well as tank and air support.[34] Moreover, some of the finest divisions in the BEF would deliver the attack, many of them coming from the Dominions (as Mangin had used Americans and Senegalese). The Fourth Army comprised four Canadian, five Australian, and five British divisions, and one American one. Since late July it had nearly doubled in strength from 54,323 to 98,716 horses and 257,562 to 441,588 men.[35] The Australian divisions had recently been consolidated into an Australian Army Corps, and for the first time would fight with their own staffs and support services and under an Australian commander, Sir John Monash, allowing them to display to the full their aggressive and democratic fighting ethos.[36] Monash, who was unusual among BEF officers both for being Jewish and for his civilian background, applied a clear brain and business experience to the problems of the Western Front; after the war he oversaw a massive hydro-electric power project in South Australia. In contrast the Canadian Corps under Sir Austin Currie had been created earlier and was used to operating as a unit: Currie and his commanders had developed a doctrine of limited attacks as a result of their 1917 experiences, but the Canadians had escaped the defensive fighting of March to July and they constituted a pool of refreshed and experienced divisions, larger and more heavily armed with automatic weapons than the BEF norm.[37] They had spent months training for open warfare, and their platoons were semi-autonomous and trained and equipped to suppress machine guns.[38] Moving them to the Amiens front, however, would unmistakably signal an intention to strike, and for this reason it was strictly concealed, the British diverting two Canadian battalions to Flanders and generating extra wireless traffic to create the impression that the attack would come there.[39] Up until the summer the Germans had been able to track British dispositions and deployments through 'traffic analysis' of wireless signals, but the British improved their signals security before Amiens and knew that the Germans were expecting an assault further north. As a final precaution, none the less, the infantry were informed only 24–36 hours ahead.[40]

The upshot was that the attack at 4.20 a.m. on Thursday, 8 August, again achieved surprise. A Ludendorff order of the day on 4 August had expressed confidence in German tactics and hoped the Allies would launch an offensive, but the German Second Army had laid down wire without fixing it with pickets; its defence rested on machine-gun nests dispersed in depth wherever the ground (a dry and open rolling plateau with a few villages and many tiny woods) provided cover. It had fourteen divisions (ten in the front line), 749 guns, and 106 aircraft. The attackers had 1,386 field guns and howitzers, 684 heavy guns, 342 heavy tanks, 72 light Whippet tanks, and 120 supply tanks, as well as 1,900 aircraft.[41] A counter-bombardment as they assembled could have caused great damage, but there was none, and little resistance during the first hour as thousands of Germans surrendered. Once more the Allies advanced under cover of a mist (intensified by smoke shells), which on balance favoured them. The infantry went forward in single file rather than waves, by-passing obstacles and accompanied by tanks. They overran the German first line before it could communicate with headquarters and with the field guns behind it, and resistance came mainly from machine guns, against which the tanks proved invaluable. The Canadians and Australians moved forward precisely on schedule, fresh divisions 'leap-frogging' through as the first echelon halted on the initial target position. Monash's and Rawlinson's thinking was that leap-frogging would enable the infantry to break exceptionally deeply into the enemy positions, operating beyond Allied artillery range with the aid of tanks and of field guns moved up on the day and guided by aircraft. It would spare the attrition on the lead formations, in contrast with the German practice of relentlessly moving them on. Even so, it meant a move towards open warfare, and units would need to operate more autonomously.[42] By the late morning this was happening, as Whippet tanks and armoured cars harassed the retreating enemy, and the cavalry – whom Haig had insisted on moving up – were able to charge them. Indeed, it was the most successful day of the war for the British horsemen, who took over 1,000 prisoners.[43] By the evening the BEF had captured over 12,000 Germans, and the French over 3,000. Out of 500 German guns south of the Somme 450 were taken intact, and the Canadians advanced up to eight miles.[44]

The day was not successful in all respects. August 1918 was not August 1944, and even so complete a breakthrough as this – the most dramatic by the Allies on the Western Front in the entire war – led neither to a rout nor to sweeping liberation of territory. On the left flank (north of the Somme) the British Third Corps faced Germans who had been reinforced and warned: its advance, with fewer tanks, was slower. On the right the French First Army under General Marie-Eugène Debeney also progressed more gradually.[45] Moreover, as on 18 July, tanks proved highly vulnerable to breakdown and artillery fire, and in the heat their crews flagged. Even though the damage and mechanical faults were often reparable, the numbers engaged fell from 453 on 8 August to 155 on the 9th, 85 on the 10th, and 38 on the 11th, and once they could no longer be used en masse their impact diminished.[46] Nor could airpower compensate. At the start of the battle much of the German air force was in Champagne and the British and French had a massive local advantage estimated at 1,904 to 365. But although the RAF had been bombing behind the German lines beforehand, its aircraft were still primarily valuable for observation and had limited value in ground attack. In any case, during the afternoon (and in an improvised departure from the original plan) the RAF was redirected against the Somme bridges, to obstruct the enemy retreat and the arrival of reinforcements. This meant fighting the Germans where the latter were close to their aerodromes, with fresh ammunition and petrol, and the RAF did no essential damage to the bridges despite making 205 flights and losing forty-four planes, fifty-two more being wrecked or damaged.[47] Hence the reinforcement could proceed. Although the German Second Army command was cut off from its front line, it knew a major attack was in progress and immediately alerted its reserve divisions. While aircraft flew in from other sectors the infantry moved up in lorries: five divisions on 8 August and three more on the following morning.[48]

On 9 August, therefore, the Allies faced a rapidly strengthening antagonist. They had lost surprise and most of their tanks, were ahead of their artillery and telephone lines, and had to use runners or horsemen and cyclists. They had no pre-prepared attack plan, and did not begin until well into the day, sixteen British units attacking at thirteen different start times.[49] Although the Canadians advanced another three miles and the French captured Montdidier, resistance from defenders hidden in villages, woods, and sugar factories was growing, and casualties rose, while air attacks against the Somme bridges again proved fruitless, forty-five more aircraft being lost. By the 10th the RAF had committed 70 per cent of its Western Front single-seater fighters to the battle zone. The French extended the line of operations to the south and Mangin again attacked on his Tenth Army front, telling his troops that 'It is time to shake off the mud of the trenches',[50] but the Allies were now running into the rusting wire of the pre-1917 front line, where the reinforced defenders had more cover and it was harder for the remaining tanks to operate; moreover, from 11 August the Germans were mounting counteroffensives. Essentially they had re-established a defence line and there was no point in carrying on. Even though the British had brought up most of their heavy artillery, it would take time to locate the German guns, and the Germans now had more divisions in line than did their enemies. If the attack encountered heavy opposition, neither Monash, nor Currie, nor Rawlinson was willing to press it further.[51]

Over the four days of fighting the British and French suffered casualties of 20,000 and 24,000 respectively; they captured 29,873 prisoners and 499 guns, and total German casualties may have been 75,000. The OHL estimated German losses between 1 and 10 August at 48,000, of which 33,000 were missing and prisoners: a very high proportion.[52] The Germans lost fewer men and less territory than in the Second Battle of the Marne, but the impact on their high command was greater, in part precisely because it was the second such event in quick succession. What really concerned the OHL, however, was the collapse in fighting spirit, as evidenced by the thousands of surrenders and by breakdowns in discipline, units moving up being jeered as 'strikebreakers'. According to the British Fourth Army War Diary, the Germans 'surrendered freely and in large numbers without any serious fighting'. Hutier, the commander of the adjoining Eighteenth Army, judged the German troops to be weak and worn out, and their nerves overstretched.[53] Further, there seemed every risk of more such debacles: even if the Germans had abandoned the Champagne bulge they were still deploying sick and weary infantry in exposed and poorly prepared positions around the 'Michael' and 'Georgette' salients. Nor was the surprise just tactical: the OHL had fundamentally underestimated the Allies' ability to prepare a major attack in much less time than Germany would have needed. With air superiority they could conceal their preparations and they no longer needed to give warning via a preliminary barrage.[54]

In a much-cited passage in his memoirs Ludendorff described 8 August as the 'black day of the German army' and the period after it as the worst he experienced until the final defeat: he offered Hindenburg his resignation.[55] Yet on 10 August he again rejected Lossberg's advice to shorten the front by a strategic withdrawal to the Siegfried Line, instead ordering 'not a foot of soil to be abandoned without determined struggle', although 'Hagen' was now shelved definitively.[56] On 10 August he briefed Wilhelm II, stressing the collapse of troop morale and saying the war had become a game of chance, the Emperor responding that 'We are at the end of our effectiveness. The war must be ended.'[57] Yet Ludendorff had not yet concluded that no mileage remained in the military option. Although the German army was ill positioned for a defensive strategy, and he resisted the measures needed to place it better for one, he told the foreign minister, Hintze, on 13 August that the only hope now was to wear down the Allies by defensive fighting, with occasional limited attacks (whereas Foch feared that the Germans would retreat to the Antwerp–Namur–Strasbourg line, half the length of the existing one, to prepare a counterstroke like that of Joffre in 1914).[58] Meeting the German civilian leaders that afternoon, the high command expressed confidence that a defensive strategy could force the Allies to sue for peace. Hintze, more doubtful, advised Hertling that a diplomatic initiative was needed and at the Spa Crown Council on 14 August he said time was on the Allies' side, that Austria-Hungary could hardly survive another winter, and the Turks were going it alone in the Caucasus. Wilhelm agreed that Germany must seek an opportune moment for an understanding with the enemy, and Hertling summarized that they must prepare to act 'after the next success in the west'. But this was a decision to postpone decision, and to reject an immediate peace appeal or a scaling down of Germany's war aims. Hence when the Austro-Hungarian leaders arrived at Spa that afternoon to press for an immediate initiative, the Germans followed the OHL's guidance and opposed them. Hindenburg and Ludendorff told the Austrian commander, Arz, that 'the possibility of a decisive blow or of decisive victory does not exist', but although secret feelers might be possible now was not the time to open negotiations.[59]

THE WIDENING BATTLE

The Spa decisions mired the Germans in a dilemma, for they had excluded political action until the military outlook improved, but the Battle of Amiens presaged further deterioration. A major reason was that the Allies now mounted offensives rapidly and at different points along the front, thus avoiding their earlier tendency to hammer too long in one place. Foch's Bombon memorandum had envisaged such a strategy, and he wound down the Champagne counteroffensive in order to facilitate operations east of Amiens. From here on began what British writers have dubbed the 'Hundred Days' of victories until the armistice – unjustly neglecting the significance of 18 July as a turning point. After 8 August, however, the Allied commanders disagreed over how to proceed, before reaffirming the new approach. Rawlinson had always envisaged the battle as limited, and on the 11th he persuaded Haig to halt it. Foch, in contrast, wanted Haig to resume as early as 15 August, but Currie induced Rawlinson to prevail again on Haig to desist. On the 14th Haig told Foch that he was ending the offensive, which would now face up to sixteen enemy divisions, backed by artillery on terrain inaccessible to tanks.[60] Foch flatly disagreed, but Haig insisted that 'I was responsible for the handling of the British forces.' Partly because the French First Army was running out of ammunition, Foch gave way.[61] It helped that Haig simultaneously proposed to bring forward an offensive by the British Third Army, on Rawlinson's left flank north of the Somme,[62] and for the next few weeks he and his commanders set the pace of BEF progress, though in conformity with Foch's general conceptions. These were for sequenced blows instead of a continuous operation, and for progressively broadening the fighting front.[63]

Under pressure from his subordinates, Haig had shown a previously uncharacteristic willingness to halt while the going was good. Over the next month Allied thrusts along the line dashed Ludendorff's hopes for a stalling defensive. On 20 August the French attacked between Soissons and Compiègne, with results that Ludendorff called a second black day. Although the French were less prominent during August, they still captured over 31,000 German prisoners, 690 guns, and the town of Noyon that had marked the closest enemy approach point to Paris.[64] Almost simultaneously, the British Third Army attack, the 'Battle of Albert', went in on the 21st. The Third Army commander, Sir Julian Byng, had been responsible for Cambrai and now planned a similar operation, dispensing with a preliminary bombardment and using tanks to capture the Albert–Arras railway. Haig was dissatisfied, as he had been dissatisfied with Rawlinson, and made the scheme more ambitious, directed at breaking the opposing line and capturing Bapaume with as much cavalry use as possible. When Byng suspended the operation Haig insisted that it resume. In what was now a well-tried formula the British attacked in the small hours, protected by mist, and achieved surprise; and on 23–24 August they did so again, capturing the railway and thousands of prisoners before repelling counter-attacks.[65] This time young British conscripts, only recently sent out, did much of the fighting, and with less artillery and tank support than on 8 August. Facing combined French and British pressure, the OHL authorized the evacuation of the Lys salient, which Rupprecht estimated would save him three divisions, and it also approved a withdrawal to the 'Winter Position' in the Somme sector, where it intended to consolidate. But the new line held for barely a week, as on 26 August the British Third and First Armies opened up another attack zone, in the 'Battle of the Scarpe' north of Albert and east of Arras. Whereas the old Somme battlefield had halted the Fourth Army, the Canadians, who had been moved up for the purpose, now fought their way through it. High Wood and Delville Wood, which in 1916 had detained the Allies for weeks, fell in three days.[66] Now the Germans were withdrawing from west of the Somme, and they used the river as a barrier. But on 31 August–1 September the Australians, in a daring and costly operation devised by Monash that Rawlinson reluctantly endorsed, established themselves across the water line by seizing the fortified hill of Mont Saint-Quentin. Further north, on 2 September the Canadians broke through the 'Drocourt–Quéant Switch', a formidable line whose fall meant that the 'Winter Position' too was outflanked.

These operations showed how the locus of authority in the Allied armies was shifting. Since the confrontation on 15 August Foch had not interfered with Haig's conduct of operations, and Haig increasingly delegated to his commanders, while Rawlinson at Mont Saint-Quentin sanctioned a Monash plan that he considered reckless, and in the battles of the Scarpe and the Drocourt–Quéant Switch Horne left much of the planning to the Canadians. Haig, who was a canny political operator, had been warned by Henry Wilson about the War Cabinet's fear of 'heavy losses', and informed Horne and Currie that he had no wish for them to attack the Drocourt–Quéant position if they doubted they could take it. In effect the decision was delegated to Currie; and the assault was launched by two Canadian divisions and one British one, starting with fifty-nine tanks at 5 a.m.[67] The Drocourt–Quéant Switch comprised two lines of trenches supported by concrete shelters and machine-gun posts, and according to Churchill (who inspected it the day afterwards) the wire was 100 yards wide and some had to be hand-cut. Yet the Germans in the forward line surrendered in large numbers, and although the second line had excellent fields of fire the position fell in seven hours. In previous years resistance would have been far fiercer, Haig commenting that German discipline even among officers was going: 'Many ... surrendered without a fight' and 'The enemy seems to be running away.'[68]

By this stage the attack front had widened to over 150 kilometres, sucking in ever more German forces. On 30 August the French estimated that Germany had forty-four reserve divisions against the Allies' seventy-five, so that in barely two months the balance of striking power had been transformed. During August the German Western Front army had 228,000 casualties – 21,000 dead and 110,000 missing – and received barely 130,000 replacements.[69] In these circumstances, after losing the Drocourt–Quéant Switch Ludendorff obtained Wilhelm's permission to withdraw some fifteen miles to the 'Siegfried Position', the movement proceeding at night between 3 and 7 September. Usually known to the British as the Hindenburg Line, the position was one of a series of defences stretching in an arc from Lille to Metz, which east of Soissons had not yet become the German front line. Opposite the British, however, the Germans had now retreated to their strongest defences, and nothing comparable lay behind. Finally persuaded that one big fallback would damage morale less than piecemeal ones, Ludendorff took a step that he had previously resisted, Hindenburg warning the army group commanders that the new line 'must be held in all circumstances'.[70]

SAINT-MIHIEL TO MEUSE–ARGONNE

The pace of the British advance now slowed. Instead, the most important mid-September battle was fought well to the east, in the Saint-Mihiel salient, and was the first to be planned and conducted by an independent American army under its own staff and commanders. The Germans had held the salient since 1914 and it was a natural fortress, especially on its western side, where forested heights towered above the river Meuse. Unlike the positions attacked on 18 July and 8 August it had long been prepared to take advantage of the terrain, and was protected by four to five successive defence lines with great belts of wire, machine-gun nests, and concrete dugouts. It severed the eastern section of the Paris–Avricourt railway and menaced the Paris–Nancy line;[71] and from it the Germans could threaten the flank of any Allied attack west of the Meuse towards Sedan. Only fifteen miles behind the salient, across the marshy plain of the Woëvre, lay the fortified region of Metz-Thionville (a pivot of the German line since 1914 and the eastern terminus of the great trunk railway that ran to Lille) as well as the Briey–Longwy iron ore basin and steel mills. Hence the salient had much to protect, and Pershing had identified it as the sector where his men could contribute decisively. For too long they had been wasted in scattered defensive fighting, and a US army should be formed to strike an offensive blow and change the course of the war: 'our officers and men are far and away superior to the tired Europeans'. After he took command on 10 August of the newly created American First Army, he established his headquarters in the region, and the main lines of the offensive (which had been envisaged in Foch's Bombon memorandum) were agreed with the French.[72] Pershing wanted a signal success with his best troops, to clear the salient, free the railway, and establish a base for further advance; Foch agreed to move three American divisions from the British zone and that France would supply artillery, tanks, air support, munitions, and lorries.[73] In early September the attack was abruptly scaled down (and now would no longer go beyond the base of the salient) in discussions about a much larger scheme for converging Allied offensives; but Pershing insisted that it went ahead. Again much of the concentration was accomplished at night, while cloudy skies inhibited overflights and the French bombarded Alsace as a distraction. Although the Germans did get wind of the attack and the Allies suspected they had done so, its commencement was again a surprise. Ludendorff had approved an evacuation, but wanted it to be drawn out: it began on 11 September but the Allied bombardment started at 1 a.m. on the following morning and the infantry assaults went in four and seven hours later.

The German commander (General-Leutnant Fuchs) had seven mediocre divisions, 560 guns, and 200 aircraft. The main Allied attack against the less imposing southern face of the salient used eight divisions, all American; the secondary attack on the western face used two: one American and one French.[74] Whereas previously American troops had fought under French or British command, now French troops fought under Pershing's. None the less, in part because of the concentration since the spring on sending over infantry and machine gunners, the Americans could not have fought without French logistical and technical assistance. The attackers enjoyed an overwhelming preponderance of 3:1 in infantry, 5/6:1 in artillery, and 7:1 in aircraft, but the 3,000 guns and 267 light tanks employed were all of French manufacture and many had French crews.[75] As the Germans were already preparing withdrawal, it was unsurprising that the elimination of the salient proceeded smoothly, with virtually no initial resistance. Fuchs ordered up reserves, but heavy rain delayed them on roads clogged by evacuation traffic. At midday he ordered a general retreat, but even in these exceptional conditions the encirclement that the Allies had hoped for failed to materialize. By the time the pincers from the south and west converged, most of the German infantry had escaped, and on 14–15 September the front settled down. Allied casualties were 7,000; German casualties 17,000, of whom 13,000 were prisoners, and the Germans also lost 257 artillery pieces and hundreds of machine guns. Two hundred square miles of territory changed hands, and the railway link was cleared. On the face of it, the operation had succeeded and on schedule. Yet Allied commentators, admittedly writing with a certain condescension, noted disquieting American weaknesses: according to French reports the Germans had got away easily and the confusion in the American communication lines had been so great that the AEF had been practically immobilized. According to a British observer, General C. M. Wagstaff, 'The show of course must undoubtedly be judged a great success', yet the Americans had been lucky that the weather improved, their treatment of horses was appalling, and their transport administration 'haphazard'. Pershing's Chief of Staff, James McAndrew, agreed: road traffic discipline had been poor, the artillery had moved up too slowly, and there had been a general slackness. In the next American operation these problems would become glaring.[76]

Saint-Mihiel was subordinated to the requirements of AEF participation in the general Allied attack unleashed at the end of September. With Saint-Mihiel the Bombon programme was completed, the salients formed between March and July eliminated, the lateral railways liberated, and the Germans driven back from Paris, the Channel ports, and the northern coalfields: Foch, earlier than expected, could prepare the 'important offensive' he had envisaged on 24 July. It was becoming so evident that the German army was crumbling that in late August Pershing advised Woodrow Wilson that the war might end that year. Haig came to the same conclusion, although the politicians in London disagreed, Milner dismissing the idea as 'ridiculously optimistic'.[77] None the less, at least two of the senior commanders perceived this possibility before the meetings that devised the biggest battle of the war. On 25 August Foch wrote to Haig to praise him for widening the British operations: Haig's reply envisaged a converging attack by the Americans from the south towards Mézières while the BEF pushed on towards Saint-Quentin and Cambrai.[78] British GHQ commented:

> The operations of these main forces should be co-ordinated in a concentric direction, with the object of defeating the enemy's forces on the whole 130 kilometre front [i.e. of active fighting] and taking the general direction of the front Verviers-Le Cateau, with a view to threatening the enemy's only lateral railway communication running from Valenciennes and Cambrai to Thionville and Metz.[79]

This would mean downgrading Saint-Mihiel, which Haig expected to lead nowhere because of the strength of German defences and its tangential orientation, pointing north-eastwards and away from the other Allied forces. Although his thinking had an evident logic, its implication was that the Allies would concentrate on enveloping the Germans in Belgium (the primary British objective) while Pershing's project for an American thrust towards the Rhineland would be marginalized.[80] But when Haig met Foch on 30 August, he won round the generalissimo, and Pétain also supported the scheme.[81] On the same day Foch wrote to Pershing that the Germans had now been driven well beyond the first objectives set on 24 July and the situation should be exploited with the British army continuing towards Cambrai and Saint-Quentin and the French continuing beyond the Aisne; but now with the extra element of a push northward along the Meuse towards Mézières. If the Germans were driven up against the forested hills of the Ardennes (which lacked trunk lines) and lost control of the Mézières–Montmédy railway, their position would be untenable. Hence the Saint-Mihiel operation should halt at the base of the salient, before French forces – and US forces under French command – launched the new operation.[82] This change of conception he put to Pershing in person on the same day.

The meeting was difficult. Pershing had been preparing for Saint-Mihiel since mid-August and could not understand the sudden alteration. However, he accepted that converging advances were desirable. He concentrated his ire on the threat to the American army's newly won independence, and it is difficult not to see the Haig/Foch scheme as an effort to curtail it, possibly for political reasons but also because the Europeans still doubted the AEF's competence. But provided Pershing's army operated autonomously he could accept the relocation, and this became the basis of a compromise. Offered the choice of operating east or west of the Meuse, Pershing chose the latter, where the communications were better, although the American First Army would have to rush its forces from the Saint-Mihiel salient as soon as the latter was overrun. In return for the principle that the AEF would fight two successive independent actions, he agreed to conditions that almost set it up to fail.[83]

A final element entered the plan after Foch proposed to Haig and to the Belgian CGS, Cyriaque Gillain, a new attack in Flanders. Apparently Foch had been approached by Belgium's King Albert, who had nursed his army since 1914 but now wished it to participate in the final act.[84] By abandoning the Lys salient the Germans had exposed their railways running north to the sea. The chance presented itself to overrun the heights east of Ypres that the British had assaulted in the previous year, and to establish a base for operations against the trunk line passing through Roulers. The proposal was accepted, and although Foch failed to persuade the Italians to strike as well the Allies were now agreed on a sequence of co-ordinated attacks before the end of September by the British eastwards against the centre of the Hindenburg Line and the French and Americans northwards along the Meuse, supported by the Flanders drive. Although Pétain still envisaged victory coming in 1919, Foch was trying to precipitate events. On 8 September he asked Haig to prepare an offensive that would hustle the Germans out of their resistance line before they could organize it.[85]

Foch had charged the Americans with leading off the general offensive and accomplishing its most difficult task. Two main railway systems linked the German armies with their homeland. The northern one, running towards Liège, could handle (in the Allies' estimate) some 300 trains a day; the southern one (from Metz towards Verdun) some 200 a day; whereas the lines across the intervening Ardennes could carry only eighty. The Lille–Hirson–Mézières–Sedan lateral railway was double-tracked for most of its length, but quadrupled between Metz and Sedan: between Carignan, Sedan, and Mézières there was no alternative east–west route.[86] This section lay only fifty kilometres from the Americans' jumping-off point, and its distance from the rearmost German defence line was eighteen kilometres, whereas opposite the British the equivalent distance was over thirty. The Americans therefore had a thinner defensive belt to fight through, and were closer than anyone else to the railway. But precisely for these reasons the Germans knew they could not retreat, and both the terrain and their defences were forbidding. On the eastern (right) flank of the attack lay the unfordable river Meuse, with wooded heights above it. On the western flank lay further wooded heights, the dense and tangled Argonne forest. In the middle of the zone between them a hogback of more high ground stretched back from Montfaucon in the centre of the German position to Romagne and Cunel in the rear. The Americans would be advancing uphill along two defiles, each commanded by German artillery, and would have to cross four east–west defensive lines with excellent machine-gun look-outs. The third and most formidable was the Kriemhilde Stellung, eleven kilometres in, which ran through the Romagne heights and formed the local section of the Hindenburg Line. The whole area was protected by barbed wire, concrete pillboxes, overlooking artillery, and machine guns deployed in depth. However, its garrison was relatively thin, so if the Americans achieved surprise they hoped to overrun the Kriemhilde Stellung before the OHL could reinforce it.

To their left, meanwhile, the French Fourth Army (which included more Americans) under Gouraud would attack west of the Argonne, and Foch gave this force the task of reaching Mézières.[87] Gouraud also faced formidable defences, which he did not expect to surprise completely, although he planned the usual counter-battery bombardment. He received fewer heavy guns than he wanted, but obtained 356 tanks: the biggest deployment since 8 August.[88] Pershing, in contrast, was taking over a new sector, and part of the surprise was to come from breaking off very rapidly at Saint-Mihiel, where he thought the Germans expected him to continue, the transports beginning from the second day of the battle there. Some 220,000 French troops were deployed out of the Meuse–Argonne sector and some 600,000 mainly American ones deployed into it, all movements proceeding in darkness along the three mediocre roads that covered the sixty miles between the two battlefields while the new attack zone received the normal paraphernalia of airfields, ammunition dumps, hospitals, signalling, and light railways. The concentration concluded on schedule, burnishing the reputation of George C. Marshall, the staff officer who played a large part in organizing it, but time was lacking to equip the new rear area with enough roads.[89] On paper, none the less, the Allies again enjoyed an immense superiority when the assault began in thick fog at 5.30 a.m. on 26 September, along a twenty-mile front after a three-hour bombardment, Gouraud following half an hour later. The Americans faced five divisions of indifferent quality and at only one third of their regulation strength, whom the attacking nine nearly full-strength US divisions outnumbered (man to man) by eight to one. Nearly 2,800 guns (most of them French) carried out the bombardment. Yet the AEF had only 821 aircraft (over 600 of which they piloted) and 189 French-built light tanks (also mostly crewed by Americans and commanded by Colonel George S. Patton, Jr), or barely half the mobile support for the much easier operation at Saint-Mihiel.[90] In the weeks to come the Americans would experience their equivalent of Britain's 1916 nightmare on the Somme.

GENERAL OFFENSIVE

On the first morning of the Battle of the Meuse–Argonne resistance was slight, but by 29 September Pershing was forced to call a pause, his troops having advanced up to eight miles and reached the Kriemhilde Stellung but not yet having taken it as they had been supposed to do on the second day. Part of the explanation naturally lay with the Germans. Although the Americans achieved initial surprise the defending commanders had readied reinforcements, six more divisions arriving by 30 September and staging successful counter-attacks. The Germans were unimpressed by American tactics, which included assaulting machine guns in dense waves, while the tanks, operating in unfavourable terrain, again proved easy targets and were mostly soon out of action.[91] Facing machine guns and shelling from the heights, the American artillery was moved up too slowly and the infantry halted, and the gamble on rushing the Kriemhilde Stellung was lost. The AEF's internal notes condemned a lack of 'markedly aggressive spirit ... advances were too slow and too cautious ... companies, battalions, and regiments sometimes remained inactive in presence of relatively small enemy forces ... Inaction is the worst military crime.'[92] Yet many of Pershing's best units had stayed at Saint-Mihiel or were serving under Gouraud, and most of the troops and officers committed had not previously fought. Major Geiger of the British liaison mission was 'convinced that the general slowness of the progress made is entirely due to the newness of the units engaged and a considerable amount of bad leadership'. Many officers were hurriedly replaced, and the 29 September pause was meant to gain time to move in experienced divisions.[93] However, a supply breakdown exacerbated the problems. Although Pershing berated Washington for not sending enough lorries and horses, Foch's change of strategy and the breakneck speed with which the offensive was planned in a remote rural location bore much of the blame – though similar chaos had developed at Saint-Mihiel. Geiger noted terrible traffic jams, many 'stragglers' in the rear, and food lorries being looted.[94] Meanwhile, men in the front line went hungry. The root of the problem may have been that Pershing was simply running too large an army (and too big divisions) for his services to support, although poor staff work and inexperience patently contributed.

In contrast, Gouraud's troops made slow initial progress but then moved forward. The situation exasperated the French and British, who had long been sceptical about AEF independence, and Foch's staff were 'terribly disappointed'. The situation came to a head with a devastating letter from Clemenceau, who had got stuck in the traffic jams behind the sector. He demanded that rather than rely on persuasion Foch should issue orders. It was questionable whether the Premier had the authority to be so peremptory, and when Foch proposed placing Pershing's left flank under French command the latter predictably objected.[95] But the upshot was that the attempt to disorganize the Germans by attacking them from the south had failed, although it had been crucial to Haig's and Foch's conception of the offensive as a whole. It had done so, moreover, in circumstances that revived old tensions within the Western alliance.

The Allied attack in Flanders on 28 September also began well before stalling. Foch had won consent for it to be conducted by the GAN (Groupe d'Armées du Nord, or Northern Army Group), commanded by King Albert with the French General Degoutte as his Chief of Staff, to which Plumer's British Second Army was subordinated. This force would drive east from Ypres across the salient and capture the Passchendaele–Clercken ridge. The GAN comprised ten British divisions (six in the attack) on its southern flank, but six French divisions (three of them cavalry) and nine Belgian ones. Plumer had wanted to by-pass the salient and attack towards Wytschaete and Messines, but Haig refused to press the case, as his main concern was to get the Belgians into action. Hence the British would cover the flank of the main advance, by establishing a defensive front along the Lys. Plumer had no tanks and although as usual he dispensed with a preliminary bombardment (the Belgians fired a brief one of three hours), the Allies did not achieve complete surprise and they attacked across the same churned up and fortified terrain that in 1917 had held up the BEF for three months – and even in similar weather conditions, of teeming rain on the first day. That none the less they progressed as far as they did is one of the outstanding pieces of evidence for how far the German army had deteriorated. On the 28th the attackers advanced up to eight miles, overrunning the salient and the area to the south, and capturing most of the ridge line, Passchendaele itself falling to the Belgians. Although the Germans held the heights their artillery fire was weak and quickly silenced, and the infantry dealt with the pillboxes and machine guns more easily than expected. On the 29th the advance continued, but so did the rain, hampering artillery observation and aircraft, while the salient became a morass across which it was almost impossible to bring supplies and heavy guns forward. On 2 October the offensive was halted, and did not resume for nearly two weeks. Although the Allies had captured 10,000 prisoners and 300 guns, reached open countryside, and were only two miles from the junction at Roulers, the forward troops were nearly starving and in a pioneering operation the RAF air-dropped 13 tons of stores. The Germans had brought up six divisions and their shellfire was becoming more dangerous, but to an extent the Belgians halted for similar reasons to the AEF: an inexperienced army operating in difficult circumstances (and unfamiliar with open warfare) ran ahead of its supplies.[96]

On 1 October British intelligence estimated the German divisions engaged since 26 September as being 12 in Flanders, 23 in Champagne and the Argonne, but 32 opposite Cambrai. Five had reinforced Ypres but 13 Cambrai and 13 the Meuse–Argonne.[97] This intelligence supports Pershing's contention that the American–French operation in the south drew off important German reserves, but still the largest German troop concentration faced the BEF in the centre, and here the Allied attacks had greatest success. Yet although the BEF in the end delivered the heaviest Allied blow, the Cabinet in London had become increasingly nervous. Henry Wilson tried to reassure the politicians that 'the impression the War Cabinet had formed some time ago, that the Amiens advance might involve us in a second Passchendaele, should now be corrected'. He pointed out that whereas during Third Ypres the British army had suffered 265,000 casualties and captured 24,000 prisoners and sixty-four guns, during August 1918 for 50,000 casualties it had captured 43,000 prisoners and 500–600 guns.[98] None the less, on the eve of the Drocourt–Quéant Switch attack he sent Haig what he described as a 'personal' telegram warning that 'the War Cabinet would become anxious if we received heavy punishment in attacking the Hindenburg Line, without success'. Haig correctly divined that the telegram did not just represent Wilson but meant that what he called the 'wretched lot of weaklings in high places' were leaving him to carry the can if things went wrong.[99] In truth the Cabinet was in a dilemma, for having supported Foch's appointment it would be difficult to block his strategy, yet on the other hand Haig's previous record gave good ground for doubting his judgements, whatever the signs that circumstances had changed. Haig rejoined that he was careful with manpower – as evidenced by his halting of the Battle of Amiens – and it was much less costly to keep the Germans on the move than to let them recover and organize a strong new position. An appreciation by Lt-Gen. Nelthorpe of Haig's staff urged that if the Germans retreated unmolested to a shorter line 'such a favourable situation as the present one is not likely to recur for some years'.[100] Haig himself told Milner on 10 September that German discipline was going and a decision was possible in the 'very near future' – although he saw the practical implication as being that British units should be up to strength by the following April. On 21 September he saw Milner again, and the Secretary warned him that if the British army were 'used up' now there would not be another one next year. But Milner left it to Haig to decide whether to attack the Hindenburg Line and Haig went ahead, advising Foch on 22 September that he was willing to carry out the operations assigned to him. He remarked that it was possible to get a decision that year and, even if not, every blow would make next year's task easier. He was aware of increasing British casualties and the political risks of failure, but also aware of declining German morale. He hoped that if he waited two or three days after the Franco-American attack the latter would draw off enemy forces, and on 26 September he told his Australian officers that 'the biggest battle of the war had commenced that morning – the enemy would be attacked by 100 Divisions in the next 3 days'.[101]

The BEF assaulted two enemy sectors: a first centred on the Canal du Nord on 27 September, and a second centred on the Saint-Quentin Canal on the 29th. The Hindenburg Line planners had integrated watercourses into their scheme, and canals and rivers had since acquired an added significance as obstacles against surprise tank attacks. In many 1918 battles the Allies fought across them, rather than toiling up slopes as in 1915–17. The Canal du Nord was an intimidating obstacle: its west bank was 10–12 feet high and its east bank 4–5 feet high, while it was 100 feet wide. Beyond it lay dense wire and marshes swept by machine guns sheltered in trenches, while the Germans also held overlooking higher ground, placing seven and a half divisions in line and four in reserve.[102] The First and Third Armies conducted the attack, but once again the Canadian Corps spearheaded it, with Currie and his staff doing most of the planning despite Byng's doubts about their proposals. The Canadians had far fewer tanks and aircraft than on 8 August – these were allocated in preference to the Saint-Quentin Canal operation – and given this and the water barrier they reverted to 1917 tactics of a set-piece advance, covered by an exceptionally heavy and accurate creeping barrage delivered by both artillery and machine guns as well as very heavy counter-battery fire against German guns that lacked shells.[103] The plan was to cross a narrow dry section of the canal, the infantry moving forward in waves and bringing up machine guns and artillery with them. The canal was crossed quite easily, and the engineers began constructing bridges on the first morning: the German defences were not continuous but an interlocking series of dugouts, which could be isolated. Once again, what should have been a strong position was guarded less stubbornly than it would have been a year before. By the evening the attackers had made a breach twelve miles wide and six deep, and had taken 16,000 prisoners and 200 guns. Having broken through to the areas fought over in November 1917, however, round Bourlon Wood and the high ground south-west of Cambrai, the operation slowed down, and in five days of continuous fighting the Canadians suffered heavily. The advance failed to assist the second British assault through a flanking manoeuvre as had been hoped, and the Canadian high command sensed that something had gone wrong.[104]

If three of the four Allied attacks lost momentum, however, the fourth broke through the German defences. This was the assault by the British Fourth Army, the last in the sequence. The Saint-Quentin Canal was thirty-five feet wide, with wire in the water and on the perpendicular slopes alongside it: it had brick-faced walls ten feet high, and was filled with mud and water up to 6–8 feet deep. Tanks could not cross it, concrete emplacements with machine guns commanded it on the east bank, it was protected by a continuous barrier of trenches, and it formed the centre of a six-line system of defences, some 6,000 yards deep.[105] None the less, it had weak points. The canal did not run the complete length of the Fourth Army sector, and to the north it passed through the Bellicourt and Bellenglise tunnels, which the Germans used as shelters. The tunnel section was only 6,000 yards wide, and as it was the obvious point for an attack the wire and machine-gun barriers there were more imposing than ever. However, on 8 August the Canadians had captured plans for the canal section, including precise locations of dugouts, headquarters, artillery, railheads, and supply dumps; and although the documentation dated from February 1917 much of it remained applicable and gave invaluable assistance in targeting the bombardment. The Germans had built additional tunnels to enable their troops to move around, but the plans disclosed their exits. Although the Fourth Army's appreciation of the captured plans described the position as 'enormously strong', its underlying principles were now outdated, with the artillery and machine guns concentrated too far forward instead of being distributed in depth. It was now nearly two years old, and the great belts of wire were starting to deteriorate.[106] Although the Germans had made improvements, so vast a system was becoming too much for their beleaguered forces to garrison.

The defenders' determination was the key to the entire position, and plenty of evidence was reaching GHQ that it was failing. Henry Wilson told the War Cabinet on 3 September that the Germans were now in 'a very bad condition', for the first-line men were reluctant to dig trenches, and only eight fresh divisions remained on the Western Front; other evidence suggested that whereas 40–45 trains had once been needed to move a German division the figure now was thirty-two.[107] All the same, the Hindenburg defences were so forbidding that Rawlinson feared that if the Germans had the chance to consolidate they might again become formidable even with reduced numbers. He warned Henry Wilson that he would have to pause while moving up the heavy guns and ammunition needed, and that the tanks were largely 'used up'.[108] Hence he laid great stress on the success of an attack on 18 September, the 'Battle of Epéhy', which confirmed that enemy morale remained low and positioned the Fourth Army to assault the main Hindenburg Line. Rawlinson had advised that it was essential to 'hustle' the Germans out of the old British 1917 front line beforehand, and this was what Epéhy achieved, a very accurate creeping barrage enabling the Australians to occupy a ridge overlooking the canal from the west.[109] Because the Germans based their defence system on the watercourse, rather than on a reverse slope as in 1916–17, the British artillery could now observe the principal position and exploit the captured documentation to the full.

This proved just as well, for artillery superiority was fundamental. While the Canadians were deployed against the Canal du Nord, Rawlinson again had the use of the Australians, and he gave Monash the lead in planning. The Australian divisions, however, were becoming tired (and their Prime Minister, William Hughes, had made representations for them to have extra leave): on 21 September 119 men of the 1st Battalion refused to attack. Hence it was decided to advance across the tunnels with two Australian divisions accompanied by two American ones that remained under British command. These latter were larger than the Australian divisions but neither had had previous battle experience, and they were required to install themselves in the German positions before the Australians followed through.[110] Even with a large accompaniment of tanks – eighty-six for the Americans and seventy-six for the Australians – this was a tall order, and Monash gambled on German demoralization. Fortunately, Rawlinson insisted – over Monash's opposition – on adding a daring crossing of the canal itself, to be undertaken by the North Midland troops of the 46th Division, who would attack with collapsible boats, mud-mats, scaling ladders, and life-belts collected from the Channel ferries. The preparations were hidden from German aircraft, and the canal assault startled the defenders. Given the strength of the Hindenburg position in general, however, the British felt they could not dispense this time with a bombardment. From 26 to 29 September a barrage by 1,600 guns, nearly 600 of them heavy, delivered 750,000 shells weighing 39 million pounds along a front of 10,000 yards. In weight this was comparable to the bombardment of June 1916, but by now British 18-pounder shrapnel shells could cut wire much more efficiently, while the heavy artillery concentrated on counter-battery fire and on machine-gun posts and dugouts, supported by the first use of British-made mustard-gas shells.[111]

Even supported by a bombardment of this intensity, all did not go well on the day. The attack forces numbered some 40,000 in eight divisions against 30,000 defenders with 5,000 in reserve, so had no great numerical edge.[112] In the north, moreover, after an American attack against the German outposts failed on the 27th the commanders feared a close creeping barrage would kill the survivors trapped in no man's land; and hence the barrage was laid down well ahead, the infantry struggling after it in thick fog and progressing more slowly than expected. On the left the attack did not reach the main Hindenburg Line, although in the centre it made more progress. But on the right flank the 46th Division accomplished one of the most arresting feats of the war. An exceptionally intense and accurate creeping barrage broke up the wire, partially smashed down the canal banks, and landed (it has been estimated) 126 shells per minute on each 500 yards of German trench for a period of eight hours. Attacking at 5.50 a.m., the Staffordshire troops reached the canal on time and by 8.30 a.m. had crossed it, capturing a bridge intact. By 3.30 p.m. the British had advanced up to three miles, taking the main enemy position and continuing into the support position beyond it, one regiment capturing 4,200 prisoners and seventy guns. By the evening of 30 September a fifty-kilometre stretch of the Hindenburg Line had fallen, and in subsequent days the British widened the breakthrough.[113] By 3 October only the flimsier defences of the 'Beaurevoir Line', the last in the Hindenburg Position, stood between them and open country. If the Germans had failed to hold the Allies on this barrier, it was hard to see how they could hold them at all.

Walking along the Hindenburg Line on 15 October Haig observed:

> The defence system is admirably sited and the wire is immensely strong – many wide belts of the thickest form of wire. Dug outs are numerous, and most of the exits are made of concrete of immense thickness. Had the Germans been in a good state of moral [sic], the position would have been impregnable.[114]

For remarkable though the 46th Division's accomplishments were, they no longer faced the opponent of 1916. German supplies of basic weapons and munitions were adequate, and equipment losses were still being made good.[115] But although the German positions in September 1918 were comparable to those that had successfully withstood earlier attacks, they needed modification for defence in greater depth, and Germany lacked manpower, both in absolute numbers and with the necessary physical strength and psychological resilience, to carry out the necessary arduous manual labour and then to hold them. German casualties in August and September were some 464,000, of whom 229,000 were missing: in other words, unprecedented numbers were surrendering. Average battalion numbers fell during August and September from 850 to 540, and were held even at this level only by suppressing twenty-two divisions. As against this, the OHL estimated that the Allies had sixty-five fresh infantry divisions and nine cavalry divisions in reserve, and some 2,000 tanks.[116] According to Allied estimates, in mid-September the Central Powers were down to 190 divisions while the Allies had 211 infantry and ten cavalry divisions; in the most active sector of the front from Verdun to the sea the ratio was 165:171, so that even in numbers of divisions the Allies had gained the edge and in numbers of men their advantage was bigger. But more fundamentally, according to the German official history 'the inner strength of the troops was no more as of old', and Boehm, the commander of the army group attacked at the Battle of Epéhy, described it as a 'Day of terror ... The troops no longer have the old firm hold, efficient officers are missing above all, and the resources of the men are tried to the uttermost.'[117]

Two further factors came into play: intelligence and transport. The OHL had lost its intelligence advantage, and not only had the balance of striking forces completely altered since July, but the Germans were being reduced to a passive defending role, increasingly failing to mount counter-attacks and uncertain where they would be hit next. Two reports by OHL officers on 23 and 24 September said the army commanders expected strong attacks soon all along the Western Front, but did not know where ('We find ourselves in dependence on the enemy'). Wilhelm Heye, who had replaced Wetzell as Chief of Operations, thought a Franco-American attack in Lorraine towards German territory would most likely be the main operation, and Ludendorff agreed, the OHL raising the forces on its eastern sector from twenty-nine to fifty-three divisions between 25 August and 21 September. A Lorraine operation was indeed what Pershing had envisaged as a continuation of the Saint-Mihiel battle, but the Allied decisions of early September shifted the axis of American advance north-westwards. Moreover, Foch's emphasis on targeting enemy communications was bearing fruit, as on 23 September the Germans started returning the divisions they had sent to Lorraine and overloading on their railways amplified the shortage once the concentric Allied attacks began.[118] Concerned though Hindenburg and Ludendorff were to reinforce the Meuse–Argonne (although Gouraud's offensive there worried them more than Pershing's), they found it difficult to do so from Lorraine, where they still feared an assault. Similarly, the Germans defending the Canal du Nord against the Canadians were reinforced one day late, by which time they had lost much of their artillery and their prepared positions.[119] In late September the Germans were under very heavy pressure indeed, and precisely in these circumstances their leaders resolved to seek a cessation of hostilities. Although the request went out on 4 October, the deliberations leading to it started when on 28 September news reached Ludendorff that Bulgaria had sued for an armistice.

MACEDONIA

Bulgaria's armistice request followed two weeks of spectacular progress for the Allies after they attacked in Macedonia on 15 September. Yet their experience in the Balkans had been chequered, and the reversal of military fortunes there was as striking as in the west. All the armies in Macedonia had to contend with heat and malaria in the summer months. But the Allies had to ship most of their troops and supplies from Taranto, through submarine-infested waters, and the port and railway infrastructure in Macedonia was rudimentary. The British estimated that the Allies could send four divisions a month by sea but the Germans could send eight to ten overland.[120] Indeed, communications were one reason for the British preferring Palestine, which was easier to supply via the Cape and from India. Macedonia never received as much equipment as the Western Front, and the Allied forces there were weak in heavy artillery (both in numbers and in calibre) and weaker still in aircraft. Conversely the Bulgarian army was quite well supplied with modern weaponry. It was not numerically much inferior to its enemies and held mountain positions overlooking them, which it protected with trenches, barbed wire, concrete gun emplacements, and shelters hewn into the rock.[121] Until recently it had been a well-motivated force that had shown it could fight hard.

During the first half of 1918 the Balkan theatre stagnated and the Allies scaled down their presence, but from the summer the situation altered, and the French pressed for an offensive. In June Clemenceau unexpectedly sent out General Louis Franchet d'Espèrey to replace Guillaumat, who became the Paris military governor. Franchet d'Espèrey had been the army group commander to whom the ill-fated General Duchêne had been responsible on the Chemin des Dames, and he left the Western Front with his reputation tarnished. But this gave him something to prove, and he both knew the Balkans and showed himself to be bold, imaginative, and forceful.[122] Further, on returning to Paris Guillaumat proved an effective lobbyist, who carried authority both with Clemenceau and with the Italians and British. The two generals took the lead in winning approval for planning and then launching the September attack.

By this stage the Serbian units in the Allied line were being reinforced by South Slav prisoners from Russia, and the new Greek divisions were coming into line, Greek numbers rising from 101,000 to 157,000.[123] On the other hand, the Germans had recalled their divisions, although German personnel still crewed much of the heavy artillery and supplied the senior staffs, including the theatre commander, General von Scholtz, with the consequence that Bulgarian resentment could be directed against the Germans both for having deserted them and for their continuing influence. Moreover, in this as in other respects, the Central Powers' successes in the east in 1918 proved a poisoned chalice, as they displayed the usual tendency of victors to fall out. The negotiations leading to the peace treaty with Bulgaria's neighbour, Romania, caused a public quarrel between Sofia and Constantinople, the Turks demanding that if Bulgaria acquired Romania's Black Sea province of the Dobrudja Turkey should regain the territory that it had ceded to Bulgaria in order to bring the latter into the war. In the end Bulgaria got the southern Dobrudja but the northern Dobrudja was placed under a condominium of the four Central Powers, the Germans distrusting the Bulgarians and hoping to cultivate Romania as a balance to them.[124] Bulgarian public opinion demanded the whole of the province, King Ferdinand bowing to it by replacing Radoslovov, the Prime Minister who had brought the country into the war, by the more pro-Allied Malinov. While Bulgaria's loyalty to the Central Powers came into question, the Allies noted faltering morale and increasing desertion in its army.[125]

After Franchet d'Espèrey arrived in Macedonia, Clemenceau instructed him that the time was ripe for a 'definitely aggressive attitude' because Germany was too committed elsewhere to help a demoralized Bulgarian army and Bulgaria was politically unstable – the aim was to break its defence system and return the Serbian and Greek armies to their lost territories, striking before the autumn when Germany might have spare troops.[126] However, an offensive would still need Allied approval, and when the Supreme War Council met on 2–4 July, it referred the issue to specialist advice. Whereas the British Foreign Office hoped to negotiate Bulgaria out of the war, Guillaumat claimed an early attack could crack the enemy lines, while the Serbs and Greeks might grow discouraged if the Allies remained inactive. The SWC's Permanent Military Representatives were sympathetic, though they opposed diverting men and materiel from the Western Front or shipping from the American troop transports.[127] The British commander, Milne, agreed that the situation had improved and that if the Bulgarians' front line were broken their army was likely to disintegrate, although he expected stubborn initial resistance. Franchet d'Espèrey won a free hand to prepare an offensive, but not yet actually to launch one.[128]

The central feature of the Macedonian theatre was the valley of the river Vardar, through which a railway ran southwards towards Salonika and northwards towards Sofia and via the Morava valley towards Serbia. Whereas Guillaumat had envisaged advancing up the valley from where it entered the coastal plain, however, the Allies' main attack in September was a Franco-Serb assault on the Moglena massif to the west, which reached the Vardar upstream at its confluence with the Tcherna at Gradsko. The conception originated with the Serbs, who were stationed opposite the Moglena, but after visiting for himself Franchet endorsed it. He hoped to gain surprise in an isolated area that the Bulgarians would find it hard to reinforce, and the Serbs were both experienced in mountain warfare and eager, provided French heavy artillery supported them. From the start Franchet saw the possibilities of knocking out Bulgaria, liberating Serbia, and threatening Austria-Hungary, but it was essential to start by mid-September before the autumn rains, and much needed doing. Serbian staff work was poor, and French officers were seconded to give assistance. Detailed maps were hastily drawn, and the supply lines improved. The assault force would be scaling precipitous heights between the Vetrenik and Sokol peaks, but Mount Floka, held by the Allies to the south-west, was higher than the Bulgarian positions, and Allied tractors hauled up nearly ninety heavy guns by night to altitudes of over 2,000 metres, while 45,000 gas shells arrived from France to silence the enemy batteries. Franchet drew on lessons from Gallipoli and the Western Front, and this would not only be better supported than any previous Balkan operation, but also more punctiliously planned.[129]

The Allies had only a small overall superiority in Macedonia, but a much larger one in the attack zone, in part thanks to the new Greek divisions, which could occupy quieter sectors and free up veteran forces. As of June 1918 the Allies had 200 serviceable aircraft against 80; 2,000 large and medium-calibre guns against 1,800; and 284 infantry battalions to 254, which on paper meant 600,000 to 450,000 men, although because of the large size of Bulgarian infantry companies the true ratio was less favourable. On the Moglena sector, however, the Franco-Serb forces achieved a 3:1 superiority of 75 battalions against 26 (36,500 infantrymen against 11,600); 580 guns against 146; 756 machine guns against 245; and 81 aircraft against 24.[130] Franchet hoped surprise would offset the difficulty of the terrain, but he also planned to disrupt Bulgarian movements by secondary attacks, principally by British and Greek forces under Milne against two high points: 'P' ridge to the west of Lake Doiran and the Blaga Panina to the north of it. The former was over 2,000 feet high, one of the most heavily fortified portions of the Bulgarians' line, and held by their best division: the Bulgarians had a railway behind them, and held a series of reinforced positions with wire and concrete gun emplacements. British attacks there had failed in 1917, and Milne was loath to repeat them, but he deferred to Franchet's insistence. He accepted the general scheme and was willing to play his part in it, though warning the War Office that he needed extra troops, heavy guns, and shells, but in fact he got no extra men and only one fifth of the munitions he requested.[131] Hence the principal attack had better prospects than the secondary one. But while the Allies concentrated their forces round the Moglena and Lake Doiran, they could safely thin the rest of the line because now, in contrast to earlier periods of the war, an enemy counteroffensive was improbable. Although aerial reconnaissance and Serbian deserters did alert the Bulgarians, they did not know when the attack would happen. They also had a spy in the Supreme War Council, but Scholtz's headquarters ignored their warnings; indeed, the Germans appear to have been deceived by a bogus Allied planning document that suggested the offensive would come further west. By September Franchet was nearly ready, but he still needed authorization to begin.

At a decisive conference at 10 Downing Street on 4 September, Guillaumat rehearsed the arguments. Lloyd George cross-questioned him before withdrawing to consult his military. Henry Wilson remained sceptical but noted that unless the Franco-Serb attack succeeded British troops would not be committed, and the Premier, who had long distrusted his advisers' Western Front preference, gave his consent. Hence on the 10th Franchet got his approval, and four days later the Serbian General Mišić opened the bombardment. At the last minute Clemenceau sent a telegram warning that responsibility lay entirely with Franchet, but the latter burned the document before his staff, and at 5.30 a.m. on Sunday the 15th the infantry attack went in.[132]

Two French divisions (one of Moroccan colonials) and one Serb division scaled vertiginous slopes with forested peaks. By the evening they had taken the crest of the range and opened an eleven-mile breach. Franchet, remembering the failed French Artois offensive in 1915, had insisted in his orders on immediate exploitation of the breakthrough and had positioned troops for the purpose, more Serb divisions passing through the first-wave units during the night. On the 16th the Allies captured the highest summit in the massif, while the Bulgarians retreated to their third position.[133] All the same, they had resisted more strongly than expected and got up fresh reserves on the first day: Bulgarian morale had in fact recovered since the summer and the Allies had over-estimated its deterioration. Moreover, the supplementary offensives on the shores of Lake Doiran on 18–19 September proved an unmitigated failure. Milne's forces attacked very strong defences without the heavy guns and ammunition he had pleaded for, and he mounted only a thin bombardment with field guns. Even so, by the second day his shells were running out. His battalions were at a low average strength of only 450, and many men were sick from flu and malaria and exhausted from pulling up the artillery.[134] They ran up into a hail of machine-gun fire and were halted with 7,000 British and Greek casualties – a forgotten massacre more comparable to the conditions of 1915 than was charac-teristic of the Western Front by this time. It is questionable whether the operation even much assisted the main assault. On the contrary, the Bulgars retreated from Lake Doiran because the Franco-Serbian attack was now dramatically gaining ground. On the 19th the Central Powers had decided on a major withdrawal, their forces retreating up the Vardar as the RAF harassed them. On the 24th the Serbs reached Gradsko, which had been Franchet's key first objective, and by now the Bulgarians' discipline was slipping and they abandoned masses of stores, though as yet few surrendered. The fall of Gradsko cut off the most direct line of retreat to Sofia, and when French cavalry reached Skopje on the 29th (after a daring cross-country trek), they isolated 70,000 of the best Bulgarian forces west of the Vardar. By this stage, Franchet's minute direction of operations in the first phase was no longer possible or necessary, and he allowed his subordinates their head.

The Central Powers had been wrong-footed, and were too slow to respond. They had prepared with a relatively thin front line and reserves deployed in depth, those behind the Moglena being some thirty kilo-metres distant.[135] When the OHL was asked for help Hindenburg replied that the Germans were fully engaged on the Western Front and could spare only a reinforced brigade from Sebastopol: the Bulgarians must do their best with what they had, abandoning territory if necessary. As the situation worsened more troops were found: by 27 September two German divisions (one from the Western and one from the Eastern Front) and several Austro-Hungarian divisions were en route.[136] They were too late. Crowds of mutinous deserters surrounded the Bulgarian GHQ and demanded trains to take them home; at Radomir a republic was proclaimed and an armed column marched on the capital, although the Sofia military governor drove it back. On the 26th a Bulgarian delegate crossed the lines to request a 48-hour suspension of hostilities, which Franchet rejected, but he agreed to receive an armistice delegation, with which he negotiated on 28–29 September, the news of Skopje's fall arriving during the proceedings. He acted on his own initiative, without reference to his government and without including Milne. The armistice was signed on 29 September and took effect on the 30th. It spared the Bulgarians from their nightmare of an enemy occupation and a partition of their homeland to the benefit of its neighbours. None the less, they had to relinquish the Serbian and Greek territory that they had seized since 1915, and the conditions reduced them to helplessness. Their troops west of Skopje were to lay down their arms: hence whereas the Allies had taken 15,000 prisoners before the armistice, afterwards they captured another 77,000. All but three divisions were to be demobilized, depriving the Central Powers of nearly 500,000 men and transferring Bulgaria's weapons, ammunition, and military transport to Allied control. The German and Austrian forces had to leave the country and the Allies would be free to use its ports, roads, and railways and occupy strategic points – stipulations not resisted by the Malinov government, which had hopes of changing sides. On 3 October King Ferdinand abdicated and fled to Germany, and his more popular son, the Crown Prince Boris, replaced him.[137]

MEGIDDO AND MOSUL

Bulgaria's fall had dramatic repercussions. It threatened Germany with the loss of its Romanian oil supplies and offered the Allies new opportunities against Austria-Hungary and Turkey. The Turkish army had reached its acme in 1916, but it had already lost many of its best troops, and the Turkish economy deteriorated earlier and more sharply than those of the other Central Powers, whereas the British poured resources into Mesopotamia and Palestine. Even so, their advance on Jerusalem in November to December 1917 had encountered determined opposition, and cost them 18,000 casualties.[138] Yet their next big Palestine offensive – at Megiddo in September 1918 – became a rout, three quarters of the remaining enemy forces being rounded up with little resistance.

Between December 1917 and September 1918 both armies in Palestine were run down for the benefit of other fronts, but the Ottoman side suffered more. The Bolshevik Revolution created glittering opportunities on Turkey's northern border, and from February 1918 Ottoman forces were advancing into the former Russian Transcaucasia, which fragmented into the three separate republics of Armenia, Azerbaijan, and Georgia. By September over half the army was in the region, including its best units. Meanwhile the Palestine force lost its German advisers and some of its ablest officers, and its unit strengths diminished, at the same time as a supply crisis afflicted it. Like the Bulgarians, the Turkish forces were rotting from within, but their decay was further advanced. In contrast, the Egyptian Expeditionary Force (EEF) coped better. During the months of Ludendorff's offensives it transferred to France the equivalent of two infantry divisions, twenty-three infantry battalions, and nine regiments of yeomanry, as well as artillery, medical units, and machine-gun companies.[139] In return Allenby received fifty-four Indian battalions, nearly half of them without previous active service, who arrived poorly trained for specialized tasks and had hardly any signallers or Lewis gunners.[140] He feared the halt in his advance would damage British prestige in Egypt, which was his main base of operations: 'The situation in Egypt is that we are surrounded by an alien and unfriendly people. The natives are nearly all anti-British ...' He asked Henry Wilson for Japanese divisions, to which Wilson replied that it was difficult enough to get Japan to send men to Siberia, and it had refused to go further afield.[141] When Allenby learned that London also contemplated depriving him of his final all-British infantry division and an Australian mounted division, he warned that this entailed 'a serious risk': he would have too few men to hold his front line or maintain contact with the Arab Revolt, with the danger that the Turks might outflank him and Britain lose Egypt. This *cri de cœur* came when the War Office was at its most nervous, in the aftermath of the Chemin des Dames attack and fearing a fresh onslaught in Flanders, Henry Wilson warning that 'for the moment the margin is very very small', but the War Cabinet decided in late June that Allenby could keep the Australians, and (after the tide turned in mid-July) that he could keep the British division as well.[142] During the summer months of relative inactivity Allenby not only instructed the Indians to his satisfaction, but also rested his men and completed a supporting railway. Unlike the Turks his troops, and their animals, were regularly fed and received high standards of medical care.[143] Even his easternmost units, who garrisoned the low-lying Jordan valley in suffocating heat, benefited from his steps to drain and oil the marshes to protect them from malaria, whereas in the Turkish-held areas, as the British would discover when they advanced, the disease was rife.

Not only was the EEF superior in health and morale, but by September it enjoyed a numerical preponderance of 2:1. Allenby estimated his combat strength at 12,000 cavalry, 57,000 infantry, and 540 artillery pieces, against 3,000, 26,000, and 370 respectively. The total British ration strength was some 346,000; that of the Turks 247,000,[144] and to the former total should be added the Arab forces operating in the interior as the Northern Arab Army (NAA), in principle under Allenby's orders although commanded by the Emir Feisal with advice from T. E. Lawrence and other British liaison officers. Political relations between the British and the leader of the Arab Revolt, Feisal's father Sharif Hussein of Mecca, were becoming delicate: Hussein knew that the Sykes–Picot Agreement had promised Syria and the Lebanon to the French, and the Balfour Declaration had pledged support for a Jewish 'national home' in Palestine. He also felt that he deserved more British backing against his rival in the Arabian peninsula, Ibn Saud.[145] But the Arab contribution mattered more to Allenby after he lost so many men to the Western Front. During the war as a whole the Arabs killed, wounded, captured, or immobilized more than 25,000 Ottoman troops: the Turks kept thousands of men in the Hejaz, where they refused to evacuate the holy city of Medina (which the Arabs blockaded) even though the Germans considered it strategically worthless. In April the Arabs finally destroyed such a large stretch of the Hejaz railway near Ma'an that the Turks ran out of rails to repair it, with the result that the link to the Hejaz was permanently broken. But Allenby was unsure whether Hussein would keep the revolt running beyond 1918, and this increased the pressure to act.[146]

Arab co-operation would be integral to the northern advance that Allenby had envisaged originally for spring 1918 and which he planned again as his confidence mounted. In contrast to 1917, when the march on Jerusalem emanated from a political decision by the Lloyd George government, the 1918 offensive was essentially Allenby's conception, which in the end he felt strong enough to implement without reinforcements. In 1917 he had misled the Turks into expecting an attempt to break through by the sea at Gaza, before turning their flank by attacking in the interior near Beersheba. In 1918, however, he feinted in the interior and launched his main attack along the coast. Of the Turkish armies that faced him, the Fourth lay east of the river Jordan and the Seventh and Eighth in a hilly rectangle bounded by the Jordan on the east, the British on the south, the sea and the plain of Sharon on the west, and the plain of Esdraelon on the north. Initially he envisaged a limited advance, but by late August he planned to follow the infantry breakthrough by a cavalry sweep that would cross the plain of Sharon and capture the passes to the plain of Esdraelon, severing the enemy communication lines while his right flank cut the Jordan crossings, resulting in 'disaster, on a great scale, for the Turkish army'. Meanwhile the Arabs would complete the encirclement by raiding the railway from Damascus, where it joined the branch running into northern Palestine at Deraa, as well as leading a tribal revolt.[147]

The plan was daring indeed, as it entailed a 50–60 mile cavalry ride from the breakthrough point in order to envelop the Turks, who were well equipped with machine guns: some 600 heavy ones west of the Jordan, and 450 light models.[148] But several factors could work in its favour. On the Turkish side, the German commander, Liman von Sanders, had a different approach from his predecessor, Falkenhayn: less inclined to the newer methods of manoeuvre, counter-attack, and defence in depth, and more inclined to station his troops well forward in continuous trenches.[149] Hence, if the opening assault pierced the front lines, it might encounter little further resistance. Allenby concentrated 35,000 infantry, 9,000 cavalry, and 383 guns in the zone running fifteen miles inland from the sea, where they faced 9,000 Turkish infantry, 1,000 cavalry, and 130 guns. Along the remaining forty-five miles or so of front, 25,000 British infantry with 157 guns faced 24,000 Turkish troops with 270.[150] The pre-attack concentration was assisted by deception measures such as leaving dummy horses and old tanks in the Jordan sector, spreading rumours of a deployment there, and carrying out all movements westward by night and eastward by day; on the coast the artillery and infantry were hidden under cliffs and in orange groves. But the key to secrecy was air superiority, which during the summer the

British achieved almost completely, only four German aircraft crossing the lines during the concentration period in contrast to over 100 during one week in June. The British were provided with two new squadrons of DH-9 and SE-5 fighters and had in total 100 serviceable aircraft, far outnumbering the fifteen German planes. While closing off their zone to enemy surveillance, they reconnoitred the territory they would cross, taking some 42,000 photographs of the area fifty kilometres north of the start line.[151] The stationary position of the lines for months before the attack enabled them to use Western Front techniques to identify the guns and wire facing them. By mid-September the preparations for the Battle of Megiddo were complete, Allenby informing Henry Wilson that 'I do not think that the Turks have, so far, any inkling of my plan.'[152]

He was correct, as the British were able to confirm from captured data soon after the battle. On the contrary, on the eve of the attack Liman was moving troops to Deraa. The Turkish commander on the coastal front wanted to pull his troops back, but permission was refused. Hence, to the attackers' relief and satisfaction, the Turks' main forces were indeed concentrated forward, presenting a target for the bombardment and the infantry assault. The EEF's Twenty-First Corps was the largest subdivision of Allenby's army and would advance along the coast, supported by the Twentieth Corps in the hill country towards Nablus. The Twenty-First Corps faced Turkish trenches on a sandy ridge, defended by barbed wire; the second and the third positions further back were not continuous and had no wire protection. For thirty minutes before the attack at 9 a.m. on Thursday, 19 September, these positions were bombarded at a rate of more than 1,000 shells per minute, by guns positioned at an average of every fifty yards (compared with the one every ten yards typical in France).[153] The bombardment was deliberately brief to ensure the element of surprise; but it was more than enough. The Turks' defence was passive, their artillery fire ragged, and they launched just one counter-attack, with one company. Heavy artillery bombarded the enemy command centres, and the RAF dropped more than 11 tons of bombs and fired 66,000 machine-gun rounds at ground targets.[154] The entire Turkish coastal defences fell in a matter of hours, and further inland the Twentieth Corps also reached its objectives. On the 20th British troops took Liman's headquarters at Nazareth, and although he himself escaped, the Turkish armies' command and control system buckled.

Meanwhile the cavalry ride began. The horsemen, whom Allenby had organized as the Desert Mounted Corps, had suffered less than the infantry from the upheavals since March. They comprised three divisions, mainly Australian and Indian, equipped with machine guns, horse artillery, and Hotchkiss rifles. Their crucial requirement was water, but the sources had been reconnoitred. Early on the 20th they reached the passes between the plains of Shalon and Esdraelon and closed the gap behind the Turks before the latter could retaliate, the Fourth Cavalry Division covering eighty-five miles in thirty-six hours. By now the Turks, leaderless, in retreat, and shot up from the air, were abandoning their equipment and surrendering in thousands. In the village of Jenin the Australian Mounted Division placed an armed guard on 120 cases of German champagne, 'some of which was later distributed to the troops'.[155] By the evening of 21 September the British held more than 25,000 prisoners and the Turkish Eighth Army had virtually ceased to exist, while the Seventh was disorganized and scattered and the Fourth had been driven from the Jordan crossings and was retreating northwards on foot, as the Arabs had cut the railway to Damascus. Allenby, properly cautious about the prospects beforehand, now wrote to his wife that 'I, myself, am almost aghast at the extent of the victory' and to Henry Wilson that 'Everything went according to plan, without a hitch.' The Indian battalions 'did grandly, in spite of their newness and short training'.[156]

Allenby had always envisaged Damascus as a goal if the first stages went well, and on 26 September he instructed his corps commanders to advance on the city, which British troops entered on 1–2 October, capturing much of the Fourth Army en route. Although assisted by armoured cars, the pursuit was still led by cavalry, who frequently charged Turkish positions. After Beirut fell on 8 October, it joined Haifa as a source of sea supply, allowing a further drive north, and on 29 October British troops arrived outside Aleppo and cut the rail link between Constantinople and the Turkish forces in Mesopotamia. With what remained of the Ottoman forces in Syria, General Mustafa Kemal conducted a fighting retreat, and the Turks prepared to hold a new position north of Aleppo that they expected to hold for four to five months in a war carrying on into 1919, while Allenby had now outrun his supply lines and needed to pause.[157] None the less, since 19 September the EEF had captured 75,000 prisoners (including 3,700 Germans and

Austrians) out of an army estimated at 104,000, as well as 360 guns and almost all the enemy's military stores. After the breakthrough and encirclement in the opening week the campaign had been dominated by rapid advances by cavalry and armoured cars with lorries trailing behind, and the occasional Turkish stands almost always being broken up quickly. Total British casualties killed, wounded, and missing between 19 September and 31 October were 5,666; figures that on the Western Front might be suffered in a day.[158] Certainly Allenby had started with a quantitative and qualitative preponderance, but he and his staff's skilful preparations had turned a likely British success into a Turkish debacle. Like Franchet d'Espèrey, Allenby conceived of innovative tactics, rapid advances, and splitting and cutting off enemy forces: both men were risk takers and provided charismatic, hands-on leadership.

In contrast, the final British advance in Mesopotamia was more a by-product than a cause of the Ottoman defeat. The Smuts mission, sent out by the War Cabinet in early 1918, had decided that General Sir William Marshall's forces there should take second priority to Allenby's, which were closer to the railway terminus at Aleppo. Moreover, Germany's and Turkey's encroachment on the Caucasus alarmed the Cabinet. For most of 1918 Marshall was required to support a British force under General Lionel Dunsterville that operated in the Caspian region at the end of a supply route via Persia that extended over 500 kilometres. Using 750 lorries, 'Dunsterforce' tied up almost all Marshall's transport, and in addition the Mesopotamia Expeditionary Force lost forces to Palestine and Macedonia.[159] For all these reasons, as well as the summer heat, Marshall was forced into inactivity.[160] Yet he faced even weaker Turkish forces than those in Palestine. Fifteen thousand (the entire local contingent) had surrendered to him with their equipment when he advanced up the Euphrates in March, and according to German reports by April 1918 some 17,000 of the Turkish troops in Mesopotamia had died of disease and hunger.[161]

Megiddo and Bulgaria's surrender transformed the situation, and on 2 October the War Office telegraphed to Marshall that the Turks might soon seek an armistice: he should therefore capture as much ground as possible. Marshall responded that as a result of the transport shortages his only possible axis of advance was up the Tigris (which was anyway for London the highest priority).[162] The Cabinet was anxious to secure the region's oil reserves, and grew impatient with Marshall's delays. In

1917 the British had advanced up the Tigris as far as Tikrit, where they established a railhead; the Turks were entrenched thirty-five miles further upstream at the Fat-ha gorge, and it was against this position that Marshall sent a column of troops who were mostly new to Mesopotamian fighting, but who none the less outflanked the Turks on 23–24 October and five days later stormed a second position at Sharqat. On 30 October, the day the Turkish armistice was signed, the entire Tigris force surrendered, the Sixth Army being virtually destroyed and some 11,322 prisoners and 51 guns falling to the British, whose own casualties numbered 1,866.[163] Mosul, the main town in the oil district, came under British occupation. As throughout the Mesopotamian campaign, the Tigris was central, as the best water source and transport artery in a land with few railways and no metalled roads, where artillery bombardments were even lighter than in Palestine, and the campaigning in consequence was more an old-fashioned affair of infantry assaults against machine guns. The Tigris advance completed the destruction of the Turkish armies outside Anatolia and it led to the Kurdish north being attributed to the post-war British mandate in Iraq. For the future politics of the region it was enormously significant, even if the British official historian acknowledged that militarily it contributed 'only indirectly to the downfall of the enemy'.[164]

VITTORIO VENETO

In contrast, the offensive in Italy that began on 24 October, and which is usually known as the Battle of Vittorio Veneto, destroyed the principal army of Germany's main ally. In the summer the Austrians, like the Germans, had thrown all their reserves into the offensive and failed to break through. But also like the Germans they had fought successfully on the defensive between 1915 and 1917, and since then had made peace with Russia and Romania. For the Italians the memory of 1917 – fruitless offensives followed by a devastating Austro-German riposte – was still raw, and under Diaz the Comando supremo remained more haunted than its British and French counterparts by the war's traumatic middle years. After his success in the Battle of the Piave, Diaz considered an immediate offensive but decided against it, confining himself to local attacks to regain the lost ground. Not only had his supply services been strained but the Italian army's troop reserve was down to four fresh divisions. At the Supreme War Council on 24 July the Italians maintained that the Austrians were still too strong, Lloyd George remarking that they had 'lost their nerve so completely' because of Caporetto. The Comando supremo claimed to be outnumbered, although its allies challenged its figures.[165] Diaz's deputy, Badoglio, said Foch was inviting them to attack while providing no extra men or equipment: he asked for the impossible figure of twenty Allied divisions. In response Foch promised 40,000 shells and seventy-five light tanks, but refused to divert any men.[166] During August, Diaz prepared a limited offensive on the Asiago plateau in conjunction with the British, but in early September he postponed this too, on the grounds that the Austrians still outnumbered him and were fighting with 'stubborn tenacity', and an offensive merely for the sake of it would waste lives.[167] Diaz wished to be ready to face another German attack in the winter (given that the Germans could transfer troops from France to Italy twice as fast as could the Allies), and for a decisive offensive in spring 1919. Unlike the French he had no reservoir of American troops as a fallback.[168]

When the deadlock changed at the end of September, it did so partly for political reasons, and once again the Allied breakthrough in the Balkans was the spur. During the summer the Italian government had supported Diaz, but the Cabinet was divided, the finance minister, Francesco Nitti, agreeing with him, whereas the foreign minister, Sidney Sonnino, sympathized with Italy's allies. The Premier, Vittorio Orlando, acted as umpire until the events of September persuaded him too that an offensive was necessary while Italy could still benefit from it. Developments in France contributed to this reappraisal, but in addition Austria-Hungary seemed on the verge of break-up. On 14 September it appealed for peace negotiations, and Bulgaria's collapse exposed it to a new frontier of danger. In addition the Italian public were criticizing the army's passivity. At the end of September, Diaz was summoned to the government's war council, although even now he was reluctant to attack and Orlando may have considered replacing him.[169] It was decided to prepare for an assault in mid-October if a 'decisive victory' seemed in prospect in the west, and on 6 October Diaz invited Lord Cavan, the British commander in Italy, to take charge of a new Anglo-Italian Tenth Army, and Graziani, the French commander, to head a Franco-Italian Twelfth Army. By this stage not only had Bulgaria surrendered but

Germany and Austria-Hungary had publicly requested an armistice, and Diaz assured a sceptical Cavan that he was now committed to an early strike.[170]

The Comando supremo's conception focused on the middle course of the river Piave, where it hoped to break through between Papadopoli island and the Monte Grappa before advancing to Sacile on the river Livenza and to Vittorio Veneto. The main task would be assigned to General Caviglia's Italian Eighth Army, supported by Cavan's and Graziani's armies on its right and left flank respectively, although the latter was also to advance up the Piave towards Feltre and the railway junction at Belluno. Once a bridgehead was established the Austrians would be split, and their western forces in the mountains and the Trentino cut off from their railways.[171] The plan entailed transferring Italian and Allied divisions from the Asiago plateau to the Piave: during the concentration period from 26 September to 10 October, 800 medium and heavy guns, 800 field guns, and 500 trench mortars were moved to the attack zone, mostly from the mountains, and 1.5 million artillery rounds collected forward. Twenty-one divisions were assembled (two British and one French), marching secretly and by night.[172] British officers and men who might be seen in the new sector were expected to wear Italian helmets and greatcoats. According to Austrian sources, on the eve of battle the Austro-Hungarian forces comprised 55 infantry and 6 cavalry divisions, with 6,145 guns; in the attack sector their divisions numbered 31.5, although their divisions were weaker than Allied ones. According to the Comando supremo, the Allies had 57 divisions and 7,700 guns. The first-line attack force comprised 22 divisions: 2 British, 1 French, and 15 Italian infantry divisions, and 4 Italian cavalry divisions. Finally, the Allies had 600 aircraft to the Austrians' 564. Quantitatively their superiority was quite small, but qualitatively greater than the figures suggested.[173]

After the Battle of the Piave, the Habsburg forces had enjoyed a respite, which they used to reconstitute the units that had suffered most severely, issue more machine guns, redistribute heavy artillery along the front, and build fortifications: rock breastworks (in the mountains) or trenches, protected by wire and flanking machine guns and with artillery positioned further behind, the whole forming successive defences in the most sensitive sectors such as the Trentino, and running between the rivers from the Piave eastwards to the Livenza and the Tagliamento on the Venetian plain. Even so, the army's front-line troops dwindled rapidly after the summer, and it never fully recovered from its June 1918 failure, even if the deserters mostly remained at home rather than going over to the enemy or mutinying. The Austrians initially supposed that they might attack in the autumn, as in the previous year, but a conference held at AOK headquarters in July decided that above all the troops must be rested and their equipment replenished. An attack would be possible only with German help, which Hindenburg and Ludendorff made plain would not be forthcoming: instead they wanted more Austrian assistance on the Western Front. By mid-October the Austrian authorities were contemplating a general retreat behind their own borders, but it was now too late. Their intelligence pointed to an impending offensive on the middle Piave, which by 20 October was considered so certain that the troops on the river and the Monte Grappa were ordered to hold ready and divisions were moved to the threatened points; with four days to go, the starting date was correctly anticipated.[174]

The Allies therefore enjoyed no overwhelming superiority in the theatre as a whole, or in the attack sector, and nor did they achieve complete surprise. In contrast to the Vardar and Megiddo, this operation would not proceed like clockwork. The Piave watercourse was nearly a mile wide, and although mostly shallow the river was broken up by shingle beds and islands, separated by icy water with fierce currents, and was so variable that no reliable maps existed. With the autumn rains the feed-waters from the mountains rose, and the river threatened to become unbridgeable. The original start date was 16 October but it had to be postponed, Cavan reporting to London a continuous downpour and water more than a metre above the level feasible.[175] As armistice negotiations between Woodrow Wilson and the Central Powers were now proceeding in public, and on 16 October Emperor Karl announced that the Austrian half of the Dual Monarchy would be transformed into a confederation, political events were moving so rapidly that the Comando supremo felt near panic that the war would end before it could act. On 19 October, Diaz therefore ordered his Fourth Army to prepare a hasty assault against the Monte Grappa, and 400 guns were moved in order to begin there on the 24th, whatever the state of the river. Retrospectively the Italian authorities presented the Grappa attack as an integral part of the plan, but actually it was a last-minute improvisation.[176]

The assault on the mountain started at 7.15 a.m. on 24 October (the anniversary of Caporetto) after a two-hour artillery bombardment, obstructed by mist and rain. The Austrians moved up two reserve divisions, so had nine in defence against seven attacking ones (though units of the Belluno army group refused to move up), and ferocious fighting continued for three days, the Italians flinging themselves against precipitous walls.[177] They gained almost no territory and as of 30–31 October the Austrians still mostly held their front lines, the Italian Fourth Army having lost over 21,000 killed, wounded, and missing in one of the war's last great bloodbaths.[178] Nor, to begin with, did the Piave attack go smoothly, Italian prisoners having disclosed its date to the Austrians. Cavan's British troops did, however, achieve tactical surprise when on the night of 23/24 October they landed on Papadopoli island, being ferried across by Italian punters in flat-bottomed boats and soon overpowering the small Hungarian garrison. By the 26th the weather was improving and the Piave waters subsided, so Diaz ordered a passage for the following day, but the French Twelfth Army and Italian Eighth Army established only small and precarious footholds and their temporary bridges were swept away. In contrast the Gordon Highlanders attacked at 6.45 a.m., after having waded between Papadopoli island and the east bank under cover of a creeping barrage, and were able to break through the defences on a sandy embankment. Afterwards they discovered that the machine guns were so sited as to be incapable of firing downwards, but in any case the unexpected crossing caused 'mass terror' among the defenders. On the following day the Allied bridgeheads were expanded, and on the 29th they joined up, while the British pierced the Austrian second line along the river Monticano, defeating fresh divisions and taking over 11,000 prisoners.[179]

According to the Austro-Hungarian official history, 29 October was the day of crisis for the entire battle. Thus far the Austrians had not only halted the Monte Grappa attack but mounted considerable resistance on the Piave, their artillery combining with the weather to smash the Allies' pontoons. Only light 30 cwt (rather than 3 ton) lorries could cross the latter anyway, and a breakdown in traffic control caused further disruption. But east of the Piave the Austrians had attempted on German lines to construct not continuous defences but 'battle belts', for zonal defence in depth, whose effectiveness depended on prompt counter-attacks. On the Grappa such counter-attacks had succeeded, and on 27 October the Austrian commander on the Piave, Boroević, likewise ordered up reserves to attack the bridgeheads, but by the following day the units concerned were refusing to obey orders. From here on, not only Allied actions but also a breakdown in Austro-Hungarian morale and discipline became the crucial variables, and the enforced delay caused by the high levels on the Piave may have worked to the Italians' advantage.[180]

Down to mid-October the Austro-Hungarian front line had held solid, although mass desertions became more frequent from trains and marching formations moving up, as did insubordination in the rear. Karl's 16 October manifesto did not immediately disturb the army, although with armistice discussions in progress and Woodrow Wilson on 20 October declaring that mere autonomy for the subject nationalities was no longer acceptable it was astonishing that the troops continued risking their lives for as long as they did. By late October National Councils were taking power in the Austrian half of the Dual Monarchy and it was no longer even clear what state the men were defending. But the critical development was the threat created by Bulgaria's surrender that the Hungarian half would be invaded. Until now its troops had tended to be more reliable, but on 24 October the Hungarian government called on the Hungarian units in the army to return home without delay, the former Premier, Stephen Tisza, acknowledging that 'We have the lost the war.'[181]

Hence the Allied offensive struck an army on the verge of break-up. On 24 October Hungarian troops refused to move up on the Asiago, demanding to be allowed to go home to defend Hungary; and when the military authorities agreed the news spread like wildfire. Hungarian troops mounted little resistance on the Piave, and others refused orders to move up. Their example spread to South Slav and Czech units, while even previously elite German–Austrian units refused to fight further if it meant they were simply substituting for Hungarians who were returning home. With every day the Allies found their progress easier and their tally of captives lengthening.[182] On the evening of the 29th the AOK ordered Boroević to evacuate the Veneto, and on the following day the Allies found their opponents in general retreat, pursued by Allied aircraft as the Bulgarians and Turks had been. Vittorio Veneto and Sacile fell on 30–31 October, and the Austrians evacuated their outflanked Monte Grappa positions. By this stage Austria-Hungary itself was in its final stages of dissolution, and an Austrian delegation crossed the lines and made contact with Diaz. The Italians played for time in order to occupy as much territory as they could, including Trent (taken by British troops) on 1 November and Trieste, occupied by an amphibious landing on 3 November.[183] By the time the ceasefire took effect at 3 p.m. on the 4th most of the Hungarian units had left for home, and some 300,000 troops from the Austrian lands became Italian prisoners.[184] As the Italians were simultaneously advancing in Albania, the largest remaining Habsburg forces were now defeated, and the armistice stipulated the demobilization of the rest of the army and the Allies' right to occupy strategic positions. As Bulgaria's collapse had exposed Hungary and Constantinople, Austria-Hungary's exposed South Germany. Although the victory resulted partly from a competent strategic plan and the Allied troops' determination (the total Italian dead, wounded, and missing were 36,498, two thirds of them in the Monte Grappa sector), it reflected also, even more than Megiddo, the disorganization of their enemies.[185]

THE END IN THE WEST

By the time of the Austrian armistice the Germans on the Western Front were in full retreat. The opening of ceasefire discussions did little to slow down operations, and the British army alone took over 100,000 casualties during October.[186] Haig's view on 10 October was that as the Germans were a beaten army and there was no risk of their counterattacking the Allies should keep on hitting. As late as 23 October, Foch supposed that Germany would hold out into 1919. On the other hand, the OHL was determined not to show weakness, Hindenburg proclaiming that the diplomacy would turn out more favourably if ground were held.[187] None the less, the Germans' positions did crumble, and the military operations were closely related to the political history of the ceasefire. Following Ludendorff's nervous breakdown at the end of September, the Allies lost momentum in early October and the OHL regained confidence. But from the middle of the month the Germans' last prepared defences yielded, and a new set of converging offensives led on to a faster Allied advance. Ludendorff himself was dismissed on 26 October, and his successor, Wilhelm Groener, decided on 4 November to retreat to a new and sketchy 'Antwerp–Meuse line', but as this manoeuvre proceeded, revolution broke out in Germany and Groener demanded a ceasefire forthwith.

The first point to consider is the pause in early October.[188] Overshadowing this period of the fighting was the second, and deadliest, wave of the 1918–19 influenza pandemic, which reached the armies in September and in the month before the armistice was at full force. During October the French army may have suffered as many as 75,000 cases, the AEF 39,000, and the BEF 14,000: an indication of the German army's growing disorganization was that it left no statistics. The symptoms of the disease – fever, intense pain in the limbs, bleeding, blueness in the face, and flooding and destruction of the lungs – were appalling, and death, visited disproportionately on young and healthy adults, could come within days or even hours. The total of 43,000 American servicemen in the army and navy who perished from it were not much less numerous than the total of American battle deaths. The massive transport movements and dense concentrations of humanity that were characteristic of wartime facilitated the spread of the infection, and the disease wreaked havoc in the training and embarkation bases in the US. It was one reason why during October the American authorities reduced the level of troop departures. None the less, Wilson reluctantly accepted the advice of his Chief of the General Staff, Peyton C. March, that shipments must continue and the priority was to finish the war.[189]

Of the four converging Allied offensive prongs, logistical difficulties had checked progress in Flanders, and German resistance combined with American shortcomings had stopped that in the Meuse–Argonne, while the Canadian advance from the Canal du Nord ran into trouble outside Cambrai. Only the British Fourth Army north of Saint-Quentin smashed completely through the Hindenburg position, overrunning the Beaurevoir line between 3 and 5 October. The process took longer than hoped, less because of the line itself than the masses of machine guns behind it (200 in one village). Characteristically, Haig hoped to accelerate matters by using cavalry; but although the British were advancing into undevastated open country without hedges or wire, and horsemen were moved up behind the Fourth Army, they had repeatedly to be withdrawn until the infantry and artillery could deal with the German rearguards. The one exception was a successful Canadian cavalry charge on 9 October, although even this did nothing that the infantry could not have accomplished, and supply for the horses interfered with that of rations and ammunition.[190] But neither could tanks provide the mobility that Haig sought, and they were less valuable in open country than against prepared positions. Although the BEF still had many available – 261 on 30 August, 317 on 19 October, and 235 on 9 November – after breaking through the Hindenburg Line it used them in smaller numbers. The biggest tank operations like Amiens took two to three weeks to prepare: the machines had difficulty keeping up, and the advance was too fast for them. The German artillery inflicted increasing losses, parts were short, and enormous stress was placed on the crews. Between 8 August and 20 October almost half the Tank Corps became casualties.[191] Furthermore, in early October the Fourth Army's Australian divisions were removed from the firing line, in part because the troops, with losses of 21,243 since the Battle of Amiens, revolted against repeated employment as a shock force.[192] Finally, when Haig asked for three more American divisions, Foch refused them on the grounds that Pershing took priority.[193]

The BEF did keep the Canadians, who were now working with the Third Army. In the Battle of Cambrai on 8 October, supported by low-flying RAF attacks, they advanced up to three miles, captured the northern end of the Beaurevoir line, and began outflanking the town. In this action alone, another 350,000 shells were fired and ninety-four tanks deployed, and Ludendorff said an Allied breakthrough had been avoided by a hair's breadth.[194] On the following day the OHL recognized that the existing line could not be held, and it authorized a retreat to the 'Herrmann Position', which was still incomplete.[195] The withdrawal proceeded at night between 9 and 11 October, and when the British came up against the next German defences along the flooded river Selle, they found the enemy had brought up heavy artillery and reinforcements. Hence another set-piece attack would be needed, and as Haig had warned Rawlinson against such enterprises unless thoroughly prepared and with all supplies brought forward, a delay was called for. In part because of German demolition work and delayed-action mines on the railways, the pause lasted a week, giving the defenders more time to ready the position at the same time as the British prepared against it.[196] Hence the main British advance was now also halted.

On the Meuse–Argonne, Pershing's memoirs recollected that the period from 1 to 11 October 'involved the heaviest strain on the army and me'.[197] Having reorganized its supply lines and brought up more experienced divisions, the AEF attacked the Kriemhilde Stellung on 4 October, running through the Romagne and Cumel heights, but even though it again had a big numerical superiority its advance, launched with mass infantry assaults, failed to reach its targets. The OHL well understood the strategic importance of the position, which it considered the 'corner pillar' of the Western Front, and the German divisions there rose from ten on 26 September to twenty-three by 4 October, some of the best formations in the army being committed and the local command maintaining them in line until they were worn out.[198] By 6 October the Americans' casualties had reached 75,000, and they could no longer replace their losses. In cold and rain the attackers faced 'desperate resistance' from mutually supporting machine guns hidden in the woods. The AEF lacked air cover because of the weather and French aircraft being directed elsewhere, and its supply difficulties persisted, above all owing to a shortage of horses. Pershing decided that before taking the central German position he needed to clear the heights of the Argonne and the Meuse through more limited attacks on his two flanks, which the Americans now started to do, but in relation to their original objectives they remained bogged down.[199] Foch's converging attacks were still far from having achieved their goals, and the OHL briefly regained faith in its men's powers of resistance.

None the less, after mid-October the Allies once more progressed. While time alleviated their supply and transport difficulties, it worked against the Germans, as did the inescapable evidence that the war was lost. Although the Allies still faced determined resistance from machine gunners and specialist units, the German infantry were surrendering in thousands. On the Meuse–Argonne, a new attack on 14 October against the Kriemhilde Stellung again fell short, but in the succeeding days the Americans captured the highest point of the ridge, breaching their enemies' main position and now facing only the last defensive line, the Freya Stellung, before they too could break out.[200] In large measure American progress resulted from attrition against numerically inferior units that the OHL was now finding it hard to reinforce. But, in addition, the Americans were becoming better organized. Pershing concentrated on the command of the AEF as a whole, delegating that of his First Army to the capable General Hunter S. Liggett, who focused on training, rounding up 'stragglers', and tightening discipline.[201]

More immediately impressive, however, was the progress on the northern flank, where the Flanders offensive resumed on 14 October. Even though the Germans were not surprised, and put down a counter-barrage, when the advance went in they were very ready to surrender. Soon British, Belgian, and French forces in the 'Battle of Courtrai' were advancing faster than expected and threatening the Germans on the Flanders coast, who had the greatest distance to retreat if the Western Front became untenable. The local commanders feared being cut off and for two weeks Ludendorff had rejected their requests to pull back, but now their position became critical and on the 15th the OHL author-ized a general withdrawal.[202] The Allies could now push up to the Dutch border, overrunning the Bruges/Ostend/Zeebrugge triangle and the bases for the Flanders U-boat force, which was recalled. Defeat on land therefore also weakened the Germans at sea, and limited their scope for falling back on submarine warfare to compensate for failure on land. The withdrawal also meant that the Allies had outflanked the Lille–Roubaix–Tourcoing manufacturing complex, which the Brit-ish occupied on 17 October, and which Ludendorff had previously intended to hold as a hostage to prevent the French from regaining Alsace-Lorraine.[203] In fact the Germans had already been preparing a withdrawal (and the prior evacuation of their equipment helps explain why their resistance was no stronger), but although they managed again to disengage their armies from the coast and Lille they had yielded crucial bargaining cards.

The OHL still hoped, however, to retrieve the situation by holding the Herrmann Position, which Hindenburg considered vital to success in the ceasefire negotiations.[204] This was the line along the river Selle where the British had halted since 10 October, and which on the 17th they assaulted. It was less formidable and more improvised than the Hindenburg Line, although the river was an obstacle to tanks, broad-ened by marshes, and protected by artillery and machine guns on its eastern slopes. Against it the British opted for the thorough advance bombardment they had used on 29 September, rather than the surprise tactics of 8 August. The BEF had no shortage of shells or guns of all calibres, with the possible exception of the 6-inch howitzer; the main task was the daunting one of getting the apparatus forward, by rail, lorry, and cart.[205] Over two days the Fourth Army fired 17 million pounds of shells from 1,320 guns – about half the 39 million pounds fired in the pre-Hindenburg Line bombardment, but against much weaker defences – concentrating against the Germans' artillery and communications and their second position on the Sambre canal. Zero hour was 5.20 a.m., the attack unfolding with four British and two American divisions, who built floating bridges. Over the week of the Battle of the Selle, from 17 to 24 October, twenty-four British and two American divisions captured 20,000 prisoners and 475 guns, and reached to within fourteen miles of the crucial railway junction at Aulnoye.[206] The Germans' first attempt at holding an improvised position had been broken, and both the Americans and the British were approaching shelling distance of the main lateral rail link.

The strategy of convergent attacks was coming to fruition; more slowly than Foch had hoped, but with some of the campaigning season still in hand. The Germans were now abandoning masses of equipment, and had failed to consolidate (as the Allies had feared) on a shorter line where they could hold through the winter. During October, Foch's strategic direction followed the lines set in September, but was modified in view of the AEF's slower than expected progress and the faster advance of the British: of whose breaching of the Hindenburg Line, he told Haig, the German armistice request was the 'immediate result'.[207] In a directive on 10 October, Foch envisaged an advance in Flanders towards Ghent, by the British in the centre towards Maubeuge, and by the French and Americans in the south towards Mézières; but now the second was 'the most advantageous to exploit'.[208] His final directive on the 19th reaffirmed this guidance, setting the Flanders group objective as Brussels; that for the British as the Ardennes, thus severing the lateral railway line; and for the French and Americans the lateral line at Sedan and Mézières. The Western Front was being truncated – especially the 'active' section of it, between the sea and the Meuse, and the portion of the active section held by the French shortened most of all, their central frontage between the British and American armies shrinking between 8 August and 11 November from 150 to forty-two miles, and enabling their Second, Ninth, and Sixth Armies to be suppressed or withdrawn.[209] Despite this advantage the British felt the French were losing impetus, and Foch agreed. He berated General Debeney, whose First Army did too little to support the British Fourth Army's attack on the Hindenburg Line, and complained to Pétain that Gouraud's Fourth Army in the Argonne slowed down in early October. After Foch's 10 October directive, however, the French First Army pushed across the Serre river, and on 24–26 October the French First and Fifth Armies pushed through the 'Hunding Position' to the south-east of the Herrmann Line.[210]

Because of the French, British, and American advances in mid-October, the Allies were now ready for another general offensive. Between 31 October and 4 November they launched sequenced attacks from the north, south, and centre. In the first, again in Flanders, British and French forces assisted by French tanks advanced to the river Scheldt. On 1–2 November the Canadians entered Valenciennes, a railway junction and the last big French town occupied by the Central Powers.[211] Also on 1 November, a breakthrough finally took place in the Meuse–Argonne, where the American First and French Fourth Army delivered a combined assault. This time the Americans had plenty of time for preparation and for aerial reconnaissance: moreover, they already controlled the strongest defences and the highest ground. Like the French and the British before them, they had learned hard lessons. According to the AEF's internal appraisals (which hitherto had been highly critical) the new attack showed a vast improvement in the infantry's ability to operate in more dispersed formations, adapting to the terrain; in the staff's speed of response; and in the handling of supply traffic.[212] Stores had been positioned well ahead, and the artillery supported the infantry more efficiently: the attack was preceded by a two-hour artillery and machine-gun barrage, including mustard gas, before the infantry went forward at 5.30 a.m., supported by strafing and bombing aircraft. For the first time they broke through completely, advancing up to five miles on the first day, and on 2 November the Germans began a general retreat. The Americans and the French Fourth Army joined up and bundled the Germans out of their last fortifications, outflanking the Brunhilde Line further west, and the Allies could now bring forward long-range guns to bombard the trunk railway.[213] The final element in the new converging offensive was the Battle of the Sambre on 4 November, in which the soldier-poet Wilfred Owen lost his life. British troops attacked across the Condé–Mons canal, the forest of Mormal, and a network of villages, orchards, and hedges that were strewn with wire. In the usual way the Third and Fourth Armies camouflaged their guns, and launched a night attack under a creeping barrage: soon the bridgehead was fifteen miles wide and two and a half miles deep. Once again the tried and tested techniques were brought to bear, and even against considerable natural obstacles they succeeded faster than ever.

In the very last week the character of the campaigning altered. The reason was a reappraisal on the German side. By mid-October Hindenburg and Ludendorff were becoming so concerned about the prospective armistice terms that they recommended fighting on after all. They lost the confidence of the new German government under Prince Max of Baden, and on 26 October Wilhelm accepted Ludendorff's resignation while commanding Hindenburg to stay. By this point the Allies were already advancing through the Herrmann Line, on which the Germans had intended to fight 'the decisive battle'. Down to his removal, Ludendorff still resisted representations from his commanders that the position was becoming untenable and they should retreat to the Antwerp–Meuse line, but although much shorter the latter too was rudimentary. Only on the evening of 30 September, after the Hindenburg Line breakthrough, had the OHL even ordered it to be reconnoitred. In mid-October Hindenburg and Ludendorff decided to use all available labour to prepare the line, directing that the Herrmann Position must be held to win time for the construction work, but when Ludendorff's successor Wilhelm Groener arrived at the OHL on 30 October the line was still very far from complete.[214] His advice from his military railway chief was that it was unsuitable to hold for long anyway, because of the lack of a developed railway network behind the Meuse; moreover, huge amounts of materiel (and 80,000 wounded) still needed to be moved behind it. But the co-ordinated French, British, and American attacks of 30 October to 1 November forced a reconsideration, and the Battle of the Sambre settled the matter, the OHL ordering a withdrawal to the Antwerp–Meuse line, although Groener believed that even this position could hold for only fourteen days.[215] Hence from 5 November the Allies found their opponents engaged in a general retreat, in places so rapid that it was difficult to keep contact. The AEF crossed the Meuse on 7 November, and American troops reached the heights overlooking Sedan. The lateral railway was now cut, and the Antwerp–Meuse position already jeopardized. Preparations were in hand for a major new Franco-American offensive, to be launched on 14 November, directed towards Lorraine and the Briey–Longwy iron ore field, a major departure from the previous converging strategy and one that would thrust towards the Rhineland. Meanwhile the British trudged on through cold and wet across the sabotaged and booby-trapped landscape that the Germans had left behind them. The BEF was at an unprecedented distance from its railheads and would soon have had to pause again to consolidate, but weather and logistical difficulties rather than the Germans were now the main obstacles to the advance and there is no reason to suppose the Antwerp–Meuse position would have held much longer than the previous such barriers.

The armistices resulted from a string of successes against all the Central Powers, which were not just defensive but also offensive. On the Western Front the Allies could overrun obstacles such as the Somme and Passchendaele battlefields that in previous years had been impassable; and could break through any German defence line. The Bulgarian and the Austro-Hungarian defences in Macedonia and northern Italy, which had previously seemed so formidable, collapsed within days. From their maritime supply lines and bases the Allies pushed uphill towards the Ardennes, the Alps, and the Balkan and the Taurus mountains that separated them from the Central Powers' heartlands. In every theatre they had the material edge, and their high commands and unit leaders had learned from years of carnage. They also had greater numbers – although in Macedonia, Italy, and on the Western Front their advantage was quite small, and partly for this reason the encirclement of the Turks in Palestine was elsewhere not replicable. Finally, they had the edge in morale, and here their lead was critical in every theatre, even though the British, French, and Italians were cautious and tired. The Central Powers' fighting prowess had everywhere disintegrated, and the German and Austrian spring and summer offensives bore much of the blame. But as in the history of any war, the record of the actual fighting tells us only so much. We must turn to the Allies' application of technology, to the quality and quantity of their manpower, to the sea lanes that united them, the production feats that sustained them, and the political cohesion and leadership that brought these advantages to fruition.

3

The New Warfare: Intelligence, Technology, and Logistics

At this moment I am a captain of industry who is working with resources at full capacity.

Philippe Pétain, autumn 1918[1]

The Great War has been described as 'the birth of the modern style of warfare'. By 1918 both sides were attacking in three dimensions, from the air as well as on the surface. Intelligence-led targeting and all-arms co-ordination made possible sudden paralysing blows delivered deep behind the enemy front in a manner more resembling France in 1940 or Kuwait in 1991 than the short-range artillery and infantry encounters of 1914.[2] During the war's middle years British troops had dubbed the Western Front 'The Great Sausage Machine': mincing both sides' manpower while remaining stubbornly in place.[3] But during 1918 it first bowed westwards with the German offensives and then eastwards as the Allies counter-attacked, foreshadowing the flow and ebb of Axis expansion in 1939–42 and 1942–5. The new tactics revived mobility.

THE CHALLENGE

The emphasis here will be on the sources of Allied success. But both sides pioneered antidotes to the 1915–17 stalemate, and the Allies borrowed from the Central Powers' offensive tactics as they had borrowed from the defensive ones. Although the Central Powers innovated for much of the war, their opponents eventually learned the lessons better than did the teachers. 'Central Powers' in this respect essentially meant

Germany, as although the Austrians tried to imitate their ally they proved a pale shadow of the original. The German revolution in tactics dated back to 1915–16, when Bruchmüller began his artillery experiments on the Eastern Front[4] and 'Stormtroop' formations were introduced in the west.[5] It reached maturity in 1917, with the battles of Riga and Caporetto and the Cambrai counter-attack. In its usual fashion, the OHL analysed these successes and built on them. It placed the commanders, CGSs, and artillery directors responsible for them in the leading positions for 'Michael'. Confidence in the new procedures encouraged the OHL to gamble on an all-out assault rather than explore a compromise peace: it would take the offensive, but not in the same way as its enemies.[6]

Central to the Germans' system was restoring surprise. Much depended on the preparatory period – which was largely under their control – rather than the battle itself. They indeed achieved substantial surprise when they struck the southernmost British line on 21 March, the Portuguese on 9 April, and the French on the Chemin des Dames on 27 May, although only by taking infinite pains. Reconnaissance of the Allied positions, expanding railways and the supporting infrastructure, and moving up and camouflaging the guns began weeks beforehand.[7] Some ranging shots were fired before 21 March and 9 April, but before 27 May, when Bruchmüller had complete control and the Pulkowsky Method was now proven, they were dispensed with. Bruchmüller's bombardments were delivered without warning by hundreds of guns in a matter of hours, firing as many rounds as Allies had done in the days-long barrages before the Somme and Third Ypres. The artillery were subordinated to a centralized fire plan – again more completely by the time of the Chemin des Dames offensive – and sub-divided into seven specialized categories.[8] By targeting in depth the enemy defences they sought disruption comparable to that achieved in later wars by aerial bombing, before silencing the enemy's artillery by accurate counter-battery fire (increasingly using gas shells) and turning to his forward positions. Bruchmüller lectured the line commanders beforehand in order to encourage the infantry to trust the gunners, although they never did so completely. Once the attack began the key task was laying down a protective fire curtain (*Feuerwalze*) just ahead of the infantry that would bewilder the defenders (Bruchmüller emphasized his measures' psychological impact) and keep them under cover until the attackers were upon them. On 21 March and 9 April the *Feuerwalze*'s successive pre-timed forward bounds advanced too quickly, but in later operations they were slower and could progress at different speeds in different sectors. But with this exception, the Bruchmüller tactics used by the Eighteenth Army on 21 March were refined but not altered in principle until the final offensive on 15 July. After the war Bruchmüller was criticized for insufficient flexibility, and once the Allies gained forewarning of the date and location of the next offensive and committed themselves to defence in depth, the advantage that he and Pulkowsky had procured was largely nullified.[9]

The counterpart to the new artillery procedures was a revised infantry attack doctrine. No one figure was as central to this process as was Bruchmüller for the sister arm,[10] but among the most important OHL tacticians was Captain Hermann Geyer, whose exposition of 'The Attack in Positional Warfare' received high command endorsement.[11] Geyer incorporated much of Bruchmüller's thinking, and likewise emphasized meticulous preparation. The key to success lay not in weight of numbers but in the intelligent application of superior firepower by well-trained specialists. The divisions moved from the Eastern to the Western Front in the 1917–18 winter allowed the Germans to create an enormous reserve, and to filter out their youngest and fittest soldiers for rest, better food, and a training period that averaged four weeks.[12] But in return for this preferential treatment, much would be expected of them. Ludendorff and the OHL believed that using artillery correctly could diminish losses, and planned for aircraft 'battle detachments' (*Schlachtstaffeln*) to give ground support. Rather than fight another Verdun the high command would call off operations that got bogged down. None the less, the attack divisions must surge ahead without relief until they reached exhaustion, in order to keep up momentum at all costs. Geyer saw the most difficult task as not the 'break in' (*Einbruch*), but fighting through the enemy main defences beyond German artillery range, in search of breakthrough before the Allies brought up reserves. Certainly the German guns must hasten forward, but the infantry should also carry their own firepower, in the shape of light machine guns, flamethrowers, rifle grenades, and portable 77 mm field artillery, as they sought out the axes of least resistance and left squads behind to overwhelm the enveloped enemy strongpoints and machine guns – which it was understood the preliminary bombardment could not completely suppress. Geyer was not prescriptive about whether the lead troops should form a loose skirmishing line or detached groups, but 'infiltration tactics' was a fair description of the procedure he envisaged, and it rested heavily on the stamina and initiative of the junior officers and NCOs. It proved a mechanism for the speedy destruction of the flower of the German army, in an enterprise prejudiced from the outset by the lack of lorries, petrol, horses, and fodder needed for sustained mobility. None the less, just as Bruchmüller adhered to his artillery system, so Ludendorff commented in memoranda of 17 April and 9 June that the attack procedure had been vindicated – indeed by the success of 'Blücher' more than ever.[13]

For the Allies to win the war they had to thwart the German attacks; and this between March and July they groped towards achieving. But in addition they needed an answer to the *defensive* tactics that the OHL had adopted before 1918 and reverted to after the mid-summer turning point, though now with demoralized troops and in improvised positions.[14] That answer prefigured later conflicts in its all-arms co-ordination and its combination of specialized units of many kinds, applying both new and more traditional technologies. It is necessary first to consider intelligence and airpower, before turning to gas, artillery, and tanks, and finally to roads, railways, and the battlefield logistics that underpinned the victors' achievements.

INTELLIGENCE

The years between 1914 and 1918 have been characterized as 'the greatest intelligence explosion in history'.[15] New technology bestowed upon the First World War commanders information that their predecessors could scarcely have dreamt of, but they had to learn to process the torrent of material, and to feed it into operational decisionmaking. New intelligence sources profoundly influenced the struggle at sea, as well as wartime diplomacy – the Zimmermann Telegram being the outstanding example. The emphasis here, however, will be on intelligence in the campaigns on land. Although the Allies held the underlying advantage, they were wrong-footed in spring 1918 and took several months to restore their lead, which, none the less, they then dramatically reasserted.

The 1918 campaigning presented different intelligence challenges from the static phase of the war, in some ways harking back to the fluidity of its opening weeks. Between 1915 and 1917 both sides had found it singularly difficult to take their enemy unawares. Intercepted Allied telephone messages forewarned the Germans of the French offensives of May and September 1915, and of British attacks during the Battle of the Somme.[16] At Verdun in 1916 the French gathered some days in advance that an attack was coming, if not its strength or its precise date.[17] In 1917 the Germans had abundant foreknowledge of the Nivelle offensive and the Third Battle of Ypres. But by the end of that year the pattern was changing. At La Malmaison, the French realized that the Germans had gained foreknowledge but anticipated them by advancing the start of the bombardment, and at Cambrai both the British attack and the German counter-attack achieved surprise. In March 1918 the British had warning of the general direction and timing of 'Michael', but not its scale or the extent of the assault front. Moreover, the Germans deceived the French by creating a phantom army in Champagne, which delayed Pétain's response to Haig's appeals. Similarly before the Lys the British expected an attack but further south, round Arras, and the size of the assault again took them aback, while on the Chemin des Dames on 27 May the French received only a few hours' notice. By contrast before 9 June the French had full foreknowledge of the Matz offensive, and before 15 July they had even earlier and fuller information about the Reims attack. On the Piave, similarly, the Allies knew the date and approximate location of the Austrian June offensive, although not the full length of the attack sector. As in other aspects of the fighting, during the summer the balance in the intelligence war tilted to the Allies' advantage.

Both sides had access to four main intelligence sources.[18] The first was information gathered at the front, from prisoners, deserters, captured documents and equipment, and simple observation, as well as by more esoteric procedures such as sound-ranging and flash-spotting to locate enemy guns. The second was aerial observation and photography, above and behind the enemy lines. The third was signals intelligence, by 1918 derived more from intercepting and decrypting radio than from telephone or telegraph messages, and the fourth was espionage, gathered from agents and informers who might operate far behind enemy lines.

The British were far from languishing in utter darkness before the 'Michael' attack. Haig's GHQ and the Directorate of Military Intelligence (under Major-General George Macdonagh) at the War Office recognized from late 1917 that the numerical balance was shifting and a major attack was likely. British and French intelligence tracked the transport of German units from the east and noted the formation of a reservoir of fresh divisions round Hirson.[19] In February Macdonogh estimated that over sixty enemy divisions were undergoing intense tactical training, and the British attached particular significance to a report that Below, whom they considered one of the best German commanders, had moved to the Western Front.[20] By the middle of the month GHQ correctly anticipated an attack in Picardy, but remained unsure of the starting date, which prisoner and deserter information disclosed on 18 and 19 March.[21] Only in the last two days was the attack known to be imminent, and even then it was expected to hit Byng's Third Army and the northern part of Gough's Fifth Army sector: the assault south of Saint-Quentin, where Gough had only recently taken over French lines, came as a very unpleasant shock. Haig had expected a slower and more methodical enemy progress, and possibly a follow-on attack further north, where he had stationed most of his meagre reserves.[22] Meanwhile Pétain's GQG feared a German attack in Champagne, and continued to do so for several days after 21 March, although in fact no such attack was in preparation.[23]

It seems that successful Allied long-range intelligence was combined with a partial failure of short-range intelligence. To monitor enemy troop movements deep behind the front lines the Allies depended in the first instance on agent intelligence, though neither side had much success in planting networks in the enemy home territories. German naval intelligence had targeted Britain, but the agents sent during the war were apprehended quickly, through a mixture of their own incompetence and the vigilance of British postal surveillance. The combination of the Security Service (named MI5 during the war) under Vernon Kell with the Special Branch under Sir Basil Thomson proved well able to cope.[24] France in contrast was targeted by German military intelligence (headed by Colonel Walter Nicolai of Department IIIb at OHL), but although the Dutch exotic dancer, Mata Hari, had liaisons with French officials (and was executed in October 1917 as a warning to others) German intelligence within France obtained no high-grade material.[25]

The Allies may have had somewhat more success in planting informers in Germany, but to what extent remains unsubstantiated.[26]

More significant was the Allies' train-watching system in occupied France and the Low Countries, to which the Germans had no counterpart. It tracked the movement of infantry and artillery, and especially that of 'constituted units' – i.e. whole divisions – which typically required forty trains each to move. Train watching in Belgium began early, much of it done by returning refugees who worked for a profusion of networks run by British, French, and Belgian intelligence. Competition and non-cooperation led several agents to disaster, as did insecure communications, secret documentation being carried by couriers from Holland to Britain on the steam packet and intercepted three times by boarders from German warships during 1916. But from here on matters improved, and after early 1917 all British intelligence reports from the Netherlands were directed for editing via Laurence Oppenheim, the military attaché at The Hague.[27] During the war the British ran some 130 networks with 4,360 agents, the French forty with 650, and the Belgians twenty-five with 500;[28] the Americans entered the field with plenty of money to poach what by now were diminishing numbers of informers, but too late to make much impact.[29] Among the British operations the dominant ones were run by the Secret Service, ultimately responsible to Sir Mansfield Cumming ('C') in Whitehall, but controlled in the Netherlands by a South African captain, Henry Landau. Landau's best-known network was known collectively as 'La Dame Blanche' – the White Lady – after a supposed apparition whose sighting presaged the death of a Hohenzollern, and by 1918 it had observers all over Belgium,[30] while other British-organized teams operated in Lille and, from 1917, in north-eastern France.[31] The latter area was crucial, as the sector where the lateral railway passing behind the German front skirted the Ardennes.[32] From February 1918 GHQ was able to establish a reporting service at the eastern end of the line in Luxemburg, whose messages reached Paris in five days (instead of three weeks via the Netherlands) by means of an ingenious code that communicated the details in a local newspaper, *Der Landwirt*, its contents seeming so innocuous that the Germans permitted its export to Switzerland.[33] All of these operations depended on civilians engaging in tedious and dangerous tasks for modest – if any – financial recompense, and risking imprisonment or execution. Of the 6,000 engaged by GHQ, at least ninety-eight lost their lives and 644 were jailed.[34] Almost a third of the members of 'La Dame Blanche' were women, and its recruits ranged from aristocrats, priests, and nuns (Catholicism proving a strong motivation) to peasants, railwaymen, and bargees.[35] The networks' contribution was vital, according to British commentators, for plotting enemy strategic railway movements and for reconstructing the 'Order of Battle' – the unit structure and deployment – of the German army that formed the principal intelligence target.

The next problem was to verify and sharpen this information (much of which came with a time lag) through correlation with more immediate sources. Prisoner and deserter interrogation was often the most valuable method, and by 1918 the BEF had developed it into a fine art. (Conversely, Allied prisoners were one of the best sources of German intelligence.[36]) A shot-down pilot on 18 March, followed the next day by prisoners and by two deserters – one Polish and one Alsatian – confirmed that the 'Michael' attack would come on the 20th or 21st.[37] The Intelligence Corps officers, who were often trained linguists, found questioning was best done during the shock and disorientation immediately following capture, and was more productive with non-German minorities and private soldiers than with NCOs and officers. A relaxed and friendly approach worked better than threats or intimidation, and 'turned' prisoners might be placed with other captives as stool pigeons. If nothing else, prisoner and deserter intelligence could confirm the identification of the units on the opposite side of the line, and might also illuminate morale and political conditions in Germany – although by 1918 GHQ had became more cautious about such information after the excessive optimism of Edgar Cox's predecessor as Haig's intelligence chief, John Charteris. Unfortunately during the quieter winter months prisoner captures were few – just 164 in January and 290 in February 1918[38] – and one of the German precautions before 'Michael' was to keep the lower ranks as ignorant as possible until the last minute. In spring 1918 prisoner intelligence was less significant than it became later.

The same was broadly true of air reconnaissance. This had rapidly proved itself in 1914, when it had traced the field grey columns marching through Belgium and the German First Army's south-eastwards turn away from Paris that triggered the First Battle of the Marne, but trench warfare offered fewer opportunities for direct observation. Instead the aeroplane became a platform for the camera, and in all the Western Front armies photographic reconnaissance came into its own during the conflict, narrowing the gap between front-line observation on the one hand and espionage on the other by mapping the enemy's infrastructure and troop movements.[39] Like prisoner interrogation, air reconnaissance helped to identify the danger point in spring 1918 – in February it detected German building projects opposite the Third Army – but for four days before 'Michael' began thick cloud and rain prevented early-morning flights.[40] Moreover, the Germans did their best to avoid disclosure, by camouflaging their new installations, covering their vehicle tracks, and by doing as much as possible in darkness. Before the attack British eyes were partially blinded.

If the BEF's vision was obscured, so was its hearing. Signals intelligence (SIGINT) was another technology whose evolution reached a turning point between 1914 and 1918. The rise of cable communication since the 1840s had required diplomatic correspondence to be encoded (cryptography), and the French in particular had developed expertise in decoding (cryptanalysis). In the 1914 campaign the French army could use cables but the invading German one resorted to radio and the French established a unit that cracked its field ciphers.[41] The British War Office had to improvise more, but also assembled an able team, many of whose members would later rise to prominence as historians and linguists. In contrast, Germany had made few preparations for a war of ciphers, and for much of the conflict was at a disadvantage.[42] Cryptography – and still more cryptanalysis – was an exacting craft that required months of dedicated training and practice. It took a while to come into its own, as once trench warfare set in both sides relied less on radio than on cable and on field telephones. By 1916 the Germans and the French had devised equipment for listening in on conversations in the opposing trenches, and the BEF, which was lax about security, owed many of its grievous losses on the Somme to German eavesdropping. Subsequently new precautions were ordered that improved matters, though to the end the British were often careless.[43]

After 1916, however, the German army on the Western Front shifted to radio as its communication mainstay at all levels, partly owing to shortages of the rubber and non-ferrous metals needed to make cables and partly because the increasingly powerful Allied artillery could sever the cables in the opening bombardment. But radio messages were far likelier to be intercepted, and the French in particular had the powerful receivers needed to do it. Both they and the British became skilled at reconstructing the German Order of Battle from 'traffic analysis' – even when unable to read the contents they could still discern where units were located from logging their call signs and the volumes and direction of wireless messages.[44] But before 'Michael' the Germans – who remembered the chaos of 1914 – again out-thought their antagonists. The relevant service, which came under the Head of Transmissions at the OHL, searched for a new code that would be both secure and easy for the clerks to use, as errors in encryption might make messages unintelligible and also frequently gave codes away.[45] From 10 March the Germans changed their call signs daily and on the 11th they introduced the ADFGX field cipher devised by Colonel Fritz Nebel, described by one historian as 'the toughest field cipher the world had yet seen'.[46] During the run-up to and course of the offensive, the Allies could not read the German traffic; while the Germans used dummy call signs and an intensified volume of bogus radio communication to create the impression of a phantom army in Champagne, which confused the French for days.[47] Not only were the Allies deprived of information: they were actively deceived.

During April and May the Allies' intelligence situation improved, though only gradually. The BEF did have warning of the 'Mars' attack on 28 March, which was one reason why it failed. But on the Lys GHQ was again surprised by the timing and location of the offensive, which started just before the Portuguese were due to be moved out. Ground and air observation on 7 April detected enemy preparations, but GHQ intelligence still thought the main attack would come south of the La Bassée canal.[48] During much of the battle itself, the weather impeded Allied overflights, and for the first few days, as during 'Michael', GHQ moved from complacency to near panic as the scale of the attack was unveiled.[49]

If 'Michael' and 'Georgette' achieved partial surprise, the onslaught on the Chemin des Dames against the hapless French Sixth Army came closer to being delivered completely without warning. Yet although the French networks in the Low Countries were weaker than the British ones, much of the intelligence gathered there was shared between GHQ and GQG and via an inter-Allied committee at Folkestone. Moreover, the French were experienced in prisoner and deserter interrogation, and they placed much stress on photography, introducing in 1918 the Salmson Sal 2 A2, a two-seater radio-equipped spotter plane, which unlike its predecessors was well armed and almost as fast and agile as a fighter. During 1918 the French took 675,000 pictures of the front, and could get them to front-line units within hours. They had developed what impressed foreign observers as a seamless system for processing and analysing the information: GQG issued lists of German units and their locations every ten days, and noted changes in call signs and traffic volumes every week, the head of the 2ème (Intelligence) Bureau briefing senior officers weekly and if necessary daily.[50] In the course of the war the French cracked some thirty German field codes, whereas the Germans had much less success in breaking Allied systems.[51] Captain Georges Painvin, a brilliant product of the elite engineering school, the Ecole Polytechnique, an accomplished cellist, and a pre-war professor of palaeontology at the Ecole des Mines, broke alone or in association some twenty enemy codes during the war,[52] but he found the ADFGX code his biggest challenge yet, not least because during March the messages and intercepts remained few. On 1 April eighteen messages were intercepted and Painvin by the 5th had managed to read the code for the 1st; but as the code changed daily the Allies never read more than about half of the ADFGX messages, even if Painvin needed shorter and shorter intervals to decrypt them. By 30 May he could crack the code in a day, and even after the Germans complicated it by adding a sixth letter (ADFGVX) he could still do so.[53]

In the interim, however, the Germans had fallen on the Chemin des Dames. This operation was the OHL's and Bruchmüller's masterpiece of concealment, even greater attention being paid to secrecy than before 21 March. During May GQG lost track of over forty-five German reserve divisions. Although Pétain insisted on day and night overflights, GQG's assessment until 25 May was that the next attack would most likely come north of the Oise.[54] From mid-May prisoner and deserter evidence pointed towards an attack on the Chemin des Dames, but in the absence of corroboration the Sixth Army commander, Duchêne, doubted anything was imminent.[55] British GHQ was similarly bemused, partly because it had evidence from aerial photographs of German preparations in many sectors, and it supposed a new attack was most likely in Picardy (whereas Foch envisaged a new effort on the Lys); on 26 May, Cox reported German movements towards the Laon sector and Haig told GQG that an attack on the Chemin des Dames was likely; but Duchêne brushed aside this warning, as he did one from the AEF.[56] Only later on the 26th did the Sixth Army's own prisoner interrogations finally convince its headquarters that the onslaught was coming the next day. Had it not been for this information, surprise would have been total.

For all the Allies' panoply of agents, overflights, and radio interceptions, they could still miss almost completely the preparations for a major offensive. The unavoidable conclusion is that the subsequent reversal in the balance of advantage reflected failures by the Germans well as progress by their enemies. The French EMA believed that the Germans' insufficiency in heavy artillery lengthened excessively the intervals between the attacks, providing more opportunity for anticipation.[57] The final Ludendorff offensives on 9 June and 15 July were not even partial surprises, and advance warning enabled the French not only to parry them but to prepare counterstrokes. In early June, as Pétain and Foch scrambled to halt the Germans on the Marne, they were desperate for information about the next blow. But aerial reconnaissance north of the Oise between Noyon and Montdidier was revealing railway stations lit up, train movements, and bivouac fires in the forests, alongside German ranging shots and more aggressive air activity. Photographs showed expanding track and ammunition dumps, and prisoners and deserters reported an attack was coming. The evidence was so glaring that GQG suspected it was a feint, or at least betrayed great haste in preparation – which was in fact the case. The interval this time was shorter than before previous attacks and the German army was getting slacker.[58] At this point the French intercepted a radiotelegram from the OHL on 1 June to a unit near Remaugies in the Matz sector, which by the following evening Painvin had decrypted as: '*Munitionierung beschleunigen Punkt Soweit nicut* [sic – *nicht*] *eingesehen auch bei Tag*' ('Rush Munitions Stop Even by Day If Not Seen').[59] As this confirmed the next attack's location Pétain sent it on to Foch. More overflights and prisoner interrogations yielded further corroboration.[60] Only one French listening station picked up the 'victory radiogram' (as the 2ème Bureau christened it),[61] but at a moment of obscurity it clarified where to look, and subsequent deserter information confirmed the timing down to the hour, allowing GQG to pull its artillery out of range, move up reinforcements, plan a counterstroke, and deliver a counter-bombardment simultaneously with the start of the Germans' artillery preparation.[62]

Before Ludendorff's 15 July offensive his cover was even more comprehensively blown. In late June the Allies were once more in uncertainty about where the attack would come,[63] but then the picture came into focus, owing to a combination of carelessness on the German side with continuing vigilance on the French. One telltale indicator came when a flurry of enemy radio messages and changes in call signs was followed by radio silence. Overflights revealed bivouac fires, new airfields, poorly camouflaged munitions dumps, and telltale digging in the Champagne chalk, but in addition the French raided very actively in the first half of July, and prisoner interrogations were crucial.[64] By 10 July it was clear that the northern Rupprecht army group's reserves were being diverted to Champagne, and Pétain persuaded Foch that the attack would be major.[65] In the end the French high command knew the precise location, strength, and timing of the assault, and was able once again to stage a pre-emptive counter-bombardment and (at least east of Reims) to hold back its forces. Yet the headquarters of the attacking armies assured Crown Prince Wilhelm and Ludendorff that 'the enemy had so far noticed nothing'.[66] Not only had the Germans lost surprise – without knowing that they had done so – but they faced an enemy who knew what countermeasures worked and was steeled to take them.

On the Italian front the Austrians had long enjoyed a cryptographic advantage, but after Caporetto the Italians tightened up and made more use of enciphered codes, advised by the Allied military missions.[67] From early June 1918 evidence from prisoners and deserters and from aircraft pointed to an impending Austrian offensive on the lower Piave.[68] Once Italian intelligence assessed that the attack was close, it stepped up raids and overflights.[69] The Austrians used field telephones regularly, and failed to protect themselves against eavesdropping, thus giving Diaz detailed information about their bombardment and attack plan. Hence the 15 June attack was no surprise, except in one portion of the British line that had expected just a bombardment rather than an infantry assault.[70]

The Allies' summer and autumn offensives continued to benefit from superior intelligence. From June the British were receiving excellent information from Luxemburg about enemy railway movements, which

1. (*top*) Kaiser Wilhelm II reviewing the army group Rupprecht, June 1918. A contrast in demeanour and apparel between reviewers and reviewed.

2. (*bottom*) Haig reviewing Canadians.

3. (*above*) Hindenburg (*at left*), Ludendorff (*front left*), the Kaiser (*back to the camera*) and Crown Prince Wilhelm (*leaning against door frame*) and staff officers at German headquarters, Spa.

4. (*left*) Foch and Pershing. Antagonists over 'amalgamation'.

5. (*left*) Boroević, Austro-Hungarian commander on the Isonzo – the man who opposed the Piave offensive.

6. (*below*) French and British infantry in newly scraped rifle pits near Nesle, 25 March 1918.

7. (*above*) British troops by the St Quentin Canal, 2 October 1918. Its storming was one of the most spectacular feats of the war.

8. (*right*) Italian infantryman, late 1917.

9. (*above*) Preparing for Megiddo: Australian Light Horse near Jericho, 17 August 1918.

10. (*left*) French interrogation of a German prisoner, by Edouard Vuillard (1868–1940). Prisoner information was a principal intelligence source.

11. (*top*) Austrian fighter squadron over the Brenta, 1917, by Max Edler von Poosch (1872–1968). The Albatros D.III, a standard German Western Front fighter, was manufactured in Austria-Hungary under licence.

12. (*bottom*) Gotha IV bomber. Gothas were the mainstay of Germany's strategic air offensive against London and Paris.

13. (*top*) American heavy artillery pounds the Meuse–Argonne.

14. (*bottom*) Royal Field Artillery at the Battle of the Canal du Nord,
27 September 1918.

15. (*top*) Machine-gun crew. The MG08, the standard German
heavy machine gun, fired up to 400 rounds per minute.

16. (*bottom*) American troops with German prisoners at the
Battle of the St Quentin Canal, 29 September 1918. The Mark V
tanks carry 'crib' fascines, used to fill in trenches.

forewarned that the Germans were targeting Champagne.[71] Before the 4 July and 8 August battles they knew that morale in the opposite lines was poor. They also got better at deception, for example by creating the impression before the Battle of Amiens that the Canadians were still in Flanders. The Germans had never established much of an espionage network behind the Allied lines; they were losing their ability not only to penetrate enemy air space but also to protect their own; they had difficulty in breaking into radio conversations; and now it was no longer the German army that was taking unprecedented prisoner hauls but its opponents. The Allies also captured crucial documents, most notably the plans for the Hindenburg Line. Nor did the arrival of the new and inexperienced AEF change this picture. In 1918 the Allies shared intelligence more than previously, and established an Inter-Allied Commission (including the Americans) in August.[72] The Americans established their own prisoner interrogation system and tried – with some success – to crack the Central Powers' codes, while denying rich pickings to German cryptanalysts. Pershing's GHQ had established a Code Compilation Section which after various experiments introduced a series of field codes named after American rivers. They could quickly be replaced if captured (as soon happened) and were more resistant to decryption than their German counterparts, although the American troops proved reluctant to delay signalling by using them.[73] Although the Germans gained warning of the Saint-Mihiel offensive and were pulling out of the salient when it was launched, the Meuse–Argonne attack achieved initial surprise.

All these factors helped the Allies in the final stages repeatedly to catch the Germans unawares, which contributed to Ludendorff's eventual breakdown. Nor was their advantage confined to the Western Front. Before the Battle of Vittorio Veneto, British divisions moved to the breakthrough sector on the lower Piave without the Austrians knowing.[74] Allenby's triumph at Megiddo followed deception operations to persuade the Turks that he intended to attack in the interior rather than along the coastal plain. By September he enjoyed complete air superiority, and he had stepped up air reconnaissance, taking twice as many pictures of the enemy positions as in the previous year. Turkish prisoners and deserters (some 3,400 and 800 respectively in the months before the attack) did much to establish the Ottoman Order of Battle, and water sources were identified in the path of the advance. The personnel in Allenby's intelligence corps rose from thirty in mid-1917 to 111 by the end of 1918, and the intelligence officers at his headquarters more than doubled; while the Commander himself devoured intelligence summaries before breakfast. Although his offensive plan was bold, he knew his enemy so thoroughly that it entailed few risks.[75] In fact he overestimated Turkish numbers, and if British intelligence in the Middle East had earlier been too optimistic, in the final stages it was too cautious,[76] as it was on the Western Front also.[77] The Allies knew that declining numbers of divisions faced them, as those that survived were rotated faster and faster into line: early in 1918 every six weeks, but by August German army leave had stopped almost completely.[78] But Edgar Cox was reluctant to repeat John Charteris's excessive reliance on prisoner testimony for estimating enemy morale, and it was easier to estimate the size of the German army than its psychological condition. Hence during the armistice negotiations themselves, Foch received political intelligence suggesting German resistance was about to collapse, whereas Haig's picture was less optimistic. Divergences in the Allies' approaches to the ceasefire largely turned on such competing assessments.[79]

AIRPOWER

Integral to the balance of intelligence advantage was air superiority, which had never been more fiercely contested than in 1918. During the war aircraft speeds and ceilings had doubled, engine horsepower quadrupled, and bomb payloads grew even more.[80] German aeroplane speeds had risen from 80 to 200 kilometres per hour, and maximum loads from 3.5 to 1,000 kilograms.[81] Since the development of fighters (or 'pursuit' aircraft as the Allies called them – 'hunter aircraft' or *Jagdflugzeuge* was the German term), combat had spread into the skies. Aircraft took up roles that they would keep through the Second World War and beyond: not just guiding the artillery but also striking ground targets as a form of flying artillery themselves. They operated at sea and in every theatre on land. They also embarked upon strategic bombing.

By 1918 'strategical' bombing existed as a concept and was discussed as such in the newly formed British Air Staff and Air Ministry. It meant attacks on home-front targets such as cities, factories, and railways rather than the enemy forces.[82] Militarily the two sides' efforts in good measure cancelled each other out, but bomber raids on Paris and London hardened Allied public opinion against Germany, and prompted reprisal raids, which if the war had continued would have become much bigger. An escalation dynamic was in evidence that anticipated later tragedies, although as yet the technology was scarcely comparable to that which a generation later laid waste to Europe.

The first Hague Peace Conference in 1899 had banned the dropping of projectiles from balloons but only for a five-year period, and before 1914 the popular press and fiction writers had foreseen air attacks on cities. London's vulnerability caused a panic in 1913.[83] After war began, humanitarian considerations caused little hesitation. The French bombed Ludwigshafen in 1914, and they and the British continued to raid enemy border towns into 1915–16, although neither had yet developed specialized bomber aircraft and the damage caused was slight. From Germany, only Zeppelin airships could reach London, and they came under the German navy. Gradually Wilhelm – who had scruples about targeting historic buildings and his cousins' palaces, while the Chancellor was worried about neutral public opinion – ceded to the navy's enthusiasm, and raids on London began on 31 May 1915.[84] For some months the British had no answer, but during 1916 new BE2c aircraft arrived that climbed higher and were stable at night, and fired incendiary 'Buckingham' bullets. Supported by better anti-aircraft guns, searchlights, and an improved ground observer system, they shot down so many Zeppelins that from September 1916 raids on London ceased.[85] Because of raw-material shortages the airships' skin was no longer rubberized, and their ribs consisted of wood rather than aluminium, making them even more flammable.[86] The danger seemed over, and in early 1917 the British authorities were winding down their civil defence arrangements.

But the Zeppelins prepared the way for bombing by aircraft. German engineers had been working on the Gotha G-IV bomber since the start of the war, and the OHL wanted it ready for raids to coincide with unrestricted submarine warfare. London, 175 miles from the Gothas' bases in Belgium, fell within their 500-mile range. Unlike French cities, it could be approached over water, without ground defences, and the Thames estuary provided a conspicuous guideline. Gothas carried a smaller payload than did Zeppelins, but they were faster (87 mph), higher (up to 10,500 feet), more heavily armed (carrying three machine guns), and harder to shoot down.[87] Moreover, whereas the British decrypted the Zeppelins' wireless code and always had warning of their arrival, the first daylight Gotha raids (codenamed Operation *Türkenkreuz*) were unanticipated.[88] They killed and injured 290 people at Folkestone on 25 May, and on 13 June they killed and injured 594 in bombing centred on London's Liverpool Street Station and the East End, including eighteen children at the Upper North Street school in the East India Dock Road; on 7 July another raid on the capital claimed 250 more casualties.[89] By this stage there was media uproar and tense discussion in the War Cabinet. Two fighter squadrons returned from the Western Front (over Haig's protests) – and a new agency, the London Air Defence Area (LADA), was created under Major Edward B. Ashmore, a gunner moved from Flanders. Ashmore added another barrier of fighters east of London and altered their tactics so that they attacked the Gothas in groups rather than singly, and the same bad weather that bedevilled British troops in Belgium assisted him. In three raids during August the Gothas failed to reach London, and in the last they lost three aircraft, one to AA fire and two to fighters. Perhaps prematurely, they switched to night attacks.

Night bomber attacks were the last and most challenging of the threats against London during the war. Now the Gothas were joined by *Riesenflugzeuge* or 'Giants', with a 138-foot wingspan (that of a B-29 Superfortress in the Second World War), a maximum height of 19,000 feet, nine crew wearing heated flying suits, six machine guns, and a payload of up to 2 tons, including 1,000-kilogram bombs that could wreck a housing block.[90] They could take enormous punishment, and none were ever shot down. During 'the blitz of the harvest moon' between 24 September and 1 October 1917 night-flying bombers visited London six times. For the British this was the most trying time: their anti-aircraft batteries were nearing exhaustion due to ammunition expenditure and deterioration of the barrels, 100,000–300,000 people took shelter in the Underground each evening, and up to one sixth of munitions production was lost, although contemporary estimates ran much higher.[91] Worsening weather and wear and tear on the bombers and their crews then provided relief, and during the winter Ashmore installed better searchlights and balloon barrages while the Sopwith Camel proved itself as an effective night fighter. As in the campaign against the U-boats, there was no one spectacular turning point but gradually the defenders inflicted greater losses and the attackers caused less damage. From October the British read German wireless messages, and once given more warning their aircraft destroyed an average of one tenth of the Gothas on each raid.[92] Terrible episodes still took place, such as the bombing of a basement shelter in Long Acre on 28 January, with over a hundred killed and wounded. But in the biggest raid of all, on 19 May 1918, forty-three aircraft took off but six were lost in action and seven in accidents, while according to a survey by the medical journal *The Lancet* the civilian mood had now improved.[93] From this point raids on London (though not the provinces) ended, in part to redirect the bombers to the Western Front. In addition the campaign was taking a growing toll of aircraft, a total of twenty-four being lost in action and another thirty-seven in accidents. Partly because of raw-material shortages the Gothas were shoddily made, and their undercarriage was liable to collapse on landing.[94] By 1918, moreover, British fighters could be mobilized much faster and Ashmore established an operations control room where observers' reports were centralized and instructions co-ordinated in a manner prefiguring the second and more celebrated Battle of Britain.

A parallel Gotha campaign against Paris began on 30–31 January 1918, leaflets dropped over the trenches justifying it on the grounds that the French had refused peace. By 15 September a total of fourteen raids had dropped 664 bombs, although the heaviest attacks came in the spring, seventy people dying on 11 March in a panic crush at the Bolivar Métro station. As against London, the Germans launched a multi-faceted attack on the city's morale, as the Gotha raids preceded the 'Michael' offensive and on 22 March the first shell landed from the 'Paris gun', the precursor to 370 more between 23 March and 8 August.[95] In fact the gun caused greater shock than the Gothas, which dropped 30 tons of bombs compared with 100 tons on Britain.[96] Fighters played a smaller role in air defence than in London, partly owing to a shortage of planes, so anti-aircraft guns were the main – and quite effective – defensive implement.[97] Even though Paris was only two hours' flying time from the enemy trenches, few of the bombers reached their destination and most got lost or turned back. Only eleven of the thirty Gothas that departed on 30 January arrived, and of 483 sent in total thirteen were shot down and only thirty-seven got through to the city.[98]

Total casualties in Paris from air raids were 266 killed and 603 wounded (the Paris gun killing a further 256 and wounding sixty-two), while British casualties in the Gotha and Giant raids numbered 856 dead and 1,965 wounded, and the property damage was estimated at £1.5m. Ashmore later compared these figures to the more than 700 lives lost annually in London in the 1920s on the roads.[99] Certainly they were small in comparison with the thousands dying daily on the Western Front, and the Germans could have pursued the campaign more ruthlessly. By August 1918 they had ready a new device based on magnesium and aluminium, the Elektron Bomb, which was incendiary enough to set off firestorms. After delays due to bad weather, a raid on London was planned for 23 September. But at the last moment Ludendorff called it off, because the German government feared reprisals, but perhaps also because he was already contemplating the ceasefire appeal that he demanded five days later.[100] Humanitarian sentiment, however, formed no particular constraint. When in 1917 Bethmann Hollweg complained that Gotha bombing was 'irritating the chauvinistic and fanatical instincts of the English nation without cause', Hindenburg replied that being conciliatory would gain nothing and the raids kept war material away from the Western Front: 'It is regrettable, but inevitable, that they cause the loss of innocent lives as well.'[101] More important as a limiting factor were technical considerations. A Giant cost over half a million marks and each one needed a fifty-man ground crew: only eighteen were built. Even the cost of a Gotha doubled between 1916 and 1917.[102] Although supposedly aircraft were second only to submarines in their claims on manufacturing resources, Germany lacked the manpower and raw materials to fulfil its construction programmes, and strategic bombing competed with the needs of army support. In addition the prevalent cloudy weather over North-Western Europe hindered all kinds of air activity (as over Kosovo as late as 1999), but especially bombing: which meant sustained attacks as in September 1917 were rare. And in comparison with their Second World War successors, 1918 bombers carried tiny payloads and delivered them inaccurately, not least because bombsights were still under development.[103] The Gothas attacking London operated at the limit of their range, under fire, and mostly at night, and achieved little beyond random terror. They hardly damaged docks and railways or the armaments industry, even the enormous complex at Woolwich Arsenal being hit just once. Hence the main practical consequence was to tie up Allied resources in air defence, which Hindenburg and the commanding general of the German air force, Ernest von Hoeppner, recognized as an objective.[104] At least in this respect they had considerable success. Britain lost forty-five aircraft and seventy-eight aircrew in the battles over its home islands, all the latter in accidents, whereas German casualties were several times heavier. But while in 1917–18 Germany committed approximately 100 Gothas, 15 Giants, and 30 Zeppelins to the British campaign, Britain committed some 200 aircraft to its defence, supported by searchlights and by anti-aircraft guns crewed by 14,000 ground personnel.[105]

Nor was this the end of the reckoning, as the Gotha raids caused a redirection in British air policy, which otherwise would not have happened at this time, nor met so little resistance. After the Liverpool Street bombing, the Cabinet decided almost to double the Royal Flying Corps (RFC) from 108 to 200 squadrons, with most of the extra aeroplanes being equipped for bombing. Although this target was never reached, production rates rose substantially.[106] Jan-Christian Smuts, the South African general and former defence minister who had joined Lloyd George's War Cabinet, reported to it on 9 August that 'the day may not be far off when aerial operations with their devastation of enemy lands and destruction of industrial centres and population centres on a vast scale may become the principal operations of war, to which the older forms of military operations may become secondary and subordinate'.[107] He recommended merging the RFC with the Royal Naval Air Service (RNAS), under an Air Ministry with its own air staff to plan for the employment of an aircraft surplus that the Ministry of Munitions – overconfidently – expected. Motivated partly by reports that Germany planned a huge bomber expansion, the government approved Smuts's recommendations and passed legislation to create the Air Ministry in January 1918, the merger into the new RAF following in April. Finally, in the wake of the 'harvest moon' raids, the Cabinet authorized immediate reprisals. The climax of the German raids on London and Paris was followed by the climax of the Allied air assault on the Rhineland.

The 1918 strategic air offensive against Germany was predominantly British. The Americans took part, using British DH9 bombers, and suffered heavily, but the French high command was ambivalent, partly because it feared retaliation and partly because it believed that bombs were better employed against the German army and its staging areas.[108] The French had developed the fast and high-flying Bréguet XIV B.2 two-seater bomber, which could be escorted over Germany by a long-distance heavy fighter, the Caudron R.XI. During 1918 they fought a battle of attrition: in the first quarter they dropped 200 tons of bombs and lost 20 aircraft; in the second they dropped 500 tons but lost 50 and the authorities hesitated over whether to continue; but in the third quarter they dropped 700 tons and lost 29 and in October they dropped 600 tons and lost 3.[109] They were slowly winning mastery of the German skies. As for the British, from October 1917 their 41st wing carried out day and night attacks on Germany from Ochey in Lorraine. In June 1918, the Independent Force, RAF (or IF) was created, under the command of Sir Hugh Trenchard, previously commander of the RFC. Now the raids were intensified and their radius lengthened. According to Sir Frederick Sykes, the Chief of the Air Staff, 'as the offensive is the dominant factor in war, so is the Strategic Air Offensive the dominant factor in air power', and the offensive would aim to dislocate the enemy munitions industries, attack the U-boats in their bases, and 'bring about far-reaching moral and political effects in Germany'.[110] Between October 1917 and November 1918, 508 raids took place, dropping 14,911 high-explosive bombs and 816,019 incendiaries.[111] In July and August the British went to the limits of their range, bombing Cologne, Frankfurt, Mannheim, and Darmstadt. The Air Staff priority for 1919 was the Ruhr's steel and chemical industries,[112] and the new Handley Page V/500 bomber, becoming available in November 1918, could reach Berlin.

Yet if anything the Allies' raids were less destructive than Germany's. German casualties from air raids during the war totalled 746 killed and 1,843 injured: the damage was valued at 24 million marks (£1.2m),[113] but industrial disruption was slight. Sykes cited photographic evidence of damage to factories and German press reports that the Rhinelanders were demanding more protection,[114] but a post-war RAF investigation was more sceptical. Although alerts and sleepless nights disheartened the workforce, few blast furnaces were damaged and the huge BASF chemical works at Ludwigshafen, a major target, never had to shut down.[115] Similarly the French tried to halt supplies from the Briey iron ore mines in Lorraine, a location close to their border that produced

80 per cent of Germany's output, but their efforts were completely ineffective.[116]

Three main explanations can be cited, the first being technical. By late 1944 Britain and America were dropping 90,000 tons of bombs on Germany per month in 18,000 sorties, as a result of which the Third Reich's armaments output finally began to decline: between October 1917 and November 1918 the British dropped 665 tons in total, and less accurately.[117] Similarly an Allied campaign in June–July 1918 dropped 61 tons of bombs over the Germans' railways but demonstrated that bombs could not destroy trains unless landing within a few feet of them.[118] Germany's fruitless efforts in June to smash the Allies' crucial railway viaduct at Etaples pointed to the same conclusion. Moreover, the Allied bombers had just five and a half hours' endurance, so only Germany's south-western corner was in reach. The weather was another obstacle, the campaign winding down as the autumn skies became more clouded. And although the British DH4 bomber was a dependable workhorse, the new DH9 proved constantly unreliable and many missions were abandoned because of engine failure.[119]

The second explanation was the Germans' countermeasures. In 1916 they introduced a centralized observation system and unified fighter defence, later supplemented by searchlights, anti-aircraft guns, and balloons.[120] In summer 1918 they reinforced their fighters to 320; and British losses became formidable: 104 day bombers and thirty-four night ones were lost to German action and 320 crashed behind Allied lines, while in September the IF lost 75 per cent of its aircraft in one month.[121] By the end of the war air defence, like the rest of German aviation, was being slowly paralysed by shortages, but until then it exacted a high price.

The third and final impediment came from the Allies' own priorities and policies. Foch shared the general French lack of enthusiasm, stating in a 1 April directive that ground attacks against the enemy troops should be the main objective (and air fighting only as necessary to achieve it) alongside bombing of key railway junctions. He wanted the IF under his authority. In October the British agreed to an inter-Allied bombing force under Trenchard that would be answerable to the Marshal, and this body would have overseen strategic bombing in 1919.[122] But Trenchard himself never carried out operations as the air staff had intended, and like the French he was a strategic bombing sceptic who as

RFC commander had seen his primary duty as assisting the army. Although Sykes instructed the Independent Force to 'obliterate' first the German chemical industry and then the Lorraine steel industry, in fact of 416 raids between June and September 1918 only thirty-four were against chemical plants and another thirty-four against steel plants, whereas 185 were against rail targets and 139 against aerodromes, objectives that Trenchard had been told to leave for other parts of the RAF. Even the locations on which effort was concentrated escaped critical damage: the 'railway triangle' round Metz and Sablon was the most heavily attacked single target, but traffic there was never halted for long. It was also true that Trenchard never received a force commensurate with the government's initial intentions, as although the IF grew from five to nine squadrons he had been required to plan for thirty-four.[123] Only 427 of the 1,817 bombing aircraft sent from Britain to France in 1918 went to the IF, and at the armistice only 140 of the 1,799 RAF aircraft on the Western Front were assigned to it.[124] Various reasons lay behind this, notably that the expected production surplus did not materialize and losses during the Ludendorff offensives were heavy. But even a much larger Independent Force would have achieved little, and airpower's most important function remained direct support of the armies.

Since 1914 reconnaissance had been a vital function of airpower, in the rudimentary period of trench warfare much of it still carried out from balloons, although sturdy two-seater observation planes increasingly replaced them. By 1916 specialized fighters were emerging, to shoot down the balloons and observation aircraft, but also to escort and defend them. By 1917 further new functions of ground attack and long-distance bombing were coming into their own. Throughout this evolution, in a microcosm of the war as a whole, the Allies had the advantage in numbers but the Germans were their equal and often their superior in quality, and regularly inflicted heavier losses. The latter's advantage arose partly from an early lead in engine technology (assisted by their development of airships), but also from the peculiar characteristics of the air campaign. Two thirds of aerial combats took place over the German side of the line,[125] the prevailing pattern being for the British (and to a lesser extent the French) to seek command of German airspace while denying Allied airspace to the enemy. According to an RFC memorandum, 'The successful performance of the roles of the

RFC in defence must primarily depend on its ability to gain and maintain the ascendancy in the air. This can only be done by attacking and defeating the enemy's air force.'[126] Thereby the Allies exposed themselves to the hit-and-run tactics of which the 'Red Baron', Manfred von Richthofen, and his 'circus' were masters. None the less, by 1918 patrols by multi-squadron units and dogfights between dozens of aircraft were not uncommon, and the exploits of individual 'aces' – many of whom perished during the year – were becoming more peripheral.[127] At times, particularly during the 'Fokker scourge' of winter 1915–16, and 'bloody April' in 1917, new aircraft types had given the Germans an extra edge, but at the end of 1917 Allied fighters such as the British Sopwith Camel and SE5a and the French Spad XIII (the most manufactured aircraft of the war), had restored near qualitative parity. Although the Germans hoped, with a new fighter generation, to tip the balance back their way, they never quite managed it.

Airpower was integral to the OHL's new offensive doctrine. Pre-attack reconnaissance would be 'of deciding importance'. Once the attack began, aircraft should hit enemy aerodromes, camps, and railway stations before turning to their infantry and artillery.[128] Preparations in winter 1917–18 included war games under Hoeppner's direction.[129] Overflights began in January, using Rumpler and LVG reconnaissance aircraft, to identify targets along the Allied lines and behind them. In keeping with their concern to avoid detection, the Germans maintained high activity even away from the attack zone, while above the latter they tried to disarm suspicion by not preventing Allied overflights. Similarly, new hangars were built all along the Western Front, not just in the designated area. None the less, over half Germany's fighters and bombers were concentrated on the 'Michael' sector,[130] as well as new and strongly armoured two-seaters that were specially designed for ground attack and gathered in thirty-eight *Schlachtstaffeln*.[131] As of 21 March along the entire British front the British had 1,255 aircraft and the Germans 1,020 while on the French front 2,590 French aircraft faced 471 German ones, but in the battle sector south of Arras the British were outnumbered by 579 to 730.[132] Whereas the British spread their airpower the Germans could focus it because they knew where the battleground would be, and their adversaries were slow to detect it. In fact, the RFC in January and February did spot preparations opposite the British Third and Fifth Armies, including railway and aerodrome construction, forward dumping of supplies, and extra railway movements. It dropped bombs night and day on German aerodromes, railways, billets, and munitions dumps, and although the German air force was deliberately inactive it engaged in dogfights, including one on 18 March over Busigny station that involved Richthofen's circus and was one of the biggest yet seen.[133] But even though the RFC could generally operate over German lines, its bombing caused little disruption, and it failed to detect the southernmost extension of the German attack opposite Gough's Fifth Army.

'Michael' was accompanied by the biggest aerial confrontation yet seen. The morning mist on the opening days impeded the Germans from exploiting their superiority while it was greatest. None the less, they monitored their infantry advance, and harassed the retreating British, the *Schlachtstaffeln* going into action on the first afternoon. On 24 March, German pilots observed the gap emerging between the British and French armies.[134] But abundant targets presented themselves to both sides, as the infantry, artillery, and supply trains emerged from cover to cross open ground in daylight, and one pre-eminent feature of the battle was ground attack. A second was that the normal liaison between aircraft and artillery broke down. On the German side this was partly due to an avoidable error, against which Hoeppner had warned: the OHL had transferred from the air service to the Signals Corps the ground crews and materiel needed to assure communication, and inexperienced and inadequately trained personnel replaced them.[135] On the British side, gun batteries in makeshift positions often failed to put up their wireless masts, so that even when the RFC reported enemy troops and batteries, no bombardments were directed against them.[136] Although aircraft-directed artillery fire might have been preferable to using the aircraft themselves for ground attack, in the confusion of the retreat it was frequently unavailable as an option.

In the opening phase the RFC lost many more airfields than expected, but it improvised new ones and moved back its supply depots, while enough reserve machines were available simply to replace damaged aeroplanes without spending time repairing them.[137] Conversely, as the Germans moved forward, they too needed to improvise new airfields, but the old Somme battlefield offered few favourable sites: a problem the more serious because German fighters (typically designed for high-performance interception) had an average endurance of only ninety minutes, whereas that of Allied fighters was 150.[138] Moreover, the RFC could reinforce any part of the British sector of the Western Front in at most one and a half hours' flying time. For these reasons, after 23 March the British (assisted by French aircraft) regained superiority, which they used to avoid dogfights and concentrate on aiding the ground troops, the Chief of the Air Staff instructing that 'very low flying is essential. All risks to be taken.'[139] Over the battle as a whole, RFC losses were twice those of the Germans and many were due to ground fire.[140] Yet even in these desperate circumstances, the British were as usual counting: so that whereas on 21 March they fired 21,000 machine-gun rounds and dropped 15.5 tons on ground targets, by 27 March the figures were 313,345 rounds and 50 tons.[141] At first the priority was to help the Third Army prevent a break-out across the old Somme battlefield, but thereafter the focus shifted south to the Fifth Army. German reports to the OHL testified to the chaos and disorientation caused by incessant Allied strafing, which forced columns to scatter and reduced the roads to chaos. In general, airpower delivered to the Germans the reconnaissance needed for Bruchmüller's bombardment, but little more: fog grounded the *Schlachtstaffeln* for much of the first two days and thereafter the Allies regained the advantage. On the other hand, aerial observation told the British much of the story about where and when the attack was coming, but missed some crucial details. At first the RFC gave the ground troops little assistance, but later its role expanded, even if the infantry and artillery played the principal part in halting Ludendorff. On 4 April Trenchard told the Cabinet that since 19 March the RFC/RAF had dropped 319 tons of bombs and fired over 1 million machine-gun rounds at ground targets. It had destroyed 244 enemy planes and driven down 122 more: 'there was a feeling at the front that we had definite air superiority over the battle zone'.[142]

'Michael' set a pattern. British overflights detected the German transport movements towards the Lys in early April, and on the 6th reported advanced preparations against the Portuguese, but GHQ supposed this attack to be diversionary and ordered only limited pre-emptive bombing. All the same, the Germans again lost numerical superiority after the first two days of the battle, partly because the swampy terrain made it difficult to create new forward aerodromes. Fog and cloud again prevented them from maximizing their advantage, and by the time the battle reached its crisis on 12 April the weather had cleared and the

RAF been reinforced. It flew more hours, took more photographs, and dropped more bombs than on any other day of the war, firing 114,904 machine-gun rounds and issuing eighty-nine calls for artillery support, while 137 aircraft harried the enemy drive towards Hazebrouck.[143] The Germans' infantry complained of inadequate protection, and they suffered another blow when Richthofen was brought down and killed on 21 April. In the later stages of 'Georgette', although German aircraft contributed to the taking of Mount Kemmel, bad weather again restricted airpower's role. Overall, as in the 'Michael' battle, it helped to stem the German tide in the critical phase, but it is hard to see its contribution as indispensable.

During 'Michael' the French had moved aircraft to Picardy to bomb the German crossings of the Somme and the Crozat Canal and to attack enemy troops in formations of up to eighty. But although the French air force was bigger than the RAF, during March and April it remained quiet.[144] Unlike the British, GQG's approach was not to maintain a continuous fighter presence but to create mixed *groupements* (groupings) of fighters and bombers for mass intervention in critical sectors. Even so, above the Chemin des Dames in May the Germans again won the initial advantage, largely due to surprise. Intensified French overflights had missed the German preparations, while British pilots in the sector had detected only clouds of dust. On 27 May itself liaison between the Allied artillery and aviation broke down along with everything else.[145] The Germans had just taken delivery of the Fokker D-VII, widely considered the best fighter of the war, and they overran many French airfields intact. In addition, communication improved between the German pilots and headquarters, so that this time the *Schlachtstaffeln* could act as intended, and delayed French reinforcements by interdicting rail traffic.[146] Yet even when the Germans held so many advantages the French still responded rapidly, Pétain ordering a *groupement* to depart early on 27 May and the first planes taking off an hour later. Between 31 May and 4 June the French shot down or damaged over 100 German aircraft and dropped 200 tons of explosives,[147] and the Chemin des Dames marked the high-water mark of the Germans' air effectiveness as of their effectiveness generally. In the Battle of the Matz French fighters commanded the skies two days after the start, and French bombers attacked the German artillery during Mangin's counteroffensive. The British also assisted, and assisted again against the final German offensive on 15 July, nine RAF squadrons flying down a day beforehand at Foch's request. Night reconnaissance – which first became important in 1918 – gave warning of this attack, and one of the most striking uses of Allied airpower was against the German bridges over the Marne.[148] In Italy, similarly, the Italians had enjoyed the air advantage before 1917, but they lost it when the Germans reinforced the Austrians before the Battle of Caporetto, only for the Allied air forces to regain it early in 1918 and add it to their other intelligence advantages before the Battle of the Piave. When the Austrians attacked, the cloud was too low for the RAF to assist the British troops in the Asiago sector, but they were redirected to helping the Italians, up to fifty British aircraft at a time in the following days attacking the Austrian pontoon bridges.[149] Repeatedly the Allies deprived the Central Powers of air superiority, and whether over the Somme, Marne, or Piave, they benefited more from airpower than did their enemies.

In the offensive phase after mid-July the Allies maintained this advantage, although it was smaller than the raw numbers might indicate. For the Battle of Amiens they assembled a crushing initial preponderance of 800 British and 1,104 French aircraft against 365 German ones, most of the German air force being still away in Champagne. During the first morning, after the mist lifted, the RAF attacked enemy artillery, rail and horse-drawn transport, and infantry columns, but in the afternoon all available aircraft were concentrated on attempting to destroy the Somme bridges. This effort continued for two days, and led to some of the fiercest aerial combat yet seen. Unusually, the Germans abandoned their guerrilla tactics and also committed their forces en masse, including the Richthofen circus, commanded since its founder's death by Hermann Goering. On 8 August the RAF lost ninety-six aircraft and on 9 August another forty-five, and by 10 August it had thrown in over 70 per cent of its single-seat fighters; yet although the Richthofen circus was pulled out and never recovered, not one of the fourteen bridges was seriously damaged.[150]

Certainly air mastery helped assure surprise, from Amiens to Megiddo, and the Allies used it to conceal their preparations – for example, flying at night to drown out tank noise – although generally like the Germans they avoided intense pre-battle activity in order to avert suspicion. By September they were shooting down great numbers of the Germans' observation balloons. On attack days they struck at enemy infantry and artillery, particularly successfully in the Drocourt–Quéant Switch battle on 2 September. On the same occasion they dropped ammunition to the forward troops by parachute, and they used air drops again when the Flanders attack got bogged down in October, delivering 13 tons of rations in one day.[151] Yet the weather continued to limit airpower's potential. In the Battle of Saint-Mihiel, for example, the Allies assembled 1,500 aircraft, but poor visibility impeded support for the advance,[152] and did so again during the British assault on the Hindenburg Line.[153] Moreover, until almost the end the German air force was a tough opponent. 30 October 1918 was the heaviest day of air fighting in the entire war, the Germans calling on all available forces against British bomber attacks on one of their principal lines of retreat, the Liège–Namur railway. They lost sixty-seven aircraft and the British forty-one.[154] Yet what the Germans were doing by this stage was concentrating their remaining fighters in formations of fifty or more to protect their communications, and when forced to fight they suffered attrition from which they could no longer recover. During 1918, the Western Front advantage slowly moved in the Allies' favour, and the surviving German pilots felt increasingly beleaguered. They kept going partly because of a qualitative advantage: the Fokker D-VII and Pfalz D-IIIa were excellent aircraft, and even the finest Allied fighters could not match them. The German official history claimed that the Germans shot down over three times as many Allied aircraft as they lost themselves; according to Hoeppner, between January and September 1918 Germany lost 1,099 aircraft on the Western Front, but the Allies 3,732.[155] But other factors weighed against them, especially a shortage of aviation fuel, which began to bite from June–July, and from September fuel was severely rationed.[156] Moreover, First World War air fighting was extraordinarily resource-intensive. By later standards 1918 airfleets seem very large, but the performance of each aircraft was very low. Enormous numbers of ground crew were needed to keep one aeroplane aloft – pilots were only 2 per cent of the British Royal Flying Corps – and by 1918 the losses meant almost entire fleets had to be replaced every few months.[157] Even if the crews usually survived their machines' destruction, the strain was immense – no fewer than 30 per cent of French pilots and observers in the war lost their lives, most of them in 1917–18.[158] The Germans were less well placed to withstand these pressures, and by the armistice their aircraft numbers had shrunk to about 2,200, from 3,668 in March, whereas Britain and France had Western Front forces of 2,600 and 3,700 and American strength was 740.[159]

The American air service was still the weakest of the three, even though the AEF built itself up from no military aviation at all to forty-five squadrons. Flying mainly French-manufactured aircraft, the Americans saw action from April 1918 onwards. They engaged in 150 bombing raids, took 18,000 photographs of enemy positions, and lost 235 killed in action.[160] French losses were heaviest during May and June, but even so they deployed more planes than the British on 8 August and provided most of the air support at Saint-Mihiel. The British believed they had brought down three times as many German machines as they had lost themselves, but this was a mirror image of the Germans' claims, and all contemporary estimates tended to be large exaggerations.[161] They also reckoned that between 1 July 1916 and 15 October 1918 they had destroyed 6,361 enemy aircraft compared with France's 4,011,[162] and it does seem that the Germans sustained most damage in the British sector, in the battles of March–April and August–October, although the British air force was smaller than the French one and more of it was stationed elsewhere. At the time of the armistice 84 British squadrons were supporting the BEF, but 4 were in Italy, 13 in the Middle East, 10 with the Independent Force, 18 engaged in home defence, and others employed in anti-submarine warfare. The Western Front was the highest British priority, but far from overwhelmingly so, and the RAF destroyed 405 enemy machines in Italy, 59 in Salonika, and 81 in Palestine.[163] And everywhere in the final phases strafing retreating columns became characteristic, whether Bulgarian, Turkish, or Austrian. In Palestine on 21 September, for example, the RAF dropped 9.25 tons of bombs and fired 56,000 machine-gun rounds.[164]

Although aircraft production was a brand-new industry, Allied manufacturers – and until near the end, also German ones – continued to make good stunning losses. But whereas in 1917 all the Western Front belligerents had placed aircraft among their highest priorities, none hit their output targets. The French in 1918 achieved the world's largest output of aero-engines and the second largest (some authorities say the largest) of airframes, but even so they fell behind schedule.[165] The

British overtook them during the year in monthly airframe output, but the goal of doubling Britain's Western Front squadrons remained unaccomplished, owing to unexpectedly heavy losses, personnel and labour shortages, and mistakes in engine procurement.[166] The American air force proved smaller than either the Germans or the European Allies had expected, in good measure as a result of production failures. Yet on the other hand, although Germany's 'Amerika Programme' of June 1917, designed nearly to double monthly aircraft output before the Americans arrived in strength, delivered an increase, it too was less than planned. Over the year as a whole the Germans' enemies outbuilt them by more than two to one.[167] This effort behind the lines – short of target for the Allies but for Germany even more so – was the story behind the story of the air superiority that the Allies finally won in the last weeks of the war.

GAS

Airpower was ancillary to the effort on the ground. The Allied advances required fire as well as movement, and the most novel element in the 1918 bombardments was poison gas. The necessary technology had evolved astonishingly rapidly since the Germans had released chlorine from cylinders to be blown by the wind in April 1915. The tonnages now were vastly greater, the principal delivery method was via the artillery, and the highest casualties came from mustard gas (dichlorodiethyl sulphate: the French term, after Ypres, was *ypérite*; the British demotic was 'Hun Stuff' or 'HS'). Of the gas tonnage employed by all sides in the war 52 per cent was used in the final year, and of some 17,000 men who died from gas on the Western Front (about 3 per cent of the total fatalities in the theatre) about half did so in 1918.[168]

The Germans remained the pacesetters. During the war they released 52,000 tons of poison gas, their usage rising tenfold between 1915 and 1917 and nearly doubling again in 1918. In comparison France released 26,000 tons, Britain 14,000, Austria-Hungary 7,900, Italy 6,300, Russia 4,700, and the USA 1,000. Seventy per cent of the British, French, and German gas casualties occurred in 1918, but Germany's total for the year of 70,000 killed and wounded was much less than for its opponents: Britain 114,000, France 110,000, and the remarkably high US figure of 75,700.[169] Between July 1917 and June 1918 the Germans alone could mass-produce mustard gas, and this was symptomatic of their lead in chemical warfare, based on a larger and more diversified pre-1914 chemical industry than any of their opponents except the United States. Moreover, Ludendorff himself prescribed the maximum use of gas, in directives that the British captured, as did Geyer's 'The Attack in Positional Warfare'.[170] Geyer assisted Max Bauer, who was in charge of gas at OHL, and Fritz Haber, the head of the Kaiser Wilhelm research institute in Berlin who became the principal director of the German chemical warfare programme, had direct access to Ludendorff.[171]

Gas could be discharged from cylinders; via shells (from 1916); and from a projector, a type of light mortar, the British introducing the Livens Projector in April 1917 and the Germans copying it. German projectors wreaked havoc at Caporetto, where the Italians' masks were virtually useless. But on the Western Front, although the German projector was more accurate and had a greater range than the Livens, its projectile carried less than half the quantity and was less likely to achieve fatal concentrations.[172] It was also more expensive: whereas Livens had invented his device in order to kill Germans cheaply. The Germans used projectors less than the British and stopped altogether after June 1918.[173] Instead shells were pre-eminent for them, and the British estimated that Germany's gas shell output rose from 11,004,000 in 1917 to 18,696,000 in 1918.[174] Shells depended less than cylinder clouds on a favourable wind – making the timing of an offensive less subject to the weather – and Bruchmüller used them as a counter-battery weapon that required less accuracy than high explosive. They were integral to his colour coding arrangement known as *Buntkreuzschiessen*, or 'colour cross shooting'. It combined Yellow Cross shells, containing mustard gas, with Green Cross (diphosgene), and Blue Cross, an arsenic-based agent that was a sternutator, intended to irritate the nose and throat and force enemy soldiers to remove their masks, thus exposing them to lethal agents. In fact the colour cross system was so complex that the gunners resisted using it except for major set-piece attacks.[175] In addition, Blue Cross was largely ineffective, as the accompanying explosive was inadequate to pulverize the substance finely enough for it to be inhaled, and the millions of Blue Cross shells that the Germans manufactured proved a notable waste of resources.[176] In contrast diphosgene was many times more deadly than chlorine,[177] and mustard gas was a blistering agent that attacked the skin (especially where moist) and eyes, producing intense pain and temporary blindness: although rarely lethal in the first instance, it might disable its victims permanently. In 1918 the Germans added a charge of high explosive to their mustard shells, in order to reduce the warning time by eliminating the distinctive 'plop' when they detonated, although by doing so they reduced how much gas the shell could carry and by scattering the gas more widely they reduced its concentration. None the less, neither gas masks nor anything else (given that few protective suits were available) offered much help against it, and it lingered for days – and even weeks in cold and dry conditions. Because it contaminated the ground it drenched, it could not be fired in front of the infantry, instead being used to seal off the flanks of an attack while the less persistent Blue and Green Cross fell on the area straight ahead, which enabled the British to work out the direction of an advance.[178]

The greatest German success with gas shells came on the Chemin des Dames on 27 May 1918. Up to 50 per cent of the munitions fired were chemical – the highest proportion in any of the offensives – and they smothered the Allied artillery and panicked the infantry, while a favourable wind drove the cloud on ahead. But the initial victory on the Lys, too, owed much to gas, which helped scatter the Portuguese. Mustard was used particularly intensively in this battle, producing lines of blinded Allied servicemen at the casualty clearing stations (the subject of a famous photograph), and a Yellow Cross bombardment forced the Allies to abandon Armentières. When the Germans assaulted Mount Kemmel, a belt of mustard gas contamination cut off the defending garrison from reinforcement, although the same belt inhibited the attackers from proceeding further.[179] For 'Michael' the ground wind was less favourable, gas accounted for only a quarter of the shells fired along a much longer front, and its effectiveness was more doubtful.[180] None the less, it forced the defenders to wear masks for the first two hours, and mustard gas deluged the British stronghold of the Flesquières salient. In contrast, in the Battle of the Matz the French countered the gas shells by moving their artillery, while on 15 July not only did Bruchmüller use fewer gas shells but an unfavourable wind blew the vapour away from the French and towards the attackers.[181] On the Piave in June the Austrians fired 175,000 gas shells, but many were Blue Cross and did little harm to Italian forces, which since Caporetto had been issued with British respirators.[182] Gas bombardment, like other aspects of the Central Powers' offensive system, lost impetus in June and July.

The most important Allied countermeasures were defensive. The French by 1918 had replaced their hopelessly deficient M2 respirator by the ARC, which, however, was still outmatched by the British SBR (Small Box Respirator), the best design of the war. In addition the British Special Brigades, led by Charles Foulkes, the BEF's Director of Gas Services, attacked the Germans using cylinders and Livens Projectors, of which the BEF had 200,000 by March 1918. German troops much feared the latter, as prisoner testimony confirmed, for only twenty-five seconds after the warning ignition flash the descending canisters could fill trenches with lethal concentrations. These, however, were harassing attacks, conducted in quiet sectors between the main battles, often against units that were resting.[183] In the battles themselves while on the defensive the Allies could mount few big counter-attacks. Nor could they counter mustard with mustard. Although they quickly identified the substance the Germans were using, the British took much longer to evolve a cheap and efficient method of mass-producing it. Clemenceau made it a matter of the highest priority,[184] and the French first used mustard gas in June 1918; the British not until September. Hence a defensive weapon par excellence was unavailable to the Allies in their greatest need, while the tens of thousands of casualties wreaked by German mustard gas exacerbated their manpower crisis.

By contrast, when the Allies went forward, they faced an enemy who still possessed large quantities of gas shells. The Germans experienced some shortages by summer 1918, but not of mustard gas until the final weeks, when colour-coded firing was breaking down. As they retreated they fired off Blue Cross (which did little damage) and Yellow Cross (which did, for example at the Battle of Albert on 21–23 August, so that British gas casualties in August and September were among the highest ever). Now the Allies were on the move, their living accommodation was flimsier, and it was harder to take precautions. All the same, Foulkes had the impression that the Germans were disposing of their stocks at will, and they could have made more of their opportunities. In the final weeks the danger diminished, although AEF casualties from mustard gas were shockingly high. Even though the German gas attacks incapacitated tens of thousands of soldiers for weeks on end, Foulkes concluded that they did not significantly delay Allied progress.[185]

As against this, once the Allies regained the initiative they could plan their own big gas attacks, and more than previously they had the wherewithal. In most of the principal war gases, Germany out-produced them over the war as a whole:

Table 3.1. Gas production (million tons), 1914–18[186]

	Germany	Britain	France	US
Chlorine	58.1	20.8	12.4	2.4
Phosgene	18.1	1.4	15.7	1.4
Diphosgene	11.6	—	—	—
Chloropicrin	4.1	8.0	0.5	2.5

Yet although Britain and France did not mass-produce the relevant chemicals before the war, the British raised their chlorine production tenfold by 1918, and with phosgene the French did even better. The British never had enough of the latter, but the French supplied it to them, and the BEF used the less effective chloropicrin for its lethal agents.[187] By 1918 for the first time it had gas shells in the quantities and varieties that it needed, the weather and the tactical situation now becoming the main obstacles to using them.[188] Although the Allies never discharged mustard gas with such abandon as their enemies, the Germans had expected retaliation less quickly, and by this stage in the war they were hard pressed to replace contaminated boots and clothing.[189] Moreover, their gas mask, which since 1915 they had modified only marginally, was reaching its limits because of the size restrictions on the removable filter in its mouthpiece, and because Germany had run out of the rubber originally used for the valves and fabric and had to substitute leather. The mask became useless if worn for more than a few hours (unlike the SBR) and by 1918 the Allies could maintain lethal concentrations for longer periods. At Hamel on 4 July, the BEF's howitzers fired over 25,000 gas shells in a morning, silencing the German batteries and creating a barrier against a Cambrai-style counter-attack, while Foulkes's Special Brigades used Livens Projectors against the German guns on the adjoining heights. The French fired gas shells before their 18 July counter-attack at Villers-Cotterêts, and on 8 August both the British and French forces used them in the Battle of Amiens. Gas was employed mainly against the German batteries on the northern (left) flank of the advance, in the Cerisy valley, and it succeeded where high explosive could not have done, by filling a defile where the guns were sheltered out of the sight line. The massive British bombardment of the Hindenburg Line also used gas shells, including mustard gas – which it was hoped would clear before the infantry advance.[190] But towards the end the Allies used gas less, to spare French civilians, and because progress was too rapid to set up projectors. Gas shells formed a lower proportion of their munitions expenditure than of Germany's,[191] and although valuable at key moments, they were not essential to them. On other fronts – for example, Macedonia, where the 15 September bombardment used French gas shells – the same applied.

Had the fighting continued into 1919, matters would have been different. The Americans treated gas warfare extremely seriously. They created a Chemical Warfare Section (CWS) of the AEF with similar functions to the British Special Brigades, and manufactured gas in a brand-new plant at Edgewood near Baltimore, which they built extraordinarily quickly: the decision was taken in December 1917, and it entered production the following summer. The USA manufactured as much phosgene as Britain and twice as much mustard gas,[192] which the AEF first used on 1 November on the Meuse–Argonne. Mustard gas production by 1 May 1919 was projected to be 200 tons a day in the US, 100 in Britain, and 80 in France, whereas German daily tonnage averaged 14.[193] There were plenty of enthusiasts for mass destruction of the surviving Germans: Haig's GHQ regularly demanded more than the Ministry of Munitions could match, despite Winston Churchill's efforts as munitions minister to maximize output. Churchill told a conference on 19 March that he hoped to treble or quadruple production: 'If you could blot out thirty miles of the enemy's front in the middle of a great battle, might it not be a staggering blow to them ...?'[194] If the front had stabilized on the Antwerp–Meuse line, the temptation to break it by a massive gas assault would have been hard to resist. Foulkes impressed such views on a government sub-committee during the run-up to the armistice, and Haber and his circle knew that if the fighting had continued German defences would have been overwhelmed.[195]

FIREPOWER

This notwithstanding, for most of 1918 Germany had the edge in chemical weapons. The 'fire' component of the Allies' advantage in fire and movement came primarily from more traditional artillery technology, though much enhanced by wartime refinements. The German artillery revolution associated with Bruchmüller and Pulkowsky had its Allied counterpart, perhaps less trumpeted but no less effective. Its preconditions were transformations in gun and shell production, and in logistics. In the final weeks Allied gunners were struck by how their opponents' professionalism was deteriorating,[196] whereas by this stage France and Britain could sustain vastly higher levels of munitions consumption than four years previously, repair and replace their cannon and howitzers, and make good from stocks their losses during Ludendorff's offensives, while all the time equipping other armies besides their own. The origins of these changes reached back into the nineteenth century, when steel breech-loading cannon with rifled barrels had replaced iron or bronze smoothbore muzzle loaders, and smokeless high explosive had replaced brown powder as the propellant for the shell and as the charge inside it. The French 75 mm quick-firing field gun, developed in the 1890s, was fitted with a hydraulic piston that absorbed the recoil from the barrel, thus enabling it to be fired repeatedly without being re-layed, delivering up to twenty rounds per minute instead of the previous four. Other armies imitated it, introducing the 77 mm gun in Germany and the 18-pounder in Britain, and quick-firing spread to heavier calibres. Moreover, whereas in the American Civil War ranges of 1,000 yards were typical, by 1914 the British artillery could already fire at 5,000–10,000.[197]

After the fighting got bogged down and the belligerents ran into 'shell shortages', the manufacturing and logistical revolutions got under way. In the French army, the artillery almost tripled in personnel during the war, rising from 18 per cent to 36 per cent of total effectives. By 1918 two thirds of its guns were new or refurbished and one third of the field artillery was motor-drawn rather than horse-drawn. Whereas the number of field guns was similar to that in 1914, that of heavy guns had risen from 300 to nearly 5,000.[198] Similarly, in 1914 the BEF had only twenty-four guns firing shells of over 60 pounds (powerful enough to suppress enemy batteries), but by 1918 it had 2,000 medium and heavy howitzers, and for the first time possessed enough heavy artillery to launch major assaults at more than one point without redeploying the rest of the army's heavy guns to the attack sector.[199] In both armies expansion went alongside centralization. In the British army, the average number of guns available to support each infantry division rose from 68 to 100 in 1914–18, but the numbers actually controlled by a division fell from 76 to 48, the vastly increased number of larger-calibre weapons being assigned to corps and army commands.[200] The French heavier calibres, similarly, were assigned in spring 1918 to a Réserve générale de l'artillerie – partly tractor-drawn – that could be shuttled rapidly around the front.[201] Not only was there a huge increase in curved-trajectory weapons (howitzers and mortars), which were easier to fire from concealed positions and of greater value against earthworks, but shell charges shifted from shrapnel towards high explosive. The British 106 fuse, employed from 1917, detonated shells on impact with the ground rather than after being buried in it, so that they spread blast horizontally and better destroyed barbed wire. Indeed, some commentators felt the change had gone too far, and in the more mobile 1918 campaigning lighter calibres and shrapnel shells (of which the French army now found it had a shortage) again became relevant.[202]

Not only had the artillery's equipment been transformed, but also its tactics. Operating at much greater ranges against infantry concealed in trenches and enemy guns behind reverse slopes obliged the gunners to practise indirect rather than direct fire. Initially this meant guidance by forward observation officers – a notably hazardous occupation – who indicated whether ranging shots were falling short of or beyond the target. As the war progressed the task passed increasingly to balloons and aircraft, whose crews by 1917 could communicate with the ground by wireless in Morse code,[203] although they could not receive radio messages in return. Such work was slow and arduous, and impeded by poor wireless reception, German fighters, and the youth and inexperience of many aircrews. The most radical form of indirect fire was 'predicted shooting', i.e. firing at a map co-ordinate, which could be done without ranging shots. Its preconditions were precise knowledge of the target's co-ordinates and an accurate map of the combat zone, but another feature of the war was a revolution in cartography. When the British arrived on the Western Front their maps were wholly inadequate, but by 1917 their Third Army headquarters was issuing 1:10,000 plans of the two sides' trench systems that were updated daily. Between 1914 and 1918 the British army's surveyors prepared and distributed some 32 million maps and their French counterparts 30 million: the Germans even more.[204]

Maps were of little use unless prospective targets could be pinpointed. Aerial photography was the key to this development: by 1917, 90 per cent of British counter-battery observation was by aircraft linked to wireless.[205] Flash-spotting – tracing a gun by the flash from its muzzle – became less useful after the Germans started using flashless powders in 1917,[206] but sound-ranging remained invaluable. The necessary equipment (the Bull-Tucker set) was French in origin but perfected by the British in 1916, and the Americans put it into mass production. It used trigonometry and an array of microphones to locate a gun from the sound of the report when it fired. By 1918 several guns could be detected simultaneously, within minutes of their first shot. The Germans had a much cruder system, relying on individuals with stopwatches, and stood at a major disadvantage. Moreover, from 1917 every BEF corps headquarters established a counter-battery staff office (CBSO), which centralized intelligence and reported daily and weekly on the location of the enemy guns and drew up fire plans against them. Before 'Michael' the system worked poorly, owing to the silence of the German guns and Allied aircraft failing to spot them; but it lay behind the successes at Hamel and on 8 August, and the Germans, once again, lacked anything comparable.[207] By the eve of the Battle of Amiens the British had located 504 out of 530 German guns in the attack sector;[208] and they had four heavy guns (with ample ammunition) to train on each battery. The suppression of the German artillery resulted from painstaking work beforehand, to be repeated in later attacks.

The two obstacles halting Allied infantry in the middle years of the war were artillery and machine guns. If counter-battery fire addressed the first of these, the second were the target of the creeping barrage, which Bruchmüller may have copied from his enemies. The British experimented with it at Loos in 1915, and adopted it more generally during the Somme, from which time the French imitated them. The basic principle was for the assaulting infantry to follow as closely as possible behind an advancing bombardment, the casualties that might result from 'friendly fire' being lower than if the troops hung back until the defenders emerged from cover. By 1918 the creeping barrage was well-established practice, although debate continued about the most appropriate speed and mix of munitions. In the British barrages of the 'Hundred Days' between August and November, shrapnel was normally the largest element, but supplemented by high explosive, and by smoke shells to impede visibility. It had become easier to regulate them as the British and French armies had each developed wireless communication, and both were much better equipped with radio as well as telephone links than were the Germans.[209] A creeping barrage was no longer a single curtain of fire but several, designed to isolate the enemy front line and fend off counter-attacks, and Canadian practice – unlike German – was to go to the limit of the barrage but not beyond it.[210] German army assessments attributed the British victories of August and September not to the infantry but the superiority of the artillery, the creeping barrage, and the curtain of fire that impeded reinforcement.[211]

Creeping barrages were symptomatic of a change in doctrine, which mirrored developments on the German side. German guidelines also stressed counter-battery fire and the *Feuerwalze*, and that the artillery's objective was less 'complete annihilation and destruction, than shattering the enemy's morale'.[212] On the Allied side, the British attack at Messines ridge in June 1917 and the French one at La Malmaison in October, both successful operations by Western Front standards, had represented the acme of positional warfare. Pétain's 31 October 1917 general instruction, issued after the latter, still envisaged that the artillery should destroy the enemy's positions prior to the infantry advance. But in contrast his Directive No. 5 of 12 July 1918 stressed the opportunity for surprise against what were now much weaker German defences.[213] The French artillery had grown adept at indirect fire without registration and could lay down smaller, shorter bombardments of only a few hours, even at night or in bad weather. Guns pulled by tractors could arrive rapidly, and using lighter 75 mm and 105 mm pieces enabled lorries to carry more shells.[214] The BEF too altered its objective from destruction towards 'neutralization', abandoning as unrealistic the goal of obliterating the enemy defences, although this trend applied only up to a point.[215] At Cambrai in November 1917 the Third Army dispensed with registration altogether, the bombardment coinciding with the infantry and tank attack. On 8 August 1918 the bombardment started at 4.20 and the attack at 4.24 a.m. Even so the British did not rely purely on surprise and hurricane bombardments, and before the attack on the Hindenburg Line – when they knew they could not conceal their intentions – the weight of munitions was formidable. By now the BEF could calculate the scale of bombardment needed, and its estimates were vindicated, as its 106 fuses cut the wire, its counter-battery fire (using twice the weight of heavy shell as on 8 August) was much more accurate than two years previously and included mustard gas, and it was no longer true as in 1916 that 30 per cent of the rounds fired were duds.[216] In short, the Allies combined neutralization of improvised positions with efficient destruction of established ones, both driving back the Germans in open country and dislodging them when they chose to make a stand. And although the American bombardments on the Meuse–Argonne were to begin with much less successful, during October 1918 the AEF too – at least at divisional level – adopted similar methods.[217]

The transformation of the artillery was accompanied by developments in infantry equipment, which commentators have insufficiently emphasized. By 1918 both sides were struggling to maintain their infantry units at anything like regulation numbers, but those units' firepower had multiplied. German machine-gun production jumped from 7,200 in 1915 to 21,600 in 1916 and 104,000 in 1917: by late 1917 it was double the Hindenburg Programme targets, and each machine-gun company could be equipped with twelve heavy machine guns and each infantry company with three to six light ones. The arrival of light machine guns after 1914 profoundly influenced infantry tactics. Portable firepower (meaning the MG08/15 light weapon) was essential to the tactical conception of the Ludendorff offensives and in summer 1918 Ludendorff increased light-machine-gun provision in consideration of the first round of experience, as well as distributing more rifle grenades.[218] In 1914 French divisions each had twenty-four heavy machine guns but by the armistice the figure was 128, plus 215 lighter and portable Chauchat/CSRG *fusils-mitrailleurs*; during 1918 the number of machine guns per regiment rose from twenty-four to thirty-six, and the men were also equipped with rifle grenades and Stokes mortars. French infantry companies were reorganized in autumn 1917 on the basis of 'combat groups' using grenade throwers and light machine guns to seize German positions once the barrage lifted.[219] Similarly in the BEF specialized bombing and rifle grenade sections disappeared in 1918 in favour of all-purpose platoons using hand and rifle grenades and mortars, advancing in skirmishing waves followed by columns, best tactical practice during the Hundred Days being for the platoon to advance in a 'blob' or 'diamond' formation, without worrying about exposed flanks. In 1917–18 the air-cooled Lewis gun, also known as the automatic rifle, became more common and to some extent supplanted the heavy water-cooled Vickers gun that many front-line troops thought a superior weapon. By 1918 Lewis gunners numbered two in a platoon (of thirty-six men), and the guns could be fired from the hip during an attack; alongside rifle grenades and trench mortars they were a crucial weapon against enemy machine guns and strongpoints. British infantry and artillery had become skilled in operating together, encircling enemy machine-gun posts and fortified villages before overrunning them by surprise bombardments and flank attacks in dispersed order, often under cover of darkness, in a way that neither arm could have accomplished in 1916.[220] Not the least of the Canadians' advantages was that of all the British army units they were most heavily armed. Canadian divisions were bigger than British ones – 21,000 men on average compared with 15,000 – and in May 1918 a Canadian division had one automatic weapon per thirteen soldiers, whereas a British division had one per sixty-one. The machine-gun battalion attached to each Canadian division was more than three times larger than its British counterpart,[221] and heavy-machine-gun barrages to accompany the artillery became characteristic of Canadian tactics. Some troops thought such barrages were wasteful, but they symbolized the plenitude of Allied supply. The British and French drove back a depleted German army with prodigious expenditure of small-arms ammunition and shells.[222]

TANKS

It is time to shift from the fire to the movement element in the equation. Traditionally the cavalry had most obviously supplied the latter, but during the war the significance of horsemen in most armies had sorely diminished. Since 1914 the German army had first moved its cavalry from the Western to the Eastern Front and then dismounted most of them, partly because of tactical experience and partly because of shortages of fodder and horses, which were needed in priority to draw artillery. Cavalry played a negligible role in Ludendorff's offensives.[223] The French in contrast still maintained two cavalry corps, each comprising three cavalry divisions, backed up by sappers and lorry-borne infantry. They used them for rapid reinforcement during the defensive phase, but when the Second Cavalry Corps was ordered up on 18 July it had great difficulty in making its way to the front line and then fought dismounted, making such slow progress that it was withdrawn.[224] In the BEF, which expanded much faster than its Continental counterparts, no new regular cavalry regiments were created and the existing ones stayed the same size, with the result that the cavalry shrank from 9.28 to 2.77 per cent of the army's combat strength between September 1914 and September 1917. It too played a limited but useful role during the March retreat, and was much more successful on 8 August than its French counterparts had been a month earlier. It continued to be used in more dispersed formations during the final advance. Except at Megiddo, however, where cavalry was essential to Allenby's tactics, it played only a minor and supplementary role in the Allied victories.[225] Instead, the most glaring novelty of the 1918 battlefields was the presence, en masse, of tanks.

A debate about their contribution existed at the time and has continued since. For all the hullabaloo that surrounded tanks (in Britain they were displayed on 'tank days' to sell war bonds), they too were useful rather than essential to Allied success. They were never used in Italy, although the French sent the Italians seventy-five and the latter were building 1,500 Renault-model light tanks in the autumn of 1918, which would have come into service in the spring.[226] A few tanks were used in Macedonia, and eight saw action in the Gaza battles of March and November 1917, though they were not employed in Palestine again.[227] If fighting had continued for another year the picture might have altered, but only the Western Front possessed both appropriate terrain and the very considerable infrastructure needed to keep 1918-style tanks operational.

Tanks were used mainly by France and Britain. Neither Germany nor the United States – despite possessing the largest mechanical engineering industries of the day – caught up with the leaders. Tanks formed part of Pershing's plans, but the AEF's tank corps (formed in June 1918) achieved little. One reason was the spring 1918 decision to rush infantry and machine gunners across the Atlantic, at the expense of other army branches. A second reason was production failure. In October a British representative in America reported to the Tank Board in London: 'Anglo-American Programme in hopeless condition here': engine gears were not under manufacture, armour plate supplies were 'chaotic', conditions in the factories 'very unsatisfactory', and the US Army's Chief Ordnance Officer was 'very disappointed'; nor without drastic action would American-produced tanks be available in spring 1919.[228] The US government placed orders in 1918 for 4,800 tanks, but the automobile industry (which remained wedded to civilian production) failed to deliver them. Output of 'Liberty' engines, a much heralded wartime design, was disappointing, and went in priority to aircraft. The French government contracted in November 1917 for America to build 1,200 Renault tanks, but in fact it built 150, of which twenty reached France by the armistice.[229] Hence the AEF got its machines from France and Britain.[230] The 301st American Tank Battalion served with the BEF and drove British tanks: during the 29 September attack on the Hindenburg Line it ran into a British minefield and twenty-four out of thirty-four tanks became casualties.[231] But the main American force served with the AEF and drove French-built Renault models. At Saint-Mihiel over 100 were deployed under Colonel George S. Patton, with a mixture of French and American crews, but they were snarled in traffic jams and on the first day the infantry went ahead of them, while on the second many ran out of petrol. They also fought in the Meuse–Argonne offensive, but intermittently and in smaller groups. After the first phase they were withdrawn and their numbers so reduced that only sixteen took part in the final general attack on 1 November. The infantry had not been trained to work with them, and the outcome was disappointment.[232]

Although British tanks were the first to see action, the French fleet was at least as numerous, and the two countries' tank projects originated independently. They had champions – Colonel Jean Estienne in France and Lieutenant-Colonel Ernest Swinton and Winston Churchill in Britain – who persevered while tanks remained unproven and divisive in the two countries' military-bureaucratic establishments. According to Major Hugh Elles, for months after he took up his post as the commander of the Royal Tank Corps in 1917–18, 'troops of other arms were divided into two parties – those who believed, and some passionately, in the possibility of the tanks and those who disbelieved entirely', and it was well into the middle of 1918 before more balanced appraisals became possible.[233] In Germany, in contrast, such champions were lacking, and in any case tanks were less relevant while the army stood on the defensive in the west and campaigned most successfully in the swampy Polish plains and the mountains of Southern Europe.

It was as well that tanks had champions, because at least until summer 1918 their contribution was patchy and small. GHQ and GQG endorsed them, but as infantry support devices, not as the mass breakthrough and pursuit forces that their more visionary proponents advocated. Even in a more modest capacity they had many deficiencies. The Mark V (the standard 1918 British tank) had a maximum speed of 4.6 mph and an average speed of 3 mph. Its radius of action was twenty-five miles. The Schneider and Saint-Chamond French medium tanks had similar speeds and endurances.[234] Tanks were thirsty – British ones consumed up to twelve gallons of petrol per mile – and supply officers were unconvinced that their calls on fuel and lubricant were justified.[235] They were prone to breakdown, on the road and in action, and suffered from component shortages, delivery of complete vehicles being more profitable and creating more impressive headlines than did replenishing stocks. During 1918 up to half the French tanks were out of service – though mostly reparable – for lack of parts.[236] Tanks had to move to the relevant sector by rail (on average twelve per train), and only for the final stage could they 'trek' across country, normal practice by summer 1918 being for them to form up by night in woodland while aircraft drowned the engine noise. The armour indeed protected the crews against machine-gun fire, but a field gun shell could easily put tanks out of action, the splinters ricocheting round the cabin and often igniting the vehicle. The early crews – in Britain commonly cavalrymen or civilians – were highly motivated, and needed to be, as conditions in the combat zone were almost unendurable. Not only was visibility inside and outside restricted, but the sweltering cabin was filled with petrol and carbon monoxide fumes, and the noise so loud that the occupants could neither hear each other nor the battle outside. Bullets hitting the tank's shell produced a 'splash' of red-hot shavings against which men had to wear chain mail masks (sometimes on top of gas masks), while the machine pitched up and down in imitation of a rough sea crossing. A few hours of such conditions were the maximum tolerable. However, the technology improved. The Mark V had double the endurance of the

Mark IV and needed just one man instead of four to drive and steer it, and lighter and faster vehicles were coming on stream. The British 'Whippet' (Medium Mark A) had a crew of three (compared with eight in the Mark V) and could reach 8.3 mph, although it was shorter (twenty feet) and could cross only a narrow trench, and carried machine guns rather than cannon. The French FT17 (usually known as a Renault, after the firm that designed it) was a remarkable vehicle with machine guns or a small cannon in a rotating turret. It was light enough to be transported by road. A mixture of the heavier and lighter models (and in the British case armoured cars) took part in the final advance.

Until the turning point of June–July 1918, tanks did little to justify the hopes placed in them. When the French attacked the Chemin des Dames ridge on 16 April 1917, 121 Schneider and Saint-Chamond tanks left the starting line but 76 were lost – 57 as a result of enemy action, of which 35 were set ablaze. They were deployed more cautiously at La Malmaison, when many broke down and their contribution was overshadowed by the artillery bombardment. Pétain's watchword was that 'We must wait for the Americans and the tanks', but for both he had to wait a long time. In September 1917 he had ordered 3,000 Renaults, but as of 21 March 1918 only one was in service. The reasons included design difficulties with the turret, and armour plate from Britain being rejected as unsuitable. The French still had 245 Schneiders and 222 Saint-Chamonds, but many had been cannibalized for spare parts and although some were concentrated in Picardy in April they played little part against the first three German offensives.[237] Similarly, British tanks were used in small numbers and with modest success as infantry support weapons on the Somme in 1916 and at Arras in 1917 but in the Third Ypres quagmire they were useless. The massed attack at Cambrai in November 1917 achieved surprise on a quiet and unshelled sector, but the tanks soon showed their vulnerability to enemy artillery, and when the enemy counter-attacked dozens were captured. Haig and GHQ did not oppose tanks in principle (and wanted more of them), but they were more sceptical than the Tank Corps enthusiasts, Hugh Elles and J. F. C. Fuller, and all agreed that tanks had limited value in defensive warfare as they could not hold ground, so were useful mainly for raids and counter-attacks.[238] Before 'Michael' the BEF positioned them in a lozenge-shaped area west of Amiens, and 180 of the 370 available went into action on 21 March, but they were too dispersed to have much impact and many wore out without firing a shot. After the first few days, and during the Lys battle, the tanks had little role and their crews fought in the open as Lewis gunners. Indeed in February and April GHQ attempted to reduce the Tank Corps and to prevent Mark Vs from being shipped. [239]

After June more tanks became available, and they were used differently. The Renaults finally arrived in substantial numbers, and on 31 May twenty-one took part in a successful counter-attack against the German advance towards the Marne.[240] From now on tanks – though at first still the older medium models – were used in most big French operations, starting with the 11 June counter-attack on the Matz. This enterprise was remarkable for the speed with which it was undertaken, and the tanks made the speed possible. After being moved up by rail they travelled 12–14 kilometres during the night before 60 Schneiders and 103 Saint-Chamonds went into action. The infantry advance soon paused and left the forward machines exposed, 73 being put out of service and 15 seriously damaged in loss rates comparable to those of the Nivelle offensive.[241] None the less, the counter-attack halted the Germans, and it provided a model for the bigger counterstroke on 18 July, when again the tanks moved up during the night before emerging from woodland at dawn. Again they helped to suppress the machine guns and to scatter the defenders, and this time they advanced much further, but the attrition rates were phenomenal. According to Fuller, on 18 July 102 out of 225 tanks that fought with the French Tenth Army were hit; on 19 July 50 out of 105; and on 20 July 17 out of 32. Taking the French forces together between 18 and 27 July, 185 Schneider, 190 Saint-Chamond, and 585 Renault tanks were engaged; and 149 of the medium and 124 of the lighter ones were seriously damaged, while 891 of their crews became casualties. These losses were so punishing that the tanks were withdrawn.[242]

Summer 1918 was also the heyday of British massed attacks. By July the Tank Corps had made good its spring losses, taken delivery of new Mark V and Whippet machines, and received new crews, while the Allies' recovery of the initiative created plausible opportunities to use them, GHQ reassuring the Corps that 'there is no intention of employing tanks for small local enterprises and that there is a definite and general plan'.[243] The Hamel operation on 4 July was the debut for the Mark Vs, sixty of which advanced in two waves behind a smokescreen and a rolling barrage after moving up under cover of aircraft noise and – unusually – reaching the start point in time. Whereas they had been scheduled to follow the infantry they actually ran ahead of them, overrunning the German first defence line and crushing the machine gun posts, and economizing both on shells and on infantry lives.[244]

As the 11 June French attack set the mould for that on 18 July, so did Hamel for the Battle of Amiens. Because of their shock effect upon the German high command, the tanks' role on 18 July and 8 August was their most important single contribution to the Allies' overall victory, although even without them both operations would have been successes. On 8 August the Allies had superiority in aircraft, artillery, and infantry, and attacked scratch positions with the BEF's finest Dominion units. They also achieved surprise – and to this the tanks contributed by making it possible to delay the creeping barrage until the attack moved off. Rawlinson, whose Fourth Army proposed and planned the battle, was a moderate tank enthusiast,[245] as indeed was Foch. Rawlinson wanted a substantial tank deployment in order to reduce losses; while the Tank Corps wanted and were allowed to use over 400 vehicles, almost all the total available.[246] This operation too was planned quickly but exceptionally efficiently, the tanks as usual moving up by rail before gathering under cover of darkness and advancing over excellent open terrain in the early mist. When the Germans witnessed the machines bearing down on them, their bewilderment encouraged the mass surrenders that were such a feature of the day. The tanks helped most in the opening phases when they silenced the machine guns, especially those in the second line as the infantry moved beyond the artillery barrage. French tanks were used in the parallel French attack to the south, and Whippets and armoured cars were able to range behind the German lines, harassing communications and command posts. But as visibility improved many tanks again fell victim to the enemy field guns, even in what might seem optimal conditions. More than two thirds of the tanks in action between 8 and 11 August were handed over to salvage. The figure overstates their vulnerability, however, as the damage was usually reparable and because the Allies were advancing the vehicles could be recovered. Many vehicles were immobilized by breakdowns or by lack of parts, or because their crews needed a breathing space: and although the Tank Corps suffered 700 casualties in the battle, between August and November some of its members went into action up to fifteen times.[247]

This mattered because although the BEF never used tanks so massively again, many were soon back in service and the French and British engaged them repeatedly. During the battles in Picardy after 8 August the French engaged over 100 tanks; in the fighting in the Argonne and Champagne between 26 September and 8 October no fewer than 852; in Flanders during October 181. They were used in smaller groups and increasingly they were Renaults, whose loss rates were lower than for the older models and whose repair times were shorter. At the time of the armistice, Pétain still had 2,700 light tanks in line.[248]

The British experience was similar. After the Battle of Amiens the War Office was concerned about casualties, and on 1 September Haig's Chief of Staff, Lawrence, warned that tank attacks had 'led to losses in this arm which were not compensated by the results attained'. He directed that they should be used only for surprise assaults against the main enemy line, and withdrawn immediately afterwards; they should be supported by artillery; and not frittered away against outposts.[249] GHQ ordered that 'no further minor operations with Tanks are to be carried out', and its new guidelines on 'Tanks and their Employment in Co-operation with Other Arms' stressed tanks' role not as independent spearheads but in infantry support. They saved infantry lives; but they themselves needed protection, and tanks, artillery, and infantry (and increasingly aircraft) should function in combination.[250] Now reserved for major operations, 183 tanks saw action in the Battle of Albert on 21 August; 81 during the Canadian attack on the Drocourt–Quéant Switch on 2 September; 181 in the Fourth Army assault on the Hindenburg Line on 29 September; 48 in the Battle of the Selle on 17 October; and 37 in the Battle of the Sambre on 4 November. Reviewing the situation at this point, Elles noted that resistance from the German artillery had stiffened and that from 8 August to 20 October 830 British tanks had become casualties, although over 300 had been repaired and reissued and 500 had been salvaged, with the upshot that only about 50 had been lost for good.[251] In the final stages, however, German resistance again diminished, though precisely because Allied progress now accelerated the tanks became less usable, as less time existed to plan assaults or move them up by rail, and there were fewer trains to convey them. Although the Whippets could travel on lorries, the Mark Vs had to crawl along the roads, which wore out both tanks and roads all the faster.[252]

The Tank Corps considered that its vehicles had been successful in almost all the operations they took part in during the Hundred Days, Haig writing that their contribution 'can scarcely be exaggerated'.[253] Undoubtedly they had helped to overrun the successive German positions, lower infantry casualties, and raise morale: the Mark V stood over eight feet tall, and even if soldiers could not ride inside it as had been intended, because they felt so ill, they could advance behind it as the machine-gun bullets bounced off. But the mass deployment on 8 August was exceptional, and the Hindenburg Line was breached by infantry crossing a fortified canal with intensive artillery backing while the tank-assisted attack on their left flank failed. Tanks lost some of their value in the concluding semi-open warfare, for which the heavier models had never been designed, although armoured cars could scout and raid behind the increasingly porous enemy front. At the time of the armistice the picture was mixed. The American Tank Corps had had to be withdrawn from the Meuse–Argonne and re-engaged in smaller numbers, while the British Tank Corps, according to Elles, had only one company still operational, and Fuller admitted that the crews were 'exhausted'. Both services needed a pause; although the French, with Renaults pouring off the assembly lines, were preparing a new mass assault in Lorraine.[254]

Had the campaigning continued into spring 1919, more tanks would have been available. A longstanding plan for mass production in an Anglo-American plant at Châteauroux was coming to fruition.[255] Though intended to come on stream on 1 August 1918 it was not ready until October. Its target was 300 'Liberty' heavy tanks per month, the first 600 going to the AEF, but thereafter providing the Allies with a successor to the Mark V. The British were working independently on a Mark VIII in Glasgow, but it was mired in production difficulties, trials showing that it was too heavy for its tracks. None the less, their programme was for 1,152 heavy tanks (Mark V** and Mark VIII) and 576 lighter ones (the 'Medium C'), although British schedules had a habit of not being met.[256] Indeed in April 1918 the War Cabinet had created an inter-departmental Tank Board to knock heads together and accelerate production and bring on new types, Lloyd George personally wishing it success. GHQ in October 1918 wanted 4,000 tanks for the spring, and in the same month tanks and gas occupied joint first place in the munitions ministry's labour and steel priorities.[257] In France the programme was for 7,000 light tanks by March 1919, together with lorries to carry them. Plans for a new heavy tank were held up by raw-material shortages, despite Pétain warning that one was desperately needed.[258] The most likely scenario is that by spring 1919 the Allies would have had many more light tanks and some more heavy ones, although they would still have been short of components and crews. Ambitious projects were afoot to use the vehicles more boldly, although Fuller's 'Plan 1919' (of May 1918) has attracted too much attention. Fuller envisaged an enormous long-range force that could pierce the enemy lines and roam at will behind them: Henry Wilson sent a modified version to Foch and Haig (proposing a surprise attack by 10,500 tanks in summer 1919 on a front of eighty kilometres), but Foch did little with it and Haig's response is unknown.[259] In any case Fuller's notions of tanks plying the land as freely as could ships the sea went far beyond the capabilities of the era, and Wilson's numbers exceeded what the Allies could manufacture. If fighting had continued into 1919, the Allies would have had more and improved machines, and they could have started the season with fresh mass attacks, but the difference would have been incremental.

What matters most in judging the tanks' contribution is less the Allies' self-perceptions than the impact on the enemy. The Germans had neglected them, and their partners never had them at all. Although pre-war German agriculture had not used caterpillar-tracked vehicles, the technicalities of design and construction should have been within the grasp of German engineers, despite the wartime fuel, oil, and metal shortages. But as the defending party on the Western Front, the Germans had less tactical incentive to develop such a device, and they lacked military entrepreneurs who were willing to push it. Even when the war ministry began work on a prototype after the British introduced tanks in 1916, the project proceeded slowly. German designers rejected the British model as too heavy and with tracks that were insufficiently protected, but had trouble devising an alternative. Nor would the OHL place tanks in its highest priority category, Ludendorff being unimpressed by a demonstration and noting the indifferent Allied tank performances during 1917. Tanks competed with lorries – of which the Germans were desperately short – and for engines they competed with aircraft.[260] After Cambrai a reassessment began, and the OHL planned to use tanks in its spring offensives. The British feared they would enter mass production, and Elles foresaw that the Allies would lose their lead.[261] In fact, the Germans had captured sixty-three usable British tanks at Cambrai and by spring 1918 they had a machine of their own, the A7V, though only some twenty were ever built. A cumbersome device with a crew of twelve, it was armed with a 1.57 mm cannon and six machine guns and could reach 5 mph on level ground, but had a range of only sixteen miles. It was poor at crossing trenches and overcoming obstacles, and had mediocre armour, so that its occupants suffered from 'splash' and artillery could easily disable it. Although arguably superior to the French heavy tanks, it was not to the Mark V.[262] In total the German tanks – A7Vs and British machines with black crosses painted on them – saw action some nine times, but their small numbers (and mediocre crews) meant operations such as 8 August were never conceivable. Tanks were used on 21 March – and made much of in the German press – and most prominently in the 24 April attack at Villers-Bretonneux. The opening of this operation suggested Allied infantry could also be shaken by tank attacks, although in the later stages during the first ever tank against tank battle the Germans knocked out two British machines but retreated after their lead tank was lost. The British were reassured, as they captured an A7V and were unimpressed.[263] Indeed the Germans themselves were so dissatisfied with it that they suspended production.[264] German tanks were also used in the Chemin des Dames attack on 27 May (where a large trench in the second French defensive system halted them), but in general their shortcomings reduced the force of the spring offensives. During the summer and autumn, they were committed only episodically, fifteen captured tanks being sent against the British on 8 October but two being knocked out.[265] After 8 August the OHL finally overcame its scepticism, and ordered 670 light tanks with a view to having 4,000 by the end of 1919. It also ordered a new heavy tank, though by the armistice this was still not even a prototype. If the war had continued, Germany would have acquired light tanks to fight the Allied ones, but the latter's edge in numbers would have persisted.[266]

Essentially the OHL woke up too late, and it was also slow to develop new anti-tank technology. Tanks themselves were not nearly mobile enough to serve as an anti-tank weapon. But experience showed that infantry weapons and artillery could be effective at close range. The Germans developed a new 13 mm single-shot gun and hastily distributed it in spring 1918, but its projectile proved too light. Hence the main riposte was field gun fire, directed from ranges of 500–1,000 yards and at great risk to the crews. During their retreat the Germans also experimented with minefields, and situated their positions along water lines, specifically as an anti-tank obstacle: an indication of how important 'tank fright' was becoming.[267]

Tanks loomed large in German military justifications for the decision to seek an armistice. Although the circumstances of 18 July and 8 August were not repeated on such a scale, the OHL feared they might be and felt it had no answer, and the element of intelligence failure and the unpredictable helped to break Ludendorff's nerve. On 11 August he blamed tank surprise for the Amiens disaster, and in October General Wrisberg of the war ministry said the same to Reichstag deputies, a radio broadcast by the war minister contending that tanks were chiefly responsible for the Allies' superiority.[268] Private briefings – for example, to the Bavarian attaché in Berlin – took the same line. It was admitted that after Cambrai the Allied tanks had been underestimated, while 8 August had shown that a massed attack in fog could panic even good infantry, and the artillery could not compensate.[269] Yet the sudden prominence of this argument raises the suspicion that its purpose was to divert attention from the OHL's deeper errors of judgement. The German front-line troops learned how to inflict enormous damage on tank forces, and compelled the Allies to deploy them more cautiously. The 8 August battle was a combined-arms success rather than one for the tanks alone, and tanks were less central to the crucial September triumphs in Macedonia and on the Hindenburg Line. These victories resulted from much wider sources of Allied superiority, underpinned by a greatly enhanced supporting infrastructure of battlefield transport and logistics.

LOGISTICS

In this latter sphere too the 1918 Western Front occupied a transition point. Essential to the nineteenth-century military revolution had been the use of railways for mobilization and concentration at the outset of hostilities: undertakings that in 1914 were vastly greater than in 1870. But once the soldiers left the frontier railheads, they had to march, their equipment being drawn by mules and horses, and only rarely (apart from in the BEF) being carried by lorries. And in the world of 1914–18, as Geoff Dyer has put it with deceptive simplicity, everything *weighed more* than it does today: plastics had yet to supplant iron and wood.[270] Twentieth-century urban dwellers transposed to open fields travelled like Victorian explorers and brought many more appurtenances than their predecessors, while their weapons devoured ammunition. Not only defensive firepower but also the sheer intractability of moving and supplying modern armies brought operations so quickly to a standstill. By 1918 the BEF needed 32.25 million pounds of forage, 67.5 million of meat, 90 million of breadstuffs, and 13 million gallons of fuel each month.[271] Standard-gauge lines could move huge masses of men and material reliably and quickly in almost all weathers, but they were inflexible instruments, and it was no accident that the Western Front stabilized between two great east–west lateral railway systems. The German trunk line ran from Thionville and Metz via Sedan and Méz-ières towards Lille and Flanders; its Allied counterpart from Nancy via Paris to Amiens and the Channel. Much of the 1918 campaigning cen-tred on a struggle for control of these systems, but with the difference from 1914 that motorized road transport was assuming comparable significance. Moreover, the military railway networks were extensions of larger networks in the hinterlands, which were crumbling after years of overload and neglect. The story of transport at the fronts formed one portion of the story of the war economies behind them.

If the Allies had superior resources on paper, many of those resources were in the wrong place: far away in overseas empires or the US. The Central Powers formed a smaller and more compact territorial bloc that benefited from interior lines of communication, and before the war the Germans had run one of the world's finest railway networks. By 1918 the conquests in Belgium, France, and Russia had enlarged it by 40 per cent, and supplying the defence of Passchendaele had taxed it.[272] None the less, it was resilient enough to support the prodigious effort of pre-paring for 'Michael'. Three east–west trunk lines transported forty-two divisions from the Eastern to the Western theatre between November 1917 and March 1918.[273] Whereas 6,591 trains had served the Fourth Army sector in Flanders between July and November 1917, 10,400 full trains ran into the new attack sector between 15 February and 20 March, and in the final phase some 345 per day.[274] Between January and October 1918 the Germans made 566 divisional movements on the Western Front, and between March and October munitions trains averaged more than 1,000 per month.[275] Although the trains ran more slowly than they once had done, the 'Michael' concentration delivered the essential quantities of men and stores to the attack front, and did so – just – on schedule. The problem was what would happen next.

The German army had an acute and worsening horse shortage, and motor vehicles could not fill the gap. Horses were fundamental for all the armies: not, as in the stuff of stereotype, because of obsolete beliefs in cavalry – in the French and German armies mounted troops largely served on foot by 1918 – but as draught animals. A horse needed about ten times as much to eat as did a man, and fodder was one of the largest categories of BEF supply.[276] In 1914 the German army had impressed 615,000 horses; it imported more from Germany's neutral neighbours, and took others from France and Belgium. But although the army's horse stock grew by 80 per cent between 1914 and 1917, its manpower rose by 140 per cent, and dismounting the cavalry made little difference, while over the same period Germany's total horse numbers fell by 30 per cent. Despite being constantly subjected to arduous and dangerous tasks, horses had their rations cut in the second half of the war, while veterinary care deteriorated and the troops increasingly lacked the knowledge and training needed to care for them. Two thirds of the German army's losses – 215,000 animals in 1917 alone – were due to illness, especially mange, for which the authorities had no remedy.[277] In addition the army estimated that 83,384 horses died from exhaustion due to undernourishment between July 1917 and May 1918, materially reducing the OHL's 'freedom of decision': in October 1917 the army was 8.3 per cent below its regulation strength in horses, and another 5 per cent were ill.[278] The 1917 oat harvest was even poorer than for other cereals, and on 8 October the war ministry reported that stocks were barely half the army's needs and the 'situation is untenable'. The daily fodder supply fell to 3 kilograms – half the regulation quantity – and according to the German official history, 'the horse stock and its preservation may have been the OHL's heaviest anxiety'. Ludendorff supported a cash incentive to oats growers, warning the finance ministry that horse shortages would endanger the army's readiness for the coming battles and 'The position is critical.'[279] The crisis became public knowledge, and Allied observers were well aware of it.[280] In 1918 the Ukraine delivered

140,000 horses, which Ludendorff said on its own justified occupying the country, but it gave no help with fodder,[281] and the problem was managed by providing only seventy of the German army's 240 divisions fully with horses, many others (especially in the east) being condemned to immobility. On the eve of 'Michael' the OHL appealed to the government for more fodder, and received a very modest increase, but the attacking divisions were warned to expect no more animals to replace those lost.[282]

The first two German offensives crossed territory where initially only men and horses could move at all – the old Somme battlefield and the Lys marshes. The Chemin des Dames terrain was better, though the ridge's steep slopes added to the wear and tear on the lorries. But in any case the army simply had too little motor transport, and nor could light railways – which the Germans had relied on during the period of attrition warfare – be pushed forward fast enough. OHL had given priority to producing lorries over tanks, and on 21 March the army had 23,000, but owing to Germany's rubber shortage most had steel tyres and hence were unsuitable for off-road work and rutted the roads still faster, while fuel shortages further hobbled them.

Before the war Germany had imported over 90 per cent of its oil requirements. Stockpiles accounted for one tenth of the country's wartime consumption, and two small domestic fields for another tenth. But this left an enormous shortfall, and neither Russia nor the USA (before 1914 the two biggest oil producers) were accessible. Nor could useful quantities be extracted from coal and lignite. Between 1915 and 1917 Germany's oil consumption doubled, and for the first three years the main supply source was a small and antiquated field in Austrian Galicia, which also provided for the Dual Monarchy and Bulgaria. Almost half of Galicia's wartime production went to Germany, but in 1918 its output fell and Romania's overtook it.[283] As the Central Powers overran Romania in November–December 1916 a British mission under the swashbuckling Colonel John Norton-Griffiths MP had wrecked the installations, destroying seventy refineries and 800,000 tons of petroleum products with sledgehammers, explosives, and fire. Romanian output had more than halved, and in 1918 was still not fully restored, although the Bucharest peace treaty gave Germany a ninety-year lease on the wells and created a distribution monopoly in which Germany would have a 56 per cent interest, Austria-Hungary 24 per cent, and

Romania only 20 per cent. Similarly, the August 1918 Russo-German supplementary agreements included a provision for facilitating supplies to Germany of oil from Baku, but although the Turks fleetingly occupied Baku, it never delivered petroleum to the Central Powers' armies.[284]

Meanwhile the intensive 1918 fighting increased Germany's requirements. When the war ended the navy still had several months' fuel for the U-boats and six for its (relatively few) oil-burning surface vessels, but German aviation had enough for only two months. Nor was fuel the only issue: from the middle of the war road vehicles and railway rolling stock were short of lubricant. In all the Central Powers civilian consumption of oil products fell drastically: in Germany by 1917 to one fifth of peacetime levels and in the winter of 1918–19 prospectively to one twentieth, so that the country was reverting to being a pre-oil economy.[285] Even before Bulgaria surrendered, a 'very serious position in the fuel question' was expected for spring 1919, and the Bulgarian armistice raised the imminent danger of Allied forces interposing themselves across the transport routes from Romania. On 19 October 1918 the army reported to the Chancellor that its aircraft depended entirely on Romanian oil production and had reserves only for another two months; as did one half of its lorries and one third of the U-boats.[286] The upshot was that the German army could never fully use even the lorries that it did possess. Although its railways delivered basic munitions and supplies – at least until October 1918 – it could fire more easily than it could move.

It is unsurprising that Ludendorff's offensives lost impetus because of supply difficulties. Moreover, his opponents' infrastructure was superior. The BEF relied on the Compagnie du Nord, which in peacetime was one of the best-performing French railway lines. But by 1916 the Nord could no longer service unaided the BEF's requirements. During the Somme offensive, it became evident that capacity was inadequate, and over the subsequent winter a wagon shortage threatened paralysis.[287] Lloyd George sent out Sir Eric Geddes, the former deputy general manager of the North-Eastern Railway, who became the BEF's first Director-General of Transport. Accompanying him, an influx of civilian experts imported management tools such as statistical forecasting.[288] The government agreed to Geddes's requests for huge investments in the supply lines, and between December 1916 and December 1918 the cranes at the BEF's ports increased from 121 to 314, nearly all of the additions coming from Britain. Handling capacity rose by 50 per cent, and between January 1917 and July 1918 the number of vessels discharged trebled.[289] In addition Britain supplied 1,205 locomotives and 54,000 wagons, which circulated over the entirety of the French network. Some were specially built or imported from America, but many were transferred from home service, while the government curtailed domestic traffic. The British also sent thousands of railway workers, built huge repair and maintenance shops, and laid 1,300 kilometres of track. By 1918 the BEF's Railway Operating Division had 18,500 personnel and operated 1,486 locomotives, and was running much of the Nord system.[290] In the spring emergency the BEF was well provided with standard-gauge lines from the ports, while lateral trunk railways could reinforce positions of need, it being possible to move two divisions simultaneously along two transverse lines that ran to Amiens from Calais and Hazebrouck.[291]

But the BEF's greatest advantage lay beyond the railhead. By August 1917 it had 368,000 horses and 82,000 mules, two thirds used for carrying rather than riding. Many came from North America, which had shipped 429,000 horses and 275,000 mules by the armistice (6,600 being lost on the voyage), but as the US had 21 million horses it could spare them. Much fodder came from the same source, despite the submarine attacks, the English Channel at times being strewn with hay. BEF horse rations were cut in January 1918, but remained much better than their German counterparts.[292] In addition, as a supplement to animal transport Geddes recommended a further investment in field railways. Sixty centimetres was the selected gauge, and the network was intended particularly for shells and road stone: but as well as easing the strain on the roads it could be pushed forward rapidly in shell-torn country where the latter were impracticable. The mileage operated rose from 100 in January 1917 to 926 in March 1918, and the tons conveyed per week from 10,000 to 250,000. The system was densest in active sectors such as Picardy and Flanders, and a north–south lateral line linked it together. In the run-up to 'Michael' it was functioning with record throughput. However, Third Ypres had shown that light railways were increasingly vulnerable to the German artillery, and they were better suited to the set-piece Allied attacks of 1917 than to a defensive, and more mobile, campaign.[293] Early in 1918 BEF transport was therefore reorganized again to make greater use of lorries. A central reserve was created, the War Office sent out two more motor transport companies, and by the armistice the BEF's stock totalled 33,560.[294] The reorganization formed part of wider contingency planning, which revealed that the sectors least well prepared were the northern part of the First Army front (where 'Georgette' struck) and the south of Gough's Fifth Army front – where 'Michael' made most headway. Conversely, the Third Army front – which was Ludendorff's main initial target, but did not collapse in parallel – had a new standard-gauge line in the rear and roads in good order further forward. The pre-existing infrastructure made predictable the pattern of German advance.[295]

When the blow fell the Germans overran the Fifth Army's field railways while the Third Army lost over 300 locomotives and 2,000 wagons: although it sabotaged most of them, as it did the railway bridges. Further north the field railways remained intact and ferried forward shells, including to the Arras sector, where the 'Mars' attack was crushed. In the rear 'Michael' gave rise to 'the most intensive series of troop movements of the whole war'. As of 21 March, of the fifty-eight British divisions on the Western Front twenty-eight were with the First and Second Armies in the north and thirty with the Third and Fifth Armies in the south, but by 18 April eighteen of the northern divisions had moved south as reliefs or reinforcements, while nineteen of the battle-weary southern divisions had moved north and nine to the rear. Almost the entire BEF had changed position, and although during the Lys battle the reverse move northwards (of seven divisions) was smaller, French divisions were being transported simultaneously.[296] This is to say nothing of supplies, GHQ estimating that for one day's intensive fighting a British division needed 1,934 tons of all kinds per mile of front held. In a war of movement animals were needed more than ever, and lorry drivers toiled for up to five days continuously, but serious ammunition shortfalls were unusual and the troops did not go hungry.[297]

Although the BEF survived through March and April, its new situation was precarious – possibly more than the Germans realized. The Channel ports of Boulogne, Calais, and Dunkirk were small. Dunkirk had the largest capacity but the German advance in April exposed it to shellfire and air attack. Half of the BEF's supplies came from south of the Somme, via Le Havre, Rouen, and Dieppe, and much of the material then had to cross the river, requiring 140 trains per day. After March and April the Albert–Arras line and those south-east of Hazebrouck became untenable. By April the Allies had eighty-six divisions north of the Somme, but to supply them only the Beauvais–Amiens line, which was now under shellfire. Losing Amiens would deprive the BEF of two of its double-tracked lines across the Somme, and losing Abancourt, south of Amiens, would deprive it of all three, leaving only a completely inadequate single-track coastal railway.[298] It was fortunate that Amiens was not at first the primary target for 'Michael', and by the time it became so the British and French had organized their defences east of the city.[299]

However, a further choke point existed where the main remaining north–south trunk line crossed the river Canche over a long and highly visible viaduct at Etaples. GHQ commented that German operations were 'obviously directed towards cutting our channels of supply' and had 'seriously affected our railway communications ... Good circulation is the essence of economical railway working: and a block at any point has an effect similar to that of an aneurism on a human artery ... The Transport system is carrying now as heavy a burden as is compatible with safety.'[300] During the night of 30/31 May bombing closed the Etaples viaduct, but within two days it was repaired, and a newly completed 'avoiding line' at once went into operation. In June attacks on British ports and communications continued and congestion round the Somme crossing at Abbeville grew so serious that for three days all but absolutely essential traffic was suspended.[301] Only in July did the pressure begin to ease, and during the summer a brand new double-track line was opened west of Amiens while the Dieppe–Eu coastal line was also doubled.[302] Soon afterwards the great advance cleared Amiens from German pressure anyway.

The British survived in part because of French assistance. In 1870 the German side had nine railways running to the common frontier and the French only four, but by 1914 the figures were thirteen and sixteen, and in addition the French had built two ring lines round Paris and two more transverse lines (*lignes de rocade*) running parallel to the border.[303] Further construction after the war began created a system of continuous double-tracked laterals, fully equipped with watering, engine sheds, and signalling. By 1916 four independent currents ran eastwards from the Somme, and in 1918 long-distance rail movements were characteristic of Foch's strategy.[304] The French were expert at using railways to support their operations, and could begin to move an infantry division (an operation requiring forty trains) six hours after deciding to do so. Their proficiency impressed the young George C. Marshall as 'a great demonstration of the highest form of troop movement'.[305]

By 1918 – and this was new – French troop movements also used road transport to an extent that rivalled rail. The French had 620,000 kilometres of trunk road to Germany's 260,000,[306] and Paris taxis had ferried reinforcements during the 1914 Battle of the Marne as during 1916 had lorry convoys along the 'sacred way' to Verdun. On the eve of war the French army had only 170 motor vehicles, but it requisitioned all it could and imported more from the US, organizing them in *groupements* of 600 lorries each. From five at the end of 1915, the *groupements* rose by the end of 1917 to twenty – enough to convey 100,000 men – and by July 1918 Pétain's lorry park numbered 37,000.[307] Loads doubled from two or three to five tons, and ranges extended to 100 kilometres per day. Although one lorry in ten might need repair after a day's travelling, assistance came from eighteen repair stations, located close to the front. In the winter of 1917–18 the military took authority over all roads within fifty kilometres of the line, so as to prioritize army traffic, and the army prepared contingency plans, one of them for a similar attack to 'Michael'.[308]

This scheme depended on oil. Lord Curzon commented in retrospect that the Allies 'floated to victory' on a wave of it.[309] Yet neither Britain, nor France, nor Italy produced much, but their consumption multiplied like that of the Central Powers, the British War Office estimating requirements on all fronts to have risen from 250,000 gallons in 1915 to 10.5 million by 1918, while French imports quadrupled from 276,000 tons in 1914 to 1 million in 1918.[310] Before the war Britain had taken 20–25 per cent of its imports from Russia and Romania, France 36 per cent, and Italy 70 per cent: but by closing the Dardanelles Turkey cut access to both countries. The Allies would have to ship from longer distances, which meant principally from the Western hemisphere and especially the US, whose output between 1915 and 1918 rose from 38.5 million to 48.8 million tons and whose exports rose from 7.6 million to 8.8 million. By 1917 America supplied two thirds of world consumption. Tankers, however, were a novelty and were rare: in 1914 Britain accounted for 55 per cent of world tonnage and the US for 16 per cent.[311] With the advent of unrestricted submarine warfare, many more were sunk or damaged, and the situation became critical.

The British pressed the panic button in summer 1917 over fuel stocks for their navy;[312] in France the crisis came over the army. Between 1914 and 1916 the French armed forces' petrol consumption quintupled while the US increased its share from one third to three quarters of French imports. Between February and December 1917 mines and U-boats sank six of the tankers supplying the country and damaged eight more. In May the leading American concern, Standard Oil of New Jersey, refused an appeal from the French importing companies to lend five tankers: Senator Henry Bérenger prodded the government to act, and was appointed chair of an inter-departmental Comité générale du pétrole. Pétain grew alarmed about army provision, and the importing firms estimated that supplies would run out on the eve of the expected attack. Hence on 15 December 1917 Clemenceau sent an urgent message to Woodrow Wilson that Bérenger had drafted.[313] He warned that 'at the decisive moment of this war when the year 1918 will open operations of capital importance on the French front, France's armies must not at any moment be exposed to a lack of the petrol needed for lorries, aviation, and tractor-drawn field artillery. Any petrol shortfall would abruptly paralyse our armies and could drive us into an unacceptable peace ...' Pétain had set the army's minimum stocks at 44,000 tonnes but they had already fallen to 28,000, and would soon be zero unless the US government released tankers that were under construction or operating in the Pacific. He had warned that he would be able to sustain an effort comparable to Verdun for just three days. But although Wilson never replied to the letter, extra tankers were made available, and this – combined with restrictions on civilian consumption – allowed Pétain's stocks to recover by 10 March to 66,296 tonnes, some 42,500 extra being made available over three weeks. In April and June, Bérenger – not by nature complacent – told his committee that stocks were 'excellent'.[314] In the newly created Conférence interalliée des pétroles the French insisted on their right to purchase from the Dutch East Indies, which would allow them greater independence from American supplies though absorbing far more tonnage than the North Atlantic run, but this demand further indicated that the emergency was over.[315]

Despite the Allies' anxiety about their port installations at Rouen and Calais, the tankers sailing up the Seine, and the filling stations behind the front line, German bombing failed to break the supply chain.[316] Given this – and given also parallel action by Pétain to top up the coal stocks of the northern and eastern railways[317] – the French army was well placed in the March crisis. On the evening of 22 March two divisions began moving northward by lorry, and by 9 April thirty had moved by rail towards the battle zone and twenty-one by road.[318] During April lateral rail links also brought up French reinforcements to the Lys. In contrast the German breakthrough on 27 May interrupted communications more gravely, overrunning two advanced transverse lines and cutting the trunk lateral railway between Paris and Châlons-sur-Marne. All strategic lateral movements would now have to go via the Paris ring line, whose capacity was hastily expanded, but no comparable east–west railway existed south of the city. This time the reinforcement plan was more improvised, but transports began on the evening of 27 May and by 2 June eighteen divisions had been moved by rail and thirty-one by road. By 12 July the divisions redeployed totalled ninety. After 28 May up to 1,500 lorries were on the roads each day – French Berliet and American Pierce-Arrow five-tonners – as well as buses, to reinforce first the Chemin des Dames and then the Matz: between 27 May and 9 June 124,000 men and 27,000 tons of equipment travelled by road. On 15 July, the opening of the final German offensive, 120,000 men and 7,000 tons of munitions were moved in one day.[319] At the climax of the summer fighting road movements exceeded those by rail, themselves at the highest level since 1914. After the war the Allies' victory was described as one of lorries over locomotives:[320] which was hyperbole, but a tribute to the French authorities' foresight.

The other most active theatre during the defensive phase was the Italian. When operations began here in 1915 Austria-Hungary had six independent railway lines running into the Venezia–Giulia sector, whereas Italy had only two; and two lines into the Trentino, where Italy's network was so poor that the CS abandoned any thought of attacking. Nor, despite Italy's interior lines of communication, did it have high-capacity lateral railways running parallel to its front, and the bottleneck of the Po crossings isolated the fighting theatre from the rest of the country. Only six bridges spanned the river's middle and lower reaches, and only one was double-tracked.[321] But by 1918 the position was altering. The Austro-Hungarian railways to the frontier shared in the general paralysis of the Dual Monarchy's network, as rolling stock deteriorated, fuel grew scarce, and congestion round Vienna intensified. Austro-Hungarian annual lorry production rose from 300 to 2,000 by

1917, but quite inadequately to compensate for the shortage of horses. The Habsburg army took 1,552,000 horses during the war, but in mountain fighting and in bitter winters without stabling losses were very heavy. Fodder rations fell to 1–1.5 kilos of oats per day,[322] and total horse numbers declined from 809,000 in June 1917 to 459,000 in June 1918.[323] This development, supplementing the railway crisis, reduced mobility in the Piave battles and particularly that of artillery. Unlike the German army, the Austrian had just sufficient oil, and its lorry fleet rose from 8,500 to 11,440 between 1917 and 1918, but coal and iron shortages and strikes prevented further growth and shortages of rubber and tyres meant the existing stock was scheduled to decline.[324] On the other hand, the Italians partially compensated for their railway deficiencies by developing road transport. By the end of the war their army had over 30,000 motor vehicles (mostly Fiats), and enough oil (in 1918, 87 per cent of it from the US) was imported to cover military needs, even though civilians were restricted.[325] In 1916 Fiat lorries had rushed up reinforcements when Austria-Hungary attacked in the Trentino, before rushing them back to capture Gorizia. But the Italians also improved their railways, adding 1,025 kilometres of double-tracked line and 10,000 wagons, while between 1915 and 1917 the capacity of the Veneto network rose from 100 trains a day to at least 240. During the November–December 1917 defensive battle on the Piave, the Italians not only supported their own forces but also handled the deployment of French and British reinforcements, whose assembly and supply required 1,500 trains with 60,000 wagons. Moving just the British divisions to Italy entailed a journey by 715 trains of up to 1,200 miles.[326] After Caporetto, thousands of goods wagons were rushed into the interior, and it took months for the authorities to restore an orderly circulation.[327] Once the new front had stabilized, however, the Italians built field railways to replace those lost, which was just as well, as the requirements of the June 1918 Battle of the Piave were by Italian standards huge. Over ten days, 4.2 million rounds were supplied to the Italian artillery, requiring an average of 900 trains a day and 20,000 wagons, whereas on the Austrian side when the offensive began much of the ammunition was still in transit, reducing the number of active batteries by fifty.[328] Before the Italians and their allies triumphed in the military battle they had triumphed in the transport one.

After July the positions were reversed, the Allies now having to adapt to the offensive. Their superiority applied in every theatre, for all the geographical contrasts between them. To take an extreme example, the East African interior had neither navigable rivers nor metalled roads, and only two railways ran in from the coast, while tsetse flies prohibited the use of horses, donkeys, and mules below 3,500 feet. The British conquest of German East Africa in 1916–17 rested literally on the heads of thousands of African carriers, who bore food, medicine, and munitions boxes in convoys across trackless bush or via roads impassable in the rainy season, equipped only with a blanket, a panga, and a cooking pot. Each soldier required ten bearers to maintain him, and over 1 million carriers supported the 120,000 British Empire forces, recruited from fifteen territories of the British African empire but particularly the present-day Kenya, Uganda, Malawi, and Zambia. Probably well over 100,000 of them died, nearly all from starvation, disease, and exhaustion rather than enemy action.[329]

Operations in Mesopotamia also took place in disease-infested territory devoid of roads and railways, where during the hot season campaigning was impossible. But the British invested in their logistical systems there after the disaster at Kut.[330] At least there were two navigable watercourses, and the 1917 advance on Baghdad was supported by a flotilla of 446 tugs and steam launches, 774 barges, and 414 motorboats.[331] Subsequently the Mesopotamian Expeditionary Force had lower priority than Palestine, and in 1918 most of its remaining transport was diverted to supporting operations in Persia and Central Asia. Once the Turks had been defeated at Megiddo, their Syrian supply routes were endangered, and the War Office pressed for a renewed advance, but General Marshall warned that all he possessed was 200 Ford vans and a mule cart supply column. He could move only up the Tigris and not up the Euphrates as well. Transport constraints also ruled out wide enveloping moves and forced the British into frontal attacks, while maintaining supplies of food, water, and ammunition proved even harder than expected. Although Marshall reached Mosul, he was very much of a poor relation compared with Allenby's Egyptian Expeditionary Force.[332]

The EEF's supply systems were impressive. The Mediterranean U-boats hampered its links with Britain, but it drew wheat, vegetables, and fodder from Egypt, and its expanded harbour at Port Said imported more wheat from India, tea from Ceylon, and meat from Argentina,

Australia, and South Africa. When the British began advancing out of Egypt in 1916, they built a coastal railway and a water pipeline as they did so. However, much of the Sinai peninsula was sandy desert, and to cross it the EEF turned again to Egypt to purchase 75,000 camels and to recruit 170,000 drivers. Camel convoys from the Red Sea port of Aqaba supplied the Arab Revolt, and camels were used in their greatest numbers during Allenby's drive from Gaza to Jerusalem in late 1917, as well as for his Jordan raids. But in 1918 their numbers per division were halved from 2,000 to 1,000. Although still useful on the slippery and precipitous paths of the Judean hills, they were less needed on the Palestine coastal plain, and other transport methods took over. The Sinai railway was double-tracked as far as Rafah, and during the summer it carried more than 2,000 tons of supplies a day. From Rafah it continued to Beersheba; and another line, linking Jerusalem to Lydda, was broadened to standard gauge. During the break-out of 15 September to 5 October, the British lost 1,270 out of 25,618 horses: a rate of under 5 per cent that was kept down by the animals' resilience (when a cavalryman with his equipment could weigh 20 stone) but also by good grooming.[333] Although the roads were poor, increased reliance on lorries was another feature in 1918, and the EEF possessed 1,744 of all types, particularly Peerless four-tonners. In the post-Megiddo pursuit the vehicles got beyond Damascus, although they often needed repair and their tyres wore out, while many drivers worked over eighteen hours per day. Finally, coastal supplies landed at Haifa and Beirut helped sustain one of the most spectacular advances of the war.[334]

The Ottomans' problems were much more acute. The Allies halted all Mediterranean coastal shipping, and the empire possessed few roads. The great Berlin to Baghdad railway project, financed since 1903 with German capital, remained unfinished. During the war the Germans lent 360 million marks to the company to save it from bankruptcy and complete the system, but it failed to provide a through connection from the capital to the fighting fronts. Along the over 500 kilometres from Aleppo to Baghdad no line ran at all: hence the Turks facing the British in Mesopotamia lacked an umbilical rail link, as did those at even greater distances from the capital in Transcaucasia. Even the most complete stretch, from Constantinople to Aleppo, included gaps in the Taurus and Amanus mountains of thirty-seven and ninety-seven kilometres. By 1917 a standard-gauge link had closed the Amanus gap and a narrow-gauge link that in the Taurus, but in the course of the journey goods were still on- and off-loaded five times.[335] The Turks had only 280 locomotives, and they burned timber, which in Palestine was scarce: in August 1918 fuel shortages reduced freight shipments from Damascus to the northern Palestinian railway junction at Deraa to barely one third of those in May.[336] In September the tunnel through the Taurus mountains was closed for ten days, to allow conversion of the track from narrow to standard gauge: this was known to British intelligence, and Allenby timed his attack to coincide with it. By the time the Taurus standard-gauge link was opened on 9 October 1918, he had delivered his blow. Meanwhile the Hejaz railway running southwards was under periodic Arab attack. Over 40,000 of the Turkish army's camels died during the war, and its starving men and horses could not tow away their artillery.[337] As the EEF moved northward, it found abundant evidence of the Turks' supply difficulties, and in cities like Damascus a breakdown in basic food and medical provisioning.

The Allied expedition in Macedonia had no alternative to sea supply via the Mediterranean, and suffered more severely from the U-boats.[338] Robertson, while British CIGS, detested the commitment in the Balkans and claimed he could save 75–100 ships by transferring the British forces there to France.[339] In early 1918 shipping shortages had reduced food stocks to less than a month, and lack of fodder meant a shortage of transport animals, and throughout the year the French forces there were acutely short of aviation fuel.[340] The Allies had improved the local roads in a remote and mountainous area, but needed more standard-gauge railway and better lateral links. During the preparations for the September 1918 offensive the docks and railways in the British sector were overstrained and the trains ran late, although the main problem was the British government's failure to send out the shells that it had promised.[341] Meanwhile the French increased capacity on the narrow-gauge railway to the attack front from 220 to 600 tons per day, and improved the roads for lorries. Using tractors to haul the guns by night up to the summits helped the attackers gain surprise. None the less, the Allies' transport advantage was less evident here than in other theatres. As the Bulgarians had neglected their roads, however, they depended on the artery of the Vardar valley railway, which they destroyed as they fell back. Once the breakthrough had begun, Allied strategy became to cut off the western Bulgarian forces and paralyse their communications by seizing the area round Skopje; and in this they succeeded. Once they had done so, the inefficiencies of the Bulgarian railways became an Allied problem, which in mid-October delayed plans to go north of the Danube.[342]

For the Battle of Vittorio Veneto the Italians could use the field railway network they had built west of the Piave, and they had now better lateral communication lines than the Austrians, as well as more lorries and fuel. In any case their logistical requirements were fewer than for the Battle of the Piave: this time only 3,260 wagons of munitions were brought up, compared with 20,000 in June. Diaz made Vittorio Veneto his objective because taking it would break up the Austro-Hungarian railway network east of the river and permit a large encircling manoeuvre.[343] Even if the latter did not occur, the Allies here as in Palestine and Macedonia obtained control of the communication bottlenecks.

Allied strategy on the Western Front showed similar concerns. Ludendorff's offensives had cut the furthest forward of the French lateral railways at Montdidier and between Château-Thierry and Epernay. The link line at Saint-Roch, one mile west of Amiens, was under fire from late April, 15–20 heavy shells falling on or near it daily. Rawlinson understood Amiens's significance for communications, and his July and August battles were meant to push the Germans away from it.[344] Similarly, Foch's Bombon memorandum of 24 July set the goal of clearing the lines required for subsequent manoeuvres (Paris–Amiens to the north and Paris–Avricourt to the east) and repelling the enemy from the Channel ports and northern coalfield in order to relieve congestion on the railways and to secure their fuel. He wanted surprise attacks at rapid intervals to disrupt German reinforcement arrangements,[345] for which the precondition was logistical flexibility, but during the summer the French continued to benefit from the changes they had made in the spring. Like Haig, Pétain avoided attacking too long in one place, and he had equipped the French front so that reserves could move rapidly.[346] From 1 August attacking units could draw men from a general reserve, without needing to borrow from other units.[347] The period from 10 to 30 July saw the most intensive French automobile movement of the war; the retreating Germans damaged the roads less than the railways, and during August the French moved up food and shells without much difficulty.[348] Meanwhile bomber attacks and congestion on the British lines also eased. By 1918 the BEF could more easily switch troops and equipment along the front, and no longer needed to continue 1916-style battering in one place.[349] Special tank transporters were coming into service, and tanks could be moved at the rate of twelve per train, the delicate task of unloading them being accomplished in as little as eighty minutes. Big troop movements still strained the system – for example, between the end of August and the end of September sixteen infantry divisions were transferred into the Fourth Army and ten out of it – but they were less intensive than in March.[350] GHQ's policy for the advance was to push the broad-gauge railways forward as quickly as possible, while improving the roads so that lorries and horses could continue from the railheads but neglecting narrow-gauge lines. This approach was controversial, but it proved itself and the British noted that the Germans in the spring had not done likewise, probably because vehicle and horse shortages had forced them to depend excessively on light railways. On 29 August, 196 trains were run to the British armies, against a 1917 maximum of 177.[351] Meanwhile the Amiens–Arras line was cleared and double-tracked and by September could move coal southward. Despite worsening weather and the need also to supply the Americans, these arrangements delivered the unprecedented quantities of ammunition needed for the assault on the Hindenburg Line, as well as moving the tanks, which went by rail for speed, to save petrol, and to spare the roads. By late September Foch's Bombon objectives had largely been met, and the Paris–Amiens, Paris–Nancy, and Lérouville–Verdun railways were all now available to support the next stage.[352]

The German official history acknowledged that by late September the Allies had a superior rail system. With their own strategic network reinstated, they could now assault their enemy's infrastructure. Foch and Pershing expressly intended the Meuse–Argonne battle to cut the German trunk line where it came closest to the front, and the Germans considered it the most dangerous Allied thrust. To counter it they first brought reinforcements from east of the Meuse, but transferring fourteen more divisions from Alsace-Lorraine proved extraordinarily difficult, partly because an Allied attack was feared there but also because of the overload and confusion in their railway network. The German railways as a whole had experienced increasing difficulties since 1916 and a retrospective analysis discerned 'a creeping transport crisis' that curtailed the army's operations and weapons supply.[353] Once the concentric Allied attacks began the system experienced 'heavy strain' and 'severe confusion'.[354] On the evening of 28 September a Hinden-burg directive warned that 'Given the shortage of battle-ready reserves and the strained [*gespannten*] railway situation the Army Groups can-not reckon with a supply of further forces.'[355] And even though American progress proved disappointing, the British were now aiming for Aulnoye, where the German lateral line intersected with the trunk line from Cologne, and by November they had taken it.[356] By this stage the French assessment was that Germany had lost three lateral lines and had only one left near the front (Brussels–Namur–Arlon–Thionille–Sarrebourg): two others lay well back to the north, and congestion on the system stretched to the Rhine. By October the Germans were aban-doning more and more stores for lack of horses and as the army jettisoned food and livestock while food trains halted further in the rear, for the first time its provisioning was endangered.[357] The impending breakdown of the army's supply arrangements was integral to the com-plex of developments forcing Germany to end the war.

Yet the Allies also faced increasing difficulties, and this too had a bearing on the ceasefire. The trains reaching the BEF's standard-gauge railheads daily fell from 153 in August and September to 133 in Octo-ber. Part of the reason was general overstretch on the French railways, but in addition the British transport services were short of personnel and running out of replacement rails.[358] By early November the Allies had recaptured 2,900 kilometres of railway, but the retreating Ger-mans not only wrecked the stations, equipment, and track, but also left delayed-action mines, which could explode weeks later, halting traffic and forcing repairs to be done again. Yet reopening the railways pre-maturely, with the tracks insufficiently ballasted, entailed more risk of accidents, whose numbers were growing. And beyond the railheads the difficulties were worse. The British no longer built field lines as they advanced, and after mid-October they were beyond the former German narrow-gauge system. On 20 October, Currie recorded that 'the enemy is making a very orderly and practically unmolested retirement. Our trouble is that the troops are very tired and that the getting forward of supplies is becoming very difficult owing to the distance away of rail-heads.'[359] By 11 November, Rawlinson's Fourth Army was fifty miles ahead of reliable railheads, and many of its roads were single carriage-ways with fragile cobbled surfaces that prevented two-way traffic and forced many lorries to be ditched.[360] Repairs could not keep up, and at the end of October, chiefly owing to broken springs, nearly a fifth of the BEF's lorries were out of action. Horses too were in short supply, the numbers on field gun teams being reduced from six to four to release more for the AEF.[361] No longer able to advance at full strength, the BEF had to send forward a covering screen, and was fortunate that German resistance was fading. After the armistice it had difficulty in advancing just a fraction of its forces to the Rhine, against no opposition at all. Yet the front-line troops were never short of food, and although ammunition caused more anxiety it did not have to be restricted. The supplies needed even for the fantastic consumption of a 1918 army were getting through. Certainly the BEF would soon need to pause, but it had also done so after breaking through the Hindenburg Line and the Selle. It needed a breathing space to bring up its standard-gauge railways and import more lorries, if not a very long one.[362]

The French were in more serious trouble. They too were advancing beyond their railheads, light railways could not make good the difference, and the distances became too great for lorries to cover in a day along dilapidated roads. Daily divisional supplies were capped at 150 tons, and transport was prioritized, first to supply Flanders during October, then for an advance in Champagne, and finally for the Lorraine offensive scheduled for 14 November.[363] Conditions on the railways alarmed not only the French but also their partners.[364] In May the eastern network could move ninety-six troop trains a day but by November only thirty; and in June the northern railway requested urgent British help yet still ran short of wagons to move BEF supplies from the ports. Whereas traffic volumes on the French lines had risen 41 per cent since July 1914, personnel numbers had fallen from 357,000 to 352,000 (and many more of them were unskilled); while although wagon stocks had increased from 373,000 to 388,000, those of locomotives had diminished from 14,047 to 13,580.[365] The German offensives had worsened matters by interrupting the lateral lines and cutting off Bruay coal supplies, but most stressful of all, according to the French authorities, was the Americans' arrival en masse.[366]

After March the accelerated American shipments destabilized both the French railways and Pershing's plans for a balanced and gradual build-up. The AEF was attempting an exercise in power projection that entailed sustaining 2 million men across 3,000 miles of ocean, and its front line lay 500 miles from its small and antiquated west coast entry ports. Although 40 per cent of its personnel came via Britain (through Liverpool and the Channel ports), 60 per cent came via Saint-Nazaire, Bordeaux, and Brest, which were also the principal conduits for its supplies. From the Atlantic coast two lines ran towards Dijon and on to the regulating station at Is-sur-Tille, but the AEF was being provisioned across the spokes of a wheel, in a peripheral section of the network that was remote from Paris and from the lateral infrastructure of the north-east.[367]

The Americans tried to improve matters. In addition to adding capacity at the ports they laid 1,002 miles of standard-gauge railway and 500 kilometres of narrow gauge. They imported 1,500 locomotives and 20,000 railway cars, assembling most of them in France though by the end also shipping locomotives intact, and they repaired 1,947 French locomotives and 57,385 cars. They brought across 30,410 railway personnel. Yet neither the rolling stock nor the railway workers equalled the AEF's needs, and it remained a net burden on the French railway service.[368] According to W. J. Wilgus, an executive from the New York Central Railroad who headed the AEF Transportation Branch, the Americans had not appreciated how poorly equipped the French lines were: American locomotives were too heavy for the track, and French sidings could not accommodate them. By August, Is-sur-Tille was so clogged that no supplies could move beyond it; in September queues of trains formed at the watering points. AEF station chiefs worsened the situation by hoarding rolling stock, and cars took ever longer to return from the interior while stocks accumulated at the ports. Had it not been for the one third shortfall on orders being delivered from the US, the problem would have been still worse. Locomotive coal supply was also 'most tense', and could not be remedied unless the British army released back home more miners from its ranks. In Wilgus's view, endorsed by James Harbord, who commanded the AEF Services of Supply, the root of the problem was the priority given to shipping American infantry and machine gunners over logistics personnel, creating an unbalanced army that could be sent more rapidly to Europe but lacked the wherewithal to get from the ports to the front. By the time of the armistice a 'crisis in transportation' was coming to a head. Foch gambled on obtaining victory before it did so, but had the war continued its consequences would have been grave.[369]

The AEF lacked not only rolling stock but also horses and lorries.

Both preoccupied Pershing, and filled the pages of his memoirs. Of 200,000 horses used by the AEF, only 40,000 came from the US. Pershing asked Washington in July for 25,000 but over the next three months he received fewer than 2,000.[370] A Spanish ban on exports exacerbated the shortage, and the horses per division were reduced in January from 6,522 to 4,712 and in August to 3,772.[371] The French government also fell short on its promises, though it contributed 50,000 early in 1918 and transferred another 13,000 from its own forces after Pershing pleaded to Clemenceau during the Meuse–Argonne battle that his artillery was almost immobile and the men were hauling their guns.[372]

In the absence of horses, the AEF became the most heavily motorized of the allied armies. But on this count too, deliveries from home fell below expectations. In September Pershing warned the War Department that 'at the present time our ability to supply and manoeuvre our forces depends largely on motor transportation', in which, despite repeated requests, he was 'woefully deficient'. The AEF kept mobile only by borrowing vehicles from the French, on whom it depended for almost all its road troop movements and half its road ammunition movements.[373] The problem was not a shortage of lorries in the US, but a shortage of ships to carry them, again in part because of the priority for infantry and machine gunners. But other factors exacerbated matters. The AEF failed to standardize lorry types and at one point was operating with 294, though eventually reduced them to thirty-four (the BEF in comparison had 154 vehicle makes).[374] An average lorry had 3,500 parts, 80 per cent being intrinsic to it, and the AEF had too few repair shops and mechanics. Many of its drivers were inexperienced, as were the military police who tried to marshal them.[375] During the Second Battle of the Marne, Pershing had commented that 'No one who has not been an eye witness can visualize the confusion in traffic conditions that exists behind the lines during the progress of a great modern battle.' At Saint-Mihiel, for which the Americans had had plenty of time to prepare, using over 100,000 tons of road rock, jams prevented many troops from reaching the front line.[376] In contrast, the transfer of forces from Saint-Mihiel to the Meuse–Argonne was impressive, and testified to the Allies' ability to ready a new battlefront far faster than had been possible earlier,[377] but the short preparation time meant too few roads could be built to the attack sector, and contributed to the chaos that followed. Whereas the British, for all their difficulties, kept their front-line troops supplied, the AEF on the Meuse–Argonne did not, some of its starving soldiers fleeing to the rear and Pershing cabling to the War Department that the prospects were 'extremely alarming'.[378] Even so, the supply services eventually got a grip, and by the armistice the AEF overlooked the Germans' lateral railway, thus rendering the Antwerp–Meuse line untenable and finally threatening its opponents with the disaster that the Allied commanders had planned.

By autumn 1918 the Allies far outnumbered the Central Powers in air-craft, tanks, and lorries, and they used that superiority to gain the edge in intelligence and mobility. Thanks to the Americans they could fuel their war machines while their enemies could not. But motor vehicles still vied with horses as the principal transport method beyond the rail-head, and tanks were too few, too slow, too vulnerable and unreliable for use as an independent spearhead, functioning more as a shield and morale booster for the infantry. Lorries could not yet supplant standard-gauge railways for long-distance supplies in the prodigious quantities needed, and photographic intelligence from aircraft, however valuable, was insufficient unless supplemented by more traditional techniques of espionage and prisoner interrogation. None the less, in all these spheres the Allies were gaining the advantage, and in 1919 would have done so more spectacularly, as hundreds more tanks and aircraft and thousands more gas shells became available. The Allies won the technological race (as they would again a generation later), and overtook their enemies not only in numbers but also in fighting power. In the process they pioneered the characteristic forms of later twentieth-century warfare – although their incomplete success in doing so made for irresolution in the hour of triumph.

4

The Human Factor:
Manpower and Morale

I think we saw clearly enough ... that we had a filthy job on hand that had to be done ... We were quite sure that we were going to win the war, but we said, 'The politicians will lose it for us afterwards.'

Lt R. G. Dixon[1]

Fundamental to the Allies' final successes was that they no longer faced the same enemies. The Turkish resistance that had halted them at Gallipoli; the Bulgarian in the hills above Salonika; the Austro-Hungarian on the Isonzo; and above all the German resistance on the Western Front had ceased to be so formidable. Once their defensive crust was broken, the Central Powers' armies crumbled into mass desertion and surrender, whereas the Allied armies – however tested – emerged intact. The usual (and entirely understandable) question raised about combat motivation in the war is that of why the troops fought. Foch's generalship would have been irrelevant had thousands of infantrymen refused to attack when he directed; and the Allies' superiority in weapons redundant without soldiers to operate them. And yet in fact by 1918 most armies on both sides were nearing breakdown, not to say open revolt. The critical question is why some overcame their crises of morale and still kept going, while others did not. The approach adopted here will be to concentrate on the Western Front, setting American enthusiasm against British and French endurance and German disintegration, before turning to the other theatres. The issue was both quantitative and qualitative, for the size of the remaining manpower reserves was vital, as well as whether the troops would continue or abandon their efforts.

AEF

During 1918 the balance between the two sides underwent two turning points. Peace with Russia enabled Germany to transfer over forty divisions to the Western Front and win numerical superiority. But by July the Allies had regained the advantage and by the autumn their lead was massive, owing partly to Germany's losses but mainly to the AEF. By November the Central Powers had 3,527,000 men on the Western Front, but the Allies and the US 6,432,000.[2] From April the Americans accelerated their troop shipments; from June they contributed substantially to the Allied defence effort; and from July they were on the attack. By November they exceeded the British in both the size of their army and their length of front, their sector rising from ten kilometres in January to 162 by October, or twenty-three more than the BEF's. Their advent overshadowed everybody else's calculations and shaped the 1918 campaign. Admittedly Ludendorff might have launched his spring offensives anyway, given the opportunity created by events in Russia, and the fading viability of a defensive strategy. None the less, the Americans' prospective deployment en masse sharpened his resolve to strike earlier than would otherwise have been prudent. Conversely, America was critical to the French and British leaders' determination to hang on, and for the growing confidence of Foch's plans. Clemenceau told French parliamentarians that against the expected German attack 'we have no other resources than to wait for the Americans', to whose arrival he attached 'a capital importance'.[3]

America's manpower pool was large though not limitless. Many of the tidal waves of recent immigrants had yet to be naturalized, and fewer volunteered than in Britain, but conscription came in quickly. Out of a male population of 54 million, 2,810,296 were called up, but as the American armed forces also included volunteers and pre-1917 regulars the total under arms approached 4 million in the army and 4.8 million in all the armed services. This represented nearly 5 per cent of US citizens, compared with 10 per cent in the Northern States during the American Civil War – impressive given the smallness of the peacetime military establishment, although well short of European levels. Of its male population aged 18–45 the US mobilized 20 per cent, compared with Britain's 60 per cent.[4]

In contrast with American tradition, Selective Service (as conscription was euphemistically entitled) was the primary recruitment procedure. In the Civil War over 92 per cent of the Union Army had been volunteers, but in the First World War, 72 per cent of the army were drafted.[5] Wilson would have preferred to give volunteering a chance, but in March 1917 he changed his mind in order to head off a plan by ex-President Theodore Roosevelt, his personal and political rival, to lead a division of volunteers to Europe. Socialists and farmers disliked the draft, but Roosevelt's scheme, with its potential for undermining military discipline and bipartisan consensus, might be even more divisive. Moreover, Britain's experience had made Wilson sceptical about volunteering, conscription seeming both fairer and more efficient. As he put it, characteristically, 'the business now at hand is undramatic, practical, and of scientific definiteness and precision'. Conscription would protect domestic output: the 'central idea was to disturb the industrial and social structure of the country just as little as possible'. Without conscription, the administration feared, 'slackers' would shirk their duty.[6] These arguments also swayed Congress, which voted resoundingly in favour, although setting the age range at 21–30 (thus excluding teenagers) and raising remuneration for private soldiers to a generous $30 per month.[7] The moderate trade unions in Samuel Gompers's American Federation of Labor backed the measure, and support for an alternative bill collapsed, in part as a result of assurances to the Southern Democrats that no units would be racially integrated.

During the Civil War anti-draft riots had shaken Northern cities, and the administration was determined – in this as in other matters – to learn from Lincoln's mistakes. General Enoch H. Crowder, who headed the Selective Service administration, operated via 'supervised decentralization', delegating to local draft boards staffed by unpaid volunteers.[8] Washington issued guidelines, but created no massive new federal agency. The first registration day, on 5 June 1917, followed an intensive propaganda campaign by George Creel's Committee on Public Information (CPI). It was a resounding success, and subsequent to it batches of registrees were called up by lot: this was the real test and although some twenty-five people died in clashes with police nationwide, Oklahoma tenant farmers offered the only organized resistance. Although over 24 million men registered on three such days during the war, the authorities estimated that up to 3 million more avoided doing so, secreted in rural fastnesses or city slums. Another 337,649 were absent from induction or deserted soon after reaching training camp, but these were manageable figures compared with the millions who did come forward, and the many more who would have done so had the war continued into 1919.[9]

At first the authorities' requirements were modest, and this caution helped delay troop shipments. The administration had underestimated Allied weakness and the size of the effort needed. Nor did the Allies ask initially for many men. In April 1917 the regular army numbered 128,000 and the National Guard 164,000: 301,000 volunteers joined up in the next three months and the first target for draftees was 687,000. The troops available by late 1917 totalled approximately 1.2 million, but building camps took until the end of the year and the men needed to be fed, clothed, and equipped, as well as trained for the five months deemed adequate before they embarked. As the Allies' 1917 disasters unfolded, both the General Staff in Washington and Pershing (who reached France in July) recommended a 1918 target for forces overseas of 1 million. But all concerned were looking to 1919 as the crucial year, and aimed to have a large and self-sufficient force ready to intervene decisively by that date.[10]

A second reason for delay was the 'amalgamation' dispute, one of the bitterest inter-Allied controversies. Pershing's arrival caused euphoria in Europe, and by November 1917 Americans were in the line in France and taking casualties. But when more failed to follow, London and Paris grew impatient, Lloyd George telling Dominion leaders that the AEF had been 'our worst disappointment'.[11] Pershing's instructions directed him to maintain his army's independence, and Wilson and the War Secretary, Newton D. Baker, feared that placing American troops under Allied command would damage their morale, be unpopular at home, and diminish American leverage at the peace conference. For all his idealism, the President foresaw that his diplomacy would lack credibility without strong armed forces. But to operate independently an American army would need artillery, engineers, medical and supply and communication troops, with stores and equipment, as well as staff officers to support the commanders, all of which would take up more than double the shipping space required just for infantry and machine gunners.[12] Moreover, although the AEF expanded its officer corps from the remarkably small starting point of fewer than 6,000 in April 1917 to

200,000 by November 1918 (and 60 per cent of its NCOs were newly created),[13] inexperience at senior levels was harder to make up for than among the rank and file. Hence the danger that even when American units deployed they would have little value, and hence also the French and British insistence that at least temporarily they must come under European commanders – an arrangement referred to as 'amalgamation' (*amalgame*) or 'brigading'. Pershing scented in it an intrigue to weaken American influence and hobble his own war plans. The Allies denied such *arrière-pensées*; and the documentation indeed suggests their main concern was getting more fighting troops to hold off the imminent German offensive. Pétain told the French government's War Committee that once America had more officers and equipment an independent AEF would be in France's interest, but 'amalgamation is at this moment the only possible form of American collaboration'.[14]

Against this background Britain took the initiative. According to Robertson, the Chief of the Imperial General Staff, the Americans 'were proceeding as if they had years to prepare'.[15] Lloyd George commented that 'Before even the Americans had fired a shot in battle their coming turned the scale of confidence and hope in favour of the Allies', and yet they seemed so leisurely that they might arrive too late.[16] He told an American mission that it might make a vital difference if the Americans deployed on the Western Front in 1918 rather than 1919. Baker then advised Pershing that the independence of US forces took second place to helping the Allies; but left Pershing with the final decision. The Commander-in-Chief, not an overtly partisan figure but a respected leader whose rise had benefited from Republican connections, could exercise a veto.

Until now the British had insisted that America must provide the shipping for AEF troops and supplies. In January 1918 they indicated that they could find extra ships but at the cost of running down their food and raw material stocks (at a time of queues in London), and they would do so only for combat troops, not for full divisions. The disclosure that ships were available after all hardened American suspicions of British duplicity, and Pershing dug his heels in. Finally the British approved a Pershing counter-proposal that still prioritized shipping whole divisions, but accepted temporary training for extra American officers with the BEF. This meant that Pershing had won for the time being, but in the emergency that followed Ludendorff's 21 March attack the issue reopened. Lloyd George sent a telegram for publication in the US: 'It is impossible to exaggerate the importance of getting American reinforcements across the Atlantic in the shortest possible space of time.' He appealed to Wilson for 120,000 men a month between now and the end of July: Britain could transport them, but they must be infantry and machine gunners and brigaded into French and British divisions. The French supported him.[17] Both countries' armies were desperately short of infantry, and when Pershing reiterated his objections, Lloyd George called on the president to overrule his commander's 'narrow obstinacy'. Wilson avoided doing so directly, but the outcome was a compromise, though it proved a breakthrough. The administration in Washington agreed temporarily to send 120,000 a month and moderated the principle of sending over what was needed for complete divisions, though still leaving the 'brigading' issue up to Pershing. After much wrangling, the latter accepted a machine gunner and infantry priority for May, June, and July. Once it became apparent that Americans were indeed arriving and in enormous numbers, the contentiousness subsided.[18]

The Allies' frustration arose in part from American working methods. They knew that Wilson and Baker were more sympathetic than Pershing, and yet the statesmen never repudiated the general. Henry Wilson regarded Pershing as 'so stupid, so narrow, so pigheaded'; Clemenceau saw him as 'terribly obstinate'.[19] In one session Pershing said he would rather see the Allies being driven behind the river Loire than sacrifice AEF independence. In fact the limited numbers of Americans who were 'brigaded' under British and French command fought at least as well as those under their own leaders, and Pershing overstated the risk that amalgamation posed to fighting spirit as well as that to his autonomy. He correctly foresaw, however, that when the hugely expanded American army went into battle its force structure would be unbalanced. The supply chaos on the Meuse–Argonne resulted partly from over-expanding the front-line forces and starving the support teams.

None the less, by November the emergency troop shipments had established an Expeditionary Force numbering over 2 million that had previously been envisaged for a year later. By attempting to strike before the Americans arrived en masse, the Germans had brought that development forward. Indeed the actual shipments exceeded the numbers in the inter-Allied agreements, and they resulted not only from the compromise with the British but also from a change of direction in Washington. In spring 1918 General Peyton C. March took over there as Chief of the General Staff. A hard-bitten, driving man, he understood the Allies' desperate straits and his absolute priority was to get soldiers over as soon as possible, 'regardless of questions of supply': in other words, even before there was equipment for them.[20] Under him troopship capacity rose by over 40 per cent, the men being packed in so tightly that they took it in turns to occupy the bunks, which were four berths high. Turnaround times for troopship voyages fell from 67 days in November 1917 to 40 in February 1918 and 33 in June.[21] Not only was more shipping available – American as well as British – but the vessels were used more intensively. A human migration on this scale and at this speed over such an expanse of ocean had no precedent

Because so many troops were being funnelled across the Atlantic, in 1918 Selective Service bit deeper. In response to Allied entreaties, Wilson won authority from Congress to draft as many men as were needed. However, there were limits. In spring 1918 the army's target was eighty divisions, which given that an American division was twice the size of a European one was already enormous. Yet in June Foch, supported by Pershing and the Allied premiers, asked for 100 divisions in France by summer 1919, claiming this was essential for achieving adequate superiority. Pershing admitted afterwards the figure was unrealistic, and Wilson and his advisers decided to stick at a target of eighty (although with another eighteen depot divisions in the US), implying an army of 4.8 million by 30 June 1919.[22] The AEF's clothes, tinned food, and horses and lorries came mostly from America and in American ships, and although the absolute quantity increased the amount sent per man fell sharply during 1918. Moreover, as General March put it, finding one or two million more men was straightforward: the problem was the economic impact.[23] In August, Congress extended the age limits to 18–45, but calling up teenagers remained controversial and it was becoming harder to conciliate agriculture and organized labour. In 1918 more exemptions were granted for farm workers, and troops were released on furlough to gather the harvest. Shipbuilders and merchant seamen were also exempted, although otherwise all occupations – even railwaymen and miners – remained liable. Protests were strongest against drafting baseball players, which Baker postponed until the season – and the war – had ended. The Selective Service administration had so far heeded trade union opposition to 'industrial conscription', but by October it was planning to compel men in productive industries to stay in their jobs or be called up.[24] At the time of the armistice reserves were less stretched than in Europe, and a more intensive effort in 1919 remained feasible, but the trawl was getting harder.

Moreover, the AEF ran into a manpower crisis. Already in the summer battles such as Belleau Wood and the 18 July Marne counterstroke American casualties had been extraordinary – up to 50 per cent in the units involved – but in the autumn the situation became much worse because of the influenza pandemic and the murderous losses on the Meuse–Argonne. Pershing's staff estimated that 103,513 infantry and machine gunners were needed and only 66,940 were available;[25] March advised that only 23,000 could be added,[26] and the huge American infantry companies had to be reduced from 250 to 175 each.[27] Although American daily losses during 1918 were substantially lower than those suffered by the British, Germans, and French, two in three of those who got to Europe came under fire, and casualties among those serving overseas totalled 244,086, including 125,000 fatalities. Many succumbed to disease, but the 50,300 deaths from combat wounds were comparable to the totals in Korea and Vietnam, and suffered in a much shorter period of time.[28] For untried soldiers this was much to demand.

Whereas in the American Civil War, however, some 90 per cent of the troops were combatants, in the AEF the figure was 40 per cent. The remainder were skilled and unskilled workers, working under military discipline, sometimes coming under bombardment, but not expected to kill.[29] Pershing described the AEF's infrastructure as 'more sophisticated than the public utility services of a great city',[30] and in a France whose villages contained only old men, *mutilés*, children, and women in mourning, it had to bring its labour with it. Much of that labour was African-American, the war intervening at a particularly dispiriting juncture in US race relations. African-Americans numbered some one in ten of the population, and were still concentrated in the Southern countryside. They were subject to the 'Jim Crow' laws, passed by state legislatures between 1890 and 1910, which disenfranchised most blacks (as well as many poor whites) and enforced segregation in schools, on transport, and in places of public entertainment. Wilson and many of his Cabinet were Southerners, and had extended segregation to the federal civil service and post office. None the less, most black political leaders supported the war and glossed over the contradictions with the President's universalist rhetoric. Southern draft boards were more likely to approve blacks than whites for military service, but the War Department acknowledged white anxieties about blacks bearing arms and only two AEF divisions – the 92nd and 93rd – were composed of black servicemen. Pershing sent the four regiments of the 93rd to serve in the French army, where many fought with distinction. The 92nd remained in the AEF, under white commanders.[31] But 80 per cent of the African-Americans became labourers, with their black NCOs and junior officers acting as overseers: a third of the US Army's labour troops were African-American, totalling some 166,000 by the end of the war. They were most conspicuous as stevedores, unloading at Saint-Nazaire and Brest, but they also put up buildings, repaired roads and railways, felled timber, and buried the dead. Their segregation at home continued abroad, although for some their encounters with the French people were emancipatory. A memorandum from the French military mission to the AEF (read out after the war, to gasps of disapproval, in the Paris National Assembly) was circulated in August 1918 to the French authorities. It warned against offending white American opinion, which was unanimous in fearing miscegenation: social contact between French white society and black Americans should be kept to a minimum.[32] Yet although the AEF authorities feared African-Americans might be susceptible to German propaganda, and despite race riots in the embarkation camps, no major indiscipline occurred overseas. One regiment of the 92nd division broke down on the second day on the Meuse–Argonne, but there were numerous mitigating circumstances and several white units behaved similarly.[33]

Pershing's final report concluded that morale and discipline were good in the AEF as a whole, and at least until October 1918 this was true.[34] After call-up, men did basic training in improvised camps under disciplinarian regular officers and NCOs who inculcated into many a lasting dislike of authority. The numbers of Military Police per division were trebled from the original provision, and on the Meuse–Argonne the police followed on the advance to urge ahead stragglers and to seek out malingerers among the walking wounded.[35] None the less those charged for desertion during the war totalled only some 5,584, of whom 2,657 were convicted but none executed, and just 4,480 Americans were taken prisoner.[36] Twenty-five soldiers were executed in America and ten in France, but all for murder or rape, offences that might well have incurred a civilian death penalty. Four death sentences for military offences were submitted to Wilson, but he approved none of them.[37] The army claimed to return the veterans to their mothers as finer men: rigorous measures contained alcoholism, brothel visits were banned, and venereal disease was remarkably rare. American troops were better paid than French or British ones, their daily calorie ration was up to one third greater, and the average AEF soldier put on twelve pounds.[38]

The AEF may have lacked skills or experience, but not willingness. Despite the remoteness of the European conflict, many voyaged with enthusiasm. Like other armies the AEF took political education more seriously in 1918: the War Department established a Morale Division, and organized films, lectures, newspapers, and religious services in the training camps. *Stars & Stripes*, produced by AEF GHQ, highlighted links with France and carried uplifting messages from US leaders.[39] American officers censoring soldiers' letters (and Germans interrogating US prisoners) detected little understanding of Wilson's idealistic objectives, but conviction of the need to win, kill Germans, help the French, avenge dead comrades, and do one's duty.[40] Veterans' responses to a survey by the US Army's Military History Research Institute in the 1970s also dwelt on feelings of duty and patriotism, and the chance to participate in great events and undergo a test of manhood. Arthur Ellwood Yensen enlisted 'for the excitement and adventure of it', and many defied orders by keeping diaries, Major Leland Garretson recording characteristically: 'Here we are sailing over the bounding ocean in search of the Great Adventure.'[41] The more literary drew on the romanticism of volunteers such as the poet Alan Seeger, who had served in France during the neutrality period. Others remembered grandfathers who had fought in the Civil War (an enormous fiftieth-year commemoration having taken place at Gettysburg in 1913, where Wilson had addressed thousands of veterans).[42] Alvin D. York, who became the most decorated American war hero, was a mountain farmer from backwoods Tennessee and a descendant of Civil War veterans, who applied unsuccessfully for exemption as a conscientious objector. A bible-reading training camp commander persuaded him that his patriotic duty was to render to Caesar what was due to Caesar. Like Horace Baker, a schoolteacher from Missouri, York read his 'testament' in the front line.[43]

Much of this picture is corroborated by the reports to AEF GHQ on the mood of the troops passing through a classification camp near Le Mans. On 6 August 1918 a consignment of machine gunners were 'openly confident of the result. The common desire was to get to the front as quickly as possible.' The optimism was common to farmers and big-city immigrants – some barely able to speak English. Westerners, though often of German parentage, were likewise 'willing to go to the front and fight. They . . . did not like to have their peaceful life disturbed by war but since they were here in the army they were going to get revenge on the cause of it.' Nor did wounding and hospitalization change matters, survivors of the summer fighting being mostly ready and even impatient to return for what they expected would be an early end to the war.[44] French soldiers' letters also admired American enthusiasm, though had reservations if it turned quiet sectors into active ones.[45] German reports found the Americans brave, physically fit, willing to take casualties, and reluctant to surrender, though also poorly trained and led. Although their earliest deployed divisions improved with experience, more greenhorn units arrived to join them, so overall combat effectiveness remained unchanged.[46]

The great test for American enthusiasm was the Meuse–Argonne. Here men stayed in line for up to three weeks in cold and rain, sleeping in the open, lacking proper supplies, seeing dead everywhere, and losing comrades.[47] They faced well-sited and determined German machine gunners and unnervingly accurate artillery, with their tanks out of action after the first day and the Allied air force rarely to be seen. Soldiers lost confidence in their officers, whom Pershing and his generals were replacing faster than in other armies (unfairly, according to many commentators) and who were often neither visible nor long in post. The previously upbeat Le Mans reports warned that the men considered the campaign a 'disaster' and blamed it on 'bad officering', troops being bunched together as targets.[48] General Hunter Liggett, who took command of the First Army, estimated that by mid-October deserters numbered 100,000, and he sent patrols to scour the woods.[49] Reports on the 26th and 77th divisions suggested that they started with good morale but became depressed and dead beat.[50]

Yet things did improve. At divisional level the AEF ameliorated its planning and co-ordination of the different arms, troops now moving forward in small steps with massive firepower and tacitly abandoning

Pershing's 'open warfare' in favour of the tactics used by other armies. American ammunition consumption was even higher than French and British, General Summerall remarking: 'If we are to be economical with our men, we must be prodigal with guns and ammunition.'[51] Morale seems to have recovered, some in the rear wanting the Allies to drive on to Berlin.[52] All the same, most front-line soldiers were relieved when the armistice came, and viewed it as the right decision. They were proud of what they had done, but there had been enough killing and they wanted to go home.[53] This was not the cynical disenchantment propagated by some American writers in retrospect, but it showed experience had not only made the AEF more effective but had also chastened it. The central point remains that it not only deployed impressive manpower reserves, but its morale and discipline were good enough for it to fight and to achieve its objectives, if more slowly than the Allies and its own commanders wished. That this was so had major implications for troop morale everywhere else.

BRITISH EMPIRE

Whereas the AEF was concentrated in France, the British Empire forces were more scattered and diverse. In November 1918 besides 4 territorial divisions in the UK and 3 in India, 19 infantry divisions were serving in Italy, Macedonia, Egypt/Palestine, and Mesopotamia, and 61 on the Western Front. Six infantry divisions were Indian (2 in Egypt and 4 in Mesopotamia); and 10 came from the Dominions – 4 Canadian, 5 Australian, and 1 from New Zealand – all of them serving in France and Belgium. Of 8 cavalry divisions (3 of them on the Western Front), 3 were British, 3 Indian, and 2 from the Dominions.[54] Britain itself had 51 infantry divisions on the Western Front, but 3 in Italy, 4 in Macedonia, 1 in Palestine and 1 in Mesopotamia.[55] In March 1918 the strength of all the British Empire armed forces was 5,559,373, of whom 3,808,990 came from the UK. In addition to a pre-1914 total of 733,514 officers and men in the Regular Army and reserves, 4.4 million more had enlisted, raising the total to 22.1 per cent of the UK male population.[56]

Seven eighths of the UK forces were recruited after war broke out.[57] Like the AEF, they were civilians in uniform. The BEF of 1918 originated from converging streams of voluntary recruitment: the pre-1914 Regular Army, which provided most of the senior commanders; the Territorial Force, established for home defence but now much expanded, though long a poor relation; the 'New Armies' raised by Lord Kitchener when Secretary of State for War; and units recruited by local or private initiative, the 'pals' battalions' from localities and workplaces up and down the country being the best known. After conscription came in, these distinctions blurred and draftees became predominant among the rank and file: in total 2,466,719 enlisted in the UK as volunteers and 2,505,183 (50.3 per cent) as conscripts.[58] From the British Isles 772,000 lost their lives; for the British Empire as a whole the official figure published in 1928 was 1,081,952.[59] The conscription system was based on the National Register for England, Wales, and Scotland compiled in 1915, and under the 1916 Military Service Acts men aged 18–41 were liable to call-up, although until 1918 those under 19 did not go overseas. On attestation men took the King's oath and a notoriously superficial medical examination, before a home training period that averaged five months.[60] Two major exceptions remained. Ireland was exempted from conscription, and although over 200,000 men from north and south joined the services during the war, the Irish mobilization level remained below that in Great Britain.[61] Still more important was the exclusion of 'protected occupations', conscription's purpose having been as much to cushion home production as to find more troops. Although the army was in majority working class it recruited disproportionately from commerce and the professions, whereas mining, munitions, shipbuilding, agriculture, and transport were shielded.[62]

If Britain relied on volunteering and then conscription, practice in its empire varied. South Africa suppressed an Afrikaner rebellion against military service, but then achieved an exceptional enlistment rate among its white population – some 160,000 out of 244,000 men aged 20–40 – and although most of them served at home or elsewhere in Africa, one brigade went to Europe. Two battalions of the British West India Regiment also served in Africa, but manpower for the campaign in German East Africa came overwhelmingly from Britain's other possessions on the continent. They provided over 50,000 askaris and over a million bearers, often coming from huge distances. Most were recruited by impressment, and perhaps one in ten of them lost their lives, principally from disease, in one of the great neglected tragedies of the war.[63]

Among the other Dominions, New Zealand introduced conscription in 1916 and kept its forces up to strength until the armistice.[64] In Canada and Australia, however, recruitment was deeply divisive. Australian volunteering tailed off after 1916; and conscription was narrowly defeated in referenda in October 1916 and December 1917, opposition centring on New South Wales, on those of Irish origin, and on the Catholic Church and the labour movement. Australia raised 416,809 volunteers out of a total male population of 2.3 million; but by 1918 the Australian Imperial Force (AIF) was a wasting asset, shrinking between February and November from 198,333 to 178,342 men, and eleven battalions being disbanded.[65] In contrast, Canada did introduce conscription, but only after a wartime election in 1917, Sir Robert Borden's Conservative government defeating the Liberal opposition. Currie pleaded forcefully for it, asserting that 'the fate of the Empire is at stake'.[66] When the draft was introduced in 1918, it provoked riots in Quebec City in which four people died, and tens of thousands of French Canadians failed to register.[67] In total 469,557 served out of a male population of 3.8 million, the great majority coming from Anglophone Canada and about half having been born in Britain. One tenth of those who served were conscripted. The Canadian Expeditionary Force (CEF) stabilized at about 300,000 men until conscription brought in extra numbers that would, if necessary, have maintained its strength into 1919.[68]

By 1918 recruitment in Britain and the white Dominions was reaching its limits. India and the Labour Corps alleviated the position. The Indian army had traditionally functioned as an imperial reserve paid for by the Indian taxpayer. In 1914 British territorials replaced the regular battalions normally stationed there, while Indian units served on the Western Front (infantry in 1914–15, cavalry until February 1918), in East Africa, and in the Middle East. Whereas the Indian army in 1914 numbered 241,934, during the war 862,855 Indians were recruited for military service and 552,311 went overseas: the largest effort of any territory in the empire.[69] Increasingly the recruitment drive used coercion, and in 1917–18 the army doubled in size, recruitment now extending well beyond the traditional 'martial races' such as the Punjabi Moslems and the Sikhs, and releasing yet further white troops for France through the 'Indianization' of imperial forces elsewhere.[70] Palestine was the leading instance, but Mesopotamia had always been a primarily Indian effort and in October 1918 Indians arrived in Macedonia. A major constraint on expansion was finding officers, and members of the British community in India took up two thirds of the 9,943 commissions created during the war: Lloyd George had difficulty in winning Cabinet approval for just 200 temporary commissions for non-whites,[71] supposedly as a precondition for raising another 500,000 Indian troops by 1919.

Palestine and Mesopotamia lacked transport and most other kinds of infrastructure, and the British campaigns there required a huge supporting effort, again much of it Indian. In Mesopotamia by October 1918, 71,000 men were serving in the Labour Corps and 42,000 in river transport.[72] But on the Western Front too the numbers working on the communication lines trebled from 42,000 in December 1916 to 124,299 by the armistice.[73] After the Battle of the Somme, GHQ created a Directorate of Labour, with powers to switch the workforce between the greatest needs (for example, building railways before an offensive and handling ammunition during it), and decided on the mass import of 'coloured' workers. British servicemen who failed the medical requirements for combat were the biggest component in the labour battalions, but other elements included the South African Native Labour Corps (who were kept completely segregated); the Cape Coloured Labour Battalion; Egyptians; and Indians. Much the largest overseas contingents, however, came from China (the British leased territory of Wei-hai-wei and the German one of Tsingtao, captured by the Japanese in 1914). By 1918 the Chinese numbered 96,000. They carried out repairs in the Tank Corps central workshops, and were indispensable for building fall-back lines after 21 March (5,000 miles of new trenches being dug within weeks of the German attack).[74] Nearly 2,000 Chinese lost their lives.[75] Finally – and swelling in numbers – came German prisoners, who did crucial work on roads and railways during the final advance. The Cabinet had forbidden their use within thirty kilometres of the front, but the Chinese could be used up to ten kilometres away, so the Germans took over as the latter moved forward. Soldiers going up were struck by the cosmopolitan appearance of the rear areas. According to Private William Francis, '. . . I'd never seen so many Chinamen, there must have been thousands of them. They . . . would do all sorts, even carrying barbed wire up to the line.'[76] Although the infantry still did much arduous manual work, without the labour battalions they would have had even less opportunity for rest and training when out of the line.

Despite these overseas contributions, manpower questions hovered constantly near the top of the British political agenda. They caused tension not only with America but also with France, and between soldiers and civilians in Whitehall. From June 1917 monthly enlistments fell sharply, while the army authorities complained the conscripts were less fit and motivated than their volunteer predecessors. In a gloomy discussion in December, Sir Auckland Geddes, the Minister of National Service, told the Cabinet that without raising the military age and conscripting the Irish he could not approach the numbers demanded for 1918: 'This country was straining all its resources to the utmost, and was nearing the breaking point.' Asking more would endanger shipbuilding and food and weapons production, or risk a coal strike if more miners were conscripted, or a confrontation in Ireland, where men would have to be 'seized'. Lord Derby, the Secretary of State for War, responded that the BEF was 100,000 below its proper strength and 'So far from there being any question of our breaking through the Germans, it was a question of whether we could prevent the Germans breaking through us.' The problem, as summarized by the Cabinet Secretary, was to prevent a military catastrophe without risking an economic one.[77] The Cabinet had to settle priorities, and it did so via a manpower sub-committee, chaired by Lloyd George himself. As the Premier put it, 'We acted on the assumption that staying power was what mattered most', and maintaining the Allies' war effort until at least 1919.[78] As that effort would collapse unless the troops and civilians were supplied, the Americans conveyed across the Atlantic, and London protected against bombing, the top priorities should be the navy and air force, followed by shipbuilding, aircraft and tank construction, food production and storage, and timber felling. The army would get only 100,000 Class I men instead of the 600,000 it wanted. Lloyd George did not conceal his view that GHQ had wasted men, and the sub-committee envisaged lowering casualties by moving to a smaller, more mechanized army, fighting defensively by choice as well as necessity.[79] According to the Prime Minister, 'Government is in part a science but it is more of an art',[80] and in weighing the imponderables he judged that Germany could not break through but he must uphold domestic morale: which meant, among other things, no conscription in Ireland. Yet he also felt that he must acquiesce at least partially in Clemenceau's demands for the BEF to take over more of the French line, which in early 1918 it therefore did at the same time as reorganizing itself and preparing its defences in order to hold, without significant reinforcement, the German attack.

It is too simple to conclude that the outcome vindicated the Cabinet's judgement because the Germans failed to break through. In fact the 'Michael' battle pushed back the BEF much faster than expected and sounded the alarm in Whitehall, widening the bounds of political possibility but also forcing the government to change tack. Lloyd George told the Cabinet that 'the Germans mean to fight the battle through to victory or defeat ... The nation with the largest number of reserves to throw in when the other is exhausted is likely to be victorious ... The strain on our reservoir of men will be beyond anything we anticipated.'[81] Three divisions were recalled from Palestine and one from Italy. Youths aged eighteen were now sent to the front and the recruiters upgraded thousands rejected earlier as unfit.[82] But these steps would take time to reinforce the firing line, as would the simultaneous breakthrough over American troop shipments. Lloyd George saw the first imperative as survival until August, by which point the additional conscripts could be rushed through training, and crucial to the British authorities' immediate response were the forces available in the UK. Typical of the more than 200,000 conveyed to France by 7 April – and 544,005 by 31 August – was gunner Sidney Edwards, who was filled with foreboding as he marched from his London barracks to a sleepless passage on a ship so crowded that he could find no floor space on which to sit down.[83]

GHQ had allowed 88,000 men to be at home on leave – responding to a legitimate grievance over backlogs, but at the least surprising in view of the expectation by mid-March that an attack was imminent. But in addition the UK had an enormous permanent home garrison of 1.5 million, which the authorities now cut by 170,000. The government had over-insured against German raids or invasion, the likelihood of which the Admiralty had just downgraded.[84] The larger question, which remained disputed long after the war, was whether Lloyd George had deliberately kept men back to prevent them from being squandered in a renewed Flanders offensive – an offensive which, be it remembered, until January 1918 was Haig's intention for the new year. This accusation appeared in Churchill's memoirs, and Churchill was both well informed and supported by much circumstantial evidence:[85] the Prime Minister indeed believed that lives had been thrown away during the Third Ypres operations, which he had authorized against his better judgement. If the men now rushed across the Channel had been in France before 21 March, the unfortunate Gough could have been reinforced faster. Yet Lloyd George vigorously defended himself against such insinuations, both subsequently and in the controversy at the time that led to the 'Maurice debate' in the House of Commons on 9 May.[86] General Sir Frederick Maurice, formerly Director of Military Operations at the War Office, alleged in *The Times* that the government had kept the BEF undermanned and held in Palestine soldiers who could have gone to France. He queried the Prime Minister's insistence that on 1 January 1918 the BEF had been larger than a year earlier. The truth was that the total numbers were slightly larger, but infantry fighting strength had peaked in 1917 and was now falling. Much of the increase had gone to non-combatant forces such as the labour battalions, and men had also been redistributed to units such as the Tank Corps, which augmented the BEF's offensive power during the advances after August but helped less in the defensive battles. By the armistice only one in three of the BEF were infantrymen.[87] Although Lloyd George won the parliamentary debate, the argument missed the point, which was that to safeguard Britain's staying power in a longer war the Cabinet had cut a finer margin than it realized in preparing against Ludendorff's attacks. As it turned out, although Haig's immediate reserve on 21 March was only eight infantry divisions, enough was available across the Channel (to say nothing of French assistance) to check the onslaught. Even so, British casualties in March and April exceeded 281,000 and the BEF's net strength fell by 53,500, so that only in the summer, when the storm centre shifted to the French front, could it rebuild its shattered units.

Lloyd George was also looking to the longer term, and another of his responses to the spring crisis was a new military service bill to raise manpower for 1919.[88] This legislation increased the maximum age to fifty but also gave the government discretion to go to fifty-six (an astonishingly high figure in view of the average life expectancy at the time) and extend conscription across the Irish Sea. Having previously resisted the latter, the Prime Minister now argued that he could not ask the English trade unions to concede more men if Ireland remained exempt. His decision was taken under pressure and without studying the matter properly. His critics warned that Irish conscription would inflame republican nationalism and antagonize America and the Dominions, without producing extra men: according to Lord Wimborne, the Lord Lieutenant, it would lead to an 'explosion'.[89] In fact the government got the worst of both worlds. It held back from exercising its new powers, instead appealing for 50,000 more volunteers though actually obtaining fewer than 10,000. But the Irish reaction against even the possibility of conscription was so ferocious that the authorities proclaimed military rule and increased the garrison from 25,000 to 100,000, most of the troops coming from Great Britain.[90] In short, the underlying manpower shortage was exacerbated.

Partly for this reason, from summer 1918 a new phase opened in the manpower question: one overshadowed by Anglo-French friction and the government's fear of ending the war prostrate.[91] In June, Lloyd George told the Imperial War Cabinet that it was 'essential that the British Empire should be adequately represented in that great [inter-Allied] army next year, not merely in order to achieve the purpose of the campaign but in order that the Empire . . . may be able to claim its fair share in the victory . . .'[92] Yet seven BEF divisions had suffered such losses in the spring fighting that they had temporarily to be reduced to 'cadre' formations and taken out of the line, while three others went back to Britain to re-form.[93] The French suspected that too many able-bodied men were being retained in the British Isles, Foch insisting that the divisions must be reconstituted: 'the situation is critical . . . we should not compromise the present on the pretext of assuring the future . . .'[94] The two prime ministers clashed publicly, Lloyd George feeling that the French (like the British army authorities earlier) did not understand the special demands made on Britain as a furnisher of coal, raw materials, and seapower to the rest of the alliance. Although Lloyd George agreed to a French representative, Colonel Albert Roure, coming to London to investigate, the mission resolved nothing. On the contrary, both Milner and Lloyd George emphatically rebutted Roure's conclusion that the British were keeping too many able-bodied men out of the front line.[95] In a most revealing letter Foch pleaded that France was keeping up its divisions and Britain must do too – 'we must win the war in 1919, with American aid that will then be at its maximum development, therefore organize all our maximum efforts for that year's battle . . . with the present number of divisions'.[96] Foch wanted to be sure of winning next

year – given the strain on France and on its influence at the peace conference if the war continued longer – and British concerns were similar.
But as the danger from the Ludendorff offensives diminished so an
array of civilian manpower needs (above all for coal) again beset Lloyd
George's Cabinet. Henry Wilson told Foch that Britain might have to
suppress 15–20 of its Western Front divisions (up to one in three):
'Agriculture, vital industries for ourselves and our Allies, coal, aeroplanes and tank construction . . . all show such significant demands
that little remains for the fighting services. The Cabinet therefore are
anxious about the future. They do not want to end the war absolutely
exhausted . . .'[97] Wilson warned Haig on 1 September that he might
have to withdraw 50,000 miners from the BEF to avoid 'a coal
disaster' and urged him to be wary of incurring heavy casualties against
the Hindenburg Line: 'the constant – and growing – embarrassment
about Man Power . . . makes the Cabinet uneasy; . . . the curiously hostile attitude, on several points, of both the French and the Americans; it
is the uneasy spirit in this country . . . the feeling that, when the end
comes, we must still possess a formidable army'.[98] For the time being,
Haig took no notice and continued operations at full tilt, but the Cabinet approached the armistice facing a personnel shortage that in a 1919
campaign would have meant a much smaller British army alongside an
enormous AEF, with disturbing implications for the peace settlement.
Both Haig and Lloyd George feared an American-dominated peace.[99]

If it was becoming harder to keep up the BEF's numbers, observers
were at one on its continuing spirit. American troops arrived with a low
opinion of the British, but on acquaintance grew more respectful.[100]
Interrogating British prisoners at a low point in June, the Germans
found a temporary demoralization but also a conviction that the war
must go on. Their intelligence concluded that the BEF had undergone a
crisis and its situation remained fragile, but that its summer successes
restored its confidence. Although the British troops were tired and their
attacks more easily halted, their *Siegeswille* – their will to victory – was
unbroken.[101] British internal assessments corroborated much of this
picture. Whereas most Americans were under fire for less than six
months, the British army was composed in part of raw eighteen-year-
olds, but in part also of men who had endured the terrible attrition
battles of 1916–17 and of some who had served even longer: more
than enough, in other words, for war weariness to set in. Although it

experienced no crisis of morale as intense as those of the French or Italians, in the winter of 1917–18 it developed disquieting symptoms, from which it mostly recovered. Its morale varied with the military prospects, but showed an underlying resilience.

This resilience rested partly on coercion. The British Military Police expanded even more than the American, from 1 per 3,306 soldiers in 1914 to 1 per 292 by 1918.[102] The BEF held 304,262 courts martial: most frequently for absence without leave, followed by drunkenness, insubordination, and desertion. The scale of punishments seemed harsh compared with other armies, and was criticized in Britain. It included imprisonment; 'Field Punishment No. 1' (tying the offender for several hours to an object such as a limber wheel); and execution, and although only one in ten death sentences was implemented the total of 346 killings still much exceeded the German army's forty-eight.[103] Desertion was the most common capital offence (1,990 cases), followed by sentries sleeping at their posts (449), and cowardice (213). When sentences were implemented they were publicized throughout the army (although not to the dead men's families), and Haig undoubtedly approved some to set an example.[104] Yet collective disobedience was rare, and only two major incidents took place during the war. One was the mutiny at the Etaples base in September 1917, which was directed against brutality by the trainers and a ban on visiting the town, although it may have reflected a wider disenchantment during the Third Ypres offensive.[105] The second, a year later, broke out when the Australians felt that they were being ordered into line too often and objected to going again; and were withdrawn from front-line service for the remainder of the war. This was the only disciplinary breakdown that bore directly on the army's willingness to fight, and in general when British units were ordered forward, they went.

Although coercion helped to glue the BEF together, sticks mattered less than carrots. Materially, British soldiers were adequately provided for, many better than in peacetime, better than civilians, and certainly better than their enemies. Their letters and memoirs made few complaints about the clothing: the food was a constant topic of conversation but as a rule nutritionally adequate, although hunger and thirst were common companions on the March retreat. A further element of solidarity was loyalty to the 'primary group' of the soldiers' squad and its NCOs and junior officers: a factor much emphasized in the theoretical literature in the light of studies of the American army in the Second World War. In fact the members of many British volunteer units had originated from the same locality, although by 1918 such territorial bonds were growing tenuous and men's initial comrades had mostly gone, even if new friendships could form quickly. But much did turn on officers and their tactical leadership. By 1917–18 many officers had been promoted from the ranks and some 40 per cent are estimated to have been of lower-middle-class or working-class origin.[106] Their superiors and their guiding texts enjoined them to show concern for their men's welfare, as well as bravery and judgement – and testimony from below suggests that many heeded the message. If they felt fear, they were expected to conceal it: as Lt R. G. Dixon put it, 'I fancy most fellows were scared out of their wits ... The thing was to try not to show it, especially to one's men.'[107] Even junior officers had privileges – servants, separate meals and accommodation, more frequent leave – and the latter especially caused resentment, but they shared the dangers and many of the hardships of the front-line troops, and to some degree formed a community with them against staff officers and non-combatants.[108]

Repression, adequate support services, and small-group loyalty formed three bases of the BEF's cohesion, and to an extent all differentiated it from the opposing side. But recent writers have placed new stress on individual and mass psychology. Crucial to morale were optimism about personal survival chances and faith that victory could be won and the cause was worthwhile. Canadian troops were sustained by a sense of individual and collective superiority, buttressed by repeated successes.[109] Coping mechanisms included soldiers' confidence – grounded in religion or superstition – that they personally would pull through,[110] which among new arrivals was supplemented by excitement, and among more experienced men by a magnetic sense of obligation: to cite Dixon again, 'One hated it but one wanted to be back in it, because it was shirking to be elsewhere.'[111] This experience, with all its tribulations, would mould men for a lifetime and many did not regret it, even if they would not care to traverse it again.[112]

None of this sufficed to save the BEF from a loss of confidence after Third Ypres: part of a pattern of morale being dashed by unsuccessful offensives. The first big British attrition battle – the Somme in 1916 – appears not, despite its miserable conclusion, to have shaken optimism.[113] Casualties, even if enormous, were offset by the evidence that the

German army had been beaten back. Nor did the Battle of Arras, despite its similarly dispiriting outcome, modify this impression: the seizure of Vimy ridge in April 1917 and of Messines ridge in June provided further evidence of progress. According to postal censorship reports for the Third Army in November 1916, morale had never been higher: a spirit of 'cheery optimism' and 'dogged resolution' continued into January, and after a dip during the bitter weather of the early spring, the mood improved again. In contrast, the report for 25 August 1917 was far gloomier – 'for the first time there is a frequent suggestion that the war cannot be won by military effort, but must end by political compromise'. The change reflected a rise in anti-war feeling at home, but the main explanation was 'uncertainty as to the progress of our army to an ultimate victory', following the unfulfilled hopes placed in the Flanders campaign.[114] R. C. McKay wrote that 'the Somme was a picnic and Arras a joke compared with Ypres now'.[115] Auckland Geddes told the Cabinet's sub-committee on manpower that recently discharged soldiers were in 'a very disgruntled state', and expressing 'extreme dissatisfaction' with the conduct of operations. A retrospective report by the Dominion prime ministers reported that after Passchendaele the army had been in 'a deplorable condition', and morale 'seriously impaired'.[116] The effects were lasting, for nineteen of the twenty-one British divisions in the Third and Fifth Armies on 21 March had fought at Third Ypres.[117] Haig himself wrote on 15 December (and Robertson agreed) that 'The whole army is ... at present much exhausted and much reduced in strength.'[118] Haig acknowledged the need to rebuild soldiers' faith in the war effort, and in February 1918 he approved a political education scheme and a plan for chaplains to run discussion groups.[119]

The scheme did not get going until the summer, however, and only some 25,000 soldiers – barely 1 per cent of the army – then took part.[120] But fortunately the BEF was less despondent than its leaders apprehended. Another censors' report based on 17,000 letters and forwarded to the Cabinet in December 1917 concluded that 'The morale of the Army is sound ... there is ample ground for the belief that the British Army is fairly convinced, not only of its ability to defeat the enemy and its superiority man to man, but also of the danger of a premature peace ...' In the Second Army, which after August had borne the brunt of the Flanders fighting, pessimistic comments matched optimistic ones;

but elsewhere the latter predominated and in general 'War weariness there is, and an almost universal longing for peace but there is a strong current of feeling that only one kind of peace is possible and that the time is not yet come.'[121] By the time of the 'Michael' attack, a further survey spoke of the 'high quality of morale', and Haig noted on 22 March, the second day of the battle, that 'all reports show that our men are in great spirits'.[122] Yet the German perspective on 'Michael' differed. Certainly there was no rout. Yet never before had so many British troops surrendered (21,000 on 21 March alone), and many British units were not resisting to the final round but giving up when they saw no further purpose in fighting.[123] Despite the weeks of rest since Passchendaele, morale was not yet fully restored, and it seems the real change came *after* 21 March. Once again casualties were in themselves not crucial, and open warfare was exhausting but at times exhilarating. Captain C. J. Lodge Patch wrote of its 'glorious thrills', and for many the adrenalin factor counted.[124] The German threat was newly evident – familiar towns and villages lost, pathetic streams of refugees, and retreat towards the Channel and nearer home – but also, for the first time in years, the Germans were venturing into the open and lining up as targets.[125] As well as hastening forward the Americans, the Ludendorff offensives galvanized the British.

According to a massive postal survey in July, based on 83,621 letters, 'the loss of ground . . . acted as a powerful tonic on the moral [sic] of the army as reflected in its correspondence'.[126] Haig's 'backs to the wall' order may have been unnecessary, as spirits in the Second Army were 'marvellously good', while in the First Army confidence grew in summer 1918 that the war might end that year. In the Fourth Army, despite distrust of the government and high command, men predicted that after holding the next German offensive they would, with American help, 'walk through the enemy'. Indeed, references to the Americans were frequent, while the new experience of fighting alongside the French had raised esteem for that army too. Although an undercurrent of cynicism and dissatisfaction lingered, the Germans were correct about the BEF's optimism on the eve of its final successes. Its advances after 8 August were intensely strenuous, men being on the move for days on end, often soaked to the skin, and lacking warm food and drink. More time was spent under fire, and leave became less frequent.[127] But it was comforting to see reconquered territory and – especially – German prisoners in unprecedented numbers, many now appearing young, half-starved, and only too glad to be out of the war.[128] Though the Germans found the British infantry cautious and reliant on artillery support, it continued to move forward, and as it now faced weaker resistance and fewer counter-attacks the recaptured ground was kept.

FRANCE

All three main Western armies made indispensable contributions to the 1918 victory. The British army was hardest hit by 'Michael', Ludendorff's heaviest single blow, and inflicted most damage on the Germans during the Allied advance. But the French army gave vital assistance to the BEF and halted largely single-handedly the three German attacks between May and July. It remained the largest of the three and held the longest sector of front, as it had since 1914. It guarded the foothold on the European mainland where the British and Americans deployed and built up for the final assault. That it could muster the necessary manpower – and its troops recover from the 1917 mutinies – was therefore critical.

France had a smaller and an older population than either Britain or the US. Its birth rate was so low that after 1870 it had maintained its population only through immigration. It was also less urbanized. Perhaps half the French army came from the countryside, and it has been estimated that peasant farmers took 44 per cent of its casualties.[129] In addition it was a maturer army than the AEF and BEF: some 50 per cent of those doing military service in 1918 were aged between thirty-three and fifty-one, and almost half the Frenchmen mobilized were married.[130] In peacetime young men joined the colours at twenty as members of a conscript cohort (or *classe*). France called up a higher percentage of each cohort than did Germany, and it entered the war with an exceptionally high proportion of its population accustomed to bearing arms. The 1913 military service law extended the term of active service in the infantry from two years to three, followed by a longer period in the reserves with continuing call-ups for training. During the war men were called up at nineteen, and up to the age of fifty: eventually all thirty-three of the 1887–1919 cohorts (i.e. men reaching twenty in those years). The 1915–19 cohorts joined up after war broke out, the

1919 one from April 1918. In total, 7.74 million men were mobilized from metropolitan France, and nearly 475,000 from its colonies.[131]

A grim destiny awaited them: 1,383,000 were killed; 506,500 taken prisoner; and 2.8 million wounded (half of them twice): 29.2 per cent of the 1914 cohort ended up as dead or missing. Most of these losses came in the first half of the conflict, whereas Britain's came in the second. After the disaster of the Nivelle offensive, 1917 was for the French the least costly year of the war, but in 1918, especially June and July, the monthly casualties were the highest since 1914.[132] Even though some two thirds of the wounded would return to active service,[133] numbers were slipping. French combatant forces on the Western Front peaked at 2,234,000 on 1 July 1916. They fell to 1,888,000 on 1 October 1917 and 1,688,000 on 1 October 1918. Even during the 1917 breathing space the army was shrinking, and the renewed fierce fighting of 1918 accelerated the process.[134]

As against this, France's navy made much smaller manpower claims than Britain's, and the army was more concentrated on the Western Front. In summer 1918 France had 103 infantry divisions there, two in Italy (reduced from six since the emergency of March 1918), and eight at Salonika, as well as three battalions in Palestine. Salonika was the one big external commitment, and French governments resisted pressure from the colonialist lobby to send troops to Africa and the Middle East. They did, however, like the British, respond to manpower stringency by looking beyond their borders. In April 1918 the authorities estimated France contained 197,573 workers from elsewhere in Europe (principally Spain) and 148,192 from Africa and Asia, including 33,643 from China but the others mainly from the empire, including 43,298 from Indochina, 37,878 from Algeria, 17,361 from Morocco, and 1,285 from Tunisia.[135] During the war as a whole over 220,000 workers from the empire came to France as factory operatives and labourers, leading in 1917–18 to a wave of racist attacks.[136] In the armed forces, France had almost 90,000 non-white troops in 1914, and during the conflict it recruited 473,300 more. The biggest contingents came from French West Africa (166,000) and Algeria (140,000), followed by Indochina (50,000), Tunisia (47,000), Madagascar (46,000), and Morocco (24,300). The high command regarded the West Africans – over 90 per cent recruited from 'warrior races' – as the finest fighters, and best deployed as shock troops.[137] One in five of those enlisted were killed:

Mangin, the leading proponent of recruiting Africans since even before 1914, believed they were best used for surprise attacks without artillery; Nivelle, Pétain's predecessor as Western Front commander, stated bluntly that using Africans would reduce white casualties.[138] Nominally, the Africans were volunteers, but the French paid bounties to recruiting agents and local chiefs for the men delivered, and many were compelled to go by village heads or were seized in night raids, fear of which drove thousands of families into the bush. According to Blaise Diagne, the African deputy for French West Africa in the French parliament, there had been 'a veritable manhunt'.[139] Indeed, the recruitment drive tied down additional forces by igniting in West Africa and Algeria in 1915–16 the most serious rebellions since the French Empire's foundation. Undeterred, Mangin persuaded Clemenceau to authorize a further effort in the final year, even though the colonial administrations warned that the empire had yielded as much as could safely be extracted. In the event, with Diagne's help, 143,200 more men were found, the best result of the war, and colonial troops bulked large in Clemenceau's contingency plans for maintaining the war into 1919.[140]

French civilians treated the African soldiers respectfully, and would remember them twenty years later when war approached again.[141] They proved to be disciplined troops who by 1918 were serving to the high command's full satisfaction. Men freshly arrived in Macedonia from Senegal took part in the September–October 1918 advance against the Bulgarians, and West African forces distinguished themselves in defending Reims and Soissons.[142] By the armistice non-white personnel constituted 6.6 per cent of France's total forces: but the corresponding figure for British forces was 16 per cent.[143] The French proportion was lower in part because the French empire's population of some 40 million in 1914 was about the same size as that of the mother country instead of being several times bigger. Moreover, the French did much less campaigning outside Europe – where most of the British Indian troops served – and the West Africans were unable to withstand winter conditions on the Western Front, and had to be quartered on the Mediterranean coast. They had been brought back prematurely before the April 1917 Nivelle offensive, hundreds dying when thrown against the German wire in freezing temperatures and blizzards. The North Africans were hardier, but judged less good fighters, while the Malagaches and Indochinese served primarily on duties in the rear. Four thousand Indochinese became lorry drivers, many transporting the Americans from the Saint-Mihiel to the Meuse–Argonne sector by careering at night and without headlights along unfamiliar and rutted roads.[144] Colonial troops alleviated shortages of manual labour, which were especially pressing during the anxious winter of 1917–18. But as combatants – though not separated from whites as were the African-Americans – they were placed under French officers and few received commissions, and the French army's general officer shortage impeded the rapid expansion of colonial infantry that Clemenceau desired.

Despite imperial recruitment, then, by 1918 the French army had too few men. Pétain and Clemenceau planned to nurture it by substituting machines for soldiers in order to amplify mobility and firepower while reducing losses, but this meant diverting men from military service into war production, and manufacturing additional weapons for the American army diverted even more. To find the necessary labour the French looked not only to their colonies, to women, and to prisoners of war, but also to conscripts serving as workers in uniform (though paid at civilian rates rather than the miserable 25 centimes per day received by a private soldier).[145] The numbers of soldiers working in factories rose from 122,000 in July 1915 to 559,000 two years later, and was still 492,000 at the armistice.[146] As in the BEF, new specialist services were needed to operate the additional weapons, whereas the proportion of infantry in the army fell between 1914 and 1918 from 80 per cent to 50 per cent.[147] Concern in parliament about the inequality of sacrifice entailed in soldiers working in munitions factories while their comrades were dying for a pittance led to legislation to transfer more soldiers to the front, but the authorities were so preoccupied with production that they diluted the measures and dragged their heels in applying them. Soldiers' letters cited 'shirkers' (*embusqués*) behind the lines as a major source of grievance, and Clemenceau came to office determined to root them out. He managed to return 88,000 from the interior to the combat units down to February 1918, but abandoned the effort after Ludendorff attacked. Even when in the emergency following the 'Michael' battle Pétain asked for 200,000 men from the interior, the government gave him only 40,000.[148] The principle of equal sacrifice took second place to modernizing the army and industrializing the war effort.

It was unsurprising that when Clemenceau took over as Premier, manpower became, in one of his advisers' words, 'a veritable obsession'.[149]

Pétain's prognoses resembled Haig's: a dismal GQG report in December 1917 predicted losses of 920,000 by October 1918 and a net shortfall of 328,000, requiring twenty-two divisions to be suppressed.[150] Much of the tension in inter-Allied relations arose from manpower shortages. In the winter of 1917/18 Pétain was determined to obtain an extension of the British line, threatening that otherwise he could not take responsibility for holding the French sector.[151] Having got it, over Haig's protests, he could allow more leave, release 75,000 older men, and constitute a forty-division reserve.[152] Similarly, the French pressed the Americans over amalgamation; and insisted that the British keep up their divisions. Behind these controversies lay a perception on all sides that their contribution to the final campaigning would shape their influence on the peace settlement. Thus in July Foch urged the drastic step of calling up the 1920 class almost two years early, from October 1918, on the grounds that 1919 would be the decisive year and 'the stronger we are and the sooner we are victorious, the better we will be listened to'. Clemenceau agreed that 'France is playing for the highest stakes in its history', and even though French blood should now be conserved 'as the most precious material', the class would have to be summoned. They could just get through 1918 with their existing resources, but if the fighting continued into 1919 they would use the 1920 men alongside the Senegalese.[153]

The French had already weakened their divisions in 1916 by reducing the battalions in each from twelve to nine (a measure implemented by the British army on the eve of 'Michael').[154] Unlike the British, during 1918 they maintained their nominal total of divisions, but at lower and lower strengths, retaining the appearance of a larger army than they could keep replenished. Three things helped. First, they delayed longer than the Germans in calling up their 1919 conscript cohort, which joined the ranks from April 1918 onwards.[155] Second, French casualties were not as bad as feared, though still terrible enough: 92,000 in March–April, nearly 160,000 in May–June, and nearly 279,000 between July and September.[156] Pétain warned Foch on 31 July that the army was 120,000 short and could expect only 29,000 over the next three months – 'we are at the limit of effort' – and perhaps for this reason Foch assigned the French army a supporting role alongside Britain and America in the battles of August to October.[157] Third, however, whereas the bulges created by Ludendorff's offensives once more extended the French line by 120 kilometres, in the final stages it was greatly curtailed. As it included the quiet stretches east of the Meuse, the British estimated that by the armistice the 'active' French sector had fallen to just forty miles.[158]

If there were just enough French troops – and now much better equipped than previously – their morale was shaky. The French army mutinies of 1917 had been one of the most dangerous Allied crises of the war, and recovery from them incomplete. Their crucial precipitant was the ill-fated April 1917 offensive. Certainly the French high command had been more neglectful than the German or British of its troops' material welfare, and the men had justified grievances about their conditions, but the mutinies were concentrated in the attack sector and among units that had taken part, a backwash of disorder also rippling along the trains carrying soldiers to and from leave.[159] Analysis of the military justice records confirms that although disproportionate numbers of the mutineers were young and came from Paris (and relatively few were industrial workers), the men came from all regions of France and were varied by age and occupation: in other words, what distinguished them was involvement in the offensive. Despite the hopes the high command had encouraged for it, from the first day it was evidently another disaster, and exacerbated by persistent further attacks. The disturbances started soon after 16 April and peaked in early June, by which stage some protests were violent and accompanied by talk of revolution and marching on Paris, but in general they were peaceful and their essence a rejection of further wasteful great attacks: some units refused to move up but others were willing to hold the line, although calling for an early peace and for France to reduce its war aims. Further, the mutinies were extensive rather than profound: some 250 incidents were recorded in sixty-five infantry divisions, but only nine divisions had seven or more incidents and the number of individuals committing mutinous acts totalled 30,000–40,000.[160]

These factors helped the authorities regain control, much of the task being accomplished by junior officers before the repression implemented by the high command.[161] To his credit, Pétain took a broader view of the problem than had Nivelle, who blamed unrest on the interior ministry's failure to control pacifist agitation. Pétain was determined to restore order and saw military justice as an essential part of that process, but he moderated its impact. Just under 3,000 mutineers were sentenced and 629 condemned to death, but forty-three were executed.

Pétain had opposed Nivelle's offensive and his Directive No. 1 renounced 'strategic breakthrough' in favour of brief surprise attacks at different points, wearing down the enemy but minimizing French losses. He advised his subordinates that officers must feel free to signal the difficulties in a proposed operation. In addition he tried to improve the men's conditions. He ensured that they had absolute rest for the first two days after a tour in the line, and he improved the quantity and quality of food. He also introduced a more transparent system of allocating home leave (which in future would be for ten days every four months instead of seven) as well as faster trains to get soldiers to their destinations, and on both scores he achieved real results that were greatly appreciated.[162]

Part of Pétain's medicine was for the army to return to the offensive, but through short, sharp blows with massive materiel support. French troops attacked in Flanders on 31 July 1917, at Verdun on 20 August, and in the Chemin des Dames sector itself at La Malmaison from 23 to 26 October, with up to three times the artillery densities used in April.[163] He commented in retrospect that after Malmaison the 'crisis of morale' was over. Yet at the time he admitted to the government's War Committee on 18 November 1917 that morale remained 'fragile': notwithstanding which the army must remain active 'until the end without failing' to ensure that France was 'paid at its price'.[164]

Foreign appraisals conformed with this equivocal view. According to a German assessment in July 1918, French troops had been depressed by Germany's breakthrough on 27 May, but once it had been halted morale recovered quickly, and although tired the men were disciplined and confident and willing to fight on for another winter. In contrast, a report on 7 November said recent successes had boosted spirits sky high, but although the men wanted to drive the Germans out and were still ready to fight, they were increasingly reluctant to attack and wanted to go home.[165] American observers found the French experienced and skilful, but very cautious, while in June 1918 Pershing doubted if they (or indeed the British) could continue for another year.[166] British assessments were more cutting. According to the official British history, General Debeney's First Army advancing alongside the BEF left flank in the Battle of Amiens made only slow progress; and the French in Flanders in October did little more than shadow the retreating enemy, leaving the fighting to their allies.[167] After piercing the Hindenburg Line, Haig's GHQ commented that the British army was mainly responsible for the Allies' success, and Lawrence noted sourly that the BEF was doing all the fighting and the French were doing nothing.[168] In the final week Haig wrote to Henry Wilson that 'few of the French divisions fight now', Wilson told the Cabinet that the French were 'extremely fatigued', and Haig noted that the men were more reluctant to risk their lives and 'next year a large proportion will probably be black'.[169] This was ungenerous in view of GHQ's own estimate that between 1 July and 24 October the British had taken 180,700 German prisoners but the French 122,000, the two armies had captured 2,000 guns each, and the French had liberated more territory.[170] In fact the French were both taking casualties and inflicting them, although it was true that after bearing the main weight of the fighting between May and July their contribution diminished. Moreover, outsiders' impressions of flagging morale were borne out by the army's internal reporting.

Typifying many of the French army's characteristics was Louis Barthas, a barrel maker from Languedoc, who in 1914 was thirty-five and married with two young sons. He had read Marx and the French classics, and was a socialist activist. As an infantry corporal he served through the worst battles of 1915–16 and in the mutinies he drafted a manifesto for a soldiers' soviet (though was too canny to accept election as leader). In 1918 he was withdrawn from the front line, exhausted. He viewed the war as a disaster, fought to benefit profiteers and jingoists, and he ended it with a 'fierce hatred' of the military hierarchy and the language of glory, patriotism, and honour, though was ready none the less to follow good officers who shared their men's hardships.[171] In contrast Paul Pireaud, a peasant from the Dordogne, was called up in 1914 six months after his marriage. Less politicized than Barthas, his thoughts centred on his home and on his wife Marie, but he too served right through, in the heavy artillery, with whom he ended the conflict serving in Italy.[172] Both men carried on despite their deep reluctance to be fighting. We know about Pireaud through the survival of more than 2,000 letters that he exchanged with Marie; about Barthas because of the remarkable memoir that he wrote up, in distinguished prose, after returning to his village. Barthas exemplifies the political consciousness of a significant proportion of the French army; Pireaud those less politically aware but well informed about the home front and anguished by reports of food shortages. And in addition to diaries and letters, many French 'trench newspapers' have survived, although these were often produced behind the lines with officers' involvement. Analysis of their content underlines the army's concern to be viewed as part of the nation and discloses little doubt that France would win. Its citizen-soldiers cared little about revenge for 1870 or regaining Alsace-Lorraine, but they did want to expel the invaders from French territory, and accepted their patriotic duty to fight.[173]

The best evidence on morale, however, comes from the postal surveillance system. Pétain's headquarters paid its findings close attention, comparing them with reports that it now required regularly from the officers of each unit.[174] The censors saw only a small proportion of the 180,000 letters sent each week from the French Western Front armies, and no doubt many correspondents – who mostly bitterly resented the intrusion – censored themselves. Yet many others were unimpeded from expressing in the fiercest terms their criticisms of the war, the high command, and the government, and there was a stronger undertow of really radical alienation in the French army than in the British. Moreover, the vast quantity of correspondence between the soldiers and their loved ones ensured that morale at the front and in the rear were interdependent.

After Pétain's reforms, the French army's basic needs were better met. Its soldiers were paid less than British or Americans (and Pétain thought they spent too much money on drink), but enough food and wine usually reached the *poilus*.[175] Barracks during rest periods were often cold, draughty, and remote, which caused much grumbling, as did the curtailment of leave forced by the 1918 emergencies. None the less, larger political and military developments did more to shape the army's mood swings. Pétain was right that the Battle of La Malmaison boosted spirits, but in November 1917 confidence dipped, owing partly to Caporetto but especially to the Bolshevik Revolution and the ceasefire in Russia. Men appreciated that these events presaged a new German assault and that considerable American assistance was unlikely until 1919.[176] Yet even now, according to a survey of the post of 922 units, morale was 'good' in 85 per cent of them and 'bad' in only 5 per cent.[177] Moreover, at the end of 1917 the mood improved, which the censors attributed to a perception that the next German offensive would be the last, and to confidence that the French army would withstand it.[178] Throughout the war, hopes that peace would return in another six months had buoyed up French morale, and this foreshortening had proved a recipe for repeated disillusionment. Yet now such hopes were stirring again, the censors warning that 'the sensititivity of the combatants to influences from whatever source is extreme: they live in perpetual fever', and 'Never, in the trenches, has there been so much talk of peace.'[179] Anxiety centred on the home front, the soldiers worrying about food shortages and the bombing of Paris, and condemning strikers in the war industries. Pétain was trusted, and his defensive preparations known to be supported by a much more powerful artillery than when the Germans had attacked Verdun. But overall, although the war had gone on far too long and its butchery was viewed as an affront to civilization, the vast majority of soldiers who expressed an opinion about peace wanted it to be victorious rather than one imposed by Germany, so that their children need not undergo this nightmare again: indeed, the censors were surprised at the strength of determination.[180] When Clemenceau told French parliamentarians that the army was in good spirits, he had foundation for his optimism.[181]

At first the 'Michael' battle affected French troops similarly to the BEF. As relieving forces, they were drip-fed into what appeared a losing battle, exposed in the open to the enemy guns, and without their own artillery to back them. The result was much recrimination against the British, but also pride that France had checked the onrush (as well as satisfaction at Foch's appointment as supreme commander).[182] The new style of campaigning was more challenging and absorbing than trench fighting, and it enabled men to shoot down Germans from behind cover, which they hoped would bring peace nearer. But precisely this perspective became dangerous when the line stabilized with the end apparently no closer, and troop morale relapsed. The German success at the Chemin des Dames on 27 May then caused astonishment and fury, much of it directed against the high command for having been surprised and unprepared. Among a minority there was a new wave of defeatism – 'better to be a living German than a dead Frenchman', and despair that the enemy could ever be beaten.[183]

This despondency too, however, was temporary, and (as German observers detected) in June and July the mood recovered again. Despite the enormous casualties in these months, the enemy were held, first on the Marne and then on the Matz, while the events of 15–18 July were universally recognized as a turning point. The road to Paris had been barred, and confidence in the army's leaders and in Clemenceau revived.[184] Of comparable importance was the deployment of the Americans. Pétain had played heavily on them as a morale booster, but until now opinions had been divided – they were coming too slowly; their fighting prowess was uncertain; they chased French women; and they would prolong the war.[185] Once they fought in the summer battles opinion moved overwhelmingly in their favour, and the censors found that confidence had never been greater.

Yet by the autumn the army's mood was darker. Open warfare was gruelling, partly owing to the heat, but also because the horses were worn out, and as in the BEF leave and rest were curtailed and men were more frequently in the line, without the protection of deep trenches or dugouts and often unable to shave or change their clothes for days on end, receiving food and water irregularly in country that was often dry and chalky and where the Germans had poisoned the wells. The infantry now once again had to go forward, against resistance that came more from machine guns than artillery, but which German aircraft still supported vigorously. The French approach to the Hindenburg Line was painfully slow, and some units refused the order to advance. Middle-rank officers were now freer to tell their superiors when the men were reluctant to attack, and the Fifth Division, for example, moving up the Aisne valley, covered barely a kilometre per day. The troops had been enthusiastic to start with, but became disheartened by the continuing resistance, the casualties, and disappointing progress, and they feared another winter campaign. In these circumstances Germany's armistice request was very welcome indeed, but again it did not lead to immediate peace. In the final weeks French soldiers very understandably did not want to get killed.[186] They did not refuse to fight, but during the October armistice negotiations morale softened still further, and if the war went on into the spring Foch and Pétain knew they would have to axe divisions, rely more on colonial forces, and operate with still more unruly soldiers, while a transport crisis intensified behind the lines. They were fortunate to be competing with a German army that was disintegrating even faster.

GERMANY

The Germans suffered from similar problems to the French and British, but more so. Unlike the Allies, they could not turn to their overseas empire, which was small enough anyway and mostly soon overrun. And although Germany occupied large tracts of territory within Europe, its efforts to recruit there failed. In 1916 it promised (nominal) independence for Poland, hoping that Polish volunteers would flood in, but it obtained only a trickle, and the French had more success in forming an army of Poles in exile. During 1918 the Central Powers overran even more of Eastern Europe, but incorporating Balts or Ukrainians into their armed forces was not considered before the defeat. Even Germany's previous European conquest, Alsace-Lorraine, was troublesome enough. Although 380,000 men were recruited there, their desertion rates were far above average and some generals refused to have them under their command, the many who were deemed untrustworthy being sent to the east. From 1917 the Alsatians and Lorrainers remaining on the Western Front were deployed only in mixed units and not in advanced patrols from which they might desert. The army deepened their alienation by discriminating against them, but they were disaffected from the beginning.[187] Similarly, in the winter of 1916/17 Germany deported thousands of Belgian civilians to Germany to work as forced labourers, but in the face of an international outcry it abandoned the project, although during the war it used some 120,000 Belgian workers in France and Belgium.[188] But its greatest source of battlefront labour was prisoners of war, as many as 400,000 of whom may have been in use by spring 1918 near and behind the front. During the year many of the Russians were repatriated, but big new hauls of British and French captives to an extent replaced them. Their treatment – especially if working in labour companies rather than held in camps within Germany – was often very harsh indeed, and deteriorated drastically during the last year of the war. In breach of an understanding between the belligerents in spring 1917, prisoners were used within shelling range of the line; they survived (and many failed to survive) on coffee, watery soup, and barley bread, and were often beaten if they failed to meet work targets. The authorities issued edicts against ill treatment but failed to police the system. German prisoners were also used in labour companies by France and Britain, but generally much better looked after, and the grim conditions of the Allied prisoners were both known of at the time and caused outrage after the armistice.[189]

Lacking imperial reserves of manpower, Germany fell back on its own population. Although it is convenient to speak of the 'German army', strictly speaking there was no such thing. Saxony, Württemberg, and Bavaria all kept separate armies and war ministries alongside Prussia's, although they copied Prussian training, organization, and equipment, and in wartime all came under the OHL. Of the empire's 68 million people in 1914, 15.6 million were men born between 1870 and 1899, i.e. aged between fifteen and forty-eight in 1914–18. During the war the army called up 13,387,000 men, of whom 4,215,662 were wounded and 1,900,876 died.[190] Yet down to 1917 it continued to grow, drawing on previously untrained men of military age and on the new young conscript cohorts as they attained maturity. The 1895–9 cohorts (1915–19 cohorts in French terminology) were called to the colours between 1915 and winter 1917/18, and the 1900 (1920) class also in 1918: a sign of desperation.[191] As of January 1918, 2.1 million older men were serving in the homeland and 2.3 million conscripts had been seconded to work in the economy, of whom 1.2 million were fit enough to fight – *kriegsverwendungsfähig* or 'k.v.', in the ubiquitous wartime abbreviation – but the Field Army had reached 5,166,000 and was close to its wartime peak. It was organized into no fewer than 239 infantry and eight cavalry divisions.[192]

Until mid-1917 the German army did remarkably well in keeping its regulation and its actual strength in line, but then a shortfall appeared,[193] and manpower projections in the autumn – like those in Britain and France – were gloomy. In December the war ministry predicted that if 1918 losses averaged 150,000 per month the gap would reach 330,000.[194] Even if Hindenburg and Ludendorff had stayed on the defensive, in other words, their army would have shrivelled, while the American presence was expected to rise by summer 1918 to 450,000.[195] As it turned out, because the OHL opted for the offensive, both German casualties and American arrivals far exceeded the forecasts. Hindenburg and Ludendorff well understood that attacking would mean enormous losses, but they judged their manpower situation favourable enough to take the risk. In part this reflected the efficiency of their medical service, the war ministry expecting 60,000 convalescents to return to duty every month.[196] Second, the men of the 1899 (1919) cohort were becoming available, and the high command directed them particularly towards the Western Front; and third, the authorities were combing out the non-combatant troops, although by the end of April they had obtained only 90,000.[197]

Essential for the offensives, then, was recalling men from other

theatres of war. Between November 1917 and 21 March 1918 the Western Army increased from 3.25 million men to over 4 million, while the
eastern and southern European forces fell from 2 million to 1.5 million.[198] It is true that most of the forces used in the offensives did not
come from other theatres – only six out of the seventy-seven attack divisions on 21 March – but by occupying quieter sectors they freed up the
Western Army's best assault divisions, much as the AEF was releasing
French manpower by taking over parts of the line.[199] In addition, all
men aged below thirty-five were taken from the east (the OHL believing that only younger men were fit enough for Western active service),
and the outcome was that on 21 March the 'Mob' divisions that spearheaded the attack were close to their regulation size. The Western Army
still barely outnumbered its opponents, but in the 'Michael' sector it
achieved an intimidating numerical advantage.

The problem now was to sustain this superiority in the face of
massive casualties. It proved insurmountable. In March and April the
German army suffered its heaviest losses on the Western Front since
1914 – exceeding those at Verdun, on the Somme, and at Third Ypres.[200]
In April alone the figures were 54,000 killed and missing, and 445,000
wounded and sick. Within days of 'Michael' starting, the OHL had to
ask the war ministry for more men.[201] On paper enough were available
to meet the Western Army's now colossal requirements, but in fact they
failed to cover the gap. The Eastern army occupied an enormous landmass and was still advancing: it gave up ten more infantry divisions in
April and May before the OHL decided it could lose no more.[202] Peace
with Russia in March released 151,700 German prisoners for repatria-
tion, but many were in poor physical shape and they were slow to
re-cross the border, subsequently being 'quarantined' for up to three
months lest they spread the Bolshevik contagion. Hindenburg and
Ludendorff raided their technical troops to sustain the infantry, moving
some 65,000 out of aviation, communications, and motor and rail
transport. They also fended off the fleet, which demanded more personnel to support the submarine campaign and claimed its establishment
was only two thirds of its needs. The OHL rejoined that at this stage in
the war the army must take priority.[203] Its focus, however, was on the
men of military age and fitness who were working in the home economy, and for months it fought a bureaucratic battle to reclaim them,
calling for superfluous industries to be closed and more male workers to

be replaced by women. It made negligible progress, while the fighting forces ran down.

In mid-May Ludendorff told his assistant, Colonel Haeften, that 'Only if the homeland soon makes available another some 200,000 usable men for the Field Army will there be a prospect of achieving militarily a decision in the war', but he added that neither Chancellor Hertling nor the war minister, Stein, could help him.[204] He went into the Chemin des Dames battle knowing he had too few troops. Matters came to a head when in June Hindenburg formally requested Hertling to raise the military service age for men to sixty and introduce compulsory non-combatant service for women. With extra powers the authorities could raise productivity by imposing wage and therefore price cuts while 'ruthlessly' confiscating war profits, with the consequences that the war industries would cease to operate on capitalist lines and more effort could be squeezed out of a feminized labour force, freeing up extra men for the army. In any case, the army's critical point of stringency was less armaments than manpower. At a meeting with Hertling and the heads of ministries on 1 July, Stein and Scheüch (who headed weapons production) said they could deliver 200,000 men but their training would be poor and arms output would suffer. As for extending liability to military service, they advised Hertling that the Reichstag was likely to dilute it and it would generate more dissension than it justified, while causing the 'collapse' of the war economy: moreover, employers preferred male to female workers.[205] The OHL therefore found itself in a minority and Hertling ruled against it. At a subsequent meeting on 20 July with leaders of the Western German heavy and armaments industries, the businessmen confirmed they could release no extra labour without harming productivity, the fit men being skilled workers who could not easily or quickly be substituted. The upshot was that the OHL combed out another 42,000 men from the rear for front-line service, but this figure was a drop in the ocean. Although the high command would have been willing to sacrifice some war production, the government shrank from confrontation with business and the industrial workforce. By July the Field Army had declined by 883,000 since March, and was down to 4,227,000. It could no longer maintain its unit strengths, and the OHL was forced to suppress divisions – the policy that the French, more or less, managed to avoid. By the time of the armistice, thirty-two had gone.[206]

In the meantime the eighteen-year-olds of the 1900 (1920) conscript cohort were being called up early and would provide 300,000 able-bodied levies from the autumn, when their training had been completed. Coupled with the return of wounded men from the hospitals, this development would bring relief if the army could hang on to the end of the campaigning season. But raw numbers were not the only issue: since the spring the OHL had also been worried about the poor quality of recruits.[207] Moreover, the army was desperately tired. Not only was leave restricted after March, but units were more frequently in the combat zone and for longer periods. British intelligence logged how what in June still seemed a massive reserve of fresh divisions melted away, leaving fewer and fewer to hold the line. Whereas the 'Michael' battle had been fought with 112 German divisions, all fresh (i.e. having rested for several weeks), and the Lys with 51, of which 41 were fresh, the Chemin des Dames was fought with 44, of which 11 were fresh, and the 15 July offensive with 37, only 4 of which were fresh. During the battles of the retreat, for the most part fewer than one in ten of the German divisions engaged were fresh and by late October the reserve was down to fifteen divisions, all of them tired.[208] In the surviving divisions, battalion strengths were falling to very low levels indeed, the OHL estimating on 5 November that the average figures were US, 1,200; Britain, 700; France, 600; and Germany, 500. Whatever Britain's and France's difficulties, Germany's were worse. And increasingly the problem was not simply to replace the 420,000 further battle losses between July and November, but also to stem outflows of manpower via capture and desertion. Between July and November, 340,000 German soldiers surrendered to the Allies or went missing.[209] The British, who captured the largest number, recorded how the surrenders mushroomed during August and remained at higher levels than ever previously.[210] The increase in desertion to the rear is harder to quantify, but probably involved similar numbers. These two developments suggest the German army was overwhelmed not only by new Allied strengths and tactics but also by an internal failure of morale and discipline.

Despite its appearance as an awesome fighting force, the German army had had problems from the beginning. The basis for Erich Maria Remarque's classic portrayal of disenchantment in *All Quiet on the Western Front* was the experience of the volunteers – a surprisingly large group who may have exceeded a quarter of a million. Most were young men who had not done military service, and they included a prominent minority of high school and university students. Many were promoted rapidly, but precisely for this reason they encountered jealousy as well as finding army life less glamorous and more gruelling than expected.[211] A much larger group, about whom less is known, were soldiers from a socialist background, many of whom suspected the war was an upper-class enterprise but were muzzled by the SPD's and the trade unions' support for it.[212] A final group – about whom evidence is more abundant – were Catholic peasants from southern Bavaria, who left their families amidst scenes of consternation in August 1914 and whose letters denounced the war as a 'swindle', although they continued to do their duty.[213] However, grousing about the soldier's lot was endemic to all the armies and hardly surprising in view of the conditions into which hundreds of thousands of civilians had been precipitated – and what mattered for the course of the war was less attitudes than conduct. In the German as in the Allied armies many stabilizing factors operated. Much of the army was non-combatant, and those who did pass through the line mostly stayed for limited periods before rotation into quieter sectors; moreover, the soldiers' letters suggest that many accepted the government's and the newspapers' contention that the war was a justified and defensive effort. Down to the end of 1915 the military authorities had no particular qualms.[214]

During 1916, however, the army fought two long and difficult attrition battles at Verdun and on the Somme, and in the latter it was on the defensive and for the first time faced an opponent with superior firepower. German casualties on the Somme approached half a million, and men's letters described the experience as a 'butchery' and a 'slaughterhouse'.[215] After it there was a mood of depression, which Hindenburg and Ludendorff for a time redressed by adopting new defensive tactics, withdrawing to the Hindenburg Line, boosting the army's equipment, and defeating the Allies' spring offensives.[216] But developments during 1917 disturbed the army still more. With Tsarist Russia defeated, the war had lost a crucial element of its defensive justification, and evidence was growing that the German government aimed at territorial expansion. The political truce established in 1914 fragmented when the Reichstag voted through the July 1917 Peace Resolution. Most soldiers seem to have disregarded the Fatherland Party, which was established to counter the Resolution and demand a victorious peace, disdaining it as a group of armchair strategists.[217] But little more success attended the programme of 'Patriotic Instruction' initiated by the OHL in July to counter subversion and enemy propaganda. It entailed obligatory lectures in each unit at least twice a week, supported by films and pamphlets: the soldiers must obey, Germany had to win, and to do so it must show unity and determination, inspired by heroes such as Schiller's Wallenstein.[218] Bavarian records suggest that soldiers were indifferent to such exhortations, and alienated by the middle-class instructors.[219] And in the meantime the Third Battle of Ypres, although endured by less of the German army than of the British, forced the soldiers who passed through it to undergo worse conditions than any yet experienced.[220]

By now the German army was in serious trouble, although its fighting performance and outward discipline were mostly intact. Ludendorff referred to it as a 'militia'. Very few 1914 veterans remained and the average age diminished: 18- to 20-year-olds were 7.6 per cent of the fatalities in 1914 but by 1918 almost a quarter. Men went to the front who would previously have been rejected, and by 1917 they did so after only two to three months of training, or half the time in the BEF.[221] Casualty rates among officers were higher than among the men, and the pre-1914 regular and reserve officers – the most respected – dwindled away.[222] The temporary officers who replaced them seem to have imbibed less than their British counterparts of the ethos of setting a good example and looking after their troops. In any case, there were simply not enough of them, and by 1917–18 many German companies were delegated to be run by NCOs – who might well, however, be more experienced than nineteen-year-old lieutenants. Although 'officer hatred' existed in all armies, it drew more comment in Germany than in Britain and France. German officers had the usual privileged access to leave and to better accommodation and food, but resentment of these privileges was concentrated against those in the rear, plus front-line officers who kept out of danger and aloof from their charges. It was a background source of tension rather than a precipitant of the German army's break-up. Resentment over inequality did, however, add an extra twist to anger over material conditions, which deteriorated much more in the German army than the Allied ones. In 1917 Hindenburg advised his soldiers to make their boots last twice as long, and the bread ration was cut by almost one third.[223] The Fifth Army postal censors reported in July that food was the critical issue, and from food shortages wider discontent followed.[224] None the less, the troops who longed for peace did not want it at *any* price, and food and rest could calm the front line down. Desertion rates increased but remained small compared with total numbers,[225] and although scattered indiscipline broke out on the Western Front in May to August 1917, none of the incidents involved an entire unit or compared with what happened on the French side. And in the winter of 1917/18 Hindenburg and Ludendorff succeeded in again raising sprits.

Among the factors contributing to this improvement, the most important were events abroad. According to the postal censors Caporetto, and especially the ceasefire with the Bolsheviks, heartened the troops. They understood that these developments portended a big offensive, but if it succeeded (and soldiers, in mirror image of their French counterparts, still trusted in the German army's superiority) they hoped to march home with honour. Most denounced the January 1918 strikes as encouragement to the Allies and likely to prolong the war.[226] They hoped an offensive could be avoided, but they had not, the censors noted, ever complained about casualties as such, and the preparations aroused excitement akin to that of 1914. On both sides of the lines, the prospect of a return to mobility and a decisive battle improved the mood. The danger, as some officers warned, was that depression would return if things went wrong.[227] R. von Dechend, a field artillery battery commander who was both an exceptionally thoughtful observer and a longstanding sceptic about the war, recorded that his unit looked forward to success: the offensive 'awoke in us a new spirit of confidence, not to say enthusiasm, and obscured the spirit of discouragement, war weariness and hopelessness'. The men took pleasure in attaining the highest pitch of efficiency, moving up huge quantities of ammunition and preparing the surprise bombardment from a position far forward that was a hallmark of the new tactics.[228]

The Germans therefore struck on 21 March with high but precarious optimism. Anticlimax set in rapidly. The Lys offensive, launched with wearier troops and less preparation, aroused fewer hopes, as this was no longer something new but instead a more familiar story of rapid initial progress followed by return to stalemate. Albrecht von Thaer, a senior officer with the Rupprecht army group, noted that the best infantry were dead and the soldiers becoming discouraged:[229] they had hoped the war would terminate, but now faced endless further fighting and during

the battle some units refused to move forward.[230] Certainly the spectacular breakthrough on the Chemin des Dames revived some of the earlier
optimism: Herbert Sulzbach, an artillery adjutant, was exhilarated by
the bombardment's accuracy and the triumph over formidable defences,
but felt less elated than on 21 March, not least because he had lost so
many comrades.[231] Assisted by the long prior pause, the Germans had
prepared the Chemin des Dames attack with similar thoroughness to
that before 'Michael', but in June and July their energy ebbed.

Not only was the army's operational efficiency slipping; its basic
discipline had started to break down. Trouble began in 1917 on the
journeys returning men from leave or transferring them from the east:
always slow, troop trains grew slower, sometimes taking days to reach
their destinations. Troops were bundled on to them in squalid conditions and with too few officers to supervise, received meals irregularly
and often at night, and frequently were not even furnished with toilets
but had to descend at each stop. They had time on their hands to take
stock of their predicament, talk endlessly, and vent their feelings on the
NCOs and railway officials. The authorities realized what was happening, but failed to contain it. In autumn 1917 Ludendorff estimated that
one in ten of those transported from the eastern theatre to France went
missing while en route. If they were caught German military justice
defined 'desertion' as opposed to 'absence without leave' more narrowly
than did British, and punished the latter relatively mildly. Over the war
as a whole executions for desertion in the German army totalled eighteen; those in the much smaller British army 269.[232] In an order of
10 June (a copy of which the British obtained) Ludendorff disclosed
that two deserters had told the French of the Chemin des Dames attack,
and captives had alerted them to the Matz offensive; yet he could do
little other than warn the troops not to disclose such information.[233]
Another Ludendorff order threatened death to all deserters when they
returned to Germany,[234] and one from a divisional commander, which
was captured by the British, urged officers to use their revolvers if necessary to secure obedience.[235] Yet when the OHL pressed the war ministry
to tighten up disciplinary procedures, the latter refused. By summer
1918 over 30,000 men had fled to Denmark, the Netherlands, and Switzerland,[236] and many more delayed their return home from leave or
lingered in the twilight zone behind the front, carrying false identity
papers or circulating from unit to unit before the police could catch

them. Stragglers congregated round hospitals and railway stations and in big cities – Brussels and Ghent in the occupation zone, but also in the homeland. The Berlin police estimated that by late September 40,000–50,000 deserters roamed the capital,[237] and by summer 1918 those separated from the army by one means or another may have totalled 90,000–100,000: in itself a sizeable rather than decisive number but about to become much bigger.[238] We also know that in May 1918 there was another sprinkling of mutinies. Several hundred Alsatians and Lorrainers planned to escape to Holland (in a conspiracy foiled by the authorities) from the camp at Beverloo near Brussels; at Erlangen, Ingolstadt, Munich, Würzburg, and Neu-Ulm units ordered to the front violently protested. In Ingolstadt they stormed and looted the town hall, and *The Times* reported the episode. Even after the trouble subsided, a sullen depression and discontent festered.[239]

Despite the mounting chaos in the rear, the front-line units maintained their discipline until the 'Michael' attack. But one of that attack's attractions – for men who spent much of their time hungry – was pillage, and captured villages and BEF depots offered plenty of opportunity. It was the German carnival season, and the food and alcohol prompted Bacchanalian scenes. Men keyed up to an intense pitch of preparation vented their feelings by gorging and celebrating in disregard of their superiors' efforts to urge them forward.[240] After the offensives halted the Germans found themselves exposed: in Picardy with the old Somme battlefield behind them, across which their engineers never established satisfactory communications, and in Champagne in an awkward salient with only one rail link. Hence the next stage of the disorder became attacks on German depots and supply trains.[241] By the summer the OHL, after initial complacency, appreciated the dimensions of the problem, and the authorities issued increasingly desperate directives.[242] The army had reached a turning point, and with its hopes in the offensives dashed the forces undermining it resurged. Although the OHL tried to recapture the mood of March by christening the 15 July offensive a 'peace storm', the troops involved had lost their spirit.[243] Following its failure, the army began deflating like a pricked balloon, new arrivals being vastly outnumbered by those leaving.

The departures fell into two main categories: desertions and absenteeism, and surrenders to the enemy. Until October the latter were probably more numerous. By recycling the wounded and summoning up the 1920 conscript cohort Ludendorff could replace his killed and injured, but not his losses through captivity, and prisoners were gone for good. The Allied victories delivered hauls previously unknown on the Western Front: 17,000 between 15 and 17 July, 20,145 in the week after 8 August, and 22,000 in the first three days of the September offensives.[244] The British estimated that 358,900 Germans surrendered to the Allies during 1918,[245] and until the end of the war captures remained at unprecedented levels. The explanation lay partly in the Allied counter-offensives, which combined technological and tactical innovation with saturation propaganda. German forward troops were repeatedly surprised, traumatized, and cut off with little prospect of relief, as the forward British redoubts had been on 21 March. But in addition the Allies' intelligence services recognized that they faced a cowed opponent. Parts of the German army remained formidable: machine gunners often expected to be killed and fought to the end, as did elite Prussian units. But according to Friedrich Altrichter, writing after the war, most troops fought until they felt that they had done their duty. This might mean holding out until the ammunition had gone or there was no prospect of escaping, but not resisting to the last man in the interest of a larger cause that was lost.[246] Haig's GHQ used captured documents to track the process. At the start of 1918 German morale was very good, partly because all ranks hoped that the peace in the east would be followed by peace in the west; but by May discipline in the rear areas was breaking down and by June it was 'seriously shaken', more and more soldiers were openly disobedient, and the Germans showed less energy in building defence lines. By September they were 'in a woeful condition' and 'great disarray' and on the 25th three officers and a hundred men gave themselves up: 'the largest numbers of Germans who have ever deserted to us at one time'.[247] German soldiers captured by the Canadians denounced the war as 'the great swindle'.[248] These were not mass surrenders – the British and French advanced too warily to achieve a Stalingrad, and down to the storming of the Hindenburg Line the German army dwindled through captures measured in dozens: repeated, however, hundreds of times.

The Allies deluged their antagonist not only with shells but also with leaflets. German propaganda – and especially organized fraternization – had helped to undermine the Russian army, but similar methods against the French army in late 1917 had little impact.[249] Conversely, the French and British (in the latter case, department MI7b of the War Office) had since 1915 been distributing propaganda to the occupied areas and to German troops. But Allied propaganda in 1918 was more co-ordinated and on a grander scale. The principal means of dissemination was via unmanned balloons (as with gas, the prevailing winds in North-Western Europe lending the Allies an advantage), as a test case in early 1918 had showed that the Germans would treat aircraft crews as criminals rather than as prisoners of war if they were captured when dropping propaganda, and in any case the air force had other priorities.[250] But although the technology might seem primitive the results were impressive. MI7b had been distributing 1 million leaflets a month at the start of 1918, but by August the Allies between them were distributing 100,000 a day, and the AEF alone disseminated more than 3 million leaflets over German lines by the armistice.[251] The British distributed 1 million leaflets in April, but 5.36 million in October.[252] The material was intended to encourage desertion, and it stressed common themes: that Germany could not hope to win (American troop shipments being used to underline the message); that its troops were dying for an exploitative and expansionist Berlin elite; and that prisoners would be fed and cared for. Alsace-Lorrainers' and South Germans' anti-Prussian resentments received special attention.[253] In short, the Allies accurately identified many of the factors eroding enemy morale, and the British regularly interrogated German prisoners who testified to the effectiveness of the leaflets and were carrying them when captured.[254] Dechend also believed that the material, written professionally and in good German (unlike some earlier productions), helped to crystallize minds.[255]

The word 'crystallize' is important. Ludendorff and Hitler stressed in retrospect the power of propaganda and of Northcliffe in particular, but they did not say it had decided the war.[256] Allied propaganda intensified at a moment when it found a receptive audience, during the critical months of mounting evidence that the Ludendorff offensives had failed. More open warfare meant constant exposure to the elements, and repeated hauling of guns and equipment. General Hutier of the Eighteenth Army noted that his men were being worn out by constant digging, that too much was asked of them, and that they had reached the limit. He believed the OHL saw just the numbers of divisions, and not the strain on the ranks.[257] In fact Ludendorff knew the men were getting no rest, but he saw no alternative.[258] Dechend, returning to his gunners in

July, found not only that his own 'good spirits' had deserted him but also that 'The mood among the officers has evidently been transformed': none expected victory and criticisms of the high command and of the government were voiced in terms that earlier would have been unthinkable. So far from the end being near, however, they feared that none of them would live to see it, yet beyond being inured to military life it was hard to explain what kept them at their posts.[259] In the words of Werner Beumelberg, writing of the German soldiers in 1918: 'To endure without belief and without hope – only from a sense of duty – that is the last, the greatest demand.'[260] But by the Battle of Amiens, duty was no longer enough. The commander of the Alpine Corps reported that when his men moved up on 8 August they were jeered as 'war prolongers' and 'stupid Bavarians' who were closing the holes that other units had opened up.[261] Ludendorff was shaken by the evidence that the spirit of the troops had given way, although denying that they had failed because too much was asked of them.[262] Similarly the Fifth Army postal censors reported that the mood had changed completely for the worse: war weariness had sharpened older grievances and men talked openly of desertion and surrender. The war would soon be lost, and there was no point in fighting it.[263] By September, Dechend noted that even previously very brave men were going over to the enemy: hunger for home, the length of the war, and especially the failure of the offensives had produced complete hopelessness and depression. Morale, according to a further censorship report, was 'really bad'.[264]

German and British evidence on the disintegration of the German army largely tallies on the nature of the process. Like the French army mutinies, it was triggered by a failed offensive, but unlike them was not an act of collective disobedience. In May–June 1918 such disobedience appeared to be developing, but it fizzled out. Instead the German army was undermined by individuals and by small groups, staying behind the line or surrendering. Many surrenders included and were even led by junior officers. After the German government on 4 October publicly appealed for a ceasefire, however, this relatively disciplined process was overtaken in importance by mass desertions. The postal censors reported that the news had been disastrous for the troops' willingness to fight. They now wanted to accept peace at any price: their sacrifices had been for nothing, and they had been lied to.[265] Figures submitted to the post-war Reichstag Committee of Inquiry suggest that by the armistice deserters may have swelled to 750,000–1,000,000, though this estimate is probably excessive.[266] Yet to the end more discipline persisted in the combat zone than behind the lines. After the ceasefire most of the Field Army marched back into Germany in good order, whereas in the rear the soldiers established soviets. Conditions were created which fostered a legend that shirkers and strikers had stabbed an undefeated army in the back. In reality, much though Hindenburg and Ludendorff were exercised over the agitation in the army by the USPD, which wanted democratization and peace negotiations, it played little part in undermining discipline.[267] Certainly, hundreds of thousands of soldiers would in peacetime have supported the left-wing parties, and others who would not have done were driven by 1918 to accept the socialist critique of the regime.[268] But most commentators now consider that the soldiers' discontent can be explained by the desperate military prospect and the sheer practical difficulty of army life. German soldiers were better fed than German civilians (although many were constantly worried about their families), but they were neither fed nor clothed adequately, and as the numbers in the fighting army dwindled the burdens on those remaining became crushing. The crises of numbers and of morale were mutually reinforcing. Although the British and especially the French armies displayed many similar symptoms they were less acute, and colonial and American assistance offset them. But the fundamental difference was that after mid-July at the latest much of the German army could no longer see how the war could be won. Further sacrifice seemed pointless and escape a matter of self-preservation, while the authorities lacked the powers to keep their men in place by terror. Neither did they execute thousands of their own troops, as the Wehrmacht would do in the Second World War; nor were the Allies so intimidating an opponent as was the Soviet Union in the later conflict. Although Allied action prior to 1918 had greatly worn the German army down, the latter had inflicted comparable damage on its opponents. Only in the final year did it become conclusive that Germany would win the race to the bottom.

ITALY

Of the other fighting theatres, the biggest was the Italian. A major difference between it and the Western Front was the absence of Americans, beyond the 332nd Ohio Regiment, a 1,000-man detachment sent as a propaganda gesture.[269] Diaz, however, had asked for two or three US divisions, and he told the British that there was 'discontent and bitterness' in Italy about it.[270] Instead, the nearest equivalent to the blood transfusion provided by the AEF came from the British and French divisions sent to Italy after Caporetto. Even though reduced in numbers after March 1918, they were prominent in the battles of the Piave and Vittorio Veneto. The French troops found conditions easy and the Austrians much less formidable than the Germans; the British were welcomed by the population and considered the theatre a 'picnic' compared with the Western Front, while their respect for the Italian soldiers – initially disparaged as 'ice-cream vendors' – eventually rose.[271] The Allied divisions were better fed, clothed, equipped, and paid than the Italians, and gained more rest and leave, which kindled jealousy, but on balance they buttressed morale.[272] On the other side, the Germans were withdrawn before the 21 March offensive and although the Comando supremo feared they would return, they did not. But the war remained primarily an Austro-Italian duel.

Although Italy's troops were mostly in the home theatre, 100,000 were stationed in Albania and 55,000 in Macedonia, while, in 1918, 48,000 combatants and 70,000 labourers served in France. Italy's colonies were small, poor, incompletely subdued, and a drain on manpower rather than a significant source of it. As for the 15 million Italians who had emigrated in the twenty years before the war, 6 million of them in 1914 had not yet become naturalized and were still Italian citizens. But only 304,000 of them (155,000 from the US) came home to do military service, many soon bitterly regretting it.[273] Hence the main resource was the population of the Italian peninsula and islands. All the age cohorts born between 1874 and 1900 were drawn on, and just over 6 million men were called up. Before the war only about a quarter of those liable had actually done military service, partly owing to lack of money and partly because so much of the population was undernourished and physically unfit. But during the war the normal medical requirements were relaxed, and about half the men in the relevant age groups served. Of those called up over a million by 1918 were working in the home economy as soldiers and under military discipline, but 5,039,000 served in the army, and 4.2 million at the front. About half were countrymen (*contadini*), who served disproportionately in the infantry, the arm that took 95 per cent of the losses.[274] 550,000 would die from battle injuries and illness – at least 100,000 from the latter, which took a much higher toll than in France – and another 600,000 were taken prisoner, of whom 100,000 died in captivity. Italy's death toll, in fact, was not far short of that for the British Isles. Like the British and German armies, none the less, the Italian army expanded until 1917, when it peaked at 2,431,000 on 1 October.[275] But after Caporetto it never regained its former strength. The 1899 cohort was called up at the end of 1917; that of 1900 was registered in 1918 but not summoned to the colours before the war ended. As this was the last reserve and the authorities preferred not to dip into it, the army's numbers declined after the Battle of the Piave and as of 1 October 1918 were down to 2,291,000. Its manpower shortage was less pressing than for the Western Front armies, but it too was reaching its limits.[276]

However, the most serious problem was not quantitative but qualitative. Like the French army, the Italian army had undergone a crisis of morale. Although it revived sufficiently to remain a fighting force, the recovery was partial and fragile. Once again the crisis followed a run of failed offensives. But in the Twelfth Battle of the Isonzo, which has gone down to history as the Battle of Caporetto, the Austrians counter-attacked with German backing, and the Italians were routed. The initial breakthrough can largely be explained by operational factors, but many Italian soldiers' subsequent conduct testified to a deep malaise – almost a festive atmosphere prevailed, as over half a million troops either surrendered to cries of 'Long Live Germany!' and 'Long Live Austria!' or broke from their units as 'disbanded' men, looted their own territory, and fled to the rear.[277] The survivors regrouped along the river Piave with only half the army's divisions still intact. Many believed that Caporetto meant the end of the war – on what terms being irrelevant – and this was cause to celebrate.

Caporetto did not come from nowhere. The Comando supremo had known something was wrong, and begun monitoring morale earlier in 1917. Cadorna (like Nivelle in France) blamed the government for failing to suppress anti-war agitation. In reality, the factors undermining morale were similar to those on the Western Front, but in exacerbated form. Italy's war entry had been a transparent act of aggression, and socialists, middle-class progressives, and the Vatican were detached or critical from the start. Italian national unity and patriotism were weaker than in Britain and France, in a country only recently unified, with high levels of illiteracy and a continuing regional and local political focus. Many could not understand why they were fighting, and, in contrast to France and Germany, Italy had very few volunteers. Soldiers' letters complained that the conflict had been cooked up by 'the higher-ups' (*i signori*), who themselves stayed out of the trenches. Moreover, the fighting proved to be no promenade to Trieste, outnumbered Austrian forces repeatedly holding off frontal attacks that were unsupported by adequate artillery preparation and drove uphill against the enemy guns. Like the French, the Italians were buoyed up by false new hopes each spring, and months of rest and re-equipment before the 1917 fighting were followed by the biggest Isonzo battles ever, and yet by little more gain.[278] Colonel Gatti, the Comando supremo's historian, thought the men endured the eleventh Isonzo offensive only because they thought it would be the last, and he wondered what would happen when they realized it was not.[279]

What happened was increasing restlessness. Mutiny in the Italian army was rare, but in May 1917 the Ravenna brigade protested against being sent back to the front, and in July the Catanzaro brigade did likewise, both outbreaks being suppressed with signal ferocity. By 1917–18 desertions were running at five times the level of the first year of the war, and in September 1917 some 25,000 deserters were estimated to be at large, in addition to 50,000 men who had defied the call-up and 34,000 who had obeyed it but deserted prior to mobilization. This made for a total of over 100,000 fugitives, some living in camps outside the cities with the complaisance of the local population, or sheltered in the countryside in return for providing farm labour. During the war as a whole 162,563 men were tried for desertion, and 101,085 convicted.[280] So worried were the authorities about men surrendering to the enemy that even after the Central Powers warned that because of the Allied blockade they would not meet the full cost of supporting prisoners of war, the Italians – unlike the French and British – refused to subsidize it by sending food parcels. One in six of the Italians who entered Austrian captivity died.[281]

The severity of Cadorna's military justice suggests that the authorities felt they were sitting on a volcano, and to contain the situation they relied primarily on repression. In response to the tide of desertion they resorted to summary executions and even to 'decimation', unknown in other armies, whereby members of an offending unit were selected at random for the firing squad. In a ferocious letter to Orlando, at that stage interior minister, in June 1917, Cadorna called for immediate summary executions 'on a vast scale', though the minister felt the commander exaggerated the danger.[282] During the war 870,000 Italians were denounced to military justice: 400,000 for failing to obey the call-up and 400,000 for offences committed while under arms. Desertion was by far the most common, followed by indiscipline and self-mutilation. 729 Italians are known to have been executed, and the official figure for the war as a whole was 107 put to death without trial – though both figures are understatements. Summary executions peaked in summer 1917, at the same time as the CS took exceptional powers, warning that men returning more than twenty-four hours late from leave were liable to be shot, while three weeks before Caporetto the government's Sacchi decree prescribed draconian fines and jail sentences for anyone propagating 'defeatism'.[283]

It is even harder than in most armies to grasp the mind of the Italian troops. The postal censorship may have covered only 2 per cent of letters sent; moreover, the penalties for expressing critical or pessimistic sentiments were severe and many soldiers did not take the risk.[284] In any case, up to 30 per cent of the older men were illiterate. Nor could troops communicate easily with their officers, Italian soldiers being disconcerted by the camaraderie between higher and lower grades among the French and British. Cadorna was ruthless with his senior commanders – he removed 217 generals – and he wanted a similar culture of fear lower down.[285] 160,191 were admitted to the officer corps between 1915 and 1918,[286] many of them lacking experience or the respect of their men. They were perceived as often harsh, incompetent, and failing to take their share of danger. The fragmentary evidence from intercepted letters suggests, however, that Italian soldiers not only shared the grievances felt in other armies, but also that many were more radically alienated. In addition to being less well fed and paid than the French and British, they were subject to a rigorous regime of work and drill when out of the line, and their leave was less frequent and often altered or cancelled. Events in 1917 – the Russian Revolution, Pope Benedict XV's peace appeal – further soured the mood. Men were looking for a way out, and Caporetto seemed to offer one.

None the less, the army survived the collapse. Cadorna wrote of 'a pacific rebellion by an inert human mass',[287] but despite the evidence of demoralization Caporetto was not a crisis of indiscipline. The mass surrenders resulted neither from mutinies nor insubordination, and officers often led them, believing as did many British officers in the 'Michael' battle that they were surrounded and further bloodshed was pointless.[288] In November and December 1917 Italian troops halted the Central Powers' advance. The 'disbanded' soldiers were mostly soon reintegrated into units. The 1899 cohort joined the colours, and the new front line was 170 kilometres shorter.[289] Cadorna was replaced and the new team of Diaz and Badoglio showed greater concern for morale and welfare, achieving much of what Pétain had done. As Diaz put it, 'The best system for fighting anti-war propaganda is the elimination, as far as possible, of the causes of discontent.'[290] He did not redraft the disciplinary regime but it operated more humanely, summary executions and decimation virtually ceasing.[291] Front-line tours of duty became shorter and more regular: to the previous one annual leave period of fifteen days Diaz added another of ten, suspending leave only during the June battle. Rations had fallen from 4,082 calories per day in 1914 to 3,067 by 1917, but now recovered to 3,580 and the meals became more varied.[292] Wounded soldiers on recovery returned to the familiarity of their original units, and battalions stayed in the same divisions instead of being moved around, while insurance policies were introduced to compensate families whose menfolk died. Pay also rose, and canteens were placed near the front to sell at discount prices.[293] The activities of the 'P' or propaganda service were generalized throughout the army.[294] These measures did more to hearten the bulk of the troops than did the role of the *Arditi*, special assault units created in 1917 that Diaz reorganized, establishing one per army corps. Under him their numbers rose to thirty-nine detachments with over 30,000 men. More heavily armed than normal infantry, specially trained, and exempted from routine fatigues, they undertook riskier tasks such as raids and clearing the way for major attacks. They helped defend the Piave in June and took part – with limited success – in the attack at Vittorio Veneto. Their significance, however, was as an eye-catching new model of the soldier for public opinion and for their later links with the Fascist movement, rather than as greatly improving general performance.[295]

Conditions in the winter of 1917/18 were difficult, the end of trench warfare meaning – as later on the Western Front – that men were out in the open, sleeping in tents in sub-zero temperatures by the Venice lagoon. Many had hoped that Caporetto would bring peace, but instead the war continued, heightening soldiers' anxiety about their families' survival on inadequate separation allowances.[296] On the other hand, the Italian political class now displayed more unity, and after December the front became quieter. Except during the battles of the Piave and Vittorio Veneto it would remain so, daily killed and wounded totals between March and November 1918 averaging 614, compared with 2,155 in the previous year.[297] Desertions fell off sharply, and soldiers' letters showed appreciation of the better food, if still much discontent about other matters. Conditions had therefore improved when in spring 1918 an Austrian propaganda offensive tested them. The Austro-Hungarian high command had identified Italy as the next target after Russia but it missed the best subversion opportunity, in the post-Caporetto chaos. Attempts at fraternization made little headway against the Italian army, whose commanders and military police were more vigilant than the Russians and circulated units more rapidly between sectors. Moreover, air drops were the principal method of delivering pamphlets, and by March the Italians and their allies had largely regained air superiority. Some 3 million leaflets were none the less distributed, using methods such as rockets, floating down rivers, and delivery by night patrols.[298] They urged that the Allies had no chance of winning and that Italian soldiers were fighting for an imperialist elite and for 'England', whereas Austria-Hungary had no claims on Italian territory. Interrogation of Italian prisoners confirmed that these themes carried conviction, but the prisoners were few, and from January the CS was organizing counter-propaganda. The test came at the Battle of the Piave, for which the Austrians had high hopes of a new Caporetto; but although the attackers took over 40,000 Italian prisoners, this time the Italian resistance held and after the battle the Austrians called off the propaganda campaign, instead now concentrating on defending their own troops against a much more intensive Allied counter-effort. None the less Diaz still feared that he could not replace his losses and might endanger the new confidence if he attacked too recklessly. He resisted Allied demands for him to attack, being concerned to save the army for what he expected to be a decisive campaign in 1919.[299] Only at the very end, and under urgent pressure from the government, which stood by him until it became evident that the Central Powers were crumbling, did he authorize an offensive against an Austro-Hungarian army that was in far more desperate straits than his own.

AUSTRIA-HUNGARY

Actually Austria-Hungary had three armies: the common army, which came under the joint Ministry of War, and the Landwehr and Honvéd, which came respectively under the governments of the Austrian and the Hungarian halves of the Dual Monarchy. The common army was the biggest and the most heavily armed of the three, which in wartime all came under the AOK (Armee Oberkommando) or army high command. In peacetime over half the officer corps were German-speakers but the composition of the rank and file mirrored closely that of the Dual Monarchy as a whole. Austria-Hungary had a bigger population than Italy, but it had been in the war for ten months longer and during the first year had suffered exceptionally even by Great War standards. By August 1915 it had lost 2.5 million killed and wounded and 730,000 prisoners and missing: one in eight officers and one in ten men had lost their lives. As the main target of the Brusilov offensive in 1916, it took another 750,000 casualties, including 380,000 prisoners.[300] Until this point the authorities kept up the army's strength by recruiting more untrained civilians, but now replacement became more difficult and by late 1917 8.42 million out of 11.8 million men aged 18–52 had been called up. 0.78 million were dead, 1.1 million were prisoners, and 0.5 million had left the army as invalids. 0.4 million were working in arms production and another 0.6 million had been released for other (mostly economic) purposes. Still available in the coming year were perhaps 100,000 who could be combed out from those previously deemed unfit, 140,000 from the 1900 conscript class, and 250,000 recovered wounded, but the army still expected a 600,000 manpower gap. Both the Austrian and Hungarian governments resisted seconding more men from the war economy, facing as they did a food crisis and industrial collapse. The army was therefore allocated only 122,000 from the civilian sector – less than half of what it had demanded – and in March 1918 it released nearly 300,000 men from the oldest age cohorts, partly because it could not feed the troops it had under arms.[301] In addition, after empire-wide strikes in January 1918, the war ministry insisted on keeping seven combat divisions at home, although in May reservists replaced them.[302]

Two factors came to the army's assistance, if assistance is the right word. The first was the return of prisoners of war from Russia. By June 1918 they numbered 517,000, but they needed 4–5 months of surveillance and retraining before they could return to the front, and many deserted rather than do so, or mutinied when ordered to go. In return for them Austria-Hungary had to send back its 908,000 Russian prisoners of war, 248,000 of whom were working directly for the army and another 660,000 on the home front, mostly in industry and agriculture. The second factor was reduced casualties, which from August 1917 were lower than in any period since the start of the war (though still reached 1,437,600 down to November 1918); but here again there was a balancing factor as the numbers falling ill were higher than ever. Eighteen-year-olds from the 1900 class were called up to fill the gaps, and in the first half of 1918 the army's strength levels improved, but in the second half they dropped. Although the regulation strength of a division was 11,567, in reality it might be less than half that figure. The 'Standesmisere' or 'manpower misery' became a staple of unit commanders' laments.[303]

As of 1 July 1918 the Austro-Hungarian forces numbered 2.85 million in the front army and 1.56 million in the territorial and reserve units.[304] Though more numerous than their Italian adversaries, they could not concentrate so exclusively on the Italian front. From July 1918 they assisted Germany by stationing four infantry divisions in France,[305] and although the 1918 peace treaties with Russia and Romania eased the strain, Austria-Hungary still maintained occupation garrisons in the east. None the less, whereas in summer 1917 Austria-Hungary had been maintaining roughly equal numbers of combatants in the Russian and the Italian theatres,[306] the latter, or 'South-West', front became its biggest commitment in the final year. As of 15 October 1918 Austria-Hungary had some 400,000 fighting men on the Italian front, as against 50,000 in the Balkans, and 150,000 occupation troops in Russia, plus 18,000 in France.[307] This commitment was increasingly difficult to sustain. During September a series of conferences took place between the Dual Monarchy's senior military officials, at which Arz and the Chief of Military Manpower pointed out that the army was now half a million below regulation strength and faced becoming no longer combat-ready in 1919. In a way characteristic of Austria-Hungary's final months, however, proposals to recall soldiers who had been released to the civilian economy were obstructed by the Hungarian government, even in the face of pleas by Karl himself.[308]

If the authorities were losing the struggle to keep up numbers, sustaining morale was even harder. The biggest and most distinctive problem of the Habsburg army was material shortage; the more serious as much of the South-Western Front was mountainous – some at a very high altitude indeed – and the supply links from a crumbling home economy across a difficult terrain were more precarious than for the Italians, who had their backs to the prosperous Po basin and could draw from the world beyond. The troops were reasonably equipped with basic weapons – machine guns, artillery, and ammunition – and received priority over the home front for food supplies, but the run-up to the harvest was extremely difficult, no meat or fat being available for months. After Caporetto the Austrian troops along the Piave pillaged and requisitioned in the newly occupied land, but within weeks they had picked it bare. Hence if Italian troops were shivering in makeshift positions in early 1918, the Austrians were still worse off. The AOK needed 219 flour wagons per day but was getting only 112.[309] Between August 1917 and July 1918 the army received less than three quarters of its flour needs, and the daily flour ration for soldiers at the front fell from 500 grams in April 1918 to 300 in August, while for men in the rear it was even less.[310] The 400-gram daily meat ration of 1914 was barely 100 grams at the start of 1918, and even for officers horse flesh had become a luxury.[311] In the mountain regions, hundreds of troops lacked proper boots or underwear, as the AOK well knew, and many presented themselves in torn and threadbare uniforms: the authorities estimated that if the war continued they could supply little more than half of the footwear that was needed, nor the blankets and coats required for a mountain winter.[312] Boroević, the commander on the Piave front, warned in February that the situation was undermining discipline; in the mountains conditions were worse.

Food shortages had already helped precipitate a wave of unrest in spring 1918. A major mutiny took place in the navy at Cattaro in February, demanding democracy and an immediate end to the war, although it was quickly put down. As elsewhere, a warning sign was disorder on the troop trains: by May this was endemic, and the AOK pressed for the soldiers to regain their weapons only after rejoining their units.[313] Collective disturbances in the army reached a climax with six outbreaks spread across the empire during May, reintegrated prisoners of war from Russia acting in almost every case as a catalyst. Despite the high command's apprehensions, the returnees did not demand socialist revolution, but they felt they had been better fed when in captivity and resented being returned so quickly to the line, instructions to move up frequently triggering the outbreaks. Although these were mutinies in the interior rather than at the front, and the authorities still had enough loyal troops to repress them, collective protests were followed as in the German army by an increase in individual desertions, which in the end proved more damaging. Desertions had gathered momentum during 1917, being centred on the South Slav areas of Croatia and Slavonia where the fugitives formed 'Green Cadres' in the backwoods. But the turning point was the Piave battle in June 1918, whose impact was comparable to the failure of the Ludendorff offensives. It followed months of preparation and at the start expectations were high.[314] But after the army demonstrated once again that man for man it was superior to most of the Italian infantry, it was outclassed by the enemy's guns and aircraft and forced to retreat. In other words, the Italians could not be routed again and the war could not be won, especially as simultaneously it was turning against the Germans. Lothar Rendulić, a career officer who had been fighting since 1914, became downcast over the food supply difficulties and still more over the offensive. For the first time he foresaw that the Habsburg Monarchy might break up.[315]

The army had little reason to hold together out of military pride. Its record in the first half of the war had been of shattering defeat, and although its situation improved in 1917–18, it did so largely as the result of German successes. With the death of the Emperor Franz Joseph in 1916 and his replacement by the young and inexperienced Karl, another unifying factor was lost. Moreover, much of the multi-lingual pre-war officer corps, whose members had known the languages of the Slav regiments, had gone. It was true that the army's ethnic composition was less of a disadvantage against Italy than in other theatres. The only unreliable minority were the Italian-speakers, all of whom were stationed elsewhere. The South Slavs (and the Croats in particular) who were unreliable in the Balkans were more dependable here and often Italophobe: they constituted 18 per cent of the front-line troops facing

Italy in spring 1917 and at Caporetto were used as assault forces.[316] None the less, the AOK (like other high commands) complained that agitation from home was infecting the army. In fact under Franz Joseph the regime in the Austrian half of the empire was highly repressive, and only under Karl in 1917 was a relaxation attempted. The effect after previously bottling up discontent was now to release it, in the midst of economic crisis and potential for revolutionary spillover from Russia. When Arz von Straussenberg took over in February 1917 he asked his army commanders for reports on the moral and physical state of their troops: the replies were generally favourable, especially for the German, Magyar, and Croat regiments, although he foresaw trouble ahead and made it standard practice to mix regiments as a check on suspect nationalities.[317] But that September, Conrad von Hötzendorff, the commander in the Tyrol, reported a big increase in desertions to the enemy, which he blamed on the relaxation of discipline under Karl and the recruitment of unreliable elements.[318] Similarly, Czech and South Slav units participated in the May 1918 mutinies with nationalist resentment against Habsburg rule as one motive.[319] Thus the 42nd Honvéd Infantry Division, a Croat unit with a previously good record, moved in January 1918 from the Eastern Front to the Asiago plateau. There it lacked food, clothing, and shelter, and by May the men's South Slav nationalism was stirring and many were deserting to the enemy or the interior. Although they took part in the June offensive they suffered afterwards from 'deep depression', and in October they mutinied.[320] Unrest over material conditions that resembled that in other armies was evolving into something more radical.

It was therefore on fertile ground that the seeds were scattered of an even more intensive Allied propaganda campaign than in the west.[321] Previously the major obstacle to it had been the Italian government's thinly disguised ambition to annex South Slav-inhabited territory, but after Caporetto the Orlando government was willing (at least in public) to downpedal this commitment. The Rome Congress of oppressed nationalities, held in April 1918, accepted the principle of an independent Yugoslavia whose frontier with Italy would be decided on the basis of national self-determination and the two countries' vital interests. The Italian government welcomed (without ever officially accepting) this declaration, which provided a basis for the Padua Commission (or Central Inter-Allied Propaganda Commission) to begin work. Although including representatives of the Austro-Hungarian subject nationalities and the other Allies, the Commission was an Italian-led operation. Between May and November 1918 it produced 60 million copies of 643 separate pamphlets, as well as eighty newsletters, translated into most of Austria-Hungary's languages and crafted to take account of each nationality's concerns and traditions. To begin with the principal targets were the South Slavs, Czechs, and Poles, but later the core nationalities – the Austrian Germans and Magyars – were added to the list. The object was to show that the Central Powers had no chance of winning, but also to highlight that Allied victory would mean freedom for the Dual Monarchy's peoples. Leaflets were air-dropped (including 150,000 in a spectacular raid on Vienna led by the nationalist poet Gabriele d'Annunzio) and delivered by patrols at the front, including by some 17,000 Czechs who had changed sides since capture and now fought alongside the Italians. In short, this was a much more sustained and sophisticated effort than the earlier Austrian propaganda campaign. Against it the AOK established an 'Enemy Propaganda Defence Agency' (Feindespropaganda-Abwehrstelle, or FAst), which was essentially a programme of orations to the troops, but it had neither the money nor the personnel to make much impact and it suffered from the very practical problem of a shortage of paper.[322]

As with Allied propaganda on the Western Front, it is difficult to evaluate the Padua Commission's contribution. If it aimed to make the enemy desert, this was happening anyway. The Italians captured about 22,000 Habsburg troops during the Battle of the Piave,[323] but the front was so inactive that more such prisoner-taking had to await the final advance after Vittorio Veneto. Instead, desertion continued to be primarily to the interior: in the summer and autumn of 1918 the numbers may have reached 230,000, and gangs of outlaws fanned out from the South Slav lands towards Galicia, Hungary, the Czech lands, and the Alps. In the meantime the army on the Italian front shrank from 406,000 (and 252,950 in the rear) on 1 July to 238,900 (and 146,650 in the rear) on 1 October.[324] According to the Austrian military occupation authorities in Serbia, their units by late July were down to 50 per cent of regular strength, and the AOK had too few men to reinforce them.[325] In the final month, from late September to late October, the local commanders reported that although the harvest had alleviated bread scarcities, meat and fresh vegetables were as short as ever. The men had only one change of underwear, and often that was full of holes. In one front-line regiment, only one soldier in three had a coat. Of the fifteen divisions on the river Piave, only five exceeded two thirds of their regulation strength, and some stood at less than one third. It was still thought that the men would fight, but they were outnumbered and outmatched in equipment, and supplying them through another winter would be very difficult indeed. None the less, although a few units mutinied during October, most of the army resisted during the opening days of the Battle of Vittorio Veneto, and only after the Allies had broken through and the Monarchy had not only sued for a ceasefire but was already fragmenting into separate units did its front-line soldiers give themselves up wholesale. Desertions to the rear had enfeebled the army, but surrender following defeat destroyed it.

THE BALKANS AND THE MIDDLE EAST

The Allies' successes in Macedonia and the Middle East can be taken together. In both theatres, they faced serious manpower problems, but worse confronted their opponents. Their Macedonian army in September 1918 totalled some 628,000 men, of whom 180,000 were French (many from the colonies), 150,000 Serbs and other South Slavs, 135,000 Greeks, 120,000 British (including Indians), 42,000 Italians, and 1,000 Albanians.[326] It was a motley force, and had had its share of difficulties. In 1917 the mutinies at home spread to some French units, and the Bolshevik Revolution to the Russians, who had to be disarmed. In 1918 it lost British and French divisions to the Western Front. Relief, however, came partly from the arrival of thousands of Yugoslav volunteers, fleeing from the Balkans, Austria-Hungary, and Russia, who supplemented the Serbian units. In addition, Greek units occupied quieter sectors, releasing other contingents, and by the summer the Allies' difficulties had diminished. In Palestine, Allenby's army included a token French contingent, a Jewish Legion of two battalions, and four mounted divisions of Indians and Australians. But its core was seven infantry divisions, only one of them all-British. The other six comprised three British and nine Indian battalions each, so fifty-four Indian battalions in all. The Indianization of Allenby's infantry was an unforeseen development forced by the crisis in Europe that meant his army stayed at the same size instead of growing to nine divisions as he had expected. He lost the British territorials who had been the backbone of his forces, and had serious concerns about their replacement: many of the Indians lacked combat experience and they required specialist training (by officers who knew no Hindustani) and he doubted the reliability of the 29 per cent who were Moslem.[327] By the eve of his September offensive, however, he was reassured and during the campaign troop morale was not a worry. British Empire troops in Palestine understood their chances of survival were better than in Flanders, and the relative smallness of the EEF made for a more informal style of soldiering – encouraged by Allenby personally – with less emphasis on petty discipline and drill. Supply to both Palestine and to Mesopotamia had much improved in the middle years of the war, and the forces there were mostly adequately cared for medically and sufficiently fed.[328] Unlike in France, however, they were isolated. They had virtually no opportunity for home leave (in 1919, 56,000 men in Palestine had been in the Middle East since 1914–15),[329] letters and parcels arrived belatedly, if at all, and rest periods out of the line offered few facilities. The lower (though far from negligible) risk of battle deaths and wounds was offset by boredom, discomfort, and the debilitation caused by malaria, heat, and humidity. None the less, the Allies managed to maintain their numbers, and their forces both held together in the face of setbacks and stagnation and obeyed orders to fight.

Their enemies were less favoured. Bulgaria's population was 4.5 million, but its men under arms numbered 500,000: a prodigious effort.[330] Its army had the reputation of being one of the best Balkan forces and in 1912 had led the defeat of the Turks in the First Balkan War. Yet by the same token, by 1918 it had been involved in major campaigning for almost six years. The Germans and Austro-Hungarians largely redeployed out of Macedonia in 1917–18, leaving it as principally a Bulgarian front though under German command. Although the Bulgars managed to preserve approximate numerical parity with their enemies, they intensely resented the better-fed foreign personnel who exercised authority over them. 1917 and 1918 were also years of food crisis, which convulsed Bulgarian politics and prompted plaintive letters to the soldiers from their families.[331] It also threatened the army's supplies, and although the troops had enough shells their food and clothing were deficient.[332] In 1917 the bread ration fell from 1,000 to 800 grams per day; by summer 1918 in some units it was 500, and its composition (barley bread mixed with straw) made the men sick. In June the Commander-in-Chief, General Nicola Zhekov, warned the government that morale had become a serious problem; by July he was using the word 'crisis'.[333] Soviets had been formed in the army in 1917, and discontent continued to rumble. Although it had always fought hard when tested, by summer 1918 Allied intelligence detected a decline in its efficiency and big increases in desertion. In the September fighting the Bulgarians defeated the Anglo-Greek attack on 'P' ridge and until the ceasefire they never surrendered en masse as the Austrians did. None the less, once driven back from their initial positions they offered only limited resistance.

A greater catastrophe overwhelmed the Turks in Palestine, where 75,000 soldiers were captured and two corps virtually ceased to exist. Here again the deterioration in fighting power was recent: the Turks had repeatedly defeated British forces between 1915 and 1917, and as recently as April and May 1918 had beaten off Allenby's Jordan raids. But the Ottoman Empire was desperately poor. Even in peacetime, although it supposedly had a conscription system, it never conducted the census needed to enumerate its manpower. Its recruiting demands fell primarily on the 18 million Moslem peasant farmers of the Anatolian interior: the Christian minorities (Greeks and Armenians) who made up a fifth of the population were less intensively conscripted, as were the Bedouin nomads, although 200,000–300,000 of the empire's Arab subjects served in its forces.[334] The Ottoman army had been fighting even longer than the Bulgarians: since Italy's invasion of Libya in 1911–12 and before that against insurrections in the Balkans and Yemen. Since 1914 it had bitten deeply into its reserves. The most authoritative estimate is that during the war 2,873,000 were mobilized, of whom 771,844 lost their lives (243,590 combat fatalities, 61,487 missing, and 466,759 dying of disease), 763,753 were wounded, and 145,104 taken prisoner. Death from combat or disease awaited nearly one in three of those mobilized.[335]

From 1916 onwards a decline in fighting power among the Arab units was becoming evident. Deserted Arab regulars (who faced execution if recaptured) formed the 3,000-man nucleus of Faisal's Northern Arab Army,[336] rather than the more picturesque Bedouin who accompanied Faisal, according to Allenby, only for as long as they were paid at a rate of £6 per man and camel and received insurance for the camel.[337] This circumstance highlights the importance of desertion, which reached immense proportions: some 300,000 in 1917 and more than 500,000 by late summer 1918. Already in September 1917 Mustafa Kemal reported to the war minister that most units were down to one fifth of regulation strength.[338] The majority of deserters stayed behind the Turkish lines, joining bands of brigands in the countryside or milling around near the depots and in cities like Damascus. According to Liman von Sanders, they outnumbered those under arms.[339] The Turkish army could not round up so many outlaws, and lost control over great tracts of its own territory. It disintegrated like those of Austria-Hungary and Germany, but faster.

This being said, besides the general deliquescence of the Turkish forces more specific factors were at work. Throughout 1918 the Ottoman Empire continued to maintain a fighting force of just over 1 million men, but its best units were advancing into the Caucasus and North Persia.[340] The Palestine army lost some of its most experienced commanders, and several of its German units moved north. Liman protested against the transfer of the 11th Jäger battalion, 'the backbone of future operations', and warned Constantinople that the Transcaucasian enterprise would cost it all its Arab provinces, but the transfer was not rescinded.[341] Simultaneously Allenby was remonstrating with the British Cabinet against plans to withdraw his last all-British division: and kept it. Although the Turks did not move any of their own Palestine units to the north,[342] they ran down their strengths and their supply situation became desperate. According to Liman, 17,000 in his army died of starvation in the winter and spring of 1917/18, and his troops were down to 3 ounces of grain per day.[343] By summer 1918 they had run out of anaesthetics and many soldiers and even officers had to wear tschariks – animal skins tied on with string – instead of boots,[344] others marched barefoot. The men were on half of meagre regulation rations and surviving on flour soup, as they lacked meat, fruit and vegetables, sugar, butter, coffee and tea.[345] The front-line forces were fed only by repeatedly cutting rations for those in the rear, with the result that by August the latter were going over to the British, enticed by assurances in air-dropped leaflets that prisoners would receive all their wants.[346] Several hundred a month went over, bringing valuable intelligence with them,[347] and the wonder is that they were not more numerous. Their officers were aware of and disheartened by Germany's defeats in Europe. Allenby's forces meticulously planned and executed an ingeniously conceived attack, but in contrast with the tenacity of previous Turkish resistance they encountered unexpectedly complete demoralization and were overwhelmed by the prisoner haul.

Considerations of manpower and morale were fundamental to the endgame. The belligerents on both sides – except for the Americans – had all but used up their men. They had to await the next cohort of eighteen-year-olds and the soldiers patched up from wounds. Indeed, the efficiency of the medical system was a major reason why manpower had not run out earlier: 29 per cent of the British wounded on the Western Front returned to serve there.[348] But in itself it did not advantage the Allies, and the Germans had better recuperation rates.[349] On the other hand, in all the main belligerents hundreds of thousands of able-bodied men were working in the home economies, and governments resisted transferring them. Striking a balance between manpower and equipment was delicate, and Germany may have produced too many weapons when the army more urgently required soldiers; while the Allies misdirected soldiers into armaments production when needs were greater for coal, food, and transport. In 1918 the politics of manpower moved up the agenda, as a return to semi-mobile warfare caused much higher losses and great volatility of mood. At first it encouraged optimism in the British, French, and German armies simultaneously, but soon it led to exhaustion, offset by satisfaction in the BEF but much less among the French, and among the Germans intensified by despair. In one sense the defeat of the Central Powers *was* the moment at which their armies ran out of men and out of willingness to carry on. None the less, even before 1918 they were beset by growing indiscipline. During the final year the problem grew, creating an outflow that could be neither stemmed nor compensated for. By the summer the German army was melting away because of surrenders at the front and an exodus to the rear: after the government sued for peace the latter became the dominant factor. Austro-Hungarian deserters also generally went homewards, mass surrenders coming after the Italians advanced. Fewer Bulgarian soldiers surrendered or deserted, but by late September they had been beaten and wanted to go home; while most of the Ottoman troops in Palestine were encircled and captured. In contrast, during

1917 the French and Italian armies – and to a lesser extent the British – had undergone morale crises that on many points resembled those experienced by their enemies (and an even greater crisis had engulfed the Russians). Often these crises followed failed offensives, but losses in themselves did not weaken discipline unless they appeared to have been futile. Similarly, grievances over leave, food, and clothing could be thoroughly debilitating and encourage desertion, but would not cripple an army. Finally, all the high commands had realized that repression was not enough. All launched political education campaigns for their own troops, often combined with propaganda drives against their enemies, and yet the effectiveness of both devices remains doubtful. Ultimately a loss of hope proved crucial, whereas to the European Allies the Americans offered hope in abundance, whatever the tardiness and limitations of the AEF's battlefield effort. After 'Michael' and the Piave offensive, realization spread ever wider through the German and Austrian armies that there was no point in carrying on. Combatant morale was not a world in isolation but was intimately linked to broader developments, and the interconnection between the military story and home front economics and politics must now be probed more closely. As a preliminary, it is necessary to consider the sea communications that were vital to the Allied victory, and the Central Powers' failure to sever them.

5
Securing the Seas:
Submarines and Shipping

For the bread that you eat and the biscuits you nibble,
The sweets that you suck and the joints that you carve,
They are brought to you daily by all us Big Steamers –
And if anyone hinders our coming you'll starve!

Rudyard Kipling, 'Big Steamers', 1911

The Allies' mastery of global resources depended on command of the seas. As 1918 began, neither side saw that command as being assured. Admiral Henning von Holtzendorff, the Chief of the Admiralty Staff in Berlin and the architect of the unrestricted submarine campaign, advised Wilhelm that 'decisive consequences are to be expected from U-boat warfare in 1918'.[1] The Allies' shipping losses still exceeded new construction, and their experts forecast worsening tonnage shortages.[2] Admiral Sir David Beatty, the commander of the British Grand Fleet, feared his margin of superiority was so fine that his best policy was simply to contain his adversary.[3] Yet by the autumn the Allies had decisively diminished not only the submarine peril to their communications but also the threat from the enemy surface fleets, and they had reorganized their shipping to the maximum logistical advantage. In the words of the British geographer Sir Halford Mackinder, 'We have been fighting ... in the close of the war, a straight duel between sea-power and land-power, and sea-power has been laying siege to land-power.'[4] This was an unspectacular struggle, fought out away from public gaze in a myriad of encounters across the expanses of the Mediterranean and the Atlantic. Yet its outcome was emphatic and underlay every other Allied achievement.

SUBMARINES

Table 5.1. Gross merchant shipping tonnage lost to enemy action, 1 January 1917–11 November 1918 (000 tons, rounded)[5]

	Jan.	Feb.	Mar.	Apr.	May	June	July	Aug.	Sep.	Oct.	Nov.	Dec.
1917												
British	154	313	353	545	352	418	365	330	196	276	174	253
World total	369	540	594	881	597	688	558	512	352	459	289	399
1918												
British	180	223	199	216	192	163	165	146	137	59	10	
World total	307	307	319	343	296	256	261	284	188	119	18	

The first imperative was to staunch the losses, and convoy was the principal instrument. To Admiral William Sims, who commanded American naval forces in European waters, a convoy 'seemed to be a rather limping, halting procession. The speed of a convoy was the speed of its slowest ship ... The whole mass was sprawled over the sea in most ungainly fashion: twenty or thirty ships, with spaces of nine hundred or a thousand yards stretching between them, took up not far from ten square miles of the ocean's surface'. Yet on to the maelstrom of Allied shipping movements convoy imposed an order that Sims likened to the trans-continental regularity of the US railroads.[6] The system's nerve centre lay in London, where an enormous map, accessed by ladders, covered one wall of the Admiralty's convoy room: a paper ship marked each convoy, and circles the suspected positions of the U-boats. As merchantmen converged on Britain from across the globe, they formed up at assembly points. Those from the Mediterranean gathered at Gibraltar, which was the busiest point of the entire network: on one day in November 1917 117 ocean-going vessels lying at anchor.[7] Steamers from the Cape, East Asia, and Australasia met at Dakar; those from Panama, the Gulf of Mexico, and the southern USA at Hampton Roads; and those from the middle Atlantic American States and Canada at New York, whence they proceeded to Sydney (Cape Breton Island) or Halifax (Nova Scotia).[8] Convoys normally left New York at eight-day intervals, cruisers or old pre-Dreadnought battleships accompanying them to the edge of the danger zone around the British Isles, where a destroyer escort took over for the final leg. Faster and slower vessels followed different routes, and the Admiralty planned for the North Atlantic convoys' destination to alternate between Britain's west-coast and east-coast ports, the latter reached via the Channel. In the reverse direction, vessels from the Channel and east coast assembled off Devonport or Falmouth; those from the west coast at Milford Haven, Lamlash on the Isle of Arran, or Queenstown (Cobh) in Ireland. Originally convoys averaged twenty vessels, but as experience grew so did the numbers: thirty became commonplace, and convoy HN73 leaving New York in June 1918 numbered forty-seven.[9]

Convoy emptied the seas. Before its introduction, merchant ships funnelling in singly through the thinly patrolled approach cones to Britain's western coasts had been easier to detect. In contrast, in Churchill's words:

> the sea is so vast that the difference between the size of a convoy and the size of a single ship shrinks in comparison almost to insignificance. There was in fact very nearly as good a chance of a convoy of forty ships in close order slipping unperceived between the patrolling U-Boats as there was for a single ship; and each time this happened forty ships escaped instead of one.[10]

Of 219 Atlantic convoys sailing between October and December 1917 only thirty-nine were even sighted:[11] and this not only because of the ocean's immensity, but also because shipping could now be better managed. The German Admiralty's espionage network in Britain failed to ascertain the routes and schedules, and by mid-1918 British counter-intelligence had broken it up.[12] Few merchant ships yet had powerful wireless apparatus, but most warships did, and the Admiralty communicated with the convoy commanders to re-route their charges away from danger. Its convoy room was the clearing house for reports of U-boats, gathered from sightings by ships and – increasingly – aircraft, but above all from the surprisingly frequent moments when the submarines broke their isolation by radioing each other or their bases. The Allies' direction-finding equipment rarely gave a precise enough location for the submarine to be attacked, but it did indicate vicinities to avoid, and frequently the messages – which might include a U-boat's bearings – could be decrypted.[13] Hence the Admiralty's Anti-Submarine

Division had plentiful information for its daily briefings, and redirecting convoys may have done as much as anything to save cargoes and lives.

Even if a U-boat did locate a convoy, the chances of a successful strike were small. The submarines were still an infant technology. Their radius of action was short, only a handful in 1918 being able to operate much beyond the British Isles. Rather than submarines proper they were submersibles. They could remain below for only a few hours before resurfacing to recharge their batteries, unless they could halt and sit on the bottom, which was possible only in shallower waters such as the Channel and the Irish Sea – in the Atlantic the pressure would crush them. They had two sets of engines: diesel for travel (at up to 15 mph) on the surface, and electric for travel (at up to 8 mph) beneath. When cruising to and from their killing grounds they were generally surfaced, and when surfaced they were most vulnerable, especially in fine weather, when visibility was unhindered. Once they were sighted, a single shot could pierce their hulls. Whereas a contest between a submarine and an isolated merchant ship was stacked against the latter, against a convoy escorted by destroyers the odds were reversed.

For the final stage into harbour a convoy zigzagged in formation, arranged in columns with the destroyers on its flanks, steaming at the highest speed it could muster. At night its lights were extinguished. Normally the destroyers parted company with an outward convoy at the edge of the danger zone, only promptly to rendezvous with an inward one, thus operating continuously though sorely trying their captains, several of whom broke under the strain.[14] Yet the destroyers needed to be worked hard, as they were the vital anti-submarine weapon. Shallow in draught so that torpedoes would pass under them, they were fast (up to fifty knots) and could accelerate quickly. As well as 4- to 5-inch guns, they carried depth charges: canisters packed with high explosive that water pressure detonated. If one exploded within a hundred feet of a U-boat it was likely to destroy it or force it to surface. The Royal Navy pioneered depth charges during the war, and whereas in 1917 destroyers typically carried three or four each, by summer 1918 they carried thirty or more, as well as hoists that would throw them well out from the ship. In 1916 the British used 100 depth charges a month; in 1917, 200; and in 1918, 500 (although in 1942, by comparison, 1,700).[15]

One consequence of convoy was that submarines attempted many fewer sinkings by gunfire, which had been their preferred method.[16]

Losses to submarine-laid mines also diminished; partly because the Admiralty re-routed convoys; partly because casualties among German mine-laying submarines had been very high indeed, no fewer than thirty-six being destroyed in 1917;[17] and partly because minesweeping improved. In addition, from late 1917 all larger British merchant ships were fitted with the 'Otter' – a mine cable cutting device akin to the 'paravane' used by warships – although their captains did not always use it. This left sinking by torpedo, but torpedoes were bulky and expensive and U-boats typically carried only eight to twelve, their captains being advised to limit themselves to one hit per victim.[18] Moreover, before firing successfully a submarine commander had first to take up position and aim, preferably from as close as 300 feet in order to inflict most damage by targeting the engine room. As a submarine's torpedo tubes were located at its bow and stern, it had to fire from a point at right angles to the merchantman, whose high speed and direction changes obscured its likely 'mean' forward course to the point where it and the torpedo might make contact. Aiming was a highly skilled art, practised in the most stressful of circumstances, and the torpedo's wake – a broad and distinctive foaming white line – would betray its originator's position. Hence a U-boat could risk only one or two shots against a convoy, or might prefer simply to track it in the hope of picking off stragglers. Convoy losses proved extremely low, and the Admiralty's statistician (a seconded railwayman, George Beharrel) quantified them.[19] In August to October 1917 the loss rate among convoyed ships was 0.58 per cent, compared with a non-convoyed rate of 7.37 per cent.[20] Even if a convoyed merchant ship were hit, the accompanying vessels might well salvage it or at least take off the crew, and inhibit U-boat practices such as taking the master and chief engineer captive. Against a form of warfare that relied on terror, convoy offered psychological reinforcement.

By early 1918, 90 per cent of the vessels sailing the Atlantic were convoyed,[21] and more than half of Britain's total overseas trade. Yet a major reason why sinkings continued high was that the system remained incomplete and the U-boats found the chinks in it, 85 per cent of the losses being independents.[22] One weak point was the mid-Atlantic islands – Madeira, the Azores, and the Cape Verdes – where new longer-range 'U-cruisers' could operate, and the Germans extended their sink-without-warning regime in winter 1917/18.[23] The prime targets

were grain ships from the river Plate, and in response the British introduced a convoy service direct from Rio.[24] A second weak point, the
Mediterranean, was more difficult to deal with. In early 1918 losses
there were rising, and the British First Sea Lord regarded conditions as
'very critical'.[25] The Mediterranean seaways were vital for Allied operations in Palestine, the Balkans, and Italy; for France to ferry troops from
Africa; for Italy to import cereals and coal; and for Britain to bring supplies from Australasia and Asia without going via the Cape of Good
Hope. None the less, the Cape route had become the norm and the shipping ministry estimated that restoring through-voyages from Suez to
Gibraltar could free up the equivalent of forty steamers.[26] Yet the Mediterranean's narrowness and shallowness made it a happy hunting
ground for the U-boats. In October 1917 fourteen Austro-Hungarian
and thirty-two German submarines were stationed in the Austrian bases
at Pola and Cattaro on the Adriatic, and four more German submarines
at Constantinople. During the whole of 1917, only two Mediterranean
U-boats were destroyed,[27] and during 1918 Mediterranean sinkings
averaged a quarter to a third of total Allied shipping losses.[28] Through-
convoys ran between Gibraltar and Egypt from October 1917, but the
heaviest traffic plied the Western Mediterranean, and key routes such as
those from Gibraltar to Genoa and to Bizerta had to wait until the
spring to be organized.[29] Yet even once the system was operating, Mediterranean loss rates averaged more than twice those for convoys as a
whole,[30] and in early 1918 shipping was so short that many units at
Salonika were receiving only half their needs.[31] Part of the problem was
that the Mediterranean was a poor relation, its convoys having fewer
and older escort vessels than those in northern waters and including
auxiliaries such as converted trawlers. Moreover, the multiplicity of
ports of call on both shores required a complex, criss-cross pattern of
routes. Whereas Britain (with increasing American assistance) managed
the Atlantic convoys, in the Mediterranean much greater international
co-operation was called for, but not always forthcoming, Italy's navy
conducting almost no escort duty outside its coastal waters. Conversely,
fourteen Japanese destroyers that had arrived in 1917 (in return for
secret Allied pledges to support Tokyo's claims to Germany's island colonies in the North Pacific) proved indispensable as troopship escorts.[32]

Even larger losses than in the Mediterranean occurred round Britain's coasts. In response to the convoys' introduction the U-boats shifted

their attention from the Atlantic towards the Irish Sea and English Channel, and between May to July 1917 and November 1917 to January 1918 the proportions of sinkings in European waters occurring within ten miles of land rose from 17.7 to 62.8 per cent.[33] The change had advantages for the Allies. Ships attacked inshore were easier to salvage and their crews more likely to be rescued. Moreover, the vessels were smaller: the German Admiralty advising U-boats that none the less these targets were worthwhile, as every loss would accentuate the Allies' overall stringency.[34] Trout being absent, minnows would do. Yet the coastal seas presented a formidable organizational challenge, as they contained not only ocean-going steamers but also shoals of short-haul vessels, and the British Isles were caught in a pincer between the German High Seas Fleet submarines operating from North Sea bases in the Heligoland Bight and the Flanders U-boats stationed at Bruges and exiting via canals to Ostend and Zeebrugge. The U-boats and U-cruisers used in Flanders were smaller, cheaper, and quicker to build, and they sank more tonnage each than did their High Seas Fleet counterparts.[35]

Convoy was the essential element in the package that would frustrate the U-boats in these new theatres, but it competed for resources with other methods, some of dubious effectiveness. 'Dazzle painting', for example, the brainchild of Lt-Cdr Norman Wilkinson, entailed decorating ships in bewildering geometrical patterns. By October 1918, 2,719 British merchant ships had been painted, as well as 251 warships, and other Allied merchant fleets followed suit. Merchant skippers found it reassuring, but whether it really confused the U-boats' aim remained inconclusive, and captured submarine crews said they failed to see its purpose.[36] Other measures included the Jarrow smoke-box, which created an obscuring cloud by expelling boiler smoke at sea level rather than through the funnel; and a scheme of masthead look-outs whereby larger British merchantmen would train and pay bonuses to crew members who kept watch from the crow's nest. More ambitious and expensive was DAMS (defensive arming of merchant ships), which entailed fitting cannon on to merchantmen and training their crews to use them (the American merchant navy, in contrast, placed service personnel on merchant vessels).[37] DAMS ranked low among the Admiralty's priorities,[38] but the numbers of armed ships more than doubled, from 1,749 in September 1916 to 4,203 by November 1918.[39] Yet although cannon were effective against surfaced U-boats, they were useless against submerged torpedo attacks, and altogether 1,784 armed British merchantmen went down.

The Admiralty's answer to the U-boats, however, was not purely defensive. Indeed, part of the reason for the admirals' lack of enthusiasm for convoy (at least in certain quarters) was the equivalent of the supposed offensive bias among the generals on land: the opinion that the navy's proper function was to go out and take aggressive action. American naval thinking was similar. Allied strategy in 1918 therefore combined convoy with more pro-active measures, the latter facilitated by convoy's success in easing the pressure. This approach achieved results, although concentrating all available vessels as convoy escorts would have done so more quickly and cheaply.

In the Mediterranean the centrepiece of the offensive strategy was an attempt to block the 45-mile exit from the Adriatic via the Straits of Otranto. Initially the Otranto 'barrage' had consisted of a courageous line of fishing vessels with nets, inadequately supported by naval patrols. On 15 May 1917 the Austrians attacked it, destroying fourteen drifters out of forty-seven. In 1918 the Allies tried to build a fixed barrier using special steel wire from Britain, but the wire arrived slowly and the new barrage was completed only in September. On the other hand, the Austrians attempted on 9–10 June to repeat their previous raid, but they withdrew after an Italian torpedo boat sank one of their most modern battleships, the *Szent István*. This success helped the Allies to station an enormous force of some 30 destroyers, 15 submarines, 18 trawlers with hydrophones, and over 1,000 drifters, as well as 36 American 'submarine chasers' – 110-feet-long wooden vessels equipped with new listening devices and depth charges.[40] Between them the nets and barrage ships destroyed two submarines, and frightened and disheartened the crews of others. And yet, according to the Allies' estimates, passages through the Straits fell by only 30 per cent. What really turned the corner in the Mediterranean was a reorganization and extension of the convoys in June, allowing more vessels to be escorted along a total of eighteen routes. Sinkings and tonnage losses fell permanently to about half the previous average, and of the fourteen U-boats destroyed in the Mediterranean during 1918, eight fell victim to convoy escorts. The Otranto barrage diverted forces from a convoy system that was losing 2 cent of the vessels it protected to a scheme that swallowed up resources to little purpose.[41] Reviewing the situation in October 1918, Commodore George Baird, the Malta-based Director of Shipping Movements, considered that the escort vessels' increased strength had destroyed more submarines and deterred attacks on convoys, especially when supported by air patrols. Better intelligence about the U-boats and convoy re-routing had also helped, as (and probably most significantly) had worsening morale among submarine crews. Yet although the methods that had succeeded in the Atlantic were now prevailing in the Mediterranean, he warned that the diversion of resources to the barrage was cutting convoy escorts to the bone, so that even at this stage in the war it would 'really be a matter of luck and successful dodging if sinkings remain at the present low level'.[42]

In British home waters too, Allied strategy included more aggressive elements. Overrunning the Flanders U-boat bases had been one goal of Haig's 1917 Third Ypres offensive, and one reason why the Germans had so tenaciously resisted it. In 1918 the Bruges–Zeebrugge–Ostend 'Flanders triangle' remained a British target, but now via naval and air action. Most spectacular was the raid against Zeebrugge and Ostend on the night of 22/23 April 1918, undertaken on St George's Day, blazoned in the press after weeks of bad news, and silencing murmurs that the navy had lost its Nelsonian daring.[43] Another attack on Ostend followed on 9–10 May. Yet although both operations aimed to close the U-boats' exit channels by sinking blockships, and although they seemed at first to have succeeded, neither matched up to expectations.[44] Three blockships were sunk at Zeebrugge, but the Germans dug fresh channels round them.[45] The sinking of the *Vindictive* closed only one third of the channel at Ostend.[46] Channel losses fell afterwards, but mainly owing to a concatenation of other measures.[47] Almost daily air attacks during the summer damaged the Zeebrugge lock gates, but they were quickly repaired, and coastal minelaying failed to close the sea exits. Second World War-style concrete pens shielded the U-boats, and eventually the Germans withdrew them because of land operations: the Allied advances in October obliged Wilhelm to order the Flanders submarines back to the homeland.[48] But by now the Flanders flotillas were in decline anyway. In the final months they fell from twenty-five to sixteen vessels, and only one in seven of those returning through the Dover Straits in August and September did so without difficulty.[49] The perils simply of getting to and from their harbours added further stresses to a nerve-racking existence.

Tighter Dover Straits security resulted from improved mines. For most of the war the Germans' mines had been much superior and they had strewn them round the British Isles.[50] Against this threat the Royal Navy and the civilians of its Auxiliary Patrol assembled an unsung armada that included sloops, trawlers, drifters, and motor launches. During the war no fewer than 3,685 auxiliary vessels enrolled in the Royal Navy's service, and 445 were destroyed: 2,304 of their officers and men lost their lives.[51] None the less, by late 1917 minelaying was diminishing and minesweeping becoming more effective:[52] German mines sank 128 British merchant ships in 1917 but ten in 1918.[53] Moreover, in autumn 1917 the British began mass production of the Mark H2, a 'horned' mine patterned on its German counterpart, which was far more reliable than its predecessors.[54] By June 1918 the Royal Navy had 32,500 in store, was producing 6,000–7,000 per month, and was laying about the same number.[55]

The 'H' mines could be moored at greater depths, and in autumn 1917 a new deep field was laid across the Channel between Cape Gris Nez and the Varne. Radio intercepts had revealed that U-boats were passing freely via the Dover Straits, and the previous barrage was useless.[56] But whereas Rear-Admiral Roger Keyes, the head of the Admiralty's Plans Division, wanted to prevent submarines from passing over the barrier at night by stationing trawlers along it with searchlights and flares, Vice-Admiral Sir Roger Bacon, the commander at Dover, refused to place ships in such an exposed position. Keyes was moved to Dover to supplant him, and he set the trawlers in place.[57] On the night of 14/15 February German destroyers then raided the barrage, sinking eight fishing vessels and killing seventy-six men from their crews.[58] Yet they never repeated the operation and the new barrage did make passage of the Straits much harder, forcing more U-boats to take the far longer alternative route round the north of the British Isles.[59] Some 14–16 U-boats were lost in the Straits during 1918, and in May they were ordered not to use them until the weather became more suitable, the Flanders bases thereby losing much of their value.[60] The new barrier did achieve something, if later than the British realized.

As the menace from Flanders receded, the burden of the campaign in

British waters fell to the North Sea submarines based with the German surface fleet in the Ems, Jade, Weser, and Elbe estuaries. But here too more mines facilitated countermeasures. The Allies laid some 15,700 mines offshore during 1917; and some 21,000 during 1918, mostly by destroyers from the Humber.[61] Extending more than a hundred miles out, the mined area became so vast and unpredictable that the Germans confined themselves to maintaining swept channels through it, but even these were repeatedly blocked.[62] During September 1918 only seven submarines were escorted out of the Heligoland Bight, in three convoys.[63] Increasingly the U-boats used the Kattegat, the strait between Denmark and Norway, which the British also mined though never succeeding in closing: but this route added 3–4 days to their travelling time and reduced their stay in the campaigning zone.[64] The Allies also tried to block the U-boats' exit into the North Atlantic by laying the 'Northern Barrage'. This scheme – an American conception – was for a minefield from the Orkneys to Norway. It would replace the Tenth Cruiser Squadron, which had patrolled the wild northern seas since 1915, but had become a target for the U-boats while assisting little in their detection.[65] An inter-Allied conference in September 1917 approved the plan: work began in March 1918 and by the autumn the British had laid 13,546 mines and the Americans 56,571,[66] assembled at Norfolk, Virginia, and shipped across the Atlantic in special vessels. But so many American mines blew up or drifted off loose that laying was temporarily suspended and Beatty feared the North Sea would become too dangerous to navigate.[67] The barrage was not completed until October, when the Norwegians submitted to Allied pressure to close a remaining gap by mining their territorial waters.[68] It may have sunk six or seven U-boats, at a cost of $40m.[69] Like the Otranto barrage it was an enormous diversion of resources, and was finished too late to make much difference.

More important than the Allies' offensive measures was the submarines' continuing lack of an answer to convoys. In British home waters, as in the mid-Atlantic and the Mediterranean, the system tightened its grip. More vessels were escorted to their assembly points, and local convoys introduced across the riskiest stretches: the Irish Sea in March and the English east coast in June.[70] Round the shoreline, moreover, aeroplanes could operate, and by November 1918 the RAF was deploying

285 seaplanes and flying boats and 272 land-based aircraft against the U-boats, more and more of them carrying radios.[71] In the last five months Allied aircraft sighted 167 U-boats and attacked 115, although sinking only two, in both cases aided by warships.[72] Unlike in the Second World War, aircraft did not themselves destroy submarines, but they could spot them from a greater distance and observe torpedo tracks, and served as a deterrent: during 1918 U-boats pressed home attacks against only six convoys with air escorts.[73] Like warships, aircraft achieved more when accompanying convoys than when engaged in general patrolling.

The argument thus far has questioned the effectiveness of the Allies' offensive measures. Although they sank 69 submarines in 1918, compared with 63 in 1917 and 46 in 1914–16,[74] new building kept the U-boat numbers at around the same level and the newly commissioned submarines were superior in performance and armament. The absolute numbers might suggest that the Allies were merely containing rather than reducing the threat. Nor did the Allies in the First World War achieve any breakthrough like that of May 1943, when the Germans called off their mid-Atlantic campaign after losing forty-one submarines in a month.[75] The nearest equivalent was May–June 1918, after which Allied shipping losses in both the Atlantic and Mediterranean permanently fell off. The naval authorities were aware of the change, which the post-war official histories highlighted.[76] However, it owed more to unspectacular modifications in convoying arrangements than to the fourteen U-boats destroyed in May, the highest monthly total of the war. Although Holtzendorff warned Wilhelm that losses were reaching a 'dangerous magnitude',[77] he correctly saw the figure as freakish, linked to fine weather and 'mirror-smooth' seas that made the submarines more visible, and he foresaw that it would diminish.[78]

Table 5.2. U-boats lost/entering commission, 1914–18[79]

	1914 (Aug.– Dec.)	1915	1916	1917	1918
Lost (all causes)	5	23	23	75	102
Commissioned	11	52	108	87	88

Table 5.3. U-boats lost/entering commission, 1918[80]

	Jan.	Feb.	Mar.	Apr.	May	June	July	Aug.	Sept.	Oct.	Nov.
Lost (all causes)	10	3	7	7	17	4	6	7	10	20	12
Commissioned		3	6	8	8	11	12	9	8	9	12	2

What mattered more was that sinkings per submarine declined relentlessly: the U-boats based in the North Sea destroyed an average of 0.55 ships each per day in March 1917 but 0.07 in June 1918, or some eight times less.[81] Even in the Mediterranean, German U-boats sank 802 tons per boat per day in April 1917 but 619 in July 1918 and 417 in August;[82] in the Atlantic convoys loss rates almost halved between May to October 1917 and May to October 1918.[83] Whereas the U-boats' key objective was to destroy carrying capacity and cargo, the Allies' was to shepherd the merchantmen safely to their destinations. The monthly totals of destroyed U-boats mattered less than that more cargo was getting through, and therefore that the Allies were winning. They prevailed as much through wear and tear upon the submarines and on their crews as through sinking them. By 1918 what the Germans had originally intended as a five-month all-out offensive had lasted four times longer, and at sea as on land men and machines were worn out. At the end of the war barely one U-boat in two remained available for front-line service,[84] as they spent ever longer voyaging to and from their hunting grounds and rarely regained harbour undamaged. In the Mediterranean the facilities at Pola and Cattaro were overwhelmed with damaged submarines, and throughout 1918 some 30 per cent of the squadron was in dock for lengthy repairs, for which increasingly the requisite materials were unobtainable.[85] Even in the better equipped yards in Flanders and Germany, the burden of repair grew heavier, and competed with the requirements of new building.[86] Moreover, increasing numbers of submarines were needed to train replacement crews.[87] The British Admiralty placed great stress on the U-boat crews' demoralization and the killing or capture of many commanders. Being depth-charged was a terrible experience, with after-effects akin to those of shell shock on land. Interrogations of U-boat prisoners during 1918 suggested that many officers were still defiant, but the ratings were mostly raw and poorly trained conscripts, much more disaffected than in 1917, intimidated by the Allies' countermeasures, and relieved to be

out of the war.[88] Loss of seasoned commanders was even more important, as their work demanded extraordinary courage, aggressiveness, and
seamanship: out of some 400 captains only twenty had been responsible
for 60 per cent of Allied shipping losses, and many had now gone.[89]
When in June 1918 British representatives negotiated an agreement for
prisoner of war exchanges, the Admiralty protested that sixty-five submarine officers and men could go to neutral countries whence they
could easily return to Germany, and 'In carrying on this submarine warfare the greatest difficulty with which the enemy is now faced is the
shortage of trained submarine officers and crews.'[90]

As the U-boat offensive lost impetus, Germany's leaders disagreed
over how to revive it. Holtzendorff wanted an offensive in American
waters, seeking softer targets and forcing Germany's enemies to disperse
their defences. The OHL, hoping for attacks on American troop transports, supported him. Reinhard Scheer, the High Seas Fleet commander,
considered long-range operations would wear out the U-boats and sink
fewer ships: he preferred to concentrate in closer waters.[91] Moreover,
Chancellor Hertling and the foreign ministry objected to proclaiming a
Sperrgebiet (prohibited zone) off America's east coast, fearing it would
inflame US opinion and draw the country more whole-heartedly into
the war. They feared a re-run of 1917, when they had caved in over
unrestricted submarine warfare, only to find the navy's optimism to be
baseless. Wilhelm shared these misgivings, and ruled out a *Sperrgebiet*.[92]
Yet although the navy exploited the issue to blame the politicians for
the U-boats' failure, the submarines actually lacked the capacity to do
much damage. Few of them could reach the American eastern seaboard,
although U-151, operating there from May 1918 onwards, sank twenty-
three ships and severed two underwater cables, while in June fear of
submarine-launched seaplanes blacked out New York City, and six submarines stationed off the American coast between July and November
sank ninety-three ships, including a cruiser.[93] The Wilson administration
responded by introducing coastal convoys but refused to recall American warships from European waters. It had expected such a campaign,
knew when the U-boats were en route, and despite the public consternation believed that random patrolling in the Western Atlantic would
be as ineffective as in the Eastern.[94]

Around Britain, where the U-boats now faced coastal convoys protected by aircraft, they returned in summer 1918 to offshore operations.

Their tactics in the final months foreshadowed those of the Second World War, with more attacks far out to sea at night (to avoid aircraft) and on the surface (for higher speed).[95] The German Admiralty Staff had envisaged that group attacks might overwhelm convoy defences, but Holtzendorff accepted that only the North Sea U-boats (rather than the smaller and slower Flanders types) were suited to such tactics, and they would need time to become familiar with them.[96] In fact the U-boats never achieved the co-ordination needed to break up convoys. For a fortnight during May up to eight submarines were stationed in the approach routes between Brittany and Ireland but during this period 183 vessels were convoyed safely inward and 110 outward, and only five (three of them in convoy) were damaged or sunk, while two of the U-boats were lost. Even in this relatively confined area, and in favourable weather conditions, the submarines had great difficulty in finding convoys, in massing attacks against them, and in landing torpedoes on their targets. In July a second attempt focused on the northern and southern approaches to the Irish Sea, but no more successfully.[97]

The U-boats of 1918 had poorer radio communication than their Second World War counterparts, both for co-ordinating movements and for taking guidance from the homeland.[98] Their numbers were much smaller, and their commanders warned Holtzendorff that to achieve much they would need more vessels.[99] In March 1943, at the climax of the Battle of the Atlantic, an average of 116 submarines were at sea; in 1918 the average monthly figure was forty-five.[100] The totals in commission were 132 in January (33 at sea), 129 in February (50 at sea), 125 in April (55 at sea), 112 in June, and 128 in September.[101] Part of the problem was that too few had been launched earlier. After war broke out the Imperial Navy Office (Reichsmarineamt, or RMA) gave U-boats priority, but still completed two battlecruisers and two battleships between 1915 and 1917.[102] It also built merchant ships, although German seaborne trade had almost entirely halted.[103] On commencing unrestricted submarine warfare in 1917, the RMA had been so confident that it suspended further U-boat orders for fear of being encumbered with masses of redundant submarines after victory.[104] In addition, it sacrificed potential gains from mass production by spreading orders between different yards and a variety of types, concentrating on larger and longer-range vessels that took longer to build. Throughout the war, only twelve U-boats were delivered by the contract date, and the lags grew longer. On 1 April 1916, twenty-five were over contract: on 1 April 1918, seventy. In May 1917 the RMA expected 142 new vessels to come into service by May 1918; in fact 93 did, so that the 1918 fleet was similar to that of 1917 instead of being substantially bigger. In December 1917 the navy tried to accelerate the building programme by creating a new U-Boots-Amt – 'U-Boat Office' – within the RMA. By the end of the war – the hubris of 1917 now long abandoned – it had contracted for 340 more vessels, none of which entered service.[105] As of 3 August 1918, no fewer than 473 submarines were on order.[106]

Extra procurement made little sense until the production bottlenecks had loosened. Under the U-Boots-Amt completions rose, but only slightly.[107] Many factors accounted for the delay, including the rival claims of repairs and of surface ship construction, and shortages of coal, transport, and non-ferrous metals, but all involved agreed the critical scarcity was of labour.[108] Yet when at a conference on 4 October 1917 the RMA chief pleaded for copper, lead, and extra labour to build 118 submarines for delivery in 1919–20, as well as for 7,000–8,000 workers to finish those under construction, Ludendorff objected both to transferring metals from the army's weapons programme and to providing more manpower. The army, he said, had already released 250,000 soldiers to the home economy and could spare no more: the key requirement was to raise the productivity of the workers already in place. In 'all probability' the war would end in 1918, and he needed to rest his troops for the spring campaigning.[109] Implicitly he discounted the Admiralty Staff's argument that more submarines were an insurance policy in case the war on land went wrong: 'the great and also only reserve for the eventuality that the military direction of the war should not – or only incompletely – achieve its objective'.[110] Although Ludendorff agreed in principle that U-boats should be the highest armaments priority, ahead of aircraft, motor vehicles, and munitions,[111] he would not relinquish soldiers or weapons from his projected offensive, and in June 1918 the OHL again refused men from the home or front armies for U-boat construction.[112] Matters only changed – and far too late – after the July turning point on the Western Front put paid to Ludendorff's hopes of a land victory, and after the naval leadership was reconstructed in August. Holtzendorff was removed while Hipper, the battlecruiser commander, replaced Scheer as commander of the High Seas Fleet, and Scheer himself became head of the SKL or Seekriegsleitung, a new overall naval command that moved out of Berlin to sit alongside the OHL at Spa. The Battle of Jutland had given Scheer some of the aura of victory that Hindenburg and Ludendorff owed to Tannenberg, and he and the aggressive young officers round him at once pressed for a massive expansion in submarine output. Assuming that the U-boats were now indeed Germany's last means of applying enough pressure to achieve a favourable peace, Scheer wanted targets comparable to those attempted for land armaments with the 1916 Hindenburg Programme. He prepared a scheme to accelerate the completion of the submarines now on the slipways and to order more, with the aim of once again sinking ships faster than the Allies could build them. Monthly completions were to rise from 12.7 in October 1918 to thirty-six by autumn 1919, continuing at that level into 1920, while the construction workforce was to double from 70,000 to 140,000, of whom 17,000 were needed at once.[113] Ludendorff, however, though recognizing 'what extraordinary importance a stronger pursuit of the U-boat war possesses', again said that neither the front nor the home army could release more men.[114] This was the position when at the end of September the OHL decided to seek an armistice, although Ludendorff agreed that Scheer should continue developing his project in case negotiations failed, and only after Germany finally recalled all U-boats to port on 21 October was the programme abandoned. Intended to rally the public and redeem the navy's reputation, it was overtaken by Germany's collapse.

The Germans intended that the British should get wind of the Scheer programme,[115] and in London the prognostications were surprisingly gloomy. In late September Sir Eric Geddes, the former railway chief who had become First Lord of the Admiralty, warned the Cabinet that because of the need to escort troopships the Admiralty had neglected anti-submarine warfare, with the consequence that U-boat numbers were higher than they had ever been, a great new submarine offensive was developing, and tonnage losses would again become 'a menace to the Allied cause'.[116] Frustration caused by failure to sink more U-boats partly explained this despondency,[117] which came to the Cabinet days before it considered Germany's appeal for an armistice. Yet even if the war had continued into 1919 and the OHL had released some of the workers Scheer requested (which Ludendorff's industrial expert, Colonel Bauer, was willing to contemplate),[118] the trebling in production the SKL envisaged was not remotely achievable. Nor would extra U-boats with unskilled and disgruntled crews have made much impact on the panoply of Allied defences. The crucial elements in Germany's dilemma – the decline in the U-boats' destructiveness and their inability to harm the convoys – continued to apply. On sea as on land, the options had run out.

SURFACE FLEETS

Similar conclusions can be drawn about Germany's surface fleet, although at the start of the year the British were far from confident. Nor did they have simply to worry about the North Sea. The Turkish fleet, assisted and partly commanded by Germans, controlled the Black Sea, and the Allies feared it would sortie into the Mediterranean: hence warships under British command were stationed off the Dardanelles. Moreover, the Bolshevik takeover made it possible that the Central Powers might seize Russia's Black Sea and Baltic fleets. The Austro-Hungarian navy at Pola was efficient and included modern dreadnoughts; the Italian battlefleet at Taranto dreaded an attack on Italy's Adriatic coast and resisted contributing to the wider Allied effort. The French squadron of seven dreadnoughts at Corfu was therefore the Allies' strongest Mediterranean contingent and their principal safeguard against an Austrian break-out.[119] None the less, the most powerful naval forces lay in the North Sea, where Germany's High Seas Fleet in the Jade estuary faced Britain's Battlecruiser Squadron at Rosyth and its Grand Fleet, which moved from Scapa Flow to Rosyth in April 1918. Characteristic of all these stand-offs was the caution observed on both sides, after repeated demonstrations of how capital ships that had taken years to build might succumb to mines and torpedoes within minutes. In the Aegean, the Adriatic, and the North Sea the Allies held numerical superiority, and they controlled all the crucial seaways except the Black Sea and the Baltic. This gave them little incentive to risk their advantage; but nor was it logical for the Central Powers to seek battle unless by some raid or trap they could destroy a portion of the Allied forces and reduce the odds. The Battle of Jutland had been the most spectacular German attempt to achieve precisely such an outcome, but Scheer had concluded from it that he had been lucky to avoid disaster and that surface action could not win the war at sea. Hence he supported making unrestricted submarine warfare the navy's primary contribution during 1917, the High Seas Fleet doing little for months and its battleships being swept in August by mutiny. None the less, the High Seas Fleet continued to justify itself as the 'backbone of the U-boat campaign', essential to safeguard the submarines' outward and inward passage, while in the longer run Wilhelm wanted to keep it in being for leverage at the peace conference.[120]

In London, likewise, the First Sea Lord, Admiral Sir John Jellicoe, advised the Cabinet that 'The Grand Fleet is the centre and pivot on which all naval operations depend.'[121] Despite its seeming inactivity, it deterred invasion and attacks on Allied convoys and troop transports, as well as supporting the anti-submarine effort.[122] Admittedly, at the end of 1917 Whitehall downgraded the invasion risk, though not by much. The Second Sea Lord, Rosslyn Wemyss, agreed in a joint report with the CIGS, Sir William Robertson, that improvements in mining, in air defence, and in fortifying prospective landing places made it reasonably probable that the largest force Germany could land was 70,000, and the navy could intercept it (if between the Wash and Dover) in 32–6 hours; up to 160,000 was possible, but unlikely. The Director of Naval Intelligence, Reginald Hall, had known beforehand of recent German landings in the Baltic and expected at least five days' warning of an enterprise against Britain: the Board of Admiralty approved the Wemyss/ Robertson report for submission to the Cabinet, which was looking for reasons to cut the counter-invasion garrison.[123] Yet the High Seas Fleet reasserted its destructive potential when its cruisers and destroyers surprised and virtually annihilated two of the British-escorted convoys that ran between the Shetlands and Norway, on 17 October and 12 December 1917. The Scandinavian convoys could not be abandoned, not only because of the fish and raw materials that they conveyed to Britain but also because protecting Norwegian merchant vessels formed part of a secret agreement that gave access to vital Norwegian tonnage. Yet the only answer to such ambushes was to guard the convoys with capital ships, which meant that Germany might up the ante and attack with battlefleet forces, so that next time a British battleship or battlecruiser might go down. Although capital ship escorts were provided, the convoys remained vulnerable. German warships could creep up towards them along the Norwegian coast, and the German consul in Bergen might report their sailing dates, while the priceless advantage that Room 40 had provided in the first half of the war was now less assured. The High Seas Fleet was increasingly circumspect in using wireless and in May 1917 it had switched to a new 'FFB' code and completely changed its call signs. By the autumn Room 40 had made progress in cracking the new code, and U-boats, minesweepers, and patrol vessels continued to use the older AFB code, which the British could read without difficulty. Hence London might still gain warning of a major operation by applying traffic analysis and direction-finding techniques to signals from the smaller German ships. In fact Room 40 did get wind of the 17 October attack, but the information reached Beatty too late for him to intercept the raiders. On 12 December, however, Room 40 got no warning at all.[124] Wemyss warned Beatty that in future there might be no notice, Beatty commenting that 'We are gambling upon obtaining accurate information.'[125] Enhancing the escort of the Scandinavian convoys meant that the Germans had effectively divided the Grand Fleet. They were close to their objective since the start of the war of whittling down British superiority by inflicting defeats in detail.

The crisis over Scandinavian convoys came when the Royal Navy was already overstretched. The apparatus built up against the U-boats required an enormous commitment. In October 1918, when the convoy system was at its maximum, some 257 British warships were involved in escort duty.[126] Pressure was acutest on the destroyers, which were essential for protecting warships as well as merchantmen. According to a gloomy memorandum by Jellicoe in November 1917, 'The whole of our naval policy is necessarily governed by the adequacy of our destroyer force', and of the 100 assigned to the Grand Fleet at least one third were always assigned to convoy work, whereas the High Seas Fleet, without the convoy distraction, could give battle with some eighty-eight. Even though building during the war had increased the British destroyer total from 102 to 283, and thirty-five American destroyers were now serving on the west coast of Ireland, the numbers were still at least ninety below requirements.[127] The Admiralty's maxim was 'It must always be anticipated that the High Seas Fleet may come out', and the Grand Fleet must be strong enough to engage it 'with a reasonable prospect of obtaining a complete and overwhelming victory', even if this meant fewer destroyers for convoy work and higher shipping losses.[128] Nor could it count on British battlecruisers not blowing up again as three had done at

Jutland.[129] In a policy statement in early 1918, Beatty took the logic further. Although Britain had more battleships, he warned, its forces were dispersed (whereas the Germans could concentrate by surprise and when they chose): in battle the Grand Fleet was likely to be outnumbered in submarines and destroyers, and to possess no clear advantage in light cruisers and battlecruisers. Germany's destroyers had been rearmed and equalled Britain's in fighting power, while the weaknesses exposed at Jutland had only partially been remedied and he preferred to avoid combat until he had received a new armour piercing shell. In view of all this, and the overriding imperative of escorting the convoys and protecting trade, 'the correct strategy of the Grand Fleet is no longer to endeavour to bring the enemy to action at any cost, but rather to contain him in his bases until the situation becomes more favourable to us'.[130] Actually the Grand Fleet had never sought battle at any cost, as Jellicoe's caution at Jutland had shown, and Beatty was elaborating on the arguments for an existing posture. But the Board of Admiralty unanimously recommended his conclusions to the Cabinet (which accepted them), commenting on 'the strength of the German Grand Fleet, from a strategic point of view' and the pressure on Britain's, especially given the reduced home defence forces. Until more destroyers and the new shells became available, the mining of the Heligoland Bight (and the Dover Straits and Northern Barrages) would serve as restraining measures. But the Admiralty also pressed the Cabinet to agree to finish building two battlecruisers in order to ensure superiority over Germany in 1920. Although eventually the balance would turn towards the Allies, it would be a very long haul.[131]

Russia's collapse and the Central Powers' offensives underlined the need for caution. The German cruiser *Breslau* and battlecruiser *Goeben*, which had joined the Ottoman navy in 1914 and helped to bring Turkey into the war, sallied out of the Dardanelles on 20 January 1918: mines sank the *Breslau* but although the *Goeben* also hit them it managed to escape, despite air and submarine attacks.[132] The British underestimated how badly it had been damaged, and the danger at the Dardanelles increased when the Germans captured part of the Russian Black Sea Fleet, posing a challenge to inter-Allied co-operation and the newly created Allied Naval Council. The ANC comprised the chiefs of staff of the French, Italian, and British navies and flag officers from the American and Japanese ones, was to meet at least once a month, and could make recommendations to the member governments.[133] Its function was consultative, and the danger at the Dardanelles broke it up, the British, French, and Americans wanting to move French battleships from Corfu into the Aegean and to place part of the Italian fleet under French command at Corfu, but the Italians refusing. Although on paper the Allies enjoyed an adequate margin of superiority in the Mediterranean, their vessels were not disposed in what the majority believed the most appropriate way, much to the British Admiralty's exasperation.[134] In northern waters the Admiralty feared that Germany would seize the Russian Baltic Fleet,[135] and Wemyss, who replaced Jellicoe early in the year, was worried that with Britain's most modern warships up in Scotland the Thames estuary was defenceless. On 26 February he commented that 'At this stage in the war one feels inclined, like a drowning man, to clutch at any proposal that holds out the slightest chance of being successful',[136] and at this point Ludendorff's offensives opened months of danger to the Channel ports and the Dover Straits, which Wemyss told the Cabinet were of 'vital importance'.[137] It was fortunate that the Germans so feared mines that Wilhelm instructed his navy to support Ludendorff's offensives primarily by intensified U-boat operations in the Channel, while the surface fleet confined itself to a night bombardment of Dunkirk on 21 March to coincide with the 'Michael' attack.[138]

Instead, the High Seas Fleet's main target during the Ludendorff offensives was again the Scandinavian convoys. Scheer understood a new attack would need support with capital ships, but if successful it would be 'an impressive military success' and oblige the British to move more forces northwards.[139] Hence he planned a sortie by the entire fleet for the first time since August 1916, observing strict wireless silence and issuing his orders in writing. The fleet adopted a new code key on 21 April, which the British did not break for three days,[140] and on 23 April it put to sea undetected. It was discovered only when an engine room accident halted the *Moltke*, a battlecruiser with Hipper's advanced force, which Hipper reported to Scheer by radio: although the British fleet now also put to sea, it did so too late to intercept the Germans before they returned to port. Luckily for the British, Scheer's otherwise meticulous preparations had failed to detect a change in the Scandinavian convoys' sailing schedule, and Hipper's battlecruisers found nothing before being forced to return for fear their accompanying destroyers would run out of fuel.[141] Had Scheer set out a day earlier or later he might have destroyed not only another convoy but also the heavy ships escorting it, causing what Beatty feared as 'a disaster of considerable magnitude'.[142] Yet in fact he had failed and the Scandinavian convoys continued, British naval dispositions remaining as before. From now on, although many tense weeks remained, the balance began to move as Beatty had anticipated, back in the Allies' favour.

Several Allied fears had been exaggerated. Not only was the *Goeben* badly damaged after its January expedition but also the Turks were furious at not having been consulted and determined not to see the warship risked again. Russia's Black Sea Fleet was dilapidated and its new German and Turkish crews did not try to turn it into a fighting squadron; nor did the Germans take over the Russian Baltic Fleet, and although peace with the Bolsheviks enabled them to move warships from the Baltic to the North Sea, the numbers were small.[143] Nor did the Austrian navy sortie out again after its abortive raid in June against the Otranto barrage. Morale among its crews was at rock bottom after the mutinies in February on its battleships at Cattaro. By the end its coal was running low, and it concentrated on escorting convoys to the Austro-Hungarian forces in Albania and on mine-laying.[144]

In the main naval theatre, by summer 1918 the Royal Navy was receiving its armour-piercing shells and the Northern Barrage reduced the risk to the Scandinavian convoys,[145] while the assignment of four modern American dreadnoughts to the Grand Fleet increased Beatty's lead in capital ships. The US Navy Department had been reluctant to spare them, but the Chief of Naval Operations, Admiral William S. Benson, decided to send them, in part to justify continuing future investments in American seapower. The vessels anchored in the Orkneys in December 1917, but they had to learn new flag signals, wireless codes, manoeuvring practice, and battle orders, and their gunnery was less accurate than was the British. Beatty used them for Scandinavian convoy duty and on sweeps through the North Sea, but until the summer he regarded them as much inferior to his own warships.[146] In July, however, a fifth American battleship joined the Grand Fleet, and in August three more were sent to Ireland, to protect the Atlantic convoys against surfaced U-boat attacks.[147] By now Beatty viewed the prospects in a clash with the High Seas Fleet much less queasily.[148]

But it was unlikely that the High Seas Fleet would fight. Between autumn 1917 and spring 1918 it had carried out amphibious operations in the Baltic and raided the Dover barrage and the Scandinavian convoys. Thereafter it relapsed into quiescence. One reason was the strategy the British had adopted as a stopgap: that of carpeting the Heligoland Bight with the new 'H' mines. British mining during 1917 had already forced much of the HSF to devote itself to sweeping entrance and exit channels and escorting submarines through them. British cruisers then tried to ambush German minesweepers, obliging the HSF to support the minesweepers with capital ships. Hence the war of attrition in the Bight occupied more and more of the German fleet's energies even before the British pursued it with larger numbers of better devices. Mining reached its peak in April to July 1918, after which Wemyss judged the Bight was pretty well filled up and the exit channels were now so long that the minesweeping forces had to anchor at sea overnight.[149] One reason why Scheer supported the Ludendorff offensives by attacking the Scandinavian convoys was that the channel leading northward was the only one still open. During July alone the High Seas Fleet lost seven boats and 200 lives in mine-clearing, and bad weather prevented it from making further progress after that date.[150] The endless anti-mining operations increased wear and tear, and whereas until 1918 the German shipyards had kept up reasonably well with repair and maintenance they could no longer cope. While the demands on them increased their labour force did not, and partly owing to undernourishment the workers achieved less.[151] Poorer coal meant cruisers could no longer reach their maximum speed, and the navy's crews were raided both to prepare for possible operations in Russia and for the U-boats, which by autumn 1918 had taken one third of the officer corps. After Hipper took over the command in August, he estimated that only five battleships and four battlecruisers would be available for action against a British attack; on 24 September he directed that keeping open the U-boat entrance and exit channels and protecting the North Sea and Baltic bases were now the fleet's sole tasks. Had Scheer's submarine-building programme gone ahead it would have made still larger inroads into the surface fleet, and in September Scheer was considering mothballing his First Squadron of the most modern battleships.[152]

Not only was the fleet being stripped of manpower, but its officer corps was losing authority, and unrest seethed below deck. The inactivity, the resentment over food and other conditions, and the gulf between officers and men that had led to the 1917 mutinies had if anything intensified. In April, Scheer foresaw that removing too many officers would lead to 'Bolshevism', but the creation of the Seekriegsleitung caused weeks of upheaval, during which nearly half the commanders and first officers of the larger warships were replaced.[153] When the navy leadership decided in the middle of the armistice negotiations in October to launch a final desperate attack, these tensions would explode.[154] In contrast the British Grand Fleet remained seaworthy to the end, and its officers from Beatty downwards worked hard to keep up morale, even in the grim surroundings of the Orkneys: men and officers combined in theatrical and sporting events and joined the Americans in baseball and boxing. Discipline was milder than in the German navy, and food better. Resentment over higher civilian wages encouraged the formation of 'Lower Deck Societies' in September 1917 and a petition was circulated against anomalies in pay scales and conditions of service, but the government helped to pacify the movement by improving pay and pensions.[155] In autumn 1918 unrest revived, and a journalist, Lionel Yexley, claimed to have evidence of great lower-deck dissatisfaction, which came to the Prime Minister's notice. Quizzed by Lloyd George, the Admiralty conceded that the men still envied civilian wages, had grievances over shore leave and pensions, and that a recent police strike had set a bad example, but denied any danger of a serious incident.[156] By now it was too late to matter anyway. Yet still the measure of this peculiar naval triumph, achieved without destroying the enemy fleet, was not apparent to the admirals, who petitioned for new building to forestall German battlecruiser superiority by 1921. When the question came before the Cabinet on 4 September Churchill objected that one battlecruiser required as much skilled labour as fifty merchant ships, and Lloyd George that they must consider the enormous expansion of the American merchant marine. The government decided to wait, and later confirmed that work on only one new battlecruiser, the ill-fated *Hood*, would go forward.[157]

SHIPPING

These discussions are a reminder that immense construction, manufacturing, and repair programmes underpinned the Allies' triumph. British mine and depth charge output trebled between 1917 and 1918; that of depth charge throwers quadrupled.[158] Convoy reduced sinkings, but damage to merchant vessels remained frequent, and commercial tonnage repaired in Britain more than doubled from 202,289 in May 1917 to 467,822 in March 1918.[159] In just one quarter at the end of 1917, 3,276 naval vessels were repaired and refitted. As for construction, the pre-war Anglo-German naval race continued into the conflict, and Britain won. When war broke out Britain's superiority in capital ships had been quite narrow, but by the Battle of Jutland the ten battleships being built in 1914 were finished, and the new *Queen Elizabeth* class with 15-inch guns outranged the largest German calibres of 13.5 inches. The anti-submarine campaign then posed a different challenge, the imperative now being no longer battleships but destroyers and escorts. According to the Admiralty Controller, who was responsible for building, Britain had to create a 'new navy' of light craft, the numbers of anti-submarine vessels under construction rising from 576 in August 1917 to 848 in May 1918. During the war as a whole, the Admiralty ordered four more battlecruisers, thirty-six cruisers, and over 300 destroyers, and added in all 842 warships and 571 auxiliary vessels.[160]

These achievements had a cost. Although Geddes complained that the navy was losing its 'first claim upon the resources of the nation',[161] it still enjoyed a privileged position. Britain possessed not only the Royal Dockyards but also the largest private shipbuilding industry in the world, and 'work badges' protected shipyard and marine engineering employees from military service. Whereas the Ministry of Munitions had to build up production for the army with a largely raw labour force, the Admiralty held on to its skilled workers, over 90 per cent of whom in 1918 were still male.[162] The merchant marine also made sacrifices, and in the first half of the war commercial shipbuilding was crowded out and fell to a third of its 1913 level. In 1916, however, the incoming Lloyd George government set up a Ministry of Shipping under a tough but shrewd and public-spirited Glasgow ship owner, Sir Joseph Maclay. In May 1917 all naval and commercial building was placed under a Navy Controller, the Cabinet agreeing that before the end of 1918 merchant shipbuilding output should rise to the equivalent of 3.11 million tons per annum.[163] The precondition would be increased allocations of steel and labour, and steel supplies did improve.[164] Yet the crucial labour shortfall was never overcome, despite the Cabinet's Committee on Man Power identifying shipbuilding as one of the highest national priorities.[165] Britain's shipbuilding output in 1918 reached 2.9 million gross tons, exceeding the 1913 record of 2.3 million, but merchant ship production accounted for barely half this total and remained well below target.[166] Both the employers and the trade unions resisted 'dilution' – a temporary relaxing of the skills level required for employment – although this was common practice in munitions ministry work (which admittedly was more suitable for it). Other measures did raise productivity, one being limiting construction to five models of 'standard ships', which accounted for 60 per cent of the total being built in May 1918. But schemes to circumvent the steel shortage by building concrete barges and to get round trade union resistance by creating 'National Yards' on the Bristol Channel (using prisoners of war and military labour to assemble ships from pre-fabricated parts) achieved virtually nothing.[167]

British shipbuilding therefore made an impressive but limited contribution. The Admiralty warned that failing to raise output above sinkings would mean 'nothing less than losing the war',[168] and by May 1918 new British building exceeded British losses.[169] This was too little to cope with the overall shortfall, however, as American output came on stream belatedly, and none of the other Allies contributed much. Japan doubled its shipbuilding output in 1918, but pooled none of its tonnage. After the Americans embargoed steel exports to Tokyo, an agreement in April allowed them to charter some Japanese vessels and to purchase more, in return for renewing steel deliveries, but neither side honoured the deal.[170] In contrast France and Italy had merchant fleets that were inadequate to satisfy even their peacetime shipping needs, and during the war both suffered big losses.

However, the crucial story – and a curious and dramatic one – unfolded in the US. During their neutrality the Americans had focused on building capital ships, for which they set ambitious targets in their 1916 navy bill. Once they entered the war, the British pressed them to concentrate on anti-submarine production, which Navy Secretary Josephus Daniels agreed to do, approving an additional 200 destroyers and deferring capital ship building.[171] Unfortunately, American destroyer output remained so disappointing that Sims and Daniels were embarrassed by it, a conference with the construction firms in July 1918 revealing that at most half were up to schedule.[172] As regarded merchant shipping, in contrast, in 1914 the US accounted for 9.5 per cent of world steamship tonnage against the British Empire's 45.2 per cent, but by 1931 the figures were 18.8 and 33.7 per cent, and the war years accounted for the difference.[173]

The United States made a prodigious effort but one that matured too slowly to affect decisively the war's outcome. This was partly because it was the continuation of a long-term plan, Geddes advising the British Cabinet that 'American shipbuilding, like the American army, is being laid out for a very long war'.[174] Already during the neutrality period, business and Congressional lobbyists had urged state action to create a big national mercantile marine, and the 1916 Shipping Act created a United States Shipping Board, which established an Emergency Fleet Corporation to purchase, build, and run a state-owned merchant navy. In 1917 Wilson appointed as head of both the USSB and the EFC Edward Hurley, who became the driving force behind the shipping programme. Hurley had earned a fortune from manufacturing machine tools and domestic appliances in Chicago: his policies were nationalist and mercantilist. On entering the war the USSB seized ninety-seven German vessels lying in American ports, totalling 638,000 gross tons. The American shipyards were already busy with navy work and over half the merchant vessels on the slipways had been ordered by foreigners, especially Britain, but the USSB took control of all the yards and ownership of all the ships being built in them. The British government was compensated, but lost orders none the less.[175]

What followed during the bitter winter of 1917/18 was a story that could have come from Stalinist Russia, as a huge new industry was forged at breakneck speed. At Hog Island, near Philadelphia, an entire city was created, with fifty slipways, hundreds of miles of railway, and 120,000 piles driven into ground that had to be blasted with dynamite because it was frozen five feet deep. Record wages attracted workers to a labour force that expanded by 1,000 a day. From 160 slipways in 1915 the US had reached 1,010 by September 1918; the workforce, less than 50,000 in 1916, reached 386,000. Hurley was an enthusiastic evangelist, boasting in March 1918 that 'The new industry we have created will make America the greatest maritime nation in the history of the world':[176] Wilson eventually asked him not to publicize the administration's post-war plans, out of concern for British sensitivities.[177] None the less, America's seagoing merchant marine rose from 2.75 million deadweight tonnes in April 1917 to 9.5 million in September 1918. On Independence Day 1918 the US launched ninety-five vessels in twenty-four hours, and in August it overtook Britain to become the world's largest builder.

From the second quarter of 1918 shipbuilding by the Allies including the United States exceeded total losses, and in the war's final months the gap was widening. Yet at the same time as adding to the supply of shipping the United States was also adding to demand for it, and it needed help both in getting its troops across the Atlantic and in supplying them once landed. Hence, according to the British Ministry of Shipping, 'as regards maritime transport the United States proved a minus rather than a plus factor in the problem, and a minus factor of considerable magnitude'.[178] Nor did Britain's increased construction close the gap, for if the remaining Allies are considered as a whole, the imbalance between their need for shipping and the diminishing tonnage available to them continued to widen. During 1918 Allied construction of seagoing steamers totalled 5.4 million deadweight tons (including 2.6 million by the US), but losses totalled 3.9 million and the demands involved in transporting and supplying American troops were by the armistice equivalent to the continuous employment of nearly 4 million tons. According to a report on inter-Allied co-operation, over the year the 'actual stringency of tonnage' continued to worsen.[179]

New building was therefore not enough. The Allies also exploited their existing shipping more intensively and used neutral fleets. These latter were crucial to the entire equation, the German Admiralty Staff estimating that before 1914 shipping owned by neutrals had brought in one third of Britain's seaborne imports, and hoping that the 'deterrent effect' of unrestricted submarine warfare would frighten off at least 40 per cent of it, the attitude of neutral ship owners being 'of decisive importance for the outcome of the war'.[180] Likewise the British shipping ministry considered that 'a satisfactory solution of the neutral tonnage question was the crux of the entire shipping problem'.[181] From 1915 the British used the leverage given by their sole ability to provide world-wide coal bunkering facilities in order to insist that neutral vessels burning British fuel must cease trading with the Central Powers and instead carry goods for the Allies. Before Greece entered the war in 1917, Britain chartered much of its merchant navy, and used it in the

Mediterranean, where more than a third of it was lost. But the Scandinavian countries mattered still more, especially Norway, which possessed the world's fourth-largest shipping fleet. After the Germans launched their unrestricted submarine warfare campaign much neutral shipping did indeed at first tie up in harbour, and Britain resorted to stringent measures, requisitioning some twenty Danish ships and refusing to let other neutral vessels leave its ports until another one arrived. It also threatened to deny the neutrals vital supplies. Hence by a secret agreement reached in summer 1917 with the Norwegian ship owners, Britain promised to supply Norway with coal at cost price, in return for access to 1.5 million tons of Norwegian tonnage. Although it promised to insure the Norwegian ships against war risks, and to move them off the most dangerous routes, Norway lost 780 ships (45.4 per cent of its merchant fleet) during the war, and 2,000 of its seamen.[182] The Germans suspected that such an agreement existed, but decided that invading Norway was not worth the cost. A similar agreement made 200,000 tons of Danish shipping available, again in return for coal, although one with Sweden came too late to make a difference. In addition, in January 1918 the Americans reached an agreement to charter Dutch shipping, but it was never implemented as the Germans threatened to torpedo the vessels, and in March the Americans and British instead seized some 130 Dutch vessels lying idle in their ports.[183] This action sparked a crisis and a risk that the two sides' demands would force Holland into the war: the OHL retaliating by demanding the right to use Dutch railways for its troop movements into Belgium, and the Dutch government refusing. The British authorities suspected Germany was bluffing but doubted if they could defend the Netherlands and preferred a limited climbdown. A compromise was negotiated whereby food and telephone and railway equipment could be transported but not weapons, Wilhelm ruling that there must be no break with The Hague.[184] The upshot, none the less, was that Norwegian and Danish tonnage very materially assisted the Allies. The Scandinavian convoys formed an essential component in a spider's web of arrangements – by delivering coal across the North Sea, by carrying fish, iron ore, and pyrites in the other direction, and by showing that neutral vessels would be protected – which explains why Beatty accepted they were a vital interest and why he ran such risks to protect them.

The neutral tonnage mattered so greatly because if the US was a net consumer of tonnage, Britain's other allies were still more so. France was the biggest single user, some 45 per cent of its imports between August 1917 and the end of the war being conveyed in British ships, and by August 1918 British vessels were likewise carrying 45 per cent of Italy's imports.[185] Maclay reported in June that of the 14.5 million tons of British shipping 1.7 million was servicing Britain's allies, 3.4 million the armed forces, and less than 7 million was available for the UK's civilian import needs. Most of the British vessels that supplied the Allies, moreover, did so at government-set 'Blue-Book' tariffs, far below the market rate. Britain was pivotal for the coalition's maritime transport, yet its merchant fleet had dropped from 4,068 vessels of over 1,600 gross tons (totalling 17,516,000 gross tons) in July 1914 to 3,123 (totalling 14.48 million) in April 1918. In explaining how, none the less, 'the danger point appears to have been passed', Maclay listed new ship-building, better defences against submarines and mines, and access to neutral tonnage, but above all he emphasized improved organization.[186] What mattered was less tonnage in the abstract than what the shipping industry's historian described as 'carrying power'.[187]

The prerequisite for reorganization was control, at both national and international level. In peacetime the shipping companies operated the largest and most modern ships as 'liners' that provided a scheduled service as common carriers at regularly timetabled intervals on the principal routes. In parallel, a mass of 'tramp' steamers voyaged speculatively for months and years away from home to wherever a profitable cargo could be found – the world that Joseph Conrad immortalized. The Admiralty Transport Department chartered hundreds of tramps from the start of the war to carry troops and supply the forces, and (as shortages developed) to import commodities such as sugar, wheat, and Spanish iron ore. In 1917 the Department was transferred to the shipping ministry and the decision taken to extend control to liners. Ship owners' profits had caused public outrage, and the Cabinet considered nationalization: but it opted for Maclay's solution of requisitioning the liners while leaving them in private hands, although their profits were severely limited and they provided freight to Britain's allies at cost price, whereas the US charged three times as much.[188]

In addition to allowing France and Italy to charter British tonnage, Britain shipped coal to both countries. But in 1917 French and Italian harvest failures combined with record tonnage losses to create a still more serious crisis,[189] and Britain's partners felt their needs were inadequately safeguarded. The British accepted the principle that providing tonnage should be a 'common charge' on all the coalition's members, and pressed for what became the Allied Maritime Transport Council (AMTC), a new agency created at the Allies' Paris conference of November–December 1917.[190] The AMTC had little tonnage under its direct control, and left the 'management and supervision' of the mercantile fleets to the national governments. Its brief was supervisory – to 'watch over the general conduct of Allied Transport', centralize information, and make recommendations. The Council itself, comprising the Allied shipping ministers and an American observer, met only four times, but it had an executive, the AMTE, which functioned between sessions, and a secretariat headed by the British civil servant, Sir Arthur Salter, which became the centre of a network of 'Programme Committees' for each commodity. This machinery was charged with identifying priorities among the Allies' import needs in order to allocate tonnage more efficiently, and during the successive crises of 1918 it had considerable success in doing so.[191]

For these arrangements to work, the British needed to reorganize their own trade and shipping. A succession of government committees cut back on non-essential imports. One big saving came in timber, more of which was felled at home; and another in textiles, the Cotton Control Board in November 1917 curtailing output by 40 per cent in mills that consumed American raw cotton. Whereas in the first half of the conflict Britain had tried to maintain its export industries, in the second half it ran them down, clouding the prospects for post-war recovery. Exports were deliberately reduced to save on shipping, though the economy's increasing concentration on war production left less to export anyway.[192] A further change, which also mortgaged the future, was concentrating the liner services on the shorter trade routes across the Atlantic, while Britain ran down its services in the Pacific and East Asia, creating opportunities for American and Japanese competitors. Thus in the case of cereals (one of the biggest claimants on space), the inter-Allied Wheat Executive planned in 1918 to supply France and Italy from Argentina and Britain from the US while grain purchased in Australia remained unshipped. A stockpile accumulated outside Melbourne, where a British official became an expert in disease control.[193] Conversely, the number of vessels carrying US goods across the North Atlantic increased from

240 merchantmen (2,078,000 tons) in April 1917 to 284 (2,469,000 tons) in February 1918 and 313 (2,775,000 tons) in April.[194] Whereas in 1917 introducing convoys had increased delays and inefficiency, by 1918 the shipping ministry's patient regrouping – based on a card index recording each steamer's speed and other characteristics – so that faster vessels could sail together was yielding fruit. Simultaneously the Liverpool and New York convoy committees slashed turnaround times in harbour, those for liner cargo vessels in US ports falling between January and September 1918 from twenty-two and a quarter to fourteen days. In spite of the diminished tonnage available, in the first quarter of 1918 the imports landed in UK ports actually rose by 200,000 tons, for the first time since January 1916.[195] By the summer, as building increased and losses fell, the pressure perceptibly eased.

It eased also in the special case of oil, which forcefully demonstrated Britain's dependence on the US. The Royal Navy had ordered oil-fuelled destroyers since 1904 and battleships since 1912, but in 1914 it still consumed less oil than coal. As the war progressed, more new oil-burning vessels joined the fleet, whose use of the two fuels came closer to 50:50,[196] while total British oil imports jumped from 424 million gallons in 1916 to 725 in 1917 and 1,199 in 1918.[197] But unrestricted submarine warfare led to heavier tanker losses, and convoying slowed down the trans-Atlantic round trip from forty days in peacetime to 70–90.[198] By May 1917 the Admiralty was ringing the alarm bells. Its guideline was to have six months' oil fuel reserves in hand, but now the figure was barely half that and – if current trends continued – by spring 1918 it would be zero. The British appealed to President Wilson, warning that without more American supplies 'there is no limit to the danger of the position'. The shipping ministry questioned the wisdom of converting to oil, as it meant that 'any failure of the United States supply, or any action by the United States government to restrict our supply, would be a determining factor in our war policy'.[199] But the Admiralty insisted on the superior performance of oil-fuelled ships and that reverting to coal would be 'a retrograde step', although acknowledging that 'the mobility of the British Navy can under present conditions be dictated' by the US.[200] Indeed in 1918 coal became scarce too, Wemyss warning the Cabinet in August that stocks were below the 'danger minimum' and shortages were interfering with shipping and with convoy patrols.[201] But by that stage the oil crisis had been alleviated by using 'double bottoms', i.e. carrying oil in the ballast tanks of ordinary freighters, even though up to thirty per cent of it was lost when being pumped out. In addition, tanker losses to submarines halved from 18,000 tons per month in 1917 to 8,500 in 1918, more tankers were built, and the US placed thirty-two of them at Britain's disposal.[202] None the less, the Admiralty reported to the Cabinet retrospectively that over 80 per cent of Britain's wartime fuel oil requirements had come either from the US or from Trinidad and Mexico, which America 'strategically dominated': only double bottoms and American assistance had saved Britain from an 'extremely critical' position, and alternative sources must be developed in Persia and Mesopotamia.[203] A paper to the Cabinet by Admiral Sir Edward Slade in July 1918 reinforced the point, the First Sea Lord hoped the peace negotiations would take account of the 'extreme importance' of secure access to Mesopotamian oil, and Sir Maurice Hankey, the Cabinet Secretary, pushed the topic up the agenda.[204] In October British forces moved into the oil-bearing region, and in December Lloyd George struck a deal with Clemenceau that transferred it from a French into a British sphere of interest.[205]

In addition to Britain's supply and shipping crises, a string of similar shortages was developing elsewhere in the alliance. The French too appealed to President Wilson in December 1917 for more oil, or their army would be paralysed on the eve of the impending German offensive.[206] In January the British, French, and Italian premiers jointly urged Wilson to accelerate American food shipments, or face famine and revolution in Western Europe.[207] Another pressing issue was coal for Italy, the other Allies accepting that 600,000 tons a month was the absolute minimum needed and which was indeed delivered,[208] though more of it than planned via the perilous waters of the Western Mediterranean rather than the overstretched French railways. Germany's advance in April towards the northern French coalfield obliged Britain to ship more coal to France too, although in this case the monthly targets were not met, the British blaming congestion at the French ports.[209] British officials now resented the AMTC as a constraint,[210] but the Council judged the Allies' situation to be further deteriorating, its experts forecasting – too pessimistically, as it turned out – that 1918 import needs would exceed capacity by some 10 million tons.[211]

Against this backdrop the Ludendorff offensives forced massive emergency troop shipments. It was fortunate that the American winter was easing, the Atlantic convoys were well established, and the U-boats becoming less formidable. Initially the British rushed extra men across the Channel, Maclay finding enough vessels to carry up to 32,000 per day, against the 6,000–7,000 sent previously, and not a single transport (every one of which was escorted) was lost.[212] But moving American troops was a much bigger challenge, which the US could not meet unaided. The Americans provided passenger liners, including the *Leviathan*, one of the largest liners in the world, a confiscated German vessel that eventually carried on its own one tenth of all the American forces. Ironically the Germans had built it (as the *Vaterland*) with potential service as a troop carrier in mind. But of a total of 2,078,880 American troops transported to Europe 46.25 per cent went in American ships, whereas 51.25 per cent went in British or British-leased vessels and 2.5 per cent in French or Italian ones.[213] During 1917 the British had refused to ship Americans, but from January 1918 they agreed to take 12,000 a month,[214] and in return for Wilson promising to send at least 120,000 a month between April and July they accepted much larger numbers.[215] The British also provided liners, notably the *Mauretania*, *Aquitania*, and *Olympic*, although many soldiers went in converted cargo ships. The fastest passenger liners travelled in threes without escorts; the US Navy escorted the converted merchantmen. Some troops sailed to Liverpool and then across the Channel, but most of the AEF went to the French west-coast ports of Brest, Bordeaux, and Saint-Nazaire, where the Americans had made extensive preparations: thirty-six destroyers were stationed there and oil storage capacity at Brest had been more than quadrupled.[216]

Table 5.4. American troops embarked per month, 1918 (000s, rounded)[217]

	Jan.	Feb.	Mar.	Apr.	May	June	July	Aug.	Sept.	Oct.
British ships	22.7	9.2	27.7	50.0	147.9	156.9	188.6	180.1	121.6	103.4
US ships	24.1	38.8	36.1	67.2	96.4	119.4	120.4	134.6	106.5	76.5
Total	46.8	48.0	63.8	117.2	244.3	276.3	309.0	314.7	228.1	179.9

As striking as the numbers conveyed was their safe arrival, given Holtzendorff's boasts that if the Americans intervened his submarines would sink their soldiers. In the event one British troopship was torpedoed on 5 February 1918, with the loss of 166 troops and forty-four crew, while on 6 October two troopships collided, with the loss of sixty-nine crew and 362 servicemen. But although five returning American troopships were torpedoed and three were sunk, none were lost on the outward voyage.[218] The routing system comprised a commercial 'lane' to the north, headed towards the British Isles, and a troopship lane further south, directed towards France, the submarines being too few for sustained attacks on both and in practice concentrating on the former. Troopships in convoy were heavily escorted, typically four to five ships being accompanied by ten to twelve destroyers, and stringent precautions were taken – soldiers could not light matches at night, and cooks had to hole tin cans before throwing them overboard – but the principal security was that the troopships travelled faster than could U-boats, zigzagged through the danger zone, and averaged no more than three a week through a stretch of water 200 miles wide.[219] Hence the Germans found them 'extraordinarily difficult' to locate,[220] especially as (despite the OHL's pressure for them to be intercepted) Holtzendorff stationed very few submarines off the French west coast, the great distance from base placing operations there at the limit of the feasible.[221] The navy hoped that stationing submarines off the American east coast might stop the troopships at source, but here too the laws of probability worked against it. Although Wemyss advised that U-boat operations in the Western Atlantic heightened the risk to British passenger liners and recommended replacing the latter by smaller ships, Geddes and Maclay warned the Cabinet that if Britain did so the Americans would withdraw *Leviathan* too, and shipments would fall by 30,000 men a month. In these circumstances ministers preferred to accept the risk and to continue; and events vindicated them.[222]

In the final weeks the most pressing question became less transporting American troops than supplying them. The initial arrangement with the British was that all the AEF's equipment would be shipped in American vessels, and over 95 per cent actually was, the quantity rising from 19,000 short tons in August 1917 to 829,000 in November 1918.[223] The US merchant fleet was growing so rapidly that from early 1919 the Americans hoped finally to be able to use it for the Allies' net benefit, but in the meantime the AEF had become so enormous that they needed assistance. In September, Newton D. Baker crossed the ocean to attend the AMTC as a supplicant, and the Council agreed to make 1.2 million extra tons available immediately, reducing to 200,000 in the spring. Yet this agreement came when the AMTC still expected a serious tonnage shortfall for several more months. It therefore decided to prioritize munitions shipments for the rest of 1918 before switching the emphasis in spring 1919 to food, profiting until then from the recent good harvests.[224] If the war had continued, the AEF manpower build-up would have slackened but the Allies' materiel build-up would have intensified for a spring offensive, while food supplies would have been held near the current level, despite pleas from the Inter-Allied Food Council that imports needed higher priority to prevent more winter shortages and to maintain civilian morale.[225] Light was finally becoming visible at the end of the tunnel, especially with more American shipping becoming available in 1919, but for the moment painful choices remained necessary.

August was the peak month for American troop shipments. In September they fell substantially, and in October even more. Historians have offered differing explanations, but that provided in the British archives is technical and related to convoy security. During the summer the slower troop convoys were routed from Halifax, Nova Scotia, but doing so meant an extra leg up the Atlantic coast while U-boats lurked offshore, and it was agreed to abandon it. The British alternative plan was to rail the troops to Montreal or Quebec, but the US War Department objected on the grounds that accommodation for the troops there was inadequate. However, private information reached the British that the War Department was anyway 'not averse to ... a falling off in the shipments of troops',[226] for reasons that included the heavy mortality from influenza, which might fall if the authorities packed the troopships less densely.[227] On the other hand, the British also wanted to reduce their transport commitment, which they had undertaken under pressure of emergency. They knew the American merchant navy was taking business from their own and were aware of Hurley's ambitions:[228] Lloyd George feared that diverting British shipping from its normal thoroughfares would lose more markets and cause unemployment after the war. By October the Cabinet favoured carrying fewer troops in order to force the US to transfer ships from other routes.[229]

In short, Anglo-American rivalry may have contributed to the falling-off in troop passages. The Admiralty suspected the Americans were not pulling their weight: in its view Britain was bearing the brunt of escort duty and anti-submarine operations, as well as providing cheap tonnage to France and Italy and transporting the majority of the AEF. It thereby jeopardized its own import requirements and its mercantile and exporting future while the Americans expanded their merchant fleet. In the Admiralty's view, 'the question of maintaining the pre-eminence of the British Navy, not only in relation to the German navy, was one of vital importance which must not be lost sight of'.[230] Both the British and the Americans were looking forward and each saw the other as a potential rival. That being said, the two navies on Atlantic convoy duty and in Scapa Flow enjoyed excellent working relations,[231] as did the Admiralty with Sims, though at the cost of making him look too Anglophile. If more slowly than the British wanted, America switched its building to anti-submarine vessels and provided destroyers for escort, battleships for the Grand Fleet, submarine chasers for the Mediterranean, and mines for the Northern Barrage. It also provided tankers and oil. Anglo-American tension resurfaced during the run-up to the armistice, but the two countries' collaboration was indispensable to the Allied victory.

It would be wrong to end with high policy. Both the Central Powers' surface fleets and the U-boats tied up enormous Allied resources. Germany operated under many disadvantages but could have exploited its assets more vigorously by striking harder against such weak points as the Scandinavian convoys and the Dover barrage. Fundamentally, however, it had no answer to the convoy system, and it is doubtful whether one existed – even if more submarines had been constructed – with the technology of the day. Churchill likened Allied command of the seas to a bridge that was strained but did not break.[232] Yet if the reasons for Allied success were multi-layered, at the heart of the struggle was a contest between two quite small groups of submarine crews and merchant seamen, the former initially mainly volunteers and the latter wholly so throughout. Both paid a grim price in an unforgiving environment where the risk of death in horrific circumstances was ever-present. Most of the U-boats that sank were lost with all hands, and 515 of their officers and 4,894 ratings gave their lives: at least 30 per cent of the total in service. The British merchant navy dead exceeded 14,000, and some men went back to sea even after surviving half a dozen sinkings.[233] Although morale among the U-boat crews faltered in the final months, that among the merchant seamen appears not to have done, perhaps because of the very ruthlessness of the U-boat captains and a determination not to be beaten by terror tactics. Not the least of the convoys' contributions were their protection and encouragement of the merchant crews, who came from all over the empire (especially India) as well as beyond. Up to 40 per cent of those who died were not from the British Isles.[234] Their sacrifice would be acknowledged by a poignant memorial on London's Tower Hill, and by the gratitude of a parliamentary resolution 'for the devotion to duty with which they have continued to carry the vital supplies to the Allies through seas infested with deadly perils'.[235]

6

The War Economies:
Money, Guns, and Butter

A picture might be drawn of the movement of materials from every climate and region under the sun, beginning with rills and rivulets in remote corners of the earth, and growing in volume as the converging streams unite in a mighty river of supply, finally directed in an irresistible torrent against the resistance of the enemy's defences.

Memorandum on the work of the British munitions ministry[1]

The scene now turns to the war between the workshops: to Pittsburgh, Birmingham, Paris, and Turin; and to Wiener Neustadt and Essen. The Allies' economic advantage was indispensable to their triumph, though at the time that advantage seemed much less certain than in retrospect, and a mere superiority in resources meant little unless managed and directed to the tasks in hand. Not only had weaponry to be manufactured – and plant, raw materials, and labour earmarked for that purpose – but also the civilian population had to be supplied and fed, and transport and finance provided. So far from the Allies enjoying an effortless advantage, they lurched from one supply emergency to another, even if the Central Powers' position was far worse. The immediate question is that of how the Allies overcame their difficulties, before considering how their enemies failed to, and the USA is the obvious place to begin.

UNITED STATES

America stood in a class by itself. In 1913 its gross domestic product was more than twice Russia's or Germany's.[2] Its pre-war steel production exceeded those of France, Germany, and Britain combined.[3] Since the Civil War the north-eastern states had become home to the greatest complex of railways, iron and steel, chemicals, and engineering in the world, and the American economy was not only big but also sophisticated, with higher levels of productivity and per capita income than any other belligerent. Yet in the First World War it did not dominate Allied armaments production as it would in the Second, and when the AEF took the field its heavy weapons came largely from French factories, even if America provided much of the steel that built them and the petrol that drove them. The Atlantic alliance of 1918 was more evenly balanced than a generation later, and the US contribution most striking not in finished manufactures but in food, raw materials, and finance.

Money was essential for everything else, and the Americans had nowhere else to go for it. Germany drew on credit from its neutral neighbours; Russia, France, and Italy drew on Britain; and Britain ran up debts with its empire and the US. But America lay at the end of the chain of dependence. The few remaining neutrals had little to lend, and after April 1917 their currencies rose in relation to the dollar, making borrowing from them more expensive.[4] In one way or another the American people would have to shoulder what Treasury Secretary William Gibbs McAdoo described as the 'stupendous' burden of financing the war.[5] While the Americans were belligerents they outspent everyone else: $42.8m per day from mid-1917 to mid-1919, compared with Britain's $32.6m, France's $32.4m, Germany's $32.2m, and Italy's $10.4m.[6] Although American war expenditure in 1917–18 (in constant dollars) was less than one sixth of that in 1941–5, it was comparable to expenditure in Indochina between 1964 and 1973, and as a proportion of GNP much greater: average daily expenditure was more than twelve times higher than by the North in the Civil War.[7] The First World War came second only to the Second World War and possibly Iraq as the most expensive in American history, whether measured in constant value or in relation to total output, and it cost vastly more in 1918 than in 1917.[8]

Table 6.1. War expenditure, 1914–18 ($m)[9]

USA	UK	France	Italy	Germany
35,731	45,307	30,009	12,892	32,388

None the less, the burden proved relatively affordable. The federal government's annualized rate of expenditure in 1917–18 was 13.8 times higher than in 1916,[10] an extraordinarily steep increase, and a sharper transition from peace than in the Second World War. But inflation in America was lower than in any other major belligerent, and only one fifth of war expenditure was met through money creation, either direct, through the government 'printing money' (5 per cent), or indirect, through commercial banks creating additional deposits without monetary reserves (15 per cent). The other four fifths came either from borrowing (58 per cent) or from taxation (22 per cent).[11]

Although the share covered by taxes was one of the highest among the belligerents, McAdoo shunned the inflationary precedent of 1861–5 and had hoped the proportion this time would be at least half.[12] An energetic and clear-thinking southern lawyer, who had come to national prominence by organizing the financing of the Hudson river tunnels linking New York to New Jersey, McAdoo had married Wilson's youngest daughter, Eleanor, and was one of the Cabinet members on whom the President most relied. After war was declared he profited from the initial patriotic upsurge by proposing to Congress expenditure on an army of a million men and an initial $3,000m of loans to the Allies. To pay for them he wanted tax increases, and the 1917 War Revenue Act shifted the federal budget away from indirect levies such as excise duties towards direct ones on incomes and war profits. During 1918 the Act tripled federal revenue.[13] Until the extra money came in, however, the federal government issued short-term (sixty-day) certificates of indebtedness and repeatedly rolled them over while mopping up the extra liquidity by issuing longer-term Liberty Bonds, which became the financial mainstay of the American – and therefore Allied – effort.

Liberty Bonds were modelled on the issues of long-term government stock that were also fundamental to German and British war finance. McAdoo planned to market them to a huge new investing public while paying interest at below the market rate, relying on patriotism and publicity to achieve the necessary subscriptions. To the Treasury's relief the formula worked. McAdoo gave the first Liberty Loan its name because it was 'issued in the name of freedom' and 'for the purpose of waging war against autocracy': according to his memoirs, 'We capitalized the profound impulse called patriotism.'[14] The books were opened on 15 June 1917 and the bonds carried an interest rate of 3.5 per cent, enhanced by tax exemption on the income. They would mature in thirty years, though were callable after fifteen. $2,000m of stock was offered but $3,035m eventually taken up: an oversubscription ratio of 52 per cent.[15] With the wind now in his sails McAdoo issued a second loan worth $3,000m in November 1917, a third for the same amount in May 1918, and a fourth for $6,000m in October 1918. All were over-subscribed, though by decreasing ratios, and the $14,000m they raised was close to half the federal government's war expenditure. To an extent the appeal to patriotism succeeded, the Liberty Loans being accompanied by similar ballyhoo to the war loan campaigns in Europe. McAdoo spoke himself hoarse in countrywide tours, and was supported by an army of volunteers – some 60,000 saleswomen just for the second loan, under a national committee that his wife chaired. The number of sub-scribers rose from over 4 million for the first loan to 22,277,680 for the fourth, representing 21.9 per cent of the population.[16] McAdoo succeeded in enlarging the investing public (encouraging an appetite for speculation that led on to the 1920s bull market) but most of the income from the loan drives came from the wealthy and from business, and they succeeded because the loans were a reasonably attractive invest-ment. McAdoo believed that for a flotation to fail would be 'equal to a crushing military disaster':[17] on the later issues he reduced the tax exemptions but raised the interest and on the fourth he offered exemp-tions plus 4.5 per cent, as by this time market prices for some earlier bonds were falling below their issue value. However, he tried to keep down interest on the bonds in order to save enormous costs to the American taxpayer from servicing them (not to mention the Allies, who would otherwise have to pay more for US Treasury loans), and to do so he needed to keep down interest rates generally. This latter the authori-ties accomplished through engineering a credit explosion by relaxing the commercial banks' reserve requirements. Between 1917 and 1919 the Federal Reserve System banks increased their loans to the commer-cial banks from less than $20m to $2,000m, much of which the latter lent on to customers to buy Liberty Bonds.[18] For the duration of the war the Federal Reserve (which had begun to operate only in 1914) accepted subordination to the Treasury, and monetary and fiscal policy comple-mented each other.

McAdoo's ability to raise huge sums at low interest allowed him to lend cheaply to the Allies, who during the period of US belligerency received $7,100m in Treasury credits.[19] He had hesitated to engage in inter-government lending, but Wilson endorsed the principle. Even so, in McAdoo's dealings with Congress and in his speeches he stressed that these were loans, not gifts; in retrospect he doubted whether otherwise they would have won approval.[20] For the time being, the Allies were grateful enough for advances that required no collateral and were cheaper than anything available on the New York money market. After the United States entered the war the Treasury began by lending the British £200m at 3 per cent interest, which was two points lower than the latter had been paying for private finance.[21] Moreover, by April 1917 the British government's collateral in gold and securities had dwindled to $219m to cover purchases of $75m per week, the Chancellor of the Exchequer, Andrew Bonar Law, warning that he could finance only three more weeks of spending.[22] When in May the Foreign Secretary, Arthur Balfour, headed a British delegation to Washington, he told McAdoo that the financial peril alarmed the Cabinet more than did the U-boats.[23]

McAdoo had gravely underestimated the Allies' difficulties and eventually lent far more than he had expected. As almost all the Treasury advances were conditional on purchases in the US, however, they also benefited American farmers and manufacturers; in addition McAdoo justified them to Congress as a 'substitute for soldiers' that would 'save the lives of the young men of America'.[24] All the same, to begin with there was chaos as the Allies competed to place contracts, boosting inflation in the process. McAdoo insisted on all their orders being cleared through a Purchasing Commission in Washington,[25] and at the Paris conference of November–December 1917 the US Treasury obtained the formation of an Inter-Allied Council on War Purchases and Finance (IACWPF), to which it sent a representative. In return for financing Allied contracts, the American government insisted on controlling the process. Moreover, after a rocky start, McAdoo accepted that arrangements must be more predictable. He began signalling to the British the monthly credits they could expect, and after a crisis in summer 1917, during which they warned they were on the verge of devaluing, he recognized that maintaining the $4.76 = £1 parity was necessary to maintain the Allies' solvency and limit the cost of their American purchases.[26] He advised Wilson that 'a collapse of exchange – particularly of British exchange, on which the whole fabric of international trade is built – would have produced disastrous consequences, both moral and material'.[27] Not only was the sterling exchange rate held (at slightly below the pre-1914 level) for the rest of the war, but the Americans and British also co-operated to support the Italian lira.[28] McAdoo did not give the Allies everything they wanted, but in addition to financing its own prodigious expenses the US met its partners' essential needs.

That being said, even America's wealth was finite, and during 1918 its resources came under increasing strain. Both the federal government's spending and its deficit rose inexorably. By November monthly outgoings were more than twice those in January, just the ammunition fired on the Meuse–Argonne offensive costing $726m.[29] Moreover, the AEF bought most of its supplies in Europe and American servicemen were now spending in sterling and francs, thus counterbalancing the Allies' foreign exchange costs (although the Treasury refused the French permission to use the income to pay off their debts). American expenditure in France in 1919 was forecast to exceed French spending in the US.[30] Whereas in January 1918 McAdoo remained confident that he could sustain the cost of the war, by May he was warning the President that 'The way in which the Estimates are climbing is appalling', and although Congress was resisting new tax legislation, it was 'unescapable ... Unless the matter is dealt with now fairly and satisfactorily, we shall invite disaster in 1919.' It would be impossible to borrow the $20,000m needed in the 1918–19 fiscal year if there were no further tax increase: trying to do so would spell inflation and high interest rates and 'bring ultimate destruction to the country'. Even if tax rises meant the Democratic Party lost control of the House of Representatives in the mid-term elections, they were essential. Fearing that further tax rises would damage industrial production and sales of Liberty Bonds, McAdoo had moved too slowly: business was protesting to Congress about the 1917 increase, and the Chairmen of the House and Senate Ways and Means Committees hesitated to act before the elections. On 3 October McAdoo advised Wilson that if Congress delayed in enacting the revenue bill 'the future financial operations of the Government will be gravely imperiled', but it was to no avail.[31] The bill passed the House in September 1918 but did not clear the Senate until the following February, and its benefit to revenues came only in 1920.[32] By the summer and autumn of 1918 McAdoo feared affairs were sliding out of his control, and that fear would encourage him to support a ceasefire.[33]

All the same, down to the armistice the US had neither to stint on its own effort nor rein in its partners. How it spent the money may be considered under the headings of food, raw materials, and manufactures. A salient feature of the surge of economic globalization that preceded 1914 had been the rise of bulk long-distance transport to the world's industrial heartlands of key commodities from the virgin territories in the western and southern hemispheres. For few crops was this development more dramatic than wheat, the mainstay of the European diet and a foodstuff laden with psychological and political significance. Before the war Europe's 'wheat deficiency' countries (practically all of them) consumed some 1,800 million bushels a year, but produced only 1,300 million: Russia made up some 160 million of the deficit and Romania and Bulgaria another 50 million, leaving 300 million to be filled by non-European suppliers, of which the chief, in order of importance, were the US, Canada, Argentina, Australia, and India. With the Central Powers cut off, the main importers became Britain, France, Italy, and Belgium (which the US took responsibility for feeding via the international humanitarian agency known as the Commission for the Relief of Belgium or CRB). In 1909–13 these four countries' wheat production had averaged 575 million bushels and their wheat and flour imports 364 million. As by 1917 their output was down to 344 million, they would need some 600 million to match their pre-war requirements, none of which could come from Russia or the Balkans. In 1917 Argentina's harvest was poor, and far more tonnage was needed to bring Indian and Australian wheat than for the Atlantic run. Hence the Allies looked primarily to North America.[34]

Yet American farmers were poorly placed to respond. Per capita cereal production in North America was much higher than in Western Europe, and in 1914 the US alone produced about one quarter of the world's wheat, although the proportion exported was diminishing as America's own urban market matured. Early in the war the US had bumper crops, a good proportion of which went to Europe; but the surpluses lowered prices and therefore earnings, and farmers moved into other lines. Whereas the 1914 and 1915 harvests totalled 892 and 1,026 million bushels, the 1916 figure was only 636 million, and the 1917 one similar.[35] These crops barely sufficed to cover American internal consumption of 640 million annually, and already in 1917 the carry-over from the 1916 harvest had fallen to a minimum.[36] And although Canada had a 1917 surplus of production over consumption of 134 million, on its own it could hardly satisfy Allied needs. But, in the event, over the twelve months down to 31 March 1918 Canada exported 150 million bushels to the Allies and the AEF and the US exported 138 million, some of which was offset by increased imports but still reflected a 110 million reduction in US internal consumption. The two North American countries almost tripled their pre-war grain exports, and this, linked to conservation measures and production increases in Britain, France, and Italy, tided the latter over.[37]

In the US the main initiative lay with the United States Food Administration (USFA), created in 1917 and headed by Herbert Clark Hoover. Hoover's reputation would be tarnished by his presidency during the Depression, but at this point he held high prestige as an orphan who had made his fortune as an engineer and mining entrepreneur, and become a food supply expert while heading the CRB. Although a Republican, he was an obvious choice to head the USFA. As he understood the problem, the US was self-sufficient in most foodstuffs (sugar, much of which came from Cuba, was a notable exception) and the problem was one of depressing its consumption to generate a surplus for Allied requirements. Action was urgent, as Allied bidding in the Chicago futures market was driving grain prices up to stratospheric levels, with a consequent danger of inflation and social instability.[38]

Hoover addressed both the supply and the demand side of the equation. The USFA established the United States Grain Corporation, which from September 1917 began operations as the purchaser of the entire grain crop. One of the American concerns in establishing it was not to leave individual grain producers at the mercy of negotiations with the Allies: Britain, France, and Italy had agreed in November 1916 to establish the Wheat Executive, which would buy, allocate, and transport their cereal needs, and which used as its purchasing agent a British body, the Royal Commission on Wheat Supplies. As a monopoly supplier the Grain Corporation was well placed to bargain with this monopoly buyer, and it offered American farmers a price for spring wheat of $2.20 per bushel that was deliberately set high enough to encourage a larger sown acreage. Government intervention ensured more stable though higher prices for the Allied and American consumer (and great prosperity for the American farmer) and the prospect of a better harvest in 1918. The USFA also offered loans for tractors, advice to farmers via a network of agents, and patriotic exhortation via speeches and posters, while the authorities were cautious about conscripting farm workers, only 1.48 per cent of whom had been called up by March 1918. None the less, price support was the most important step.[39]

Hoover began too late to improve the *1917* yield, and the problem remained of covering the gap until the following summer. His remedy was consciously different from the bureaucratic and coercive methods that he had seen (and abhorred) in Europe, and he rejected compulsory rationing both on ideological grounds and as being impractical – he did not believe it enforceable in a country whose population was still half rural. He did not wish to be a 'food dictator', and he operated through a campaign of propaganda and education, paralleling that for McAdoo's Liberty Bonds (and little love was lost between the two officials). 750,000 citizens (mostly women) joined local committees of consumers and distributors; 14 million families, 7,000 hotels and restaurants, and 425,000 dealers signed pledges to abide by the USFA conservation programmes, which included 'wheatless' days (first one then two per week), as well as 'meatless' days, although the biggest single saving came from requiring millers to use more of the grain when making flour so that less was discarded. In 1917–18 American domestic consumption fell from around 5.3 to around 3.9 bushels per head, allowing a sufficient margin until the 1918 harvest, which at over 921 million bushels exceeded that of 1917 by nearly 50 per cent.[40]

None the less, the 1917/18 winter was extremely anxious. Hoover feared 'social cataclysm' unless Allied civilians were fed, but he was unsure whether his voluntary programme would work (and the Allies urged him to adopt compulsory rationing). He resisted any commitment to his partners, saying the US was a last resort and their demands exceeded what America could grow and its railways could carry.[41] Difficult negotiations in November and December established a provisional export programme of 1.1 million metric tons of cereal products each month (1 metric ton = 36.74 bushels), which would cover more than half of the Allies' expected deficit. They still considered this figure dangerously inadequate, and the Wheat Executive warned the Grain Corporation that unless strictly adhered to 'it would mean disaster for the Allied cause'.[42]

In fact the programme was not adhered to, and frantic telegrams criss-crossed the Atlantic. Grain deliveries fell 900,000 tons behind schedule in December and 400,000 tons in January: on 31 January

Clemenceau, Lloyd George, and Orlando jointly cabled to Wilson that 'the need of bread cereals in Europe cannot be exaggerated ... food shortage, with the effect it may produce on the moral [sic] of the population, which has been one of the principal causes of the breakdown of Russia, is the greatest danger at present facing each of the European Allies'.[43] According to Allied representatives in Washington, the Italian army had cut its rations twice, the French army once, and unless adequate food supplies arrived immediately the Allies' civilians would starve and their armies be defeated.[44] When a further telegram from the Allied ambassadors on 22 February warned that 'nothing short of calamity' would befall their countries unless more grain were shipped immediately, Hoover promised extra deliveries as he understood this to be the President's wish, even at the risk of placing America itself in difficulties. Quizzed by Hoover, Wilson confirmed that 'I am afraid that there is no choice in the matter': America must maintain shipments. Similarly, McAdoo accepted that the US Treasury must finance them, even though doing so imposed 'extraordinary demands'.[45] American leaders were willing to supply and pay for the food, at risk to their own country, but the root of the problem lay with transport.

In early 1918 the economy was gripped by a 'winter crisis'. Freak weather coincided with paralysis on the railroads, much of whose rolling stock was in the wrong place for food exports. Since the neutrality period enormous Allied orders had been shipped out of New York and the north-eastern ports, and – as commercial operations – the railroad companies hesitated to move box cars back westwards without goods for them to carry there. By December 1917, when Wilson placed the railroads under federal control and appointed McAdoo Director-General of the newly formed United States Railroad Administration, 180,000 more cars than normal were standing on the tracks in the east, enough to stretch from Paris to Warsaw.[46] Goods had to be unloaded in open country, miles from the docks, and jams stretched back into the interior, while shortages developed elsewhere. Before McAdoo could grapple with the situation the harshest winter for fifty years descended, the freeze-up of the Great Lakes also halting Canadian grain movements. Weeks of recrimination followed in an atmosphere of rising panic. Finally on 8 February McAdoo ordered absolute priority for shifting box cars to the grain-producing states. His powers enabled him to move them empty, and the Grain Corporation briefed the Railroad

Administration on where they should go.[47] By 15 March he could tell the Allied representatives that so much food had accumulated on the eastern seaboard that he would have to forbid additional consignments until they could provide ships to collect them, but this they managed to do, thereby surmounting their provisioning crisis just before the military crisis opened.[48] By the autumn, with the new harvest garnered, the primary constraint again became shipping, and a high-level debate about priorities for the coming year was settled in favour of a munitions priority for now and a food priority – if the war continued – for spring 1919. Hoover and the Allied food controllers still feared demoralization and unrest if food supplies were held to their present level for another year, but the prospect ahead was no longer one of starvation.

Wheat formed part of a broader programme of commodity shipments. In 1917–18 the US exported 125.3 million bushels of oats, mostly to Britain and France, both of whose armies were hard pressed to feed their draught animals and for whom America became the leading overseas source of fodder. American pork and lard exports rose from a pre-war average of 941 million pounds to 2,279 million in 1918, and Hoover assisted with a British meat shortage (and an American glut) by furnishing huge quantities of bacon: more, indeed, than the British could adequately store, and much of it was wasted. Between 1915 and 1918 condensed milk exports rose from 37 million pounds to 530 million. Sugar was a particular pressure point, as occupation of France's best beet-growing regions had turned it from an exporter into an importer, and Germany and Austria-Hungary had supplied two thirds of Britain's pre-war requisites. The USFA created a Sugar Equalization Board that purchased the Cuban crop, and distributed both this and America's own output to the American and the Western European markets. Although American per capita consumption fell, the alliance's needs were satisfied. In other sectors the US could do less – its cotton exports fell and it lacked time to expand its cattle herds – but in key selected sectors the difference that it made was vital.[49]

The same applied to industrial raw materials, which included copper – the US supplying France with 50,000 tons for shell production[50] – and, outstandingly, oil. The European governments informed the newly created Inter-Allied Petroleum Conference that their estimated 1918 oil needs were 6,655,100 tons for Britain (much of this for the navy and 4,928,600 coming from the US), 1,644,000 for France (1,239,000 from the US), and 836,400 for Italy (400,000 from the US).[51] Without American supplies the Royal Navy's finest warships would have been confined to harbour, and kerosene was essential for Allied aviation fuel, as were petrol and lubricating oil for the lorries transporting Pétain's strategic reserve. France's American oil purchases in 1917–18 were ten times higher than in 1913, but its armies did not go short.[52] Fortunately the Americans could meet these requirements fairly easily, Navy Secretary Daniels advising Wilson that Californian production comfortably exceeded consumption.[53] The administration was more concerned about Mexico, which at that time contained the world's largest known reserves, and whose radical President, Venustiano Carranza, increased taxes on the oil companies in February 1918. Partly because of anxieties about Mexico but also because of heavy demand, American reserve stocks fell and crude oil prices tripled between August 1917 and April 1918, but the United States Fuel Administration opposed price controls and when the State Department proposed readying 6,000 marines to seize the Mexican fields, Wilson took Daniels's advice that such a move would be unjustified. Indeed, the greatest danger foreseen by administration planners was rivalry with the British for control of oil after the war.[54]

We turn from commodities to manufactures. Without American supplies the French army could not have held the line. According to Clemenceau the US delivered not only enough food to feed 12 million French people for one and a half years but also enough steel for 160 million field gun shells.[55] In 1918 American steel output hit the record total of 39 million tons, of which 959,778 tons went to Britain, 1,279,298 to France, 400,565 to Italy, 168,811 to Canada, and 107,755 to Japan, while much of US home consumption also assisted the military effort: as rails, projectile steel, or plate for locomotives, merchant vessels, and warships.[56] As for armaments themselves, among the most impressive results came in high explosive and propellants (i.e. materials respectively for shell charges and firing the projectile from the gun). Between April 1917 and November 1918 America's propellant output equalled that of Britain and France combined, and by November 1918 its high-explosive production was more than 40 per cent above Britain's and nearly double France's.[57] To get this far, American industry had to overcome great difficulties. The War Department's Ordnance Department built fifty-three new plants for propellant and high explosive and worked with the steel firms to double production of toluol, a coke by-product that was essential for TNT and 11 million pounds of which were dispatched to the Allies. The most critical restraint on explosives production, however, was the supply of nitrates for nitric acid. The Americans decided to emulate the Germans in 'fixing' nitrogen from the atmosphere, and constructed two huge installations for the purpose: the Nitro plant in West Virginia and the Old Hickory plant in Tennessee.[58] By the armistice both were generating enormous quantities, but in the interim manufacturers depended on nitrates from the Chilean guano fields. American agriculture was deprived of fertilizer, contributing to the origins of the 1930s Great Plains 'Dustbowl', and in May 1918 the Americans were down to six weeks' reserves and France nearly ran out altogether.[59] It has been stated that the loss of just one steamer on the Pacific coast could have halted French explosives production.[60] None the less, the gap was bridged.

American shell output was less impressive. Between April 1917 and November 1918 the US delivered 17.26 million completed shells against Britain's 121.74 million and France's 149.83 million. By the armistice its monthly total had risen to about half theirs (and in shell casings the three were about equal), but the Americans purchased some 10 million shells from their partners and the rounds the AEF actually fired were almost all of French manufacture.[61] In small arms the Americans did better. They produced 226,556 machine guns of their own and bought 39,300, mainly from France. In April 1917 they had nearly 600,000 model 1903 Springfield rifles and by November 1918 about 900,000; but most of their production (some 2–3 million pieces) was of Enfields, made in America but based on a British design. Output of complete artillery pieces, however, came on stream much later than expected. By the armistice the Americans had completed 2,008 guns, the monthly total rising from fifty-three in July 1918 to 420 in October, but over the same period the British completed 8,065 and the French 11,056. The Americans gained momentum, but too late, producing mainly field guns modelled on the French 75 mm, while for heavier guns they turned to Europe. By November 1918 France had delivered to them 1,828 75 mm field guns and 938 155 mm guns and howitzers; Britain 163 8-inch and 9.2-inch howitzers.[62] Similarly, although American industry produced sixty-four light tanks by November 1918, the AEF's main force of 227 light vehicles was purchased from the French, as were sixty-four heavy tanks from the British.[63] Most mortifying, in the land of the Wright brothers, was the record in aircraft, which caused a storm of indignation and multiple Congressional inquiries. The success story was the Liberty twelve-cylinder aero-engine, 13,574 of which were turned out by the armistice: 73 per cent of the engines received by the American air service were of US manufacture. But out of 2,698 aircraft delivered to the AEF in the zone of action, only 667 were American-built. Of the foreign-built planes, nine tenths were French. Although by the end American airframe ouput was gathering momentum, the AEF, which now rivalled the French and British armies in size, disposed of 860 front-line machines against Britain's 2,100 and France's 3,000.[64] Without European Allied assistance, it could not have gone into battle.

There were many reasons for this situation, so different from in the Second World War, when America produced almost two thirds of the military equipment used by the victors, including 297,000 aircraft, 193,000 artillery pieces, 86,000 tanks, and 2 million lorries.[65] The obstacles were partly geographical, for everything was complicated by the vast distance between the Americans' fighting front and their manufacturing base. One commentator likened the problem to a fire bucket chain: the longer the chain, the more water at any one time was en route via the buckets rather than dousing the flames. Thus the army's rule for clothing was that each man at the front should have one three-month reserve in France, a second in the US, and a third in transit, and the demands even for basic items were enormous: in the year from April 1917 to May 1918, for instance, 131.8 million pairs of socks and 21.7 million blankets.[66] By the armistice the War Department had reluctantly taken possession of all the wool in the US. In contrast with clothing, armaments raised not only logistical but also major technological obstacles. Americans had little background in manufacturing complete artillery pieces and few experienced engineers. The most difficult task was building the 'recuperator', the hydraulic recoil system that kept a gun static while it fired its rounds. Even though the Allies gave advice, French patterns were difficult to copy because they used the metric system, and French workshops still relied more on the expertise of individual artisans than on mass production with rigid tolerances: American industry's preference for machinery over skilled labour slowed conversion.[67] By the end of the war the Americans had nineteen plants (mostly built by private firms) engaged in full-time artillery production, but in this as other areas they were gearing up when the ceasefire intervened.[68] Likewise in aviation, although their motor industry gave the Americans expertise in engine design, they had been on the sidelines of the dramatic evolution in European combat aircraft and they underestimated the challenges. Not least among the latter were spare parts: of every 100 aircraft sent to France the equivalent of another 80 had to go as spares. Spruce, for the airframe, came from the Pacific North-West, where the lumbermen needed special training and many, incited by the syndicalist gospel of the International Workers of the World, opposed the war effort. In the end 180 million feet of timber were cut, and two thirds went to the Allies. But Britain produced too little linen for the fabric that was stretched over the skeleton, and cotton had to be substituted, while the chemical industry had to make up 'dope' (a form of varnish) with which to treat the fabric. In view of these difficulties American manufacturers concentrated on building trainers for use at home. They copied combat planes from Allied designs, and made observation and bomber aircraft rather than the faster-evolving fighters. The most successful was the De Haviland 4, a British bomber, of which 3,272 were completed and 667 reached the battle zone; but few Caproni and Handley-Page night bombers were ever finished and the adapted Bristol fighter, made heavier by the insertion of an American engine, was a failure.[69]

In addition to the technical barriers, production was limited by resource constraints and policy choices. Despite the ravages of the Great Depression, America by 1939 produced five times more petroleum than in 1914, and twice as much steel.[70] Although in both neutrality periods (1914–17 and 1939–41) the economy grew rapidly, it started in 1914 with lower unemployment and less spare capacity, so that by April 1917 it was already close to its output limits. In contrast to the Second World War, during the First America grew faster before it intervened:

Table 6.2. American gross domestic product, 1913–18:[71]

1913	1914	1915	1916	1917	1918
100.0	101.0	109.1	111.5	112.5	113.2

It is true that war-related capacity had expanded before 1917, partly the result of investment financed from Allied contracts: thus Bethlehem Steel had enlarged its facilities and the Allies had built up a TNT capability in the US of 5 million pounds per month.[72] None the less, expanding weapons production after American entry meant redirecting resources, and McAdoo's tax increases and Liberty Bonds were the fiscal instruments for this process. Whereas in 1914–16 the private profit-making sector had expanded its labour force fastest, in 1917–18 the public sector set the pace,[73] and official judgements about priorities became crucial. American industry had accepted $2,200m of Allied contracts during the neutrality period, and a basic decision was made to honour them.[74] The administration's military advisers recommended that the Allied armies should receive what they needed, and the forces assembling in America be supplied from what was left over, though once the latter reached the front they should have first claim. War Secretary Baker endorsed the principle, and that the Allies and the US government should be charged the same prices.[75] As American industry needed conversion time, it was accepted that at first the AEF must purchase in Europe, and the French were willing to sign artillery and aircraft contracts both for financial reasons and in the hope of political influence. Eventually the AEF bought 10 million tons of equipment in Europe and received 7 million tons from home.[76] Finally, the inter-Allied gatherings in London and Paris in November–December 1917 approved the 'international ordnance agreement'. The Americans would send food for Allied civilians and equipment for the Allied armies, and as many men as they could transport in American ships, while preparing for a huge American army that they would supply themselves in 1919. In the meantime Britain and France would supply the AEF with its artillery of all types while asking the Americans to concentrate on propellants and explosives and to maintain the shell production already under way for the Allies. During 1918 this division of labour was largely adhered to, except regarding troops, but the agreement envisaged that in the longer term America would tool up to supply its army independently, thus providing an insurance if France were overrun.[77] Because hostilities ended unexpectedly early, much of the $7,000m that the War Department spent on ordnance created underused capacity and stocks of weapons that never left American shores.[78]

The American economy was preparing and acquitting a wide variety of missions, and its central allocation arrangements were inadequate. The consequences included production crises in winter 1917–18 and the following summer. Unlike Britain, France, and Italy, America had no separate Ministry of Munitions or Armaments. The War and Navy Departments were the primary contractors, and they jostled with the Allied orders routed via the Purchasing Commission. Although the Navy Department was relatively efficient, the War Department spent much more and its personnel were inexperienced and divided between competing bureaux over which the Chief of Staff had too little authority. In 1916 the Wilson administration had created a Council of National Defense, charged with 'the coordination of industries and resources for the national security and welfare'. The CND established an Advisory Commission of industrialists and technicians,[79] and its leading lights were engineers, determined that America should catch up with Germany's supposedly superior national organization. The President sympathized: he believed that modern conflicts were decided not only by numbers and by national spirit but also by 'the scientific conduct of war, the scientific application of industrial forces'.[80] However, the administration (and particularly Baker, who had the greatest influence on industrial mobilization) was notably reluctant to coerce the business community; and the CND was a consultative body that lacked statutory powers, as did the agencies created under its auspices, the most important being the War Industries Board.

The WIB comprised civilian and service representatives. Under its aegis 'commodity sections' were developed for fifty-seven branches of industry, alongside 'war service committees' that represented business interests in the sectors concerned. It was to:

> act as a clearing house for the war industry needs of the Government, determine the most effective ways of meeting them and the best means and methods of increasing production, including the creation and extension of industries demanded by the emergency, the sequence and relative urgency of the needs of the different Government services, and consider price factors, and in the first instance, the industrial and labour aspects of the problems involved . . .

The WIB stood at the apex of a planning system of sorts, but one that delegated many decisions to corporate leaders. Although it created a Priority Committee in September 1917, the committee lacked both guidance on government requirements and the authority to prevent the army and navy from disregarding it.[81] Confusion at the top contributed to the 'winter crisis'.

The crisis was industrial as well as agricultural, and the railroads were at its centre. A modern wonder of the world, and the great engine of nineteenth-century American expansion, by the outbreak of war the railroads had passed their peak. Partly owing to government ceilings on their tariffs, the companies' income was declining and they had cut expenditure on permanent way and rolling stock. Repairs were neglected and locomotives kept in service too long. In 1915 the new mileage built was the smallest since the Civil War, and one sixth of the network was in receivership, but now it faced a prodigious growth in traffic. In April 1917 the companies undertook to co-operate under an executive committee that liaised with government agencies, but like the WIB system this arrangement pushed the voluntary principle to its limits, and according to McAdoo, 'In the fall of 1917 the President was more disturbed over the condition of the railroads than he was over any other problem of the Administration.' Moreover, in 1916 Congress had intervened, at Wilson's behest, to head off a threatened rail strike by passing legislation to impose an eight-hour day, and the companies applied to the Interstate Commerce Commission for a tariff increase to pay for the shorter hours and for new investment. The ICC rejected the case, but in December 1917 it recommended that railroad operations must be unified. Hence it placed the problem squarely in the government's lap, at the same time as the notoriously underpaid railroad workers were leaving for munitions jobs or being called up.[82] Although progressives in the administration saw an opportunity to demonstrate the advantages of state intervention, Wilson acted only when the thousands of boxcars standing idle outside the eastern ports showed incontrovertibly that the private sector had failed.

On 26 December 1917 the President transferred 'possession and control' of the railways to the United States Railroad Administration, and henceforth the companies would operate under McAdoo's instructions as Director-General. But by the time McAdoo assumed his new responsibilities (while continuing at the Treasury), the combination of the rail crisis with the winter weather had affected almost every sector of the economy and shipments of all kinds threatened to come to a halt. Fifty thousand African-Americans in New York City were reported to have no fuel; in Philadelphia the poor broke through police cordons to raid coal cars in scenes one hyperbolic commentator likened to Petrograd. The government may have been partly responsible for the coal shortage, as production had fallen since Wilson set a maximum price below the market level.[83] However, in the opinion of the United States Fuel Administration, headed by Harry A. Garfield, the basic problem was too few freight cars.[84] In turn the coal shortage and the extreme weather disrupted not only coal-burning industry but also electricity generation. American production already depended heavily on electric power, and no one had considered the consequences if supplies failed, but fail they now did over wide sections of the north-east. The problem began near Niagara Falls, where it was worsened by the freezing of the Niagara river that drove the hydro-electric plants;[85] it spread to the mid-Atlantic states and New England. The War Industries Board learned that shells for France were caught in rail jams, that 'numerous munitions plants' were in a 'serious condition', and by February that steel production was down by two thirds.[86]

An economic crisis was becoming political, and Congressmen of both parties assailed the administration. Two chairs of the WIB resigned, partly from frustration at its lack of power: their successor, Bernard Baruch, detected an atmosphere of 'drifting and indecision'. Wilson strengthened Baruch's authority and asked other government agencies to co-operate with him, but the real difference Baruch made was as an effective political operator, who won the confidence of business leaders such as Judge Elmer H. Gary of the huge United States Steel Corporation.[87] Baruch's background – as a self-made Jewish millionaire who had speculated successfully on Wall Street, but was also a Democrat – made him something of an outsider, but also gave him an independence from the business establishment that allowed him to win the administration's confidence. Under his chairmanship the WIB became a noticeably more effective co-ordinator, though this was partly because the tide was turning anyway.

In a dramatic order on 17 January Garfield ordered a five-day suspension of manufacturing production east of the Mississippi in order to win time to clear the backlog at the collieries and alleviate the rail and fuel bottlenecks.[88] But more important were a series of steps taken by McAdoo. 'Coal zoning' divided the country into traffic zones, within each of which local railways would move fuel from the local pits, minimizing long-distance hauls. A permit system prevented cars from embarking for the seaports unless their consignees were ready to receive them. Shipments to the ports fell from 177,904 tons in December 1917 to 118,752 in January 1918, but recovered to 233,317 in February and

809,779 by November. The frequency of passenger trains was drastically cut, yet passenger numbers rose; the 1918 figure for freight-ton miles was a record, but accomplished using fewer trains and cars.[89] Efficiencies did therefore result from the USRA's authority to remove unnecessary duplication of terminals and insist on use of the most appropriate routes, even though the railroads ran at a loss.[90] By April the congestion in the north-east was clearing, fuel was on the move, and power supplies and industrial output were recovering.

In the aftermath of the winter crisis, a different set of constraints began to operate, more akin to those in the European belligerents. Shipping shortages preoccupied the WIB,[91] even though American shipbuilding was coming on stream. Troop movements taxed the railways, which during 1918 moved an average of 616,276 service personnel a month, and in July a maximum of 1,147,013: McAdoo estimated that transporting one of the super-size American divisions required fifty-eight trains.[92] As conscription bit more deeply, so the economy felt the shortage of men, and McAdoo pressed Wilson unsuccessfully for a waiver for the railroads, while call-ups of miners reduced coal output.[93] Even the American steel industry was inadequate to the demands now piled upon it. According to J. Leonard Replogle, the head of the WIB's steel section, in September 1917 it had been supposed that 17 per cent of steel production would suffice for the war programme, but by June 1918 practically the entire national output was needed directly or indirectly for war necessities.[94] At a conference with business leaders on 7 May, Replogle reported that deliveries were on average thirty-one weeks behind order dates, and 'Deliveries to some of our allies are in frightful shape ...' In Baruch's words, 'We have an important situation.'[95] The WIB moved inexorably towards demanding a shutdown and a reconversion of the civilian automobile industry, but the most the motor manufacturers would agree to was a 25 per cent cut on 1917, pending a total transfer into war production in 1919.[96] At this juncture Wilson himself intervened, expressing deep concern that war output was consuming so much steel production, and desiring civilian industries to be respected as much as possible.[97] In the circumstances, this plea amounted to a warning that industrial mobilization had proceeded far enough, and as the armistice approached, not only was the United States nearing the limits of its fiscal capacity and facing an uncomfortable choice between big tax increases or accelerated inflation, but it also had too little manpower for the key domestic industries. It faced the prospect that in the coming winter its rail, coal, and steel sectors would again come under strain, while if deprived of nitrate fertilizers its agricultural yields would stagnate.[98] Continuing the war into 1919 would have meant a larger AEF and a torrent of American weapons, but would have intensified the pressure at home.

BRITISH EMPIRE

The economic prospect was much bleaker for America's allies, the British Empire among them. Like the American economy, the British one expanded during the war, especially in its first half:

Table 6.3. United Kingdom gross domestic product, 1913–18[99]

1913	1914	1915	1916	1917	1918
100.0	101.0	109.1	111.5	112.5	113.7

British government spending rose from 8.1 per cent of GDP in 1913 to 11.4 per cent in 1914, 31.2 per cent in 1915, 35.6 per cent in 1916, and 38.7 per cent in 1917, before dipping to 37.7 per cent in 1918: proportions that fell below the 49.7 per cent of 1943 but far exceeded those in any previous conflict.[100] Although the estimates of total war expenditure are crude, they suggest that Britain outspent every other belligerent,[101] and within these totals, despite the enormous contributions made by Britain's overseas possessions, the preponderance of the home base still stands out. The output of the 46 million inhabitants of the British Isles before 1914 was similar in value to that of the 380 million in the British Empire, and the United Kingdom accounted for almost nine tenths of imperial war expenditure.[102] Even in Canada and Australia government spending peaked at less than one sixth of national income, compared with Britain's two fifths.[103] The Dominions paid for their own armed forces, and Canada became a net creditor to Britain; but this was a unique case and the UK's outstanding loans to the empire as a whole rose from £39.5m in 1914/15 to £194.5m in 1917/18. Moreover, the

UK lent on a grander scale to its European allies, to whom its outstanding loans by 1917–18 totalled £1,333.2 m.[104]

Britain's financial challenge had domestic and external aspects. The former, the Chancellor of the Exchequer advised the Imperial War Cabinet, was relatively simple; the latter more complex.[105] As in America the nub of domestic war finance was the government's success in borrowing, but this in turn depended in part on respecting financial orthodoxy. Sterling remained on the gold standard and as a convertible currency internationally, even if the link with gold was broken at home. Chancellors presented annual accounts and budgets as normal, and taxation rose to a level where for most of the war it not only covered the equivalent of peacetime expenditure but could also service the interest on the mounting National Debt, thus meeting the expectations of economic commentators and of parliament. In total, taxation met 22.9 per cent of the cost of the war,[106] the key figure in raising it being Reginald McKenna, the Chancellor in 1915–16. Unlike most of the Continental countries, Britain had in place the machinery and personnel for collecting income tax. McKenna increased the rate and lowered the threshold from £160 to £130 a year (for the first time bringing many skilled workers into the net), and the numbers of income tax payers tripled from 1.1 million in 1914 to 3.5 million in 1918. In addition, as part of a pact by which the trade unions accepted the deskilling of labour in war industries, McKenna introduced the Excess Profits Duty, a levy on exceptional wartime profits that came in earlier in Britain than elsewhere, and which because it rested on self-assessment by the firms involved was cheap to collect. By 1918 it rivalled income tax as a revenue source.[107] McKenna's successor, Andrew Bonar Law, raised income tax to 30 per cent and Excess Profits Duty to the almost confiscatory rate of 80 per cent, but believed that taxes had now gone as high as they should, with business, farmers, and the Unionist Party in parliament all opposing further increases.[108] Additionally, the government faced working-class resistance to income tax, which many South Wales miners refused to pay, and although the Labour Party called for a levy on wealth the Treasury believed that such a step would harm the government's creditworthiness. Its ability to find additional funds therefore depended on borrowing.

Despite some danger signals, even in 1918 the government remained able to do so. During the war the national debt rose tenfold, from

£706m to £7,481m,[109] but in 1914 Britain had had very low indebtedness by international standards, and during the first half of the conflict the Treasury floated three major issues of long-term War Loan, that of January 1917 raising nearly £1,000m and attracting nearly 8 million subscribers.[110] However, it was having to offer increasingly generous interest rates, and in 1917–18 it resorted more to medium- and short-term loans, which it placed at diminishing rates of return but to the accompaniment of a faster increase in the money supply, which more than doubled over the war as a whole. National War Bonds, carrying interest of 4–5 per cent and repayable after 5–10 years, were the most important financial vehicle in 1917–18, and from 1920 the government would face a daunting redemption problem, but in general the size and sophistication of the London money market allowed borrowing of comparable amounts to those in Germany but with a smaller inflationary impact, the more so as much of the debt was held abroad.[111] The upshot was that domestic financial considerations did not curtail the war effort. As Churchill put it, reviewing his work as Minister of Munitions, 'finance is not a limiting factor. I do not mean it is not a factor which is not very carefully considered, but we are held up before we reach the limit of money by the supply of materials.'[112]

Britain's external finances were another matter. Whereas Bonar Law in April 1917 was almost complacent about the domestic position, he described the financial situation in North America as 'a very bleak one indeed' – had the USA not been entering the war Britain would be forced off the gold standard, which would be a 'very dangerous' shock to the Allies: 'our financial position was a source of great anxiety . . . to the whole Government', which had 'deliberately gone ahead with the knowledge that danger in this direction was in front of them which we might be unable to face'.[113] Britain purchased in America not only for itself but also for Russia, Italy, and France; and devaluing sterling would raise the cost (and/or reduce the quantity) of supplies to the entire coalition. Although without American intervention the British might have covered their own dollar needs, they could not cover those of their partners; and without their partners they could not win.

In the event, by autumn 1917 the British both had some advance assurance of what America would provide and enjoyed American backing for sterling. This relieved the Treasury of enormous anxiety, although foreign exchange remained finite. In December the Cabinet's Restriction of Imports Committee advised that shortages of dollars as well as of shipping threatened to halt imports from the US; the Food Controller, Lord Rhondda, warned that Britain risked being unable to purchase the Argentine grain surplus, as well as American butter and meat.[114] The War Cabinet agreed to absolute priority for food imports, but at the price of restricting imports for munitions.[115] Hence although Bonar Law told the House of Commons that American entry had delivered what he had hoped from it, awkward choices were still needed, and the Chancellor feared that Britain was acting as a 'conduit pipe' by borrowing from America in order to on-lend to France and Italy. He would have preferred Washington to lend more to Paris and Rome direct, and he warned McAdoo that 'if the war is to continue for another year or more the existing arrangements will put us in an impossible position'.[116] But his proposal got nowhere, and Britain continued in appearance to provide as much support to France and Italy as America did, the Washington and London Treasuries becoming 'joint paymasters of the alliance'.[117] At the end of the war the UK's overseas borrowing totalled £1,365m, of which 75 per cent was owed to the USA and 9.9 per cent to Canada; its lending totalled £1,741m, of which 25 per cent was owed by France, 23.7 per cent by Italy, and 10 per cent by the empire, but 32.6 per cent by Russia and therefore unlikely to be recoverable. Britain's liabilities exceeded its credits, and its role as Allied banker was American-funded. Moreover, its balance of payments was deteriorating. Down to 1917 Britain remained in payments surplus, a deficit on trade in goods being compensated by a surplus on 'invisibles' such as profits from investments and shipping. By 1918, however, it had liquidated many of its American holdings and was transferring its remaining shipping on commercial work to war-related transport on the Atlantic run, while its balance of payments current account showed a deficit.[118] For Britain even more than the US, if the war dragged on into 1919 or 1920 the penalty would be grave.

Food and armaments were the principal categories of spending. In retrospect Lloyd George singled out the difference between the Allies' and the Central Powers' food supplies as a war-winning advantage,[119] and whereas in the first half of the war working-class living standards in London, Paris, and Berlin all held up reasonably well, after 1916 those in the German capital fell further and faster.[120] Certainly Britain had pockets of great hardship: some children in the countryside and the

East End of London survived on scraps of bread, potatoes, and turnips.[121] But William Beveridge, who worked in the Ministry of Food, estimated that total daily calorie consumption dipped at worst (in 1917) to 3–4 per cent below the pre-war figure, and in 1918 it slightly recovered. At no time did the average fall below a minimum of 3,200 calories.[122] Overall the ministry judged the population had been better fed than in peacetime, as well as far better than in Germany, and modern research has confirmed that civilian life expectancy and infant mortality rates improved.[123] The reasons included declining pauperism and unemployment, and government subsidies for servicemen's dependants, but also that adequate food was available. Yet the total demand for food increased because of the expanded numbers in the army (who ate better than civilians), and the outcome seems the more surprising in view of Britain's unique pre-war dependence on overseas imports. By the eve of the First World War it has been estimated that 58 per cent of its calorie consumption was shipped in, the proportions in 1909–13 including 78.7 per cent for wheat and flour, 35.7 per cent for meats, 56.2 per cent for cereals, 68.7 per cent for bacon and ham, 62.3 per cent for butter, and 74.7 per cent for cheese.[124]

Food policy may be divided into supply and distribution. Despite the government's efforts to raise the former by stimulating agriculture, the benefits came too little and too late to make much difference. In 1917 a Food Production Department was created in the Board of Agriculture to consider schemes submitted by county committees for distributing labour, machinery, and other supplies, and for revising land use.[125] Underlying its mission was a bias towards arable farming (the most efficient means of feeding the population), and the 1917 Corn Production Act set guaranteed prices for wheat and oats, while during the war the county committees issued some 100,000 orders requiring land to be brought back into cultivation.[126] Thousands of tractors, mostly from America, made their debut in the English landscape. But more important was labour: from 1917 most agricultural workers were protected from conscription, and by the armistice 79,000 released soldiers were working in farming alongside over 30,000 prisoners of war, while the Women's Land Army provided a further 16,000 pairs of hands. The overall effects might seem undramatic (the index of gross farm output in constant prices moving from 100 in 1909–13 to 103.2 in 1914, 101.3 in 1915, 97.7 in 1916, 97.5 in 1917, and 93.2 in 1918), but this total concealed a redistribution towards cereals, the wheat harvest rising from 1.598 million tons in 1909–13 to 1.706 million in 1914, 1.961 million in 1915, 1.559 million in 1916, 1.654 million in 1917, and 2.428 million in 1918. Almost half the area that had switched from arable to pastoral since the onset of the Victorian agricultural depression in the 1870s was reconverted to the plough. All the same, the growth in calorific value of British home output has been estimated as only 1 per cent between 1909–13 and 1918, compared to the 91 per cent achieved by similar policies between 1938/9 and 1943/4.[127] Britain's import dependence continued, and it would feed its population by using more efficiently the supplies already available and by distributing them more equitably.

It was during the second half of the war that food imports were squeezed. Net imports of all foodstuffs totalled 18.3 million tons in 1913, 16.7 million in 1914, 17.0 million in 1915, and 16.3 million in 1916; but 13.8 million in 1917 and 11.89 million in 1918. By weight the largest component was cereals, which fell from 9.32 million in 1916 to 8.65 million in 1917 and 6.59 million in 1918, twice causing great anxiety.[128] The first wheat crisis came in spring 1917, when the climax of the U-boat offensive followed poor American and British 1916 harvests. In March the Cabinet approved a new guideline of maintaining at least thirteen weeks' supply; but in April and May stocks stood at barely five and a half weeks, perilously close to the four-week level at which distribution might break down. Diverted extra shipping and the harvest raised the margin in August to fourteen weeks,[129] but by November a second alert impended, in the light of dollar shortages and Hoover's warnings that American deliveries would fall short. The root of the problem, according to the Food Controller, was a drastic and unprecedented decline in imports, and a crisis as severe as in spring 1917 lay ahead.[130] Yet as matters turned out, once the Americans had sorted out their transport congestion stocks never fell so low as previously and Britain remained outside the danger zone, Lord Milner briefing the Cabinet that the situation was much better than anticipated.[131] Enough came in to maintain supplies, but at the price of greater dependence on North America – which meant Canada as well as the US. In 1917 Canada exported no less than 72 per cent of its wheat harvest, and in volume 50 per cent more than America, although in 1918 the latter exported twice as much and the proportion of Canada's harvest exported fell to what was still a remarkable figure of 51 per cent.[132] Whereas in 1913 the US and Canada accounted for 34.7 per cent and 22.5 per cent of Britain's wheat and flour imports, by 1918 the figures were 52.3 per cent and 25.1 per cent. For bacon and ham the percentages rose from 44.9 and 5.8 to 83.7 and 15.2; for other meats from 1.6 and 0.1 to 31.2 and 5.0; for dairy produce from 0.2 and 10.4 to 37.8 and 20.6. According to a food ministry appraisal of the 1918 prospects, 'supplies from North America ... are vital'.[133]

Even so, 1917–18 imports remained below the pre-war level, and home production rose too little to compensate. It became essential to use food more efficiently. Like the Americans, the British authorities required more of the grain to be incorporated when milling wheat into flour; in addition, they imposed 'dilution': i.e. an admixture of other cereals (principally barley), as well as pulses and potatoes. The precondition was government control of the mills, which in 1917 came under official direction. The extraction rate rose from 70 per cent in peacetime to 77.8 per cent in October 1917 and 92.01 per cent in March 1918; the proportion of other grains from 17.9 per cent in October 1917 to 32.57 per cent in June 1918. The resulting concoction, 'war bread', was distasteful to a population used to white loaves, though arguably more nutritious, and the millers and bakers learned to make it more palatable. The Royal Commission on Wheat Supplies estimated that these measures provided another thirteen weeks of grain supply, equivalent to 1.8 billion extra calories in 1917 and 3.7 billion in 1918.[134]

It was as well that enough grain was available, as breadstuffs were central to food policy. Bread was never rationed in Britain in 1914–18 (or in 1939–45), uniquely among the European belligerents.[135] The Cabinet considered the possibility, but as late as October 1918 the Food Controller warned it would be 'very dangerous', given 'the degree of unrest at present existing', and ministers dreaded Russian-style queues.[136] Yet they were also advised that rising bread prices fuelled working-class unrest, including nationwide engineering strikes in spring 1917, subsequent to which the government introduced a bread subsidy in order to hold the quartern loaf (4 pounds) at 9d. The decision was contested in Cabinet, and the Treasury agonized about the expense of £50m a year, but in the Second World War it was implemented again.[137] Even if the staple foodstuff was adulterated, it remained freely available at an affordable price.

Instead the most acute food crisis centred on other commodities. It reached its peak in February 1918, and compulsory rationing overcame it: it was, therefore, caused largely by a distribution failure. Lord Rhondda's acts as Food Controller contributed, for he was appointed to underpin domestic consensus by restraining food price rises, and for a while he managed to do so through the bread subsidy and by ceilings imposed on other products.[138] But by autumn 1917 price controls on butter, lard, bacon, tea, and cheese were reducing their availability in the shops, and still more serious was a meat shortage, which the government exacerbated by approving a new price schedule that encouraged farmers to slaughter their herds before Christmas, leading to an absence of freshly butchered stock in the New Year.[139] The consequence was food queues, familiar on the Continent, but in Britain previously little known. Their mood was often one of anger against the better off, the press reporting that at the Ritz six-course meals remained on the menu. The queues reached their peaks on Saturdays, the police estimating that during February over half a million people were standing in them,[140] while soldiers' meetings at the front demanded 'why, while they risked their lives for their country, she could not even manage to feed their wives and children at home'.[141]

The government feared that rationing would exacerbate unrest, and the food ministry was divided over whether to administer it centrally or via local initiative. However, hundreds of local food committees already existed, and when the local authorities, led by Birmingham, introduced rationing schemes, the Cabinet pressed Lord Rhondda to follow. Sugar was rationed nationally from the start of the year, and from February meat was also, followed in July by jam, tea, butter, lard, and margarine. The system backed up the local food committees with directives from the centre and with nationwide consumption standards, and it applied to everyone, from Buckingham Palace downwards. It was rigorously enforced, with over 50,000 prosecutions in 1918–19 for offences against control orders,[142] and it immediately banished queues and restored consumer confidence. Unlike in Germany, moreover, the weekly amounts to which ration cards entitled their holders were actually available, although rationing would also have facilitated the authorities' task if supplies had really run down. Britain still benefited from its access to food sources worldwide, and from – just about – sufficient shipping. And for as long as these conditions applied, its peculiar supply pattern had advantages. Because it had a much smaller peasant farming class than the other belligerents, and shipped in more of its food, it could regulate distribution more tightly. What might seem vulnerabilities proved factors in success.[143]

By the time Ludendorff's onslaughts hit the British armies, American food deliveries were recovering and the food queue crisis had subsided. Britain seemed to have turned the corner, though if the war continued into 1919 the prospects remained uncertain. Yet another of the proliferating inter-Allied agencies, the Inter-Allied Food Council, which represented Hoover and the other food controllers, first met in London in July 1918.[144] It entered on a dialogue with the Allied Maritime Transport Council, querying the latter's priorities for American troop shipments and for a munitions build-up for a 1919 offensive if they held down civilian food supplies. But the AMTC's authority over shipping gave it the upper hand, and Hoover believed that Britain was stockpiling too much food and should release more to the Continental countries. Although he failed to achieve a formal restriction on Britain's food imports, the new AMTC priorities achieved much the same result. The food ministry had asked the AMTC for shipping to import 13.5 million tons of food into Britain in the cereal year 1918–19 (compared with 12.4 million in 1917–18), but the AMTC proposed only 10.5 million, the remaining shipping to go to the other Allies, the AEF, and armaments. Although the food ministry considered 12.2 million an absolute minimum, Lloyd George and the Cabinet decided on 6 September to go provisionally with the AMTC figure and run down Britain's food reserves, gambling that American shipbuilding would allow the Americans to take over more of their shipping from the spring (and gambling also that the U-boats really were beaten). Within a fortnight of this decision, grain imports were dropping rapidly.[145]

The implications were the gloomier because domestic cereal production could not take up the slack. On the contrary, the 'plough policy' that had raised grain output between 1916 and 1918 had been suspended. The turning point here, as in so many ways, was the spring 1918 emergency, the Ministry of National Service on 30 April withdrawing the exemption from military service for agricultural workers aged 18–23 and setting a quota of 30,000 recruits. Although few were actually called up, the change of tack reduced the farming community's willingness to co-operate with government targets, shown especially when the House of Lords vetoed the powers in the Corn Production Act for requiring changes in cultivation. In the Board of Agriculture's opinion, just maintaining 1919 production at the 1918 level necessitated ploughing up new land (as fertilizers were lacking to replenish the existing arable soil) and hiring tens of thousands more workers; but in view of the labour shortage a long-range programme to achieve self-sufficiency in breadstuffs was abandoned.[146] Meanwhile, in August the Food Controller warned the Cabinet of 'the gravity of the situation' created by lack of feedstuffs, with the risk that running down livestock herds would cause milk shortages and another and more serious meat crisis, to say nothing of the 'dangerously short' provisions for working horses. But Hoover refused to provide fodder until human requirements had been satisfied, and on 14 October Britain commenced feedstuff rationing. Soon after, its livestock herds were reported to be shrinking.[147] As the armistice approached, therefore, the government had abandoned further expansion in home cereal production, gambled it could run down food stocks, and was headed for a graver meat and dairy crisis than it had just surmounted. The policies that had protected civilians were being redressed in favour of the fighting front.

Subsistence had to be balanced against arms production. In the latter domain the British had impressive achievements. Their output in certain categories was less than Germany's (notably machine guns, and possibly rifles and explosives),[148] but generally it met their armies' needs in the climactic 1918 battles, and left a surplus to assist their allies. In the March 1918 emergency the munitions ministry speedily replaced artillery and machine guns out of stocks, while simultaneously releasing workers to the BEF; even aircraft losses were made good with what the official history termed 'astonishing rapidity' and by 8 April more planes were in service than when the battle began.[149] In the autumn advance, BEF shell expenditure reached extraordinary levels. Twenty-eight thousand tons a week were fired off during the 1916 Battle of the Somme, but in the week ending 29 September 1918 (when the Hindenburg Line was breached) the BEF fired 83,140 tons (3,383,700 rounds); and on 29 September itself 943,837 rounds, worth £3.871m. Even so, at the armistice 555,390 tons of filled shell remained in hand, enough for at least three weeks' campaigning.[150] In fact the 'shell shortage' (the top priority when the munitions ministry was established) was largely over by 1917, and in the final year the ministry's efforts focused elsewhere.

Explosive, shell, and rifle output peaked in 1917, but that of guns, gas, tanks, and aircraft in 1918.[151] The latter amounted to a new wave of innovation, which as munitions minister in 1917–18 Winston Churchill promoted, and which went in hand with the revolution in tactics.

Moreover, whereas down to 1917 the British had had little surplus to deliver to their allies, now they sent both finished munitions and raw materials. It is true that the dependence worked both ways. By 1918 Britain no longer drew so heavily on America for finished shells as it had done in 1915–16, but the US still delivered propellants and raw materials such as copper and aluminium, as well as machine tools and shell steel: 15 per cent of the munitions ministry's imports in 1918 came from America, and it acknowledged 'our dependence on the United States for the vital elements in our Munitions programme'.[152] Britain also brought equipment from the French, notably aero-engines,[153] though overall it supplied more to its allies than it received from them, and if the war had gone on into 1919 it would have done still more. France received machine guns and cartridges, as well as an emergency delivery of 1,200 mortars in spring 1918. Britain was France's major wartime foreign steel supplier, delivering some 3 million tons, and the British Empire was France's prime source of tin. Italy had vast replenishment needs after Caporetto, Britain sending 160 artillery pieces, 2,000 Lewis light machine guns, and 2.5 million gas masks. During 1918 not only Italy (which mined hardly any coal) but also France (after Germany's advance into its northern colliery area) depended on British coal supplies, which in the summer and autumn of 1918 to France alone averaged 17,000 tons a month.[154] Even the US turned more to British industry as the AEF grew. When in summer 1918 discussions took place of an AEF expansion to at least eighty divisions in 1919, the French said they could kit out up to thirty but Churchill offered to equip the remaining fifty, the Americans agreeing to accept more than 2,000 British guns at a cost that would eliminate over £100m of British debt to the US. Although an expanded AEF would have given America greater military prominence if the war had gone on, financially it would have helped restore British and French independence. Churchill was confident that British industry could do the work, and already during 1918 the UK was delivering to the AEF guns, ammunition, aviation gear, and trench warfare equipment, including 1.5 million steel helmets.[155] By 1919 Britain would have been bidding to replace France as chief armourer to the coalition.

The empire played its part in these achievements. Malaya sent tin, South Africa chromium, and Australia by 1918 was supplying two thirds of the munitions ministry's demand for lead, as well as delivering copper and zinc, although (partly owing to distance) plans for it to become a significant shell producer failed to materialize. India was the primary supply base for Mesopotamia, as well as for the Indian troops on the Western Front, and possessed a small but sophisticated armaments sector. It could make its own steel and explosives and during the war it manufactured 176 guns, 145,758 new and converted rifles (which required a notoriously complex manufacturing operation), 1.36 million shells, and 583 million small-arms rounds.[156] By 1918 the Indian government had spent some £200m on goods for Britain and its allies without being reimbursed, the result being what the Secretary of State for India warned was 'the gravest currency crisis' and a threat to the rupee's convertibility.[157] Yet the most significant imperial economic contribution came from Canada, which not only rivalled the US as a wheat supplier but was also a major armaments manufacturer. From 1915 its war industry was supervised by the Imperial Munitions Board, which was an arm of the Ministry of Munitions in London rather than answering to the government in Ottawa, and spent more than £200m of British taxpayers' money. By the end of the war the Board was responsible for seven state plants and had issued contracts to over 600 private firms, and more than 250,000 people worked for it. Before 1914 Canada had had virtually no armaments sector, yet it turned out over 65 million shells, nearly 30 million fuses, and 47 million cartridge cases, and in the first half of 1917 was scheduled to produce half the shells fired by the standard British 18-pounder field gun on the Western Front. This was the peak, however, and in 1918 Canada's industrial contribution diminished, mainly as a result of shipping shortages and the inability of the British authorities to find the currency to pay for it, though Canadian capacity was redirected to supplying shells to the US. Although the payments crisis caused Lloyd George's Cabinet great soul-searching, it saw no choice but to cut Canadian supplies.[158] One in four of the shells produced in the empire during the war came from Canada, but most of the BEF's equipment came from the home islands.

In contrast to the United States, the British armaments industry by 1918 was reaping the benefits of conversion and expansion. As the first Minister of Munitions in 1915–16 Lloyd George was less of a miracle worker than he later suggested, but he elaborated a system that survived for the rest of the war and became a model for Lord Beaverbrook's Ministry of Aircraft Production in 1940.[159] Private industry was re-equipped with new machine tools (many imported from the US), and mobilized under Boards of Management, each supervising a regional Area of Organization. The ministry built new state-owned National Shell Factories, National Projectile Factories (for heavy artillery), and National Filling Factories, as well as enlarging the government plants at Enfield, Waltham Abbey, and Woolwich. Woolwich became one of the largest arms establishments in the world, rivalling Krupp at Essen: by 1918 its central complex covered 285 acres and was fed by nearly 150 miles of railway, its workforce rising between 1914 and 1917 from 15,559 to 96,325. After 21 March 1918 it produced 48 million small-arms rounds for each of three consecutive months, some of its employees working for nearly 100 hours a week. In general, firms moving into weapons production concentrated on the less skilled work of producing shell casings, while rifles, machine guns, and artillery remained with the state arsenals and with established companies such as Birmingham Small Arms, Vickers, and Armstrong, the last alone producing 9,000 guns for the army during the war (and 4,000 for the navy), alongside 14.5 million shells and more than 1,500 aircraft. By 1918 Britain had solved the problem of shell production so completely that even the enormous quantities delivered to the BEF did not fully engage capacity, and the cost of the standard 18-pounder field gun shell had halved.[160] Quality control, which earlier had been downgraded in the interests of attaining volume, was now excellent, GHQ being well satisfied with the deliveries.[161] Similarly, the munitions ministry had accumulated so much high explosive by December 1917 that by the following August it had halved its output, before boosting it again to supply the AEF.[162] By 1917 it had to give more attention to repairing artillery pieces already in service that were wearing out, but the guns lost in the German spring offensive could be replaced as effectively as the shells; and the rifle reserve was enormous.[163]

In contrast, gas was a creation of the war, and a new industry with complex and dangerous processes was established to manufacture it (including the Porton Down establishment created in 1916). Nine thousand tons were used against Germany during 1918 but the ministry envisaged quintupling that figure in 1919. Tank plans were similarly ambitious, it being intended to build 4,000 (including the new Mark VIII model) in 1919, triple the 1918 number.[164] The third, and biggest, new field was aircraft, which Haig and the Army Council agreed should have priority over all other 1918 munitions orders. During 1917 the ministry had reduced the standard types from fifty-one to thirteen, in preparation for mass production, and the 32,018 delivered in 1918 were more than double the 1917 number (and dwarfed the 1914 output of 245).[165] Aviation was an industry of gigantic proportions – Churchill said it was almost as big as ordnance and shell – and it too was scheduled to expand even more in 1919, although engine supply was a bottleneck. If the war had continued, British industry would have delivered far more tanks, gas shells, and aircraft to the BEF, and become of prime importance to the Americans.

In such an expansion, plant capacity would not have been the principal limiting factor. Nor would finance, except for certain categories of import, particularly from Canada. In February 1918 the Cabinet had decided that in the present military situation the munitions programme must be as large as tonnage, raw materials, and labour would permit.[166] Although the Admiralty always enjoyed priority claims on the latter two categories, another of Lloyd George's legacies had been to negotiate 'dilution' with the engineering trade unions, enabling unskilled workers – chiefly women – to take for the duration of the war employments that were normally reserved to skilled men. By 1918 Britain's war industries (including the Admiralty plants) employed some 3.4 million people; the munitions ministry and its 5,500 'controlled establishments' (i.e. privately owned but state-regulated factories) accounting for 2.75 million, of whom 0.75 million were female.[167] During the March–July emergency some 120,000 men aged 19–20 were released to the army, though many were substituted for, but thereafter Churchill claimed he was reaching the limit and prevented further cuts. In contrast to other sectors of British industry the strike rate was low (reducing output during the last fifteen months by only 0.2 per cent), and although labour shortages began to bite in sectors such as tank production they were not a big constraint overall.

Potentially more important as restrictions were transport and raw materials, and yet British industry escaped an American-style winter crisis. Its railway system withstood the stress of war better than the North American or Continental networks, in good measure owing to something that in peacetime had been criticized: the surplus capacity built by competing operators. From Inverness southwards, all pairs of towns of any size were connected by at least two routes, and Britain had a denser concentration of rolling stock per mile than Germany, nearly twice that in France, and nearly three times that in Austria-Hungary and Russia.[168] In 1914 a Railway Executive Committee had been formed, comprising the General Managers of the twelve leading companies, which received financial compensation but became a state-directed system, prioritizing the armed forces and the war economy. One consequence were the 'Jellicoe specials' hauling South Wales coal to Grangemouth, whence it was shipped to the fleet, thus shortening its passage through coastal waters. Even so, in 1917–18 domestic passenger services were cut back, and danger signals began flashing. More people used suburban trains because of the exodus from London due to air raids; but the curtailment of coastal shipping meant the railways carried more goods traffic and their rolling stock deteriorated, over 4,000 locomotives lying idle and being denied repairs for lack of steel.[169] By the armistice some 20 per cent of the major companies' locomotives needed attention: Churchill acknowledged that the railways were operating on a very fine margin and if the war continued into 1919 the munitions ministry would have to find more steel for them.[170] None the less, they operated reasonably efficiently during 1918. Those in the empire were less fortunate, the Canadian railway companies becoming as financially hard pressed as their American equivalents.[171]

Raw materials were an anxiety for the explosives industry, which could extract benzol, toluol, and phenol from the coalfields but imported most of its other supplies, including pyrites from Spain and sodium nitrate from Chile.[172] Like Baruch in Washington, Churchill was haunted by the dependence on Chile, via a voyage so long that a freighter could manage it only two and a half times per year. He reported that Britain held the only reserves on its side of the Atlantic, and France and Italy feared 'complete breakdown' in their shell filling factories.[173] Unlike America's, moreover, Britain's nitrogen-fixing plants did not come on stream before the armistice. None the less, when the war ended it had big stockpiles of high explosive. Steel, however, proved more intractable, Churchill telling workers in a September 1917 circular that this was 'a steel war'.[174] In 1913 the UK had been the world's third-largest steel maker with 14 per cent of global output, but came well behind

Germany's 25 per cent and America's 40 per cent.[175] The industry was composed of smaller companies with older equipment than either of its rivals, and it relied heavily on the Bessemer rather than the basic process, so that much of it smelted non-phosphoric ores. Because Britain had abundant phosphoric ore in the East Midlands but much smaller non-phosphoric deposits, it continued to depend on imports, principally from Spain, with whom relations were delicate. According to the munitions ministry's Director of Steel Production, Spanish iron ore imports had caused intense anxiety during 1916, and 'I had hoped that never again would the country have to escape disaster by so narrow a margin', but in July 1917 the situation was again 'of the utmost gravity'.[176] In November the Cabinet therefore agreed to supply Spain with coal and buy its oranges in return for ore, overriding the Treasury's reservations.[177] The government also approved investment at home, and output using the Midlands ores did expand, but although total production rose from 7,664,000 to 9,717,000 tons between 1913 and 1917, in 1918 it dipped to 9,539,000, whereas demand was growing. The shortfall arose partly from labour scarcity (which was more serious than in the armaments plants),[178] but also because shipping shortages led the Cabinet's committee on the restriction of imports to reduce deliveries for munitions, forcing the munitions ministry to revise its 'steel budget'.[179] To keep its arms industries busy in 1918 Britain had to import steel from the US, but it also cut its deliveries to France and Italy. None the less, it achieved record shipbuilding levels, and equipped its forces better than ever before.

In many ways British manufacturing performed better in the First World War than in the Second: its artillery, tanks, and aircraft compared with the best models of the time, and even an apparently simple item like the infantry steel helmet, made from manganese steel produced by Hadfield of Sheffield, was lighter and yet more resistant to impact than its German counterpart.[180] Britain suffered no production crisis as grave as that in several branches of its war economy in 1942–3,[181] and it created new output lines such as optical glass for binoculars and rangefinders (before 1914 imported from Germany) and magnetos (used to start internal combustion engines and previously supplied by Bosch of Stuttgart).[182] It bore most of the burden of equipping its own armed forces as well as greatly assisting its partners. Nor did its railways seize up like the Russian ones, and as the German, American, and

French ones all threatened to. None the less, in the final months one major industry caused great concern: coal. In the Second World War coal output drifted downwards after 1939, partly because the labour force declined, but also because productivity per worker fell.[183] A generation earlier, output also slipped: from 287.4 million tons in 1913 to 265.7 million in 1914, 253.2 million in 1915, 256.4 million in 1916, 248.5 million in 1917, and 222.7 million in 1918. In addition, the coal became 'dirtier', the element of stone and shale doubling to more than 10 per cent, and productivity, as measured by tons per man per shift, dropped to 4 per cent below the 1913 level in 1917 and 6 per cent below in 1918. Unlike munitions, steel, or the railways, the mines were dogged by labour unrest, 134 disputes between January and November 1918 involving 356,000 workers and costing 1,081,000 working days.[184] Indeed, precisely an impasse between employers and workers in the South Wales field (which was crucial for the navy) persuaded the government to appoint Sir Guy Calthrop as Coal Controller in February 1917, the existing managements staying in place but the owners' profits being regulated. Under Calthrop's aegis the industry and the railways adopted the 'Coal Transport Scheme', which eased pressure on transport by minimizing long-distance coal movements. Of 1.16 million employees in the industry on the eve of war, 289,700 (24.97 per cent) had joined the armed forces by January 1917. But that autumn the government decided that the industry could spare 50,000 Grade I (i.e. fit and unmarried) men for the army, and despite a ballot by the miners' union, the MFGB, voting against, Lloyd George ruled that the transfer must go ahead. After the 21 March offensive, the government decided to take a further 25,000 men, and by August the mines had lost 69,094 fit workers in return for 8,588 unfit ones, while output in July was the lowest since the war began.[185]

The fall came at a point when the shipping ministry warned that France and Italy faced a coal crisis, that Britain's shipping-for-coal agreements with neutrals such as Norway might break down, and that bunker stocks for the Mediterranean and elsewhere were endangered: Calthrop rejoined that if Britain maintained its deliveries to others, its own munitions works would go short.[186] None the less, on 13 June a meeting chaired by Lloyd George agreed to cut supplies to industries such as textiles, shoes, and pottery, in order to maintain deliveries to Italy and France, and a week later the Cabinet decided to ration households' fuel and light. These steps were inadequate to solve the problem, and the American, French, and Italian delegates on the Allied Maritime Transport Council jointly warned the Cabinet of 'the extremely grave consequences' of the coal shortage, as a result of which France and Britain could not stockpile for the winter, supplies to the Atlantic coaling stations were endangered, the French and Italian navies were in a 'most serious' position, British Admiralty stocks stood at 'danger level', and Italian steel production had dropped by a quarter.[187] Calthrop and Lloyd George made personal appeals to the miners, but output recovered little and at the end of the year the country still faced a 16.5 million ton deficit, only the armistice saving it from a 'coal famine'.[188] Admittedly, part of the problem was that the government's attempt to close down non-essential industries had been frustrated. Three quarters of the operatives in the Lancashire cotton industry were still engaged on civilian rather than war-related tasks, but the Cotton Control Board (CCB) representing the employers and unions in the industry rejected Calthrop's proposal to concentrate production and cotton was treated much less ruthlessly than in 1941, when much of it was mothballed.[189] In the light of the coal dearth Churchill warned that he could expand aircraft, tank, artillery, and machine-gun production in 1919 only by cutting shell output from 52,000 to 40,000 tons a week.[190] As the Inter-Allied Munitions Council, created in June, had agreed with the AMTC that munitions shipments and AEF supplies should take precedence over food imports,[191] British civilians faced a grim winter in 1918/19, with fuel, rail travel, and food all restricted at the same time as industrial unrest increased.

FRANCE

France's gross domestic product in 1913 was barely half of Britain's and less than a quarter of America's. During the war its GDP fell: according to the most recent estimates, from 100 in 1913 to 84.0 in 1914, 71.6 in 1915, 80.6 in 1916, 78.9 in 1917, and 66.2 in 1918.[192] It struggled under exceptional disadvantages due to its smaller manufacturing base than Britain's, America's, or Germany's, the dislocation created by invasion, and the intensity of its 1914 mobilization. Yet its estimated total war expenditure was not far behind America's,[193] and by concentrating on land- and aerial-weapons production it became the Allies' biggest arms exporter. In the year to 1 March 1918 French daily shell production averaged 261,000 to Britain's 229,400; both countries produced 3,200 rifles a day, and during 1917 France produced 681 guns of all types against Britain's 449 (although Britain produced more of the heaviest pieces and over twice France's monthly average of machine guns).[194] In April 1918 France's aircraft output averaged 496 a week against Britain's 570, but in total France produced 90,000 aero-engines: more than twice as many as Britain or Germany.[195] France's industry equipped its army and air force and needed little foreign assistance, the main exceptions being American propellants, British machine guns, and Italian aero-engines. In the first half of the war it also became the main supplier to Russia and the Balkan Allies, and in the second to the AEF[196] (although Britain might have overtaken it if the war had gone on into 1919). The price was increasing overseas dependence not just for industrial raw materials but also in areas such as finance and even agriculture that had been traditional French strengths. It encouraged the country's leaders to seek an early armistice, and jeopardized their ability to exploit the fruits of victory.

In 1914 the French called up the highest proportion of their manpower of any great power. To begin with their army was not especially well equipped, but by 1918 it was on a par with those of the other belligerents. Between 1914 and 1918 its park of lorries and cars rose from 164 to 98,000; of aircraft from 170 to 3,600; of machine guns from 5,100 to 60,500; of wireless sets from 50 to 28,000; and of heavy guns from 308 to 5,128.[197] The initial priority was 75 mm field gun shells, whose consumption far exceeded expectations, most of the peacetime reserve being fired off in the opening weeks. By autumn 1915 output was meeting the army's demands, and production peaked in May 1917 when 7.01 million 75 mm shells were delivered in one month. On the first day of the Battle of La Malmaison 520 tons of field gun shells were fired per kilometre, but the heaviest 1918 bombardment, of 420 tons per kilometre on 26 September (the first day of the Franco-American offensive), was lower, and during the final year production fell back. After the initial shell crisis, the pressure point became repair and replacement of the field guns, partly because defective rounds exploded in over 600 of them in 1915 alone. But this problem too was solved, and as of 1 April 1918 France had 5,152 75 mm guns at the front (against 4,000 in

August 1914) while between July and September it produced 2,000 in three months.[198] To drive the Germans out, however, the crucial requirement was heavy artillery, for which the high command established a production programme in May 1916 and Pétain an accelerated one a year later.[199] For heavy guns the manufacturing processes were more complex, and France produced only one new design during the war, but by 1917–18, according to Loucheur, the army was 'beginning to receive the fruits of the mass production embarked on for heavy artillery pieces'. Heavy-gun production peaked in the second half of 1917, and that of 155 mm shells in April 1918.[200] By the latter date the French had over 3,000 heavy guns along their sector and outnumbered the Germans. They no longer needed to expand their field artillery and focused on replacing their older pieces; similarly they replaced the 1907 model heavy machine gun by the superior Hotchkiss.[201]

In the final phase, new frontiers opened. One was gas, particularly mustard gas shells, output of which Clemenceau ordered to be accelerated 'at all costs'.[202] A second was tanks, a priority for both the high command and the government, Loucheur commenting that 'we must sacrifice other manufactures to that of tanks, as the infantryman will not want to march unless tanks precede him'.[203] After the failure of the earlier French heavy models in the April 1917 Nivelle offensive, tanks meant above all the lighter two-man design. In all, the French authorities ordered 7,820 light tanks, and although production ran behind schedule they took delivery of 3,940, the peak delivery month for Renault (the largest manufacturer) being 278 in July 1918.[204] But, as in Britain, the biggest new story was in aircraft. Under Clemenceau's predecessor, Paul Painlevé, the government had set an initial target of 2,870 and a subsequent one of 4,000, telling the aviation department that 'every means of realization would be placed for this purpose at your disposal'. Although the reality fell short, between January and October 1918 monthly output rose from 1,714 to 2,362 and by the armistice France not only had the world's largest air force but was also the world's biggest aero-engine maker and second only to Britain as an airframe manufacturer, completing one aeroplane every fifteen minutes and one engine every ten. During 1918 as a whole it produced 24,652 aircraft and 44,563 engines.[205]

In August 1914 the French arms industry had employed some 50,000 workers, mainly in the state arsenals; by 1918 the total was 1,675,000, some four fifths in the private sector. The 1918 workforce was much more heterogeneous than its 1914 predecessor, including 430,000 women, 108,000 foreign and 61,000 colonial workers, and 40,000 prisoners of war, as well as 425,000 male civilians and 492,000 released soldiers.[206] With an army now desperately short of effectives, the French like the British were juggling with a labour force that was too small to go round. Yet labour shortages were not the most important production constraint, and neither were shortages of plant and machinery, despite the industrial significance of the territories lost in 1914. The areas invaded or remaining subject to bombardment had covered 8–9 per cent of France's territory and contained 14 per cent of its industrial population. They had accounted for 41 per cent of the steam power in French manufacturing, 74 per cent of coal production, 63 per cent of steel production, 81 per cent of woollen textile production, and 44.5 per cent of chemicals output. Yet despite this apparently crippling loss, industrial production in the rest of France increased between 1914 and 1917 to 74 per cent of the pre-war level, falling back to 50.5 per cent only in the final year.[207]

Until 1918 the war industries were shielded from the overall economic contraction. Geographically this was achieved by industrializing previously underdeveloped areas in the west and south: Bordeaux and Rouen gained over 50,000 inhabitants; Lyons over 200,000; and Marseilles nearly 400,000.[208] Organizationally, it meant converting general engineering firms to 75 mm shell production, and while the state arsenals concentrated on heavy artillery they offloaded field gun manufacture to big arms firms in central France such as Schneider and Saint-Chamond. The arsenals were also enlarged, but the government operated principally by giving private industry generous contracts. Legislation in 1915 enabled it to lend to firms to invest in facilities for weapons manufacture, and Citroën, for example (which produced 24 million 75 mm shells), built its brand new Javel plant in western Paris. Similarly Renault (which besides tanks made shells, lorries, aircraft, and aero-engines) more than doubled its factory floor space and machine tool numbers, while Loucheur's own firm filled a converted exhibition hall at Lyons with women workers and imported American machinery that by the end of 1916 turned out 30,000 field gun shells a day.[209] In contrast, the new wave of war industries that developed in 1917–18 was centred on the capital. This was true of Hotchkiss, the principal heavy-machine-gun manufacturer, and of Renault, the largest tank builder. Over 90 per cent of French aircraft came from the Paris region, much of the output coming from subcontractors.[210] War production would have suffered greatly if the capital had fallen, and steps began in April 1918 to decentralize out of it.[211] Yet it did not fall, and neither did German bombing and shelling cause much disruption.

The most critical constraint, instead, was raw material supplies. Like Britain, France had depended on Germany for many chemicals, and had now to find alternatives. For propellants the main source was at first America, but by April 1918 France was manufacturing 290 tons a day itself and importing only 100. By 1917–18 French high-explosive capacity exceeded what was needed, and although some raw materials such as nitrates remained critically short, powder and explosives were less of a bottleneck than across the Rhine.[212]

Steel and coal were another matter. France's pre-war steel production was about one half Britain's, and most of it came from the occupied regions. The government helped what remained of the industry to invest in extra facilities, and French steelmakers expanded capacity by 1.76 million tons, but between 1916 and 1918 the utilization rate fell from 94 to 59 per cent. A major reason was that France lost its principal iron ore deposits to German occupation: output dropped from 21,918,000 tonnes in 1913 to 620,000 in 1915 and in 1918 was still only 1,672,000. Imported ore could not begin to cover the gap, and to ship in this bulky commodity was a poor use of tonnage.[213] In these circumstances imported steel became critical to the French war effort: the quantity rising from 7.5 million quintals in 1915 to 19.5 million in 1917 and over 13.5 million in 1918. In the first half of the war Britain was the main supplier but in 1917–18 the US overtook it.[214] In 1918 both imports and domestic production fell, partly owing to shipping shortages, and Loucheur had to cut 75 mm shell output.[215] He told French parliamentarians that the biggest problem was armour plate, for all the pre-war capacity had gone, though also short were special steels for munitions and aircraft.[216] None the less, he managed to cover the army's shell needs, reviving daily production of 75 mm shells from 145,000 to 210,000 after what he described as 'a fearful consumption' during the Second Battle of the Marne, when 600,000 were fired per day during the 18–20 July counterstroke. He was helped by Baruch, who rushed steel to France in autumn 1918 to avert a shortfall. With foreign aid, the gap was covered, and according to Loucheur not steel but coal was 'the dominating question'.[217]

French coal output in 1913 was 40,844,000 tonnes: far lower than in Britain, the US, or Germany. Two thirds of it came from the coalfields of the Nord and Pas de Calais, most of whose mines were overrun. By 1915 the figure had halved to 19.53 million, before climbing to 28.9 million in 1917 after the army released over 100,000 miners. Even so, output per man declined by 31.7 per cent between 1913 and 1920. Moreover, after the Germans in spring 1918 occupied or made unworkable still more of the northern field, output dropped again – over the year as a whole to 26.26 million. Imports of coal and coke therefore now accounted for about one half of consumption instead of one third as before the war, and in the second half of the conflict they tailed off, from 28.06 million tonnes in 1914 to 20.92 million in 1916, 17.45 million in 1917, and 16.86 million in 1918.[218] Britain continued in its traditional role as main supplier, and without British coal the French war economy could not have functioned:

Table 6.4. British coal exports to France, 1913–18 (million tons)[219]

1913	1914	1915	1916	1917	1918 (Jan.–July)
12.8	12.3	17.6	17.3	17.5	9.4

As with steel, in 1918 coal output and imports dipped simultaneously, and in this case America could not fill the gap. Germany's offensives between March and July interrupted the rail routes bringing steel and iron ore from Lorraine and coal from the north to Paris. In August Loucheur reported that he had been 'very much hindered' by losing control of the Paris–Amiens and Paris–Nancy lines, and forced to close down blast furnaces: the fuel shortage in the east had been 'critical', France had had to run down its coal stocks, and 'the recapture of the lines has an enormous importance'. But by forcing Britain to recall miners to the BEF, the German offensives also cut British supplies. It was unsurprising that the French joined the Americans and Italians in urging that increased British coal output was needed for the entire alliance, but although an agreement in April 1918 provided for British deliveries of 1.74 million tonnes per month, in September and October they attained only 1.24 and 1.25 million. As the armistice approached, France like Britain faced a difficult winter if the war went on. [220]

The French survived by importing fuel and raw materials, most of which came in foreign ships and at ever higher prices. Like the British, they financed their domestic more easily than their foreign purchases, but even at home their funding was among the most inflationary of any major belligerent. When war broke out the legislature had only just approved the introduction of income tax, a reform that the finance minister in 1914–17, Alexandre Ribot, disliked and was glad to postpone implementing. Tax increases might upset political consensus and were difficult to implement in the chaos of invasion when many revenue collectors had been called up. Although income tax was collected from 1916 it contributed little revenue, and the war profits tax, introduced in the same year, yielded less than in Britain. Receipts rose slowly and only because of fiscal drag resulting from inflation, and together with sales of assets they covered only 16.5 per cent of expenditure. Revenue was still too low even to cover normal non-war expenditure, and at the end of 1918 France had not yet paid off a centime of its war costs.[221]

Even as regarded borrowing, Ribot was slower and more cautious than the British and Germans in floating issues of government bonds, and when he did so he offered a particularly generous combination of high interest with tax exemptions, such was his fear (with German forces barely fifty miles from Paris) that they could fail. This made them an expensive form of fundraising, and although four took place the last was much the most remunerative, issued in September–October 1918 when victory was practically won. Instead, the biggest support of French domestic finance was short-term borrowing via 'national defence bonds', intended to be less prominent, but proving popular with the investing public. Typically maturing in three to twelve months and earning annualized interest rates of up to 5 per cent, they were widely available and supported by intense propaganda. The government would have been in trouble if the public had attempted to redeem them en masse, but fortunately confidence held up and enough continued to be sold to keep the debt rolling over, so that such devices covered over 76 billion francs of spending.[222] But a second characteristic of French war finance was the finance ministry's reliance on credits to the government from the Bank of France, totalling 17,150 million francs by the end of 1918 and accompanied by a trebling in the note issue between 1914 and 1918 from 10,042 million francs to 30,250 million. As Clemenceau put it, 'one can always find money', and indeed the government neither went bankrupt nor ran out of funding for its domestic purchases, although under Clemenceau's finance minister, Louis-Lucien Klotz, both short-term borrowing and the note issue grew faster than ever.[223] The priority was to find the wherewithal to win the war, leaving the bill to be settled afterwards – and as much as possible at Germany's expense.

While France stored up a monetary overhang and floating debt, it accumulated indebtedness abroad. It had started the war with a high level of government borrowing at home, but no foreign debt. Indeed, it was second only to Britain as a foreign investor, and a surplus on invisibles such as services and tourism offset its deficit on merchandise trade. Between 1913 and 1918, however, French exports diminished in real terms by more than two thirds, while imports rose by a quarter (and in money terms by much more). France's merchandise trade deficit of 1,500 million francs in 1913 widened to 21,600 million by 1917 and exceeded 60,000 million for the war as a whole, but trade with just two countries accounted for more than two thirds of the total. From Britain, which supplied coal, steel, textiles, machinery, and chemicals, France imported 23,000 million francs' worth of goods, creating a visibles deficit of 18,000 million; from the US, which supplied cereals, steel, explosives, copper, oil, and machinery, it imported 27,000 million francs' worth of goods and created another 18,000 million deficit. No other country rivalled the Anglo-Saxon powers, even imports from Italy totalling only 3,000 million.[224]

In general French economic policy was less interventionist than in Britain and America. The authorities held off from raising taxes, and were slower than the British to confiscate holdings of overseas assets. Gradually, however, under the impact of the shipping crisis and of pressure from London and Washington, they changed tack and were drawn into the thickening network of inter-Allied financial and supply agreements. From 1915 the British Treasury extended sterling credits to finance French purchases from the British Empire; after 1916 Britain also paid for France's purchases in the US. Despite France's ballooning payments deficit, the franc was held at much the same parity against the dollar from 1915 until the end of the war. The British and Americans believed the French were too lax, and in 1917–18 French governments extended their powers, at any rate on paper. They took over merchant shipping and introduced exchange control; imports were prohibited except by authorization. To implement the system the commerce ministry under Etienne Clémentel established 'consortiums' for each main import category: specially constituted limited companies representing manufacturers and importers who identified to the authorities the needs of their group and took responsibility for distribution among their members.[225] In the final year the balance of payments crisis was alleviated, partly by import restrictions and partly by the offsetting franc purchases of the hugely expanded AEF. None the less, British and American government credits were essential to finance the coal and steel and oil imports that powered France's armaments and military effort, and they gave it access to vastly enhanced resources, albeit at the cost of $3bn of debt to Britain and nearly $4bn to the US by the end of the war.[226]

Unlike Britain, France was traditionally a great agricultural producer, and yet it too became dependent on imported food. Though not particularly efficient – wheat yields per hectare were about one third lower than in Britain and Germany – before 1914 it grew more than 90 per cent of its wheat and was self-sufficient in most other foodstuffs. Yet compared with a 1904–13 average of 100, the wheat harvest fell to 87 in 1914, 68.5 in 1915, 63.6 in 1916, and a catastrophic 41.4 in 1917, before recovering to 69.4 in 1918. By 1918 the potato crop was less than half the pre-war average and barley not much better, while numbers of horses fell to 69.5 per cent, cattle to 82.9 per cent, and pigs to 56.7 per cent, and milk production declined by two thirds.[227] The loss of the occupied territories, which were excellent wheat and sugar beet producers, was a contributory factor but more important was declining productivity even in unoccupied France. The fundamental reason was lack of labour. Nearly two in three male agricultural workers were called up, and unlike miners or factory operatives few were released. Women, children, and the elderly bore the brunt of the work needed to keep French farms going, helped to some extent by Spanish and Portuguese immigrants and by prisoners of war. They faced shortages of fertilizer (superphosphate production collapsed, potash could no longer be imported from Germany, and nitrate of soda was diverted to explosives) and rising costs for labour, implements, and transport. Moreover, bread prices had long been sensitive – in 1789 a price surge had coincided with the storming of the Bastille – and from 1915 the authorities held them at a little above the pre-war level, empowering the prefects to requisition grain and flour for the civil population. As meat, dairy, and potato prices remained unregulated, the consequence was a producer exodus from cereals and a fall in the sown area. In 1918 an increase in the prices offered for wheat would check this trend, but until then domestic production plummeted while submarine warfare and bad harvests across the northern hemisphere inhibited imports.[228]

In 1917 matters came to a head. Maurice Long, the Minister of Food Supply, told the Chamber of Deputies Budget Commission on 10 October that bread supply was 'particularly agonizing'. He had faced 'an extremely critical and tense situation', the Paris granaries falling to one day's supply (compared with a norm of fifteen) and the army's to one week's. Even after the harvest had been gathered in, farmers had delayed marketing their crops in the hope of a price rise, and he had had to scrabble for emergency shipments from the Americas at the expense of supplies needed for armaments. He had increased reserves in Paris (where major strikes in the aircraft industry were in prospect), but at the cost of lowering army stocks to two days.[229] The British Cabinet learned that according to Clémentel France faced the danger of 'a food revolution . . . and she would go out of the war'; in retrospect the commerce minister commented that 'France no longer lived from day to day, but from hour to hour . . .'[230] Fortunately Clemenceau's government, as usual, acted vigorously. Flour mills came under state supervision, and extraction rates, which had already gone up from 70–72 per cent before the war to 85 per cent, now rose to the point where almost everything was milled. A bread ration card was introduced in Paris from February 1918 and in the rest of the country from June, and the daily allocation reduced to 14 ounces for adults in active occupations, monthly consumption falling from 650,000 tons in 1915–17 to 430,000.[231] While foreign observers noted fewer patisseries were available, during the summer the authorities imposed three meatless days a week and restrictions on hotel and restaurant menus, nearly all frozen meat imports being directed to the army.

The government still needed foreign supplies. In 1917 France imported nearly 17 million quintals of wheat (5.5 million from the US), and in 1918 12 million (over 9 million coming in roughly equal amounts from America and Argentina). The USA became its main supplier of flour, oats, and sugar, and sent large quantities of meat.[232] Hence the French were as nervous as the British when the North American winter threatened grain shipments, which André Tardieu (the French commissioner-general in Washington) warned were down to a third of the planned level. Clemenceau joined the appeal to Woodrow Wilson by the three Allied prime ministers on 31 January, and followed up with a message of his own.[233] In view of the shortfall in American deliveries the agriculture minister, Victor Boret, wanted an 80,000–100,000 reduction in the army's horses, to conserve supplies of oats, saying the choice lay between feeding the horses and feeding civilians, but Pétain categorically refused, saying that 'if the number of horses is allowed to fall below 700,000 it will be impossible to continue the war'. Hence, on the eve of the German offensive the French put first priority on their army's mobility and gambled on civilian grain stocks, and in March the alarm subsided, Boret now estimating that supplies were just about adequate.[234] The 1918 harvest eased conditions in France as well as Britain, though by 1919 the authorities would have faced renewed shortages.

The abiding impression is that the French were leading a hand-to-mouth existence. By securing an early lead in industrial conversion, they concentrated their restricted industrial resources on finished weapons and on munitions production, but at the price of depending on their maritime partners not just for steel, coal, and finance but also for food. A similar fragility characterized the French railways, for here too the country had been living on its capital and could do so no longer. Before the war this had been one of the finest systems in the world, divided into six regional networks. It became pivotal to the logistics of three great armies as well as to France's industrial effort. By 1918 the railway companies had replaced the rolling stock lost during the German invasion and their workforce was only slightly less than at the start of the war, having been broadened to include foreigners, returned soldiers, and women (whose proportion of the total rose to 35 per cent), although it included too few skilled drivers. But traffic had risen by 50 per cent, and its distribution was skewed, unbalancing a system that lacked transversal connections and was based on trunk lines radiating from the capital.[235]

None the less, the railways coped until a series of shocks in the winter of 1917/18. One was a dangerous fall in coal stocks:

Table 6.5. Coal stocks of French railway networks, 1916–18 (tons)[236]

	1916	1917	1918
East:	132,892	155,748	77,411
Paris–Lyons–Marseilles	190,000	68,000	84,000
Paris–Orléans	302,548	137,400	16,450

Hence Pétain faced not only shortages of petrol for his army's lorries and oats for its horses, but also coal for its railways. He warned the government in February that the eastern network was down to four days' supply.[237] The problem was also one of quality, as the imported wartime coal was rougher and of lesser calorific value than the fuels supplied in peacetime by the northern and Belgian fields. Partly for this reason the number of breakdowns due to malfunctioning locomotive furnaces rose from 671 on 1 July 1913 to 2,051 by 1 January 1918. France constructed no wagons or locomotives during the war, and for three years repairs were postponed or neglected, but a day of reckoning was approaching and the number of wagons immobilized for repair rose from 17,275 on 1 January 1917 to 27,443 on 1 January 1918 and 38,561 by 1 January 1919. The numbers of locomotives held for repairs rose to 873 in July 1918 and 1,007 in November (or nearly 10 per cent of the total). This enfeebled system had to carry men and supplies to Italy after Caporetto; then to cope with the Ludendorff offensives, which not only entailed intensive rail movements but also severed key trunk lines; and finally to transport men and materials for the AEF, via poorly equipped peripheral routes. Another sign of strain was the increase in 'refused' trains, i.e. formed up but then cancelled for lack of a locomotive. Before the war such instances were almost unknown, but they numbered 163 in July 1918 and 272 in October, while locomotive breakdowns, averaging 150 a month before the war, were running at more than three times that level by July to November 1918.[238]

That the system was seizing up was well understood. Ministers discussed 'the current crisis of the railway networks' on 15 July and

16 September in the War Committee, and the Chamber of Deputies Public Works Commission heard testimony from the company directors. The high command was well aware of the problem.[239] Yet the railways' condition was of vital concern to the Allies as a whole, for sustaining the French industrial effort, the Western Front, and the Italian theatre, and by autumn 1918 they appeared to be slipping into the sort of breakdown that had paralysed Russia and Austria-Hungary. The French railway crisis, in other words, would present yet another major claim on the Allies' resources if they had to continue through a fifth winter of war.

ITALY

Although Italy's population of 35.6 million in 1913 was similar to France's 39.8 million, its gross domestic product was one third less. It was evenly matched against Austria-Hungary, whose population of 50.6 million was 42 per cent larger but whose gross domestic product was only about 10 per cent bigger. In terms of output per head, Italy and Austria-Hungary were both second-division powers rather than ranking alongside France, Britain, Germany, and America, and Italy's war expenditure totalled about one half of France's and one third of Britain's.[240] None the less, and although Italy began its economic mobilization more gradually than the other belligerents, by 1917–18 its war-related expenditure had reached 33.1 per cent of GDP, and some of the armaments figures were impressive.[241] Italy, France, and Britain were on a par in monthly rifle output; during the war Italy produced 37,029 machine guns to Britain's 240,000, but 16,000 artillery pieces to Britain's 21,000; 70 million shells to Britain's 195 million; and 12,021 aircraft to Britain's 55,000. Though outclassed, it was not overwhelmingly so.[242] And despite the rout that followed Caporetto, when Italy's losses included some 3,000 artillery pieces, by August 1918 it had replaced them with more modern substitutes and largely through its own efforts.[243] The most significant foreign contribution was British gas masks, and Britain also sent 2,000 Lewis and 400 Vickers machine guns. But the 481 French and 170 British artillery pieces delivered to Italy after Caporetto were few compared with domestic output.[244] Over the war as a whole Italian industry supplied the Italian army with nearly all its small arms, guns, shells, and motor vehicles, and in 1918 orders were placed with Fiat to manufacture light tanks of Renault design. As elsewhere, new industries sprang up to manufacture poison gas and aircraft, the latter often built under French licence, although Fiat developed the A12 aero-engine that eventually accounted for over 50 per cent of Italy's output.[245]

Labour and plant were not particularly pressing constraints. By 1918 the workforce in the war-related industries had risen to over a million, 100,000 of them in aircraft. Italy made less use than France of foreign and colonial workers, but tens of thousands of women were recruited and 441,000 men returned to industry and transport from the army, many continuing to work under military discipline.[246] Strikes were forbidden, and safety requirements relaxed. As for buildings and equipment, unlike in France the country's dominant manufacturing region lay well behind the lines, in the Milan/Genoa/Turin industrial triangle, which in 1918 contained over 80 per cent of the employees of the 'auxiliary' firms placed under war ministry authority. Italy's problem was more its industrial weakness to begin with, particularly in chemicals and engineering. The authorities responded by pouring money into the private sector, and indeed deliberately used the war to build up capacity at the taxpayer's expense.[247] The main conduit was the Under-Secretariat for Arms and Munitions (originally in the war ministry and later a ministry in its own right), headed by General Alfred Dallolio from 1915 until in 1918 a corruption scandal removed him. Within this department an Industrial Mobilization Office directed procurement and the industrial war effort, in liaison with Regional Mobilization Committees. Industrialists were represented both at the centre and in the localities and Dallolio plied them with lucrative contracts and tax waivers. When Italy introduced a war profits tax, business could pass the bill back to the state by charging higher prices. Hence the assets, workers, and reported profits of the key concerns grew spectacularly. Ansaldo, which made 46 per cent of Italy's artillery pieces during the war (importing its machine tools from the US), expanded its labour force from 6,000 to 56,000; Caproni came from nowhere to become the biggest aircraft producer; and Fiat became the principal vehicle builder and aero-engine manufacturer, quadrupling its motor vehicle output and multiplying its workforce ten times. The profitability of limited companies in iron and steel rose from 6.3 to 16.55 per cent; in chemicals from 8.02 to 15.39 per cent; and in automobiles from 8.2 to 30.51 per cent.[248]

Although much of the extra income went into building capacity, it financed acquisitions that consolidated the new producers' dominance.

Even more than France, however, Italy depended on imported raw materials. Output in many of its industries peaked in 1917 and dipped in the final year,[249] the reasons including cuts in Allied coal and steel shipments, which in turn reflected the difficulties in the British coalfields, losses to the Mediterranean U-boats, and the shipping shortage. British iron and steel deliveries were 188,279 tons in 1916 and 208,907 in 1917 but 126,878 in January–July 1918.[250] Italy's steel output moved correspondingly from 934,000 tons in 1913 to 1,332,000 in 1917 but 933,000 in 1918;[251] its automobile output from 6,670 vehicles in 1913 to 25,280 in 1917 but 22,230 in 1918. Other categories affected included shells, railway wagons, and shipbuilding, and the situation caused the British government 'considerable anxiety'.[252] The coal problem was even more damaging: during the war imported British coal multiplied in price, while its volume fell from 9.647 million tons in 1913 to 8.625 million in 1914, 5.788 million in 1915, 5.71 million in 1916, 4.14 million in 1917, and 1.952 million in January–July 1918. In the first years of the war British deliveries ran at half the pre-war level, and subsequently they fell further.[253]

The Italians tried to alleviate their situation by doubling hydro-electric power generation and increasing the output of electrically produced steel. But blast furnaces had to be extinguished, hospitals were deprived of heating, and goods traffic was confined to what was needed for the war. Indeed the railway network was a prime victim, as little of it had yet been electrified, and many locomotives had to burn olive wood.[254] In order to cut their shipping losses, the Allies planned for Britain to supply more coal to France in return for France sending more to Italy, but the French coal was of inferior quality, and increased the numbers of locomotive breakdowns. Whereas railway traffic had risen from an average of 7 billion ton-kilometres in 1910–14 to over 11 billion in 1916, it fell to 10.6 billion in 1917 and 10.3 billion in 1918. A bottleneck developed round Genoa, the port for Italy's manufacturing districts: in February 1918 the chief executive warned that he could load only half the number of wagons per day that were needed, goods were piling up on the quays, and the head of Ansaldo complained about 'the total paralysis of transports through insufficient allocation of wagons'. Although the problem was partly incompetence by the transport minister, who was forced to resign, it seemed that in spring 1918 Italy was sliding into a vicious circle of fuel and transport paralysis.[255]

The Italian leaders' top economic priority in the 1917/18 winter, however, was food. Unlike France, Italy had not been self-sufficient even before the war, importing nearly 20 per cent of its wheat consumption. Much came from the Black Sea coasts of Russia and Romania, and dried up when Turkey became a belligerent. On the other hand Italy's home production dropped off. Conscription bore more heavily on the rural south and islands and on agriculture rather than industry, only 163,090 of the 603,985 soldiers released by September 1918 going back to farming. Fertilizer use declined, and manure supplies diminished because nearly half the cattle herd was requisitioned. Remittances from Italians who had emigrated or moved to the towns dried up, and prices for agricultural produce rose more slowly than the overall index. The authorities attempted to requisition grain at a fixed price, further discouraging cereal production. From a pre-war average of 49.3 million quintals, wheat output fell to 46.4 million in 1915, 48.0 in 1916, and 38.1 in 1917, before recovering to 49.4 million in 1918. For all cereals average annual production fell from 100 in 1909–13 to 93 in 1915–18; for vegetables from 100 to 90; and for animal products from 100 to 95. Hence there was a perceptible drop in output, especially in 1917, and both the sown area and yields per hectare diminished.[256]

Several factors exacerbated matters. Many peasants in uniform enjoyed better subsistence than as civilians (even though less well fed than other Allied armies). At the end of the war soldiers' rations were 136 kilos of meat per annum against civilians' 15, and a kilo of bread per day, against civilians' 100–400 g. Indeed, TB and malaria caused the civilian death rate to soar during the war, and excess fatalities may have been over 500,000. A second factor was a drop in imports, those of wheat dipping in 1917, which as everywhere was the dangerous year, not least because 400,000 tons of cereals were abandoned after Caporetto.[257] The shortage was partly one of fodder for army horses, the British Cabinet agreeing to divert American oats to Italy after Lloyd George urged that 'in the existing strategical position of the Italian army, the maintenance of their transport was of great importance to the whole alliance'.[258] But still more the question was of human consumption, as supplies in Italy's industrial cities were low even before the disappointing 1917 harvest, and bread riots broke out that summer in

Milan and Turin. In December the slow formation of a convoy bearing Indian wheat from Port Said endangered the supplies to the army.[259] When Orlando joined Clemenceau and Lloyd George on 31 January 1918 in appealing to Woodrow Wilson, the Italian leaders were close to panic. Nitti, the finance minister, told the Allies that the queues outside the bakeries endangered public order: as of 10 January Palermo and Calabria had lacked bread for days and Rome was without pasta. Crespi, the minister responsible for food supply, thought revolution imminent unless matters improved, and Nitti told the press that Italy depended on Allied food supplies and would face 'revolutionary consequences' if it broke with them by leaving the war. Hence ministers prioritized food over all else in allocating shipping, despite Dallolio's protests that raw materials for armaments were curtailed.[260] By summer 1918 Italy too had turned the corner and food supplies were more secure,[261] but munitions output had suffered and the country's precarious economic situation contributed to both its leaders' reluctance to take the offensive and their determination to stay with the Allies.

This determination was reinforced by financial dependence. Like the British and French, the Italians found it easier to handle domestic than external war finance. After spring 1916, when Austria-Hungary's Trentino offensive threatened to cut off Italy's armies, Paolo Boselli's government agreed to much higher arms expenditure, and Dallolio – who put equipping the armed forces above financial considerations – was given his head. His methods did deliver the goods, but expensively. Yet also in part because Italy had entered of its own volition, the pro-war consensus was shallow, and governments hesitated to raise tax rates. The upshot was that taxes paid for somewhat more of Italy's war costs than of France's – possibly 23 per cent – but like everyone else its government drew primarily on borrowing, and its stance became increasingly inflationary. Increased spending after the 1916 emergency caused a big increase in floating debt; after Caporetto the Bank of Italy feared a run on the banks and expanded the money supply by 11 per cent in ten days.[262] Although the government issued five national loans during the war, the largest in early 1918, it had to offer increasingly generous terms, and a large proportion of the debt was taken by the commercial banks, which used it as collateral to issue loans.[263] The money supply rose faster than in Britain, France, or Germany, and especially in the second half of the conflict: in 1914 by 23 per cent, 1915 by 31 per cent,

1916 by 27 per cent, 1917 by 59 per cent, and 1918 by 38 per cent. By 1918 the note circulation had gone up from 100 to 443 since 1914, and the retail price index also rose faster than elsewhere (from 100 in 1914 to 134 in 1916, 189 in 1917, and 264 in 1918). The authorities met their needs, but they created preconditions for post-war chaos.[264]

Some 29 per cent of the cost of the war, however, was represented by external borrowing.[265] Like the French, by borrowing abroad the Italians gained access to resources unavailable at home. They too had a deficit on merchandise trade before 1914, compensating by receipts from tourism and emigrant remittances, both of which withered after war began. During the war exports as a percentage of GDP halved, but imports rose, first from Britain and then from the US, which in 1918 accounted on its own for 43.4 per cent.[266] Italy could continue only by means of foreign borrowing, which by October 1918 totalled 13,116 million lire: 4,403 million owed to America and 8,713 million to Britain. By this stage, in fact, Italy's and Britain's foreign debts were comparable.[267] Yet whereas previous Italian governments had tried to limit indebtedness, Nitti, as finance minister from October 1917, pressed for more, in order to increase the Allies' stake in assisting the country's post-war reconstruction.[268] One reason help was needed was the currency, which had been allowed to float freely and was drifting downwards: in contrast to the French franc, the lire fell in relation to all the major Allied currencies from 100.5 per ounce of gold in 1914 to 149.4 in 1918. In 1918 Nitti introduced exchange controls, but the depreciation was checked only by a series of agreements whereby America, Britain, and France undertook to support the currency and finance Italy's imports, the US Treasury paying for purchases of South American meat and Chilean nitrates and the hire of neutral shipping.[269] In the war's final months, Italy achieved greater security of supply at the cost of greater dependence on London and on Washington. None the less, and in contrast with the French, it had no pressing economic need to end the war in 1918.

Although this account has considered the major allies individually, their coalition should be seen as a bloc: and as one that also aided smaller partners such as the Belgians, Greeks, Serbs, and Arabs. Before 1917 Tsarist Russia had also benefited financially, although providing little economic assistance in return and – in a remarkable but very costly achievement – largely manufacturing its own armaments.[270] The alliance benefited from having four centres of arms production, Italy more or less providing for its own needs and Britain and France supplying the AEF and the smaller countries while American war production came on stream. Underpinning these accomplishments were British shipping and American and British Empire food and raw materials. In 1917–18 an array of inter-Allied committees came into being – the AMTC, the IACWPF, the Munitions and Food Councils, and the programme committees for each commodity, on top of the existing blockade machinery – but they were the visible expression of a more fundamental willingness by governments to take a collective view and pursue mutual interests through co-operation.[271] This Allied willingness contrasted sharply with the weakness of collective arrangements among the Central Powers, who not only had fewer resources to begin with but also by 1918 were suffering disastrous contractions in their agricultural and armaments output. However great the Allies' difficulties, they were at least managed difficulties, whereas those of their opponents were spiralling out of control.

BULGARIA

Bulgaria's collapse started the process that led to the ceasefires, and much of the reason for it lay in a supply crisis. In 1910 three quarters of Bulgaria's people were rural. The peasant proprietor was the norm and large estates were rare, as were fertilizers and even metal (as opposed to wooden) ploughs. Among the few infrastructural assets were the state-owned coal mines at Pernik, and a sketchy railway network linking Sofia and other interior cities to the Black Sea. Industry was mainly confined to building and food processing: Bulgaria could make explosives, cartridges, and grenades, but had to import anything more complex.[272] When it joined the Central Powers it had drawn down its equipment stocks in the Balkan wars, and not yet replenished them. The army was short of rifles, coats, and boots, and one third of its artillery not yet quick-firing. The government expected a short war and was unprepared for a long one. None the less, the 1915 and 1916 campaigns went well enough, and left the Bulgarians occupying the Morava valley from Serbia and part of the Dobrudja from Romania. But in the south they provided most of the defenders for a frontier hundreds of miles long in Albania and Macedonia, much of it in remote and mountainous terrain. To supply it they had to requisition one quarter of Bulgarian agriculture's carts and draught animals. Cereal output fell from 26 million quintals in 1912 to 18 million in 1916, 17 million in 1917, and 12 million in 1918; potato and fodder output by even more.[273] Because of labour and raw material shortages, by late 1916 only 60 per cent of factories were still working. Bulgaria also faced a transport crisis. The army used the railways intensively, locomotives running twice as many kilometres per year as in peacetime, and freight cars six times more. Overuse and neglect of maintenance produced the usual deterioration, and by the end of the war 41 per cent of locomotives were unfit for operation.[274] By this stage Bulgaria, like wide tracts of Eastern Europe, was reverting to a pattern of all but autarkic local sub-economies.

State policy exacerbated the situation. Bulgaria had little private wealth that it could access via borrowing or taxation, and the government financed most of its expenditure by printing money. The mechanism was borrowing from the National Bank, where the government's indebtedness rose more than sixfold, enabling the note circulation to expand from 226,515 million leva in 1914 to 2,298,619 million in 1918. Retail prices, as measured by the cost in Sofia of a selection of necessities, rose from 100 in 1914 to 200 in 1916, 505 in early 1918, and 847 after the bad harvest later in that year. Supply became a constant issue of political contention, and the opposition parties belaboured Radoslavov's government, which adopted a succession of expedients. In 1915 it created the Central Committee for Public Welfare to control the distribution and price of food, replacing it in 1916 by the Central Committee for Economic and Social Welfare, which had broader powers and included the main political parties but confessed to parliament its ineffectiveness. Finally in 1917–18 both civilian and military supply came under the Directorate of Economic and Social Welfare, which soldiers ran as a branch of the General Staff. These organizations banned food exports, 'diluted' bread with maize, and extended rationing, but they neither halted the deterioration nor addressed one of the public's biggest grievances: the illegal export of goods by German and Austro-Hungarian soldiers, who were better paid than their Bulgarian counterparts and outbid them in the black market.[275]

Symptomatic of this trend was that Bulgaria became the Central

Powers' main provider of tobacco, output more than doubling between 1915 and 1918 while that of food crops fell. But overall the balance-of-payments deficit widened. After Bulgaria entered the war the German government allocated it a monthly credit of 50 million levas: an arrangement that parliament had never approved and which enabled the authorities to accumulate 1,500 millions of unconstitutional debt.[276] At the end of 1917, however, the Germans unilaterally suspended it, and from April 1918 they cut off supplies to the army. On the other hand the Directorate of Economic and Social Welfare was responsible for supplying the German and Austrian forces as well as the Bulgarian ones, and in some months it supplied much more to its allies' troops than to its own. Germany and Austria-Hungary contributed to Bulgaria's destabilization, and all but halted their assistance when its economy was entering free fall.[277]

Already in the 1916/17 winter thousands had died from hunger, but now worse loomed: too little seed corn was left over from the 1917 harvest, and that of 1918 was smaller still. By 1918 the peasants were hoarding or destroying their remaining surpluses, as the prices they received were so inadequate, and the American grain provided after the armistice may alone have forestalled mass starvation. The bread ration of 500 grams per day until December 1917 fell to 200 grams per day for the rich (who were thought to have easier access to the black market) and 400 for the poor, while meatless days by 1917 were three per week, and urban wages fell far behind price increases. In January 1918 demonstrations against the war and the low bread ration began, and spread through the country after May in the form of a 'women's revolt'; by now many prefects had no food reserves left.[278] Nor was the army spared, supply failure being probably the most important single reason why once the Allies broke through the crust of the Bulgarian defences, their opponents melted away.

OTTOMAN EMPIRE

If the Bulgarians reached the brink of mass starvation, the Ottoman Empire crossed it. By 1918 Turkey's economy, like Bulgaria's, was on the skids, but it was minimally equipped to fight a modern war anyway. Most of the statistics are unreliable – itself a commentary on the

Ottoman administration – but the empire's gross domestic product in 1914 is estimated to have been one quarter of Austria-Hungary's and one tenth of Germany's; during the war it diminished by a further 30–40 per cent. The modern sector of the economy was tiny: only 35,000 workers before the war in industrial establishments employing more than ten people.[279] The one domestic coalfield, at Eregli on the Black Sea, produced 826,000 tons of coal in 1913. But when the Russians advanced along the Black Sea coast in 1916 they bombarded it and sank the transport ships: by 1917–18 its output averaged less than a quarter of what it had been before the war.[280] Turkey had one cannon and small-arms plant, one powder plant, and one shell and bullet plant, all in the Constantinople area; and it lacked the capacity for expansion, as it had no significant steel or chemicals production. During the war the army's modern weapons came largely from Germany. After the Central Powers overran Serbia in 1915 they could run through-trains to Constantinople, but beyond that point Ottoman communications were rudimentary. Not only did the empire lack telegraph lines and paved roads, but the rail network in 1914 totalled only 5,759 kilometres: that of British India, with a 50 per cent greater area, was ten times longer (55,000).[281] Moreover, the railways had been built by British, French, and German enterprise, with a multiplicity of gauges and rolling stock. The Berlin–Constantinople–Baghdad railway, started with German capital before 1914, still had 825 kilometres to be completed when the war began, and over 600 when it ended. Two links north-west of Aleppo through the Taurus and Amanus mountains were not completed until 1917–18.[282] After the Eregli coal was lost, the locomotives still running in Syria were often forced to burn wood, leading to massive deforestation.[283] Even without the Arab raids against it, the narrow-gauge Hejaz railway was a flimsy lifeline.

The Ottoman financial infrastructure was still less developed. The empire's nineteenth-century efforts at industrialization had led it into de facto receivership and financial control by its European creditors, represented on the Ottoman Public Debt Administration (OPDA). In 1914 nearly half government revenue was being used to service external debts. It was harder for the Ottomans to tap into a taxable surplus than the Western countries, and like Bulgaria they lacked a prosperous middle class that could subscribe to war loans. They issued only one (in May 1918), and its take-up was disappointing. Although tax rates were raised and new taxes introduced, government revenue fell during the first years of the war, probably because of economic contraction as well as increased evasion of the tithe (a levy on agricultural production) by farmers.[284] Meanwhile, between 1914–15 and 1917–18 expenditure more than doubled, and the deficit yawned wider. To diminish it the Turks resorted to foreign borrowing. In good measure they were sealed off: by 1916 foreign trade was one fifth of its pre-war volume and overwhelmingly conducted with the other Central Powers, to whom Turkey supplied cotton, wool, oil, and leather, as well as chrome, which was important to Krupp.[285] None the less, much of the material delivered by Turkey's allies was on credit, the equivalent of 56 million Turkish lira being borrowed from Germany and 8.5 million from Austria-Hungary. The money was used to back what became the principal source of government liquidity. The pre-war currency had been mainly coin, but the Germans pressed the Ottomans to expand the note circulation and they did so, using the OPDA as the issuing agency and German treasury bonds as collateral.[286] This procedure cost the German government nearly 4 billion marks, on top of half a billion to pay for war materials and a further half-billion for imports such as coal and grain and the credits to the Baghdad railway. If the Turks had been reluctant to issue paper currency, however, once having started they proceeded with abandon, the circulation rising from 8 million lira in 1915 to 46 million in 1916, 124 million in 1917, and 161 million in 1918. Bad money drove out good, and coin was hoarded and became difficult to find at all.[287]

The predictable consequence was inflation. In 1918 the finance minister, Djavid Bey, admitted prices had risen nearly twenty times. An index of key consumer goods in Constantinople rose from 100 in 1914 to 130 in 1915, 212 in 1916, 1,465 in 1917, and 2,205 in 1918.[288] Such an increase far exceeded anything in Western and Central Europe, and resembled conditions in revolutionary Russia. It reflected not just the depreciation of the currency but also deeper problems. Before the war the empire had imported little food except to feed Constantinople, whose overseas suppliers were now cut off. The railway from Central Anatolia could not compensate, and even with rationing the capital remained vulnerable. In the provinces conditions were worse. Perhaps a million people in the north-east died from starvation and disease as a result of the Armenian genocide in 1915 and the flight by Moslem peasantry when the Russians invaded in 1916. Famine may have killed another half-million in Syria, the Lebanon, and Palestine, which had been a grain surplus region. By 1918 the draught animals available for agriculture had more than halved; locusts struck in 1915 and drought in 1917, and wheat production fell from 100 in 1914 to 80 in 1915, 73 in 1916, 64 in 1917, and 62 in 1918.[289] Nor could the food be moved. The Allies blockaded the Mediterranean ports, and roads were few. The Arab Revolt exacerbated the problem, as did German troop reinforcements in Palestine in 1917–18, which competed for supplies. The Turkish army requisitioned crops but failed to extract enough, and as farmers had little incentive to part with grain in return for depreciating paper currency, barter took over. In the winter of 1917/18 starvation and cannibalism were reported on the coast, and Damascus received thousands of desperate refugees. By the end of March the city was down to its last reserves, and its governor had to bribe the neighbouring Druze chieftains with gold to release their grain stocks. Nor, although the authorities tried to shield the armed forces, could the commanders feed their men. The Ottomans' manifest inability to solve the crisis (and the involvement of many officials in grain speculation) discredited their authority and incited Arab nationalism. In September 1918, like the Allies in the Balkans, Allenby's troops advanced into a humanitarian crisis.

AUSTRIA-HUNGARY

Germany's remaining ally, Austria-Hungary, appeared stronger. Research on pre-war economic development has revealed it as an unheralded success story. Its 1913 gross domestic product was two fifths of Germany's, and it was the world's sixth-largest iron and steel producer.[290] Yet it mobilized its economy less intensively than did others, and even so by 1918 faced runaway inflation, industrial and transport collapse, and looming famine. Its situation was worse than in any of the Allied countries, and even had it not broken up in late October it could hardly have continued fighting for much longer.

This was the more ironic in that in contrast to other belligerents Austria-Hungary was winding down its war effort. In 1918 it signed peace treaties with Russia and Romania. As Serbia and Montenegro had been defeated and occupied, the only major active military commitment was against Italy, and for long periods even that front was quiet. Austria-Hungary's military spending in constant prices fell from 7,382 million crowns in 1914–15 to 6,191 million in 1915–16, 4,536 million in 1916–17, and 4,039 million in 1917–18: as a proportion of its diminishing GDP from 30.2 to 26.8, 22.2, and 17.2 per cent. Even at its maximum the percentage was lower than in Western Europe, and financially, at any rate, Austria-Hungary fought on the cheap.[291] None the less, the war proved more than it could afford.

The Habsburg Monarchy's only direct sea access was via the Adriatic, which the Allies closed off. It could import from Germany and from neutrals adjoining German territory. Before the war it ran a large trade deficit, which after 1914 expanded as it sucked in food and raw materials. Germany gave assistance, but inter-governmental agreements and institutions as developed on the Allied side were lacking, and the Austrians financed much of their importing through loans from a German banking consortium.[292] Additionally the Berlin government provided credits worth 100 million marks a month, but in 1918 it first cut them and then stopped them altogether.[293] The Austrians also obtained credits from the neutrals – Sweden, the Netherlands, and Denmark – and to pay for imports they ran down their central bank's gold reserves. None the less, they had to tighten up trade controls, and from 1917 all import contracts required official approval. In 1917–18 the balance of payments deficit narrowed because imports shrank substantially, although this meant the Dual Monarchy was drawing less on foreign resources to compensate for its intensifying domestic shortages. Overall, external borrowing's contribution to the Austro-Hungarian economy was between one seventh and one half of its contribution to Britain's.[294]

Austria-Hungary would have to finance its war effort primarily from its own resources. But here too it was handicapped. Really it was two states linked by a hyphen in the shape of the Habsburg dynasty. Decisions required interminable prior discussion and accommodation between the centre and the two halves, and partly for this reason taxation covered hardly any military spending. The Austrian government did introduce a war profits tax, but the Hungarian one made virtually no changes to taxation policy, for fear of antagonizing the country's farmers. By 1917–18 revenue was covering less than one fifth of spending and did not even service the interest payments on government debt; the authorities therefore had to borrow more in order to continue borrowing.[295]

War loans did not fill the gap. Eight were floated (the last in June 1918) and their proceeds divided between the two halves, but the lack of depth in the investment market meant increasingly that only the banks took them up.[296] If this was inflationary, it was as nothing compared to the authorities' use of credits from the central bank, in exchange for state obligations, which directly expanded the note issue. From mid-1917 in the Austrian half (in the Hungarian one restraints were stronger) this process was getting out of control, in a mechanism that contemporaries well understood and the Viennese press condemned.[297] In July 1916–June 1917 the two governments borrowed 4.5 million crowns from the central bank; in July 1917–June 1918, 9 million; and in July–October 1918 over 15 million. Between late 1917 and late 1918 the note circulation doubled, and the Austrian cost of living index rose from 129 in December 1914 to 829 by December 1917 and 1,589 by October 1918, which was far worse than in Germany, France, or Britain.[298]

Inflation was only one element in the Dual Monarchy's predicament. Its industry supported its fighting forces adequately at first, but only until 1917. Before the war the Austrian half was home to the state-owned Vienna arsenal and a sophisticated private armaments sector, including companies such as Škoda for artillery and Steyr for small arms, while at Trieste a yard built dreadnought battleships. In 1914 skilled workers were drafted and raw material supplies and railway traffic disrupted as right across Europe, but in 1915–16 industry, fuelled by war ministry orders, recovered. Under German pressure, the authorities introduced the 'Centrals' (*Zentralen*): privately owned and financed joint-stock companies for most branches of industry that obtained and distributed raw materials and set prices and production quotas. Most of the commodities required were furnished from the Monarchy's continuing modest imports or from home sources. During the war the army's stock of artillery pieces nearly trebled, from 3,666 to 9,585. The production effort, led by Škoda and the Vienna arsenal, rose from a monthly total of seventy-five finished guns in the first half of 1915 to 288 in the first half of 1917, but in the first half of 1918 it fell to 128.[299] Shell production followed a similar course, rising from 375,000 a month in 1914 to 1,476,000 in the first half of 1917, but in the second half of 1918 falling to 400,000.

In 1917 the arms industry reached its peak, but it also overstretched itself. As part of the German-led Hindenburg Programme, the common war ministry in autumn 1916 had set ambitious new targets, including more than doubling munitions output, but was obliged to scale them down. The Joint Council of Ministers learned that shortages of transport, labour, explosives, coal, and non-ferrous metals had all got in the way:[300] the war ministry had thrown 454 million crowns into a programme that the finance ministers could not afford and industry could not implement. The aircraft industry (much of it German-owned) continued to expand, its output rising from 1,272 aircraft in 1917 to 1,989 in 1918, although even this barely made good losses. Machine-gun output also rallied in 1918, because it gained top priority. But overall arms production declined from 1917, in this mirroring output as a whole: gross domestic product by 1918 was only 61.5 per cent of the 1913 level.[301] There was less of everything to go round, and armaments shared in the stringency.

Falling labour productivity contributed to this situation, but the most serious pressure point was raw materials. War production entered a vicious circle of decline, embracing steel, coal, and transport. Thus Austria-Hungary's crude steel production, averaging 100 in 1912–13, fell to 80 in 1914 and rose to 98 in 1915 and 126 in 1916, but fell to 106.5 in 1917 and 68.5 in 1918.[302] Most of the steel industry was located in the Austrian half, especially in the Czech and Alpine German provinces. Its technological prowess was comparable with anywhere in Europe, and in peacetime it supplied most of the Monarchy's needs, while drawing most of its raw materials from the home territories. Hence it proved relatively invulnerable to the Allied blockade: low-grade manganese and tungsten ore mines were opened up, although copper was more of a problem and the authorities had to replace copper locomotive fireboxes by inferior iron ones, as well as extracting the metal from roofs, lightning conductors, and church bells.[303] Iron ore production, on the other hand, exceeded pre-war levels by 1916, but by 1918 had halved and was a good example of the damage done by the Hindenburg Programme, during which preparing new seams was neglected in the interests of maximum extraction from existing ones. During 1917 steel output per worker fell by a third, indicating that the Hindenburg Programme levels had not been sustainable. With the winter weather from November the industry was paralysed, as transport congestion hampered fuel supplies and plants were shut down. From now on it had constant difficulties in meeting military orders. By this stage the military authorities had become deeply involved in managing steel production, establishing inter-ministerial *Eisenkommissionen* ('iron commissions') to set priorities in conjunction with business representatives. But soon all they could do was repeatedly set pauses in placing new orders, to allow the companies to cope with overstrain caused first by the Hindenburg Programme and then by fuel and transport shortfalls.[304]

By 1918 the armaments industry was short of coal. In peacetime Austria-Hungary produced enough coal and lignite (mostly in the Austrian half) to satisfy over 90 per cent of its needs, but little of the coking coal needed for iron ore smelting, which had to be imported. After 1914 output declined, and consumption fell in pace with it.[305] Here again an unsustainable burst of activity accompanied the Hindenburg Programme, and although in 1917 the army released miners they were less well fed than before the war and their productivity was lower, while Germany, whose Upper Silesian coalfield had been the main peacetime source of imports, delivered barely half of what it had done previously.[306] All the same, on production grounds the Monarchy's situation should not have been desperate. Characteristically, however, the Austrian half increased supplies to the Hungarian half (the latter claiming that without enough coal it could not meet its commitments to feed the army) and Cisleithania, where most of the war industries lay, had to bear the burden of adjustment. In the 1916/17 winter, armaments got priority because of the Hindenburg Programme but households went short and reserves ran down.[307] In the 1917/18 winter conditions were worse, though even now coal was accumulating at the pitheads and the crucial problem was the railways' inability to move it; indeed some stockpiles were lost through spontaneous combustion. Numbers of wagons at the major coalfields had been declining since 1914, and some had only half the normal numbers available. The Vienna city authorities introduced a coal ration card, but could not deliver the quantities it promised and had to forbid sales to consumers: in February 1918 the Steyr small-arms works needed 100 wagonloads of coal per week but received only forty-five. Hence while households went unheated, flour mills, steel works, and armaments plants were on short time or shut. Although conditions eased in the spring, by September shortages had reappeared and the prospects for the coming winter were worse than ever.[308]

A transport breakdown therefore exacerbated the fuel shortage. Although the Danube brought food supplies from Romania, the Dual Monarchy – unlike Germany – had few big inland waterways, and railways were critical. Trunk lines from Vienna radiated northwards to the coalfields, the industrial centres, and the Russian front; southwards to the Balkan and Italian theatres; eastwards to Hungary; and westwards to the Alpine provinces and Bavaria. Most of the system was state-owned, and in 1914 the common war ministry took over the Austrian part, Hungary grudgingly accepting central control over its rolling stock. Subsequently the railways' experience mirrored that of the economy as a whole: a generally successful performance to early 1917, and thereafter steepening decline. None the less, the later problems originated from earlier developments: many skilled men called up in 1914 never returned; steel fireboxes replaced copper; the quality of coal deteriorated; and oil shortages meant less frequent lubrication (or resort to olive oil), while timber scarcity meant less frequent replacement of sleepers. By 1918 one third more coal was needed to travel a given distance than in peacetime. At the core of the crisis, however, was a shortage of rolling stock. The Austrian half increased its locomotive and wagon production, but not by enough to meet demand. The Hungarian network received more than its entitlement, but a bigger culprit was the army, which hoarded wagons as living quarters, offices, and even hospitals.[309] By the end of the war 30 per cent of the Hungarian locomotives needed repair, and in Austria conditions were worse. In August 1917 the war ministry's Transport Directorate warned of the danger that coal shortages might soon have 'near catastrophic consequences'.[310] That November the autumn cold, following the extra demands of the Caporetto campaign, indeed provided the final ingredient needed to jam the system. The problem centred on the Nordbahn, the artery linking Vienna to the Polish front and the northern coalfields. On it, the authorities suspended movements of everything except food. Lack of coal slowed down the railways, and meant they could move still less of the fuel, which in turn shut down the steel production needed to make wagons and locomotives. The numbers of stationary wagons on the

Nordbahn rose from 3,556 to 8,294 between August and October 1918, and by the end of the war one tenth of all goods wagons were blocked. The authorities had no answer to the problem, and if the war had continued conditions would have further deteriorated.[311]

Industrial and transport difficulties eventually impinged on military operations. In 1918 armaments firms received 62 per cent less coal than in 1917.[312] By September 1918 the army had only half the Italians' numbers of medium and heavy guns, and although machine gun output was adequate, that of rifles needed to be doubled.[313] In textiles, the Allied blockade really hit home, as Austria-Hungary had enough sheep but could not substitute for imported cotton, and the dualist system again exacerbated the problem, as Hungary received more fibre than its textile industry justified. By 1918 industry was producing less than half the footwear that the army needed, one quarter of the pairs of trousers, and one sixth of the numbers of coats; in some units only the troops in the line had uniforms, and many lacked serviceable boots or even a change of underwear. The stock of field blankets fell from 9.5 million in 1914 to 2.7 million in 1917 and 232,000 in October 1918: yet these were essential in mountain conditions and the coming winter threatened mass freezing and frostbite.[314]

Yet the most damaging internal deadlock (and the gravest of all of Austria-Hungary's economic crises) centred on food. On the eve of the war the Dual Monarchy was normally self-sufficient in wheat and rye, the more urbanized and industrialized Austrian half running a deficit that a Hungarian surplus offset. Hungary exported about a quarter of its harvest, almost all to Austria, but during the war output in both halves declined. Wheat and rye production fell from 90.2 million quintals in 1914 to 79.4 million in 1915, 62.9 million in 1916, 62.2 million in 1917, and 52.7 million in 1918, the gap between these figures and consumption requirements widening each year. The weather contributed: drought in 1917, and a cold and wet June in 1918. But more directly related to the war was Russia's 1914 invasion of Galicia, which had grown about a third of the Austrian crop, and even after the Austrians regained the province much of it was abandoned or devastated. In non-invaded regions the same factors as all over Europe were at work: above all loss of manpower, but also a lack of draught animals (in the Hungarian half down by a third by 1915), and of imported fertilizers, machinery, fuel, and seed corn. In contrast, the demand for food if anything rose, for the usual reason that many of the millions called up were (at least initially) better fed in the army than they had been outside it. The Allied blockade cut off the Dual Monarchy from alternative sources, and the war entry of Romania (in 1914–16 Austria-Hungary's biggest external supplier) was a particularly serious blow, for although grain was extracted from occupied Romania it never approached the quantities purchased while the two countries remained at peace.[315]

The grain shortage was therefore real enough, but political decisions worsened it. The Austrian authorities introduced bread rationing as early as 1915, and followed up with a system of maximum prices, but as these bore down hardest on cereals and were most lenient for animal products they created an incentive to switch to fodder crops. Whereas the Austrians were guided by consumer rather than producer interests, in the Hungarian half the opposite applied, and a widening price differential between the two deterred Hungarian farmers from selling to Austria and encouraged them instead to grow fodder for their own livestock. Although prices were higher in the Hungarian half, the permitted rations were larger, and it remained legal to buy more than the ration quota, while 'self-providers' – a very widely defined category of farmers and agricultural businesses – were protected from the requisitioning adopted in both halves as the war progressed. The Austrian leaders protested unavailingly to Budapest, which was determined to protect its farmers and to maintain high rations in order to pacify its non-Magyar minorities. The Hungarians rejected any obligation to Austrian civilians, although from 1916 onwards they undertook to meet the whole of the army's needs, which might seem to ease the burden on Austria but also practically eliminated the surplus available to it when its own production had halved and no outside source could compensate. Thus Hungary's cereal exports to Austria, which had averaged 13.298 million Meterzentner in 1909–13, fell to 10.212 in 1914, 5.194 in 1915, 0.464 in 1916, and 0.277 in 1917, and deliveries of fruit, vegetables, and animal products fell equally drastically.[316]

For the remainder of the war the Austrian half lived from hand to mouth during the run-up to each harvest. Emperor Karl was greatly concerned, but like Franz Joseph he held back from issuing orders to Budapest. Machinery was introduced to control imports and exports, and although it helped to eke out supplies the Austrians' demands for a single food policy for the whole Monarchy were unavailing. The

Gemeinsamer Volksernährungsausschuss (Common National Subsistence Committee), created in February 1917, was a co-ordinating body without executive powers, and the spring 1917 discussions in the Joint Council of Ministers were gloomy but ineffectual, the Austrian government warning that it faced 'an imminent subsistence catastrophe'. Both the troops' and the Austrian civilians' rations were cut, but an agreement with the Germans that allowed Austria-Hungary a larger share of the grain from occupied Romania tided things over until the harvest.[317]

This was only a dress rehearsal. As in all the belligerents, the 1917 crop fell below expectations and by the autumn the authorities faced a still larger deficit. The common war minister reported that the army had virtually no reserves. But by now Hungary's surplus had also disappeared, and Budapest called in 50,000 troops to aid with requisitioning against, in some places, armed resistance.[318] The best prospect seemed the Ukraine, with which Austria-Hungary and Germany concluded a separate peace in February 1918 in exchange for the promise of at least 1 million metric tons of grain by August. But this hope too proved false: supplies came late and erratically and were primarily eggs, sugar, and animal products rather than bread grain, which counted for only 9,700 of the 43,000 wagons of food eventually delivered (and only 4,800 of which went to Austria-Hungary rather than Germany).[319] The authorities' remaining recourse was to cut the bread ration, which they did in January and in June (in the latter case halving it), both times unleashing strikes and protests. Even so, parts of the Austrian half went for weeks without flour and bread, at a time when all foodstuffs were short. Austrian herds of cattle and pigs had fallen respectively by 20 per cent and 60 per cent, milk supplies to Vienna were only a quarter of the 1915 level, and in the summer the city's meat supplies broke down and Hungary and Germany rushed in emergency aid. The 1918 harvest brought little relief, as the Austrian government could no longer afford to subsidize the bread price and in August doubled it. The financial and the subsistence crises had interlocked.[320]

Austria-Hungary's food crisis was more serious than anything on the Allied side. Deaths among Viennese women rose from 15,390 in 1913 to 20,816 in 1917 and 23,898 in 1918. A 1919 study by Viennese doctors found that starvation caused directly 7–11 per cent of civilian mortality and contributed to another 20–30 per cent, alongside diseases such as tuberculosis. By 1918 many were dying in their apartments or dropping in the streets, while armed gangs ransacked food trains in the suburbs.[321] In some of the provinces conditions were still worse, and by autumn 1918 the economy was fragmenting on ethnic lines – foreshadowing the political fragmentation that would follow – as Bohemia and Galicia prevented cereal shipments outside their borders. German observers saw food shortage as a major reason for the central authorities' loss of control over the subject nationalities,[322] but it also sharpened antagonism between the two halves of the Monarchy and strained relations with Berlin. Moreover, in return for the elusive Ukrainian grain, Austria-Hungary accepted Kiev's claim to the Polish-inhabited territory of Cholm, which so antagonized its own Poles as to render them uncontrollable except by coercion.[323] Yet coercion too was becoming impossible, as the economic crisis sapped the army's readiness. Not only could the army not feed its horses or fuel its trains and lorries, but its soldiers also suffered, their daily bread rations falling during the war from 700 to 250 grams, and the content being increasingly adulterated. The troops whose positions crumbled at Vittorio Veneto were hungry as well as cold. In 1917–18 the gap between cereal production and demand had been 14 million tons, but in 1918–19 it was expected to be 23 million, meaning that the domestic harvest would cover only eight months' instead of ten months' supply.[324] By spring 1919 Austria-Hungary's cities and industrial districts would simply run out of food, with no remedy apparent.

GERMANY

The evidence on the German war economy suggests that its position was little better. Its circumstances were not so dire, however, as to oblige Berlin to end the war when it did. Germany was less well placed than its enemies, but less far down the road to collapse than its allies. It did not, as of autumn 1918, face hyper-inflation, mass starvation, or the collapse of its fighting forces for lack of weapons. The effect of Allied pressure was cumulative and the country's difficulties were extremely serious, but it could have continued into the following spring, if not for much longer. This point is fundamental for a judgement of the circumstances that led to the end of the war, and will be examined more closely under the headings of finance, industry, and food. But the timing and the manner of the Central Powers' defeat (if not the defeat itself) were determined by political and morale factors.

Germany was Europe's manufacturing powerhouse. It had a very big economy and it spent a lot on the war. Its 1914 GDP was larger than Britain's and almost twice that of France:

Table 6.6. Gross domestic products, 1914 ($bn)[325]

Austria-Hungary	France	Germany	Italy	Russia	UK	US
100.5	138.7	244.3	91.3	257.7	226.4	511.6

None the less, although Germany's war expenditure was comparable to those of France and the US, it spent only two thirds as much as Britain.[326] Its economic mobilization was less intense, and, like Austria-Hungary's, it diminished in 1918. According to the most recent estimates, military spending rose from 3 per cent of GNP in 1913, to 14.9 per cent in 1914, 36.8 per cent in 1915, 37.3 per cent in 1916, and 56.7 per cent in 1917; but fell in the final year to 38.8 per cent. Not only was the percentage falling, but German national income (approximately equivalent to GDP) also fell, from 100 in 1913 to 90 in 1914, 81.1 in 1915, 75.8 in 1916, 73.5 in 1917, and 71 in 1918.[327] A sharp drop at the outset was not made good, and further deterioration followed. Whereas the British and American economies expanded during the war, Germany's followed a trajectory similar to France's, but without France's mid-war rally: though also without the French experience of invasion and devastation.

The outstanding difference between German and Allied economic conditions was the blockade. But even after the Allies declared a total blockade, Germany imported Norwegian pyrites, Swedish iron ore, Romanian oil, and food from Switzerland, Denmark, and Holland. Although the value of its exports collapsed from 1915 to barely a quarter of pre-war levels, its decline in imports was slower, falling (in constant prices) from 10.8 billion marks in 1913 to 8.5 in 1914, 5.9 in 1915, 6.4 in 1916, 4.2 in 1917, and 4.2 in 1918. Over the war as a whole its trade deficit averaged 5.6 per cent of net national product, and it represented a very useful supplement to domestic resources, albeit one that diminished in 1917–18 and was half the British figure of 11.3 per cent.[328] But Germany's ability to import was limited by its capacity to pay. The Allies had confiscated much of its merchant fleet and its overseas assets, and without exporting it could not earn foreign exchange. In the first half of the war it was able to deliver iron and steel, but in the second half all of its output of these goods was needed at home. Hence to finance its purchases Germany exported gold bullion – twice as much as Britain – and relied on short-term commercial credits.[329] A Dutch banking consortium lent repeatedly to a German one in 1916–18, and by the end of the war Germany owed 1,600 million gold marks to the Netherlands, as well as smaller amounts to Switzerland, Sweden, and Denmark.[330] Moreover, the Germans reduced import costs by manipulating the exchange rate in order to uphold the mark. Foreign currency transactions had to be cleared with the authorities and the government began appropriating private holdings of overseas assets. The mark depreciated more slowly in relation to the neutral currencies than the expansion of the money supply would have justified, and during the period of Austro-German military successes in 1917–18 it rose, suggesting the key influence on it was foreign assessments of Germany's chance of victory. Conversely, after Ludendorff's offensives faltered it tumbled,[331] and it ended the war at about half its 1914 value. As Britain, France, and Italy broadly maintained their currencies' exchange value until the armistice, this depreciation was a telling sign that the authorities were losing their grip. By 1918 not only were Germany's imports by volume less than a third of their pre-war level, but also their price was rising sharply. As the Reichsbank's gold reserves dwindled, Germany found it harder not only to secure its imports, but also to subsidize its allies, and in consequence Bulgaria, Austria-Hungary, and Turkey all felt the pinch.[332]

Most of Germany's war expenditure had to be financed from internal resources. In real terms this was a major disadvantage, though it simplified debt management and during the first half of the war the economy seemed up to the task. War-related spending (in current prices) rose from 6,936 million marks in 1 April 1914–31 March 1915 to 23,909 million in 1915–16, 24,739 million in 1916–17, 42,118 million in 1917–18, and 33,928 million in 1918–19.[333] The Reich Treasury shunted this expenditure into its 'extraordinary account', categorizing it as a long-term investment that it did not attempt to cover from current revenue. Tax yields covered non-war expenditure and serviced the debt on war loans, but not much more. Taking the Reich and state governments together, taxation covered 17.7 per cent of war-related expenditure in 1914–18, whereas the British figure was 22.9 per cent.[334] The difference was real, although less than contemporaries supposed, the German Treasury Secretary actually praising in the Reichstag the British taxpayer's 'heroism'.[335] In truth the British had been slow to respond to the conflict's fiscal demands but the Germans were even slower. Karl Helfferich, the first wartime Treasury Secretary, relaxed his department's monitoring of war expenditure – which as an 'extraordinary' item also largely escaped Reichstag scrutiny. The constitution permitted the Reich government to levy indirect taxes, but the authorities suspended customs tariffs in order to keep down import prices, and they hesitated to raise consumption taxes for fear of increasing working-class living costs. On the other hand direct taxes were a jealously guarded prerogative of the states, with whom the imperial government steered clear of conflict. Like the French, it hoped that post-war reparations would save it. In 1916 Helfferich belatedly introduced a war profits tax, but it generated much less than in Britain. Other devices such as a sales tax on coal were re-absorbed by the state in the form of higher payments for military contracts.[336] Although revenue quadrupled from 2.1 billion marks in 1916 to 8 billion in 1917 and 7.4 billion in 1918, much of this growth was due to inflation, and most of Germany's war would have to be paid for by other methods.[337]

Chief among these methods were the nine war loans (*Kriegsanleihen*) issued at six-monthly intervals from September 1914 to September 1918. In total they yielded almost exactly 100,000 million marks, or more than half Germany's war spending.[338] The authorities had not expected such success, but promoted the loans with a fanfare of publicity, including posters, speeches, and wooden statues of Hindenburg in town squares, to which subscribers hammered in nails: the Reichsbank used 100,000 sales agents.[339] The loans offered a rate of return of approximately 5 per cent and were redeemable after ten years, so money placed in them risked both falling behind inflation and being lost altogether if Germany were beaten. None the less, millions of middle-class and farming investors (and increasingly working-class ones too) gambled their savings on a German victory.[340] Down to 1916, demand was strong and the war loans' proceeds helped consolidate Reich debt because they comfortably exceeded the authorities' short-term liabilities. The turning point came in September 1916, with the disappointing outcome of the fifth issue, mirroring the downturn in Germany's military fortunes over that summer. Thereafter inflation eroded the loans' attractiveness, and anxiety over Germany's military prospects made demand more volatile: the eighth loan, in March 1918, was the most successful yet, but the ninth, in September, the least. But the trend was for the proceeds to fall further and further behind the growth of floating debt.[341]

If a first warning signal was the depreciation of the mark, and a second the weakening demand for *Kriegsanleihen*, a third was accelerated growth in the money supply. To cover the gap between expenditure and revenue the government deposited short-term liabilities with the Reichsbank in return for currency, thus facilitating (once the requirement for note convertibility for gold was dropped) a prodigious expansion in the note issue. The monetary base rose from 100 in 1913 to 131 in 1914 and 165 in 1915 before leaping to 220 in 1916, 343 in 1917, and 604 in 1918. The rate of debt monetization hovered round 15 per cent for most of the war, but in 1918 it rose to 18 per cent: in other words, more spending was being covered by printing money.[342] It was unsurprising that prices also rose: indeed, whereas the government had previously censored the word 'inflation', Helfferich's successor, Roedern, himself used it in the Reichstag in April 1918, and said reducing it would have to wait until peace. Wholesale prices increased by 2 per cent in 1914, 14 per cent in 1915, 14 per cent in 1916, and 19 per cent in 1917, though at a slower pace of 9 per cent in 1918, probably because the velocity of monetary circulation slowed and Germans saved more.[343] In August 1918 the government also took direct action to uphold the exchange value of the currency and to bear down on prices. The resulting conjuncture has been described as one of 'suppressed inflation'. A monetary 'overhang' of liquidity could (and would) generate more dramatic price increases once the wartime controls were lifted: the Reichsbank president was anxious about the huge floating debt, and the public were starting to sell off old war loans to purchase new ones. After Germany appealed for a ceasefire, in October–November there was a run on the banks.[344] But although the authorities knew inflation was taking root and monetary stability was imperilled, financial considerations did not compel them to stop when they did.

Nor was Germany unable to produce more armaments. On the contrary, it appears to have manufactured more in many major weapons categories than did any other power, and to have satisfied until the end most of the needs of a very large army. In 1917 Germany produced 115,200 machine guns compared with Britain's 79,700; and in 1916 it produced 3 million rifles to Britain's 1 million; although also in 1917 Britain overtook Germany in explosives output (with 186,000 tons to 144,000).[345] Not only did German industry produce the artillery and infantry equipment needed for trench fighting, but it also shared in the innovations of the final phase: although Germany opted not to mass-produce tanks, it delivered the gas shells for Bruchmüller's bombardments and came not far behind Britain and France in aircraft. According to retrospective staff assessments, the German army's most serious problem in spring 1918 was mobility – it had too few horses and lorries – and, secondly, too few heavy guns. But it had big stockpiles of all shell categories and more than enough machine guns and field artillery, while during 1918 production of helmets, *Minenwerfer* ('mine throwers'), and hand weapons could actually be reduced.[346] Arguably Germany was overproducing rifles and trench warfare items to an extent that wasted labour and raw materials that were needed elsewhere,[347] but it also had a surplus for its partners. During the war it supplied to Austria-Hungary 447 aircraft, 182,747 rifles, 100,000 helmets, 632 machine guns, 4,135 artillery pieces, and 1,827,700 shells; to Bulgaria 230,000 rifles, 1,950 machine guns, and 403 artillery pieces; and to Turkey 559 cannon, 557,000 rifles, 1,600 light and heavy machine guns, 200,000 shrapnel shells, 930 million cartridges, 1,000 vehicles, and 300 aircraft.[348]

Germany's war production history fell into two main phases, before and after summer 1916. Like the other belligerents it had made few preparations for a long conflict, and the German army like the French ran short of shells in autumn 1914, but German industry responded quickly. Much was owed to the husbanding of raw materials through the system headed by the Kriegsrohstoffabteilung (KRA) or War Raw Materials Department at the war ministry. The initiative that led to it came from Walther Rathenau and his colleagues at the Allgemeine Elektrizitäts Gesellschaft (AEG). The KRA was a planning and statistical agency that commissioned prospecting for raw materials on Germany's home territories, and efforts to devise substitutes. It left purchasing and distribution of raw materials in each branch of industry to *Kriegsroh-stoffgesellschaften* (war raw material associations) that were normally joint-stock companies, supplied with initial capital by the member firms and staffed by businessmen. The government guaranteed their debts and placed representatives on their boards, and the KRA could vet their decisions, so the system was state-supervised, but private ownership and profit remained intact.[349] For the first two years the war ministry continued as in peacetime to oversee arms production, placing contracts with a widening circle of firms and at first allowing generous profits. For a while this arrangement worked well enough, monthly output of field guns rising from 100 to 480 in the year after December 1914, and of their shells from 1.2 million to 2.1 million.[350] Explosives were the bottleneck. Substitutes were needed for imported cotton and nitrates, but the Haber–Bosch process of 'fixing' nitrogen from the atmosphere gradually built up enough nitrates for the army, though not enough for agricultural fertilizer: a good example of how military needs took precedence. Monthly powder production rose from 1,200 tons in August 1914 to 6,000 in July 1916, and copper – one of the metals in shortest supply – was imported from Scandinavia, extracted from pots and pans, or replaced by iron, of which there was plenty. Similarly manganese, which was used to harden steel, was simply added in smaller quantities, though at the price of heavier shell casings that contained less explosive and wore out the gun barrels faster.[351] By these devices Germany kept ahead until 1916, but the troops fighting in the Battle of the Somme faced an unprecedented weight of Allied firepower, and for the first time found their own artillery support inadequate.[352]

The Hindenburg/Ludendorff team that took over in the summer 1916 crisis believed Germany needed a reorganization comparable to that achieved under the munitions ministry in Britain: to meet a renewed Allied offensive in 1917 output must rise drastically. In addition they knew that German heavy industry now felt the war ministry curtailed profits too severely and was too sympathetic to organized labour. The outcome was the most radical change in economic policy in the course of the war, a package of new departures known collectively as the Hindenburg Programme. At its core were new weapons targets set by the OHL and the government for May 1917, Hindenburg demanding a doubling of munitions and a tripling of artillery and machine gun output irrespective of the cost, which would include a crash programme of new investment.[353] Purchasing was transferred to a new Weapons and Munitions Procurement Agency (Waffen und Munitions Beschaffungsamt, or WUMBA), which, along with the KRA and labour supply, came under another new agency, the War Bureau (Kriegsamt), thus hiving off from the war ministry many of its economic responsibilities. A new committee was created to close down smaller factories, and new legislation – the Patriotic Auxiliary Service Law – established the principle of compulsory labour service for all men aged 17–60, although in practice during 1917 many more men were released from the army for war industry work than moved in the other direction.[354]

The Hindenburg Programme overstrained the rest of the economy without hitting the spring 1917 targets. In February Ludendorff ordered work to cease on all factories that could not be finished by May. In September Hindenburg complained the targets had twice been cut, and still not reached.[355] None the less, output did increase, though as much despite the programme as because of it, for the war ministry had planned a more balanced expansion anyway. Powder production rose to 9,200 tons in July 1917 – 50 per cent more than a year earlier – against a target of 12,000 by May. In April 1918 it reached 12,000 tons and in October 1918 14,315, and by now had become less of a constraint than was steel.[356] Similarly field gun output averaged 2,000 pieces per month during 1918, and in June, with 2,489, reached its highest level of the war, while monthly machine-gun production rose from 1,608 in July 1916 to 8,676 in July 1917 and 11,354 in August 1918.[357] Among newer technologies, aircraft received special attention. The Hindenburg Programme set a target of 1,000 per month by March 1918, but for most of 1917 output remained below this level. In June 1917 Ludendorff proposed doubling it to 2,000 aircraft (and 2,500 aero-engines) by January 1918, in view of American entry into the war, although the objective eventually set for the 'Amerika Programme' was 1,600 aircraft (and 1,800 engines). It was fortunate that the American air peril turned out to be less than feared, as neither even of the revised targets was reached on time, although aircraft production did rise to 1,360 in March and 1,478 in July 1918, while that of engines reached 1,530 in April; and in October aircraft production hit 2,195, thus fulfilling Ludendorff's recommendation at the last moment.[358]

Germany's belated success in attaining the targets owed much to its steel industry, which before 1914 had been by far Europe's strongest.

Production dipped at the beginning of the war but recovered well, before faltering at the end:

Table 6.7. German crude steel output, 1914–18
(million metric tons)[359]

1914	1915	1916	1917	1918
13.81	12.28	14.87	15.50	14.09

At first the industry received adequate coal and coke, and Germany was not short of iron ore. It relied more on its low-grade Lorraine deposits to compensate for the loss of higher-grade Spanish imports, but it also shipped high-grade ore from Sweden and used more scrap. After the Hindenburg Programme iron and steel entered the KRA system, but unlike other metals were never subject to wholesale requisitioning. Steel was more difficult than pig iron production owing to shortages of non-ferrous metals, but by continuous searches for the latter and by economizing on their use, the German authorities met most of the army's needs. In the case of copper, for example, which was one of the most acute shortage materials, the artillery's workshops were using 10,000–12,000 tons per month at the start of the war but only 5,000 in mid-1917 despite vastly expanded production. Only at the end, in autumn 1918, did a lack of special steel for tool bits force a quarter of the machines at Krupp to stand idle.[360]

While weapons production belatedly responded to the stimulus, however, the burden of adjusting to shortages was passed on to the civilian sector. Thus, in the case of textiles, German army uniforms (unlike Austro-Hungarian ones) became shabby but adequate, whereas for civilians the authorities turned to substitutes such as nettles for cotton fibre.[361] Moreover, the whole of the economy suffered from two winter crises, resembling those in Austria-Hungary and the US. Before 1914 the state-owned German – and especially Prussian – railway system had been profitable and efficient, and for the first two years of fighting it matched up to requirements, but after 1916 it was less successful and gave the fighting fronts priority over the home economy. The Allied blockade closed the ports and reduced the traffic on the waterways; mobilization cut the railways' workforce at the same time as redirecting traffic flows.

Germany's western and eastern conquests expanded the network (the greatest frontier to frontier distance in 1913 was 1,300 kilometres, but by 1917 Antwerp to Bucharest measured 2,400), without a commensurate growth in rolling stock. By 1 April 1918 the total extent was 62,758 kilometres, of which 24,309 were in the occupied territories, and like other railway systems Germany's suffered from labour shortages, wear and tear from lack of lubricants and maintenance, and poorer coal. Whereas the railways used 32 million kilograms of lubricating oil in 1913, in 1918 they used only 16.7 million, and of inferior quality; 5.23 per cent of the track was replaced in 1914 but only 2.53 per cent in 1917; and before the war the proportion of stones in the coal delivered to the railways was 7–10 per cent but by 1917–18 it was 20–30 per cent. By 1919 almost 50 per cent more coal was needed to achieve the same level of railway output as in 1913, while the network's coal reserves fell from fifty-eight days in September 1916 to twelve a year later. Against this backdrop, the Hindenburg Programme entailed more coal and steel movements as well as construction traffic for new plants, in an icy winter that froze the canals. By February 1917 the system was in paralysis, with widespread jams and delays. In winter 1917/18 the problems returned, and more intensely. Whereas passenger services in 1916 were running at 70 per cent of peacetime levels, they were now only at 43 per cent; and although the total rolling stock increased during the war the proportion of locomotives being repaired rose from 19.3 per cent in 1915 to 29.5 per cent in 1916 and 33.7 per cent in 1918, so that the numbers actually available fell from 21,962 in 1913 to 19,223 in 1918.[362]

As usual, the transport crisis interlinked with one in energy. In 1914 Germany had been the world's largest coal producer after America and Britain as well as a major exporter. For the first two years coal supplies were adequate, but after the 1916/17 winter stringency increased.[363]

Table 6.8. German coal and lignite production, 1913–18
(million tons)[364]

	1913	1914	1915	1916	1917	1918
Coal	190	161	147	159	168	161
Lignite	87	84	88	94	96	101

Lignite went overwhelmingly to the chemical industry; but the army and navy, weapons production, heavy industry, and the railways all needed coal, whose output fell in 1914 and again in 1918. The railways' difficulties made the problem one of distribution as well as production. The OHL was well aware that transport and coal difficulties had delayed the implementation of the Hindenburg Programme, and pressure from business and the high command led the government to appoint an Imperial Coal Commissioner in February 1917, the Chancellor taking powers to requisition the fuel.[365] None the less, in August 1917 supplies to armaments and heavy industry were cut by 10 per cent to build up household coal for the winter, although in the autumn munitions became the priority, in order to rebuild stocks after the Flanders battles.[366] In September the Commissioner, Stutz, advised there was a 2-million-ton shortfall that could not be made good, the railway minister telling Hindenburg and Ludendorff that only 60 per cent of the wagons needed for coal transport were available. The OHL protested to the Chancellor about the vicious circle of transport and energy crises that was directly affecting the war industries; and asked the navy to reduce its coal reserves, while during the winter shortages of coal contributed to drops both in powder and in steel production, which in turn forced a cut in steel for the railways in order to sustain munitions output in the run-up to the 1918 offensives. On 18 March, Hindenburg and Ludendorff called for more locomotives and railway coal: 'In the last months the position of our war economy has become increasingly unfavourable.'[367]

This leads on to the connection between Germany's industrial predicament and the end of the war. The British Ministry of Munitions well understood the impact of the Hindenburg Programme, and the shortages of coal, lubricating oils, and non-ferrous metals.[368] Extraordinarily detailed monthly reports on the German and Austro-Hungarian economies were prepared in London by W. G. Max Müller, collating material from the enemy press and from intelligence sources. Max Müller highlighted the interlocking coal and railway crises in the winter of 1917/18, and noted their prominence in the Reichstag and the press. But he was a careful observer who also recorded the improvement in the following spring, doubted Germany's war industries were critically short of raw materials, and questioned whether blockade alone could ever bring the Reich to its knees.[369] Similarly, the secret history of the blockade prepared after the war for the British Cabinet Office concluded that Germany had enough iron ore and could eke out its non-ferrous metals, so that the blockade's greatest impact fell not on industry but on food.[370] On the German side, Hindenburg and Ludendorff monitored the economy closely and were well aware of the winter crisis, which was at its worst precisely during the deliberations that led to the 1918 offensives. Yet by the time they attacked, powder production was back on schedule and abundant quantities of the basic weapons had been accumulated. The most serious shortages were of transport and of soldiers, but partly because so many men had been released back into industry. Germany's economic circumstances, as well as peace with Russia, pointed to a last opportunity to attack as opposed to a defensive effort in which circumstances could only worsen.[371]

This is not to say, however, that Germany's industrial situation was so bad by September 1918 that it was obliged to seek an armistice.[372] In fact the KRA had decided by September 1917 that it must organize Germany's raw materials 'from the viewpoint of a possible duration of the war until the end of 1919'.[373] From March 1918 the winter crisis eased, powder and coal and steel production improved, and Ludendorff could release some manpower from munitions production, to the benefit in the first instance of the railways, clothing, and footwear. Even so, in summer 1918 munitions production was still on an upward trend: 'In May all raw material crises were overcome; the highest war economy productivity was again reached.'[374] Although replacing some categories of equipment lost during the autumn retreat proved difficult, until the end the Germans had plenty of machine guns and ammunition and the real sticking points were where they had always been: especially in transport and due to shortages of horses, rubber (for tyres), and petroleum. It was in this respect that Bulgaria's surrender dealt the heaviest blow to Germany's chances, threatening a loss of Romanian oil that would ground its aircraft and strand the U-boats.[375] None the less, the coal, steel, and railway industries could have operated into the spring of 1919. The condition of Germany's war economy does much to elucidate Ludendorff's gamble on the offensives, but less to explain his gamble on an armistice.

There remain the questions of agriculture and food. Although Germany's subsistence situation was less desperate than those of its allies, it was signally more difficult than those of its opponents, and for three reasons: the blockade, declining home production, and government policy. Pre-war Germany depended less on imports than did Britain, but was also less self-sufficient than Austria-Hungary or France. Continuing purchases from its neutral neighbours gave it a breathing space in the first two years, but then the screws were tightened and British agreements in 1916 with the Netherlands marked a milestone: London undertook to buy up surplus Dutch produce at guaranteed prices, but the Dutch agricultural co-operatives had to halve their German deliveries. The understanding was one of the reasons for Germany's decision for unrestricted submarine warfare, whose repercussions made matters much worse.[376] The U-boats cut the shipping entering neutral ports and by bringing in America made possible still tougher Allied trade arrangements with the neutral governments.[377] Germany's imports of bread grains fell from 240,750 tons in 1916 to 42,598 in 1918; of flour from 8,179 to 2,224 tons; of livestock from 356,229 animals to 130,643; of meat and meat products from 119,913 to 8,005 tons; of butter from 95,730 to 15,149 tons; and of fish from 435,770 to 88,642 tons. By 1918 its imports from Scandinavia were well below pre-war quantities.[378]

None of Germany's partners could help it much: on the contrary, it had to rush supplies to Austria in summer 1918, much to the German public's disgruntlement. The occupied territories were also a disappointment. Romania was the most valuable acquisition, although its 1917 and 1918 harvests were smaller than expected. Poland supplied the German army with 120,000 cattle in 1918 but had no spare grain. German public opinion centred its hopes on the Ukraine, whose prospects aroused much press speculation, but proved illusory. Although the government in Kiev promised 1.22 million tons of bread grains, the 1917 harvest had been poor and the peasants were loath to part with their produce. The Germans had neither consumer goods nor hard currency with which to purchase it, and as the Ukrainian government lacked the authority to requisition the crop, the Germans would have to do it themselves. The Rada government's resistance to orders to suspend land redistribution and start the spring sowing was one of the reasons why the Germans replaced it by the Skoropadsky regime, but this change made little difference.[379] By November 1918 the Ukraine had delivered

only 120,000 tons of cereals of all kinds, along with (to Germany)
40,000 cattle, 10,000 sheep, 29,000 tons of sugar, and 67 million eggs:
one for each member of the German population.

German agriculture proved unable to fill the gap.

Table 6.9. German agricultural production, 1913–18
(million tons)[380]

	1913	1917	1918
Rye	12.13	6.98	8.01
Wheat	4.42	2.23	2.4
Oats	9.5	3.63	4.68
Potatoes	52.85	34.41	29.47

Even though the cereal crop recovered in 1918, by comparison with
1913 it was down by 34 per cent for rye, 45.7 per cent for wheat, and
51 per cent for oats. And if arable production nearly halved, Germany's
livestock herds also contracted. Pig numbers fell between 1914 and
1918 from 25 million to 6 million, and cattle numbers from 22 million
to 17 million, average weights of pigs and cattle halved, and milk output per cow fell by 30 per cent. The overall agricultural production
index fell from 100 in 1913 to 89 in 1914, 85 in 1915, 65 in 1916, 60
in 1917, and 60 again in 1918.[381]

The reasons were partly common to all the Continental countries
and partly specific to Germany. In 1913 about 10 million worked in
agriculture, of whom 3.4 million were men aged 16–50.[382] Two fifths of
the male agricultural workforce were called up, and in Westphalia
40 per cent were still doing military service in July 1918, although a
third of them were released to help with the harvest.[383] During the war
women ran two thirds of the country's farms. They were helped by
other women (some from the cities), temporarily released soldiers,
youths, and prisoners of war: by 1918 up to 900,000 POWs (mainly
Russians on the big eastern estates), although their productivity was
low and generally the new and more diverse labour force was too small
and inexperienced.[384] It also lacked draught animals, as the army called
up over 1 million horses during the war and those remaining were
poorly fed, as a shrinking oat harvest was drawn down for human

consumption. By 1918 daily rations for horses were down to 1.5 kilograms.[385] The blockade exacerbated the problems. British and American farm machinery was no longer available and the existing stock was halted by lack of fuel, or could not be repaired if it broke down. By 1918 lack of paraffin for lamps cut daily working hours during the winter from fourteen to eight.[386] But the most serious shortage was of fertilizer. Before the war German arable yields had been among the highest in the world, and were linked to a quadrupling in fertilizer use since 1890. Germany used three times as much as France, and much of it was imported.[387] During the war, in contrast, the application of nitrates and phosphates approximately halved; that of potash, which was available domestically, increased, but not enough to compensate; and nitrogen from the Haber–Bosch process went mainly to explosives. After the war crop yields stayed low even after the farmers were demobilized, rising only later when nitrate and phosphate imports recovered. Between 1915 and 1918 yields fell from 2,350 to 1,720 kilograms per hectare for wheat; from 1,910 to 1,390 for rye; from 2,190 to 1,430 for oats; and from 15,860 to 10,800 for potatoes; but in addition the area under crops fell by 15 per cent.[388] Lower yields from a smaller cultivated area lay behind the decline in arable output, and this in turn led to fewer and thinner animals, producing less manure.

As supplies of foodstuffs shrank, demand for them increased, the millions of men doing military service enjoying a prior claim. Moreover, whereas in Britain the state could control much of the food chain from the time produce was purchased abroad, in Germany (as in Austria-Hungary) the government decided to leave the agricultural sector with enough to feed itself, and to set aside a portion as seed corn. In simple figures the armed services counted for about one sixth of the total population and the rural population one third, and if each of these maintained a similar calorific intake to peacetime the burden of adjusting to the loss of imports and of output would fall on everyone else.[389] Posed in these terms, the problem of maintaining civilian food supply was insoluble from the outset.

This being said, aspects of official policy intensified the hardship. Before the war the government had stockpiled little. In 1914–15, however, it moved quickly to create a War Grain Association (Kriegsgetreidegesellschaft – KGG), through which it took responsibility for purchasing and distributing wheat, also introducing a system of bread rationing with maximum prices. It adopted similar arrangements for potatoes,[390] and later for meat, fruit, and vegetables. On balance the system meant that arable prices were restricted whereas those for live-stock products were not, thus (as elsewhere) encouraging farmers to move towards the latter and diminish the crop acreage, whereas they resisted pressure to reduce their livestock herds. A further, and more serious, consequence was the early emergence of a black market as an alternative channel for selling produce, which soon undermined the official rationing system and in the latter part of the war became enormous.[391]

Government policy was incoherent. The German Empire was divided into twenty-six military districts, each under a Deputy Commanding General (DCG), who in wartime took on numerous decree powers, including over public order and food distribution. The DCGs tended to favour low prices whereas the rural local authorities would have pre-ferred to raise them.[392] To these conflicts at local level was added a multiplicity of some forty agencies established by the Reich authori-ties.[393] Most prominent was the Kriegsernährungsamt (War Food Office), created in May 1916 to act as a co-ordinating agency in place of the Ministry of the Interior, but it lacked the directive powers needed for the role until August 1917, when it became a full ministry. Weakness at the centre became more damaging as food grew scarcer. The 4 million inhabitants of the Ruhr conurbation, for example, could not be fed from the surrounding districts: they needed meat and potatoes from Germany's surplus regions, but it was more profitable for the farmers there to feed the potatoes to their livestock. Conversely, in 1916 Bavaria and Hesse did not supply Frankfurt with potatoes, and it had to resort to the much more distant Pomerania. Some of the tensions that existed in the Habsburg Monarchy between Austria and Hungary were mir-rored between the German states.[394]

According to the Eltzbacher commission of officials and academics, which published its findings in December 1914, 19 per cent of the calo-ries consumed in pre-war Germany had come from abroad, but the country ought (for example by switching from meat to more vegetable products) to be able to compensate for losing them. The report was a bestseller, but gravely over-optimistic.[395] As early as 1915 shortages emerged in cities such as Berlin, leading to queues and riots, but the turning point, as for the industrial economy, was the 1916/17 winter, and the precipitant was the failure of the potato crop. Pre-war per cap-ita potato consumption was much higher than in France and Britain, and became more crucial as bread grains ran down. But in 1916 heavy rains fell in late summer, followed by an early frost. The wet and cold ruined the crop, and yields were down on peacetime by nearly 60 per cent.[396] With too little coal to heat their homes, and much of industry coming to a standstill, Germans substituted turnips for bread and pota-toes, and the DCGs' monthly reports recorded the most serious blow yet to civilian optimism, as well as a wave of anti-Semitism against Jew-ish traders. The agony drew out into the spring, as the bread ration was cut and food supplies remained precarious until the 1917 harvest. A modern urban population relived the subsistence crises of pre-industrial times, and the 'turnip winter' permanently soured the public mood, even if conditions were never quite so bad again.[397]

During the 1917–18 harvest year, meat and fat rations continued to be reduced, and conditions for civilians remained thoroughly miserable. Even if depriving the population of meat and fats was nutritionally the most efficient procedure, it created a deep sense of grievance. Moreover, undernourishment contributed to the falling output in key industries such as coal that so alarmed the OHL: in November 1917 agricultural deliveries to the Ruhr were at record low levels.[398] As in Austria-Hungary, food shortages created a war of all against all, exacerbating tension between workers and wealthy, between town and countryside, and between west and east. Also as in Austria-Hungary, they undermined authority. The DCGs' surveys of civilian morale found that dearth in itself caused less discontent than did perceptions of inequity, but the fall in imports and in home production placed the distribution system under intolerable strain.[399] After the Hindenburg Programme more inequality was built into that system anyway, as 'heavy' workers in sectors such as armaments received preferential rations, or could supplement their diet by eating in workplace canteens.[400] Although the government intro-duced a national scale for meat rations, the ration in cities of over 50,000 was twice that in villages of less than 2,000, and Berlin in par-ticular was treated generously, to the vexation of the southern states.[401] For those without particular advantages, the weekly rations for a big city dweller in early 1918 were 3 kilos of potatoes, 1.5 of bread, 325 grams of sugar, 250 of meat and bones, and 62.5 of butter and fats.[402] But whereas the British authorities could deliver the rations that they allocated, the German ones could not, and the meagre official quantities were subject to reduction. The authorities admitted that the rations were inadequate for subsistence, and citizens who had no access to canteens or public soup kitchens (or to friends and relatives in the countryside) had little alternative to the black market, via which it has been estimated that up to one third of food supplies were being channelled by 1918,[403] even though its prices were soaring beyond family budgets. Big firms and the public authorities themselves resorted to black market purchases, as became open knowledge. For those at the end of the queue, the consequences meant sickness and worse. By 1917 the female death rate was 23 per cent higher than before the war, largely because of pneumonia and TB; in Germany's seventy largest cities 18,659 people died in 1914 but 32,737 in 1918 and the overall death rate was 37 per cent higher than in 1913, regressing to the level of 1901–5 and reversing a decade of public health progress.[404] According to a report from the Erzgebirge in May 1918, 'There is a degree of hardship here that I had never imagined. In districts with a predominantly industrial population ... they receive over ten days 1 kilogram of potatoes – that is two potatoes per day – very little bread, the people are gradually starving ... Crowds of beggars go through the agricultural villages ... There are very many cases of people falling dead in the street ...'[405]

In summer 1918 the authorities underwent another very nervous period before the belated gathering of the harvest. Research on Düsseldorf has shown that conditions were the most difficult since spring 1917.[406] In June the Reich flour ration was cut to 160 g per day, which was the lowest level yet,[407] and although food supply overall was less critical than in 1917 the bread shortage was worse. Indeed the government had known in the spring that grain stocks were inadequate to stretch until the harvest at current consumption rates,[408] but it had postponed action, perhaps hoping for an early victory or for help from the Ukraine, before cutting the ration drastically. By August the harvest enabled it to restore the ration to 200 grams, but the authorities' assessment was that they had had a narrow escape, with dangerously low bread and potato stocks in many cities and meat supply also problematic. The DCGs reported that public opinion, still seared by the memory of the 'turnip winter', feared worse ahead, and although the public had been willing to endure great hardships while they saw a chance of victory, once that chance was lost rapid demoralization would set in.[409] Max Müller, observing from London, made the same comment, summing up that Germany's meat supplies were much scarcer than in 1917, its food stocks lower than in any previous autumn, and if the war lasted another twelve months it would almost certainly face famine.[410] This is not to say that mass starvation was imminent when the Reich sued for an armistice; but as on the industrial front it faced disaster within a few months and the loss of its allies even before then. Even supplying the army was increasingly difficult, and the armistice appeal – which raised the possibility that the Ukraine garrison must be withdrawn and fed at home – exacerbated matters. Once the Allies' military success cracked the OHL's willingness to resist, internal developments soon made it impossible to carry on.

This chapter began with the United States and ended with Germany, the two alliances' lenders of last resort and economic backstops. By 1918 the former was in a far superior position. Closer examination underlines how vital American assistance was to the European Allies, even if the US contribution was less spectacular than a generation later. But it also brings out the European Allies' own strengths: theirs really was a coalition effort. Italy largely made good its losses after Caporetto; France manufactured most of the AEF's armaments and equipped the smaller countries; the British Empire not only provided for its own land and naval forces but also contributed shipping and finance and was preparing to overtake France as the Americans' main armourer. Among the Central Powers, Austria-Hungary manufactured most of its own weaponry, but Bulgaria and Turkey mainly contributed manpower, and in 1918, as America's assistance to its partners expanded, Germany's was cut back. Whether in finance, transport, or agriculture, the Central Powers' position was far less favourable. They had begun with smaller resources, which had further diminished. Yet in many ways both blocs adopted similar solutions to similar problems. Both relied heavily on borrowing (though more long-term in Germany, Britain, and the US); both overtaxed their railway networks, and both neglected agriculture, as well as civilian industries, in the interests of war production. By 1918 the resulting strains had produced a hierarchy: the United States and Britain best placed, France and Italy less so, Germany less so still, and Germany's partners desperate. Yet the victors had their own difficulties, and analysis of the prospects for a 1919 campaign underlines the complexity of the trends. During 1917 and 1918 one supply crisis after another had given the Allied leaders a roller coaster ride and underlined the precariousness of what seemed on paper to be an enormous preponderance. If the war continued even America risked overstretch, and for France all the trends were worsening. The war's multiple economic costs not only predisposed the Central Powers to seek an armistice but also predisposed their enemies to grant one. Before returning to the decision-making that ended the fighting, however, it is necessary to consider a final element in the compound making for Allied victory: the politics of the home fronts.

7

The Home Fronts:
Gender, Class, and Nation

Of all the problems which Governments had to handle during the Great War, the most delicate and most perilous were those arising on the home front . . .

David Lloyd George[1]

Whenever I think of the War today, it is not as summer but always as winter; always as cold and darkness and discomfort, and an intermittent warmth of exhilarating excitement which made us irrationally exultant in all three. Its perennial symbol for me is a candle stuck in the neck of a bottle, its tiny flame flickering in an ice-cold draught yet creating a miniature illusion of light against an opaque infinity of blackness.

Vera Brittain[2]

In 1918 the Central Powers were not only defeated militarily: they were also convulsed politically. Revolution overthrew the Hohenzollern monarchy, Austria-Hungary broke up, King Ferdinand of Bulgaria abdicated, and the Young Turk party left government and dissolved itself. Military defeat set the collapse in motion, but internal upheaval completed it. Yet when the war began it had been far from obvious that the Allies could better withstand a prolonged struggle. Italy was socially polarized, and the Catholic Church as well as the Left and liberal progressives opposed its intervention. Pre-1914 France had been riven by the Dreyfus Affair and over rearmament, while Britain had suffered vicious party strife, unprecedented labour unrest, the most militant women's suffrage campaign in Europe, and the threat of civil war in Ireland. Nevertheless – with Russia the glaring exception – the Allies outlasted their opponents, and liberal political systems proved more resilient than their authoritarian rivals. The emphasis here will be on the wellsprings of that resilience, on gender, the working-class and the Left, and nationalism and the Right, before concluding with leadership.

GENDER

Without co-operation from millions of women, neither side could have continued fighting. Most feminist organizations supported the war effort, including the Bund der Frauen (BDF) in Germany – with some 500,000 members – and Emmeline and Christabel Pankhurst's Women's Social and Political Union in Britain. The WSPU suspended its direct-action suffragist campaign, and in 1915 its leaders (in collaboration with Lloyd George as munitions minister) marched through London on behalf of 'Women's Right to Serve'. By 1917, 40 per cent of the British Expeditionary Force were married men,[3] and in Continental armies the ratio was higher. All over Europe women not only managed families but also took over businesses and farms or filled the jobs their partners had vacated. Their role in sustaining morale and patriotism was vital, and they directly supported the armed forces. The French army eventually employed some 30,000 women as nurses, and 90,000 more served via the French Red Cross; the German army employed 92,000.[4] In 1917–18 Britain, uniquely, set up uniformed women's auxiliary services under military discipline, and by the armistice the WAAC (Women's Auxiliary Army Corps), WRNS (Women's Royal Naval Service), and WRAF (Women's Royal Air Force) had between them over 90,000 members, undertaking everything from clerical work to driving, repairs, and signalling.[5]

Joffre acknowledged that without the women in the war factories France would have lost.[6] Asquith, the British Prime Minister from 1908 to 1916, and a notorious opponent of women's suffrage, now admitted in the Commons that 'Some of my friends may think ... my eyes ... at last have been opened to the truth';[7] the British Representation of the People Act of 1918 enfranchised women over the age of thirty (which balanced a simultaneous enfranchisement of working-class men, while excluding many of the munitions workers because they were too young and deliberately kept women as a minority of the electorate). In

September 1918 Woodrow Wilson urged the Senate to approve a constitutional amendment allowing women to vote in federal elections, on the
grounds that it was 'vitally essential to the successful prosecution of the
great war ... This war could not have been fought had it not been for
the services of the women ...', and although the votes for the measure
fell two short of the two thirds majority needed,[8] the Nineteenth Amendment became law in 1920. Allied and American propaganda claimed to
be defending women and families against a barbarism manifested in
the 1914 invasions, the sinking of the *Lusitania*, and the execution in
Belgium of the British nurse Edith Cavell for helping prisoners of war to
escape.[9] More prosaically, women received separation allowances. In
Britain up to 1.5 million service wives and several million children did
so, at a cost between 1914 and 1920 of £414.75m. By late 1915 in Germany 4 million families (and 11 million individuals) received similar
assistance, whose cost during the war totalled 4–4.5 billion marks.[10]
America was most munificent, its combination of allowances with combatant war-risk insurance giving many women higher incomes than in
peacetime.[11] But in Europe life on allowances was more straitened,
and in the second half of the conflict, when women might spend hours
each week in queues or struggling with black market prices, it got
harsher still.

In many ways women played similar roles on both sides, rather than
giving either an advantage. By 1917–18 many were writing 'letters of
lament' (as the Germans called them) to their spouses,[12] and thousands
protested for higher wages, better food, and peace. But still larger numbers did not, and in one crucial respect historians have seen the Central
Powers as disadvantaged: that of women's war employment.[13] This
issue had a major bearing on the growing exhaustion and labour shortage in all the belligerents, and on relations between governments and
male workers, for everywhere the female proportion of the workforce
rose to unprecedented levels – even in remote Australia, from 24 to
37 per cent.[14] In general, this phenomenon was temporary, and expected
to be such: in the 1920s women returned to pre-war participation ratios
across most sectors, like a tide subsiding after rising. But while the
phenomenon lasted, contemporaries were startled by its novelty, women
attaining a new visibility in public places – as tram conductresses or in
ticket offices – and in tasks of which they had previously been judged
incapable.

It is true that much of this applied in the Central Powers. In Austria-Hungary a million women entered the labour force, their numbers growing by 40 per cent.[15] After an early rise in female unemployment the metalworking and chemical industries expanded, drawing in women as they did so, although when Austro-Hungarian industry contracted in 1917–18 women's employment fell with it. Arms plants such as Steyr and Škoda increased the women in their workforces to 10 per cent; in Vienna the proportion rose from 31.5 per cent in 1913 to 53.4 per cent by 1918. But the big story was arms production in Lower Austria, round Baden and Wiener Neustadt. Here private firms clustered round two great state plants, the bigger of which, at Wöllersdorf, rose from 8,000 to over 30,000 employees, about half of them female. Many came from farms and textile mills in Bohemia but did not stay, worn down by fourteen-day stints of twelve-hour days in conditions of deafening noise, monotony, and danger. On 18 September 1918 an explosion in a fuse-making building killed 277 workers, incinerated as they crushed towards the exits. As much of the male workforce comprised soldiers under military discipline, women became the most militant element, striking successfully in 1917 for a shorter working week and in 1918 against ration cuts.[16] In the resourcing debates at the beginning of 1917 and 1918 the Austrian and Hungarian governments refused to release many men from agriculture and industry, and the scope for reinforcing the army by substituting women reached its political limits.[17]

In Germany too, at the outbreak of war, unemployment rose in traditional female sectors such as domestic service, clothing, and textiles. Women seeking work exceeded vacancies until 1916–17.[18] None the less, between 1913 and 1917 the numbers of women workers in the Berlin machinery industry trebled, from 29,000 to 101,000; in Ruhr metalworking they rose from 5 to 34 per cent; and in the steel giant Thyssen they attained one in three.[19] Nationally, the authorities estimated that by 1916 women in the iron and steel and engineering and machinery industries rose from 7 to 23 per cent; in the electrical industry from 24 to 55 per cent; and in chemicals from 11 to 77 per cent: the absolute numbers of women in engineering, chemicals, iron and steel, and mining climbing more than six times between 1913 and 1917, from 113,750 to 702,100. In armaments women reached three quarters of the workforce making shells and fuses and over half that making army vehicles;[20] in April 1918 they numbered 38 per cent of the Bavarian munitions workforce.[21] In the biggest arms firm, Krupp, which employed only 2,000–3,000 women before the war, the workforce by January 1918 was 28,000 women and 75,000 men.[22] Women's labour made possible the Bruchmüller bombardments.

And yet these figures fell short of aspirations. The German government was slow to make employing women a matter of policy, and when it did so the spur was to catch up with the British. In the 1916 discussions leading to the Hindenburg Programme, Hindenburg demanded a law requiring all able-bodied women to contribute: countless thousands of childless war wives were doing nothing useful while costing the state money, and those who did not work should not eat. The trade unions and women's organizations opposed the demand, and Bethmann Hollweg ruled that it was economically, morally, and socially objectionable, would infringe personal rights, and make little practical difference.[23] The government preferred to encourage further volunteering, entrusting the task to the Kriegsamt, the new agency headed by Wilhelm Groener that under the Hindenburg Programme took primary responsibility for war production. A ministerial meeting in November 1916 agreed 'to introduce with the greatest acceleration all requisite steps to replace men by women in all work domains', and the Kriegsamt established a Women's Department under Marie-Elisabeth Lüders (a prominent BDF member), with sub-agencies in each military district and an inspectorate responsible for over half a million women in 538 factories, its remit including health, workplace facilities, training, and generally removing barriers to women's work.[24] At the same time the army tried itself to employ more women in offices, clubs, and aerodromes in the *Etappengebiet* (staging region) behind the front line.

The results were disappointing. The female labour force did increase, but Lüders resigned in 1917 from impatience with lack of military co-operation. Although the OHL had backed the 1916 Auxiliary Service Law as a means of getting more men into the ranks, in fact by 1918 the number of men in war production had more than doubled, many employers dismissing their women employees once they could obtain more skilled male workers.[25] In June 1918 Hindenburg renewed his demand for compulsory labour service for women (and men up to sixty), arguing it would make it easier to discipline and raise the output from the male labour force.[26] But a meeting on 1 July between Chancellor Hertling and his department chiefs again concluded that such a step might do more harm than good, antagonizing the workforce for a gain of only 100,000 soldiers, and that employers still preferred to take on men. When government officials met representatives of heavy industry on 20 July, almost all the business spokesmen objected to taking on more women: they wanted to keep their skilled male workforce, with military backing for imposing discipline.[27]

One obstacle to recruitment was employers' opposition. But many women themselves were resistant. In Bavaria, businesses complained about high turnover, women finding the work not what they had expected and injurious to their health, or having to return to care for family members or gather the harvest. In particular, married women remained at or below one third of the female factory workforce, as they had before the war.[28] Although separation allowances were worth little enough, many women receiving them found it pointless, after deducting travel costs, to take employment: in contrast, in Hamburg home working for the army (such as sewing uniforms) almost doubled. None the less, the government rejected OHL demands to cancel allowances in order to force women into the factories, not least for fear of alienating the troops. In total, women's employment nationally expanded by 17 per cent between 1 July 1914 and 1 July 1918, which little exceeded the peacetime growth rate.[29] Much of the recruitment into war industries was offset by declines in domestic service and textiles, so that the female labour force relocated rather than greatly enlarging. Even this relocation was limited, only one quarter of the unemployed women in textiles finding positions elsewhere, and in 1917–18 the female workforce may actually have declined while its turnover became faster than ever.[30] Not only was the female workforce – in employers' opinion – of questionable value, but it also failed to release a continuing inflow of men into the army.

Many of these generalizations also applied to the victors, but the overall experience was more positive. In the US pre-war female employment was surprisingly low: in 1910, 24 per cent of women over sixteen worked for wages, most being young and single and withdrawing after marriage.[31] In addition, America came in too late to expand its female workforce as much as the European countries, although in 1917–18 the numbers of women in industry rose two and a half times to 1 million.[32] White women moved into armaments, chemicals, and consumer goods, operating lathes, driving cranes, becoming inspectors and streetcar conductresses; black women replaced them in textiles and domestic service. The aircraft industry expanded from 211 workers in 1914 to 27,000 by 1918, of whom over 6,000 were women; they also exceeded one fifth of the workforce in electrical machinery, optical goods, food, paper and printing, and motion picture equipment.[33] Female employees on the railroads rose by 70,000 in 1917–18, and over 10,000 women produced gas masks, often chosen for the role because they had men at the front. Jones and Lamson of Springfield, Massachusetts, a precision engineering firm that carried out the highly skilled manufacture of howitzer recoil mechanisms, trained and employed 100 women by 1918 in a workforce of over 700. Yet although these figures were substantial, they came largely from a redistribution of the existing labour force. In autumn 1918 the authorities began a campaign to urge non-working women into munitions plants, but the armistice intervened.[34]

Among the European Allies, Italy was the most hesitant, partly owing to conservatism about women's social role, and partly because male workers feared conscription, if replaced, for a war the socialists and trade unions abhorred. After Austria-Hungary's spring 1916 offensive Italy stepped up its war effort, and the women and juveniles employed by the state mobilization authority rose from 76,000 in December 1916 to 258,000 by August 1918, but these numbers remained smaller than elsewhere, as did the 22 per cent proportion of women in the total workforce.[35] Although the government urged firms to employ more women, it found them extremely reluctant: Fiat, for example, employing only a few hundred among a total in June 1918 of over 20,000. After legislation made it easier to use women at night and on feast days, employers became more willing, but especially in the South and Sicily women were reluctant to enter the plants, where conditions were extremely poor (not even toilets being provided) and male workers resented them. Although the government set up an inspectorate, it was ineffective and by 1918 absenteeism was rife and protests broke out among women workers in Milan and Brescia. Yet disciplining them was difficult, as if they were imprisoned their children became parentless.[36]

Women were most intensively mobilized in France and Britain, which were also the biggest Allied arms producers. France already had one of the highest female employment rates in the world before 1914, and a stronger tradition than in Britain and America of employing wives.[37] In 1914 it faced the emergency of invasion while its trade unions (much weaker than in Britain and Germany and frequently denied recognition) had their officials conscripted and their membership and dues income collapsed. The metalworkers' leader, Alphonse Merrheim, protested that substitution harmed women and meant 'sending men to the slaughter',[38] but few obstacles prevented authoritarian managements from transferring tasks traditionally accomplished by skilled male workers to more perfunctorily trained women operating machinery imported from the US. In so far as the armaments division at the war ministry (later a ministry in its own right) under the socialist Albert Thomas intervened, it was to accelerate the process, while seeking (unavailingly) to ameliorate working conditions. Although a bill was introduced for female conscription, it never passed the Senate:[39] none the less, a Chamber of Deputies resolution asked the government 'to utilise the feminine labour force to replace the military labour force wherever possible', and in 1916 Thomas confirmed this was official policy.[40] According to the factory inspectorate, the female labour force halved in 1914 but regained the pre-war total by 1916 and by early 1918 was 25 per cent above it: as a percentage of the industrial workforce women rose from 32 per cent in 1914 to 40 per cent by early 1918. In metallurgy the ratio increased from 5 to 25 per cent; in private munitions plants numbers rose by 288 per cent, and in state ones by 195 per cent.[41] In the Department of the Seine (i.e. Paris) women constituted almost one third of the munitions workforce in 1917–18, and in André Citroën's ultra-modern Javel works half.[42] They continued working in traditional sectors such as making uniforms but also entered new ones like the Metro.

French women workers tended to be older and therefore possibly steadier than in Britain, and to endure the conditions they needed to be. In 1914 health and safety requirements and restrictions on working hours were largely waived for the duration, and a typical workday ran from 7.00 a.m. to 6.45 p.m., most of the time spent standing, while shifts alternated between two weeks on days and two weeks on nights. Workshops were often cramped and poorly lit with unfenced machinery, and explosions killed more than 100 women in Paris alone. Discipline was severe, and friction with male workmates and with coarse and even violent foremen happened frequently.[43] Women earned only a half to two thirds of civilian male workers, although the gap did narrow, and in early 1917 Thomas introduced a minimum wage, but only after strikes by women workers in summer 1917 did legislation bring in the 'English week' of five and a half days. On the other hand, subsistence allowances were meant to do no more than supplement income, and were cut if a woman received unemployment compensation. This incentive structure may therefore have encouraged women's work more strongly than in Austria and Germany, and although employers complained as elsewhere about high turnover, many were very satisfied.

In Britain, Churchill, as munitions minister, addressed the House of Commons on 25 April 1918. He explained how the equipment losses in the 'Michael' offensive had already been more than replaced, despite the shipping shortage and despite – a key contrast with Germany – his having released over 100,000 skilled and semi-skilled men to the army during the last year. 'Of course, we have had at each stage in this process to replace these men by less physically efficient male substitutes and by women, both of whom, in most cases, have had to be trained', but rationalizing production had yielded 'immense economies and simplifications' and the 750,000 women working for the munitions ministry produced more than nine tenths of its shells. Their contribution was 'beyond all praise … they constituted today an additional reserve in labour-power without which we could not carry on'.[44]

Yet Britain had been slower than France and Germany to bring women into armaments manufacture, beginning after the BEF's 'shell scandal' in spring 1915 and accelerating the process after imposing conscription.[45] Before the war female employment had been lower than across the Channel, but as a percentage of the workforce women rose from 26.5 per cent in 1915–16 to 46.9 per cent in 1916–17 and 46.7 per cent in 1917–18. The big increases came as Britain settled down to a long war: 382,000 in July 1914–July 1915, but 563,000 in 1915–16, 511,000 in 1916–17, and 203,000 in 1917–18.[46] In January 1918 the total workforce in government plants and Ministry of Munitions 'controlled establishments' was 2,298,950, of whom 1,666,418 were men and 632,532 women: since July 1914 the men had risen by 31.9 per cent but the women by 515.8 per cent. In government establishments only, out of a total workforce of 278,009 men numbered 132,165 and women 145,844, whereas in 1914 the state plants had employed 14,648, only 357 of whom were women. In the biggest state plant, Woolwich Arsenal, of 70,845 employed in January 1918, 34.82 per cent were women; in the government-owned National Shell Factories 75.8 per cent; and in the National Projectile Factories (making shells for heavy guns) 54.2 per cent.[47] In transport, women employed rose from 18,000 to 117,000, and in industry generally from 2,197,000 to 2,971,000, while the total numbers of British working women rose by 22.5 per cent from 5,966,000 to 7,311,000.[48]

The British authorities confronted a more highly unionized workforce than existed in France, and the tight wartime labour market strengthened the unions further. Between 1910 and 1914 union membership had shot up and the expansion continued, by 12 per cent in 1913–16, 18 per cent in 1917, and 19 per cent in 1918, while between 1913 and 1918 the Amalgamated Society of Engineers (ASE), the voice for engineering craftsmen, grew by 90 per cent.[49] In contrast to Paris's combination of small workshops with big modern plants, British engineering was dominated by medium-sized enterprises in which the skilled men organized the shop floor: their apprenticeship lasted 5–6 years as against 2–3 across the Channel[50] and the men's relationship with their unions became increasingly fraught when the latter – again unlike in France – were not sidelined but co-opted. In March 1915 the unions negotiated with the employers and the government the Treasury Agreement, which bound them to accept changes in working arrangements needed to accelerate war production, although the government undertook to use its influence to restore the previous conditions once peace returned.[51] The agreement was embodied in the 1915 Munitions of War Act, and followed up by the munitions ministry's Circular L2, which provided that women undertaking skilled men's work would receive equal piece rate payments though not the same time rates if men were still required to do the setting-up – as normally they would be.[52] These texts set the basis for 'dilution'.

G. D. H. Cole defined dilution as 'the introduction of less skilled workers to undertake the whole, or a part of the work previously done by workers of greater skill or experience, often, but not always, accompanied by simplification of machinery, or the breaking up of a job into a number of simpler operations'.[53] It did not necessarily entail replacing men by women, although in practice, according to the munitions ministry, 'dilution fundamentally means increased employment of women with a view to releasing men'.[54] Although intended to apply just for the war, it had much in common with the 'scientific management' of the American engineer Frederick Winslow Taylor, whose approach also entailed dividing skilled craft work into processes that unskilled or semi-skilled employees could accomplish with the aid of machines. In France dilution started earlier,[55] and the employers could impose it, but in Britain the workplace balance was more equal and the state intervened more directly. Despite the celebration of women's contribution in photographs and propaganda, the munitions ministry found 'in the early stages a very great reluctance on the part of employers to engage women at all'.[56] Businesses feared unrest, losing craftsmen, and having to invest in extra facilities, and they took on women – and especially married women – as an unknown quantity and a last resort, much of the union movement sharing their suspicion.[57] Hence the ministry not only circulated a 'Dilution of Labour Bulletin', which tracked the growing evidence that most skilled jobs could be split up and that after 1–8 weeks' training women could undertake almost all aspects of men's work,[58] but also sent out dilution-of-labour officers to check on implementation and the number of men released. If skilled men were still doing tasks that should be done by unskilled men or women, the employer could be fined.[59] Once conscription was introduced the issue became not only dilution but also 'substitution', i.e. replacing even unskilled and semi-skilled men by women, in order less to expand output than simply to release every single potential combatant.[60]

There are grounds for seeing dilution and substitution as symbolic as well as substantive, a demonstration that the government was responsive to pressure over manpower from the army, the Unionists, and the press. Women's employment expanded most dramatically in the National Shell and National Projectile Factories, which were state-run establishments that started from scratch. The Admiralty did not want dilutees building ships, and its yards remained a male bastion. Dilution also figured relatively little in that heaviest of heavy industries, steelmaking. It was most relevant to engineering and to items such as machinery and heavy artillery, repetitive tasks being assigned to women while skilled men continued making the tools and setting them up and repairing them.[61] None the less, more than 700,000 of the new wartime jobs entailed dilution, and 363,000 women in engineering directly replaced men.[62] By the end of the war some women in Britain (unlike France) were carrying out skilled tasks themselves, and managers were more willing – although as elsewhere they complained that women had higher turnover – to accept a permanent change, especially after many had provided canteens, rest rooms, and even nurseries, so that French visitors to London found conditions much better than in Paris.[63] After a difficult start, employers grew more satisfied with their women workers, commenting retrospectively they found women better than men in some positions, although using them did entail higher costs.[64] Pay differentials were wider than in France, and women workers lost fingers in machinery, were poisoned by TNT, and were killed in explosions such as that at Silvertown in January 1917, but the hours were shorter than on the Continent and many, at least in later years, viewed wartime employment as a good time in their lives.

On both sides women began as about a third of the workforce – more in France, less in Germany and Britain – and female war workers came mostly from sectors such as textiles, the land, and domestic service, although many younger women took jobs for the first time. In agriculture women were crucial as managers of family farms. In manufacturing, conditions at first got worse, as governments waived pre-war restrictions. Later, they set up inspection regimes, although the German authorities, for example, failed to replace the two-shift day by the more humane three-shift one. Broadly, conditions – particularly working hours – were better in the Allied countries and especially in Britain and America (as well as France after 1917), though not in Italy. In 1917–18 female employment everywhere grew more slowly (and in Germany and Austria-Hungary it probably declined), but the Allies still obtained more men for the front than did their enemies. Statistical shortcomings inhibit precise comparison, and the female workforce grew less than contemporaries imagined, but it seems to have expanded more in France and Britain than in Germany, providing the Allies with additional leeway when labour power commanded a premium and their peoples neared the limits of effort.

CLASS

Women's employment in the factories formed one element in a wider pattern of relations between governments and labour and socialist organizations. In Russia a breakdown in these relations caused near disaster for the Allies, and everywhere they were strained. Yet eventually revolution came to Germany, and not to its opponents, who proved more successful in co-opting the moderate against the extreme Left and in winning the battle of ideas. After Nicholas II's abdication and American intervention, the Allies could claim more plausibly to be crusading against autocracy, and the struggle became more ideological. Two points of reference were provided by Lloyd George's Caxton Hall speech of 5 January 1918, and, especially, by Woodrow Wilson's Fourteen Points address on 8 January, followed by the President's 'Four Principles' on 11 February and 'Five Particulars' on 27 September. Collectively, Wilson's speeches became the basis on which the Central Powers would request an armistice.[65]

Both Lloyd George and Wilson offered programmes of war aims, and war aims had become central to political debate. In late 1917 the Bolsheviks published the annexationist secret treaties that the Allies had negotiated before America entered the war. When the Central Powers paid lip service to Bolshevik peace principles in their 'Christmas Declaration', a response was imperative or the Allies would face a public relations disaster. But Wilson wanted not only to answer Lenin (and if possible keep Russia in the war) but also to undercut the enemy governments by appealing to their opposition movements, and to cultivate the Left in Western Europe and the US.[66] When at the inter-Allied Paris Conference of November–December 1917 his envoy, Colonel House, failed to secure an Allied declaration repudiating the secret treaties, the President decided to go it alone.[67] Lloyd George was less concerned about Russia, but rather by conversations held in Switzerland between Smuts and an Austrian diplomat, Count Mensdorff, and a representative of the Turkish opposition, Dr Parodi, both of whom called for a statement of Allied objectives. In addition, a letter to the *Daily Telegraph* from the former Foreign Secretary Lord Lansdowne had demonstratively broken ranks by advocating more moderate goals, as did a December 1917 agreement between the Labour Party and the TUC on a joint war aims programme. Furthermore, the Premier wanted trade union agreement to release men from protected domestic occupations for the army, and it was to a trade union audience that he gave his Caxton Hall speech.[68]

Although the two statements had much in common, they were drawn up separately. Lloyd George's was drafted by Smuts and by Sir Robert Cecil of the Foreign Office, discussed intensively in Cabinet and referred to the leaders of the Labour and Liberal parties and the Dominion premiers. Wilson worked primarily just with Colonel House (whose suggestion the speech was), allowing only small last-minute changes by Robert Lansing, his Secretary of State. However, the Fourteen Points also drew on memoranda from the progressive publicist Walter Lippmann, who wrote up recommendations from 'The Inquiry', a commission composed mainly of academics whom Wilson had appointed to gather materials on a future peace settlement. But neither leader consulted the other Allied governments, and instead they fired shots across their bows. Both made their strongest declarations yet in support of France's claims to Alsace-Lorraine, although neither was unequivocal, and neither mentioned French aspirations to the Saar coalfield and in the Rhineland. Similarly, both supported Italy's claims to ethnically Italian areas, but neither mentioned its strategic demands for German-speaking territory in the South Tyrol and for Slovenian- and Croatian-speaking territory in the Adriatic. Both wanted Serbia (like Belgium) to be fully restored, but were silent on Serbian and Romanian territorial expansion, and both envisaged that Austria-Hungary would survive, albeit with autonomy for its nationalities. In the Middle East, Lloyd George's government was determined to control Mesopotamia and Palestine, and he opposed restoring Ottoman rule to non-Turkish areas, whereas Wilson (who was not at war with Bulgaria or Turkey) envisaged only autonomy for them. Both speeches supported a liberated Poland (Wilson's more emphatically), but whereas Lloyd George was willing to abandon Russia if it made a separate peace, Wilson called on all parties to leave Russia to determine its future. On this point the President was notably more idealistic, as he was in his demands for a new world order based on open diplomacy, free passage on the seas, arms limitation, non-discriminatory customs tariffs, and a League of Nations. None the less, Lloyd George also spoke of international organization (as an antidote to arms racing) and more explicitly favoured basing territorial rearrangements on self-determination, Wilson moving in the same direction only in his Four Principles a month later.[69]

Both leaders therefore laid out sanitized sets of war aims, less imperialist than the inter-Allied secret treaties, and accompanied by a restructuring of global politics to reduce the risk of war. The Central Powers were wrong-footed, and slow to respond. Czernin, the Austro-Hungarian foreign minister, welcomed the Fourteen Points and was willing to negotiate on their basis, although secret American and Allied contacts with

Vienna led nowhere. Chancellor Hertling in the Reichstag denied seeking annexations, but on Wilson's general principles his language was evasive.[70] But neither Wilson nor Lloyd George had intended to start peace negotiations, which neither regarded as yet being opportune; rather, their speeches were manoeuvres in a contest for hearts and minds.

Left-wing opposition to the war took two overlapping forms. The first was resistance based on principle: either on pacifism or on suspicion that men were dying not for self-defence and liberation but to serve the interests of an expansionist elite. Such opposition might be socialist in inspiration though it could also be liberal or Christian. At its core were often the radical critics of pre-war foreign policy: marginal in Germany,[71] though more significant in Britain, France, and America. The second source of opposition centred on the trade unions and the labour and socialist parties that claimed to represent the working classes. To begin with almost all supported the war, but they shifted their position once it damaged their constituents' interests and they began to doubt its justification. By 1917 the labour movement was threatened with schism, or at any rate with its pro-war leaders being ousted. But whereas in Germany the SPD split into two opposed factions, in France and Britain nominal unity was preserved and the patriots kept control (though on the condition of shifting their ground) until the eve of the armistice.

To an extent the United States participated in the shift to the Left. During the war its main trade union organization, the American Federation of Labor (AFL), rose to 3 million affiliates. In 1917, strikes totalled 4,450, the highest figure in American history.[72] Autumn stoppages hit the mountain copper mines and the Pacific shipyards and spruce forests, all vital to war production. Although the AFL supported American intervention, the syndicalists of the Industrial Workers of the World (IWW), condemned it, as did the Socialist Party of America. In 1917 the SPA had nearly 70,000 members, and its candidate in the 1916 presidential election had won 600,000 votes.[73] Unlike its European counterparts it denounced the war as soon as it was declared, as 'a crime against the people of the United States'. Although several of the SPA's intellectuals broke with it and supported Wilson, the party established a People's Council for Democracy and Peace that made inroads into the Irish communities of Boston and Chicago and among the Jewish garment workers of New York City. The latter, whose economy was not geared towards armaments and did not particularly prosper from the war effort, was the most important centre of opposition to the conflict, and ideological and ethnic sources of anti-war feeling became interconnected. In the city's mayoral elections in November 1917, the Socialist candidate, Morris Hilquit, gained the unprecedented voting share of 22 per cent.

The administration responded with repression, conciliation, and persuasion. Against the IWW Wilson personally approved police raids that led to mass trials and convictions of nearly 200 of its leaders. When its loggers downed tools in the North-West 10,000 troops were sent to cut the lumber, and the government organized a tame alternative union. In 1918 the number of strikes diminished,[74] but as the labour market tightened the administration got tougher. The War Department's 'work or fight' order in May envisaged immediate drafting for any deferred registrant found to be idle or in an unproductive occupation,[75] and in September Wilson halted a strike among machinists at Bridgeport, Connecticut, by warning the workers that they were showing 'disloyalty and dishonour' and might be called up.[76] Moreover, new legislation restricted civil liberties, notably the Espionage Act (June 1917), the Trading with the Enemy Act (October 1917), and the Sedition Act (May 1918). Although censorship proceeded (as in Britain and unlike in Germany) in the first instance by voluntary engagement with the press, the first two of these measures empowered the Justice Department to prosecute, which it did in 2,000 cases. The Espionage Act also empowered Wilson's Postmaster-General, Albert Sidney Burleson, to prevent the distribution of socialist and pacifist literature via the cheaper second-class inter-state mails, and Burleson, a Southern conservative, did so energetically, the President querying some of his excesses but not overriding him. The Sedition Act, which Wilson said he agreed to in order to prevent something even more draconian, forbade any words or deeds intended to restrict the sale of US war bonds, any deed intended to curtail production of war material, any utterance intended to induce contempt for the constitution, government, or flag, or any word or act favouring any country at war with the US: convictions carried fines of up to $20,000 (an enormous sum at the time) or twenty years' imprisonment.[77] If implemented literally the Act could have closed down criticism of the war altogether, although in practice freedom to oppose the government survived.

Even so, the administration bought off much unrest (though if the war had gone on into 1919 it might well have grown more coercive). It permitted a big pay increase on the government-run railways, passing on the cost through higher tariffs,[78] while government-backed arbitrators awarded similar rises elsewhere. In addition it insisted on labour commissions in sectors where it purchased heavily, such as camp construction, shipyards, docks, and clothing: the commissions included union representatives and required eight-hour days, equal pay for women, and respect for existing craft rules, the employers passing the expense back to the state through 'cost-plus' contracts. This arrangement formed part of a strategy of co-operation with Samuel Gompers, the redoubtable AFL president, a British-born cigar maker who denounced any compromise peace. At the AFL's 1917 Buffalo Convention the Left had endangered his leadership, but his support for the administration restored his position.[79] He met the President regularly, and co-operated with the administration against his SPA and IWW rivals.[80] In particular Gompers worked closely with George Creel, whose Committee on Public Information (CPI) deluged the home front with pro-war propaganda. Creel's background was as a muckraking journalist in Kansas and Denver, and he brought a certain idealism to his role, as well as driving ambition: he was intensely loyal to the President and one of the few who remained so until Wilson's melancholy end.[81] Creel was concerned about the labour movement, to which the CPI devoted more attention than it publicly acknowledged. He secretly subsidized the American Alliance for Labor and Democracy, which Gompers established as a counter to the SPA's activities, and which in its first six months distributed 2 million pamphlets and set up 150 branches.[82]

Although censorship and wire-pulling formed parts of Creel's role, he emphasized his commitment to persuasion. The CPI proselytized on an unprecedented scale.[83] During its life it issued 6,000 press releases and delivered a weekly digest to over 12,000 papers, its services remaining open twenty-four hours a day and seven days a week to answer inquiries. Its pamphlets had a circulation of over 75 million, while its speakers during cinema reel-changes, the 'Four-Minute Men', numbered 75,000 (all volunteers) and may have spoken to audiences of over 314 million.[84] One CPI film, *America's Answer*, was shown in nearly half the 12,000 cinemas in the US; and the committee held exhibitions in twenty cities, that in Chicago receiving nearly 2 million visitors.[85] Leaflets from leading scholars were commissioned on the war's origins and purpose and on the American and German governmental systems, but Wilson's speeches were a focus of Creel's pamphleteering and he intensively exploited the Fourteen Points, which had been drafted with home opinion as one target. They constituted evidence that the United States, at least, was not fighting for annexations and indemnities, and resuscitated the President's support among progressive intellectuals and the labour movement, the SPA leader Eugene Debs offering the Points his 'unqualified approval'.[86] Sympathy from the American Left for Bolshevism was evanescent, and the Brest-Litovsk Treaty and the Ludendorff offensives further damaged the anti-war movement. In the final months Wilson's main domestic political problem became the growth of super-patriotism.

Like the USA, Italy had intervened after war began, but unlike France and Britain it patently had not been responding to aggression. Its war aims conflicted glaringly with self-determination, and the disclosure of the secret treaties made them public knowledge. Its claims to Slovene- and Croat-inhabited areas in Istria and Dalmatia clashed with Serbia's objectives and with Yugoslav ambitions. To the chagrin of the foreign minister, Sidney Sonnino, not only did Wilson – who had never been a party to the London Treaty – dissociate himself from gains beyond the ethnically Italian areas, but so too did Lloyd George – although in private the British reassured the Italian government that they still considered their treaty commitments binding, the Foreign Secretary explaining that it would not be 'good propaganda' to base a public declaration on a secret treaty.[87] The watchword of the Italian Socialist Party (Partito Socialista Italiano, or PSI), more radical than its counterparts north of the Alps, was 'Neither sabotage nor adhesion': although it did not obstruct the war, it consistently condemned it.[88] Nor did the Vatican support an attack by Italy (with which it remained in dispute for having annexed papal territory in 1870) on the more devotedly Catholic Habsburgs. Finally the former Premier, Giovanni Giolitti, who in 1915 had opposed intervention, retained a large parliamentary following. In 1917 these elements came together: Pope Benedict XV appealed for peace, and Giolitti declared that foreign policy must change after the war. During August food shortages in Turin caused days of rioting.

Although in October 1917 a new and more broadly based coalition government was formed under Vittorio Orlando, it took defeat at Caporetto to reconsolidate the home front. In December a Fascio di Difesa Nazionale (National Defence League) was formed in parliament, committed to victory and to standing by the Allies, and 158 deputies joined it. In a secret debate Orlando gained the Giolittians' backing and won a majority of 345:50.[89] According to the British Ambassador in January, the 'general spirit' had already greatly gained in constancy and determination.[90] Two reformist socialists – Leonida Bissolati and Ivanoe Bonomi – served in the government, Orlando giving the appearance of mediating between the Bissolati and the Sonnino positions (though really favouring the latter) by welcoming the creation of a Yugoslav state and being willing to compromise over its borders. The appearance of a defensive war fought for moderate objectives helped other socialists to come round, and moderates in the PSI and in the trade union confederation, the CGIL (Confederazione Generale del Lavoro), preached resistance to the enemy and were willing to support a crusade for Wilsonian ideals, although the majority of the party persisted in its anti-war stance.[91] The government continued its struggle against 'defeatism' and broke up recalcitrant socialist groups, war critics being imprisoned or placed under house arrest in remote areas, while the authorities by-passed parliament and resorted more to decrees, military administration extending over much the north of the country. But food rationing became more efficient and trade union membership and real earnings (at least for some workers) increased. Although Italy's coal and food supply remained very difficult, labour relations improved, the number of industrial disputes having risen from seven in 1915 to 115 in 1916 and 504 in 1917, but now falling to 280.[92] In 1917 General Dallolio had taken responsibility from the military for labour relations in the armaments sector, and he conceded large wage increases until pressure from industrialists and a corruption scandal led to his being removed in May 1918. Reports from south and central Italy by the carabinieri indicated nationwide discontent in the autumn of 1917 over food prices and the war, from which the government's socialist and clerical critics profited. After Caporetto, however, the mood changed. By May 1918, although agitation over food prices continued in cities such as Florence and Rome, the protests were more subdued and had lost their political edge, while a secret PSI meeting was reported to have rejected the option of a general strike as certain to fail.[93] Prefectoral reports suggested that the war remained unpopular, but by a mixture of carrots and sticks the unpopularity was contained.[94]

In many ways developments in France were similar: after a crisis in 1917 the Ludendorff offensives rallied opinion, though in the final weeks strains re-emerged. In May–June 1917 the army mutinies had coincided with nationwide strikes. Industrial unrest persisted, including a September 1917 stoppage in the aircraft industry,[95] while the prefects' reports on home morale suggested that after a first trough in the summer it plumbed another in the autumn, especially in working-class areas, because of the continuing military stalemate, pressure on living standards, and bad news from Italy and Russia.[96] And at this moment of uncertainty, politicians were poorly placed to lead. The French Third Republic was notorious for ministerial instability, its pre-war governments enduring on average only nine months, but between August 1914 and March 1917 René Viviani and Aristide Briand headed two relatively enduring cabinets. In contrast, the two subsequent governments led by Alexandre Ribot and Paul Painlevé lasted only from March to November 1917, and the latter was the first wartime administration to lose its parliamentary majority. A succession of scandals was a further symptom of malaise. Jean-Louis Malvy, the Minister of the Interior, was alleged to have had dealings with shady partners in German pay, and Joseph Caillaux, a pre-war premier who had not concealed his willingness for a compromise peace and had sympathizers among the Radical Party in parliament, believed his hour was approaching. After Painlevé fell, President Raymond Poincaré believed he must choose between Caillaux and Clemenceau, and by selecting the latter he confirmed that France would go on.[97] By this stage better food and leave and an end to great offensives had calmed the army, pay rises and shorter hours had pacified the strikers, and judicial proceedings against the treason suspects had been instigated. When Clemenceau came to office, his task was the more straightforward one of withstanding the expected onslaught until American assistance came on stream.

'My entire policy', Clemenceau told the Chamber of Deputies, 'has this sole objective: to sustain the morale of the French people through the worst crisis in its history.'[98] Against the scandals he took a very firm line. He considered it essential to show that no one, irrespective of seniority, would be shown indulgence, and the backbeat to political life became a succession of proceedings, revelations, and verdicts.[99] Some of the accused, such as Emile-Joseph Duval – the finance director of the left-wing newspaper *Le Bonnet Rouge*, which was revealed to have been receiving German subsidies – were executed. Caillaux was imprisoned, and Malvy exiled. The latter was found not guilty of treason but to have been culpably inadequate in conducting his duties – which came down to a political accusation that he had been too lenient towards the Left and the unions. As interior minister he had indeed instructed the prefects not to harass the working classes, and the socialists protested against the sentence.[100] And yet, as Malvy pointed out, Clemenceau continued to permit opponents of the war to organize and express themselves. His government transferred four cavalry divisions to home security, stepped up police surveillance, and suppressed rather than merely suspending newspapers, but – perhaps because a longstanding rebel himself – he circumscribed civil liberties instead of terminating them.[101] For all his intransigent rhetoric, his approach was flexible and he was harsher on the socialist politicians than he was on the industrial workers.

Anti-war opposition among intellectuals had existed from early on. By 1915 it was making wider inroads. The metalworkers' union, headed by Alphonse Merrheim, challenged the policy of co-operation with the government adopted by the main trade union federation, the CGT (Confédération générale du travail), and by the GCT's secretary, Léon Jouhaux. The socialists of the Haute Vienne department, deep in the interior, challenged the official party line. Dissident French and Allied socialists met in Switzerland with others from the neutrals and the Central Powers, at Zimmerwald in 1915 and at Kienthal in 1916. By the latter date the SFIO's conferences and its parliamentary delegation were polarizing into a 'majority' supporting the government and a 'minority' that favoured opening peace negotiations and opposed voting war credits. In June 1917 the Ribot government's decision to refuse passports for the SFIO to attend the proposed international socialist conference at Stockholm brought matters to a head. After learning from the Russians about the secret treaties the party leaders felt they had been duped, and they and the 'majority' switched in favour of going. Although the party continued to vote war credits, it left the government in September and became vociferously critical. However, its co-operation was a luxury for Clemenceau rather than a necessity, and he did little to accommodate it. He continued to prohibit the SFIO from meeting enemy socialists, and ignored its demands to clarify war aims. Instead, his inaugural ministerial declaration finessed the latter issue: 'My war aim is to be the victor.'[102] In parliament his foreign minister, Stephen Pichon, welcomed Caxton Hall and the Fourteen Points, but France made no such declaration of its own and French objectives beyond Alsace-Lorraine remained unspecified.[103] During 1918 the Chamber of Deputies became a bear garden, the scene of repeated bruising confrontations between the Premier and his critics.

Yet socialist alienation little damaged the war effort. France had become a powerhouse of arms production, and totals of strikes and working days lost remained lower than in Britain or Germany. Although the CGT was much smaller than its British and German counterparts, and its membership fell from 350,000 to 50,000 after war broke out, by 1918 it had climbed to 600,000.[104] Clemenceau well knew that labour was scarce and his government's War Committee spent much time adjudicating inter-ministerial tussles over how to allocate working German prisoners between industry, agriculture, and the army.[105] He remained in private contact with Merrheim of the metalworkers, and for all the trade unions' ideological detestation of the French state its ministers and officials often ruled in their favour. Between March and July 1918 industrial unrest subsided, and police reports ascribed the calm to the German offensives.[106]

To this generalization there was a dramatic exception, in the shape of the May 1918 strikes in the war industries of Paris and the Centre: Roanne, Saint-Etienne, Grenoble, and Vienne. Although smaller than that of June 1917 nationally, this strike wave was the biggest of the war in Paris, and it exemplified the participants' paradoxical outlook: supporting national defence and yet resenting their employers and the state as well as the trade union leadership. For whereas the CGT condemned the strike, the initiative for it came from shop floor delegates who were influenced by the socialist *minoritaires*, those at Renault leading the way in the capital. Government plans to conscript more younger men were the trigger (it being rumoured that Americans would replace them) and compared with 1917 the motives were less economic and more political. The strikers demanded neither revolution nor higher wages, and they denied wanting to lose the war. But first and foremost they were making a gesture on behalf of peace, and they called for clarity over war aims, for fear that France was fighting for its capitalists.

Between 13 and 18 May over 100,000 were on strike in Paris, but many opposed the stoppage and a drift back to work began at once. Merrheim and Albert Thomas met Clemenceau and Loucheur, and found them surprisingly sympathetic but unyielding over substance. The Premier insisted that the call-up went ahead, and again avoided greater explicitness about war aims.[107] The Paris strike failed, as did its provincial counterparts. Beginning during a relative lull in the fighting, they continued until 28 May, by which time the Germans were pushing forward from their Chemin des Dames breakthrough and the emergency helped to end the stoppage.[108] Indeed, according to the British Embassy, from the government's viewpoint, 'Fact of it occurring in present circumstances makes it easier for the President of the Council to deal with it', and after imposing a news black-out, the authorities faced it down calmly.[109]

Once the situation at the front improved, the Left became more militant. Strikes returned to the levels of the previous winter and spread to new sectors such as clothing and food processing. Shop stewards rather than the union leaderships were responsible, many of the strikers were women, and the main issue was pay. The most damaging dispute, however, halted the Parisian railway repair shops between 6 and 8 November, at a moment when transport was on a knife edge. Yet railway employees had been one of the most disciplined and patriotic workforces, and their main demand was for a cost of living increase: it was characteristic that the stoppage ended once the transport minister interceded with the companies to grant an award.[110] The pattern therefore was of short, sharp actions that generally succeeded. Even so, both the trade unions and the SFIO were tilting further towards the anti-war camp. In July at the CGT's confederal congress supporters of national defence were accused of having sold out the working class, and told to go to the trenches themselves. Jouhaux and Merrheim reached a compromise, but Jouhaux made most of the concessions and the new programme repudiated annexations and indemnities and demanded passports to an international conference, though still supported fighting on for moderate objectives.[111] Concurrently in the SFIO, the former minority became the new majority. In July the party's National Council approved a resolution from the leading *minoritaire*, Jean Longuet (a grandson of Karl Marx), and called on the SFIO deputies to cease voting war credits. In October its policy-making body, the National Congress, voted

1,528:1,212 for an immediate compromise peace, and the *minoritaires* took over the executive and the party newspaper, *L'Humanité*. For the moment, the damage to Clemenceau was small. Outside parliament the SFIO was tiny, its pre-war membership of 72,000 having halved to 34,000; and forty of its 100 deputies ignored the turnaround and continued to vote war credits.[112] The government's majority was massive, resting on virtually all the non-socialist parties, and by the time of the National Congress armistice negotiations were in progress. If the conflict had continued into 1919, however, Clemenceau would have faced resurgent industrial unrest and much stronger anti-war opposition.

On the other hand, the government was secure with wider public opinion, which according to the police, regional army commanders, and prefects had recovered from the uncertainties of 1917. During the spring the picture remained mixed and the overall picture no better than satisfactory: determination in the rural areas but instability in the towns, where workers were monitored closely for fear of contagion from Russia. In March there was an exodus from Paris and much anxiety, as again in early June. But after July and especially by September, as the Germans retreated and the AEF deployed in strength, the mood improved, and it was hoped that Germany would soon be driven out.[113] In contrast to the earlier part of the war, when the government left propaganda on the home front to the Church, the press, lobbying groups, and political parties, in 1917–18 the state took a lead. The most impressive example was the Union des grandes associations contre la propagande ennemie (UGACPE), which was established in March 1917 under the joint headship of the President of the Chamber of Deputies, Paul Deschanel, and the historian Ernest Lavisse, at a gathering attended by President Poincaré and Prime Minister Ribot. It disseminated its message through primary schools and a network of affiliated patriotic organizations, but the government was represented at its weekly executive meetings, and Clemenceau was much interested in it. In its first year it distributed 5 million tracts and 2 million brochures, postcards, and posters, and organized over 3,000 meetings; in its second it stepped up its activities. It insisted on fighting until victory and the achievement of French war aims, although on what these were (except for Alsace-Lorraine) it remained vague, in keeping with the government's concern to avoid a topic that was divisive both within France and between France and its allies.[114] Its efforts reached into the most remote departments, and were stepped up during the Ludendorff offensives. None the less, propaganda would be ineffectual unless the military circumstances were auspicious. After the national *crise de nerfs* in 1917, by the time Clemenceau came to office the issues were clearer: if France survived the onslaught made possible by Russia's withdrawal, the Americans were likely to bring victory.

The British government operated in scarcely easier circumstances. The Labour Party was smaller than the SFIO in its share of votes and seats; and nor was it constitutionally socialist, although it contained many socialists in its affiliated groups, the Independent Labour Party (ILP) foremost among them. But the bulk of its affiliated membership and finance came from trade unions, and the TUC was much stronger than the CGT. In 1914, 22.5 per cent of male manual workers were unionized, and among key groups such as coalmining faceworkers and shipbuilding craftsmen the proportion rose to 100 per cent. The pre-1914 labour unrest, which had included strikes by miners, railwaymen, and dockers, had underlined to everyone from Lloyd George downwards that organized labour was a force to be reckoned with. And whereas in 1914 trade union membership dipped, in the second half of the war it rose to record figures: from 2.6 million in 1910 and 4 million in 1914 to 6.5 million in 1918.[115]

The Prime Minister understood that he led a population predominantly composed of urban wage earners and their families. He wrote afterwards that in Russia and the Central Powers the home front broke down, and 'To guard against it happening to Britain was the most anxious preoccupation of statesmanship here ... the contentment and co-operation of the wage-earners was our vital concern, and industrial unrest spelt a graver menace to our endurance and ultimate victory than even the military strength of Germany.'[116] Like Clemenceau's War Committee, Lloyd George's War Cabinet confronted a complex of dilemmas rooted in labour scarcity. Milner said demands for men were coming at them from all sides, and the Cabinet's War Priorities Committee found that competition for manpower was causing 'chaos and confusion'.[117] In 1914 the trade unions had called for strikes to be suspended and the number of stoppages had dropped to a fraction of the pre-war level, although in July 1915 the miners had struck in the South Wales field, which delivered steam coal to the navy, and Lloyd George had undertaken one of many interventions that gave them most of what they wanted. As in France, wartime conditions favoured workplace-elected part-time shop stewards at the expense of salaried union officials, and by 1917 the stewards were forming an independent network with its own national conferences. In America they existed in some AFL-represented sectors, but were not in revolt against their officials,[118] whereas in Britain Lloyd George attributed almost all the government's difficulties to them, in contrast with the patriotic responsibility of official trade unionism.[119]

Dealing with economic demands was challenging enough: but the greatest danger would arise if labour unrest combined with political opposition. That possibility existed from August 1914, when Ramsay MacDonald resigned as Labour Party chairman. Although not calling for withdrawal from the war, he denounced the secrecy of pre-1914 foreign policy. MacDonaldites came together with Liberal intellectuals and backbenchers to form the Union of Democratic Control (UDC), with E. D. Morel, a stubborn and gifted organizer, as its secretary. It became an exceptionally effective lobby organization, nine members of the first Labour Cabinet of 1924 having belonged to it.[120] By 1918 it had over 300 affiliated organizations, with a membership exceeding 750,000.[121] Although much of its funding came from Quaker families such as the Buxtons, Cadburys, and Rowntrees,[122] its approach like MacDonald's was not one of absolutist pacifism but centred on a demand for accountability in foreign policy formulation. The struggle against conscription radicalized it, and by 1917–18 it resembled the Continental minority socialists in its suspicion that the authorities had a hidden agenda and they must disclose their war aims to facilitate a negotiated peace.[123]

By 1917 UDC influence was growing. Although Labour was not as alienated as the SFIO, a majority in a Consultative Conference voted to attend the Stockholm conference and therefore meet with enemy socialists. After hesitation the Cabinet withheld passports, and Arthur Henderson, MacDonald's successor as party chairman, left the government. Once out of office Henderson made up with MacDonald, and at a special conference at Westminster in December the party and the TUC's Parliamentary Committee adopted a 'Memorandum on War Aims' that reflected UDC and Wilsonian views. The memorandum endorsed the creation of a League of Nations, and condemned secret diplomacy, 'every form of Imperialism, and 'economic aggression'.[124]

Although the Labour Party continued to be represented in the War Cabinet (by George Barnes from the ASE), it was increasingly at variance with the government. In addition, in April–May 1917 Britain had experienced its biggest strike wave of the war, centred in the engineering industry, and claiming more than 5 million working days. The strikes were shop-steward-led and aimed partly to keep pace with inflation and partly to protect craftsmen from conscription. But although the government arrested twenty-two stewards – without a warrant – it also negotiated an agreement with the ASE that conceded nearly all the strikers' demands.[125]

The authorities' response to the situation has been described as 'domestic appeasement',[126] and it indeed included concessions extracted under duress and against the Cabinet's better judgement – though also an authoritarian element, directed more against the pacifists than the labour movement. Britain lacked scandals as dramatic as the French *affaires*, and pacifist agitation was untainted by German involvement, much as ministers suspected it. So did Basil Thomson, the Director of Criminal Investigation at Scotland Yard, who began centralizing information on pacifist and revolutionary organizations and reporting to the Cabinet, although he found no confirmation for his surmises. From October 1917, the Home Office expected chief constables of county police forces to report regularly on pacifism, and to forward their reports on industrial unrest to the local military commanders.[127] While sparing MPs such as MacDonald and Philip Snowden, the authorities acted against the UDC early in 1918: Morel was imprisoned for evading censorship regulations and the philosopher Bertrand Russell arrested. By 1917 declining imports had caused a shortage of newsprint, and whereas the patriotic press had preferential access, opposition titles ran short of paper, the authorities also preventing UDC material from being exported or reaching the Western Front. The police and Home Office turned a blind eye to patriotic violence against pacifist meetings, and the Home Secretary, Sir George Cave, drew more frequently on his powers to ban assemblies, notably one scheduled for Hyde Park on May Day 1918 that he feared would lead to 'gross disorder', and which was moved to Finsbury Park in June.[128]

The government also repressed industrial workers, but relied more on persuasion and concession. The centrepiece of the persuasion effort was the National War Aims Committee (NWAC), launched in August

1917 in the wake of the Russian Revolution and the May 1917 engineering strikes, and in the midst of the Stockholm conference affair. After the strikes the Cabinet resolved that 'the time had come to undertake an active campaign to counteract the pacifist movement, which at the present had the field to itself'. The NWAC's organization bore resemblances to the UGACPE's in France, but also to that of the UDC, which it was intended to counter.[129] In appearance it was non-partisan – Lloyd George, Asquith, Bonar Law, and Barnes were joint presidents – but the government's chief whip, F. E. Guest, became its chairman, and a secret Treasury grant was indispensable to it.[130] Although it suited it to appear at arm's length from the government, its target was antiwar propaganda and its guidance to its speakers was 'to keep before our nation both the causes which have led to this world war and the vital importance to human life and liberty of continuing the struggle until the evil forces which originated this terrible conflict are destroyed for ever'. In September it noted the 'general disposition of organized labour to stand aloof from our local Committees', which it believed was primarily because 'our war aims have not been clearly defined', and in December it reiterated that although 'there is no weakening of public opinion on the war', it could campaign more effectively if British war aims were specified: indeed, given the organization's title it is surprising this issue had not been attended to.[131] The NWAC helped persuade the government that a war aims statement was needed, and contributed to the Caxton Hall speech, which Lloyd George followed up on 18 January by reiterating at a conference with trade union representatives that Britain's goals were moderate – 'I would not have this war for a second on my soul if I could stop it honourably.'[132] The organization was central to the government's efforts to carry the labour movement.

Armed with an official war aims statement as well as public funding, the NWAC continued its activities into 1918. Unlike the UGACPE, it was based on war aims committees organized round the Liberal and Unionist party organizations in the constituencies, and it functioned like an election campaign, producing leaflets (distributed free of charge by W. H. Smith & Son), posters, and films, but operating above all through speaker meetings, between three and seven every day across the country by July 1918. The speakers' notes on their receptions survive, ranging from coastal resorts to industrial centres, and with suspect uniformity reporting enthusiastic or at least polite and interested audiences, although attendance depended greatly on the weather and could be small, whereas the NWAC's film propaganda may have reached 6 million people every week.[133] In Britain, like the US, a torrent of government-backed advocacy reinforced the efforts of private societies and war-loan campaigns to resist a premature peace, while the authorities inhibited expressions of dissent.

The third element in the response to the home front challenge was concession. It included promising a reconstructed and a better Britain after victory, and the 1918 Representation of the People Act, which enfranchised not only women over thirty but also almost all the adult male population (compared with only two thirds before 1914). It also meant addressing more immediate grievances, foremost among which, according to the reports of the regional commissions that investigated the 1917 strikes, was the cost of living. The bread subsidy, Lord Rhondda's restraints on food prices, and the introduction of rationing all fell under this head. But there were limits. A continuing issue during the 1917/18 winter was the government's effort to comb men for the armed forces out of the protected occupations, which was the immediate reason for the Caxton Hall speech, and over which negotiations with the ASE failed. None the less, the Cabinet resolved to implement a 'clean cut' of men under twenty-three and face down strikes rather than give way.[134]

At this point the 'Michael' offensive intervened. The extra hours volunteered by munitions workers more than compensated for the days lost through disputes in the industry, the Miners' Federation of Great Britain (MFGB) co-operated with the call-up of miners, and strikes dwindled away. For a time, a weary labour force worked flat out. But the underlying level of strike activity and lost working days was much higher than in Germany, and as soon as the crisis eased unrest revived. The trend was international, the French and Canadian authorities also noting an upsurge of discontent.[135] Union membership rose by 19 per cent in 1918, and real wages, which had fallen in the first half of the war, rose rapidly. The number of strikes (many in the aircraft industry) rose from 730 in 1917 to 1,165 in 1918, the highest figure since 1913.[136] On 21 June, Churchill warned the Cabinet's War Priorities Committee that 'For the last three months Labour had behaved with great loyalty and had been less disturbed than at any previous time, but during the last week a reaction had set in ...'[137] Sure enough, a week later the Cabinet discussed an MFGB demand for 9 shillings more per week, which exceeded the rise in prices and which labour and munitions ministries officials opposed because granting it would be unfair to other workers. None the less, ministers believed the impact of a coal stoppage on munitions, shipping, and supplies to allies and neutrals would be 'disastrous', and they conceded the claim in full.[138] On 23–26 July thousands of engineers came out in Coventry and Birmingham, demanding protection against conscription, and although the government broke the strike by threatening to call up the leaders, Lloyd George was so concerned that he received situation reports almost hourly.[139] At the end of August a strike over pay and recognition brought out most of the Metropolitan Police, and Lloyd George settled it with the men's representatives, refusing to recognize their union but consenting to their second war bonus in eight months.[140] Finally, a stoppage on the Great Western Railway on 24–26 September, over a bonus the men deemed insufficient, halted traffic between South Wales and London. The government declared it illegal and readied six battalions of troops, but the movement collapsed before they were used.[141] As the armistice approached, the British government like the French one faced escalating militancy, to much of which it yielded, especially when pay was the grievance. Moreover, in June a Labour Party conference voted to abandon the political truce and contest by-elections, and in October the party executive recommended withdrawal from the government. Labour had now reorganized itself, adopting a socialist constitution and an internationalist foreign policy; and it embarrassed its remaining ministers by behaving as the principal opposition.[142] Had the war continued Lloyd George's Cabinet would have faced an invidious choice between repression (and prospective disruption in vital industries) and increasingly expensive conciliation. It would have had to support an overstretched and even unreliable police force by holding back extra troops, to say nothing of the conscription crisis in Ireland.

Yet whatever the Allies' difficulties, the confrontation between the socialist and labour movements and the authorities in the Central Powers outmatched them. The Ottoman Empire lacked significant modern industry, and Bulgaria had little, although by 1918 food shortages there caused both parliamentary uproar and street protest.[143] But

Austria-Hungary had a substantial industrial workforce and a socialist movement. In 1914 the socialists and trade unions in the Austrian half declared a 'truce' for the duration of a 'just defensive war',[144] but their reward was military repression and dwindling membership, that in the Vienna region falling by 1916 from 50,000 to 16,000 while trade union affiliations to the party declined from 156,367 to 60,583. After Franz Joseph's death civil liberties were partially restored, but now in a far more difficult environment of resentment and deprivation, enormous casualties, and meagre military success, and the socialists and trade unions grew more radical. By 1917 real wages had fallen by 64 per cent, and the industries of Vienna and its suburbs offered long hours and harsh conditions to a workforce whose wages were set by decree and which was forbidden to strike or move from plant to plant. In April the foreign minister, Czernin, warned Berlin that revolution would spread from Russia to Austria-Hungary by the winter. Although the Germans rightly suspected Czernin of exaggerating in order to frighten them, the Austrian authorities had reason to fear that food supplies would run out before the harvest.[145] May 1917 saw the first big strikes, the metal-workers demanding elected shop stewards to distribute food: the government agreed to control rents, to allow complaint commissions in the militarized factories, and to permit meetings, and socialist and trade union membership began to recover.

In 1918 the challenge to authority was more formidable, and centred again on the nervous months before the harvest. In Hungary the social-ists had also moved leftwards, and strikes took place in March, May, and June,[146] but the starving cities of the Austrian half experienced the big-gest upheaval. Although triggered by a cut in the flour and bread ration, the strike that spread out after 14 January from the Daimler works at Wiener Neustadt was centrally against the war, at a moment when the Central Powers' demands threatened breakdown in the Brest-Litovsk negotiations. Surprised, the socialists moved to take the lead, appealing to the workers to demand an early peace without annexations and based on self-determination, though also calling unsuccessfully for the stop-page to be suspended.[147] At the peak about a million workers were out across the Dual Monarchy, including over 100,000 in Vienna: the strik-ers set up workers' councils on the Soviet model and drew up a four-point programme which the authorities agreed to meet, and by the 24th work had resumed.[148] The government was so alarmed that it held back seven divisions to secure the home front. Finally, in mid-June yet another unexpected cut in the bread ration provoked a further strike wave in the metal and armaments industries, and the socialists formed a Vienna workers' council, although this stoppage was smaller and less politicized and after the authorities promised more food and higher wages the council appealed for it to end. In the final months the industrial areas were quieter, although sullen discontent lingered.[149]

The Austrian strikes set an example for Germany. The distinctive feature of German socialism – which proved enormously important for the armistice – was its schism between reformist and radical parties, one of which would co-operate in seeking an orderly disengagement from the conflict while the other fomented revolution behind the lines. Yet although pre-war factional conflicts within the SPD foreshadowed such a division, in 1914 its Reichstag delegation had voted almost unanimously for war credits. Moreover, the Free Trade Unions (the largest of the three union federations) under their summit organization, the Generalkommission (GK), were as tightly tied into the party as were the British trade unions into Labour. The GK chairman, Karl Legien, belonged to the SPD executive, and a third of the party's Reichstag deputies were union officials. The unions co-operated with the war effort, the authorities regularly consulted them, and the first two war years were a time of relatively stable living standards and industrial peace.[150]

In 1916–17 the internal situation abruptly deteriorated. The cause was partly economic: the privations of the turnip winter and the paralysis caused by the Hindenburg Programme. Moreover, the summer 1916 military emergency jolted confidence, and surveys of opinion by the deputy commanding generals in charge of Germany's military districts disclosed a new unease, which unrestricted submarine warfare dispelled only temporarily.[151] The SPD's position was especially difficult because war feeling among much of the working class had been tepid even in 1914,[152] and the apparent threat from tsarist Russia had been the principal rationale for the party's decision to co-operate. Yet by 1917 enough had leaked out to prove the German government had expansionist objectives, and the February Revolution not only paralysed Russia militarily but also left Germany as Europe's most authoritarian regime.

Despite its rhetoric of social transformation, the SPD's immediate commitment was to political reform, and in particular to replacing the

17. (*top*) A German transport column on the Albert–Bapaume road during Operation 'Michael'. A staff car accompanies wagons stretching into the distance.

18. (*bottom*) French supply trains. For both sides, carriage beyond the railhead was largely horse-drawn.

19. (*top*) Overturned British locomotive in snow.

20. (*bottom*) The newcomers: American troop train in Lorraine.

21. (*top*) Senegalese by a field kitchen on the Aisne.
France would have depended ever more on colonial
forces in a 1919 campaign.

22. (*bottom*) British and German wounded at an
advanced dressing station during the Battle of Epéhy,
18 September 1918.

23. (*left*) Austro-Hungarian infantry sergeant captured by the British in Italy. Troop surrenders were a key indicator of the Central Powers' decline.

24. (*below*) *A Convoy, North Sea, 1918*, by Sir John Lavery (1856–1941). In 1918 convoys – often with aerial escorts – were extended from the Atlantic into British coastal waters.

25. (*top*) *In the Gun Factory at Woolwich Arsenal, 1918*, by Sir George Clausen (1852–1944). Woolwich became one of the biggest manufacturing complexes in Europe.

26. (*bottom*) *Shop for Machining 15-inch Shells*, by Anna Airy (1882–1964).

27. (*top*) Train carrying heavy artillery shells to the Front
near Bourg-et-Comin (Aisne).

28. (*bottom*) Moroccans quarrying under supervision.
Demand for road stone was voracious.

29. (*top*) Women peat diggers in Alsace.

30. (*bottom*) Two WAACS (members of the Women's
Auxiliary Army Corps) lay wreaths at the British
cemetery, Abbeville, February 1918.

31. (*top*) Aftermath: British troops at Valenciennes station.

32. (*bottom*) French troops and civilians in the textile town
of Fourmies (Nord), 9 November 1918.

property-weighted three-tier franchise for the Prussian lower house of parliament. Democratizing the franchise would help to make the Prussian and Imperial authorities responsible to an electorate in which the socialists were the largest element, and the Prussian Conservatives and the OHL were set against it. Whereas in Britain franchise reform was uncontentious, even on the previously polarizing issue of the women's vote, in Germany it deepened divisions. In April 1917 Wilhelm II, advised by Bethmann Hollweg, issued his 'Easter Message', which promised Prussian franchise reform: but by direct and secret, not necessarily equal, ballots, and not until after the war. And to take effect the measure must pass the Prussian Landtag and House of Peers (Herrenhaus), which were disinclined to vote away their privileges. Until revolution dislodged this obstacle, it proved insurmountable.

The SPD leaders were challenged not only by the ultra-Left Spartakus League under Rosa Luxemburg and Karl Liebknecht, but also by a larger minority within the party who denied that Germany's war was defensive and opposed granting credits for it. In spring 1917 the leaders resolved that the minority's position was incompatible with SPD membership, and the latter reconstituted themselves as the German Independent Social Democratic Party (Unabhängige Sozialdemokratische Partei Deutschlands, or USPD), headquartered in Leipzig. The USPD included both the Spartakists and more moderate elements who wanted a peace without annexations and indemnities and approved of the Zimmerwald and Kienthal conferences. In summer 1917 the mutineers in the German navy made contact with the party, which counselled them to use passive resistance rather than violence.[153] A parallel industrial movement led by shop stewards who were mostly USPD supporters was centred on Berlin and on the turners' branch of the metalworkers' union. As in France and Britain, trade union officials – who were exempted from conscription – were increasingly seen as privileged and out of touch.[154] In April 1917 the shop stewards led the largest strike wave yet, prompted by cuts in the bread ration. They called for cheaper coal and food, and in Leipzig they also demanded a peace without annexations, civil liberties, the release of political prisoners, and equal and direct suffrage across the empire.[155] Not only was the number of strikes and working days lost increasing, but compared with the pre-war period fewer stoppages were trade-union-led and a growing proportion were political. In 1910–13 four fifths were trade-union-led, but in 1917–18 only one fifth.[156]

Table 7.1. Workers on strike in Germany, 1916–18 (000s)[157]

	1916	1917	1918
Number of strikers	124	651	1,304
Number of 'political' strikers	65	275	925

The stage was set for a political realignment. The precipitant was growing evidence that the submarine campaign was not delivering the predicted results, while the Austro-Hungarian government disclosed its dire circumstances to the German (Catholic) Centre Party. A new majority coalition in the Reichstag comprising the Centre, the two liberal groups (National Liberals and Progressives), and the SPD, liaised through an inter-party committee and passed the 19 July Peace Resolution, renouncing – although in equivocal terms – a peace based on annexations and indemnities, and seeking a 'peace of understanding'. Coming after the Easter Message, this was too much for Hindenburg and Ludendorff, who by threatening to resign forced Wilhelm II to replace Bethmann Hollweg by their own candidate, Georg Michaelis. Michaelis was unacceptable to the Reichstag majority, and was soon replaced by Count Georg von Hertling, with a liberal, Friedrich von Payer, as his Vice-Chancellor. But this outcome was still very far from democratization, and the Prussian parliamentary reform bill remained blocked, while the OHL's ability to oust officials it disliked remained untrammelled. The 1917 realignment failed to restore stability, and early in 1918 a second realignment reversed it, its essential features being a strike wave and the Brest-Litovsk Treaty. Between them these two events were a defeat for the Left, though they also prepared it for its later role in disengaging Germany from the war.

The second realignment followed another difficult winter. Lenin's takeover had less resonance in Germany than in Austria-Hungary, and much of the Left and the labour movement viewed the Bolsheviks with distaste, but by January it was evident that the struggle between the OHL and the foreign minister, Kühlmann, was impeding peace.[158] The strike wave began on 28 January, four days after the Austro-Hungarian one had ended, and although the USPD had pleaded for action in support of the Russians and Friedrich Ebert, the SPD's co-chairman, had declared solidarity with the Austrian strikers, the German movement still surprised both the SPD and the Generalkommission. Like its French counterpart in May, it was primarily a political gesture, conceived of as a moral demonstration that would last three days, but in fact enduring longer. It was non-violent and profoundly impressive: 400,000 joined it in Berlin and in the Ruhr over a million.[159] It centred on big arms plants where the workforce had grown rapidly and the official unions were weak: the Generalkommission did not denounce it but declared its neutrality in a political strike and condemned the 'anonymous' agitators who led it.[160] The impetus came again from the shop stewards, and the 'action committee' that the strikers elected comprised mainly USPD members. It called for better food supply, civil liberties, and democratization, but its first demand was for a peace without annexations and indemnities and based on self-determination. When the SPD accepted an invitation to join the committee, however, hoping 'to keep the movement within orderly paths and . . . rapidly bring it to an end', they tried to invert the order of the demands, putting food supply first and a non-annexationist peace at the end.[161] It made no difference. Even though the strikes were almost entirely orderly, they met a harsher response than in Austria. Representatives of the action committee met Hertling, but achieved nothing: press reporting was censored, the leaders were called up, and many factories were placed under military control.[162] The OHL was enthusiastic for repression, and munitions stocks were already so big that the stoppage scarcely impeded preparations for the offensive.[163] Ludendorff had stationed reliable troops near Berlin, and a Hindenburg warning – 'To strike is treason' was posted on billboards.[164] The strike had no prospect of succeeding, and the authorities were little concerned by it. Its failure dashed the Bolsheviks' hopes of revolution spreading to the Central Powers and soon left them with no choice but to save their regime by submitting to the Central Powers' peace terms.

The strike's defeat was also a setback for Woodrow Wilson, and the hopes he had invested in the German opposition.[165] It divided the new Reichstag majority, as the SPD's partners opposed its participation in the action committee, although they kept the inter-party liaison committee going. Indeed, the parties represented on the latter agreed on 22 February that provided Germany lost no territory (including Alsace-Lorraine) the Fourteen Points would be an acceptable basis for peace.[166] But the liberal parties and the Centre voted for the Brest-Litovsk Treaty, while the SPD, although denouncing Brest-Litovsk as a 'peace of violence' incompatible with the July 1917 resolution, abstained, and voted in favour of the associated peace treaties with the Ukraine, Finland, and Romania, thus leaving the USPD alone in opposition. The SPD understood that the treaties created a chain of buffer states resting on military power rather than their inhabitants' wishes, but at least they offered an end to the fighting, promised food for German workers, and ended Russia's domination over its border peoples.[167] It appeared that the Reichstag front in favour of democratization and a peace of reconciliation had broken up.

This appearance was deceptive, but during the Ludendorff offensives the industrial scene was quiet, even though – unlike in France, Britain, and America – real wages were falling.[168] The DCGs reported that public opinion was buoyed up by the peace with Russia and the western victories, producing a euphoria unknown since 1914 and an outburst of agitation for expansionist war aims.[169] Down to June, despite anxiety over food shortages, the mood was confident, and further military blows were expected to end the war by the winter. Then the bubble burst. In July food shortages before the harvest dampened spirits; and the Allies' Marne counter-attack dashed peace hopes and pointed to another war winter, causing 'dullness and indifference' even if 'the will to hold on' was mostly unbroken.[170] By August both the DCGs and the Berlin police said the mood had never been worse, owing to the economic situation and the unexpected retreats from the spring gains on the Western Front, the gloomy military prospect making privation harder to bear. Finally, in September food supply improved as the harvest came in, and at first there were hopes that the front was stabilizing, but soon the combination of defeat with political uncertainties caused unparalleled disorientation and confusion.[171] Allied observers were in agreement. A graph of German civilian morale maintained by the American General Staff recorded it as plummeting after June,[172] while W. G. Max Müller, collating intelligence for the British Foreign Office, registered a dramatic change between July and September: Germans would endure intolerable hardship if cheered by hopes of victory, but now such hope was gone and 'the whole machinery of national life is running down ... I have all along insisted ... that the enemy would endure privations, that might otherwise have proved intolerable, so long as they were buoyed up by the assurance of ultimate victory, but that when once that hope was gone their powers of resistance would collapse, and that is the situation in Germany today.'[173]

Unsurprisingly, unrest revived. After July strikes resumed, and significantly the main demand was for shorter hours.[174] The SPD began repairing its networks in the Berlin factories, which in the autumn would prove important. In a spectacular by-election it won back from the USPD the industrial constituency of Niederbarnim, near Potsdam, and although its membership had fallen by three quarters during the war, its voting strength had held up better.[175] On the political scene until July, when the OHL was able to force Kühlmann out of office, business appeared to continue as usual, but in late August the state governments, led by Bavaria, began pressing for peace negotiations.[176] The Generalkommission sent a delegation to demand of Hertling that the government control black market food supplies and unambiguously support a compromise peace (on which the Chancellor remained evasive).[177] On 11 September the SPD executive called for immediate Prussian elections and franchise reform and on the 23rd, in a very considerable step, it announced its willingness to enter a government committed to the Reichstag Peace Resolution. In the Reichstag Main Committee on 24 September Hertling said he accepted the Fourteen Points and Four Principles, and the war minister acknowledged that the Ludendorff offensives had failed.[178] The SPD and the Generalkommission, reasonable men in an unreasonable time, still pushed for a moderate peace and for democratization, accepting as patriots their duty to support national defence, voting war credits to the end, and trying to contain extra-legal action. While Hertling was weakened and the SPD willing to enter government, the events of the previous winter had brought the spectre of USPD-led revolution to the forefront of the German leaders' minds. The elements of the dénouement were falling into place.

At this point a further factor must be integrated. In 1917–18 the Allies stepped up the war of ideas, not only at home with the CPI, the NWAC, and the UGACPE, but also via intensified propaganda against their enemies. The British took the lead – and particularly Lloyd George, who was advised that the Foreign Office was too timid and had directed propaganda towards an elite rather than a mass audience. In neutral America this approach had worked well, but now something more incendiary was needed.[179] After a succession of reorganizations, in early 1918 the Prime Minister called in his press contacts. Lord

Beaverbrook (Sir Max Aitken), the owner of the *Daily Express*, headed a new Ministry of Information, dealing with propaganda in the Allied and neutral nations and at home, while Lord Northcliffe (Sir Alfred Harmsworth), the owner of *The Times* and the *Daily Mail*, became Director of Propaganda in Enemy Countries. Initially Northcliffe focused on Austria-Hungary, where he hoped to incite the subject nationalities against the Habsburg regime, although in line with the cautious Caxton Hall approach the Cabinet authorized him to promise only autonomy rather than independence. In May Lloyd George asked him to give the German army similar priority, although down to September the main agency for propagandizing in Germany continued to be division MI7b of the War Office.[180] Northcliffe envisaged stressing Allied determination and warning the German people that fighting on would mean a continuing post-war blockade (which was indeed a sensitive point); he also hoped to turn the Germans against the dynastic and military caste who ruled them, and Allied caricaturists gave this theme particular prominence.[181] Moreover, whereas each ally's effort had previously been independent, in the final months an Inter-Allied Board for Propaganda against the Enemy met regularly in Northcliffe's London headquarters at Crewe House. But the effectiveness of any propaganda remained limited by the principal delivery method, which was via balloons.[182] Alternatives included floating material down the Rhine from Switzerland, planting it in the Dutch press,[183] and a French attempt to purchase the Rhenish newspaper the *Kölnische Volkszeitung*, but as none of these promised wide dissemination the Allies' best hope was that their propaganda among the enemy troops would spread to the home front.

The German reaction was slow and poorly co-ordinated. No central domestic propaganda agency existed, the civilian and military authorities having agreed in 1917 that the main responsibility for it should rest with the DCGs, whose effectiveness varied from district to district.[184] Until July 1918, the DCGs' reports on German opinion were reassuring, possibly because they placed an optimistic gloss on them, which lulled Wilhelm and the OHL into complacency.[185] Ludendorff did not believe revolution could happen in Germany,[186] although he was worried about civilian morale and he and his staff officer, Colonel von Haeften, repeatedly urged the creation of a central propaganda agency, but successive Chancellors turned them down. Bethmann Hollweg

feared an OHL-dominated publicity machine would hem him in politically, and Hertling, who wished to work with the SPD and the
Generalkommission to isolate the USPD, had similar reservations. After
the January 1918 strikes, Hertling approved a scheme by Major Erhard
Deutelmoser, the head of his press office, to create a new agency,
the Zentralstelle für Heimataufklärung (Central Office for Homeland
Enlightenment – ZfH), which was specifically designed to remotivate the
working classes, but Deutelmoser worked just with the unions and the SPD
and excluded the OHL from the directing committee. The episode indicated the limits to Ludendorff's influence, even in a matter he considered
pressing, but in any case the ZfH started work in April with only two
employees, and although it set up an autumn lecture programme it was
now all far too late.[187] In a gloomy correspondence that summer, regional
commanders and central officials agreed that much of the urban working
class had remained impervious to their efforts.[188] Indeed, German propagandists suffered from an inferiority complex, and believed their enemies
had better punchlines.[189] In a letter in September that the British noted,
Hindenburg openly acknowledged the Allies' impact: perhaps because he
needed a scapegoat.[190] The German authorities faced an uphill struggle,
but they could have tried harder to wage it were it not for fundamental
disagreements over how domestic propaganda should be orchestrated.

NATIONS

The nearest German equivalent to the NWAC and the UGACPE was
not a state initiative at all but an independent (and anti-governmental)
enterprise, the German Fatherland Party or Deutsche Vaterlandspartei
(DVLP). Its originator was Wolfgang Kapp, a conservative deputy in
the Prussian Landtag and former state official who had become a right-
wing activist and in 1916 had challenged Bethmann Hollweg to a duel.
He secured support from the Agrarian League of East Elbian Junker
landowners, and finance – though not nearly enough – from the Ruhr
coal mining syndicate. He advised Hindenburg beforehand, and Ludendorff welcomed the initiative. The DVLP's three presidents were Kapp,
Tirpitz (who had become an embittered critic of the government), and
Duke Johann Albrecht of Mecklenburg. It was launched in September

1917 in reaction to the Reichstag Peace Resolution: many members regretted calling it a 'party' and in reality it was another ultra-nationalist league of the kind that had proliferated in pre-war Germany, intended to propagandize and to co-ordinate activity in favour of its objectives. These objectives were to combat disunity and 'partisanship' (*Parteiung*), and to rally the nation behind 'a strong imperial government, which knows how to interpret the signs of the times not in weak concessions at home and abroad but in Germanic steadfastness and unshakeable faith in victory'.[191] It demanded a 'Hindenburg Peace', which its members understood as controlling Belgium, taking the Briey–Longwy iron ore basin from France, acquiring settlement land along the Baltic, and extra-European expansion. It wanted the Peace Resolution rescinded, the Reichstag suspended or at least dissolved for new elections, and Tirpitz as Chancellor.[192] It proselytized via press inserts, meetings, pamphlets, and films and its activities contributed to political tension before the January strikes.[193] None the less, after its dissolution in December 1918 its leaders acknowledged that it had failed. Although it claimed a membership of 800,000 by September 1918, probably at least half were affiliates from other organizations. It set its dues low, and ran out of money. The more far-sighted industrialists foresaw how the war would end and severed their contacts: it had to lay off staff, and its expenditure fell from 86,000 marks in March to 9,900 in September. The national press refused to carry its communications, and its lectures were too long and academic: it too could make few working-class converts. Most of its members came from Protestant small-town and rural eastern Germany, beyond the Elbe; it lacked Catholic and southern backing, and its members were predominantly upper-middle-class officials and professional men. Although its geographical base resembled the Nazi party's in 1933, its social composition was much more restricted.[194]

This point leads to a larger conclusion: that by 1917–18 nationalism divided Germany rather than unifying it. It is conventional to distinguish between patriotism – a feeling of attachment and defensive loyalty to one's country – and nationalism as a more aggressive and expansionist ideological commitment as a matter of overriding priority to the independence, unity, and greatness of the nation.[195] Germany's 1914 unity had been based on patriotism: on the government convincing the public (including Catholics and the Left) that the homeland was endangered and that the war was a response to aggression. By 1918 the

German Right – and more mutedly the government – had acknowledged that the war was not just to defend the status quo but was also
imperialist. Germany's unification was still recent, and identification
with the Reich in the non-Prussian south and among workers and Catholics remained weaker. Behind the struggle over propaganda lay the
issue of whether to rally the population (as desired by the OHL) round
an expansionist project with which dissenters must collaborate or be
repressed; or, as Hertling (a Bavarian Catholic, though no socialist) preferred, to seek a more inclusive consensus that acknowledged progressive
forces at home and preserved negotiating flexibility towards America
and the Allies: what Bethmann Hollweg had dubbed a 'policy of diag-
onals'.[196] For the latter approach, the DVLP was a complication. In
1917–18 Germany failed to match the patriotic remobilization accomplished by its enemies.

The role of nationalism in Bulgarian politics resembled that in Germany; in the other two Central Powers it was not merely divisive but
also disintegrating. In Sofia, King Ferdinand and Premier Radoslavov
pursued annexationist expansion in all directions: against Serbia, Greece,
Romania, and their own ally, Turkey. The opposition wished to confine
expansion to ethnically Bulgarian regions. Bulgarian political life had
traditions of Pan-Slavism and Russophilia, and an undercurrent of
Germanophobia. In 1918 resentment against Berlin over the peace
treaty with Romania brought Radoslavov's government down.[197] In the
multi-national Ottoman Empire, in contrast, the authorities bore down
on their subject nationalities with great violence. In addition to the
massacre and repression of the Armenians, almost half the Christian
communities in Syria known as the Assyro-Chaldeans lost their lives
during the war, at least 150,000 Greeks were expelled to Greece or
deported from the coast to the interior, and hundreds of thousands of
Kurds were forcibly resettled. As the British advanced into Syria in the
final weeks, rebellion spread among the Arab population. Yet until then,
although dissident officers from Syria and Mesopotamia joined the
Arab Revolt, Hussein's following was small and confined to an area that
had long been marginal. Independence movements in the empire were
weak by European standards and repression so thorough that although
by 1918 the Turkish authorities were losing control over their dominions, separatist nationalism was less important as an explanation than
were desertion and famine.[198]

Austria-Hungary's national movements were more evolved, and its government less draconian, especially after Karl's accession. Once Germany sought an armistice, its principal ally was liable to fly apart. Admittedly Karl had started as a species of Habsburg Gorbachev, seeking to end external confrontation and base his rule internally on greater openness and consent, but not to break up his inheritance. Yet his power in the Hungarian half was more circumscribed, and in his coronation oath he pledged to respect its constitution. By insisting on a broader franchise there, he obtained the resignation of the redoubtable Hungarian Premier, Count Stephen Tisza, who opposed it. But Tisza's followers still dominated the Budapest Diet and his weaker successors still needed his goodwill, and in 1918 his supporters re-entered the government. A modest suffrage reform was passed only in July 1918.[199] Until almost the end, the Magyar authorities kept their grip on most of their half of the Dual Monarchy, including the Slovak area, whose nationalist movement was weak, and the Romanians in Transylvania, 80,000 of whom had left with the retreating Romanian army in 1916. The exception was Croatia, which already had a separate assembly, although its leaders were too cautious to commit themselves to seeking independence. By summer 1918 large areas of the Croatian countryside were falling to the 'Green Bands', which began as groups of deserters in the forests but were swelled by local people and reached up to 200,000. They were, however, as much an agrarian revolutionary movement against the landlords and clergy as a nationalist one against Hungarian rule.[200]

The Hungarians were tough bargainers. In 1917–18 they not only resisted concessions to nationalism in their own domains, but they also defended their economic interests, lowered their recruitment quota, and obtained the promise of a separate post-war army.[201] The 1867 compromise enabled them to veto constitutional changes in the Austrian half, and they were unlikely to endorse reforms that set a precedent for their own kingdom, especially as the Czech and South Slav nationalists in Austria hoped for union with the Slovaks and Croats under Magyar rule. Yet in the absence of rapid devolution little chance remained of keeping the nationalities' allegiance to Habsburg rule in any form, leaving no middle course between autocracy and break-up.

Before the war, in contrast, the Austrian half (Cisleithania) had been a half-way house between authoritarian and constitutional rule. Although the parties representing the nationalities wanted greater administrative autonomy and language rights, only isolated individuals demanded independence, and in 1914 most of the nationalities rallied with unexpected warmth to the Monarchy's support. Their reward, however, was two years of repression, especially in the Czech and South Slav lands, during which the press was censored, parliamentary life ceased, and many national leaders were imprisoned.[202] Karl came to the throne in the bitter 1916/17 winter, with its economic chaos and food shortages, soon followed by the Russian Revolution, which promised autonomy for the nationalities on Austria-Hungary's eastern border. Hence his experiment with liberalization unfolded at an extraordinarily difficult moment, and within a year his authority over the Poles, Czechs, and South Slavs in Cisleithania was breaking down.

The Poles had traditionally been among the most loyal of the ethnic groups. They were less harshly treated than their brothers under German and Russian rule, and Vienna acknowledged their control over the Ruthenes (Ukrainians) in Eastern Galicia, where Catholic Polish landlords dominated an Orthodox peasant population. In 1914 the Polish politicians split. Roman Dmowski, the conservative leader of the National Democratic Party, pursued an understanding with Russia and went into exile in order to lobby the Allies. Josef Piłsudski believed Russia must be defeated before Poland could regain its independence, and he helped recruit a Polish Legion that served with distinction in the Austro-Hungarian army. However, his allegiance was not to Vienna but to creating Polish armed forces, including a clandestine organization, the POW, and in 1917 he fell out of favour with the Central Powers and was imprisoned, while the POW went underground.[203] In the meantime, the 'Polish Club' of sixty Reichsrat deputies remained loyal to the Austro-Hungarian government, which pursued a union between Russian and Austrian Poland under Habsburg sovereignty. When Karl reconvened the Reichsrat in May 1917, the Polish Club called for a united and independent Poland and the lifting of military rule in Galicia,[204] but the real parting of the ways came in early 1918. It was now that Czernin, appalled by the January strike in Vienna and desperate to find extra food, promised to the Ukraine the ethnically Polish territory of Cholm. In reaction, the Polish Club went over to the opposition, mass demonstrations and a general strike broke out in Galicia, and Polish soldiers serving in the Austro-Hungarian army deserted to the Russians. Moreover, in return for the Ukrainians dropping their claims to Eastern Galicia, Czernin agreed that it should become a separate crownland within Austria-Hungary and the Ruthenes' rights protected. When in June news of this promise leaked out, the Polish Club withdrew from negotiations with the government.[205] At the same time the Habsburg administration was losing control on the ground in Galicia, a breadbasket province before 1914 but heavily damaged in the campaigning, and now facing desperate food shortages with much land left uncultivated.[206] The authorities lost the support not only of the Catholic clergy but also of Polish telegraph, telephone, and railway workers, and in October the Poles led the way in taking over the administration and seceding from the Habsburg Monarchy.[207]

The Poles acted, however, only a few days before similar action by the Czechs, who were located not on the Dual Monarchy's border but at its heart. The Czech lands included major manufacturing and arms-producing complexes, as well as the two and half million German-speakers of the Sudetenland, whose fate preoccupied the German-Austrians of Vienna and the Alpine provinces. Bohemia and Moravia were the Ireland of the Habsburg Monarchy, divided between a Slav majority and a German minority, and unlike the Poles the Czechs in the Reichsrat had long been in opposition. None the less, the repression in 1915–16, which shut down much of the press and arrested key radical leaders, kept the lid on until Karl took over.[208] In spring 1917, however, the reconvening of the Reichsrat and the relaxation of press censorship forced a debate in the Czech lands and among the Czech Union of Parties in the Reichsrat about where they stood. The resulting 'May Declaration' was a compromise, in that it envisaged remaining under Habsburg rule but in 'a federal union of free and equal national states', among them a Czech and Slovak state that included the Sudetenland: an arrangement as objectionable to the Hungarians as to the Germans.[209] The Czechs were therefore making their allegiance conditional on concessions by the leading nationalities that Karl was in no position to offer. His further gestures such as releasing activists in a July 1917 amnesty only encouraged greater intransigence: the Czech Union removed its more moderate leaders, and its 'Epiphany Declaration' of January 1918 demanded Czechoslovak independence.[210]

The Czech lands had a powerful labour movement, but the Czech Social Democratic Party had broken with its German-Austrian counterpart and belonged to the Czech Union. The January strikes in Vienna were followed in Plzen and Prague, but only weakly and with a delay, the Czech working-class leaders blaming economic hardship on the war and on the union with Vienna.[211] During 1918 industrial unrest was endemic, including at the Škoda armaments plant, and the Habsburg authorities used troops to repress it, but Czechs were also prominent in the May mutinies in the army.[212] As in Galicia, the authorities were losing their grip, the more so as during 1918 the Cisleithania government tilted emphatically towards the Czechs' rivals, the Austrian Germans. The war had upset the balance between the nationalities, and German-Austrian opinion was also becoming more hard-line, increasingly favouring an *Anschluß* or union with Germany,[213] while the alienation of the Poles made the government more dependent on German support for getting any business through the Reichsrat. Thus in May 1918 the government of Ernst Seidler conceded a major German-Austrian demand and prepared to partition Bohemia by announcing plans to redraw its administrative districts, establishing Czech majorities in seven but German majorities in four. When forced to resign in July, Seidler defiantly described the Germans as the 'backbone' of the Austrian state, and his successor, Baron von Hussarek, promised to implement the reform that autumn.[214] The Czech parties wanted the kingdom of Bohemia within its historic borders, but now that demand was challenged. Hence the Czech National Council, representing the Czech politicians on the ground in Bohemia, began preparing to seize power from the Dual Monarchy's failing grasp.[215]

In 1918 (as in 1848 and 1989) nationalism was infectious, as the Habsburg authorities well understood, and radicalization of the Czechs set a precedent for that of the South Slavs. But a basic preliminary issue was whether the Serbs, Croats, and Slovenes would pursue their separate destinies or join a state of Yugoslavia that would unite them with Bosnia-Herzegovina and the independent kingdoms of Serbia and Montenegro. National consciousness was less developed in Bosnia-Herzegovina (especially among the Moslems) and in Croatia (which was under Hungarian authority) than among the Slovenes, and both the Slovenes and the Croats felt threatened by Italy. None the less, they moved (though more slowly) along a similar trajectory to the Czechs and Poles. In May 1917 the South Slav deputies in the Reichsrat demanded union for the Croats, Serbs, and Slovenes within Austria-Hungary, and the May Declaration became the foundation document for a grass-roots 'declaration movement' of rallies and mass-petitions in support of it. Backing came from the clergy and from women, and a similar dynamic to that in Bohemia established itself, as the German-speakers in the partially Slovene province of Carinthia felt threatened. In May 1918 the Seidler government opposed Slovenia's inclusion in a South Slav entity and tried to ban further agitation, but by so doing it antagonized a movement of which much had so far not been anti-Habsburg. In August a National Council was established in Ljubljana for the Cisleithanian South Slavs.[216]

In its final months Habsburg authority was losing the will to survive. Karl and his wife Zita were vilified in the press as Franz Joseph had never been. Seditious speeches were tolerated in the Reichsrat and published uncensored in the official transcripts. Efforts to counter Allied subversion in the army were weak and late, and among civilians the government never attempted a propaganda campaign. It would have been difficult to see what such a campaign could be based on. Czernin had insisted that the Central Powers' Christmas 1917 Declaration should reserve 'self-determination' as an internal question – the slogan might be useful against the Russians, but was dangerous for the Monarchy itself to adopt.[217] Nor was the dynasty a focus of union. Karl lacked the age and authority of Franz Joseph, and he lost much of his remaining prestige as a result of the disastrous 'Czernin incident', which exposed him as a liar who had negotiated clandestinely with the French, and obliged him to accept the May 1918 Spa agreements that bound Austria-Hungary to Germany more firmly than ever.[218] The disclosure of his bad faith shook confidence in him even among the Austrian Germans and the officer corps, including the army high command. Yet on the other hand by summer 1918 little scope remained for an opening to the Slav nationalists, while the Spa agreements bolted the door to an Austro-Hungarian separate peace.

For a time such a peace had greatly tempted the Allied and American leaders. The Caxton Hall and Fourteen Points speeches had deliberately left open the possibility of a reformed Habsburg Monarchy surviving, to the disappointment of nationalist intransigents. Lloyd George heeded his Cabinet's reservations and dropped the phrase 'national self-determination' (partly because of its implications for the British Empire): at Caxton Hall he spoke instead of 'Government with the consent of the governed'.[219] Wilson likewise avoided the phrase in the Fourteen Points, though a month later the last of his Four Principles proposed that 'all well defined national aspirations shall be accorded the utmost satisfaction that can be accorded them without introducing new or perpetuating old elements of discord and antagonism'.[220] The Allies hesitated to commit themselves to fighting on for the nationalities of Central Europe, the British Foreign Secretary, Arthur Balfour, advising Wickham Steed that 'As far as we are concerned we should gladly recognize proclamations of independence made by subject nationalities in Austria-Hungary, though we could not pledge ourselves to securing it.'[221] But after the Czernin incident they became less guarded. Since early in the war, committees of Polish, Czech, and South Slav exile politicians had lobbied the Allies for independence. The Czechs, led by Tomáš Masaryk and Edvard Beneš, were the most persuasive, and had the closest links with the Czech parties at home; the Poles were more divided, and handicapped by Russian hostility to them; the South Slavs' position was complicated by their relations with Serbia and Italy. None the less, during 1917 the Allies moved closer to making commitments to the nationalities, both for propaganda purposes and to encourage the formation of pro-Allied volunteer forces in exile, and they had to balance these considerations against the possibility of a peace with Vienna. A Polish army was established on the Western Front under French command in 1917, providing a useful manpower supplement, and the French recognized Dmowski's Polish National Committee as having authority over it; in 1918 the Italians formed Czech and Yugoslav contingents. The most significant fighting force for the Allies, however, was the Czech Legion, recruited among prisoners of war in Russia, which in summer 1918 clashed with the Bolsheviks and established control over much of the Trans-Siberian Railway, thus opening the possibility of a new front in the east. Russia's exit also removed an obstacle to commitment to the Poles, and the Fourteen Points backed a united and independent Poland with sea access. In June 1918 the Allies made a similar collective undertaking to the Poles, though extended only 'warm sympathy' to the Czechs and South Slavs: so weak a declaration that to avoid discouragement the Americans clarified that in their view 'all branches of the Slav race should be completely freed from German and Austrian German rule'.[222] This statement was followed by a British commitment to Czech independence, a French one to Czech independence within the historic Bohemian frontiers, and a more cautious Italian commitment to a new state of Yugoslavia. Hence before their final advances the Allies endorsed self-determination in Central Europe, and this clarification encouraged the Poles, Czechs, and South Slavs to secede. None the less, the crucial development was neither Allied diplomacy nor the activities of the exiles, but rather the radicalization of the politicians and peoples within Cisleithania.[223] By autumn 1918 not only did Germany face a rising revolutionary tide within its own borders, but its principal ally stood on the brink.

Nationalism worked in contradictory ways. In Germany, as represented by the DVLP, it complicated the authorities' task in maintaining the patriotic, defensive consensus needed for their country's endurance. In Austria-Hungary Slav nationalism reacted against that of the Germans and Magyars, and alienated all parties from the Habsburg institutions. In contrast on the Allied side, centripetal integral nationalism was less disruptive, and centrifugal separatist nationalism better contained, even in the multi-ethnic United States. The issue was least problematic in France, one of the oldest states in Europe, with traditions of national mobilization extending back to the 1790s. Although the army high command considered men from the south were less motivated to fight, the evidence about civilian morale in summer 1917 is that the problem was less regional than urban, portions of the working class being most disaffected from the war effort.[224] In 1914 French public opinion was mobilized behind the war mainly on the patriotic basis that the country must be defended against attack, whereas regaining Alsace-Lorraine and revenge for 1870 were secondary. And if compared with Germany, the case for viewing French policy as defensive was much stronger. The experience of invasion underlined it, as did the new German advances in 1918 and the shelling and bombing of Paris. Although Clemenceau was not by background a right-winger, the far Right in French politics – as represented by organizations such as the authoritarian and royalist Action Française – backed his onslaught against treason. On the other hand – and again in contrast to Germany – expansionist pressure groups such as the Ligue des Patriotes and the Comité pour la Rive gauche du Rhin, which wanted to control the Rhineland, kept their heads down until after the armistice. On this basis a consensus that united most political tendencies except the socialists was relatively easy to maintain.

In Italy the task was more complex. The Italian state was a much newer creation than the French one, and national consciousness weaker than in Germany. Nor, because it had taken the initiative in going to war, could the government appeal to a reflex of patriotic unity against aggression. Moreover, its ambitions extended well beyond simply completing national unification, as the publication of the Treaty of London disclosed. At least, however, unlike Austria-Hungary, it faced no separatist movements within its borders. The south and islands were less committed to the war, and many soldiers recruited there felt no common identity with the inhabitants of the Trentino,[225] but the north was the centre both of interventionism (in Milan) and of anti-war protest (in Turin). The government formed by Vittorio Orlando, formed in October 1917, ranged from moderate socialists to annexationists. Although criticized for not being tougher with the socialists, it co-operated well with the new high command and faced little pressure from the ultra-nationalist Right.[226] Indeed, it was able to invest not only in a powerful campaign of front propaganda against the Habsburg army, but also to launch a more modest campaign at home. During the Caporetto emergency an Under-Secretaryship for Propaganda Abroad and the Press was created and placed directly under Orlando; by March 1918 its head, Romeo Gallenga Stuart, had a budget of 9 million lire.[227] In 1917 Italy's patriotic organizations merged into the Opere Federate di Assistenza e di Propaganda Nazionale, which though supposedly unofficial was headed by a minister, Comandini, in a relationship resembling those with the UGACPE and NWC in France and Britain. The 'P' Office, intended for propaganda at the front, ran posters and leaflets throughout Italy, and another co-ordinating body for civilian work, the Commissariat for Civilian Assistance and Propaganda, was created in February 1918, while 'war lessons' were taught in schools.[228] In short, although Italy in 1918 saw the beginnings of a German-style radical Right,[229] for the time being the evidence that defeat and occupation were real dangers created an uncharacteristic semblance of unity.

Britain like Germany had seen the emergence before 1914 of nationalist pressure groups and demagogic publicists who had harried the Liberal government. But it lacked a large and vociferous 'war aims party' baying for expansion. Far-Right agitation concentrated on other demands, such as interning enemy aliens, on which subject Lloyd George received in August a petition two miles long and bearing 1.25 million signatures.[230] Agitation centred in the Home Counties, where the British Empire Union, merged with the Anti-German Union, had a network of branches, and where in 1917–18 the government fought a series of by-elections in a climate embittered by the Gotha raids. 'Vigilante' candidates weakened the government majorities, though they failed to win seats: anti-Semitic rioting in Bethnal Green in 1917 had targeted Jews from Russia who were allegedly escaping military service, and in summer 1918 the press was filled with the libel trial of the radical-Right MP, Noel Pemberton-Billing, who claimed to have a 'Black Book' of sexual perverts in the Establishment who were susceptible to German blackmail.[231]

Given its backing from the Unionist Party, the Lloyd George government could largely ignore the far Right in England. Across the empire the demands of military recruiting and supply strengthened discontent from Quebec to Egypt and India (despite the promise in 1917 to the last of 'the progressive realisation of responsible government ... as an integral part of the British Empire') and laid the basis for a post-war upsurge of nationalist unrest.[232] Only in Ireland, however, did conditions become critical during the war itself, and the British authorities there faced the gravest separatist challenge in any Allied country. The common identity of England, Wales, and Scotland had been forged in a century of wars against the French and a subsequent century of prosperity and imperial grandeur. But the British Crown was an entity from which many Irish Catholics had long been alienated, and in the two years before the war the Liberal government had tried to pass a Home Rule Bill devolving powers from Westminster to an assembly in Dublin, which the Ulster Protestants had resisted with Unionist backing. Both sides formed militias tens of thousands strong, many of whose members joined the British army after war broke out. In 1914 Home Rule was placed on the statute book, although not to be implemented for the duration of the war. Even in the 1914–16 honeymoon period, however, although Ulster recruiting rates resembled those elsewhere in the UK, rates in the south were substantially below.[233] And after the Easter 1916 Rising by the Irish Republican Brotherhood and the Irish Citizen Army in Dublin, and still more after the executions of its leaders, the British lost the adherence of the southern counties. The 1918 conscription crisis accelerated the process, as the Sinn Feín separatists, the more moderate nationalists of the Irish Parliamentary Party, and the Catholic hierarchy united in opposition to compulsory service, and British authority in the countryside crumbled. In the December 1918 general election the Lloyd George coalition obtained a landslide on the mainland; but Ireland outside Ulster voted for Sinn Feín, which before 1914 had been a marginal element.[234] In many ways Ireland resembled Bohemia, where the demands of the German minority reduced the government's ability and willingness to accommodate the Czechs, and the nationalist movement also progressed from seeking autonomy to demanding independence. But Ireland was on the western fringe of the United Kingdom, and accounted for only a tenth of its population, whereas shared war experience strengthened the bonds between England, Scotland, and Wales.

Potentially more serious questions about patriotic identity were raised in the United States. Before he entered the conflict, Wilson had feared strain on national cohesion. Since the Civil War the US had experienced massive immigration from southern and eastern Europe, areas culturally remote from the British Isles, Scandinavia, and Germany, which – along with Africa – had been the original sources of settlement. In 1917 over 14.5 million inhabitants of the country had been born abroad (compared with a total 1914 population of 92 million), and many could barely speak English.[235] The influx had caused much agonizing among the political and intellectual elites, and during the neutrality period the debates about preparedness and intervention to some extent polarized on ethnic lines. Even if the majority sympathized with the Allies, many Jews were hostile to Russia, many Irish felt similarly about Britain, and German-American loyalties were split. In considerable measure the socialist anti-war movement was ethnically based. The administration responded to this challenge with persuasion but also with an admixture of coercion, in the process undermining Wilson's political support.

Alongside the socialists and labour, the 'hyphenated Americans' were Creel's principal focus. The CPI's Division of Work with Foreign Born organized societies for twenty-three ethnic groups, including not only German-Americans but also Austro-Hungarian minorities such as Hungarians and South Slavs. Its 'Four Minute Men' across America were expected to speak on the same topic at the same time, and in New York City in 1918 they addressed 500,000 people a week, in English, Italian, and Yiddish. On 4 July 1918 the CPI arranged patriotic rallies by forty-four organizations representing twenty-nine ethnicities. The committee's work became a great nationalizing enterprise, raising the visibility of the federal government and promoting an ideology of democracy.[236]

Creel was particularly concerned with the German-Americans, whose fate would have its tragic elements. Before the war they were among the oldest and most successful of the hyphenated groups. In 1910 some 2.5 million Americans had been born in Germany and 5.78 million had one or both parents born there: in Chicago, San Francisco, Los Angeles, Detroit, Baltimore, and Pittsburgh they were the biggest ethnic element, and in Milwaukee they were over half the population.[237] In 1917, 522 German-language newspapers and journals were in circulation. Politically they were far from united, many having left Germany as socialists who opposed Bismarck; but in the 1916 election campaign their organizations tended to support Charles Evans Hughes, Wilson's Republican opponent, while the National German-American Alliance, although urging loyalty to the US, campaigned against intervention.[238] Wilson warned in his War Message that although he hoped the German-Americans would be loyal, if they were not they would be firmly repressed; in his Flag Day speech of 14 June 1917, which became one of Creel's most widely circulated pamphlets, he warned that 'the military masters of Germany have filled our unsuspecting communities with vicious plots and conspirators and sought to corrupt the opinion of our people'. His Navy Secretary, Daniels, threatened to 'put the fear of God into those who live among us, and fatten upon us, and are not Americans'.[239] Although Wilson warned against vigilante justice, the administration's statements encouraged the wave of xenophobia that descended on German-American communities from the autumn of 1917 and reached its peak in April 1918 when Robert Prager was lynched in Collinsville, Illinois. No other German-Americans were killed, but many were assaulted, tarred and feathered, or abused, had their homes broken into or daubed with yellow; and even the respectable press savagely lampooned them while small-town papers were full of anti-German insinuations. The National German-American Alliance dissolved itself before Senate hearings on it were completed; half the German-language periodicals closed and their circulation fell by two thirds; and hundreds of local societies shut down or were renamed, while half the states passed measures against using German in schools. Sauerkraut was renamed 'liberty cabbage', and German music not performed.[240] In general the German-Americans suppressed their culture and language, and followed their leaders' advice to subscribe to Liberty Loans and assert their Americanism, losing much of their distinctiveness in the process. The process was brutal.

No other ethnic minority was treated so severely. The Irish were another large and old-established community, who dominated the politics of east-coast cities such as Boston and Philadelphia and Midwestern centres like Chicago. After the Easter Rising the British Foreign Secretary urged immediate implementation of Home Rule for fear of irreparable damage to Anglo-American relations, although unavailingly. Because of the Irish diaspora, not only in the United States but also in the Dominions (especially Australia, where Irish opposition helped to defeat conscription in two referenda), the Irish Question took on international ramifications and could do great harm to Britain's reputation. Once the United States was in the war, however, Lloyd George won a year's delay by referring discussion to an all-party Irish Convention, while Wilson, though privately sympathetic to Home Rule,[241] refused to intervene officially for fear of causing 'serious international embarrassment'. The imperative of winning the war re-ordered his priorities,[242] as it did those of the American press, while Burleson excluded some of the Irish nationalist papers from the mails.[243] The same imperative moved the Irish-Americans, whom British observers reported were mostly intensely loyal to the United States, and once their relatives were at the front Sinn Feín's influence diminished.[244] American reaction to the Irish conscription crisis was moderate, and it remained so when the British arrested Sinn Feín leaders on suspicion of communicating with the Germans. The Church discouraged anti-British politics, and when the Lord Mayor of Dublin presented Wilson with a petition against conscription the President shelved it.[245] None the less, during the final months the British Cabinet hardened its mood against the Irish, while American opinion became impatient over the lack of progress towards Home Rule.[246] Although so far the British had finessed the issue, if the war had continued into 1919 it would have added a further element to the many clouding the Anglo-American relationship.

If the Germans were repressed and the Irish bided their time, the conversion of the Jewish-American community was more complete. This was important for the American Left more generally, as much of the dissidence against Gompers within the AFL came from Jewish garment workers, and Morris Hilquit, who did so well in the New York City mayoral elections, was a Latvian-born Jew who led a coalition of Jewish-, German-, Irish-, and African-Americans. But during the winter of 1917/18 the situation altered, partly because of the Balfour

Declaration, which Ludendorff considered British propaganda's cleverest stroke,[247] and was indeed intended to win round Jewish opinion to British objectives. Membership of American Zionist groups rose from 15,000 in 1914 to 200,000 by the armistice, and 500 volunteers from New York City went to fight in Palestine under British command. Even more important, however, were the Bolshevik Revolution and German occupation of most of the Jewish Pale of Settlement in western Russia, while the Fourteen Points lowered the head of steam behind left-wing Jewish opposition to American involvement.[248] In this respect too, by taking the offensive the Central Powers rallied their enemies, and Caporetto had similarly strengthened war enthusiasm among Italian-Americans.[249] American public opinion moved from cautious and divided acceptance of the war towards hypertrophied enthusiasm, while war weariness grew in Europe. Not only this, but the Republicans, who had been split and defeated in 1916, were reunited early in 1918, and now could challenge Wilson more seriously in the upcoming mid-term elections.[250] Although until October the two big parties remained more or less united, the Republicans criticized the administration for not waging war more vigorously and efficiently. As the armistice approached, the progressive coalition that had voted for Wilson in 1912 and 1916 had been gravely weakened, a development that reduced his leverage in seeking a moderate peace. If the war had continued into 1919 it would have been weakened even more. Domestic unity sustained the outpouring of transatlantic energies that assured an unexpectedly early victory; but Wilson obtained it at a price that jeopardized his objectives.

LEADERS

No discussion of the home fronts can overlook the victors' superior leadership. In 1918 Germany, Austria-Hungary, and Bulgaria were still governed more or less as autocratic monarchies, their rulers owing their position to accidents of birth, in contrast to their main opponents. France and the US were republics; Italy and Britain constitutional monarchies under Victor Emmanuel III and George V. Victor Emmanuel was a stumpy man of unmilitary bearing, who in 1915 had carried the day for intervention after the government that had signed the Treaty of London resigned, and he helped to steady the public and the cabinet after Caporetto. Normally, however, apart from morale-boosting visits to the home and fighting fronts, his political contribution was limited. Similarly George V, and his German-born wife, Mary of Teck, had a role in visiting industrial areas to which Lloyd George – no natural sympathizer with monarchy – paid tribute:[251] they set an example by sharing in rationing restrictions and staying in London under air attack. In 1917 George anglicized his dynasty's family title from Saxe-Coburg and Gotha to Windsor. Although the British monarchy had long relinquished most of its executive powers, George V remained titular Commander-in-Chief of the armed forces, and in 1915 had exerted his personal influence in favour of Haig's appointment to command the BEF. In 1918 his sympathies were with Robertson and with Trenchard when the Cabinet insisted on their removal as CIGS and Chief of the Air Staff, but Lloyd George warned the King's private secretary that he 'was encouraging mutiny by taking up the cause of those officers … whom the government had decided to get rid of', and George desisted.[252] The contrast with Wilhelm II's submissiveness to the OHL at the expense of his civilian ministers is glaring.

By 1918 the European Allies and America had effective constitutional leadership, albeit more collegial in Italy and Britain and centred on a single personality in France and the US. All their heads of government had roots in the non-socialist progressive Left, though all enjoyed support – or at least co-operation – from most of the Right. Vittorio Emmanuele Orlando, the Italian Prime Minister from October 1917 to June 1919, was a Sicilian from a gentry family, born in 1860 during the march of Garibaldi's patriots that attached the south to Italy. He had Mafia connections that in 1925 he proudly acknowledged; he combined them, perhaps incongruously, with a career as a professor of law and in left-liberal politics as a follower of Giolitti. In November 1914 he became Minister of Labour; in the Boselli cabinet of 1916–17 he was promoted to Minister of the Interior, in which position Cadorna assailed him as being too lenient towards socialists and pacifists, but Orlando maintained his balance.[253] He continued to hold the post after becoming Prime Minister, and his government represented a mildly leftward political shift, while at the same time the more moderate socialists and non-socialist progressives such as Giolitti became more supportive of the war effort. Orlando became Premier at a moment of disaster but also one of opportunity for greater political unity: which he built on. It is true that he bore down on the PSI intransigents. In February 1918 the authorities arrested (and later fined and imprisoned) Lazzari and Bombacci, the PSI Secretary and Deputy Secretary, for issuing circulars that maintained the party's anti-war line, and long sentences also fell on the leaders of the 1917 Turin riots.[254] But in other respects Orlando was less drastic than Clemenceau: in particular Giolitti, sometimes accused of being the Italian Caillaux, was left untouched. In his memoirs Orlando prided himself on having followed a middle course and presiding for a while over a party truce.[255] He discouraged manifestations by the extreme nationalists, and in May 1918, when he feared the French strikes would spread to Italy, he urged his officials to avoid provoking the Left.[256] In civil–military relations his principal contribution was removing Cadorna (which Britain and France urged on him, but he was keen enough to do) and choosing a more competent successor team. He then supported Diaz until almost the last moment in resisting Allied pressure to attack before he felt ready.[257] In cabinet, Orlando acted as a skilful chairman between opposing views. He spent much time fine-tuning the Italian government's war aims to make them in appearance more accommodating to South Slav pretensions, at least supporting the principle of a Yugoslav state if remaining ambiguous about its borders.[258] In dealing with the Allies – on whom by 1918 Italy was unprecedentedly dependent – he showed restraint over the silence about Italy's claims in the Caxton Hall speech and the Fourteen Points, and good grace when British divisions were recalled to the Western Front.[259] Though less prominent as an orator and a figurehead than were Clemenceau, Lloyd George, and Wilson, he quietly restored harmony among Italy's politicians, between government and high command, and between his country and its partners, at the price of a calculated ambiguity over war aims. At the 1919 peace conference, in contrast, he would straddle both camps once too often by making contradictory claims based both on national self-determination and on the 1915 Treaty of London, uniting Clemenceau, Lloyd George, and Wilson against him.

Georges Clemenceau came from an older generation than Orlando, and had a more turbulent past. Born in 1841 into a gentry family, he trained as a doctor, although soon transferred into a lifelong career as a politician and journalist. He maintained both rural and provincial connections with his homeland in the west and familiarity with the intellectual circles of the capital. He also knew the Anglo-Saxon world:

he lived in America as a young man, married (briefly) an American wife, and spoke excellent English. During his first political career from the 1870s to the 1890s he combined patriotism – he was mayor of Montmartre during the siege of Paris in 1870 and opposed the 1871 peace treaty – with a reputation as an extreme left-winger. After losing his seat, amid accusations of financial impropriety and that he was an English agent, he remade his reputation during the Dreyfus Affair as a defender of Republican and secular values and civil liberties against the Church and army. As a senator after 1903, and Premier in 1906–9, he pursued a second and more successful career, although during the first three years of the war he was again out of office. He had long believed another war against Germany to be inevitable, but he relentlessly criticized both governments and the high command for their conduct of it, in his newspaper (which was often censored) and as chair of the Senate's Army and Foreign Affairs Committees. His arguments were so vehement (and some of them so outlandish, such as his insistence on bringing Japanese troops to the Western Front) that his return to office seemed ruled out by erratic judgement and inability to work with others. All the same during 1917 his star rose, given the difficulties of the politicians – whom he cordially despised – who had led France since 1914, and his focus on treason and defeatism. By November, Poincaré saw no alternative but to try him, as an appointment that signified a break with a failing system but was the absolute opposite of a peace ministry.

In government Clemenceau proved more flexible and prudent than expected. His appointment brought little institutional innovation, although it transformed political practice. He was concerned to restore the state's effectiveness, and he made decisions rapidly and saw that they were executed. Poincaré had been an activist president but now was marginalized as he had feared: informed but consulted only perfunctorily. His precise and legalistic manner (and his letters in a tiny, meticulous hand) infuriated Clemenceau. The Council of Ministers was also sidelined, meeting once a week to register decisions taken elsewhere. Ignoring France's political veterans, Clemenceau headed his ministries with second-rankers, mostly from the Radical Party, as well as with technicians (such as Loucheur at Armaments) who were able but no threat to him. His principal confidants were his private office advisers such as Jean Mordacq for military affairs and Georges Mandel for domestic, whom he saw after rising early every morning and in the evening before retiring to bed. Nor did he come frequently to parliament, although when there he faced down socialist barracking, and his ministry enjoyed commanding majorities.

With limited reserves of strength, Clemenceau had to concentrate on the essentials. Despite his instinctive cynicism, his assessment was optimistic, if France could hang on until American power was brought to bear. His highest priority was not technical – he left armaments to Loucheur, finance to Klotz, and the scandals to the justice ministry – but upholding civil and military morale. This meant punishing defeatism and treason while upholding working-class living standards. It also meant rejecting socialist demands for exploring compromise and reformulating war aims. But his principal focus was on the army, and he combined the premiership with the war ministry. He and Mordacq spent much time on personnel questions and the high command. Initially he had a high regard for Pétain, supporting his defensive posture and opposing further Nivelle-style adventures, while eking out French manpower by extracting larger contributions from Britain and the US. But he lost patience with Pétain and eventually subordinated him to Foch, who in Clemenceau's view made mistakes but was more often right than not, and above all had the necessary faith in victory whereas Pétain was loyal and competent but best in a subordinate position. Even more pressing than the high command was the condition of the *poilus*, and Clemenceau's front-line visits in his waders and floppy hat became legendary. Between March and October 1918 he spent one third of his time visiting troop commanders, often venturing into the forward positions.

A frequent duellist in his youth, Clemenceau was morally and physically courageous, but experience had curbed his impetuosity and he was determined to avoid 'stupidities'. He rightly vetoed Foch's schemes for pre-emptive attacks, and kept his nerve during the crises of March and May 1918. By the autumn his popularity was enormous. The British Embassy described him as being 'honest, straightforward and as pro-British as a French politician could be' and very considerably responsible for public confidence.[260] Admired by both Winston Churchill and Charles de Gaulle, and an exemplar to them in a later conflict, Clemenceau's terse, stark speeches, delivered as a succession of epigrams, became emblems of defiance; but he was profoundly conscious both of his country's suffering and of its weakness. He understood how victory needed British and American assistance, but was suspicious of Wilson, and his relations with Lloyd George deteriorated. This was the more serious as his ministry was taken by surprise when the Central Powers requested an armistice, having not only avoided public discussion of war aims but also failed to formulate its objectives. None the less, he so dominated public life that he was bound to be central in France's response to the ceasefire request, only Foch enjoying enough prestige to challenge him.[261]

Lloyd George had much in common with Clemenceau in his background and approach to politics. Yet although the Cabinet Secretary, Maurice Hankey, capitalized the Prime Minister in his memoirs as 'THE MAN WHO WON THE WAR',[262] Lloyd George conducted a collective effort and his authority was more circumscribed than his French counterpart's. The orphaned son of an elementary school headmaster, he was raised in modest circumstances and a bilingual environment in North Wales by his shoemaker uncle, whom he revered and who propelled him forward. After training as a solicitor he entered politics on a local stage and, after his election as MP for the Caernarfon Boroughs, on the national one. While his family remained in Wales, his liaison after 1912 with his secretary, mistress, and eventually second wife, Frances Stevenson, maintained the adulation that he needed. Like Clemenceau, he had both provincial and metropolitan allegiances, even if his background was radical and anti-establishment. If the Dreyfus Affair re-launched Clemenceau, opposition to the 1899–1902 South African War brought Lloyd George to national prominence, although he criticized this particular conflict as uncalled for rather than condemning all wars on principle. After 1905 he became the star performer in the Liberal government, the architect of the People's Budget and National Insurance, but he was not drawn intellectually to the New Liberalism and was suspicious of trade unions and antithetical to socialism, being repeatedly attracted to centrist coalitions and admiring practical men of action. These tendencies increased after 1914 with the advent of a war whose necessity he accepted, Germany's invasion of Belgium providing according to Frances Stevenson a 'heaven-sent excuse' for doing so.[263] Like Clemenceau, he was a risk taker, rarely more than when he left the Treasury to create the Ministry of Munitions, and although arms production 'miracles' took place in every belligerent his methods were distinctive and successful. He became – in this again like Clemenceau – the principal critic of the lack of energy and focus under Asquith, but he did so from within, aligning himself with similar criticisms by the Unionists and facilitating the first coalition (in May 1915) with himself at Munitions and the second (in December 1916) with himself as Premier. For the Unionists, who feared a divisive election in the middle of a struggle for survival, and doubted the viability of a single-party government, backing him promised a more vigorous direction of the war while retaining mass support. It does not seem that in December 1916 Lloyd George planned to oust Asquith from Downing Street or to split the Liberal Party, but both consequences resulted, given Asquith's resistance to being shunted to a figurehead position and the preference of most of the Liberal ministerial talent to leave office rather than serve under his successor.

Unlike Clemenceau, Lloyd George made big additions to the structure of government – the War Cabinet (initially comprising a five-man team mostly without departmental responsibilities), the Cabinet secretariat, the Prime Minister's secretariat, and new ministries for matters ranging from food to shipping and headed by technicians. He surrounded himself – partly perforce – with top-rank politicians and outside experts, and encouraged frank criticism: he was resilient, buoyed up those who worked with him, and kept a clear head in crises. Yet he persistently aroused distrust among his colleagues (whereas Clemenceau quarrelled habitually and alienated many but was respected for his directness). Crucial for the survival of his government – backed by half the parliamentary Liberal Party, most of Labour, and the Unionists – was the role of Andrew Bonar Law as leader of the Unionists and of the House of Commons as well as Chancellor of the Exchequer and a member of the War Cabinet. Not being a regular ministry, the coalition had to work hard to pass legislation, and Law benefited from a reputation for integrity. Like Clemenceau, Lloyd George himself was mostly absent from parliament, although he also was an accomplished (if more florid) orator, and his speeches were both frequent and widely reported. He visited the battle zone much less, and stayed away from the front line, but he was imbued with the importance of civilian morale and many of his government's achievements – convoys, rationing, air defence – bear witness to his concern for it. Like Clemenceau too, he wished to nurture his country's endurance, which led him not only into friction over burden sharing with Paris and Washington but also into endemic conflict with his military chiefs. After having weakened his position in February 1917 by subordinating Haig to the ill-starred Nivelle, he felt unable to prevent or halt the Third Ypres offensive, over which he rightly questioned Haig's strategic judgement, and which left him ever afterwards with blood on his conscience. In 1918 he succeeded in replacing Robertson as CIGS – a necessary step, as although Henry Wilson provided no better advice he at least respected civilian authority – and faced down the military-inspired resistance in the Maurice debate. He would have liked to remove Haig also, and on the record would have been justified in doing so, but Haig displayed more competence in 1918, partly because his role was more circumscribed. In general, Lloyd George proved an energetic and resourceful innovator who rarely shrank from even the most difficult personal and policy issues, as well as a spokesman who retained attention from the Left while being respected on the Right for his managerial qualities. But like the Unionists he worked with – Lords Curzon and Milner in particular – he was an imperialist, and he strengthened Britain's connections with the Dominions while pursuing Middle Eastern expansion. He also understood the drain the war imposed on Britain's resources and global position and viewed France and the United States as past and prospective future rivals, whereas although he considered Germany an aggressive threat to British interests he was never so convinced of its irrevocable enmity as was Clemenceau. All of these considerations shaped the direction he gave to British deliberations on the armistice.[264]

Churchill remarked on Woodrow Wilson 'that the action of the United States with its repercussions on the history of the world depended, during the awful period of Armageddon, upon the workings of this man's mind and spirit to the exclusion of almost every other factor'.[265] The last phrase goes too far – but had Wilson not called on Congress to declare war the United States would not have done so and the Allies would most likely not have won; nor, without Wilson's personal role, would the fighting have ended when and in the circumstances that it did. Wilson both enabled Allied victory to happen and set that victory's limits. Despite the debacle in which his presidency ended, with Wilson incapacitated by a stroke and his cherished League of Nations unratified by Congress, until November 1918 he was remarkably successful both in pursuing his goals and in galvanizing his home front to support them.

Like Clemenceau and Lloyd George, Wilson had begun as an outsider, but his rise to prominence was more recent and sudden. He was a Southerner, born in Virginia in 1856, in comfortable surroundings as the son of a Presbyterian minister: his father's family originated from Scotland. Although from youth he thought of a political career, he trained as a lawyer before transferring to academic life and publishing on history and political science. By 1906 he was President of Princeton, but after defeat in two major university battles he accepted an invitation to run as Democratic candidate in 1910 for the governorship of New Jersey, having obtained which he publicly broke with the party bosses who had backed him, transferring from the Right to the Left of the party. On this basis he gained the presidential nomination in 1912 and won decisively, leading the Democrats to control of the White House and of Congress and ending decades during which they seemed condemned to opposition. He rose in part because the Republicans were divided, but he appealed both as a progressive, untainted by compromise with the party machine, and yet more cautious and moderate than the Democratic candidate in 1896, 1900, and 1908, William Jennings Bryan. Once in office he co-operated with Congress in carrying out a major programme of reforming legislation, lowering tariffs, and establishing the Federal Trade Commission and Federal Reserve Board.

Foreign policy, in contrast, Wilson regarded as primarily for the executive branch, despite his inexperience of it. After the *Lusitania* went down he steered – against protests from Bryan, who resigned as Secretary of State – into a series of confrontations with Germany over submarine warfare, making demands that were not required by international law and were more rigorous than his parallel policy towards the Allied blockade. Yet although the Germans regarded his neutrality as partisan, the guiding thread behind his actions was his interpretation of American national interest rather than any pro-Allied bias. He admired British Liberal statesmen such as Gladstone, was proud of his Scottish Covenanter ancestry and steeped in English literature, and had made several visits to the British Isles, but he had few acquaintances among British statesmen or sympathies for British imperialism, and neither knew nor liked France and Italy. He wrote to Daniels that 'The English persist in thinking of the United States as an English people, but of course they are not.'[266] He was hostile to the balance of power and arms race system of European politics generally, and not merely to German militarism, although by 1917 he agreed with his advisers that a German victory would force the United States to enter the *Realpolitik* game, endangering its free institutions.[267] On the other hand his mediation efforts had sharpened his views about a just and lasting settlement, and whetted his ambition to attend the peace conference. After Germany resumed unrestricted submarine warfare in February 1917 the Zimmermann Telegram affair created for the first time a potential majority in Congress and public opinion in favour of intervention and Wilson became persuaded of the righteousness and compatibility with national interest of doing so. He acted without relish and in awareness of the human cost: 'I hate this war! I hate all war, and the only thing I care about on earth is the peace I am going to make at the end of it.'[268]

Lloyd George was an admirer of Abraham Lincoln but disliked Wilson and insinuated in his memoirs that the President so hated the war that he minimized America's contribution to it.[269] Certainly Wilson intended to disrupt the home front as little as possible, and play things long with a view to contributing decisively at the finish in 1919–20. In the meantime the US should preserve its diplomatic independence, build up a self-sufficient AEF, increase its financial leverage over its partners, and cultivate Allied public opinion. In September 1917 Lloyd George, after long consideration with his Cabinet, sent a message envisaging closer Anglo-American co-operation both in fighting the war and in making the subsequent peace, but Wilson never responded: as nor did he to many high-level messages from his partners.[270] He supported the creation of inter-Allied institutions such as Foch's command, the SWC, the AMTC, and the IACWPF, but normally he restricted American participation to observer status, and he shunned any limits on his freedom of action. Despite now being at war against Germany, Wilson continued to balance between Allied and German imperialism, and the Fourteen Points, with their warning that a moderate peace programme was the 'only' one conceivable, were directed against both sides. None the less, the Brest-Litovsk Treaty and the Ludendorff offensives compelled a further recalibration and a stronger commitment against Vienna as well as Berlin. This harsher line continued until the military successes of the autumn drove Wilson once more to distance himself from his partners, most notably when in his New York speech on 27 September he warned against excessive economic demands.

Wilson's handling of the home front was subordinate to his international vision. Always a good hater and habitually attributing unworthy motives to his opponents, since a mild stroke in 1906 he had become less tolerant of contradiction and little inclined to cultivate friends unless on terms – such as those with Colonel House – of unconditional admiration for him. His stamina and his memory were beginning to fail, and compared with Lloyd George he had minimal secretarial support. He was the last American President to type out his own speeches, and he consulted little about their content. He expected the legislature to defer to him, and unlike previous presidents he repeatedly addressed it in person. He took poorly to Congressional scrutiny and made few concessions to the Republican opposition, despite its loyal (though critical) support for the war effort. Men of Republican sympathies, such as Pershing and Hoover, held senior positions in the administration, but not the Republican chiefs. Reserving his energies for foreign affairs, Wilson left his cabinet members to run their departments, acquiescing in the assault on freedom of expression by Burleson, who stood to the right of him, although defending the War Secretary, Baker, against Congressional criticism. His personal interventions – such as deciding on conscription, taking over the railroads, and strengthening the War Industries Board – were important but rare. In contrast to Lloyd George's War Cabinet, his cabinet was not an overseeing agency, although in March 1918 he did establish a war cabinet of himself and the most important foreign policy, military, and economic heads.[271] He had less need than the European Allies to worry about pacifism and defeatism: on the contrary, the danger for him was that American opinion would become too xenophobic, playing into the hands of his Republican antagonists, undermining his progressive constituency, and jeopardizing his League of Nations project. Indeed, he discouraged discussion of the League, avoided going into detail, and became increasingly proprietorial about it. This was the more serious as integral to his political style, from Princeton onwards, was reliance on his exceptional cogency with the written and spoken word in order to mobilize a wider opinion against his enemies. In this he was the antithesis of Lloyd George, who impressed Beatrice Webb (an acute observer) as an instinctive fixer, ever on the look-out to cut a deal.[272] Down to November 1918 Wilson strengthened the Allies enough to overcome the Central Powers while not delivering an overwhelming victory. But the strain on US resources, in terms of finance, manpower and pressure on domestic living standards, would intensify if the conflict went on. His supporters had been scattered and demoralized while his opponents were regaining strength. Having always viewed armed conflict with fastidiousness, he found himself increasingly isolated, the preacher's son in a rough neighbourhood.

In the Central Powers monarchs ruled as well as reigned, even if none did so particularly effectively. Admittedly in Constantinople the Sultan was a marginal figure, sidelined by the Young Turk collective leadership. But Ferdinand of Bulgaria had been central in the decisions that brought his country into war when public opinion was unenthusiastic, and in maintaining the Radoslavov government until 1918. He made his will prevail, if being neither liked nor trusted, and stayed in control until his army was beaten. In contrast, Karl I, who became Austrian Emperor and King of Hungary after the death of his great-uncle Franz Joseph in November 1916, fell under the shadow of one of the longest reigns in European history, and took over a *damnosa hereditas* of war and repression. Born in 1887, he acceded when aged twenty-nine: by far the youngest wartime executive leader in any of the powers. He was the eldest son of Otto, who was the second son (the first being Franz Ferdinand) of Franz Joseph's second-youngest brother, Karl Ludwig. After the suicide of Franz Joseph's only son, Rudolph, at Mayerling in 1889, and the assassination of Franz Ferdinand in 1914, Karl became the heir apparent. Until then he had had a conventional Habsburg upbringing: journeying round the empire, learning several of its languages, and training to become a conscientious army officer, before in 1911 he married Princess Zita of the Bourbon-Parma family. He appears to have been pious, cautious, and good-natured, and after 1914 he held more senior command posts and saw a good deal of the reality of war, as well as being regularly briefed by senior officials and by Franz Joseph. Despite his relative youth he had had two and a half years to prepare, and at least for the first year of his reign – to judge by popular reaction on his travels – he and Zita were well liked.

Karl made radical changes of direction, but after first liberalizing he returned to a conservative course, ending up with the worst of both worlds. Both at home and abroad, his room for manoeuvre was severely circumscribed and he hesitated to test the limits. None the less, he removed the core officials of the previous regime, Conrad being replaced by Arz von Straussenberg as CGS, Tisza resigning as Hungarian Prime Minister, and Burián being replaced as foreign minister by Count Ottokar Czernin. Czernin agreed with Karl that peace was urgent, and was willing to press Germany to moderate its war aims and to sound the Allies out, though not to negotiate separately. But Karl went further. He told Czernin that a German victory would spell Austria-Hungary's 'ruin',[273] and he did venture into separate negotiations, both via Prince Sixte de Bourbon and when in February 1918 he indicated to President Wilson through the King of Spain that he would accept a peace based on autonomy for the subject nationalities. Personal diplomacy led him into the error of committing himself more than his enemies, and Clemenceau's publication of his letter promising support for France's claims in Alsace-Lorraine was a blow from which he never recovered.

Karl wanted peace urgently for many reasons – humanitarian and religious scruples, and awareness of the damage war was wreaking on the fabric of his monarchy. He feared food shortages would lead to revolution, and he moved his family out of Vienna.[274] Peace went in parallel with domestic reform, which might remove a barrier to it and reduce the Monarchy's vulnerability to Allied propaganda. Before 1914 Karl had discussed reform with the Archduke Franz Ferdinand, and he was influenced by Professors Förster and Lammasch, who envisaged a federal structure and equal status for the different nationalities, within the framework of continuing Habsburg sovereignty. Karl's Chief of Cabinet, Count Arthur Polzer-Hoditz, drafted proposals for such an arrangement, which Karl confirmed reflected his own views.[275] Yet when he reconvened the Reichsrat in May 1917 he offered it not autonomy within the empire but only a much vaguer promise of constitutional change. Facing resistance from the Austrian Prime Minister to anything more concrete, he had backed off, and although he urged on Tisza a franchise reform that would properly represent the non-Magyars in Transleithania, no majority for anything substantial existed in the Budapest parliament. Part of Karl's problem was that in desperate circumstances he was too scrupulous, and he rejected the option of a military dictatorship to force through change. Moreover, after German troops rescued Austria-Hungary at Caporetto, his government began to realign itself more closely with Berlin and with the German-Austrians and Magyars at home, Czernin urging a gamble on a German victory.[276] Polzer-Hoditz was dismissed, Karl telling him that he regretted it but that Czernin and both prime ministers insisted. But Karl's own views seem also to have hardened, and he replaced Polzer-Holditz by Seidler, the former Austrian Prime Minister who provocatively declared that the

German-Austrians were the backbone of the government. By summer 1918, in fact, Karl had forfeited his initial goodwill, and he was blamed not only for the Sixte affair but also for the failure of the June offensive. By first trying to liberalize and then identifying himself with the dominant nationalities he lost the confidence both of the latter and of their opponents. His authority was squeezed between conflicting national demands, while the army and the bureaucracy that had sustained it atrophied. More might have been salvaged if he had either continued Franz Joseph's policy of repression or broken with the dominant nationalities and withdrawn from the war, but he lacked the ruthlessness for either course. Almost at the end, however, once it was clear that the wager on a German victory had been lost, he first urged a new peace initiative on the Germans, and when they failed to act he unilaterally appealed on 14 September for a peace conference, following up with a manifesto on 16 October announcing the federalization of Cisleithania. It was far too late, and while the Allies rejected his peace appeal the federalization manifesto initiated the Dual Monarchy's break-up.

If Karl took over the wheel of a ship that was headed for the rocks, Wilhelm II had gone far to cause Germany's pre-1914 encirclement, and then approved a war he could have averted. He also approved the unrestricted submarine campaign, despite fully expecting it to bring America in.[277] Although by 1918 his influence had diminished, and the attacks by Allied propagandists were oversimplified, they were not wrong in seeing him as peculiarly responsible for the ruin that had befallen his country and the world.[278]

Wilhelm had been born in 1859 and had acceded as King of Prussia and German Emperor in 1888. Unlike Karl, he had been expected from birth to assume the role and had been groomed for it, including a brief spell at the University of Bonn and training as an officer cadet. Under the Prussian and Imperial constitutions he and not the Reichstag appointed the Chancellor; and dozens of senior armed forces positions, including that of CGS, were directly answerable to him. In his first two decades he tried to rule as well as reign, initiating the naval construction programme that so worsened Germany's international position by antagonizing Britain. After 1908, however, when a characteristically indiscreet interview with the *Daily Telegraph* caused uproar, he delegated much more, and during the war he left land operations almost entirely to the OHL, receiving daily briefings but almost never contesting decisions. Although nominally Commander-in-Chief, and authorizing the 'Michael' offensive, he was absent from the conferences that preceded it.

Wilhelm was more important in naval strategy, prescribing that the High Seas Fleet must show caution in venturing out of port and should avoid a pitched battle with the British, while endorsing unrestricted submarine warfare and its extension in 1918 into American waters. Indeed, Scheer's Seekriegsleitung in August 1918 was intended to distance the Emperor from naval policy, but was established too late to make much difference. Wilhelm also retained a leading role in foreign affairs, chairing the April 1917 and July 1918 war aims conferences at Kreuznach and Spa, that at Bellevue in September 1917 which approved a peace sounding to Britain, and that at Bad Homburg in February 1918 which decided to dictate peace to the Bolsheviks. Finally the Emperor, advised by the chiefs of the Civil, Naval, and Military Cabinets in his household, retained a crucial say in top appointments, for example nominating and retaining Falkenhayn as CGS despite fierce opposition from within the army. After Hindenburg and Ludendorff took over the high command, however, this power too was eroded, a turning point being reached when the two generals forced Wilhelm to dispense with Bethmann Hollweg. They used similar threats in order to pick off other officials, including the foreign minister, Kühlmann, and Valentini, Wilhelm's Chief of the Civil Cabinet, whom they replaced with the ultra-conservative Friedrich von Berg. The underlying pattern was that Bethmann, Falkenhayn, Valentini, and Kühlmann all recognized that total victory was impossible and Germany must extricate itself by combining military power with concession and negotiation, while the civilians among them wished to keep on board the majority SPD and were willing to reform the Prussian franchise. If less enthusiastic about the latter, Wilhelm generally accepted that the war would not end in a great victory,[279] but despite disliking Ludendorff as brutal and power-hungry and feeling that the general threatened his prerogative[280] the Emperor still ended up by parting with men who shared his own views.

Hence Wilhelm's officials were encouraged to trim their sails, including Georg von Hertling, the Chancellor from November 1917 to October 1918. Hertling was in many ways a sensible appointment and by no means an OHL stooge: he made it a condition of serving that the high command should respect government decisions. He had spent thirty years as a Reichstag deputy, including as head of the Centre Party, before becoming Bavarian Premier. He had a reputation for being pious and upright, held a doctorate and had taught logic at Munich University: he was given to retreating to his study to read Aquinas. To begin with he asserted his independence, bringing in a Progressive, Friedrich von Payer, as his deputy and during the Brest-Litovsk negotiations obtaining Wilhelm's backing for a written warning to Hindenburg to respect the government's rights in foreign policy.[281] Yet he failed to back up Kühlmann at the Bad Homburg conference, or to defend the foreign minister in the summer when Kühlmann was attacked over a speech that the Chancellor had cleared beforehand, and was replaced by Paul von Hintze, another OHL candidate. Hertling was not a believer in parliamentary government and he did not pursue the Prussian franchise reform when it became blocked. Although two years younger than Clemenceau, he was, as many round him noticed, very tired. In his final months he coasted.

The latter also applied to Wilhelm himself. Conversation with the Emperor could be disconcerting: he had a capacious memory and quick understanding, and could be charming and humorous. Yet an undercurrent of menace lurked close to the surface, and he was given to petulant and vindictive rages. He was singularly ill suited to constitutional responsibilities that required him to co-ordinate and arbitrate and take a strategic view. His attention span was short, his familiarity with the paperwork limited, and his leadership skills were poor. Many commented on his startling inconsistency, and those who worked with him ended up neither respecting nor liking him. His personality had not changed fundamentally since adolescence: he learned little from experience and from early in his reign rumours circulated that he was mentally unstable.[282] His erratic behaviour made him unfit to serve as chief executive. And by 1918, in the expressive indictment lodged by the English parliamentarians against King Charles I, he was a man of blood.

The victors' superiority in leadership applied not only to confidential decisionmaking but also to public presentation. Orlando was more self-effacing, but Lloyd George, Clemenceau, and Wilson were all compelling spokesmen for their respective countries' will to victory. No one in the Central Powers equalled them. Karl and his wife lacked the aura of Franz Joseph; Hertling was a competent parliamentary performer but his public statements were rare and his response to the Fourteen Points was uninspired and ponderous. Wilhelm enjoyed a new-found popularity in 1914, but for most of the conflict (to his advisers' relief) he took a lower profile. He spoke occasionally – for example for three quarters of an hour to unimpressed Krupp workers in September 1918 – but in the same rambling and ill-judged fashion as in private. Increasingly he absented himself from Berlin and from General Headquarters, retreating to private life with his nervous and ailing wife. Nor did he put on a show of abstemiousness, in contrast with his duty-bound cousin in London, but continued to eat well and consume scarce coal for the royal train's visits to relatives.[283] In September 1918 criticism of him broke into the open in Reichstag circles and in the press, and his son, Crown Prince Wilhelm, had faults that were almost as glaring. Not only were the Hohenzollerns a gift to Allied propagandists, but also – as the Tannenberg victors – Hindenburg and Ludendorff enjoyed a warrior prestige that Wilhelm lacked, and Hindenburg filled a vacuum as symbolic father of the nation.

The Allied governments made terrible mistakes in running the conflict, particularly during its early years. None the less, as a generalization they made more use of female labour, less radically alienated their working classes, and faced less formidable secessionist movements and ultra-nationalist pressure groups. Some of these advantages they started with, but certainly by 1918 they were intensely conscious of the home front's importance, and deliberately managed it by a combination of persuasion and of economic and political concessions, combined with a hard edge of repression. They benefited from superior co-ordination and more uplifting oratory, in addition to their advantages in natural resources, industrial production, and land and sea logistics, better use of military technology, and more harmonized and intelligent strategic oversight. Their politicians bore much of the credit, even if their war efforts ultimately depended on millions of ordinary individuals. Clemenceau, Lloyd George, Wilson, and Orlando – all of whom, whatever their faults, were men of superior and even exceptional abilities – provided direction that neither Karl nor the unstable triangle of Wilhelm, Hertling, and Hindenburg–Ludendorff could match. And as the autumn nights drew in, and the drama reached its climax, the leaders on both sides would face the most testing choices of all.

8

Armistice and After

While we were going through the formalities of disembarking a strange and unreal thought was running through my mind. I had a future. It took some getting used to, this knowledge. There was a future ahead for me, something I had not imagined for some years. I said as much to Captain Brown. He smiled at me; he was a man of about forty. 'Yes', he agreed. 'You've got a future now, Dickie. And so have I. I wonder what we'll do with it, and what it will be like. Because, you know, things are not going to be the same as they were before.'

Lt R. G. Dickson[1]

The process that began the First World War had started in the Balkans: so did the process that ended it. The Allied offensive in Macedonia launched on 15 September 1918 led to a ceasefire with Bulgaria on the 29th, and that ceasefire led on to Germany's request to Woodrow Wilson on 4 October to terminate hostilities. From there the steps towards the armistice were Wilson's decision to recommend one, his partners' decision to acquiesce, and that of the Central Powers to accept the victors' demands. Consent from all the warring powers was needed, and while governments deliberated the fighting proceeded with scarcely a loss in tempo, casualties during the five weeks of negotiations reaching another half-million.[2] Although the American and Allied leaders were anxious to prolong the bloodshed no longer than was necessary, they also feared that halting prematurely might lay insecure foundations for the peace.

The Central Powers' unity collapsed with disconcerting speed. The ceasefire with the Bulgarians was settled in a rush: they did not consult their partners before signing, and Franchet d'Espèrey dictated terms without referring to his allies. Bulgaria's surrender deprived the Central Powers of fourteen combat divisions, enabling the Allies to liberate Serbia and advance to the Danube, which they reached on 1 November. Severing the Danube shipping route and cutting overland communications prevented Germany from supplying Turkey (the rail connection being broken on 12 October) and as the best Turkish units were in the Caucasus, Constantinople lay exposed.[3] Romanian oil was also vulnerable, the more so as Romania had never fully disarmed and now was poised to rejoin the Allies. The Hungarian portion of the Habsburg Monarchy faced invasion both from this direction and from Serbia, and in late October the Budapest government announced the withdrawal of its forces from the Italian front. For the Central Powers, the implications of Bulgaria's surrender were all bad.

The OHL (having previously told the Bulgarians that it could not help them) diverted to the Balkans units in transit from Russia that had been earmarked for the west. It had carried out such fire-fighting operations before, transferring troops in 1916 and 1917 to help Austria-Hungary against Romania and Italy. But the new emergency coincided with a larger crisis. So far from demonstrating that the Allies should all along have concentrated against the weaker Central Powers, the Macedonian breakthrough had such impact because it came after two months of German setbacks in the west and at the climax of Foch's general offensive. Indeed, the Bavarian military plenipotentiary at the OHL suspected the German high command of using Bulgaria as a pretext for conceding defeat.[4] A military reassessment at headquarters converged with a political one in Berlin, and Germany's note to Wilson asked not only for an armistice but also for a peace based on the Fourteen Points and the President's subsequent speeches. It was addressed not to the Allies in general but to the President alone, and was issued in the name of a new government, headed by a man known as a moderate, Prince Max of Baden, and including representatives of the Centre, SPD, and Liberal parties that since the 1917 Peace Resolution had formed the Reichstag majority. Not only did Germany seek to end the fighting, but it was simultaneously scaling down its war aims and democratizing its institutions, thus modifying all three elements in the military, diplomatic, and domestic political stalemate that had endured for so long.

This process had begun in the summer. After the 18 July Allied counterstroke the OHL had shelved its 'Hagen' plan but assumed it could still return to the attack. After the second shock, at Amiens on 8 August, which laid bare how army discipline was failing, Hindenburg and Ludendorff informed the government at Spa on 13–14 August that Germany was no longer strong enough to win the war by an offensive, but a strategic defensive might still bring the enemy to terms. Ludendorff reiterated that the Allies could not break through, and although the Spa meeting agreed to launch a new peace feeler, this should await the next military success.[5] In September Ludendorff changed the latter precondition to one of Germany stabilizing its defensive position – at the same time as his army fell back to the Hindenburg Line – but although the foreign minister, Hintze, made preparations for a diplomatic initiative he had still not launched it when at the end of the month the Allies attacked. Part of the explanation for Hintze's delay was that the foreign ministry was busy discouraging the Austrians from publishing a peace appeal of their own – until Vienna lost patience and on 14 September invited all sides to send delegates to a neutral capital for peace discussions, only to receive a peremptory Allied rejection.[6] But, in addition, whereas the Germans had initially intended using Holland or Spain, increasingly Hintze viewed the best prospect as Wilson, who in his Five Particulars address in New York on 27 September (which the Germans noted) attempted publicly to rein in his partners by condemning imperialism of any kind. As repeatedly since the pre-war origins of Germany's 'encirclement', the foreign ministry hoped to split the country's adversaries. Hintze's officials devised a plan to ask the American President for a peace based on his speeches, while replacing Hertling's government by a broader-based one.[7] The revolutionary potential in Berlin had disturbed the foreign minister, who wished to head it off by a 'revolution from above',[8] while simultaneously the Reichstag majority parties were renewing their attacks on the government and the SPD had declared its willingness to serve in a replacement. Hintze had moved slowly because the OHL had concealed the situation's gravity, and on 26 September Ludendorff's staff officers took the initiative in inviting him to headquarters.[9] A hard-bitten naval officer whom the OHL had chosen to replace Kühlmann, Hintze became a pivotal figure whom both civilians and military respected, and the principal author of Germany's peace appeal.

Before the appeal could go out it needed the OHL's blessing, given the veto that the high command had established over major foreign policy initiatives. The second strand leading in to the September turning point was the growing strain on Ludendorff, as the more volatile, activist, and decisive element in the OHL partnership. During the spring offensives he had already become intolerable to work with. After 18 July he quarrelled with Hindenburg and relations between the two men suffered permanently: he also drank to excess. Hindenburg's physician arranged for a consultation on 4 September with a specialist in nervous disorders, Dr Hochheimer, who recommended shorter working hours, walks, roses in Ludendorff's office, and the singing of Germanic folksongs 'to soften a soul hardened by the weight of war'.[10] Colonel Wilhelm Heye, who proved to be a pessimist about the military prospects, was brought to the OHL to lighten Ludendorff's load. Hochheimer found that Ludendorff responded, sleeping better and growing calmer, which would imply that what happened next was not a psychological breakdown. The more charitable alternative explanation is that Ludendorff, never one to do things by halves, threw his weight into the scales in order to get diplomacy moving. None the less, many observers felt the change of direction was precipitate and the high command had lost its nerve.[11] At any rate in retrospect, Wilhelm himself agreed.[12]

During 28 September Ludendorff appears first to have undergone his own conversion before finding that Hindenburg, a steadier man, agreed with him.[13] If the foreign ministry looked to the politics of war termination, Ludendorff's starting point was that his army required a respite. He knew he had no spare divisions, and as unit strengths diminished the troops were spending ever longer in the line: the manpower shortage was fundamental. But in addition he had been unnerved by the July and August massed tank attacks, which had demonstrated that the enemy could suddenly disrupt his defences at any time. The campaign had become a 'game of hazard', and for several days he had been predicting to Heye a wholesale Allied breakthrough.[14] Of Foch's convergent blows, as of 28 September the AEF had opened up in the Meuse–Argonne and the Flanders offensive was progressing (the latter's success particularly impressing the OHL) even before the British pierced the Hindenburg Line.[15] Ludendorff also feared that the army would become unreliable for domestic repression: it was imperative to save it from becoming a rabble. He was attracted by the plan to broaden the government, shifting blame onto those who had agitated so long against the

war effort.[16] All the same, according to the Bavarian military representative at headquarters, the Prussians hated democracy as much as ever,
and envisaged that after the transition they would return to the saddle.[17]
Yet if cynical about domestic politics Hindenburg and Ludendorff were
naïve about Wilson. They had not read the Fourteen Points,[18] and imagined that Germany could avoid losing territory. Ludendorff admitted
that if he were Foch he would not agree to an armistice, but none the
less it was worth trying. He also introduced a note of pathos, saying
that further sacrifice was pointless if the struggle could not be won: and
he himself had lost two stepsons who were dear to him. Given his disregard for human life thus far, the remark was revelatory.

Once the OHL had shifted, the rest of the government followed.
Wilhelm II had been favourable since August to exploring peace, and
was susceptible to the argument that concessions were needed to preserve the throne. Hintze still had to fight hard to convince him of the
merits of democratization, but on 29 September the Emperor was
brought round.[19] Hertling, who had no wish to stay in post, was sidelined and submitted his resignation, which was part of the Hintze
strategy: although the foreign minister felt that to add to the credibility
of the initiative he must resign too. All rejected the alternative of imposing a dictatorship.[20] As for the Reichstag parties, a secret briefing
conducted on 2 October on behalf of the OHL by Major von dem
Bussche stunned them.[21] Bussche dwelt on the German shortage of reserves
and on the Allied tanks – the latter to an exaggerated degree. He concluded that although the defensive battle was proceeding successfully
the war could not be won. From the parliamentarians' perspective the
OHL had lurched from underplaying the position to broadcasting its
danger. But the only serious opposition came from Max of Baden, the
man designated as Hertling's successor. He warned that accepting the
Fourteen Points would mean territorial cessions and questioned whether
a ceasefire, as opposed to a peace feeler, was needed.[22] Wilhelm overrode these reservations, telling him that he was not being brought into
office to make difficulties for the high command, but Max still smelt a
rat and obtained a written declaration by Hindenburg that an armistice
was urgent.[23] Although the new Chancellor remained unconvinced, the
appeal went out under his signature.

The appeal was a none-too-subtle effort at damage limitation. The
Germans had considered simply rejecting Wilson's Eighth Point, that

'the wrong done to France by Prussia in 1871 in the matter of Alsace-Lorraine ... should be righted', but in the end they finessed the issue by accepting the President's speeches not outright but as 'a basis for negotiation'.[24] They were evidently seeking to exploit their enemies' differences, and to cultivate Wilson with a stage-managed democratization, Max promising to introduce constitutional reform. Hindenburg and Ludendorff wanted above all to win a breathing space, while not being inhibited from resuming hostilities once the army had reconsolidated on a shorter line. The Reichstag politicians behind Max had imagined that taking over would enable them in Dantonesque fashion to prosecute the war more vigorously. They were startled by the revelations about the military situation and reluctant to be saddled with the responsibility for defeat that they rightly suspected the OHL envisaged for them.[25] Germany's decision to *request* a ceasefire was therefore by no means tantamount to a decision to *accept* one, and yet it started an avalanche, so fracturing military and civilian morale and the Central Powers' cohesion that within weeks the Germans had to accept whatever conditions were dictated to them. The OHL was right that Germany could not win, either by attacking or on the defensive, but as of the end of September it could still have carried on for several more months, without Bulgaria and if necessary alone. Its food supplies (apparently not cited in the September discussions) were better than a year before, its armaments production adequate, the OHL was determined to hold the Briey iron ore basin, and the only really pressing raw material shortage was oil, although even for that the navy's stocks made the situation less dire than the OHL assumed.[26] And it would soon become evident that a wholesale Allied breakthrough was not imminent. That the war ended when and in the circumstances that it did was in the first instance owing to Ludendorff's embracing of the Hintze plan, but whether a ceasefire actually resulted would depend on Wilson's response.

Max's note was sent via Switzerland on the night of 4/5 October. It reached a Washington where Wilson had begun another of the periodic rebalancings in his foreign policy. After the Treaty of Brest-Litovsk and the March offensive he had inclined towards the Allies, increasing troop shipments, intervening in Russia, championing the Austro-Hungarian nationalities, and suspending his pressure on his partners over the secret treaties and war aims. But by September he was rowing back on troop departures (admittedly partly for technical reasons, including the influenza pandemic), and limiting further economic mobilization. Colonel House, his closest foreign policy adviser, warned that military success would make the 'reactionaries in authority' in the Allied countries harder to deal with and that it was time to commit them to American terms.[27] The President's 27 September speech condemned 'selfish and exclusive economic leagues' and opposed continuing inter-state alliances once a League of Nations had been created.[28] If he was looking for an opportunity to bind the warring parties to his vision of the peace settlement, the German note presented one.

It mattered that Wilson was in charge. The Republicans attacked the German note and called for unconditional surrender: their foreign policy spokesman, Senator Henry Cabot Lodge, wanted to go on to Berlin. The American press demanded rejection, and speakers in a Senate debate vociferously expressed the same opinion.[29] The President was shaken: he told House that he had not realized 'how war mad our people have become'.[30] Viewed in retrospect, Wilson's armistice diplomacy appeared as a calculated and consistent drive to corner the Germans into submitting, but in fact his actions were less purposive. Especially to begin with he was feeling his way. The President was never afraid of courting unpopularity, however, and he decided not simply to issue a rebuff.[31] Before replying he read editorials in favour of negotiation in two standard bearers of English progressivism, the *Manchester Guardian* and the *Daily News*,[32] but he did not consult the Allied governments. According to France's consul-general in New York, de Billy, Wilson was reverting to his ambition to be an 'arbiter'.[33]

The President's 8 October reply was brief and interrogatory, asking for confirmation that Berlin accepted his peace conditions and that any discussion would be simply about the 'practical details of their application', as well as stipulating that a precondition for an armistice would be a withdrawal to Germany's borders.[34] If this meant what it appeared to mean, the Germans would stay in control of Alsace-Lorraine and could retreat to a shorter line. It was unsurprising that they felt relief,[35] and their reply on 12 October affirmed their willingness to evacuate. Berlin and Washington were now engaging in a public dialogue while fighting continued and Wilson's European partners remained on the sidelines. As Henry Wilson put it, his namesake's conduct was, to put it mildly, 'irregular'.[36]

But Wilson did listen to his allies. Perhaps the vagueness of his first note was misleading, as he reassured the French Ambassador that he had no thought of being close to an armistice.[37] Clemenceau was at first remarkably insouciant about Wilson's lack of consultation and commented that it meant the Allies were not bound, but Lloyd George thought the Fourteen Points 'very dangerous' and 'very nebulous',[38] and at once foresaw that the President might confront his partners with a fait accompli. The British led the European Allies in insisting that their military advisers must be consulted on the ceasefire conditions, and these must make it impossible for Germany to renew hostilities.[39] This point was crucial, for it made it likely that the terms would be so rigorous as to wreck Ludendorff's hopes of gaining a breathing space, and in response to it Wilson upped his demands in his second note, on 14 October, which was the decisive text in the exchanges. The Germans did not help their cause when on 12 October they torpedoed the *Leinster*, a British passenger liner that sank in fifteen minutes with the loss of 450 lives, 135 of them women and children,[40] thus reinforcing the image of ruthlessness and duplicity that had antagonized the Americans in the first place. When pressed by Senator Ashurst, who wanted unconditional surrender and told Wilson bluntly that public opinion feared he would sign away what American soldiers had conquered, the President rejoined that he was not 'a damned fool' and he did not take the enemy at face value.[41] But determined in his usual way to wage war dispassionately and with self-control, he did not wish for Allied armies to ravage German territory as Germany had ravaged their own.[42] He had no intention of marching on Berlin and imposing democracy: he had said as much to foreign journalists on 8 April, and he reiterated it to his cabinet now.[43] Moreover, fearing that Germany would go Bolshevik,[44] he did not call directly for Wilhelm's abdication, and his preferred solution would probably have been for the Emperor to remain but as a constitutional monarch.[45] America's first war against Germany was never explicitly for regime change, although Wilson's premise was that autocratic government was partly responsible for Germany's conduct, and destroying it formed part of the cure. Yet he acknowledged the arguments for severity, and if in his first note he had gone with a clear conscience against public opinion and his own advisers, he was now less sure. It was like entering a maze, he confided to House, with no clear indication of the right way through.[46] The upshot was that the 14 October message stipulated that inhumane and illegal practices (including not only unrestricted submarine warfare but also the devastation being carried out during the retreat from France and Flanders) should cease forthwith. But in addition Wilson required 'arbitrary power' in Germany to be rendered impotent and that the conditions of the evacuation and the armistice conditions must be left to the American and Allied military authorities and must guarantee the coalition's 'present military supremacy'.[47]

This pill was far harder for Berlin to swallow, and only after a desperate political debate did Germany's reply on 20 October suspend torpedo attacks on passenger ships and accept that the Allies' military advisers should decide the ceasefire terms. Wilson still felt more clarity was needed, and before his third note he conferred more widely. On 22 October he met his cabinet, telling them, 'I do not know what to do. I need your advice',[48] but now the second note had demonstrated he was not irresponsibly lenient, American opinion was swinging behind him and only one cabinet member pressed for unconditional surrender.[49] McAdoo, who was one of the closest to the President, felt 'there is a limit to our ability to finance this expensive war and our allies for two years more', and he reminded Wilson of the foreign exchange costs of maintaining an expanded AEF. In addition he commented on the 'Terrible responsibility to carry on the war if it could be ended on our terms', and these words reflected the consensus of the meeting. Daniels, the Navy Secretary, who was at the centre of the growing tension with Britain, felt America would have more influence if the war stopped now: 'If we continue to win their [the Allies'] selfish aims will be asserted.'[50] Wilson similarly wrote to House on 28 October that 'too much success or security on the part of the Allies will make a genuine peace settlement exceedingly difficult if not impossible'.[51] He told the cabinet he was aware of public feeling, as a mid-term election campaign proceeded in which his opponents were making political capital, but he was willing to shelter in the 'cyclone cellar' until the storm had passed, and his principal concern was that ousting Wilhelm would lead to Bolshevism.[52] All the same his third note (on 23 October) represented a further sharpening of his position, for it specified that the armistice must make it impossible for Germany to renew hostilities, and if the Allies had still to deal with 'the military masters and monarchical autocrats' who had previously ruled it they must demand 'not peace negotiations, but surrender'.[53] These comments appeared as a concession to American anti-Wilhelm feeling and a warning against attempts to double-cross the President, but he took it that he now had a clear assurance from a government representing the majority of the Reichstag and the German people that it accepted his speeches as the basis of the peace settlement and he was forwarding the matter to the Allies – whom, he had told his cabinet, 'needed to be coerced: they were reaching for far more than they should have in justice'.[54] A German–American bargain on the contours of the peace was coming into being, and, as de Billy and Lloyd George had predicted, Wilson's partners found the onus placed on them as to whether to continue the fighting.

The precondition for this fait accompli was Berlin's readiness to accept a ceasefire that would cripple German bargaining power. This readiness in turn required a reversal in the balance of strength between the civilians and the military, which took place between 5 and 26 October in tandem with the debate over the war. Max had doubted whether publicly applying for an armistice was wise, foreseeing that it would paralyse the Central Powers' resistance. Many in the army, notably Crown Prince Wilhelm's Chief of Staff, Schulenberg, thought Ludendorff had panicked, and Walther Rathenau, the architect of Germany's wartime raw materials planning, expressed the same view openly in a 7 October newspaper article that urged a *levée en masse* – a fight to the finish with every available man on the precedent set by the French revolutionaries in 1792.[55] Initially the Reichstag majority parties who entered Max's government, including even the SPD, were more inclined to fight on than was the OHL, but once Max raised the *levée en masse* possibility Ludendorff dismissed it.[56] Instead, when quizzed on 9 October, Ludendorff was less alarmist, saying that if the army could cover its shortfall of 70,000 men per month it could hold the frontiers for a long time, although the troops needed rest and an enemy breakthrough was still possible. He opposed ceding either Alsace-Lorraine (with its great fortress at Metz) or Prussian Poland, although the Fourteen Points contested Germany's right to both territories.[57]

Max's government was losing confidence in the OHL even before Wilson's second note, which dashed hopes that an easy ceasefire was on offer and required Germany either to accept defeat or fight on in the most unpromising of circumstances.[58] The government decided that before replying it must conduct a thorough review (which Hertling and Hintze had signally failed to do), but its key members already suspected that continuing was impossible. Wilhelm Solf, the new foreign minister, saw no alternative to accepting Wilson's terms: a 'struggle of desperation' (*Verzweiflungskampf*) would be pointless as Germany lacked reserves. Max felt similarly that they must salvage what they could: the German people had the right to live rather than 'die in beauty'. As the heir to the throne of Baden, Max wished to spare his inheritance from invasion, and he was privately advised by Crown Prince Rupprecht, whose military appreciation was consistently more pessimistic than Ludendorff's. The crucial question was whether prolonging resistance had any chance of improving the peace conditions or whether it would simply delay the day of 'annihilation' of all resistance.[59]

The bulk of the cabinet's marathon sitting on 17 October was taken up with a further hearing of the First Quartermaster-General, and once again it failed to pin him down. Ludendorff now made light of the Americans and the tanks, said the army had enough equipment and enemy pressure was slackening, and saw the key shortage as manpower, but the new war minister, Scheüch, confused the issue by promising 600,000 more soldiers, Ludendorff rejoining that with these numbers the Western Front crisis would never have arisen. His testimony implied that Germany's interest was to fight on, especially if it could survive the next four weeks, and Scheer, the SKL chief, took the same line. Several ministers were sympathetic; but none the less, as Vice-Chancellor Payer summed up, they could not afford to break off negotiations. According to the SPD co-leader Philip Scheidemann, who was Ludendorff's most forthright critic, combing out extra men from the homeland would not improve the army's morale: it was 'a potato question' and the working classes had had enough. Secretary Waldow, who was responsible for food supplies, said deliveries to the front had worsened the situation and it was not viable for long. The cabinet also turned to oil supply, which now seemed less precarious as Romania had not yet fallen and the navy was willing to share its stocks, although even so Scheüch estimated they would last only one and a half months.[60] Although the meeting reached no formal conclusion, the politicians accepted both Wilson's second and his third notes. By implication they discarded Ludendorff's advice.[61] Indeed, they suspected that the general's reborn optimism reflected not a genuine improvement in the military situation but an effort, now the armistice request would not yield the expected benefits, to distance the OHL from the project. Max prepared to 'sacrifice himself' in order to end the conflict, while Payer brooded: 'We are the ones who must make the lost war lost. We bear the responsibility before history.'[62]

Since 1916 the normal method of resolving such a confrontation would have been for Hindenburg and Ludendorff to demand Max's dismissal. This time events went the other way. In response to Wilson's demand for unrestricted submarine warfare to be suspended, the cabinet resolved to recall the U-boats whereas Ludendorff, who considered the submarine campaign a valuable means of pressure, supported the SKL in wishing to continue it. By now the cabinet were incensed against him and although Wilhelm was sympathetic to the navy, Max turned the tables on the OHL by threatening to resign unless the Emperor backed the government.[63] Hindenburg and Ludendorff unilaterally published an army order rejecting Wilson's third note, and travelled without imperial permission to Berlin, where on 26 October they met in heated confrontation with Wilhelm, and the Emperor accepted Ludendorff's resignation while ordering Hindenburg to stay.[64] One of Wilhelm's final, and uncharacteristic, acts of authority, this smoothed the way towards an armistice, as Ludendorff's successor, Wilhelm Groener, whom in 1917 Ludendorff had removed from the Kriegsamt for being too indulgent to the labour movement, was a Württemberger rather than a Prussian, with a background in economic management and logistics, and was much more of a realist. As the bond between Ludendorff and Hindenburg had snapped (the two men never speaking again), the military veto over German foreign policy was lifted, and few domestic obstacles now remained to Berlin acknowledging defeat.

Doubtless the politicians were right. Foch's general offensive did not yield a breakthrough comparable to 8 August, but it ousted the German army from the Hindenburg Line, and the Battle of the Selle, on the same day as the German cabinet held its crucial session, overran the first improvised German position. In mid-October the Americans were still held in the Argonne, but the Flanders advance had resumed and in Northern France and Belgium the Germans were falling back from water line to water line. Provided that the Americans and the Allies kept up the pressure, the demolition of the German army required at most a matter of months. Yet this prospect – so different from that of a year before – took time to register. As recently as 22 September the British Ambassador in Washington had reported that 'the general view among military chiefs in France is that with great effort the war might be ended in 1919',[65] but now the European Allied governments faced grave and painful judgements about whether to adhere to the emerging American–German bargain. That they did so – albeit with reservations – meant that all three sides in the American–German–Allied triangle decided to call a halt. If the first stage in the ceasefire process was the German application to Washington and the second an American–German dialogue, the third was centred on the Paris conference of 29 October–4 November and a grand bargain between the European Allies and the US. Fundamentally absent, however, was a united European front on the political conditions of the armistice, even though Lloyd George, Clemenceau, and Orlando had secured Wilson's assurance that their military advisers would decide the technical terms. When the French Embassy in London suggested seeking a joint interpretation of the Fourteen Points, the Foreign Office scented a manoeuvre to distance Britain from Washington and its instinct was that 'we must clearly temporize'.[66] Hence each Allied capital went its own way. Italy was challenged most directly by the Fourteen Points, and during the armistice negotiations Orlando concentrated on persuading Diaz to create facts on the ground by attacking.[67] The Comando supremo had planned for victory in 1919, and neither Orlando nor Diaz would have accelerated that schedule had it not been for the danger of the war ending with Italy's leverage diminished because it had made no contribution. Although they had no particular interest in an early armistice, to block one they needed backing from Paris and London, and here the policy debates inclined in favour of accepting a ceasefire now.

From the beginning Clemenceau viewed the German approach as a serious initiative that the Allies must consider carefully. He wanted 'to demand the necessary and no more. We must not lay ourselves open to the charge of having, by excessive demands, prolonged the war and caused the deaths of hundreds of thousands of men.'[68] He was maddened by a letter from Poincaré that protested against 'cutting our soldiers' hamstrings'[69] – though the President too was willing to accept as a second best a ceasefire that guaranteed French interests. Yet Clemenceau and his ministers had given little thought to designing an armistice, and initially they underestimated the danger from Wilson.[70] Hence the key input came from Foch, who like Diaz had envisaged a decisive campaign in 1919 but who understood that France's strength was failing and that the longer the war continued the greater was the risk of a disappointing peace.[71] Within three days of the first German note Foch had drafted proposals not only for the Germans to evacuate France, Belgium, and Luxemburg, but also for the Allies to occupy Alsace-Lorraine, the west bank of the Rhine, and bridgeheads east of the river.[72] On 16 October he told Clemenceau and Pichon that the ceasefire must 'put in our hands sanctions that will guarantee that in the peace negotiations we obtain the conditions that we wish to impose upon the enemy', by which he meant that France must occupy the Rhineland in order to annex it or at least detach it from the rest of Germany. Clemenceau and Pichon warned him against meddling in politics, but acknowledged that the peace settlement must have 'support positions' (points d'appui) in the armistice.[73] Moreover, both Foch and the foreign ministry were receiving intelligence, including from decrypts, that the Germans could not resist much longer and would submit, as Pichon put it, to 'practically any terms we liked to impose'.[74] According to the government's postal surveillance, only 5 per cent of the French population wanted peace at any price, and a larger minority wanted to reject the German note on the grounds that it was a trick or because they wished to invade enemy territory, but a majority would accept a ceasefire if it guaranteed that Germany could not strengthen its position and that France could fulfil its war aims.[75] Majority opinion and Foch and Clemenceau were therefore moving in the same direction, and the Council of Ministers gave the Premier and Pichon carte blanche to settle the matter at the Paris conference, a new set of terms devised by Foch being their principal terms of reference. Moreover, by the time of Wilson's third note Clemenceau was 'very much annoyed' by the President's unilateral actions, and he was determined that any ceasefire must safeguard his country's interests.[76]

Britain's position was similar, if arrived at by a process in which neither the Premier nor the military were so dominant. On the contrary, at a meeting at Lloyd George's country residence at Danny on 13 October the Prime Minister queried whether terms should be offered until Germany was more thoroughly beaten, lest it renew the struggle in twenty years. He asked whether Britain should emulate Rome in the Second Punic War by visiting fire and sword upon the enemy's homeland, but he found himself alone.[77] On the other hand, Haig commanded far less respect in London than Foch did in Paris, yet whereas Foch became more hawkish over the armistice Haig moved in the opposite direction, particularly after the Battle of the Selle, when the British broke through the German defences with more difficulty than he had expected. Haig was no longer buoyed up by his former intelligence chief, Sir John Charteris, who in 1916–17 had fed him misleadingly optimistic appraisals, and instead he absorbed the pessimism of his Chief of Staff, Sir Herbert Lawrence. Indeed (and belying his impassive exterior) the British commander proved surprisingly mercurial.[78] Whereas during August Haig had been among the earliest Allied leaders to foresee that the war might be ended that year, now his appraisal was downbeat. He had a poor impression of both the French army, which he considered worn out, and the AEF, which he regarded as incompetent and inexperienced, with the consequence that the British infantry were bearing the brunt. He advised that the Germans could regroup and defend their border beyond the end of the campaigning season. Long in favour of moderate peace conditions, on 19 October he recommended to the Cabinet lenient armistice terms: German evacuation of France and Belgium and Allied occupation of Alsace-Lorraine, but not the Rhineland. He suspected French claims to occupy the latter were motivated by a desire to settle old scores, and that doing so would actually leave the enemy in a stronger defensive position.[79] The Army Council in the War Office, which expressed 'grave concern' to the Cabinet on 24 October about shortages of manpower and of railway troops, took a similar view.[80]

However, Haig's was not the only military voice: Henry Wilson was tougher, as was Milner, who wanted to occupy the west bank of the Rhine. Wilson also doubted if a crushing victory was possible before the winter, but he considered any ceasefire must make it impossible for Germany to renew operations.[81] Consequently the Cabinet had a range of advice on the land terms, and its naval advice was draconian. Wemyss and Beatty demanded the surrender of most of Germany's warships and all its submarines, the admirals saying that even though these demands were likely to be rejected the ceasefire conditions must approximate to those in the peace treaty.[82] Foch had used the same contention, rightly assuming that once hostilities stopped it would be extraordinarily difficult to start them again, and Lloyd George agreed that the armistice should anticipate the peace terms.[83] Beatty deployed a version of the German admirals' argument that the High Seas Fleet was the backbone of the U-boat campaign, maintaining that the submarines were best intercepted when leaving their bases, and therefore Germany must lose its battlecruisers, battleships, and destroyers.[84] Ministers, however, though accepting that it would be difficult to drive Germany back behind its borders, took this as a reason for demanding more than Haig envisaged, whereas the Admiralty programme seemed tantamount to unconditional surrender. Meeting again on the 26th, the Cabinet steered a moderate course, again rejecting Lloyd George's wish to dictate peace on German soil in order to demonstrate that war could not be waged with impunity, and mandating the Prime Minister and Foreign Secretary to seek at the Paris conference 'a good peace if that is now attainable'. Smuts, supported by Reading, the Ambassador in Washington, feared that if the war dragged on another year the smaller countries would be weakened and Germany become inherently more dominant, and the US 'would dictate to the world in naval, military, diplomatic, and financial matters'.[85] Whereas Woodrow Wilson feared that prolonging the fighting would weaken his bargaining hand, the British Cabinet – and Foch in France – foresaw the opposite. Given that simultaneously Max of Baden was prevailing over Ludendorff, a conjuncture was emerging in which all parties saw it as in their interest to settle now; and once the political dynamics altered, humanitarian considerations of preventing unnecessary bloodshed carried more weight.

These prior re-evaluations made it likely that the 29 October– 4 November Paris conference would reach accord. In essence the European Allies paid lip service to Wilson's political peace programme, while the Americans accepted the Allies' military and naval demands. Compromise was facilitated by Wilson sending as his representative Colonel House, a man of the world who got on well with the Allied leaders and was inclined to flattery and to glossing over disagreement. Wilson omitted to give House specific instructions and his telegrams to his envoy, though favouring firmness, were brief, vague, and garbled in transmission. None the less, to start with tension was high, the Allied leaders resenting American high-handedness and the pressure on them to accept a programme over which they had never been consulted by a power that had entered the war late. Woodrow Wilson was ready, or so he said, to denounce 'selfish' demands; he believed Britain was dependent on America and the other Allies needed America against Britain. He was also ready to recommend to Congress that the US not fight on for excessive claims: a threat that House passed on to the prime ministers with 'a very exciting effect on those present'.[86] Yet the threat was hollow, given Congress's belligerence, and unnecessary, given the Allies' disunity. The issue was largely settled on 30 October when House endorsed a memorandum drawn up by Lloyd George. The British Premier had decided that most of the Fourteen Points were vague enough for him to live with, and his text accepted them, while reserving Britain's position on the freedom of the seas and enlarging the scope of claims for financial compensation. The French felt particularly strongly about the latter item and inserted an armistice clause that specified their right to reparations. But in general Clemenceau went along with Lloyd George's memorandum, and although Sonnino had prepared a statement of protest, Orlando overrode him and pigeonholed it.[87] From here on the Point that caused most friction was Number Two, on the freedom of the seas. Lloyd George refused to accept what he regarded as a limitation on Britain's right of blockade, and the threat of an American naval build-up did not move him. Eventually Wilson agreed to postpone the issue to the peace conference, which in fact did not return to it. But with this exception, the European Allies had accepted Wilson's programme largely intact, and within a matter of days first Berlin and then London and Paris had agreed to make peace on his terms. House had justification for telegraphing that the outcome was 'a great diplomatic victory'.[88]

In contrast, the armistice's military and naval provisions appeared much more as a ratification of Allied triumph. Wilson had conceded that the coalition's military advisers would draft these clauses and House largely deferred to them, even though all the European governments expected the ceasefire terms to prefigure the peace treaty. Most obviously this applied to the terms for Austria, which envisaged Italian occupation up to a line almost exactly matching the Treaty of London promises of 1915 and going far beyond the ethnically Italian territory envisaged in the ninth of the Fourteen Points. Yet House made no objection, while Orlando urged Diaz to create a 'fait accompli' and 'for high political reasons' to overrun as much of the area as possible.[89] Even more striking was American acceptance of Foch's programme for an occupation of both banks of the Rhine, despite British suspicions that such an occupation was politically motivated: which Lloyd George voiced but House failed to support. In fact it seems likely that the American did a deal, heading off an Anglo-French combination against him by agreeing both to Lloyd George's Fourteen Points memorandum and to Foch's occupation scheme.

This outcome meant that the land armistice conditions represented a middle position. At a preliminary meeting held at Senlis on 25 October between Haig, Pershing, Pétain, and Foch, Haig had set out pessimistic arguments resembling those he had presented to the British Cabinet. He maintained the Germans could still retreat in good order and maintain an organized resistance. The Allies could not progress fast enough to stop the enemy from destroying the communication lines and regrouping on the German border.[90] Conversely, Pershing, who remarkably had received no guidance from Washington, was the most robust, claiming that 'the German armies were so badly beaten that they would have no other recourse than to surrender if called upon to do so'.[91] After Senlis President Wilson questioned whether Germany needed to evacuate the east bank of the Rhine and even whether the Allies should occupy Alsace-Lorraine, and it was probably in response that on 30 October Pershing recommended at his own initiative to the Allied premiers that the military position was so favourable that they should 'continue the offensive until we compel her [Germany's] unconditional surrender ...' A ceasefire now would 'possibly lose the chance to secure world peace on terms that would insure its permanence ... It is the experience of history that victorious armies are prone to overestimate the enemy's strength and too eagerly seek an opportunity for peace.'[92] Pershing's superiors in Washington, March and Baker, frowned upon his letter as politicking, even though March had previously advised the administration that American military opinion favoured continuing hostilities.[93] But by the time Pershing sent it the Paris conference had already reached substantial agreement, and House told the general's aide that the ceasefire was a political question and the Allied leaders were in favour of it.[94] Certainly neither Clemenceau nor Lloyd George had much time for the American commander, Clemenceau dismissing the letter as 'theatrical' and Lloyd George surmising (wrongly) that someone had put Pershing up to it. Although Lloyd George had earlier sympathized with Pershing's arguments, the advice now was tainted by its source. Pershing was (mildly) reprimanded, but his opinion did not go further, as House and the American War Department accepted not his but Foch's recommendations.[95]

In addition, although unconditional surrender was an arresting slogan, Pershing, like Poincaré, acknowledged as an alternative a ceasefire strong enough to prevent Germany from taking up arms again. This was what he had proposed at Senlis and was what Foch (supported by Pétain) recommended to the Paris conference in the wake of that meeting. The French thus held the controlling position between Pershing and Haig, and Foch ignored the latter's views when making his recommendations.[96] Subsequently Haig rallied to Foch's position anyway.[97] Foch's advice to the Paris conference resembled the position he had discussed beforehand with Pichon and Clemenceau: the Allies should end the war now, without fighting into Germany. Nor did he call for the German army to surrender or be demobilized, but he did require it to evacuate France, Belgium, Alsace-Lorraine, and the west bank of the Rhine as well as east bank bridgeheads (leading into central Germany) at Mainz, Coblenz, and Cologne, and to withdraw within rigorous time delays – a crucial point that would oblige it to abandon much of its heavy equipment while the Allies occupied the railway networks on both sides of the Rhine. In its final version the text agreed required the Germans to hand over 5,000 guns (2,500 of them heavy), 2,000 aircraft, and 30,000 machine guns – i.e. most of their airpower, including their best D-VII fighters, and the bulk of their offensive artillery. They were also to deliver 5,000 railway locomotives, 150,000 wagons, and 10,000 lorries. In addition, they must evacuate the territories in the east beyond their 1914 border, which would bring their eastern empire crashing down.

None of this caused much controversy at the Paris conference, partly because of House's deference to the military over technicalities but also because Clemenceau promised the Americans that France would not occupy the Rhineland permanently. Indeed, the naval clauses were more contentious. The American representatives feared that Britain would become too strong if German warships ended up in the Royal Navy's possession, and Foch questioned if they should risk prolonging the war to capture a German fleet that never put to sea. Although the British took the lead in drafting the naval terms as the French had in drafting the land ones, they compromised to the extent that all the U-boats and much of the enemy surface fleet would be interned in a neutral port under Allied supervision rather than simply surrendered. Subsequently they ensured that negotiations with Spain were unsuccessful, and the German navy ended up in Scapa Flow as a default.[98] The upshot was that the armistice terms would deprive Germany of control not just over its western conquests (as it had expected) but also Alsace-Lorraine, the Saarland, and its eastern conquests. It would lose its offensive capability on land and surrender most of its air and naval forces. These terms would be more than adequate to prevent it from renewing hostilities and would place it at an extreme negotiating disadvantage, as the Allies' armies would occupy every region that their governments had aspired to dominate. Even if the Fourteen Points excluded French annexation of the Rhineland, some less obtrusive measure of control there remained on the cards. British interests were protected in that Germany had to evacuate Belgium and its colonies remained in Allied hands. Moreover – and a most important means of additional leverage – the blockade of Germany would continue. The victors would gain most of the practical advantages of a German surrender and would be strong enough to impose their wishes at the peace conference. The difference between all this and unconditional surrender was one of symbolism and psychology rather than substance: which is not to say that it was trivial.

At the close of the Paris conference, its outcome was embodied in the 'Lansing Note', communicated to the Germans by the American Secretary of State on 5 November. Britain and France declared their willingness also to accept a peace based on Wilson's speeches, subject to Lloyd George's reservations over the freedom of the seas and reparations; while for the military and naval conditions the Germans must apply to Foch. But by the time this note arrived, events had moved on and the Germans were relieved to receive it as an alternative to simply surrendering.[99] The advance on the Western Front was accelerating, the British breaking through the Sambre barrier on 4 November while the offensive that began on 1 November finally brought Franco-American forces within striking distance of the German lateral railway at Sedan. Ceasefires with the Ottoman Empire and Austria-Hungary left Germany alone amidst a world of enemies, and – above all – the long-dreaded revolution had started. Between them these developments placed the Berlin government in a position where it believed it had to liquidate the war immediately on whatever conditions were available.

In autumn 1918 the Turks still had occupation forces deep in enemy territory. They had diverted their best divisions to drives into Persia and Transcaucasia, and towards the oil wells of Baku. Yet they had lost control of most of Palestine and Mesopotamia, their Arab provinces were in revolt, brigands and deserters roamed in the interior, and famine and hyper-inflation stalked the land. They had quarrelled with the Germans and Bulgarians over the division of the spoils, and in summer 1918 the regime began relaxing its controls on political activity at home. Although periodic contacts took place with Allied diplomats in Switzerland, however, the Turks were Germany's most dependable partners and made no serious effort to leave the war until a triple blow hit them. Allenby's advance from 19 September routed their army in Palestine and expelled them from southern Syria. Admittedly, the Palestine front collapsed so quickly in part because it was a second-order Turkish priority. But on 20 September the Bolshevik government informed Constantinople that because of Turkish violations of the Brest-Litovsk Treaty it rejected the document as null and void, effectively resuming hostilities in the north.[100] And finally, Bulgaria's surrender allowed the Allies to sever the rail connection with the other Central Powers and exposed Constantinople to Allied attack via Thrace, supported by the Allied naval squadrons in the Aegean. Although the Turks began to organize the defences of their capital along the Chatalja line, and to disengage from the Caucasus, only one Caucasus battalion had arrived by early November. Meanwhile just four under-strength divisions separated Constantinople from the Allies in Macedonia.[101] It was true the Allies would need time to advance, across difficult country with poor transport and with winter approaching. Further time was lost because Franchet's initial plan was to concentrate against Austria-Hungary and send only a small force against Constantinople, under French command, until the British forced changes. None the less, by 31 October two British and two French divisions had reached the Maritsa river separating Bulgaria from Turkey,[102] and the threat of an advance from the Balkans led to the replacement of the Young Turk government by a new ministry that requested an armistice. Bulgaria's surrender and Germany's defeats in Europe impelled Constantinople to sue for peace.

Disunity among the Young Turk leaders had been rife since 1917, and during 1918 opposition to the regime had become more vocal in parliament and even in the CUP itself.[103] The Young Turk cabinet resigned on 7 October and the party dissolved itself. The new government headed by Izzet Pasha was encouraged by the promise in the Fourteen Points to respect the integrity of the ethnically Turkish portions of the Ottoman Empire (it was willing to allow autonomy to the rest), and lulled itself with hopes of leniency from the British. In fact the Turkish armistice caused serious friction between Lloyd George and Clemenceau, but although the British took the lead the terms they drafted incorporated French and Italian demands. On the other hand, when the Turkish negotiators met with the British Admiral Calthorpe off the Aegean island of Mudros they lost radio contact with their government. They accepted conditions that were much worse than the latter had envisaged and were more rigorous than those imposed on Germany. The armistice of Mudros signed on 30 October required Turkey to demobilize its army, hand over all its warships, and break all relations with the Central Powers, the Allies being entitled to occupy the Dardanelles and Bosphorus forts, control the railways, and occupy 'important strategical points' while all Turkish forces in Arab-inhabited areas were to surrender.[104] The ceasefire shut down a theatre that had distracted enormous Allied forces, and it closed off all chance of German access to Baku oil, but its impact on Berlin decisionmaking was overshadowed by that of Austria-Hungary's collapse.

The Austrians had been desperate to find an exit. Although by 1918 their own soil had been cleared and their armies occupied Ukrainian, Italian, Romanian, Serbian, Montenegrin, and Albanian territory, their economy was deteriorating even faster than was Germany's and mass starvation impended. After the Piave defeat in June their army in the Veneto was melting away. At least at one level, concern to save the Dual Monarchy had brought Germany into the war in the first place, and Austria-Hungary was helping it to garrison the Ukraine and hold the Western Front, as well as providing U-boat bases in the Mediterranean and shielding Germany on the south and east. But the Bulgarian surrender laid open the Dual Monarchy's Balkan frontiers, and when its Common Ministerial Council met on 27 September and 2 October all present – the foreign minister, Burián, the CGS, Arz von Straussenberg, and the Austrian and Hungarian premiers – agreed they could not continue beyond the end of the year. According to Burián, 'We are like a fortress whose provisions have run out.'[105] Once the Germans asked Wilson for a ceasefire, Austria-Hungary immediately followed suit, the lifeline represented by the Fourteen Points appearing the only alternative to capitulation.[106] But whereas Point Ten had spoken of 'the freest opportunity of autonomous development' for the Austro-Hungarian nationalities, even now a political consensus in favour of decentralization was lacking. Although the common war minister insisted that a solution to the South Slav problem was critical to the army's effectiveness, the idea of uniting Austria-Hungary's South Slavs into a single entity within the Monarchy fell foul of – yet again – disagreement between the two halves.[107] When Karl issued a manifesto on 16 October proclaiming the federalization of the Austrian half he could not extend the measure to the Hungarian half, whose government felt so threatened that it proposed to withdraw from all the common institutions. To the bitter end the Magyars resisted devolving power to the nationalities under their rule. But nor could federalization placate the nationalities in the Austrian half, still more so after Wilson announced on 19 October that Point Ten was superseded and the Czechs and South Slavs must decide for themselves what would satisfy them.[108] During the summer the USA, in common with France and Britain, had strengthened its commitment to the nationalities, following the Czernin incident and the evidence that Karl was inextricably bound to Wilhelm. In fact the Habsburg authorities *were* now, finally, prepared to break with Germany in the interests of survival, but as they could no longer make their writ run either by consent or by coercion this change of direction had become irrelevant. By the time of the final Common Ministerial Council of the Empire, held on 27 October, the Vittorio Veneto offensive was in progress. Arz declared 'we must make peace at any price and as rapidly as possible'. If Romania entered and the Italian offensive continued they would reach the end of their strength, but already the army's cohesion was 'at least questionable' and the 'very precarious' transport conditions ruled out rapid redeployments.[109] As even now Burián thought Wilson had not completely slammed the door, however, a final note to Washington conceded the right of self-determination and requested an immediate ceasefire, thus formally breaking with the German alliance.

It was too late. Over the next week a national committee in Cracow took over the Polish areas; one in Prague did the same in the Czech lands; and one in Zagreb declared the independence of the Serbs, Croats, and Slovenes and their union with Serbia and Montenegro. Karl absolved his officers from their oath of loyalty and neither attempted resistance nor was capable of it, as the troops in Italy were now surrendering or deserting in hundreds of thousands. A new ministry representing the Hungarian liberal opposition took office in Budapest, but the Czechs overran Hungary's Slovak lands and Romania occupied Transylvania while a further revolution terminated Habsburg authority in Vienna itself. By the time the armistice of Villa Giusti, near Padua, was signed on 3 November, Austria-Hungary had ceased to exist. The terms, agreed by the Allies at the Paris conference, required the Habsburg army to demobilize and surrender half its artillery and equipment, and gave the victors freedom of movement across all former Austro-Hungarian territory.[110] Not only did Germany lose the services of its largest associate army, but Saxony and Bavaria were now menaced.[111] The tide of conflict was lapping round Germany's frontiers, and the Allies initiated planning for a two-pronged invasion across the Alps and up the Danube in spring 1919. Even before Austria-Hungary broke up, it was no longer able to sustain resistance.

Within a week Germany would be in the same position, the key new factor being the outbreak of revolution. In the end the German home front did collapse, although only after the armistice appeal had publicly acknowledged that the struggle was lost. During October surveys demonstrated that the appeal had catastrophically damaged troop morale;[112] by November commanders were reporting a breakdown of discipline and a danger of Bolshevism.[113] The impact on the home front was equally damaging: according to the Berlin president of police, the public wanted peace at any price,[114] and the Left now argued publicly that removing Wilhelm II would elicit better terms. The war ministry began an emergency call-up of the remainder of the 1900 conscript cohort, and according to the Bavarian military attaché the authorities were attempting a secret *levée en masse*.[115] The call-up exacerbated working-class unrest, as the SPD had warned it would,[116] and propaganda from the Soviet Embassy fanned the flames, but the navy brought matters to a head. From early October the reorganized SKL and naval high command were planning a desperate sortie against the Thames estuary, partly because they hoped to improve Germany's situation but more to salvage the honour of a fleet that had sat in port while the army bled, and to strengthen its claims for funding in post-war rearmament.[117] Unlike the army, the navy had no need of an armistice, and may have wished to sabotage it. Scheer endorsed the plan, as did Ludendorff, but neither Max nor Wilhelm were consulted, and whereas the Chancellor – or so he said in retrospect – would have approved the project, Wilhelm, if consistent to his previous restraining influence, would not have done. Once the battleships began to get up steam on 29 October, however, the social tensions in the fleet exploded. A first mutiny had already been harshly suppressed in August 1917, and the crews had not forgotten it: on the capital ships, especially, life in port was dreary, inaction sapped morale, and resentment festered against the privileges of the officers, many of the best of whom had gone to command U-boats while since the SKL reorganization in August almost half had changed post. The ratings had no wish for useless sacrifice or to see the armistice negotiations interrupted and they began refusing orders. Rather than repress them, Hipper, Scheer's successor as High Seas Fleet commander, gave the rebellious Third Squadron the chance to rest by putting into port at Kiel, where the sailors made common cause with munitions workers on shore. 'Red Monday' on 4 November was the beginning of a revolutionary upsurge, largely non-violent, by workers' and soldiers' councils that usurped authority in city after city across North Germany, while soldiers' councils did likewise in the home army.[118]

The movement resembled the workers' soviets of the January 1918 strike, and its objectives were democratization and peace. As it spread towards the Rhineland, the railways, bridges, and depots in the rear of the Western Front army fell under revolutionary control. This development not only made it inconceivable for the Emperor (who had left Berlin for General Headquarters at Spa) to lead a counter-revolutionary march back on the capital, but also jeopardized the war effort. On 5 November, Groener could still brief Max's government that resistance to the Allies was possible for a while: munitions would last until the spring, although the divisions could get no rest, and the railway situation was 'stretched to the extreme'. The shorter Antwerp–Meuse line, to which he ordered withdrawal on the same day, could be held, but not for long, as the head of the army rail service, Colonel von Oldershausen, had warned him that its transport infrastructure was inadequate.[119] So rapidly were events moving, however, that by the following day Groener said that whereas he had hoped to wait for 8–10 days to establish a new line, now the news from Kiel, the developing American drive towards Verdun, the threat of invasion from the Tyrol, and his information about home opinion had persuaded him that Germany must ask Foch for terms at once.[120] By 8–9 November, Oldershausen reported that the insurgents had occupied the railway stations and controlled the domestic supply depots, so that sending loyal troops against rebel ones would cut off food supplies to the whole of the army. Groener agreed, advising that his troops had only eight days' food stocks and that supply and transport factors ruled out operations against the rebels.[121] While envoys crossed the lines to receive the Allied terms, the revolution reached

Berlin on 9 November and Wilhelm fled to Holland while Max handed over to a Council of People's Commissars headed by Friedrich Ebert and comprising equal numbers of SPD and USPD delegates, although Hindenburg and Groener remained at the helm of the army. This hybrid new authority approved the signature of the ceasefire.

In the first instance the armistice resulted from Ludendorff's loss of nerve in the face of Bulgaria's collapse and Foch's converging offensives. At a second level of analysis, the German army ran out of men. Partly this was due to errors in planning: too few women and too many able-bodied younger males were committed to war production. The problem was not merely numerical, however, for morale and discipline had been decaying since the spring, and the surges in surrenders and desertions intensified the strain on those who stayed. In contrast, domestic shortages and anti-war opposition weighed much less on the decision to appeal to Wilson, although Ludendorff wanted to conserve the army for domestic repression and the revolution would bring forward Groener's decision to recommend an immediate cessation of hostilities. In the Ottoman Empire, where conditions at home and supplies to the armies were catastrophic, the Young Turk regime hung on regardless until Constantinople was exposed, and the Allies' Balkan offensive (rather than the dire domestic situation) was similarly critical in bringing Bulgaria to terms. In Austria-Hungary, on the other hand, food shortages combined with national separatism were central in driving the Vienna leaders towards a ceasefire, even before Vittorio Veneto. But Germany dominated the Central Powers, and once it sued for peace its partners were bound to follow.

The Germans found themselves in this predicament in good measure because of their own errors, foremost among them being to have launched the conflict in the first place. In 1914 the Berlin leaders had overestimated both Austria-Hungary's vulnerability – the Dual Monarchy was far more resilient than they feared – and the threat from the Triple Entente, a fissiparous grouping that had no intention of committing aggression. But even once the war had started, it was far from predetermined that it would end so badly for the Central Powers as it did. A victory over France in the opening weeks on 1870 lines was improbable – if not inconceivable – but if in 1916 the Germans had renewed their eastern advance instead of assaulting Verdun they might well have forced a ceasefire with Russia before the United States became a belligerent. Less speculatively, if Germany had refrained from unrestricted submarine warfare in February 1917 America would not have declared war, while the Russian Revolution, the Nivelle offensive, and the French army mutinies would still have occurred, the Allies would have been hamstrung by a foreign exchange crisis, and most likely they would have had to resign themselves to a compromise in the west and to German hegemony in Eastern Europe. Even with America in the war, Russian paralysis enabled the Central Powers to achieve a new run of successes, so that the winter of 1916/17 did not become a turning point like that of 1942/3, and the flood tide in the Germans' military fortunes came later. They might still have extricated themselves more successfully than they eventually did if in spring 1918 they had accepted the Fourteen Points in the west, although to do so would have needed statesmanship of Bismarck's – or Lenin's – bravura. Renouncing Belgium would have risked a backlash from the German public and the army against abandoning such a crucial piece of territory that had been defended at such cost, but would have enabled Germany to enter peace negotiations in a much more favourable position than it occupied in September. If Berlin had accepted the American peace programme as a bloc, offering a compromise over Alsace-Lorraine, it would have divided its opponents, as Wilson could not have justified fighting on for more, and neither France nor Britain could have continued without his aid. Even later, if the Ludendorff offensives had been delayed until April and the main blows delivered against Hazebrouck, the Channel ports, and Amiens, wrecking the BEF's supply lines, the Germans might still have been able to negotiate from a stronger basis. Until the triumphs of the 'Hundred Days' it remained uncertain how the Allies could eject their enemy from France and Belgium – to say nothing of Germany's eastern conquests – without prohibitive cost. But right to the end the behavioural pattern persisted, Ludendorff's premature insistence on an armistice and the navy's abortive last-ditch sortie eliminating such bargaining power as Berlin retained.

If Germany's mistakes were essential to the outcome, the thread that linked them was excessive influence for formidable technicians consumed by hubris, inadequately restrained by politicians whose judgements, if also deficient, were generally superior, but who could not depend on the Emperor.[122] Both sides committed errors, and the Allies to begin with almost as grievously, but by 1918 their leadership was more sure-footed. Notwithstanding previous stumbles, they were still standing when their opponents fell. By 1918 America, Britain, France, and Italy all had capable and determined leaders with enough support to see the effort through, whereas Russia had lacked both and in 1917 France and Italy's political stability had also been in question. None of the big four Western powers had problems of national separatism comparable to Austria-Hungary's, either at home or in their empires, although repression – of the German-Americans, the Irish, the Québecois, the Senegalese – was part of the explanation. In contrast their labour and socialist movements were courted as well as repressed, and accommodated by wage increases, price controls, and promises of social reform and idealistic war aims, in economic circumstances that in all the Allied countries were better than in those of their opponents. It also made a difference that all four had civilian-dominated governments, whose heads came from the centre or progressive Left. Despite their leaders' fears of revolution, in autumn 1918 none were close to it.

Besides feeding their populations and their servicemen, the belligerents had to manufacture weapons and equipment and get them to the front line. The German and Bulgarian armies had adequate supplies of basic equipment, but the Austrians and Ottomans did not, whereas the Allies had no serious shortages and quickly made good their losses at Caporetto, during 'Michael', and on the Chemin des Dames. The victors reaped the benefits of a revolution in war production, in which France and Britain led but Italy shared and for which the United States was indispensable as a furnisher of machinery, raw materials, and credit. Undoubtedly their resilience arose in part from a preponderance in resources – in population, raw materials, manufacturing, food production, borrowing power, worldwide empires – that if tabulated in bald statistical fashion might seem overwhelming, though in fact was far from being so. It was also necessary to transport the material, and the Allied and American logistical achievement has been too little appreciated. Supply was an incessant preoccupation for governments and for military chiefs, and the war's last eighteen months were peppered with crises: over oil for the Royal Navy in summer 1917 and the French army in the autumn; over food for Western Europe in the winter of 1917/18, when the entire American economy ran into trouble; and over coal in the following summer. At the end of 1917 shipping tonnage and tanker capacity seemed wholly inadequate to meet the next year's needs, and at times during 1918 the American, Italian, and French railways verged on paralysis. None the less, the Allies managed not only to keep the railway traffic moving but also to marginalize the dangers from the U-boats and the German surface fleet and to maximize their shipping efficiency. In fact strategic sealift was a striking instance of how their successes rested not just on resource abundance but also on organization and on management.[123] The British shipping ministry's card index furnished one example; the Belgian railway spotting teams, Pétain's lorry *groupements* for rapid reinforcement, and the counter-battery staffs attached to every BEF corps provided others.

By 1918 the Allies had built a superstructure of intergovernmental institutions. To quote Hankey, 'The war was won primarily by a tremendous combined system of coordination and goodwill, which focused all the efforts of the Allies on the supreme task of defeating the enemy, but which only reached its zenith in the last year of the war.'[124] Actually the contribution of this system is difficult to gauge. Many agencies were formed too late to accomplish much, but the AMTC had real authority in determining shipping priorities and the SWC was valuable as a forum for discussing plans and troop movements, although the most important innovation for coalition strategy was appointing a generalissimo. By the time Foch took over, the 'Michael' battle was already turning in the Allies' favour, but he was largely vindicated in refusing to commit reserves prematurely during the defensive fighting and in husbanding his forces for a successful scheme of counter-attacks, directed to clearing the Allies' coalfields and strategic railways before assaulting the Germans' defences and overwhelming the enemy reinforcement system by sequenced blows. This conception was not Foch's alone – Haig also shaped it – but the Frenchman gave a lead and set a direction and by autumn 1918 the Allies' Western Front strategy was far better orchestrated than twelve months previously and the orchestration magnified its impact. To an extent Foch – who had also favoured a counteroffensive in early 1918, when it would have been disastrous – was fortunate in finally matching the march of circumstances, as indeed was Haig. Pétain, in contrast, who had been exactly right as French commander during the mutinies, appeared at a disadvantage in spring 1918, although actually he had foreseen the requirements both for defence in depth and for a strategic reserve with road and rail mobility, as did Diaz in Italy.

Pershing made a smaller contribution in part because the AEF was ready later, though after running risks with Allied survival during the amalgamation controversy he fell in loyally with the Meuse–Argonne plan despite the danger to his own and to his army's reputation. By the final year the Allied commanders were technically proficient and mostly avoided gross errors of judgement, and some of their Western Front subordinates such as Mangin and Rawlinson possessed an eye for opportunities and the boldness to act on calculated risks, as in other theatres did Allenby and Franchet d'Espèrey.

First World War commanders, even in the new more mobile campaigning, were unavoidably remote from the front line (though by no means never coming under fire) and much of their work was political and bureaucratic. It is a truism that the hard and dangerous task of actually occupying terrain and overpowering hostile forces fell to the field units and their NCOs and junior officers. By 1918 the Allies' combat forces had dwindled from their peak dimensions (the French in 1916; the British and Italians in 1917), but were much better equipped, and their gunners, especially, more skilled in using their weapons. But the big improvements in French and British tactical effectiveness had come in 1915–17, and innovations such as the creeping barrage and counter-battery fire were principally of value for offensive warfare. Although coming into their own after July 1918 they were less significant for the spring defensive battles. Yet it was during the defensive phase that German fighting power was crippled, and the British had little experience of such warfare, trying at first a variant of the German 1917 tactics but finding – before Arras on 29 March or to the south of the Lys salient – that old-fashioned line defences often worked better. The French, in contrast, despite their debacle on 27 May, had learned from Verdun and developed a system of elastic defence with rapid reinforcement and followed by a counterstroke that first on the Matz and then east and west of Reims stopped the Germans in their tracks. But both these formulae for defensive success and the phased offensives that followed them depended on an intelligence advantage (much of it derived from airpower) and on more flexible battlefield logistics than had been available to the commanders of 1916–17. Both sides were in transition towards a new model of warfare, but the Allies took the lead.

None of these innovations would have made a difference had the Allied troops refused to fight: but they first resisted the enemy onslaughts and then, time after time, jumped cover and attacked. Both the French and the Italian armies had endured morale and discipline crises in 1917, and in the 1917/18 winter the BEF manifested warning symptoms. Yet all three forces recovered, partly because of commonsense concessions by their high commands, and partly because of the return to defensive warfare and to repelling the enemy in what were widely understood to be the culminating campaigns of the conflict. The AEF's arrival in strength also helped enormously, and its impending deployment first panicked Ludendorff into a precipitate offensive and then disheartened his men. But morale in France's army remained precarious, and after August 1918 its contribution diminished, while Britain's manpower scarcity threatened the future of the BEF. Manpower considerations weighed heavily in both countries' willingness to accept the armistice. None the less, at every link in the chain from domestic politics and production, through seapower and rail and road logistics, to command, intelligence, equipment, and unit strengths in the front line, by 1918 the victors had the edge.

From this narrative, several insights stand out. On 20 October Sir William Robertson commented that 'our present successes are the result of the past two years of hard fighting', and Haig agreed with him. Haig's final despatch reiterated that 'the victories of the summer and autumn of 1918 will be seen to be directly dependent on the two years of stubborn fighting that preceded them'.[125] This judgement was discerning but narrow. In reality the Allies' strategy of attrition was redeemed by German blunders. Among the most striking features of the story is the manner in which the March–July 1918 offensives not only wasted the substance of Ludendorff's armies but also galvanized their opponents. British reinforcements poured across the Channel and American ones across the Atlantic, Allied combatant morale revived, Foch took over the supreme command, and diplomatically and on their home fronts the democracies closed ranks. All these developments confirm the acuity of Clausewitz's observation that the defensive is stronger than the offensive. It may seem counter-intuitive, as no war can be won without moving forward. But until summer 1918 the Allies' fundamental problem was how to defeat and dislodge the German army, and only when Ludendorff attacked in the west did he so weaken his forces as to render them incapable of repelling the subsequent counterstroke. Like Harold Godwin's housecarles on Senlac Hill, Napoleon's Imperial Guard at

Waterloo, or Pickett's Confederates at Gettysburg, they were most vulnerable when they sallied forth, and most imposing as they sealed their downfall. A further insight comes from American political science: that a war is normally terminated when all parties acknowledge that its outcome has become irreversible.[126] For many German front-line troops this realization came after the failure of 'Michael', the heaviest blow their army delivered and one that it could never equal again. For the OHL matters were less obvious, and only on 28 September did Ludendorff acknowledge that neither defensively nor offensively could Germany prevail and that further effort was pointless. Although within days he backtracked, that perception remained valid.

Ruminating at the close – in not dissimilar circumstances – of the Kuwait war in 1991, President George H. W. Bush commented how unlike at Tokyo Bay in 1945 'It hasn't been a clean end – there is no battleship *Missouri* surrender.'[127] The First World War also lacked such a surrender, its termination being arbitrated by a power that was simultaneously a belligerent. Whereas between 1914 and 1918 the leaders on both sides had insisted that only a decisive, smashing victory would lay the basis of a lasting peace and protect succeeding generations from renewed armed conflict, the actual ending was more ambiguous. The German public, whose press had concealed from them the gravity of the military situation, were presented with the unprecedented spectacle of their army's voluntary withdrawal and abandonment of its heavy equipment when it still stood everywhere on enemy territory. Yet the army mostly stayed loyal to its officers even after the revolution, and marched back in good order. Flowers and festivities attended its homecoming, and in Berlin on 10 December Ebert declared to the returning columns that 'No enemy has conquered you.'[128] Although the Allies insisted that the 1919 Treaty of Versailles was compatible with the basis on which the Germans had agreed to the armistice,[129] even the parliamentary politicians who had taken Germany out of the war and led the new republic dissented and felt double-crossed. Their sense of betrayal fed the intellectual and political xenophobia of the Weimar years.

In these circumstances the notion that there was something suspect about the defeat quickly gained currency. The term *Dolchstoß* ('stab in the back') appeared first in the Swiss daily, the *Neue Zürcher Zeitung*, in December 1918, but was soon in circulation in Germany too, and Hindenburg bestowed it with his authority when in November 1919 he testified to the Reichstag's Commission of Inquiry into the disaster. The genie was now out of the bottle, and not only did the German army and navy plan throughout the 1920s to renew hostilities, but propaganda from ex-officers, from paramilitary and ultra-nationalist agitators, and from the Protestant clergy accustomed middle-class opinion to the idea that the outcome had been a cheat. If Germany had not been properly beaten (and if, as a further propaganda campaign asserted, it bore no guilt for the outbreak of war) it would be justified on grounds of both morality and practicality in re-enacting the enterprise.[130] Adolf Hitler, the decorated soldier who (according to his own, implausible, account) decided directly after hearing of the armistice that he would enter politics[131] and the veterans who surrounded him were committed from the moment they gained office to staging a second round. From autumn 1918 onwards the ultra-nationalists of the Pan-German League deliberately identified the internal enemy who supposedly had betrayed the country as not just the democratic and socialist Left but also, and behind them, the Jews.[132]

Pershing's warning that the victors were underestimating the enemy's collapse and failing to secure the future peace therefore seems prescient. But it poses the question of exactly how and when his masters should have acted differently. Two turning points stand out, at the beginning of the ceasefire process and at its end, for the timing of the latter was indeed unfortunate. As early as 12 November, First Sea Lord Sir Eric Geddes – doubtless smarting over the naval clauses – wrote to Beatty that 'Had we known how bad things were in Germany, we might have got stiffer terms.'[133] In the following February, Clemenceau testified to a parliamentary commission that 'If we had been better informed we would have imposed much harsher conditions.'[134] While the Paris conference was deliberating the German Revolution had yet to begin, and although the Ottoman Empire and Austria-Hungary were falling away the German army was still conducting an orderly retreat and portions of it were fighting hard and daily inflicting thousands of Allied casualties. Haig's gloom at Senlis was a minority viewpoint, but at the Paris conference Foch predicted that if the Germans rejected the terms another one to three months of fighting would be needed.[135] Admittedly, at the same time he was also saying if the Germans refused to sign he could get them to capitulate in three weeks, and subsequently he told an unconvinced Haig that he would have needed just one week.[136] None the less, good grounds exist for saying that the Allies arrived at their conclusions before they knew the full measure of Germany's predicament. Had they waited even two weeks longer the logistical collapse that Groener dreaded might have materialized. This does not necessarily mean, however, that the victors would have driven deeper into enemy territory. Lloyd George and Henry Wilson wanted to keep British troops out of Germany for fear of ideological contagion, the Prime Minister characterizing the country as a 'cholera area'.[137] Although Clemenceau professed to believe that France was safe against Bolshevism, on 9 November the Paris press censors were told to prevent all mention of soviets spreading east of the Rhine.[138] Woodrow Wilson was consistently averse to occupying Germany, feared revolution there, and tried to limit political upheaval.[139] Statements by the Allied leaders that if they had known more they would have exacted harsher armistice conditions should be treated sceptically, especially as both the President and the European Allied leaders considered the actual terms so stringent that a refusal was probable.[140]

On the other hand, at the beginning of the ceasefire process Poincaré, Lloyd George, and Cabot Lodge all sensed that halting now would be premature. If Wilson had simply rejected the first German note, the consequence, given the initial bellicosity of Max of Baden's government, might well have been to postpone the German Revolution and continue the war into a spring campaign, ending in an Allied triumph on German territory and the demobilization of the enemy army on terms resembling those imposed on the other Central Powers. After mass surrenders and invasion German nationalists would indeed have found it harder to contend that it should all be tried again. As against this, six more months of combat would have inflicted tens of thousands of additional casualties (and the human cost of prolonging the fighting weighed with Allied leaders from McAdoo to Foch), whereas the armistice conditions already furnished both securities and bargaining assets. Nine months later they proved adequate for Germany to be compelled to accept the reviled Versailles Treaty even after the victors had begun demobilizing, Groener again advising his government not to resist. Given that none of the Allies intended to impose democratization at gunpoint or to occupy the German heartland, the difference embodied in an unconditional surrender would have been primarily symbolic and, in a revealing moment during his meeting in October with Senator Ashurst, Wilson had queried whether such symbolism was relevant.[141] The French leaders, who inhabited a different emotional universe from the President, had fewer illusions about their enemies, and fully acknowledged the symbolic significance for their own country of revenge for 1870 and the return of Alsace-Lorraine, yet they too believed the substance was what mattered.[142] As Foch summarized on 9 November, 'to continue the struggle would be to ... kill 50,000 or 100,000 Frenchmen for results that are problematical'. Such a judgement contrasted starkly with the OHL's hubris at the start of the year.[143]

The Allied leaders underestimated the sheer derangement that was spreading in Germany, and the demonic energies unleashed by defeat.[144] At the outset of the Second World War, Hitler predicted to the Reichstag that there would never be another 11 November 1918: by which he meant that even if beaten Germany would fight to a finish. But his enemies with their 'unconditional surrender' doctrine resolved likewise not to re-enact the Fourteen Points and the armistice. Both sides rejected the previous model, and after 1945 the outcome was indeed – after bombardment, invasion, occupation, and the destruction of the German state – a more durable peace. Yet the foundations of that durability were not only a transparent demonstration that war did not pay but also Anglo-American involvement in rebuilding Europe and tacit co-operation for another forty years between the Western allies and the Soviets in keeping Germany occupied and divided and its armaments limited. A combination of coercion with conciliation of the defeated and long-haul commitment among the victors made the difference, rather than simply the circumstances of the ceasefire. After 1918, even if the German army had been routed and its homeland invaded, it is difficult to credit that the Versailles settlement could have been upheld without a similar long-term engagement. And had it been upheld Europe would have been spared a second great conflict, as by permanently disarming Germany, demilitarizing its western border, and by providing for an Allied occupation of the Rhineland that could last at least fifteen years, the 1919 treaty contained enough to make it impossible for Berlin to resort to violence again. The melancholy implication is that even though the Allies had undoubtedly triumphed, to translate their triumph into an enduring peace necessitated years more of unrelenting and concerted vigilance.[145] This requirement proved too much for an Atlantic bloc that was as yet a novelty, whose members were unused to working together, and whose traumatized citizens and leaders yearned to return to normalcy. By conciliating first the Weimar Republic and then the Nazi regime, Britain and America bear the primary responsibility for dismantling the disarmament and security provisions of the Versailles Treaty, inter-war French governments being obliged to follow behind them.[146] Moreover, the appeasement of Germany resulted not just from misplaced idealism but also from the startling depths of hostility and rivalry that divided the Western democracies, and did so already as they fought alongside each other in 1918. Even so, the armistice terms were adequate for their purpose, and the decision to settle for them was defensible. The real mistakes came later.

Such considerations were for the future when in the small hours of Wednesday, 6 November, the Germans radioed Foch for terms. Their delegation crossed the French lines on the following morning and after a sombre passage by road and rail through ravaged landscapes its members pulled into a siding in the Compiègne forest, near the village of Rethondes on the river Aisne. Foch had sought 'a place of solitude assuring calm, silence, isolation, respect for the beaten adversary',[147] and his conduct of the closing chapter tempered magnanimity with rigour. His officers had identified a clearing from which the French railborne artillery had pounded the German lines, and the two trains drew up in parallel a hundred metres apart. The principal German coach had belonged to Napoleon III's consort, the Empress Eugénie, but the delegates met in Foch's train, in wagon 2419D, a dining car that had entered service with the Compagnie internationale des Wagons-lits in 1914. Between the wars the clearing and the dining car would be a place of pilgrimage, a stone tablet bearing the epitaph:

HERE,

ON 11 NOVEMBER 1918,

SUCCUMBED THE CRIMINAL PRIDE OF THE GERMAN EMPIRE,

VANQUISHED BY THE FREE PEOPLES

THAT IT SOUGHT TO ENSLAVE[148]

Following its reincarnation for Hitler's armistice in 1940 wagon 2419D became a victory trophy in the Lustgarten in Berlin. Later it was transferred to Thuringia, where in April 1945 its SS guards torched it. It was assumed to have been lost completely, until after German reunification fragments resurfaced from concealment and were returned home.

In these sequestered confines Foch, accompanied by Weygand, Wemyss, and the British Rear-Admiral George Hope, confronted the Germans, headed by Matthias Erzberger of the Centre Party (the inspirer of the 1917 Peace Resolution), while Captain Ernst Vanselow, Count Alfred von Oberndorff, and Major-General Detlev von Winterfeldt respectively represented the navy, the foreign ministry, and the army. Wemyss kept a record of his recollections. Erzberger was 'a common looking man. Typical German bourgeois'; Winterfeldt 'a horrid-looking man, with a cruel face'; the Germans looked 'very much distressed' whereas the French were 'all naturally very elated but dignified and calm'.[149] Foch had no mandate to bargain and he rebuffed Erzberger's efforts to do so: the Germans accepted the conditions in principle, though they were shocked by the severity and feared for their ability to keep order. A courier re-crossed the lines, with difficulty, on 9 November, and Ebert's new governing council agreed unanimously that they must yield. Two messages went to Erzberger, one from Hindenburg asking for concessions on certain points but if these were refused advising him to sign regardless; the other from the government also authorizing him to sign but to protest that the consequence would be famine. In the last discussion before the signature at 5 a.m. on Monday the 11th of the text that took effect six hours later, Erzberger did extract modifications, nearly all designed to fend off chaos. The Germans would deliver 25,000 machine guns (instead of 30,000), 1,700 aircraft (instead of 2,000), and 5,000 lorries (instead of 10,000), they had six more days to retreat behind the Rhine, and the neutral zone east of the river was narrowed from thirty to ten kilometres so that their soldiers would remain in the Ruhr.[150] Although finally Foch had heeded his antagonist's entreaties, there was no doubt who had won. In that grey November daybreak the termination seemed an anticlimax, an occasion at once strange and subdued; and yet its setting, in the means of transport that had propelled so many to their destinies, was apposite. 'It is a curious scene in the middle of the forest', Wemyss mused, 'raining & leaves falling & yet there is nothing sad – at any rate for us.'

Notes

PREFACE

1. G. Bonnefous, *Histoire politique de la Troisième République*, II (Paris, 1967), 380.
2. W. Schücking et al. (eds.), *Die Ursachen des deutschen Zusammenbruchs im Jahre 1918* (12 vols., Berlin, 1925–9).
3. B. Barth, *Dolchstoßlegenden und politische Desintegration: die Trauma der deutschen Niederlage im Ersten Weltkrieg 1914–1933* (Düsseldorf, 2003), 324, 335–7, 502–6.
4. A. D. Chandler, *The Visible Hand: the Managerial Revolution in American Business* (Cambridge, Mass./London, 1977); A. Bucholz, *Moltke, Schlieffen, and Prussian War Planning* (New York, 1991).
5. E. M. Coffman, *The War to End All Wars: the American Military Experience in World War I* (Lexington, Ky, 1998), 129.
6. S. Weintraub, *A Stillness Heard Around the World: the End of the Great War, November 1918* (New York, 1985).
7. B. Pitt, *1918: the Last Act* (Barnsley, 2003); J. Terraine, *To Win a War: 1918 the Year of Victory* (London, 2000); M. Brown, *The Imperial War Museum Book of 1918: Year of Victory* (London, 1998); R. Paschall, *The Defeat of Imperial Germany, 1917– 1918* (New York, 1994); P. Hart, *1918: a Very British Victory* (London, 2008).
8. F. Cailletau, *Gagner la Grande Guerre* (Paris, 2008).
9. D. Donald (ed.), *Why the North Won the Civil War* (Binghamton, 1960); R. E. Beringer, H. Hattaway, A. Jones, and W. N. Stil, Jr, *Why the South Lost the Civil War* (Atlanta, 1986); R. J. Overy, *Why the Allies Won* (London, 1995); M. J. Gilbert (ed.), *Why the North Won the Vietnam War* (New York, 2002).
10. S. Broadberry and M. Harrison (eds.), *The Economics of World War I* (Cambridge, 2005); M. Harrison (ed.), *The Economics of World War II: Six Great Powers in International Perspective* (Cambridge, 1998); P. M. Kennedy, *The Rise and Fall of the Great Powers: Economic Change and Military Conflict from 1500 to 2000* (London, 1989).
11. Beringer et al., *Why the South Lost the Civil War*.
12. A. R. Millett and W. Murray (eds.), *Military Effectiveness. Vol. I: The First World War* (Boston, Mass., 1988).
13. C. von Clausewitz, *On War*, eds. M. Howard and P. Paret (Princeton, NJ, 1976), 358.
14. H. F. A. Strachan, *The First World War. Vol. I: To Arms* (Oxford, 2001), 633–43.

PROLOGUE: DEADLOCK, 1914–1917

1. D. Lloyd George, *War Memoirs*, II (2 vols., London, 1938), 1986.
2. I. Kershaw, *Hitler, 1889–1936: Hubris* (London, 1998), 102–3.
3. G. Wormser, *La République de Clemenceau* (Paris, 1961), 341.
4. On the Victorian communications revolution, E. J. Hobsbawm, *The Age of Capital, 1848–1875* (London, 1975), ch. 3; cf. C. A. Bayly, *The Birth of the Modern World, 1789–1914: Global Connections and Comparisons* (Malden, Miss./Oxford/Carlton, Vic., 2004), chs. 5, 7, 12.
5. Kühlmann memorandum, 3 Sept. 1917, A. Scherer and J. Grünewald (eds.), *L'Allemagne et les problèmes de la paix pendant la Première Guerre Mondiale* (4 vols., Paris, 1966–78), doc. 235.
6. M. Dugast-Rouillé, *Charles de Habsbourg: le dernier empereur 1887–1922* (Paris/Louvain-la-neuve, 1991), 108.
7. The Conservative Party was normally referred to in this period as the Unionist Party because of its commitment to upholding the union between Great Britain and Ireland and its opposition to Liberal plans for Home Rule: i.e. devolution to an autonomous parliament in Dublin.
8. Bertie–Balfour, 2 Mar., Townley–Balfour, 4 Mar. 1918, FO/371/3217.
9. J.-J. Becker, *1914: Comment les Français sont entrés dans la guerre* (Paris, 1977); J. Verhey, *The Spirit of 1914: Militarism, Myth, and Mobilization in Germany* (Cambridge, 2000).
10. S. Förster, 'Der deutsche Generalstab und die Illusion des kurzen Krieges, 1871–1914: Metakritik eines Mythos', *Militärgeschichtliche Mitteilungen* (1994); H. F. A. Strachan, *The First World War. Vol. I: To Arms* (Oxford, 2001), 1005–14.
11. D. Stevenson, *1914–1918: the History of the First World War* (London, 2004), 92–3.
12. J. Horne and A. Kramer, *German Atrocities 1914: a History of Denial* (New Haven, Conn./London, 2001); A. Kramer, *Dynamic of Destruction: Culture and Mass Killing in the First World War* (Oxford, 2007).
13. R. T. Foley, *German Strategy and the Path to Verdun: Erich von Falkenhayn and the Development of Attrition, 1870–1916* (Cambridge, 2005).
14. W. Philpott, *Bloody Victory: the Sacrifice on the Somme and the Making of the Twentieth Century* (London, 2009); J. Sheldon, *The German Army on the Somme, 1914–1916* (Barnsley, 2005).
15. R. Gregory, *The Origins of American Intervention in the First World War* (New York, 1971), 43; K. Burk, 'The Treasury: from Impotence to Power', in K. Burk (ed.), *War and the State: the Transformation of British Government, 1914–1919* (London, 1982), 90–91.
16. I. F. W. Beckett, *The Great War, 1914–1918* (Harlow, 2001), 210.
17. J.-J. Becker, *The Great War and the French People* (Leamington Spa/Heidelberg/Dover, NH, 1985), 105–11.
18. D. Bloxham, *The Great Game of Genocide: Imperialism, Nationalism, and the Destruction of the Ottoman Armenians* (Oxford, 2007), ch. 2.
19. Strachan, *To Arms*, ch. 12.

20. On German war aims, F. Fischer, *Germany's Aims in the First World War* (London, 1967); G.-H. Soutou, *L'Or et le sang: les buts de guerre économiques de la Première Guerre mondiale* (Paris, 1989).

21. D. Stevenson, *French War Aims against Germany, 1914-1919* (Oxford, 1982).

22. V. H. Rothwell, *British War Aims and Peace Diplomacy, 1914-1918* (Oxford, 1971); D. French, *British Strategy and War Aims, 1914-1916* (London, 1986).

23. M. Aksakal, *The Ottoman Road to War in 1914: the Ottoman Empire and the First World War* (Cambridge, 2008).

24. D. Lloyd George, *War Memoirs*, II (2 vols., London, 1938), 712.

25. K. Epstein, *Matthias Erzberger and the Dilemma of German Democracy* (Princeton, NJ, 1959), 193-206.

26. Prince Sixte de Bourbon, *L'Offre de paix séparée de l'Autriche (5 décembre. 1916-12 octobre 1917)* (Paris, 1920), 96-8.

27. War Cabinet, 2, 13, 14 Nov. 1917, CAB/23/4.

28. Minutes of Rapallo meeting, 6 Nov. 1917, 57 1528, Orlando MSS, ACS.

29. Orlando-Diaz, 9 Nov. 1917, 67 1562, Orlando MSS, ACS.

30. For recent assessments, M. A. Morselli, *Caporetto 1917: Victory or Defeat?* (London/Portland, Ore., 2001); V. Wilcox, 'Generalship and Mass Surrender during the Italian Defeat at Caporetto', in I. F. W. Beckett (ed.), *1917: Beyond the Western Front* (Leiden/Boston, Mass., 2009).

31. R. A. Doughty, *Pyrrhic Victory: French Strategy and Operations in the Great War* (Cambridge, Mass./London, 2005), 387-9.

32. M. Goya, *La Chair et l'acier: l'invention de la guerre moderne (1914-1918)* (Paris, 2004), 373, 388.

33. R. Prior and T. Wilson, *Passchendaele: the Untold Story* (New Haven, Conn./London, 1996); P. H. Liddle (ed.), *Passchendaele in Perspective: the Third Battle of Ypres* (London, 1997); J. Sheldon, *The German Army at Passchendaele* (Barnsley, 2007).

34. Presentation, 'German Defences', by F. Bostyn, at conference, 'Dead Reckoning', *In Flanders Fields* Museum, Ypres, 15 Nov. 2007.

35. H. H. Herwig, *The First World War: Germany and Austria-Hungary, 1914-1918* (London/New York, 1997), 332.

36. J. P. Harris, *Douglas Haig and the First World War* (Cambridge, 2008), 382.

37. War Cabinet, 5 Dec. 1917, CAB/23/4; T. Travers, *How the War was Won: Command and Technology in the British Army on the Western Front, 1917-1918* (London/New York, 1992), 24-31.

38. W. S. L. Churchill, *The World Crisis*, Part 2: *1916-1918* (6 parts, London, 1923-31), 377.

39. M. Hankey, *The Supreme Command, 1914-1918*, II (2 vols., London, 1961), 705-6.

40. R. N. L. Poincaré, *Au Service de la France. Neuf années de souvenirs*, IX (10 vols., Paris, 1926-33), 305.

41. B. Millman, *Pessimism and British War Policy, 1916-1918* (London/Portland, Ore., 2001), ch. 5.

42. Ibid., xiv.

43. Lloyd George in War Cabinet, 11 Oct. 1917, CAB/23/13.

1. ON THE DEFENSIVE, MARCH–JULY 1918

1. T. Travers. *How the War was Won: Command and Technology in the British Army on the Western Front, 1917–1918* (London/New York, 1992), 175.
2. G. Fong, 'The Movement of German Divisions to the Western Front, Winter 1917–1918', *War in History* (2000), 227; W. Deist, 'The Military Collapse of the German Empire', *War in History* (1996), 188; Kuhl diary, 20 Sept. 1917, W-10/50652, BA-MA; *WK*, XIV, 1.
3. W. J. Astore and D. E. Showalter, *Hindenburg: Icon of German Militarism* (Dulles, Va, 2005), ch. 1; R. Asprey, *The German High Command at War: Hindenburg and Ludendorff and the First World War* (London, 1994), 61–8.
4. On the organization of the OHL, M. Kitchen, *The Silent Dictatorship: the Politics of the German High Command under Hindenburg and Ludendorff* (London, 1976), ch. 2.
5. E. Ludendorff (ed.), *The General Staff and Its Problems* (2 vols., London, 1920), 524–39.
6. H. E. Goemans, *War and Punishment: the Causes of War Termination and the First World War* (Princeton, NJ/Oxford, 2000), 114; R. Schütz, 'Einführende Bemerkungen', in J. Duppler and G. P. Groß (eds.), *Kriegsende 1918: Ereignis, Wirkung, Nachwirkung* (Munich, 1994), 46.
7. D. Storz, '"Aber was hätte anders geschehen sollen?" Die deutschen Offensiven an den Westfront 1918', in Duppler and Groß (eds.), *Kriegsende 1918*, 54–5.
8. J. B. Scott (ed.), *Official Statements of War Aims and Peace Proposals, December 1916–November 1918* (Washington DC, 1921), 159.
9. Schütz, 'Einführende Bemerkungen', 42, 45; Bruno Thoß, 'Militärische Entscheidung und politisch-gesellschaftlich Umbruch. Das Jahr 1918 in der neueren Weltkriegsforschung', in Duppler and Groß (eds.), *Kriegsende 1918*, 27; cf. I. Hull, *Absolute Destruction: Military Culture and the Practices of War in Imperial Germany* (Ithaca, NY/London, 2005), 299–301.
10. *WK*, XIV, 15.
11. Storz, 'Die deutschen Offensiven', 54–5.
12. Ludendorff memorandum, 14 Sept. 1917, D. Lloyd George, *War Memoirs*, II (2 vols., London, 1938), 1225–8.
13. Wetzell memorandum, 30 Sept. 1917, PH/3/267, BA-MA.
14. Hindenburg–Michaelis, 15 Sept. 1917, R. H. Lutz (ed.), *The Causes of the German Collapse in 1918* (Stanford, Calif., 1934), 46.
15. G.-H. Soutou, *L'Or et le sang: les buts de guerre économiques de la Première Guerre mondiale* (Paris, 1989), 572.
16. Schütz, 'Einführende Bemerkungen', 46.
17. Ibid., 41–5; ibid., 44–5. My italics.
18. *WK*, XIV, 15.
19. M. Bauer, *Der Grosse Krieg im Feld und Heimat: Erinnerungen und Betrachtungen* (Tübingen, 1921), 175, 177.
20. Schütz, 'Einführende Bemerkungen', 44–5.
21. E. Ludendorff, *Meine Kriegserinnerungen, 1914–1918* (Berlin, 1919), 430–32.
22. P. von Hindenburg, *Aus meinem Leben* (Leipzig, 1933), 248–9; Bauer, *Der Grosse Krieg*, 176–7.

23. G. Martin, 'German Strategy and Military Assessments of the American Expeditionary Force (AEF), 1917–18', *War in History* (1994), 179; Ludendorff, *Meine Kriegserinnerungen*, 432.

24. Kuhl diary, 6 Oct., 1, 22 Nov. 1917, W-10/50652, BA-MA.

25. Ibid., 31 Dec. 1917; Hindenburg, *Aus meinem Leben*, 233–4.

26. Hindenburg memorandum, 10 Sept. 1917, W-10/50397, BA-MA.

27. *WK*, XIV, 38.

28. Fong, 'Movement of German Divisions', 226–30.

29. D. T. Zabecki, *The German 1918 Offensives: a Case Study in the Operational Level of War* (London/New York, 2006), 91; *WK*, XIV, 92.

30. 'Deutsche Rüstung 1918', 26–30, W-10/50421, BA-MA; report on Hindenburg Programme, W-10/50397, BA-MA.

31. *WK*, XIV, 243.

32. Bauer, *Der Grosse Krieg*, 177; Ludendorff, *Meine Kriegserinerungen*, 460ff.

33. D. T. Zabecki, *Steel Wind: Colonel Georg Bruchmüller and the Birth of Modern Artillery* (Westport, Conn., 1994), 66; Zabecki, *German 1918 Offensives*, 54–7, 126–30.

34. *WK*, XIV, 43–8.

35. Ibid., 51–4.

36. Ibid.; Zabecki, *German 1918 Offensives*, 107.

37. *WK*, XIV, 54; M. Kitchen, *The German Offensives of 1918* (Stroud, 2001), 35; Storz, 'Die deutschen Offensiven', 59, 61.

38. *WK*, XIV, 59, 61, 74–83; Kitchen, *German Offensives*, 30–40.

39. Hauptmann–Ludendorff interview, Aug. 1923, W-10/51833, BA-MA.

40. *WK*, XIV, 85.

41. Kuhl diary, 30 Jan. 1918, W-10/50652, BA-MA.

42. Storz, 'Die deutschen Offensiven', 61.

43. *WK*, XIV, 91; Zabecki, *German 1918 Offensives*, 136.

44. Hauptmann–Ludendorff interview, Aug. 1923, W-10/51833, BA-MA.

45. *WK*, XIV, 54; Kuhl diary, 4 Feb. 1918, W-10/50652, BA-MA.

46. Storz, 'Die deutschen Offensiven', 63; *WK*, XIV, 15, 92.

47. W. S. L. Churchill, *The World Crisis*, Part 2: *1916–1918* (6 parts, London, 1923–31), 412.

48. M. Middlebrook, *The Kaiser's Battle* (London, 2000), 308.

49. Storz, 'Die deutschen Offensiven', 61; Zabecki, *German 1918 Offensives*, 134–6; *WK*, XIV, 104.

50. Zabecki, *German 1918 Offensives*, 130.

51. Ludendorff, *Meine Kriegserinnerungen*, 468; B. I. Gudmundsson, *Stormtroop Tactics: Innovation in the German Army, 1914–1918* (Westport, Conn./London, 1989), 151; *WK*, XIV, 41.

52. G. Pedroncini, *Pétain: Général en chef, 1917–1918* (Paris, 1974), 179; D. Trask, *The AEF and Coalition Warmaking, 1917–1918* (Lawrence, Kan., 1993), 42, 53.

53. Trask, *AEF*, 11–12, 24, 39; J. J. Pershing, *My Experiences in the World War* (London, 1931), 265.

54. Pershing, *My Experiences*, 263, 85; D. R. Woodward, '"Black Jack" Pershing: the American Proconsul in Europe', in M. Hughes and M. Seligman (eds.), *Leadership in*

Conflict, 1914–1918 (Barnsley, 2000), 145–6; T. K. Nenninger, 'American Military Effectiveness in the First World War', in A. R. Millett and W. Murray (eds.), *Military Effectiveness*, I (3 vols., Winchester, Mass., 1988), 125.

55. Comité de guerre, 26 Dec. 1917, 3N2, SHA.
56. Pershing, *My Experiences*, 260.
57. Trask, *AEF*, 37, 40–41.
58. 'Note on British Effectives', 28 Jan. 1918, WO/158/2; G. D. Sheffield and J. M. Bourne (eds.), *Douglas Haig: War Diaries and Letters, 1914–1918* (London, 2005), 375–6.
59. Pershing, *My Experiences*, 253, 280.
60. GQG 3rd Bureau memo, 17 Sept. 1917, 16N1712; directive, 27 Nov. 1917, 16N1690, SHA.
61. K. Jeffery, *Field Marshal Sir Henry Wilson: a Political Soldier* (Oxford, 2006), 205ff.
62. D. French, *The Strategy of the Lloyd George Coalition, 1916–1918* (Oxford, 1995), 190–92.
63. M. Weygand, *Mémoires: idéal vécu*, I (2 vols., Paris, 1953), 462–9; Jeffery, *Sir Henry Wilson*, 214–20.
64. Sheffield and Bourne (eds.), *Douglas Haig*, 382–3.
65. Milner memorandum, 14 Feb. 1918, MLN 374; War Cabinet, 12, 14, 16 Feb. 1918, CAB/23/13.
66. Sheffield and Bourne (eds.), *Douglas Haig*, 381.
67. Clemenceau hearing, 27 Mar. 1918, C7500, AN.
68. F. Foch, *Mémoires pour servir à l'histoire de la guerre de 1914–1918*, II (2 vols., Paris, 1931), liii–lvii.
69. Haig diary, 2 Jan. 1918, Sheffield and Bourne (eds.), *Douglas Haig*, 370; J. P. Harris, *Douglas Haig and the First World War* (Cambridge, 2008), is an outstanding biography.
70. G. Pedroncini, *Pétain: le soldat, 1856–1940* (Paris, 1998), 15–27; R. B. Bruce, *Pétain: Verdun to Vichy* (Dulles, Va, 2008), ch. 1.
71. Pedroncini, *Pétain: Général*, 141.
72. Lloyd George, *War Memoirs*, II, 1655–6; J. E. Edmonds, *Military Operations: France and Belgium. 1914–(1918)*, I (London, 1933–48), 47; Harris, *Douglas Haig*, 433.
73. Edmonds, *MOFB, 1918*, I, 117, 101–2.
74. D. R. Woodward, 'Did Lloyd George Starve the British Army of Men prior to the German Offensive of 21 March 1918?', *Historical Journal* (1984), 242; Harris, *Douglas Haig*, 433.
75. 'Note on British Effectives', 28 Jan. 1918, WO/158/2.
76. Edmonds, *MOFB, 1918*, I, 51; Travers, *How the War was Won*, 36.
77. Churchill, *World Crisis*, Part 2: *1916–1918*, 378–84.
78. Edmonds, *MOFB, 1918*, I, 53–5; Middlebrook, *Kaiser's Battle*, 85–8.
79. Haig in War Cabinet, 2 Jan. 1918, CAB/23/13; Sheffield and Bourne (eds.), *Douglas Haig*, 385; Woodward, 'Did Lloyd George?', 251.
80. M. Samuels, *Command or Control? Command, Training, and Tactics in the British and German Armies, 1888–1918* (London, 1995), 208–15; Travers, *How the War was Won*, 57–8.
81. 'Situation 1918', WO/158/2.
82. Churchill, *World Crisis*, Part 2: *1916–1918*, 389.
83. Davidson memo, 12 Feb. 1918, WO/158/2; Edmonds, *MOFB, 1918*, I, 122.

84. Haig in War Cabinet, 2 Jan. 1918, CAB/23/13.
85. Edmonds, *MOFB, 1918*, I, 236.
86. Stafford–Edmonds, 7 July 1930, CAB/45/187; cf. Travers, *How the War was Won*, 57–8.
87. Samuels, *Command or Control?*, 217.
88. Edmonds, *MOFB, 1918*, I, 116.
89. Ibid., 115–17.
90. D. Winter, *Haig's Command: a Reassessment* (London, 1991), 181.
91. Edmonds, *MOFB, 1918*, Appendix vol., 28–30, 45–7, 51–2.
92. Zabecki, *German 1918 Offensives*, 140.
93. *AFGG*, VI, i, 231; Middlebrook, *Kaiser's Battle*, 398–9.
94. Middlebrook, *Kaiser's Battle*, 164.
95. Edmonds, *MOFB, 1918*, I, 255; *WK*, XIV, 131
96. *WK*, XIV, 132; Middlebrook, *Kaiser's Battle*, 339–41; Sheffield and Bourne (eds.), *Douglas Haig*, 389–90.
97. Middlebrook, *Kaiser's Battle*, 322.
98. Ibid., 207–8, 278; L. MacDonald, *To the Last Man: Spring 1918* (London, 1999), 151.
99. Kitchen, *German Offensives*, 69.
100. *WK*, XIV, 163.
101. Sheffield and Bourne (eds.), *Douglas Haig*, 390–91; Haig–Wilson, 24 Mar. 1918, WO/158/25; Churchill, *World Crisis, Part 2: 1916–1918*, 423; J. J. M. Mordacq, *Le Ministère Clemenceau: journal d'un témoin*, I (4 vols., Paris, 1930), 231.
102. MacDonald, *To the Last Man*, 192; S. Pope and E.-A. Wheal, *The Macmillan Dictionary of the First World War* (London/Basingstoke, 1995), 355; H. W. Miller, *The Paris Gun: the Bombardment of Paris by the German Long-Range Gun and the Great German Offensives of 1918* (London/Bombay/Sydney, 1930).
103. *AFGG*, VI, i, 236, 248–66.
104. Pedroncini, *Pétain: le soldat*, 221–2.
105. Ibid., 218, 233.
106. Ibid., 235, 250–51; ibid., 223.
107. Edmonds, *MOFB, 1918*, I, 117.
108. Haig–Edmonds, 18 Nov. 1920, CAB/45/183; Lawrence minutes, 23 Mar. 1918, WO/158/48.
109. *AFGG*, VI, i, 287–8. My emphasis.
110. Travers, *How the War was Won*, 78–81.
111. Haig–Wilson, 24 Mar. 1918, WO/158/25.
112. Dury conference minutes, 24 Mar. 1918, WO/158/48; MacDonald, *Last Man*, 236–7.
113. Sheffield and Bourne (eds.), *Douglas Haig*, 392n; Pedroncini, *Pétain: le soldat*, 223–4.
114. Haig memo, 25 Mar. 1918, WO/158/20.
115. *WK*, XIV, 678.
116. Kuhl diary, 25, 27, 29, 31 Mar. 1918, W-10/50652, BA-MA.
117. *WK*, XIV, 166–8; Zabecki, *German 1918 Offensives*, 143–5.
118. C. Barnett, *The Swordbearers: Supreme Command in the First World War* (London, 2000), 311; *WK*, XIV, 199.
119. *WK*, XIV, 149; Kuhl diary, 26 Mar. 1918, W-10/50652, BA-MA.
120. Hauptmann–Ludendorff interview, Aug. 1923, W-10/51833, BA-MA.

121. *WK*, XIV, 147.
122. Edmonds, *MOFB, 1918*, II, 28.
123. *WK*, XIV, 199; Zabecki, *German 1918 Offensives*, 171.
124. Zabecki, *German 1918 Offensives*, 160; *WK*, XIV, 237–9, 253–4.
125. *WK*, XIV, 217–20; Edmonds, *MOFB, 1918*, II, ch. 3.
126. E. Greenhalgh, *Victory Through Coalition: Britain and France during the First World War* (Cambridge, 2005), 194, 201–2.
127. M. S. Neiberg, *Foch: Supreme Allied Commander in the Great War* (Dulles, Va, 2003), ch. 1.
128. W. Philpott, 'Marshal Ferdinand Foch and Allied Victory', in Hughes and Seligman (eds.), *Leadership in Conflict*, 50.
129. Foch, *Mémoires*, II, xlvii; Weygand, *Mémoires*, I, 460; Trask, *AEF*, 34.
130. Foch, *Mémoires*, II, 16–17; Foch–Clemenceau, 24 Mar. 1918, 1K/129/1, Foch MSS, SHA.
131. Milner memorandum, 27 Mar. 1918, MLN 374; Loucheur, 'Le commandement unique', 1K/129/1, SHA; Weygand, *Mémoires*, I, 480–84; Foch, *Mémoires*, II, 21–4; Greenhalgh, *Victory Through Coalition*, 195–7; R. Recouly, *Marshal Foch: His Own Words on Many Subjects* (transl., London, 1929), 27.
132. Pershing, *My Experiences*, 322; Trask, *AEF*, 53–5.
133. Barnett, *Swordbearers*, 327.
134. Foch, *Mémoires*, II, 28, 39; *AFGG*, VI, i, 326; Weygand, *Mémoires*, I, 500, 398.
135. *AFGG*, VI, i, 322; Pedroncini, *Pétain: le soldat*, 232–4.
136. *WK*, XIV, 164, 197; *AFGG*, VI, i, 254, 357.
137. Edmonds, *MOFB, 1918*, I, 116.
138. *AFGG*, VI, i, 294, 276, 289, 316, 341, 348, 358, 390.
139. Haig–Edmonds, 18 Nov. 1920, CAB/45/183; Hindenburg, *Aus meinem Leben*, 250.
140. Edmonds, *MOFB, 1918*, II, 483.
141. Zabecki, *German 1918 Offensives*, 161.
142. Edmonds, *MOFB, 1918*, II, 4, 9–11; I, 335.
143. Weygand, *Mémoires*, I, 497.
144. Zabecki, *German 1918 Offensives*, 84–5, 95; *AFGG*, VI, i, 521.
145. Milner minute, 18 July 1918, WO/32/5097.
146. Zabecki, *German 1918 Offensives*, 160; Travers, *How the War was Won*, 53.
147. *WK*, XIV, 244–5; CGS Abt. 1a, 4 Apr. 1918, MKr/1835, KAM.
148. *WK*, XIV, 310.
149. Zabecki, *German 1918 Offensives*, 160.
150. *AFGG*, VI, i, 429; Edmonds, *MOFB, 1918*, II, 156.
151. Hauptmann–Ludendorff interview, Aug. 1923, W-10/51833, BA-MA; Churchill, *World Crisis, Part 2: 1916–1918*, 433.
152. *WK*, XIV, 53, 56, 68, 72–4, 80; Kuhl diary, 11 Nov. 1917, 9 Feb. 1918, W-10/50652, BA-MA; Zabecki, *German 1918 Offensives*, 126; Edmonds, *MOFB, 1918*, II, 153.
153. Zabecki, *German 1918 Offensives*, 181; *WK*, XIV, 265–9, 207.
154. Kuhl diary, 29, 30, 31 Mar. and 2 Apr. 1918, W-10/50652, BA-MA; Hauptman–Ludendorff interview, Aug. 1923, W-10/51833, BA-MA; *WK*, XIV, 269.
155. Kuhl diary, 2, 5 Apr. 1918, W-10/50652, BA-MA; Zabecki, *German 1918 Offensives*, 182; *WK*, XIV, 208–9; Carlowitz report, 3 May 1918, HGr/91, KAM.

156. Zabecki, *German 1918 Offensives*, 185, 199; *WK*, XIV, 279, 260; A. von Thaer, *Generalstabsdienst an der Front und in der OHL* (Göttingen, 1958), 182, 188.

157. Edmonds, *MOFB, 1918*, II, 157–60.

158. Ibid., 147–8; Sheffield and Bourne (eds.), *Douglas Haig*, 400.

159. G. Powell, *Plumer: the Soldiers' General: a Biography of Field-Marshal Viscount Plumer of Messines* (Barnsley, 2004), 260–61; B. Pitt, *1918: the Last Act* (Barnsley, 2003), 114; Asprey, *German High Command*, 394; Edmonds, *MOFB, 1918*, II, 165.

160. Edmonds, *MOFB, 1918*, II, 144; *WK*, XIV, 264–5; Wilson–Haig, 7 Apr. 1918, WO/158/25.

161. Edmonds, *MOFB, 1918*, II, 139, 145; Asprey, *German High Command*, 392; War Cabinet, 9 Apr. 1918, CAB/24/4.

162. Foch, *Mémoires*, II, 46–8; Greenhalgh, *Victory Through Coalition*, 202; Edmonds, *MOFB, 1918*, II, 141.

163. Kitchen, *German Offensives*, 99; Wilson diary, 4 Apr. 1918, IWM.

164. Pitt, *1918*, 117; *WK*, XIV, 273–5; Kitchen, *German Offensives*, 102; Edmonds, *MOFB, 1918*, II, 181.

165. Edmonds, *MOFB, 1918*, II, 204 and ch. 11; *WK*, XIV, 275–8.

166. Sheffield and Bourne (eds.), *Douglas Haig*, 402; Zabecki, *German 1918 Offensives*, 198; War Cabinet, 19 Apr. 1918, CAB/23/6.

167. Edmonds, *MOFB, 1918*, II, 245; Zabecki, *German 1918 Offensives*, 189.

168. Wilson diary, 11–21 Apr. 1918, IWM; War Cabinet, 26, 30 Apr. 1918, CAB/23/4.

169. Edmonds, *MOFB, 1918*, II, 189; Lloyd George, *War Memoirs*, II, 1766.

170. V. Brittain, *Testament of Youth: an Autobiographical Study of the Years 1900–1925* (London, 1978), 419–20.

171. Sheffield and Bourne (eds.), *Douglas Haig*, 402; Harris, *Douglas Haig*, 469–70; Greenhalgh, *Victory Through Coalition*, 206; *AFGG*, VI, i, 454ff.

172. *AFGG*, VI, i, 447, 454–7; Mordacq, *Ministère Clemenceau*, I, 298; Foch, *Mémoires*, II, 51, 59–60.

173. Lloyd George, *War Memoirs*, II, 1766; Edmonds, *MOFB, 1918*, II, 284, 314.

174. Travers, *How the War was Won*, 96; Edmonds, *MOFB, 1918*, II, 289–90, 512.

175. Powell, *Plumer*, 259ff.; Zabecki, *German 1918 Offensives*, 190.

176. Sheffield and Bourne (eds.), *Douglas Haig*, 404; Edmonds, *MOFB, 1918*, II, 323, 347, 351, 354, 494; Wilson diary, 11 Apr. 1918, IWM.

177. Greenhalgh, *Victory Through Coalition*, 209; *AFGG*, VI, i, 460–63, 470–71, 480–81, 488; Weygand, *Mémoires*, I, 514–15; Pedroncini, *Pétain: le soldat*, 242.

178. Foch, *Mémoires*, II, 58–9, 65; Haig–Wilson, 20 Apr. 1918, 2/7A/22, Wilson MSS, IWM.

179. *WK*, XIV, 275–6, 281; Ludendorff, *Meine Kriegserinnerungen*, 488–9.

180. Kuhl diary, 14, 15 Apr. 1918, W-10/50652, BA-MA; Carlowitz report, 3 May 1918, HGr/91, KAM.

181. *WK*, XIV, 283; Kuhl diary, 18 Apr. 1918, W-10/50652, BA-MA.

182. Zabecki, *German 1918 Offensives*, 191; *WK*, XIV, 289.

183. Zabecki, *German 1918 Offensives*, 202–3.

184. Hutier diary, 11 Apr. 1918, W-10/50640, BA-MA.

185. *WK*, XIV, 307–8; Edmonds, *MOFB, 1918*, II, ch. 21.

186. *WK*, XIV, 293–8; *AFGG*, VI, i, 497–517; Edmonds, *MOFB, 1918*, II, chs. 22–4.

187. *WK*, XIV, 300; Weygand, *Mémoires*, I, 516.

188. *AFGG*, VI, i, 520–24.

189. Weygand, *Mémoires*, I, 518.

190. Zabecki, *German 1918 Offensives*, 199.

191. Wetzell, 19 Apr. 1918, PH/3/267, BA-MA; *WK*, XIV, 312–14.

192. Thaer, *Generalstabsdienst*, 188, 196, 202; *WK*, XIV, 315, 321.

193. *WK*, XIV, 315, 326; Hutier diary, 20 May 1918, W-10/50640, BA-MA.

194. Pitt, *1918*, 137; Ludendorff, *Meine Kriegserinnerungen*, 494–6; *WK*, XIV, 317.

195. *WK*, XIV, 319–21; Zabecki, *German 1918 Offensives*, 280–85.

196. Edmonds, *MOFB, 1918*, III, 38; *WK*, XIV, 330; Ludendorff, *Meine Kriegserinnerungen*, 496.

197. Edmonds, *MOFB, 1918*, III, 33; Hindenburg, *Aus meinem Leben*, 256; *WK*, XIV, 327.

198. *WK*, XIV, 330–32; Pitt, *1918*, 138.

199. Wilson proclamation, 11 May 1918, Vol. 84, Borden MSS, NAC.

200. Edmonds, *MOFB, 1918*, III, 18–22; *AFGG*, VI, ii, 7–9, 35.

201. *AFGG*, VI, ii, 15–18, 38–41; Weygand, *Mémoires*, I, 523–5.

202. Clemenceau hearing, 3 June 1918, C7500, AN; J. de Pierrefeu, *GQG Secteur I: trois ans au Grand Quartier Général; par le rédacteur du 'communiqué'*, II (2 vols., Paris, 1920), 168–71; P. Miquel, *Le Gâchis des généraux: les erreurs de commandement pendant la guerre de 14–18* (Paris, 2001), 187.

203. Pedroncini, *Pétain: le soldat*, 186–90; *AFGG*, VI, ii, 71–3.

204. Pedroncini, *Pétain: le soldat*, 245–6; *AFGG*, VI, ii, 70; Greenhalgh, *Victory Through Coalition*, 212.

205. Edmonds, *MOFB, 1918*, III, 31, 37, 44; Pitt, *1918*, 144.

206. Pitt, *1918*, 139–40; Pershing, *My Experiences*, 408; *AFGG*, VI, ii, 77.

207. General Staff report, 13 June 1918, MKr/1835, KAM.

208. Zabecki, *German 1918 Offensives*, 213–18; *WK*, XIV, 371.

209. *WK*, XIV, 330, 337; *AFGG*, VI, ii, 87.

210. *WK*, XIV, 348; Miquel, *Gâchis*, 195–6; *AFGG*, VI, ii, 104.

211. *AFGG*, VI, ii, 115; Edmonds, *MOFB, 1918*, III, 84, 122–3; *WK*, XIV, 390.

212. Hauptmann–Ludendorff interview, Aug. 1923, W-10/51833, BA-MA; *WK*, XIV, 351–6; Zabecki, *German 1918 Offensives*, 227.

213. Zabecki, *German 1918 Offensives*, 219; *WK*, XIV, 353; *AFGG*, VI, ii, 385; Edmonds, *MOFB, 1918*, III, 103–4, 134.

214. Pierrefeu, *GQG*, II, 179; *AFGG*, VI, ii, 82, 101, 206–8.

215. Mordacq, *Ministère Clemenceau*, I, 46; Edmonds, *MOFB, 1918*, III, 133; Pedroncini, *Pétain: le soldat*, 248.

216. Weygand, *Mémoires*, I, 534; Mordacq, *Ministère Clemenceau*, I, 54; *AFGG*, VI, ii, 211, 216.

217. Edmonds, *MOFB, 1918*, III, 132; Mordacq, *Ministère Clemenceau*, I, 42–58; Foch, *Mémoires*, II, 92, 96–100; *AFGG*, VI, ii, 138, 177–8, 226.

218. Pershing, *My Experiences*, 411, 426; Sheffield and Bourne (eds.), *Douglas Haig*, 416; War Cabinet, 28, 29 May 1918, CAB/23/6.

219. Zabecki, *German 1918 Offensives*, 223; Edmonds, *MOFB, 1918*, III, 17.

220. *AFGG*, VI, ii, 237–8; Edmonds, *MOFB, 1918*, III, 146; Milner–Haig, 7 June 1918, MLN 374.

221. Edmonds, *MOFB, 1918*, III, 147; Pitt, *1918*, 150–51; *WK*, XIV, 364–6.

222. *WK*, XIV, 308, 374–7; *AFGG*, VI, ii, 233–4, 241.

223. Trask, *AEF*, 70–73; *WK*, XIV, 14, 385.

224. Pierrefeu, *GQG*, II, 189–91; Clemenceau hearing, 3 June 1918, C7500, AN; Edmonds, *MOFB, 1918*, III, 141.

225. *WK*, XIV, 380; Zabecki, *German 1918 Offensives*, 226.

226. *AFGG*, VI, ii, 214; *WK*, XIV, 380; Mordacq, *Ministère Clemenceau*, I, 56.

227. Pershing, *My Experiences*, 430; Mordacq, *Ministère Clemenceau*, I, 51.

228. *WK*, XIV, 308; Zabecki, *German 1918 Offensives*, 287, 221.

229. Zabecki, *German 1918 Offensives*, 235–6; *WK*, XIV, 395–6.

230. *AFGG*, VI, ii, 262–4; Zabecki, *German 1918 Offensives*, 238; Edmonds, *MOFB, 1918*, II, 172.

231. *AFGG*, VI, ii, 270–73.

232. Churchill, *World Crisis*, Part 2: *1916–1918*, 456–7; *AFGG*, VI, ii, 275–94.

233. *WK*, XIV, 397, 400.

234. Weygand, *Mémoires*, I, 543–4; *AFGG*, VI, ii, 322–3, 329–39; C. E. Mangin, *Comment finit la Guerre* (Paris, 1920), 184–5.

235. *Erfahrungsbericht*, 18 June 1918, HGr/91, KAM; *WK*, XIV, 403–5.

236. Zabecki, *German 1918 Offensives*, 242; *AFGG*, VI, ii, 341; *WK*, XIV, 410.

237. E. Michels, 'Die "Spanische Grippe" 1918/19: Verlauf, Folgen, und Deutungen in Deutschland im Kontext des Ersten Weltkrieges', *Vierteljahrshefte für Zeitgeschichte* (2010), 7–10.

238. G. Fassy, *Le Commandement français en orient (octobre 1915–novembre 1918)* (Paris, 2003), 304; *WK*, XIII, 402–7, 421.

239. Fong, 'Movement of German Divisions', 234; *WK*, XIII, 397–8; W. Baumgart, *Deutsche Ostpolitik 1918: Von Brest-Litovsk bis zum Ende des Ersten Weltkrieges* (Vienna/Munich, 1966), 142, 149n.

240. Baumgart, *Ostpolitik*, 23, 25, 378; R. von Kühlmann, *Erinnerungen* (Heidelberg, 1948), 546; W. Baumgart and K. Repgen (eds.), *Brest-Litowsk* (Göttingen, 1969), 57–62.

241. F. Fischer, *Germany's Aims in the First World War* (London, 1967), 531.

242. V. G. Liulevicius, *War Land on the Eastern Front: Culture, National Identity, and German Occupation in World War I* (Cambridge, 2000), chs. 3, 4.

243. *WK*, XIII, 371–3; Baumgart, *Ostpolitik*, 93–8; H. H. Herwig, 'German Policy in the Eastern Baltic Sea in 1918: Expansion or Anti-Bolshevik Crusade?', *Slavic Review* (1973), 341–3.

244. Herwig, 'Eastern Baltic Sea', 348–56.

245. O. S. Fedyshyn, *Germany's Drive to the East and the Ukrainian Revolution, 1917–1918* (New Brunswick, NJ, 1971), 194–211.

246. Baumgart, *Ostpolitik*, 176.

247. Ibid., 181.

248. Ibid., 127–8; Fedyshyn, *Germany's Drive*, 133ff.; Fischer, *Germany's Aims*, 534–45.

249. Ludendorff–Kühlmann, 9 June 1918, Z. A. B. Zeman (ed.), *Germany and the Revolution in Russia, 1915–1918: Documents from the Archives of the German Foreign Ministry* (London, 1958), 134–6.

250. Fedyshyn, *Germany's Drive*, 184ff.; Baumgart, *Ostpolitik*, 150; *WK*, XIII, 399.

251. *WK*, XIII, 435; Baumgart, *Ostpolitik*, 197n.

252. D. Rossini, *Il mito americano nell'Italia della Grande Guerra* (Rome, 2000), 108–10.

253. Nenninger, 'American Military Effectiveness', 124–5.

254. *WK*, XIII, 403; C. Seton-Watson, *Italy from Liberalism to Fascism, 1870–1925* (London, 1967), 498; G. H. Cassar, *The Forgotten Front: the British Campaign in Italy, 1917–1918* (London/Rio Grande, O., 1998), 132.

255. C. Falls, *History of the Great War Based on Official Documents. Egypt and Palestine*, II (London, 1930), 449; Fassy, *Commandement français*, 341.

256. Wilson–Cavan, 5 May 1918, 2/28A/14, Wilson MSS, IWM.

257. B. Schwarz, 'Divided Attention: Britain's Perception of a German Threat to Her Eastern Position in 1918', *Journal of Contemporary History* (1993), 109–16; Milner–Wilson, 6 Mar. 1918, 2/11/9, Wilson MSS, IWM.

258. D. Omissi, *The Sepoy and the Raj: the Indian Army, 1860–1940* (Basingstoke/London, 1994), 132.

259. Wilson memo, 30 Apr. 1918, AC/14/1/61, AC.

260. J. F. Moberly, *History of the Great War Based on Official Documents. The Campaign in Mesopotamia, 1914–1918*, IV (London 1927), 255; A. J. Barker, *The Neglected War: Mesopotamia, 1914–1918* (London, 1967), 145.

261. Barker, *Neglected War*, 442, 453–4.

262. M. Hughes, *Allenby and British Strategy in the Middle East, 1917–1919* (London/Portland, Ore., 1999), 60–64.

263. Falls, *Egypt and Palestine*, II, 411–20.

264. Allenby–Wilson, 5 June 1918, 2/33A/4, Wilson MSS, IWM.

265. Allenby–Wilson, 6 Apr. 1918, 2/33A/1, ibid.

266. Hughes, *Allenby*, 79–88.

267. D. Dutton, *The Politics of Diplomacy: Britain and France in the Balkans in the First World War* (London/New York, 1998), 13.

268. A. J. P. Taylor, *The First World War: an Illustrated History* (London, 1963), 101.

269. Fassy, *Commandement français*, 7.

270. Ibid., 276, 341; C. Falls, *History of the Great War Based on Official Documents. Macedonia*, II (London, 1935), 76; Milne–Wilson, March 1918, CAB/45/3.

271. Falls, *Macedonia*, II, 187–90; M. Rauchensteiner, *Der Tod des Doppeladlers: Österreich-Ungarn und der Erste Weltkrieg* (Graz, 1993), 553–60.

272. Rauchensteiner, *Tod*, 564, 570; Ludendorff, *Meine Kriegserinnerungen*, 497.

273. Rauchensteiner, *Tod*, 566; J. E. Edmonds, *Military Operations: Italy 1915–1919* (London, 1949), 188.

274. G. W. Shanafelt, *The Secret Enemy: Austria-Hungary and the German Alliance, 1914–1918* (New York, 1985), 197.

275. Rauchensteiner, *Tod*, 567; A. A. Arz, *Zur Geschichte des Grossen Krieges 1914–1918* (Graz, 1969), 262–4, 267.

276. Edmonds, *Italy*, 188.

277. Rauchensteiner, *Tod*, 564; Arz, *Zur Geschichte des Grossen Krieges*, 269.

278. Regio esercito italiano, Comando supremo, *La battaglia del Piave (15–23 giugno 1918)* (Rome, 1920), 23; C. Falls, *Caporetto 1917* (London, 1965), 116.

279. Regio esercito, *Piave*, 21–3; Arz, *Zur Geschichte des Grossen Krieges*, 258; Ludendorff, *Meine Kriegserinnerungen*, 407; Cavan–Wilson, 19 June 1918, 2/28A.22, Wilson MSS, IWM.

280. Regio esercito, *Piave*, 34–6; Rauchensteiner, *Tod*, 572.

281. Edmonds, *Italy*, 146; Arz, *Zur Geschichte des Grossen Krieges*, 262; I. Deák, 'The Habsburg Army in the First and Last Days of World War I: a Comparative Analysis', in B. K. Király and N. F. Dreisziger (eds.), *East Central European Society in World War I* (New York, 1985), 309.

282. Regio esercito, *Piave*, 22; R. Wegs, 'Transportation: the Achilles Heel of the Habsburg War Effort', in R. A. Kann et al. (eds.), *The Habsburg Empire in World War I: Essays on the Intellectual, Military, Political, and Economic Aspects of the Habsburg War Effort* (New York, 1977), 130.

283. A. Baldini, *Diaz* (transl., London, 1935), 202.

284. A. Curami, 'L'Industria bellica italiana dopo Caporetto', in G. Berti and P. del Negra (eds.), *Al di qua e al di là del Piave: l'Ultimo Anno della Grande Guerra* (Milan, 2001), 557.

285. Edmonds, *Italy*, 176–82; Cassar, *Forgotten Front*, 142–6.

286. Cassar, *Forgotten Front*, 119; Falls, *Caporetto*, 51.

287. Regio esercito, *Piave*, 36–7; Edmonds, *Italy*, 197.

288. Regio esercito, *Piave*, 28–33.

289. N. Gladden, *Across the Piave: a Personal Account of the British Forces in Italy, 1917–1919* (London, 1971), ch. 7. Vera Brittain's brother Edward was killed in the battle.

290. Ibid., 39–40; Edmonds, *Italy*, ch. 15.

291. Rauchensteiner, *Tod*, 574–6; Edmonds, *Italy*, ch. 16.

292. Seton-Watson, *Italy*, 501; Regio esercito, *Piave*, 58; Cavan–Wilson, 19 June 1918, 2/28A/22, Wilson MSS, IWM.

293. Edmonds, *Italy*, 236; Rauchensteiner, *Tod*, 576. M. Isnenghi and G. Rochat, *La Grande Guerra 1914–1918* (Milan, 2004), 465, give higher figures.

294. Arz, *Zur Geschichte des Grossen Krieges*, 276–8; Rauchensteiner, *Tod*, 580.

295. W. Etschmann, 'Österreich-Ungarn zwischen Engagement und Zurückhaltung. K.u.k. Truppen and der Westfront', in Duppler and Groß (eds.), *Kriegsende 1918*, 104.

296. Ludendorff, *Meine Kriegserinnerungen*, 511.

297. Zabecki, *German 1918 Offensives*, 252, 258–9.

298. *WK*, XIV, 380.

299. Hohenlohe–Burián, 9, 15 July 1918, Preußenberichte 1918, HHStA.

300. Fischer, *Germany's Aims*, 622–3.

301. Zabecki, *German 1918 Offensives*, 253; *WK*, XIV, 415; Hauptmann–Ludendorff interview, Aug. 1923, W-10/51833, BA-MA.

302. *WK*, XIV, 414–18.

303. Ibid., 421; Zabecki, *German 1918 Offensives*, 246; Hindenburg, *Aus meinem Leben*, 265.

304. Zabecki, *German 1918 Offensives*, 251; Ludendorff, *Meine Kriegserinnerungen*, 516.

305. *WK*, XIV, 441–2, 439; Zabecki, *German 1918 Offensives*, 300–301, 290; Hindenburg, *Aus meinem Leben*, 264.

306. Hindenburg, *Aus meinem Leben*, 265; *WK*, XIV, 444; Zabecki, *German 1918 Offensives*, 254–5.

307. Zabecki, *German 1918 Offensives*, 257, 260; *WK*, XIV, 441; Kitchen, *German Offensives*, 177.

308. Pétain–Foch, 17 June 1918, 6N53, SHA.

309. *WK*, XIV, 456.
310. Comité de guerre, 26 June 1918, 3N2, SHA; Greenhalgh, *Victory Through Coalition*, 221.
311. Comité de guerre, 2 June 1918, 3N2, SHA.
312. Geddes–Milner, 16 July 1918, MLN 374.
313. *WK*, XIV, 462, 444, 456-9; Edmonds, *MOFB, 1918*, III, 232, 221-4; Foch, *Mémoires*, II, 139-40.
314. Ibid.
315. Sheffield and Bourne (eds.), *Douglas Haig*, 428.
316. War Cabinet, 11 July 1918, CAB/23/4; Wilson–Foch and Lloyd George–Clemenceau, 12 July 1918, 2/24A/28, Wilson MSS, IWM.
317. Sheffield and Bourne (eds.), *Douglas Haig*, 430-31; Greenhalgh, *Victory Through Coalition*, 224-7.
318. Kitchen, *German Offensives*, 182; Pitt, *1918*, 175.
319. Weygand–Liddell Hart, 22 Oct. 1931, 1K/129/1, SHA.
320. Zabecki, *German 1918 Offensives*, 239.
321. Ibid., 260; cf. R. Binding, *A Fatalist at War* (London 1929), 234.
322. *WK*, XIV, 451.
323. *WK*, XIV, 464.

2. ON THE ATTACK: JULY–NOVEMBER 1918

1. WO/157/36.
2. C. M. Seymour (ed.), *The Intimate Papers of Colonel House*, IV (4 vols., London, 1926-8), 57.
3. War Cabinet, 11 July 1918, CAB/23/4; Lloyd George–Clemenceau, 12 July 1918, 2/24A/28, Wilson MSS, IWM.
4. *AFGG*, VII, i, 1; B. Liddell Hart, *Foch: the Man of Orléans* (London, 1931), 334.
5. G. Pedroncini, *Pétain: le soldat, 1856-1940* (Paris, 1998), 268; Weygand–Liddell Hart, 22 Oct. 1931, 1K/129/1, SHA; F. Foch, *Mémoires pour servir à l'histoire de la guerre de 1914-1918*, II (2 vols., Paris, 1931), 142-4.
6. C. E. Mangin, *Comment finit la Guerre* (Paris, 1920), 192-4; R. A. Doughty, *Pyrrhic Victory: French Strategy and Operations in the Great War* (Cambridge, Mass./London, 2005), 467-9.
7. G. Martin, 'German Strategy and Military Assessments of the American Expeditionary Force (AEF), 1917-18', *War in History* (1994), 179; D. Trask, *The AEF and Coalition Warmaking, 1917-1918* (Lawrence, Kan., 1993), 89-90; *USAWW*, V, 678-9.
8. *AFGG*, VII, i, 43, 55, 60, 67; J. J. Pershing, *My Experiences in the World War* (London, 1931), 496-7.
9. 11th Bavarian infantry division, 18 Aug. 1918, HGr/1, KAM.
10. E. M. Coffman, *The War to End All Wars: the American Military Experience in World War I* (Lexington, Ky, 1998), 241-3; Trask, *AEF*, 91.
11. *AFGG*, VII, i, 88, 132.
12. Ibid., 120-21; Pedroncini, *Pétain: le soldat*, 270; B. Pitt, *1918: the Last Act* (Barnsley,

2003), 187–8; M. S. Neiberg, *The Second Battle of the Marne* (Bloomington, Ind./ Indianopolis, Ind., 2008), 140, 142.

13. *AFGG*, VII, i, chs. 4–5; Pitt, *1918*, 189–91.

14. *WK*, XIV, 536; Pitt, *1918*, 197; *AFGG*, VII, i, 152; Weygand–Liddell Hart, 22 Oct. 1931, 1K/129/1, SHA.

15. Köberle reports, 22 July, 8 Aug. 1918, MKr/1832/1, KAM; Foch, *Mémoires*, II, 160; R. Asprey, *The German High Command at War: Hindenburg and Ludendorff and the First World War* (London, 1994), 441.

16. Haig diary, 18 July, 4, 6 Aug. 1918, MF/861, LHCMA.

17. *WK*, XIV, 530ff.; Du Cane telegram, 20 July 1918, WO/158/102.

18. *WK*, XIV, 532.

19. C. Barnett, *The Swordbearers: Supreme Command in the First World War* (London, 2000), 341–6; Neiberg, *Second Battle of the Marne*, 130.

20. *WK*, XIV, 536–9.

21. Neiberg, *Second Battle of the Marne*, 190.

22. Haig diary, 24 July 1918, MF/861, LHCMA; Pershing, *My Experiences*, 504ff.; Foch, *Mémoires*, II, 162–8; *AFGG*, VII, i, 111ff.

23. Ibid., 111, 113; Foch, *Mémoires*, II, 168.

24. Foch, *Mémoires*, II, 169; *AFGG*, VII, i, 114; Pétain–Foch, 31 July 1918; Pétain circular, 19 July 1918, 16N1698, SHA.

25. Pershing, *My Experiences*, 506; Haig diary, 24 July 1918, MF/861, LHCMA.

26. W. Philpott, *Bloody Victory: the Sacrifice on the Somme and the Making of the Twentieth Century* (London, 2009), 519.

27. A. Montgomery, *The Story of the Fourth Army in the Battles of the Hundred Days, August 8th to November 11th 1918* (London, n.d.), 1–5.

28. J. E. Edmonds, *Military Operations: France and Belgium. 1914–(1918)*, IV (London, 1933–48), 12, 14–15; *WK*, XIV, 549.

29. Rawlinson–Wilson, 12 July 1918, 2/13A/24, Wilson MSS, IWM; Rawlinson memo, 17 Aug. [sic] 1918, 49, IWM.

30. R. Prior and T. Wilson, *Command on the Western Front: the Military Career of Sir Henry Rawlinson, 1914–1918* (Oxford, 1992), ch. 27.

31. J. P. Harris and N. Barr, *Amiens to the Armistice: the BEF in the Hundred Days' Campaign, 8 August–11 November 1918* (London/Washington DC, 1998), 66, 76.

32. Montgomery memo, 22 July 1918, Fourth Army Papers, 49, IWM.

33. Prior and Wilson, *Command on the Western Front*, 314; A. Palazzo, *Seeking Victory on the Western Front: the British Army and Chemical Warfare in World War I* (Lincoln, Nebr./London, 2000), 178.

34. Edmonds, *MOFB*, *1918*, IV, 8; *AFGG*, VII, i, 67; Prior and Wilson, *Command on the Western Front*, 310–11.

35. Harris and Barr, *Amiens*, 73; Edmonds, *MOFB*, *1918*, 22.

36. J. Monash, *The Australian Victories in France in 1918* (London, n.d.), 1, 10; C. E. W. Bean, *The Australian Imperial Force in France during the Allied Offensive, 1918* (Sydney, 1942), ch. 1.

37. I. M. Brown, 'Not Glamorous But Effective: the Canadian Corps and the Set-Piece Attack, 1917–1918', *Journal of Military History* (1994), 425–31; D. Winter, *Haig's Command: a Reassessment* (London, 1991), 148.

38. B. Rawling, *Surviving Trench Warfare: Technology and the Canadian Corps, 1914–1918* (Toronto/Buffalo, NY/London, 1992), 189; S. Schreiber, *Shock Army of the British Empire: the Canadian Corps in the Last 100 Days of the Great War* (St Catharines, Ont., 2004), chs. 1–2.

39. Currie–Fraser, 7 Dec. 1918, Box E100, MG30, Vol. 1, Currie MSS, NAC.

40. Edmonds, *MOFB, 1918*, IV, 20, 8; J. Ferris (ed.), *The British Army and Signals Intelligence during the First World War* (Stroud, 1992), 16–21.

41. Edmonds, *MOFB, 1918*, IV, 38, 23–4; *WK*, XIV, 552.

42. Monash, *Australian Victories*, 86–9.

43. S. Badsey, 'Cavalry and the Development of Breakthrough Doctrine', in P. Griffith (ed.), *British Fighting Methods in the Great War* (London/Portland, Ore., 1996), 163; Harris and Barr, *Amiens*, 98.

44. Prior and Wilson, *Command on the Western Front*, 371.

45. Edmonds, *MOFB, 1918*, IV, ch.5; *AFGG*, VII, i, 175–8; Philpott, *Bloody Victory* 525.

46. J. P. Harris, *Men, Ideas, and Tanks: British Military Thought and Armed Forces, 1903–1939* (Manchester/New York, 1995), 179.

47. Edmonds, *MOFB, 1918*, IV, 26, 83–4.

48. *WK*, XIV, 556–8.

49. Edmonds, *MOFB, 1918*, IV, 93; Prior and Wilson, *Command on the Western Front*, 320–22.

50. Edmonds, *MOFB, 1918*, IV, 120; *AFGG*, VII, i, 192.

51. Edmonds, *MOFB, 1918*, IV, 124, 144–6.

52. Ibid., 154–5; *WK*, XIV, 567.

53. 'Summary of Operations', 8 Aug. 1918, Fourth Army Records, 44, IWM; Hutier diary, 9 Aug. 1918, W-10/50640, BA-MA.

54. *WK*, XIV, 564–5.

55. E. Ludendorff, *Meine Kriegserinnerungen, 1914–1918*, II (2 vols., Berlin, 1919), 679.

56. Asprey, *German High Command*, 444; *WK*, XIV, 568; Köbele report, 8 Aug. 1918, MKr/1832/1, KAM.

57. Barnett, *Swordbearers*; *WK*, XIV, 568.

58. H. Rudin, *Armistice 1918* (New Haven, Conn., 1944), 23; Foch, *Mémoires*, II, 185–7.

59. Asprey, *German High Command*, 452; Rudin, *Armistice*, 24–7; minutes of Spa meeting, W-10/50290, BA-MA.

60. Prior and Wilson, *Command on the Western Front*, 333–6; *AFGG*, VII, i, 206–8.

61. J. Terraine, *To Win a War: 1918 the Year of Victory* (London, 2000), 119–20; Haig diary, 15 Aug. 1918, MF/861, LHCMA.

62. *AFGG*, VII, i, 199, 208; Foch, *Mémoires*, II, 181–4; Edmonds, *MOFB, 1918*, IV, 166–70.

63. Cf. S. Robbins, *British Generalship on the Western Front, 1914–18: Defeat into Victory* (Abingdon/New York, 2005), 79–81, 128–31, 139–40.

64. Ibid., 173; *AFGG*, VII, i, 228–9, 245–56.

65. Haig diary, 19–22 Aug. 1918, MF/861, LHCMA; Edmonds, *MOFB, 1918*, IV, chs. 10–15.

66. Harris and Barr, *Amiens*, 138; P. Simkins, 'Somme Reprise: Reflections on the Fighting for Albert and Bapaume, August 1918', in B. Bond et al. (eds.), *'Look to Your Front':*

Studies in the First World War by the British Commission for Military History (Staplehurst, 1999), 153–8; Edmonds, *MOFB, 1918*, IV, 310, 387.

67. Haig diary, 31 Aug. 1918, MF/861, LHCMA; Pitt, *1918*, 220.

68. Pitt, *1918*, 230; Edmonds, *MOFB, 1918*, IV, 396–400; Haig diary, 3, 4 Sept. 1918, MF/861, LHCMA.

69. *WK*, XIV, 584–6; *AFGG*, VII, i, 256.

70. *WK*, XIV, 590, 593; Pitt, *1918*, 212.

71. Pershing, *My Experiences*, 584–5; *USAWW*, I, 42.

72. Pershing, *My Experiences*, 520, 540.

73. *AFGG*, VII, i, 221–4.

74. *WK*, XIV, 600; *AFGG*, VII, i, 293.

75. *WK*, XIV, 601.

76. Ibid.; 'Notes on American Offensive Operations', WO/106/528; Wagstaff report, 15 Sept. 1918, WO/106/529; McAndrew, 'Notes on Recent Operations No. 3', 12 Oct. 1918, WO/106/519.

77. Pershing, *My Experiences*, 565; Haig diary, 21 Aug., 10, 32 Sept. 1918, G. D. Sheffield and J. M. Bourne (eds.), *Douglas Haig: War Diaries and Letters, 1914–1918* (London, 2005), 448, 458, 463.

78. Edmonds, *MOFB, 1918*, IV, 315–16; Haig–Wilson, 27 Aug. 1918, 2/7B/7, Wilson MSS, IWM.

79. 'Notes on the General Situation', 28 Aug. 1918, WO/158/20.

80. P. Miquel, *Les Poilus: la France sacrificiée* (Paris, 2001), 431.

81. Haig–Wilson, 30 Aug. 1918, 2/7B/9, Wilson MSS, IWM; Terraine, *To Win*, 131–2; Du Cane, 31 Aug. 1918, WO/158/102.

82. *AFGG*, VII, i, 266–8.

83. Ibid., 268–9, 273; Pershing, *My Experiences*, 568–77.

84. G. Powell, *Plumer: the Soldiers' General: a Biography of Field-Marshal Viscount Plumer of Messines* (Barnsley, 2004), 272.

85. *AFGG*, VII, i, 271–2; Foch, *Mémoires*, II, 208ff.; Edmonds, *MOFB, 1918*, IV, 457.

86. Foch, *Mémoires*, II, 214; 'A' Branch daily summary, 13–14 Sept. 1918, Appendix B, WO/157/35; Pershing report, 1 Sept. 1919, *USAWW*, XII, 40.

87. Ibid.; Trask, *AEF*, 122.

88. *AFGG*, VII, i, 330–38.

89. Pershing report, 1 Sept. 1919, *USAWW*, XII, 41; Pershing, *My Experiences*, 603–5; F. C. Pogue, *George C. Marshall: Education of a General, 1880–1939* (New York, 1993), 175–9.

90. Coffman, *War to End All Wars*, 302; Pershing, *My Experiences*, 612, 608; Trask, *AEF*, 123.

91. Pershing, *My Experiences*, 616; *WK*, XIV, 618; Trask, *AEF*, 128.

92. McAndrew, 'Notes on Recent Operations No. 3', 12 Oct. 1918, WO/106/519.

93. Geiger reports, 29 Sept. 1918, WO/106/5309.

94. Geiger reports, 28–30 Sept. 1918, ibid.; Pershing, *My Experiences*, 623–5; 'Notes on American Offensive Operations', WO/106/528.

95. Haig diary, 5 Oct. 1918, MF/861, LHCMA; Pedroncini, *Pétain: le soldat*, 275; Pershing, *My Experiences*, 622.

96. Powell, *Plumer*, 273–5; Terraine, *To Win*, 161; Edmonds, *MOFB, 1918*, V, chs. 5, 6.

97. 'A' Branch daily summaries, 30 Sept./1 Oct., 1/2 Oct. 1918, WO/157/36.

98. Ibid., 29/30 Aug., WO/157/34; 1/2 Sept. WO/157/35.

99. Sheffield and Bourne (eds.), *Douglas Haig*, 453.

100. Haig diary, 3 Sept. 1918, MF/861, LHCMA; Haig–Wilson, 1 Sept. 1918, 2/7B/11, Wilson MSS, IWM; Nelthorpe, 'Appreciation', 10 Sept. 1918, WO/158/20.

101. Edmonds, *MOFB, 1918*, IV, 507–9; Haig diary, 21, 26 Sept. 1918, MF/861, LHCMA.

102. Rawling, *Surviving Trench Warfare*, 208; Terraine, *To Win*, 158; Harris and Barr, *Amiens*, 192.

103. Edmonds, *MOFB, 1918*, V, 115; T. Travers, *How the War was Won: Command and Technology in the British Army on the Western Front, 1917–1918* (London/New York, 1992), 161.

104. Travers, *How the War was Won*, 164–5; Harris and Barr, *Amiens*, 196; Edmonds, *MOFB, 1918*, V, 46, 155.

105. Edmonds, *MOFB, 1918*, V, 102; Harris and Barr, *Amiens*, 206; Prior and Wilson, *Command on the Western Front*, 396.

106. Harris and Barr, *Amiens*, 209; German report on Hindenburg Line, Aug. 1918, Fourth Army Records, 53, IWM; Terraine, *To Win*, 141.

107. 'A' Branch daily summaries, 6/7, 9/10 Sept. 1918, WO/157/35; 1/2 Oct. 1918, WO/157/36.

108. 'A' Branch daily summaries, 30 Sept./1 Oct. 1918, WO/157/36; Rawlinson–Wilson, 9 Sept. 1918, 2/13A/29, Wilson MSS, IWM.

109. Rawlinson–Wilson, 18 Sept. 1918, 2/13A/31, Wilson MSS, IWM; Edmonds, *MOFB, 1918*, IV, 459; Prior and Wilson, *Command on the Western Front*, 356.

110. Terraine, *To Win*, 163; Prior and Wilson, *Command on the Western Front*, 360.

111. Prior and Wilson, *Command on the Western Front*, 362–6; 'Instructions for Operations', 23 Sept. 1918, Fourth Army Papers, 45, IWM.

112. Prior and Wilson, *Command on the Western Front*, 351–2.

113. Ibid., 373; Harris and Barr, *Amiens*, 224; Travers, *How the War was Won*, 173–4; *WK*, XIV, 620.

114. Haig diary, 15 Oct. 1918, MF/861, LHCMA.

115. *WK*, XIV, 608.

116. Ibid., 608, 610.

117. Ibid., 610, 603–4; Edmonds, *MOFB, 1918*, V, 5.

118. *WK*, XIV, 605–9, 614, 617ff.

119. Ibid., 614.

120. Wake memorandum, 24 July 1918, WO/106/1385.

121. C. Falls, *History of the Great War Based on Official Documents. Macedonia*, II (London, 1935), 145.

122. Ibid., 331–3.

123. Ibid., 341.

124. Wake memorandum, 24 July 1918, WO/106/1385.

125. R. J. Crampton, *Bulgaria, 1878–1918: a History* (New York, 1983), 464–7; Otto Czernin despatches, 26 May, 30 June 1918, Bulgarien Berichte 1918, HHStA.

126. Clemenceau–Franchet, 23 June 1918, Falls, *Macedonia*, 321.

127. G. Fassy, *Le Commandement français en orient (octobre 1915–novembre 1918)*

(Paris, 2003), 354–64; Guillaumat report, 19 July, PMR report, 3 Aug. 1918, WO/106/1385.

128. Milne–War Office, 22 July, and Spiers–Wilson, 31 July 1918, WO/106/1385.
129. Falls, *Macedonia*, ch. 7; Fassy, *Commandement français*, ch. 15.
130. Fassy, *Commandement français*, 383, 393; Falls, *Macedonia*, 131, 128.
131. Falls, *Macedonia*, 117, 161–2; Fassy, *Commandement français*, 375, 385; Milne–War Office, 22 July 1918, WO/106/1385.
132. D. Lloyd George, *War Memoirs*, II (2 vols., London, 1938), 1917–19; Fassy, *Commandement français*, 397.
133. Falls, *Macedonia*, ch. 8.
134. Ibid., 163, 167.
135. Fassy, *Commandement français*, 392.
136. Falls, *Macedonia*, 348, 237.
137. Ibid., ch. 11.
138. C. Falls, *The First World War* (London, 1960), 308.
139. C. Falls, *History of the Great War Based on Official Documents. Egypt and Palestine*, II (London, 1930), 413–14, 421.
140. Chetwode–Wavell, 28 Mar. 1939, 6/IX & X, Allenby MSS, LHCMA.
141. Allenby–Wilson, 5, 22 June, Wilson–Allenby, 4 July 1918, 2/33A/4, 12, 10, Wilson MSS, IWM.
142. Allenby–Wilson, 1 June, Wilson–Allenby, 21 June, 26 July, 1918, 2/33A/7, 8, 13, Wilson MSS, IWM.
143. Falls, *Egypt and Palestine*, II, 438–41.
144. Ibid., 452.
145. 'A' Branch daily summary, 5/6 August 1918, WO/157/34; Falls, *Egypt and Palestine*, II, 410.
146. Falls, *Egypt and Palestine*, II, 406; Allenby–Wilson, 5 June 1918, 2/33A/4, Wilson MSS, IWM.
147. Allenby–Wilson, 14, 21 Aug, 11 Sept. 1918, 2/33A/18, 20, 22, Wilson MSS, IWM; A. Bruce, *The Last Crusade: the Palestine Campaign in the First World War* (London, 2003), 213.
148. Falls, *Egypt and Palestine*, II, 453.
149. C. Falls, *Armageddon 1918: the Final Palestinian Campaign of World War I* (Philadelphia, Pa, 2003), 22.
150. Bruce, *Last Crusade*, 215.
151. Falls, *Egypt and Palestine*, II, 462–3; Y. Sheffy, *British Military Intelligence in the Palestine Campaign, 1914–1918* (London/Portland, Ore., 1998), 315.
152. Sheffy, *British Military Intelligence*, 307–9; Allenby–Wilson, 18 Sept. 1918, 2/33A/22A, Wilson MSS, IWM.
153. Bruce, *Last Crusade*, 215; Falls, *Armageddon*, 36.
154. Falls, *Armageddon*, 55–6; Falls, *Egypt and Palestine*, II, 488.
155. Falls, *Egypt and Palestine*, II, 631.
156. Allenby–Mabel, 24 Sept. 1918, 1/9/6, Allenby MSS, LHCMA; Allenby–Wilson, 23 Sept. 1918, 2/33A/23, Wilson MSS, LHCMA.
157. E. J. Erickson, *Ordered to Die: a History of the Ottoman Army in the First World War* (Westport, Conn./London, 2001), 303; E. J. Erickson, *Ottoman Army Effectiveness in World War I: a Comparative Study* (Abingdon/New York, 2007), 163.

158. Falls, *Egypt and Palestine*, II, 618.

159. A. J. Barker, *The Neglected War: Mesopotamia, 1914–1918* (London, 1967), 453–4.

160. Marshall despatch, 1 Oct. 1918, WO/106/916.

161. Barker, *Neglected War*, 442; Lloyd George, *War Memoirs*, II, 1925.

162. J. F. Moberly, *History of the Great War Based on Official Documents. The Campaign in Mesopotamia, 1914–1918*, IV (London, 1927), 259–60.

163. Moberly, *Mesopotamia*, IV, 319.

164. Barker, *Neglected War*, 467–8; Moberly, *Mesopotamia*, IV, iii.

165. Lloyd George, *War Memoirs*, II, 1929; J. E. Edmonds, *Military Operations: Italy 1915–1919* (London 1949), 243–5.

166. Cavan–Wilson, 29 July 1918, Delmé–Radcliffe–Wilson, 17 Aug. 1918, WO/106/852; Edmonds, *Italy*, 244, 246.

167. Cavan–Wilson, 9 Sept. 1918, WO/106/852.

168. M. Isnenghi and G. Rochat, *La Grande Guerra 1914–1918* (Milan, 2004), 466; Edmonds, *Italy*, 245; C. Seton-Watson, *Italy from Liberalism to Fascism, 1870–1925* (London, 1967), 501.

169. Diaz–Orlando, 14 Sept. 1918, 67 1562, Orlando MSS, ACS; P. Melograni, *Storia politica della Grande Guerra, 1915–1918* (Bari, 1969), 549; Walker–Wilson, 25 Sept., Delmé–Radcliffe–Wilson, 28 Sept. 1918, WO/106/852.

170. Cavan–Wilson, 28 Sept., 6 Oct. 1918, WO/106/852.

171. Edmonds, *Italy*, 266–7; C. Falls, *Caporetto 1917* (London 1965), 179.

172. Comando supremo report on Vittorio Veneto, WO/106/837.

173. Ibid., and Edmonds, *Italy*, 264; E. Glaise von Horstenau, *The collapse of the Austro-Hungarian Empire* (London, 1930), 342–3; A. Livesey, *The Viking Atlas of World War I* (New York, 1994), 176.

174. Edmonds, *Italy*, 249–50; M. Rauchensteiner, *Der Tod des Doppeladlers: Österreich-Ungarn und der Erste Weltkrieg* (Graz, 1993), 613; Comando supremo report on Austrian army, WO/106/846.

175. Cavan–Wilson, 19 Oct. 1918, WO/106/852.

176. Edmonds, *Italy*, 269; P. Pozzato, 'Il ruolo del Grappa e le operazione della 4ª armata nella battaglia di Vittorio Veneto', in G. Berti and P. del Negra (eds.), *Al di qua e al di là del Piave: l'Ultimo Anno della Grande Guerra* (Milan, 2001), 346–7.

177. Rauchensteiner, *Tod*, 612; Glaise-Horstenau, *Collapse*, 346.

178. Edmonds, *Italy*, 283; G. Pieropan, *Storia della Grande Guerra sul fronte italiano 1914–1918* (Milan, 1988), 848; Pozzato, 'Il ruolo del Grappa', 344–6.

179. Edmonds, *Italy*, 286–96, 305; Cavan–Wilson, 29 Oct., 2 Nov. 1918, WO/106/852.

180. Edmonds, *Italy*, 311, 270, 314.

181. Rauchensteiner, *Tod*, 614, 608.

182. Glaise-Horstenau, *Collapse*, 346–9; Rauchensteiner, *Tod*, 617.

183. Orlando–Diaz, 2, 3 Nov. 1918, 67 1562, Orlando MSS, ACS.

184. Rauchensteiner, *Tod*, 621, 673.

185. Pieropan, *Storia*, 848.

186. C. R. M. F. Cruttwell, *A History of the Great War, 1914–1918* (London, 1982), 577; J. Terraine, *Douglas Haig the Educated Soldier* (London, 1963), 470.

187. Haig diary, 10 Oct. 1918, MF/861, LHCMA; Edmonds, *MOFB, 1918*, V, 384; WK, XIV, 689–90, 649.

188. Köberle report, 7 Oct. 1918, MKr/1832/1, KAM.
189. E. Michels, 'Die "Spanische Grippe" 1918/19: Verlauf, Folgen, und Deutungen in Deutschland im Kontext des Ersten Weltkrieges', *Vierteljahrshefte für Zeitgeschichte* (2010); H. Philips and D. Killingray (eds.), *The Spanish Influenza Pandemic of 1918–19: New Perspectives* (London/New York, 2003), 5–8; A. W. Crosby, Jr, *Epidemic and Peace, 1918* (Westport, Conn./London, 1976), 125, 140–59.
190. Terraine, *To Win*, 191–3; Edmonds, *MOFB, 1918*, V, 172, 195, 215–16, 235.
191. T. Travers, 'Could the Tanks of 1918 Have been War-Winners for the British Expeditionary Force?', *Journal of Contemporary History* (1992), 349; Travers, *How the War was Won*, 170; Harris, *Men, Ideas, and Tanks*, 183–6.
192. Edmonds, *MOFB, 1918*, V, 178; Terraine, *To Win*, 185–7.
193. Edmonds, *MOFB, 1918*, V, 186; Haig diary, 6 Oct. 1918, MF/861, LHCMA.
194. Edmonds, *MOFB, 1918*, V, ch. 14 and p. 267; Prior and Wilson, *Command on the Western Front*, 379.
195. *WK*, XIV, 647.
196. Haig diary, 5 Oct. 1918, MF/861, LHCMA; Edmonds, *MOFB, 1918*, V, ch. 16.
197. Pershing, *My Experiences*, 634.
198. *WK*, XIV, 648; Trask, *AEF*, 140.
199. Pershing, *My Experiences*, 634–7, 648; Trask, *AEF*, 141.
200. Trask, *AEF*, 149–51; Pershing, *My Experiences*, 650–52.
201. *WK*, XIV, 648; H. S. Liggett, *A.E.F.: Ten Years Ago in France* (New York, 1928), 206ff.
202. *WK*, XIV, 651–2, 690.
203. Edmonds, *MOFB, 1918*, V, 293.
204. *WK*, XIV, 639, 655.
205. Edmonds, *MOFB, 1918*, V, 595, 384.
206. Ibid., chs. 21–4; Prior and Wilson, *Command on the Western Front*, 363, 384.
207. Haig diary, 10 Oct. 1918, MF/861, LHCMA.
208. Doughty, *Pyrrhic Victory*, 497; Foch, *Mémoires*, II, 236.
209. Doughty, *Pyrrhic Victory*, 500; Edmonds, *MOFB, 1918*, V, 324–5, 231.
210. Doughty, *Pyrrhic Victory*, 490–91, 499; Pitt, *1918*, 21.
211. Edmonds, *MOFB, 1918*, V, chs. 28–9.
212. McAndrew–Pershing, 22 Nov. 1918, WO/106/519.
213. Pershing, *My Experiences*, 677–81; Trask, *AEF*, 161.
214. *WK*, XIV, 650–59.
215. Ibid., 693–4, 700; Köberle report, 1 Nov. 1918, MKr/1832/1, KAM.

3. THE NEW WARFARE: INTELLIGENCE, TECHNOLOGY, AND LOGISTICS

1. J. de Pierrefeu, *GQG Secteur I: trois ans au Grand Quartier Général; par le rédacteur du 'communiqué'*, II (2 vols., Paris, 1920), 212.
2. J. Bailey, *The First World War and the Birth of the Modern Style of Warfare* (Strategic and Combat Studies Institute Occasional Paper No. 22, Camberley, 1996), 3–5.
3. J. H. Morrow, Jr, *German Air Power in World War I* (Lincoln, Nebr./London, 1982), 1.

4. D. T. Zabecki, *Steel Wind: Colonel Georg Bruchmüller and the Birth of Modern Artillery* (Westport, Conn., 1994), ch. 4.

5. B. I. Gudmundsson, *Stormtroop Tactics: Innovation in the German Army, 1914–1918* (Westport, Conn./London, 1989), 43–87.

6. M. Bauer, *Der Grosse Krieg im Feld und Heimat: Erinnerungen und Betrachtungen* (Tübingen, 1921), 177; D. Storz, '"Aber was hätte anders geschehen sollen?" Die deutschen Offensiven an den Westfront 1918', in J. Duppler and G. P. Groß (eds.), *Kriegsende 1918: Ereignis, Wirkung, Nachwirkung* (Munich, 1994), 65; E. Ludendorff, *Meine Kriegserinnerungen, 1914–1918* (Berlin, 1919), 460.

7. M. Schwarte (ed.), *Die militärischen Lehren des Großen Krieges* (Berlin, 1920), 311; G. Bruchmüller, *Die deutsche Artillerie in den Durchbruchschlachten des Weltkrieges* (Berlin, 1921), 21–3.

8. Zabecki, *Steel Wind*, 37–44.

9. Ibid., 96.

10. T. T. Lupfer, *The Dynamics of Doctrine: the Changes in German Tactical Doctrine during the First World War* (Fort Leavensworth Paper, Fort Leavensworth, Kan., 1981), 8–11.

11. E. Ludendorff (ed.), *Urkunden des Obersten Heeresleitung über ihre Tätigkeit 1916/18* (Berlin, 1920), 641ff.

12. 'A Survey of German Tactics 1918' (Historical Sub-Section, General Staff, AEF, Washington DC, 1918), 12–15.

13. Ludendorff memoranda, 17 Apr. and 9 June 1918, Ludendorff (ed.), *Urkunden*, 672ff. and 677ff.

14. R. T. Foley, 'The Other Side of the Hill: the German Army in 1917', in P. Dennis and J. Grey (eds.), *1917: Tactics, Training, and Technology* (Canberra, 2007), 162–77.

15. D. Porch, *The French Secret Services: from the Dreyfus Affair to the Gulf War* (London/Basingstoke, 1996), 112.

16. J. Ferris (ed.), *The British Army and Signals Intelligence during the First World War* (Stroud, 1992), 14.

17. Ibid., 102.

18. J. Beach, 'British Intelligence and the German Army, 1914–1918', University College London, Ph.D. dissertation, 2004, chs. 1–4.

19. Ibid., 107; Porch, *French Secret Services*, 107; C. M. Andrew, *Secret Service: the Making of the British Intelligence Community* (London, 1985), 170.

20. 1 Mar. 1918 entry, WO/157/29; D. French, 'Failures of Intelligence: the Retreat to the Hindenburg Line and the March 1918 Offensive', in M. L. Dockrill and D. French (eds.), *Strategy and Intelligence: British Policy during the First World War* (London/Rio Grande, O., 1996), 88.

21. Ibid., 91, 93; Beach, 'British Intelligence', 242–4; J. E. Edmonds, *Military Operations: France and Belgium. 1914–(1918)*, I (London, 1933–48), 107–9.

22. Beach, 'British Intelligence', 245–9; French, 'Failures of Intelligence', 93–5.

23. French, 'Failures of Intelligence', 90; *AFGG*, VI, i, 250–55.

24. C. M. Andrew, *The Defence of the Realm: the Authorized History of MI5* (London, 2009), 53–83.

25. W. Nicolai, *The German Secret Service* (transl., London, 1924), 82; T. M. Proctor, *Female Intelligence: Women and Espionage in the First World War* (New York/London, 2003), 126–31.

26. M. Occleshaw, *Armour Against Fate: British Military Intelligence in the First World War* (London, 1989), 237; Porch, *French Secret Services*, 22.

27. Occleshaw, *Armour Against Fate*, 170–87.

28. LDB, Box 2, farde 12.

29. Drake, BEF Intelligence History, 15, WO/106/45.

30. LDB, Box 1, farde 7; and generally, K. Jeffery, *MI6: the History of the Secret Intelligence Service, 1909–1949* (London/Berlin/New York/Sydney, 2010), ch. 3.

31. Beach, 'British Intelligence', 69.

32. S. de Lastours, *1914–1918: La France gagne la guerre des codes secrets* (Paris, 1998), 68.

33. J. Morgan, *The Secrets of the Rue St Roch: Intelligence Operations behind Enemy Lines in the First World War* (London, 2004), 209–11, 295; Drake, BEF Intelligence History, 19–20, WO/106/45.

34. Occleshaw, *Armour Against Fate*, 144.

35. Proctor, *Female Intelligence*, ch. 4.

36. Nicolai, *German Secret Service*, 130–31; German prisoner interrogation records are used extensively in C. Duffy, *Through German Eyes: the British and the Somme 1916* (London, 2007).

37. Andrew, *Secret Service*, 171.

38. Beach, 'British Intelligence', 32–5, 243.

39. Ibid., 66, 70–78.

40. Ibid., 244; French, 'Failures of Intelligence', 92.

41. Porch, *French Secret Services*, 73; D. Kahn, *The Codebreakers: the Story of Secret Writing* (London, 1966), 28ff.

42. Ibid., 309ff.

43. Ferris (ed.), *Signals Intelligence*, 25–37; Beach, 'British Intelligence', 81.

44. Ferris (ed.), *Signals Intelligence*, 53; Kahn, *Codebreakers*, 300; Porch, *French Secret Services*, 104.

45. De Lastours, *1914–1918*, 34.

46. Kahn, *Codebreakers*, 343; cf. Porch, *French Secret Services*, 108–9.

47. French, 'Failures of Intelligence', 90.

48. Edmonds, *MOFB, 1918*, II, 144–5.

49. Beach, 'British Intelligence', 249.

50. Porch, *French Secret Services*, 83, 88–90, 93–5, 83–4.

51. Nicolai, *German Secret Service*, 130–31.

52. De Lastours, *1914–1918*, 225–6.

53. Ibid., 39–45; Kahn, *Codebreakers*, 34, 345.

54. *AFGG*, VI, ii, 8–9.

55. Ibid., 76–7.

56. Edmonds, *MOFB, 1918*, III, 17–22, 187A, 39; Beach, 'British Intelligence', 258; J. J. Pershing, *My Experiences in the World War* (London, 1931), 408.

57. Zabecki, *Steel Wind*, 97.

58. *AFGG*, VI, ii, 262–3.

59. Kahn, *Codebreakers*, 346.

60. De Lastours, *1914–1918*, 46–57.

61. Ibid., 70.

62. Edmonds, *MOFB, 1918*, III, 172; *AFGG*, VI, ii, 286–94.

63. *AFGG*,VI, ii, 383; De Lastours, *1914–1918*, 64.

64. Porch, *French Secret Services*, 110–11; Pierrefeu, *GQG*, II, 197.

65. G. Pedroncini, *Pétain: le soldat, 1856–1940* (Paris, 1998), 256; M. Weygand, *Mémoires: idéal vécu*, I (2 vols., Paris, 1953), 501.

66. M. S. Neiberg, *The Second Battle of the Marne* (Bloomington, Ind./Indianopolis, Ind., 2008), 91.

67. Kahn, *Codebreakers*, 316–20.

68. J. E. Edmonds, *Military Operations: Italy 1915–1919* (London 1949), 183.

69. Regio esercito italiano, Comando supremo, *La battaglia del Piave (15–23 giugno 1918)* (Rome, 1920), 32.

70. C. Falls, *Caporetto 1917* (London 1965), 151; G. H. Cassar, *Forgotten Front: the British Campaign in Italy, 1917–1918* (London/Rio Grande, O., 1998), 150–54.

71. Morgan, *Rue St Roch*, 303.

72. Occleshaw, *Armour Against Fate*, 177.

73. Kahn, *Codebreakers*, 326–33.

74. Edmonds, *Italy*, 274.

75. Y. Sheffy, *British Military Intelligence in the Palestine Campaign, 1914–1918* (London/Portland, Ore., 1998), xvi.

76. Ibid., 318, 327.

77. Beach, 'British Intelligence', 282.

78. 'A Survey of German Tactics', 12.

79. See Chapter 8.

80. L. Kennett, *The First Air War 1914–1918* (London/Toronto/Sydney/Singapore, 1991), 93.

81. H. Freiherr von Bülow, *Geschichte der Luftwaffe: eine kurze Darstellung der Entwicklung der fünften Waffe* (Frankfurt-am-Main, 1934), 125.

82. N. Jones, *The Origins of Strategic Bombing: a Study of the Development of British Air Strategic Thought and Practice up to 1918* (London, 1973), 13.

83. A. Gollin, *The Impact of Air Power on the British People and Their Government, 1909–1914* (Stanford, Calif., 1989), ch. 13.

84. N. Hanson, *First Blitz* (London, 2008), 21–3.

85. E. B. Ashmore, *Air Defence* (London/New York/Toronto, 1929), 15–28.

86. P. Darmon, *Vivre à Paris pendant la Grande Guerre* (Paris, 2002), 349.

87. Hanson, *First Blitz*, 35ff.

88. J. Ferris, 'Airbandit: C³I and Strategic Air Defence during the First Battle of Britain, 1915–18', in Dockrill and French (eds.), *Strategy and Intelligence*, 37–40.

89. Ashmore, *Air Defence*, 33–6; Hanson, *First Blitz*, chs. 5–6.

90. Hanson, *First Blitz*, 158–61.

91. Ibid., chs. 10–12; Ashmore, *Air Defence*, 80, 84.

92. Ferris, 'Airbandit', 43–4; French, 'Report on the Air Defences of London', 17 Jan. 1918, AIR/9/69.

93. Kennett, *First Air War*, 62.

94. Ferris, 'Airbandit', 60; Hanson, *First Blitz*, 48.

95. Darmon, *Vivre à Paris*, 353, 378.

96. C. Christienne and P. Lissarague, *A History of French Military Aviation* (transl., Washington DC, 1986), 174.

97. Ashmore, *Air Defence*, 127.

98. R. Martel, *L'Aviation française de bombardement (des origines au 11 novembre 1918)* (Paris, 1939), 299; Dorman, *Vivre à Paris*, 358.

99. Ashmore, *Air Defence*, 130, 106; Hanson, *First Blitz*, 341.

100. Hanson, *First Blitz*, 308–12, 330–33.

101. J. F. Wise, *Canadian Airmen and the First World War: the Official History of the Royal Canadian Air Force*, I (Toronto, 1980), 257.

102. Hanson, *First Blitz*, 160; Morrow, *German Air Power*, 116.

103. Kennett, *First Air War*, 51.

104. Wise, *Canadian Airmen*, I, 257; E. von Hoeppner, *Germany's War in the Air: the Development and Operations of German Military Aviation in the World War* (transl., Nashville, Tenn., 1994), 107.

105. Ferris, 'Airbandit', 61.

106. H. A. Jones, *The War in the Air (Being the Story of the Part Played in the Great War by the Royal Air Force)*, VI (6 vols., Oxford, 1922–37), 2, 90.

107. J. Sweetman, 'The Smuts Report of 1917: Merely Political Window-Dressing?', *Journal of Strategic Studies* (1981), 169.

108. Martel, *L'Aviation française*, 271; A. Barros, 'Strategic Bombing and Restraint in "Total War", 1915–1918', *Historical Journal* (2009), 414–23.

109. Ibid., 286, and viii–x.

110. Sykes, 7 Aug. 1918, AIR/1/30/15/1/155.

111. Wise, *Canadian Airmen*, I, 319.

112. Jones, *Origins of Strategic Bombing*, 181–7.

113. Jones, *War in the Air*, VI, 152.

114. Sykes, 7 Aug. 1918, AIR/1/30/15/1/155.

115. 'Effect of [Allied] air raids', Oct. 1919, AIR/1/2690; Hanson, *First Blitz*, 326–8.

116. Christienne and Lissarague, *French Military Aviation*, 174.

117. Wise, *Canadian Airmen*, I, 323, 320.

118. Jones, *War in the Air*, VI, 409–11.

119. Ibid., 139.

120. Ashmore, *Air Defence*, 119–26.

121. Jones, *Origins of Strategic Bombing*, 198; Wise, *Canadian Airmen*, I, 325.

122. Jones, *War in the Air*, IV, 456, and VI, 106–17; Air Council, 3 Oct. 1918, AIR/6/13.

123. Wise, *Canadian Airmen*, I, 296–7, 320.

124. M. Cooper, *The Birth of Independent Air Power: British Air Policy in the First World War* (London/Boston, Mass./Sydney, 1986), 136.

125. Kennett, *First Air War*, 77.

126. Jones, *War in the Air*, IV, 286.

127. P. Hart, *Aces Falling: War above the Trenches, 1918* (London, 2007), 1–7.

128. Ludendorff (ed.), *Urkunden*, 661–4.

129. Hoeppner, *Germany's War*, 140.

130. Bülow, *Geschichte der Luftwaffe*, 103.

131. Jones, *War in the Air*, IV, 274.

132. Wise, *Canadian Airmen*, I, 488.

133. Hart, *Aces*, 90–91.

134. Bülow, *Geschichte der Luftwaffe*, 106; Hoeppner, *Germany's War*, 147; Christienne and Lissarague, *French Military Aviation*, 125.

135. Hoeppner, *Germany's War*, 142, 150.

136. Jones, *War in the Air*, IV, 360.
137. Ibid., 353–7.
138. Wise, *Canadian Airmen*, I, 502.
139. Jones, *War in the Air*, IV, 320.
140. Wise, *Canadian Airmen*, I, 512.
141. Jones, *War in the Air*, IV, 336.
142. War Cabinet, 4 Apr. 1918, CAB/23/6.
143. Jones, *War in the Air*, IV, 376–86.
144. Christienne and Lissarague, *French Military Aviation*, 125; Wise, *Canadian Airmen*, I, 506.
145. Jones, *War in the Air*, IV, 387–9.
146. Hoeppner, *Germany's War*, 133.
147. Christienne and Lissarague, *French Military Aviation*, 124–6.
148. Jones, *War in the Air*, IV, 412; M. Maurer (ed.), *The US Air Service in World War I. Vol. I: the Full Report and a Tactical History* (Washington DC, 1978), 81.
149. Jones, *War in the Air*, IV, 273–83.
150. Ibid., 435–6, 442–65.
151. Ibid., 492, 534.
152. Christienne and Lissarague, *French Military Aviation*, 128; Maurer (ed.), *US Air Service*, I, 88.
153. Jones, *War in the Air*, VI, 526–9.
154. Ibid., 544; Hart, *Aces*, 342.
155. WK, XIV, 721; Hoeppner, *Germany's War*, 160.
156. Hoeppner, *Germany's War*, 164, 167.
157. Kennett, *First Air War*, 85, 94.
158. Christienne and Lissarague, *French Military Aviation*, 591.
159. Morrow, *German Air Power*, 140; Kennett, *First Air War*, 44; Maurer (ed.), *US Air Service*, I, v.
160. Ibid., 23, 27.
161. 'British Air Effort', Apr. 1919, AIR/8/13.
162. 'Comparison of French and British Results', 10 Nov. 1918, AIR/1/109/15/16.
163. Ibid.
164. Jones, *War in the Air*, VI, 225.
165. Christienne and Lissarague, *French Military Aviation*, 146–51.
166. Jones, *War in the Air*, VI, 28ff.
167. Morrow, *German Air Power*, ch. 5; J. H. Morrow, Jr, *The Great War in the Air: Military Aviation from 1909 to 1921* (Washington DC/London, 1993), 371.
168. O. Lepick, *La Grande Guerre chimique: 1914–1918* (Paris, 1998), 311, 317.
169. Ibid., 310, 315; C. H. Foulkes, *'Gas!' The Story of the Special Brigade* (Edinburgh/London, 1934), 329.
170. Ludendorff directives, WO/142/266; 'Der Angriff im Stellungskriege', 26 Jan. 1918, Ludendorff (ed.), *Urkunden*, 649.
171. Lepick, *Grande Guerre chimique*, 68; L. F. Haber, *The Poisonous Cloud: Chemical Warfare in the First World War* (Oxford, 1986), 127.
172. 'The Liven's [sic] Gas Projector' (n.d.), WO/188/143.
173. Tables of British gas casualties, WO/153/988.
174. Report on German Chemical Warfare (n.d.), WO/33/1072.
175. Haber, *Poisonous Cloud*, 213.

176. A. Palazzo, *Seeking Victory on the Western Front: the British Army and Chemical Warfare in World War I* (Lincoln, Nebr./London, 2000), 123–4.
177. Ibid., 82.
178. Foulkes, 'Enemy Use of Gas Shell' (n.d.), WO/158/127.
179. Lepick, *Grande Guerre chimique*, 251–2.
180. Ibid., 248–9; Foulkes, '*Gas!*', 329.
181. Report on German Chemical Warfare (n.d.), WO/33/1072.
182. Foulkes, '*Gas!*', 328.
183. Ibid., 336.
184. J. J. M. Mordacq, *Le Ministère Clemenceau: journal d'un témoin*, I (4 vols., Paris, 1930), 158.
185. Foulkes summaries of enemy gas activity, Aug.–Nov. 1918, WO/158/128.
186. Haber, *Poisonous Cloud*, 170.
187. Ibid., 169; Palazzo, *Seeking Victory*, 125, 137, 220n.
188. Palazzo, *Seeking Victory*, 156.
189. Lepick, *Grande Guerre chimique*, 230–31.
190. Palazzo, *Seeking Victory*, 167–87.
191. Lepick, *Grande Guerre chimique*, 251.
192. Haber, *Poisonous Cloud*, 167–70.
193. Palazzo, *Seeking Victory*, 193.
194. GHQ conference, 19 Mar. 1918, WO/32/5178.
195. Foulkes, '*Gas!*', 334; Haber, *Poisonous Cloud*, 226; Palazzo, *Seeking Victory*, 193.
196. Général Gascouin, *L'Evolution de l'artillerie pendant la guerre* (Paris, 1920), 256–7.
197. P. Griffith, *Battle Tactics of the Western Front: the British Army's Art of Attack, 1916–18* (New Haven, Conn./London, 1994), 136.
198. P. Guinard, J.-C. Devos, and J. Nicot, *Inventaire sommaire des Archives de la Guerre, Série N: 1872–1919*, Vol. I (Troyes, 1975), 153, 157; M. Goya, *La Chair et l'acier: l'invention de la guerre moderne (1914–1918)* (Paris, 2004), 412.
199. A. Palazzo, 'The British Army's Counter-Battery Staff Office and Control of the Enemy in World War I', *Journal of Military History* (1990), 58; A. Simpson, 'British Corps Command on the Western Front, 1914–1918', in G. D. Sheffield and D. Todman (eds.), *Command and Control on the Western Front: the British Army's Experience, 1914–1918* (Staplehurst, 2004), 113
200. Griffith, *Battle Tactics*, 147.
201. Gascouin, *L'Evolution de l'artillerie*, 221.
202. Ibid., 224–6.
203. P. Mead, *The Eye in the Air: History of Air Observation and Reconnaissance for the Army, 1784–1945* (London, 1983), 102ff.; Griffith, *Battle Tactics*, 155.
204. Griffith, *Battle Tactics*, 155; R. MacLeod, 'Sight and Sound on the Western Front: Surveyors, Scientists, and the "Battlefield Laboratory", 1915–1918', *War and Society* (2000), 42.
205. Moore–Brabazon memorandum on photography, 26 Oct. 1918, AIR/1/724/91/2; S. Bidwell and D. Graham, *Fire-Power: British Army Weapons and Theories of War, 1904–1945* (London, 1982), 143.
206. Griffith, *Battle Tactics*, 152–3.
207. Palazzo, 'Counter-Battery', 34–5.

208. R. Prior and T. Wilson, *Command on the Western Front: the Military Career of Sir Henry Rawlinson, 1914–1918* (Oxford, 1992), 314.

209. Goya, *La Chair et l'acier*, 379; Griffith, *Battle Tactics*, 174; 'Deutsche Rüstung 1918', 31, W-10/50421, BA-MA.

210. Griffith, *Battle Tactics*, 141–6; I. M. Brown, 'Not Glamorous But Effective: the Canadian Corps and the Set-Piece Attack, 1917–1918', *Journal of Military History* (1994), 441–2.

211. Infantry regiment 175, 4 Sept. 1918, HGr/91, KAM.

212. Ludendorff (ed.), *Urkunden*, 648, 672.

213. Gascouin, *L'Evolution de l'artillerie*, 218, 238.

214. Goya, *La Chair et l'acier*, 388–90, 403.

215. Griffith, *Battle Tactics*, 142; J. Bailey, 'British Artillery in the Great War', in P. Griffith (ed.), *British Fighting Methods in the Great War* (London/Portland, Ore., 1996), 37.

216. Prior and Wilson, *Command on the Western Front*, 362–5, 384, 388.

217. M. E. Grotelueschen, *The AEF Way of War: the American Army and Combat in World War I* (Cambridge, 2007), 346, 351.

218. WK, XIV, 33; 'Deutsche Rüstung 1918', 30, W-10/50421, BA-MA; Ludendorff, *Meine Kriegserinnerungen*, 496.

219. Guinard et al., *Inventaire*, 102ff., 122–5; Goya, *La Chair et l'acier*, 382–5.

220. Griffith, *Battle Tactics*, 95–8, 129–34; G. D. Sheffield, *Forgotten Victory. The First World War: Myths and Realities* (London, 2001), 216–18.

221. S. Schreiber, *Shock Army of the British Empire: the Canadian Corps in the Last 100 Days of the Great War* (St Catharines, Ont., 2004), 20–21.

222. See generally, P. Cornish, *Machine Guns and the Great War* (Barnsley, 2009), chs. 4–6.

223. S. Badsey, *Doctrine and Reform in the British Cavalry, 1880–1918* (Aldershot/Burlington, Vt, 2008), 243–4; 'Deutsche Rüstung 1918', 16, W-10/50421, BA-MA.

224. Goya, *La Chair et l'acier*, 386–7, 400–401.

225. Badsey, *Doctrine and Reform*, 248–9, 262, 294–302.

226. F.-J. Deygas, *Les Chars d'assaut: leur passé, leur avenir* (Paris, 1937), 265.

227. J. F. C. Fuller, *Tanks and the Great War 1914–1918* (London, 1920), chs. 11, 17.

228. Tank Board, 3 Oct. 1918, WO/158/867.

229. Deygas, *Les Chars*, 261–8; Fuller, *Tanks*, 277.

230. Pershing, 'Final Report', 60, para 26, *USAWW*, XII.

231. D. Fletcher (ed.), *Tanks and Trenches: First Hand Accounts of Tank Warfare in the First World War* (Stroud, 1994), 185; Fuller, *Tanks*, 280–82.

232. Fuller, *Tanks*, 280; Pershing, 'Final Report', *USAWW*, XII; Captain Dutil, *Les Chars d'assaut: leur création et leur rôle pendant la guerre 1915–1918* (Nancy/Paris/Strasbourg, 1919), 192–8.

233. Elles–Edmonds, 4 Sept. 1934, CAB/45/200.

234. Fuller, *Tanks*, 44; Goya, *La Chair et l'acier*, 341.

235. D. J. Childs, *A Peripheral Weapon? The Production and Employment of British Tanks in the First World War* (Westport, Conn./London, 1999), 182; Elles–Edmonds, 4 Sept. 1934, CAB/45/200.

236. Deygas, *Les Chars*, 277.

237. Ibid., 173–5; Goya, *La Chair et l'acier*, 351–4.

238. Kiggell circular, 18 Jan. 1918, Elles–GHQ, 3 Jan. 1918, WO/158/835; Lawrence circular, 13 Feb. 1918, WO/158/832.

239. Fuller, *Tanks*, 173; T. Travers, *How the War was Won: Command and Technology in the British Army on the Western Front, 1917–1918* (London/New York, 1992), 44.

240. Deygas, *Les Chars*, 186.

241. Ibid., 188, 303–4.

242. Fuller, *Tanks*, 192–4; Goya, *La Chair et l'acier*, 355.

243. Dill–Fuller, 21 July, Elles–Davidson, 12 June 1918, WO/158/835.

244. Fuller, *Tanks*, 205–6; Fletcher (ed.), *Tanks and Trenches*, 124–31.

245. Capper–Elles, 29 Apr. 1918, WO/158/816.

246. Fuller, *Tanks*, 223; J. P. Harris, *Men, Ideas, and Tanks: British Military Thought and Armed Forces, 1903–1939* (Manchester/New York, 1995), 176–9.

247. Fuller, *Tanks*, 225–7; T. Travers, 'Could the Tanks of 1918 Have been War-Winners for the British Expeditionary Force?', *Journal of Contemporary History* (1992), 392–5.

248. Goya, *La Chair et l'acier*, 354–61.

249. Lawrence circular, 1 Sept. 1918, WO/158/832.

250. Karslake conference notes, 12 Aug. 1918, WO/158/840; GHQ, 'Tanks and Their Employment', Aug. 1918, WO/158/832.

251. 'Summary of Tank Operations', Aug.–Oct. 1918; Elles memorandum, 29 Oct. 1918, WO/95/94.

252. Harris, *Men, Ideas, and Tanks*, 183–4; Childs, *Peripheral Weapon?*, 45.

253. 'Summary of Tank Operations', WO/95/94; Fuller, *Tanks*, 288.

254. Fuller, *Tanks*, 285; Elles–Edmonds, 4 Sept. 1934, CAB/45/200; Childs, *Peripheral Weapon?*, 175; Dutil, *Les Chars*, 216.

255. E. Greenhalgh, 'Errors and Omissions in Franco-British Co-operation over Munitions Production, 1914–18', *War in History* (2007), 209–10.

256. Tank Board, 5, 12 Sept. 1918, WO/158/867; Deygas, *Les Chars*, 257–9.

257. Tank Board, 15 Aug. 1918, WO/158/867; Childs, *Peripheral Weapon?*, 192, 189.

258. Deygas, *Les Chars*, 197; Goya, *La Chair et l'acier*, 363–5.

259. Harris, *Men, Ideas, and Tanks*, 167–70; Fuller, *Tanks*, 306; Wilson–Foch, 20 July 1918, WO/158/842.

260. *WK*, XIV, 33; 'Deutsche Rüstung 1918', 25, 81, W-10/50421, BA-MA.

261. Elles–GHQ, 3 Jan. 1918, WO/158/835.

262. *WK*, XIV, 34, 525; Fuller, *Tanks*, 213; 'Deutsche Rüstung 1918', 81, W-10/50421, BA-MA.

263. Fletcher (ed.), *Tanks and Trenches*, 15; Lawrence circular, 6 May 1918, WO/158/835.

264. *WK*, XIV, 525.

265. Fuller, *Tanks*, 215.

266. 'Deutsche Rüstung 1918', 83–4, W-10/50421, BA-MA.

267. Ibid., 89–90; Fuller, *Tanks*, 263–5.

268. Fuller, *Tanks*, 237–41.

269. Köberle report, 12 Oct. 1918, MKr/1832/1, KAM.

270. G. Dyer, *The Missing of the Somme* (London, 1994), 60.

271. Edmonds, *MOFB, 1916*, I, 99–100.

272. A. Sarter, *Die deutschen Eisenbahnen im Kriege* (Stuttgart, 1930), 114; M. Schwarte (ed.), *Der Weltkampf um Ehre und Recht*, VI (8 vols., Leipzig/Berlin, 1927), 258.

273. A. M. Henniker, *Transportation on the Western Front, 1914–1918* (London, 1937), xxi.

274. Schwarte (ed.), *Weltkampf*, VI, 258, 264.

275. D. T. Zabecki, *The German 1918 Offensives: a Case Study in the Operational Level of War* (London/New York, 2006), 36; H. Rohde, 'Faktoren der deutschen Logistik im Ersten Weltkrieg', in G. Canini (ed.), *Les Fronts invisibles: nourrir – fournir – soigner* (Nancy, 1984), 106.

276. J. Singleton, 'Britain's Military Use of Horses, 1914–1918', *Past & Present* (1993), 196; I. M. Brown, *British Logistics on the Western Front, 1914–1919* (Westport, Conn./London, 1998), 240.

277. Singleton, 'Horses', 184; *WK*, XIV, 31–2.

278. Generalintendant–War Minister, 10 Aug. 1918, W-10/50435; 'Deutsche Rüstung 1918', 26–7, W-10/50421, BA-MA.

279. War Ministry memorandum, 8 Oct. 1917; Ludendorff–Finance Minister, 15 Feb. 1918, W-10/50435, BA-MA; *WK*, XIV, 32.

280. Reports on German economic situation, 26 Dec. 1917, 23 Jan. 1918, *BDFA*, XII, 35–6, 61.

281. Singleton, 'Horses', 189; 'Deutsche Rüstung 1918', 43, W-10/50421, BA-MA.

282. Storz, 'Die deutschen Offensiven', 68; Zabecki, *German 1918 Offensives*, 88.

283. Hildebrand, 'Rohstofflage', W-10/50494, BA-MA; F. Friedensburg, *Das Erdöl im Ersten Weltkrieg* (Stuttgart, 1939), 82–3.

284. Hildebrand, 'Rohstofflage', W-10/50494, BA-MA; D. Yergin, *The Prize: the Epic Quest for Oil, Money, and Power* (New York/London/Toronto/Sydney, 1992), 180–82; F. Venn, *Oil Diplomacy in the Twentieth Century* (Basingstoke, 1986), 37.

285. Hildebrand, 'Rohstoffversorgung', 12, W-10/50493; Hildebrand, 'Rohstofflage', 44, W-10/50494, BA-MA; Friedensburg, *Erdöl*, 74–9.

286. 'Deutsche Rüstung 1918', 67, W-10/50421; Ludendorff circular, 19 Oct. 1918, W-10/50400, BA-MA.

287. Henniker, *Transportation*, chs. xi, xv.

288. K. Grieves, 'The Transportation Mission to GHQ, 1916', in B. Bond et al. (eds.), *'Look to Your Front': Studies in the First World War by the British Commission for Military History* (Staplehurst, 1999), 63–78; Brown, *British Logistics*, 142.

289. Henniker, *Transportation*, 231–8; 'Report on Quartermaster-General's Branch', WO/107/69.

290. Henniker, *Transportation*, 255–63; Brown, *British Logistics*, 144.

291. Henniker, *Transportation*, 342–51.

292. Singleton, 'Horses', 186, 190, 198.

293. 'History of Light Railways', WO/158/852.

294. 'Report on Quartermaster-General's Branch', WO/107/69; Henniker, *Transportation*, 358; M. G. McCoy, 'Grinding Gears: the AEF and Motor Transportation in the First World War', *War in History* (2004), 195.

295. Henniker, *Transportation*, 355–71.

296. Ibid., 393ff.

297. Quartermaster-General's Branch, 'Explanatory Review', April, May 1918, WO/95/38.

298. Henniker, *Transportation*, 398; I. M. Brown, 'Feeding Victory: the Logistic Imperative behind the Hundred Days', in P. Dennis and J. Grey (eds.), *1918: Defining Victory* (Canberra, 1999), 33–9.

299. Zabecki, *German 1918 Offensives*, 31.

300. Quartermaster-General's Branch, 'Explanatory Review', May 1918, WO/95/38.

301. 'War Diary QMG' (5 June 1918), WO/95/39.

302. Henniker, *Transportation*, 400–404.

303. D. Stevenson, 'War by Timetable? The Railway Race before 1914', *Past & Present* (1999), 175.

304. Henniker, *Transportation*, 396–8.

305. *AFGG*, XI, 514; F. C. Pogue, *George C. Marshall: Education of a General, 1880–1939* (New York, 1993), 163.

306. Friedensburg, *Erdöl*, 9.

307. *AFGG*, XI, 535, 650–52.

308. A. Doumenc, 'Les Transports automobiles pendant la guerre de 1914–1918', in Canini (ed.), *Fronts invisibles*, 371–9.

309. Venn, *Oil Diplomacy*, 35.

310. S. Fay, *The War Office at War* (London, 1937), 180; W. G. Jensen, 'The Importance of Energy in the First and Second World Wars', *Historical Journal* (1968), 543.

311. Friedensburg, *Erdöl*, 107, 6.

312. See Chapter 5.

313. R. Nayberg, 'Qu'est-ce qu'un produit stratégique? L'exemple du pétrole en France 1914–1918', in C. Carlier and G. Pedroncini (eds.), *Les Etats-Unis dans la Première Guerre mondiale, 1917–1918* (Paris, 1992), 100–109; text in Bérenger report, 11 Jan. 1918, F¹²7715, AN.

314. Text in Bérenger report, 11 Jan. 1918, F¹²7715, AN; also Bérenger report, 11 Dec. 1917, F¹²7715, AN; Comité générale du pétrole, 30 Apr. 1918, F¹²7715, AN.

315. Tardieu–de Billy, 3 June 1918, F¹²7715, AN.

316. Friedensburg, *Erdöl*, 117.

317. Comité de guerre, 16 Feb. 1918, 3N2, SHA.

318. *AFGG*, XI, 622–4.

319. Ibid., 763–4, 769.

320. Yergin, *The Prize*, 171.

321. O. Bovio, 'Le ferrovie italiane nella prima guerra mondiale', in Canini (ed.), *Fronts invisibles*, 156–8.

322. H. Loewenfeld-Russ, *Die Regelung der Volks-Ernährung im Kriege* (Vienna/New Haven, Conn., 1926), 67; G. Gratz and R. Schüller, *Der wirtschaftliche Zusammenbruch Österreich-Ungarns: die Tragödie der Erschöpfung* (Vienna/New Haven, Conn., 1930), 48.

323. R. G. Plaschke, H. Haselsteiner, and A. Suppan, *Innere Front: Militärassistenz, Widerstand und Umsturz in der Donaumarchie 1918*, I (2 vols., Vienna, 1974), 52; CGS report on the army's material situation, 18 Aug. 1918, app. 10, KMPräs 1918 25–1/9, 1918, KAW.

324. CGS report on the army's material situation, 18 Aug. 1918, app. 9, 15, KMPräs 1918 25–1/9, 1918, KAW.

325. V. Gallinari, 'La produzione dei materiali militari in Italia durante la guerra', in Canini (ed.), *Fronts invisibles*, 200; Friedensburg, *Erdöl*, 100–101.

326. R. Cruccu, 'L'organizzazione generale dei servizi logistici nell'esercito italiano durante la prima guerra mondiale', in Canini (ed.), *Fronts invisibles*, 87; Henniker, *Transportation*, 297–302.

327. Director of Transport–Diaz, 4 Apr. 1918, 57 1531, Orlando MSS, ACS.

328. Cruccu, 'L'organizzazione', 88; Bovio, 'Le ferrovie italiane', 163; R. Wegs, 'Transportation: the Achilles Heel of the Habsburg War Effort', in R. A. Kann et al. (eds.),

The Habsburg Empire in World War I: Essays on the Intellectual, Military, Political, and Economic Aspects of the Habsburg War Effort (New York, 1977), 130.

329. G. Hodges, *Kariakor: the Carrier Corps. The Story of the Military Labour Forces in the Conquest of German East Africa, 1914 to 1918* (Nairobi, 1999), 5, 15-19.

330. K. Roy, 'The Army in India in Mesopotamia from 1916 to 1918: Tactics, Technology, and Logistics Reconsidered', in I. F. W. Beckett (ed.), *1917: Beyond the Western Front* (Leiden/Boston, Mass., 2009), 134, 156.

331. P. M. Kennedy, 'Britain', in A. R. Millett and W. Murray (eds.), *Military Effectiveness*, I (3 vols., Winchester, Mass., 1988), 71.

332. J. F. Moberly, *History of the Great War Based on Official Documents. The Campaign in Mesopotamia, 1914-1918*, IV (London, 1927), 259-60, 266; A. J. Barker, *The Neglected War: Mesopotamia, 1914-1918* (London, 1967), 454.

333. C. Falls, *History of the Great War Based on Official Documents. Egypt and Palestine*, II (London, 1930), 599-600.

334. G. E. Badcock, *A History of the Transport Services of the Egyptian Expeditionary Force 1916-1917-1918* (London, 2005), 25, 95, 198, 244, 248.

335. U. Trumpener, *Germany and the Ottoman Empire 1914-1918* (Princeton, NJ, 1968), 287; M. Hughes, *Allenby and British Strategy in the Middle East, 1917-1919* (London/Portland, Ore., 1999), 34.

336. E. Zürcher, 'Little Mehmet in the Desert: the Ottoman Soldier's Experience', in H. Cecil and P. H. Liddle (eds.), *Facing Armageddon: the First World War Experienced* (London, 1996), 235; Falls, *Egypt and Palestine*, II, 445.

337. Falls, *Egypt and Palestine*, II, 445; Badcock, *Transport Services*, 56.

338. See Chapter 5.

339. Fay, *War Office*, 71.

340. G. Fassy, *Le Commandement français en orient (octobre 1915-novembre 1918)* (Paris, 2003), 227, 229-39.

341. C. Falls, *History of the Great War Based on Official Documents. Macedonia,* II (London, 1935), 116, 140; Fassy, *Commandement français*, 375.

342. Fassy, *Commandement français*, 370-71, 420-21; Falls, *Macedonia*, II, 221-2, 246.

343. Bovio, 'Le ferrovie italiane', 163; J. E. Edmonds, *Military Operations: Italy 1915-1919* (London, 1949), 265.

344. Brown, 'Feeding Victory', 142-3.

345. F. Foch, *Mémoires pour servir à l'histoire de la guerre de 1914-1918*, II (2 vols., Paris, 1931), 164-6.

346. Général Laure, *Le Commandement en chef des armées françaises du 15 mai 1917 à l'armistice* (Paris, 1937), 113.

347. Général Debeney, *La Guerre et les hommes: réflexions d'après-guerre* (Paris, 1937), 37-8.

348. *AFGG*, XI, 763-4, 769, 777, 788.

349. Brown, *British Logistics*, 197.

350. Henniker, *Transportation*, 305-13, 425.

351. Quartermaster-General's Branch, 'Explanatory Review' and 'Diary', Aug. 1918, WO/95/39; 'Explanatory Review', Sept. 1918, WO/95/40.

352. Henniker, *Transportation*, 433-7; *AFGG*, XI, 729.

353. *AFGG*, XI, 617; Sarter, *Die deutschen Eisenbahnen*, 121; 'Deutsche Rüstung 1918', 70, W-10/50421, BA-MA.

354. *WK*, XIV, 606, 617.
355. Ibid., 619.
356. Henniker, *Transportation*, 438.
357. *AFGG*, XI, 834–40; *WK*, XIV, 699; Schwarte (ed.), *Weltkampf*, VII, 30–31.
358. Henniker, *Transportation*, 456, 492, 506; Quartermaster-General's Branch, 'Explanatory Review', Nov. 1918, WO/95/40.
359. Currie diary, 20 Oct. 1918, Box E100, MG30, Vol. 43, Currie MSS, NAC.
360. *AFGG*, XI, 754; Henniker, *Transportation*, 439–40, 448, 451–5, 461.
361. Quartermaster-General's Branch, 'Explanatory Review', Oct., Nov. 1918, WO/95/40.
362. Henniker, *Transportation*, 461, 487; Brown, *British Logistics*, 237; J. P. Harris and N. Barr, *Amiens to the Armistice: the BEF in the Hundred Days' Campaign, 8 August–11 November 1918* (London/Washington DC, 1998), 290–91.
363. *AFGG*, XI, 737, 742–9.
364. Fay, *War Office*, 217, 249.
365. Henniker, *Transportation*, 433, 424; *AFGG*, XI, 757–8.
366. Claveille hearing, 16 Oct. 1918, F^{12}C7501; Leboucq report, 22 Oct. 1918, F^{12}7641, AN.
367. J. G. Harbord, *The American Army in France, 1917–1919* (Boston, Mass., 1936), 473, 478; *AFGG*, XI, 812–16; cf. C. Wolmar, *Engines of War: How Wars were Won and Lost on the Railways* (London, 2010), 187.
368. *AFGG*, XI, 56–7; ibid., 816–18.
369. W. J. Wilgus, *Transporting the AEF in Western Europe 1917–1919* (New York, 1931), 72–4, 307, 311, 506, 522–7, 555; Harbord, *American Army*, 347.
370. Harbord, *American Army*, 500, 624.
371. Pershing, *My Experiences*, 501; McCoy, 'Grinding Gears', 198–9.
372. *USAWW*, XII, 56; Pershing, *My Experiences*, 667, 685.
373. Pershing, *My Experiences*, 683–4.
374. Report on work of Quartermaster-General's Branch (n.d.), WO/107/69.
375. McCoy, 'Grinding Gears', 199–204.
376. Pershing, *My Experiences*, 498, 582.
377. Pogue, *George C. Marshall*, 175–9.
378. Harbord, *American Army*, 472.

4. THE HUMAN FACTOR: MANPOWER AND MORALE

1. 92/36/1, Dixon MSS, IWM.
2. A. Watson, *Enduring the Great War: Combat, Morale, and Collapse in the German and British Armies, 1914–1918* (Cambridge, 2008), 188–9.
3. Chamber Army Commission, 12 Dec. 1917, C7499, AN.
4. L. P. Ayres, *The War with Germany: a Statistical Summary* (Washington DC, 1919), 13; J. W. Chambers, *To Raise an Army: the Draft Comes to Modern America* (New York/London, 1987), 200.
5. Chambers, *To Raise an Army*, 42, 73.
6. *PWW*, XLII, 214, 325.
7. Chambers, *To Raise an Army*, 170, 166–7.
8. Ibid., 181.
9. Ibid., 211–13.

10. A. Kaspi, *Le Temps des Américains: le concours américain à la France en 1917–1918* (Paris, 1976), 16–24, 37–45; Chambers, *To Raise an Army*, 144.

11. Imperial War Cabinet, 11 June 1918, CAB/23/43.

12. Wilson–Derby, 23 Apr. 1918, 2/3A/14, Wilson MSS, IWM.

13. E. M. Coffman, 'Militärische Operationen der US-Armee an der Westfront 1918', in J. Duppler and G. P. Groß (eds.), *Kriegsende 1918: Ereignis, Wirkung, Nachwirkung* (Munich, 1994), 146.

14. Comité de guerre, 26 Dec. 1917, 3N2, SHA; R. B. Bruce, *A Fraternity of Arms: America and France in the Great War* (Lawrence, Kan., 2003), 148–54.

15. D. Lloyd George, *War Memoirs*, II (2 vols., London, 1938), 1806.

16. Ibid., 1793.

17. P. C. March, *The Nation at War* (Garden City, NY, 1932), 79–80.

18. Generally: Lloyd George, *War Memoirs*, II, ch. 81; D. Trask, *The AEF and Coalition Warmaking, 1917–1918* (Lawrence, Kan., 1993), 37ff., 53ff., 61ff., 74ff.; D. Smythe, *Pershing: General of the Armies* (Bloomington, Ind./Indianapolis, Ind., 2007), 100–104.

19. Wilson diary, 24 Apr. 1918, Wilson MSS, IWM; Chamber Army Commission, 3 June 1918, C7500, AN.

20. March, *Nation at War*, 3–4; E. M. Coffman, *The Hilt of the Sword: the Career of Peyton C. March* (Madison, Wis./Milwaukee, Wis./London, 1966), 54.

21. March, *Nation at War*, 70–76; Ayres, *War with Germany*, 44.

22. War Cabinet, 5 June 1918, CAB/23/6; Smythe, *Pershing*, 146–8; Pershing–March, 25 June 1918, 22/2, Pershing MSS, LOC; March–Bliss, 26 Sept. 1918, 22/1, Pershing MSS, LOC.

23. March–Pershing, 5 July 1918, 22/2, Pershing MSS, LOC.

24. Chambers, *To Raise an Army*, 196–9.

25. *USAWW*, XII, 55.

26. March–Pershing, 2 Oct. 1918, RG120/100, NARA.

27. Trask, *AEF*, 142.

28. Coffman, 'Militärische Operationen', 155; G. Mead, *Doughboys: America and the First World War* (London, 2000), 347–52.

29. J. D. Keene, *Doughboys, the Great War, and the Remaking of America* (Baltimore, Md/London, 2001), 5, 39.

30. J. J. Pershing, *My Experiences in the World War* (London, 1931), 578.

31. A. Barbeau and H. Florette, *The Unknown Soldiers: Black American Troops in World War I* (Philadelphia, Pa, 1974), 70, 83, 111.

32. Ibid., 114–15; 'Au sujet des troupes noires américaines', 7 Aug. 1918, 16N1698, SHA.

33. Barbeau and Florette, *The Unknown Soldiers*, 150ff.

34. Pershing–Baker, 1 Sept. 1919, *USAWW*, XII, 62.

35. M. Meigs, *Optimism at Armageddon: Voices of American Participants in the First World War* (Basingstoke, 1997), 61; Keene, *Doughboys*, 66.

36. Mead, *Doughboys*, 207, 349.

37. Keene, *Doughboys*, 65; Meigs, *Optimism at Armageddon*, 60.

38. Mead, *Doughboys*, 196–201.

39. Meigs, *Optimism at Armageddon*, 32.

40. Keene, *Doughboys*, 72, 77; German General Staff report on American troops, 2 July 1918, MKr/1775, KAM.

41. Mead, *Doughboys*, 79, 81; Meigs, *Optimism at Armageddon*, 27; Garretson letter, 29 May 1918, 95/6/1, Garretson MSS, IWM.

42. D. M. Kennedy, *Over Here: the First World War and American Society* (New York/Oxford, 1980), 178–82.

43. T. Skeghill (ed.), *Sergeant York: His Own Life Story and War Diary* (Garden City, NY, 1928), 152, 155, 169, 202; H. L. Baker, *Argonne Days in World War I* (Columbia, Mo./London, 2007), 13, 34.

44. Classification camp reports, 6 Aug., 8, 15 Oct. 1918, RG/120/195/1, NARA.

45. Keene, *Doughboys*, 108.

46. G. Martin, 'German Strategy and Military Assessments of the American Expeditionary Force (AEF), 1917–18', *War in History* (1994), 181–90; German General Staff report on American troops, 2 July 1918, MKr/1775, KAM.

47. Baker, *Argonne Days*, 49, 80.

48. Classification camp report, 3 Nov. 1918, RG/120/195/1, NARA.

49. Keene, *Doughboys*, 66–7; H. S. Liggett, *A.E.F.: Ten Years Ago in France* (New York, 1928), 207–10.

50. Reports on 26th and 77th divisions, RG/120/590/1–2, NARA.

51. M. E. Grotelueschen, *The AEF Way of War: the American Army and Combat in World War I* (Cambridge, 2007), 346, 358.

52. Classification camp reports, 30 Oct., 1 Nov. 1918, RG/120/195/1, NARA.

53. Meigs, *Optimism at Armageddon*, 51; Baker, *Argonne Days*, 140; Skeghill (ed.), *Sergeant York*, 284.

54. J. E. Edmonds, *Military Operations: France and Belgium. 1914–(1918)*, V (London, 1933–48), 589–90.

55. Army Council memorandum, 24 Oct. 1918, WO/106/315, TNA.

56. Lloyd George, *War Memoirs*, II, 1591–2; I. F. W. Beckett, 'The Real Unknown Army: British Conscripts, 1916–1919', in J.-J. Becker and S. Audoin-Rouzeau (eds.), *Les Sociétés européennes et la guerre de 1914–1918* (Paris, 1990), 339.

57. Beckett, 'The Real Unknown Army', 339.

58. G. D. Sheffield, 'The Indispensable Factor: the Performance of British Troops in 1918', in P. Dennis and J. Grey (eds.), *1918: Defining Victory* (Canberra, 1999), 72ff.; I. R. Bet-el, *Conscripts: Forgotten Men of the Great War* (Stroud, 2003), xiv; C. Messenger, *Call to Arms: the British Army 1914–1918* (London, 2005), 10, 287, 497.

59. B. Bushaway, 'Name Upon Name: the Great War and Remembrance', in R. Porter (ed.), *Myths of the English* (Cambridge, 1992), 137.

60. Bet-el, *Conscripts*, 33–4, 59.

61. Watson, *Enduring the Great War*, 156; D. Fitzpatrick, 'The Logic of Collective Sacrifice: Ireland and the British Army, 1914–1918', *Historical Journal* (1995).

62. P. E. Dewey, 'Military Recruiting and the British Labour Force during the First World War', *Historical Journal* (1984), 205, 213ff.; on the conscription system, A. Gregory, *The Last Great War: British Society and the First World War* (Cambridge, 2008), ch. 3.

63. H. F. A. Strachan, *The First World War. Vol. I: To Arms* (Oxford, 2001), 499.

64. F. W. Perry, *The Commonwealth Armies: Manpower and Organization in Two World Wars* (Manchester, 1988), 176.

65. Ibid., ch. 5; L. L. Robson, *The First AIF: a Study of Its Recruitment, 1914–1918* (Melbourne, 1970).

66. Currie–Creelman, 30 Nov. 1917, Box E100, MG30, Vol. I, Currie MSS, NAC.

67. Report on Quebec situation, 2 Apr. 1918, Vol. 104, Borden MSS, NAC; Burrell–Béland, 13 Aug. 1918, Vol. 100, Borden MSS, NAC.

68. Perry, *Commonwealth Armies*, 158; J. Granatstein, *Canada's Army: Waging War and Keeping the Peace* (Toronto/Buffalo, NY/London, 2002), 129.

69. Perry, *Commonwealth Armies*, ch. 3; K. Roy, 'The Army in India in Mesopotamia from 1916 to 1918: Tactics, Technology, and Logistics Reconsidered', in I. F. W. Beckett (ed.), *1917: Beyond the Western Front* (Leiden/Boston, Mass., 2009), 158, for slightly different figures.

70. D. Omissi, *The Sepoy and the Raj: the Indian Army, 1860–1940* (Basingstoke/London, 1994), 124–5.

71. War Cabinet, 12 June 1918, CAB/23/6.

72. Perry, *Commonwealth Armies*, 96.

73. Report on BEF labour, 14 Nov. 1919, WO/107/37.

74. C. Barnett, *The Swordbearers: Supreme Command in the First World War* (London, 2000), 312.

75. Report on BEF labour, 14 Nov. 1919, WO/107/37; M. Summerskill, *China on the Western Front: Britain's Chinese Workforce in the First World War* (London, 1982).

76. R. Pullen (ed.), *Beyond the Green Fields: the Final Memories of Some of the First Men of the Tank Corps* (Lincoln, 2008), 60; J. S. Bramley diary, 14 Feb. 1918, 81/14/1, IWM.

77. War Cabinet, 3, 6 Dec. 1917, CAB/23/4; Hankey memorandum, 8 Dec. 1917, CAB/27/14.

78. Lloyd George, *War Memoirs*, II, 1562.

79. Draft report, 1 Mar. 1918, CAB/27/14.

80. Lloyd George, *War Memoirs*, II, 1588.

81. War Cabinet, 6 Apr. 1918, CAB/23/6.

82. P. Simkins, *Kitchener's Army: the Raising of the New Armies, 1914–16* (Manchester, 1988), 217–18.

83. Messenger, *Call to Arms*, 272; Watson, *Enduring the Great War*, 181; S. L. Edwards diary, 27 Mar. 1918, 94/5/1, IWM.

84. B. Millman, *Managing Domestic Dissent in First World War Britain* (London/Portland, Ore., 2000), 272; War Cabinet, 21 Dec. 1917, CAB/23/4.

85. W. S. L. Churchill, *The World Crisis, Part 2: 1916–1918* (6 parts, London, 1923–31), 377–8.

86. J. Gooch, 'The Maurice Debate 1918', *Journal of Contemporary History* (1968); D. R. Woodward, 'Did Lloyd George Starve the British Army of Men prior to the German Offensive of 21 March 1918?', *Historical Journal* (1984).

87. J. G. Fuller, *Troop Morale and Popular Culture in the British and Dominion Armies, 1914–1918* (Oxford, 1990), 4.

88. War Cabinet, 6 Apr. 1918, CAB/23/6.

89. War Cabinet, 3 Apr. 1918, CAB/23/6.

90. A. J. Ward, 'Lloyd George and the 1918 Irish Conscription Crisis', *Historical Journal* (1974), 125–6; Wilson memorandum, 2 Oct. 1918, WO/106/315.

91. E. Greenhalgh, 'David Lloyd George, Georges Clemenceau, and the 1918 Manpower Crisis', *Historical Journal* (2007), passim.

92. Imperial War Cabinet, 11 June 1918, CAB/23/43.

93. Messenger, *Call to Arms*, 281-2; Wilson memorandum, 12 June 1918, 2/24A/24, Wilson MSS, IWM.

94. Foch-Wilson, 6 Apr. 1918, 1K/129/1, SHA; Foch-Wilson, 9 June 1918, 2/24A/24, Wilson MSS, IWM.

95. War Cabinet, 5 June 1918, CAB/23/6; Greenhalgh, '1918 Manpower Crisis', 407-10.

96. Foch-Wilson, 17 Aug. 1918, 2/24B/3, Wilson MSS, IWM.

97. Wilson-Du Cane, 1 Aug. 1918, 2/36/10, Wilson MSS, IWM.

98. Wilson-Haig, 1, 2 Sept. 1918, 2/7B/10-12, Wilson MSS, IWM.

99. Haig diary, 19 Mar. 1918, G. D. Sheffield and J. M. Bourne (eds.), *Douglas Haig: War Diaries and Letters, 1914-1918* (London, 2005), 388-9.

100. Classification camp reports, 18, 20 Oct. 1918, RG/120/195/1, NARA.

101. German General Staff report on BEF, 30 June 1918, MKr/1776, KAM; 6 Nov. 1918, Militärbevollmächtiger/128, KAM.

102. Watson, *Enduring the Great War*, 59.

103. C. Jahr, '"Bei einer geschlagenen Armee ist der Klügste, wer zuerst davonläuft": das Problem der Desertion im deutschen und britischen Heer 1918', in Duppler and Groß (eds.), *Kriegsende 1918*, 253, 265.

104. Messenger, *Call to Arms*, ch. 12.

105. D. Gill and G. Dallas, *The Unknown Army: Mutinies in the British Army in World War I* (London, 1985), ch. 6.

106. G. D. Sheffield, 'Officer-Man Relations, Discipline, and Morale in the British Army of the Great War', in H. Cecil and P. H. Liddle (eds.), *Facing Armageddon: the First World War Experienced* (London, 1996), 417.

107. R. G. Dixon, 'The Wheels of Darkness', p. 72, 92/36/1; H. F. Bowser memoir, p. 69, 88/56/1, IWM.

108. G. D. Sheffield, *Leadership in the Trenches: Officer-Man Relations, Morale, and Discipline in the British Army in the Era of the First World War* (Basingstoke, 2000); Watson, *Enduring the Great War*, ch. 4.

109. Memorandum on Canadian Corps, E100, MG30, Vol. 37, Folder 168, Currie MSS, NAC.

110. Watson, *Enduring the Great War*, ch. 3; M. Snape, *God and the British Soldier: Religion and the British Army in the First and Second World Wars* (Abingdon, 2005), 179.

111. R. G. Dixon memoir, p. 88, 92/36/1, IWM.

112. J. Lodge Patch memoir, p. 80, 66/304/1, IWM.

113. Reports on Third Army morale, 23 Nov. 1916 and (?) Jan. 1917, 84/46/1, Hardie MSS, IWM.

114. Ibid., 25 Aug. 1917, 84/46/1, Hardie MSS, IWM.

115. R. G. McKay diary, 2 Aug. 1917, Liddle Collection, Leeds University Library.

116. Draft report, 15 Aug. 1918, Vol. 122, Borden MSS, NAC.

117. Barnett, *Swordbearers*, 310.

118. Cabinet Committee on Man Power, 11 Dec.; Haig-Robertson, 15 Dec. 1917, CAB/27/14.

119. S. P. MacKenzie, 'Morale and the Cause: the Campaign to Change the Outlook of Soldiers in the British Expeditionary Force, 1914-1918', *Canadian Journal of History* (1990), 224-5.

120. Ibid., 229.

121. Robertson–Cabinet, 18 Dec. 1917, WO/106/401.
122. Report on BEF morale, 12 July 1918, p. 1, WO/256/33; Sheffield and Bourne (eds.), *Douglas Haig*, 390.
123. M. Middlebrook, *The Kaiser's Battle* (London, 2000), 332–8.
124. C. J. Lodge Patch memoir, p. 42, 66/304/1, IWM; L. MacDonald, *To the Last Man: Spring 1918* (London, 1999), 11.
125. C. H. Dudley-Ward memoir, V, 22 Mar. 1918, 94/30/1, IWM.
126. Report on BEF morale, 12 July 1918, p. 1, WO/256/33.
127. Fuller, *Troop Morale*, 58.
128. R. Cude memoir, II, p. 180, 22 Aug. 1918, PP.MCR/C48, IWM.
129. D. Englander, 'The French Soldier, 1914–1918', *French History* (1987), 67; M. Hanna, *Your Death Would be Mine: Paul and Marie Pireaud in the Great War* (Cambridge, Mass./London, 2006), 10.
130. J. Norton Cru, *Du témoignage* (Paris, 1997), 24; Hanna, *Your Death Would be Mine*, 9.
131. P. Guinard, J.-C. Devos, and J. Nicot, *Inventaire sommaire des Archives de la Guerre, Série N: 1872–1919*, Vol. I (Troyes, 1975), 204.
132. Ibid., 208–9, 213.
133. Hearing of M. Mourier, 16 Oct. 1918, Chamber Army Commission, C7501, AN.
134. Guinard et al., *Inventaire*, 206.
135. 'Mouvement de la main d'oeuvre étrangère et coloniale', April 1918, F^{14}1332, AN.
136. M. Michel, 'Mythes et réalités du concours colonial: soldats et travailleurs d'outremer dans la guerre française', in Becker and Audoin-Rouzeau (eds.), *Les Sociétés européennes*, 394; T. Stovall, 'The Color behind the Lines: Racial Violence in France during the Great War', *American Historical Review* (1998).
137. R. S. Fogarty, *Race and War in France: Colonial Subjects in the French Army, 1914–1918* (Baltimore, Md, 2008), 27.
138. M. Michel, *Les Africains et la Grande guerre. L'appel à l'Afrique (1914–1918)* (Paris, 2003), 250, 95.
139. Chamber Army Commission, 25 Sept. 1918, C7501, AN.
140. Fogarty, *Race and War*, 47, 49; J. J. M. Mordacq, *Le Ministère Clemenceau: journal d'un témoin*, II (4 vols., Paris, 1930), 178.
141. C. J. Balesi, 'From Adversary to Comrade-in-Arms: West Africans and the French Military, 1885–1919', Ph.D. dissertation, University of Illinois at Chicago, 1976, 296.
142. Michel, *Les Africains*, 105.
143. Michel, 'Mythes et réalités', 394.
144. Fogarty, *Race and War*, 65.
145. Englander, 'French Soldier', 57.
146. Guinard et al., *Inventaire*, 206; G. Hardach, 'Industrial Mobilization in 1914–1918: Production, Planning, and Ideology', in P. Fridenson (ed.), *The French Home Front, 1914–1918* (Providence, RI/Oxford, 1992), 62.
147. S. Audoin-Rouzeau, 'The French Soldier in the Trenches', in Cecil and Liddle (eds.), *Facing Armageddon*, 222.
148. *AFGG*, VI, ii, 46.
149. Mordacq, *Ministère Clemenceau*, I, 318; G. Clemenceau, *Grandeur and Misery of Victory* (transl., London, 1930), 58.
150. R. A. Doughty, *Pyrrhic Victory: French Strategy and Operations in the Great War* (Cambridge, Mass./London, 2005), 416.

151. Wilson–Haig, 18 Dec. 1917, 2/7A/1, Wilson MSS, IWM.

152. J. Horne, 'L'Impôt du sang: Republican Rhetoric and Industrial Warfare in France, 1914–18', *Social History* (1989), 214; G. Pedroncini, *Pétain: Général en chef, 1917–1918* (Paris, 1974), 268–70, 275.

153. F. Foch, *Mémoires pour servir à l'histoire de la guerre de 1914–1918*, II (2 vols., Paris, 1931), 168; Clemenceau in Chamber Army Commission, 26 July 1918, C7500, AN.

154. Guinard et al., *Inventaire*, 203.

155. M. Weygand, *Mémoires: idéal vécu*, I (2 vols., Paris, 1953), 454; *AFGG*, VII, i, 20.

156. Weygand, *Mémoires*, I, 544; Foch, *Mémoires*, II, 230.

157. Pétain–Foch, 31 July 1918, 16N1698, SHA.

158. Foch, *Mémoires*, II, 79; Edmonds, *MOFB, 1918*, V, 584.

159. G. Pedroncini (ed.), *1917: les mutineries de l'armée française* (Paris, 1968), 8.

160. G. Pedroncini, *Les Mutineries de 1917* (Paris, 1967), 98, 62, 308; A. Loez and N. Mariot (eds.), *Obéir/désobéir: les mutineries de 1917 en perspective* (Paris, 2008), ch. 20.

161. L. V. Smith, *Between Mutiny and Obedience: the Case of the Fifth French Infantry Division during World War I* (Princeton, NJ, 1994), 201–5.

162. Pedroncini, *Mutineries*, 234–40; P. Pétain, *Une crise morale de la nation française en guerre 16 avril–23 octobre 1917* (Paris, 1966), 110–30.

163. Pedroncini, *Pétain: Général*, 88–108.

164. Ibid., 167–8.

165. German General Staff reports on French army, 13 July, 7 Nov. 1918, MKr/1777, KAM.

166. Classification camp report, 15 Oct. 1918, RG/120/195/1, NARA; Pershing–March, 19 June 1918, 22/2, March MSS, LOC.

167. Edmonds, *MOFB, 1918*, IV, 114–15; ibid., V, 281, 584.

168. 'A' Branch daily intelligence summary, 8/9 Oct. 1918, WO/157/36; Haig diary, 10 Oct. 1918, Sheffield and Bourne (eds.), *Douglas Haig*, 472.

169. Haig–Wilson, 4 Nov. 1918, 2/7B/21, Wilson MSS, IWM; 'A' Branch daily summary, 21–22 Oct. 1918, WO/157/36; War Cabinet, 19 Oct. 1918, WO/158/25.

170. 'A' Branch daily summary, 8/9 Nov. 1918, WO/157/37.

171. R. Cazals, *Les Carnets de Louis Barthas, tonnelier 1914–1918* (Paris, 1997), 551.

172. Hanna, *Your Death Would be Mine*.

173. S. Audoin-Rouzeau, *Men at War, 1914–1918: National Sentiment and Trench Journalism in France during the First World War* (Providence, RI/Oxford, 1992), ch. 6; L. V. Smith, *The Embattled Self: French Soldiers' Testimony of the Great War* (Ithaca, NY/London, 2007), ch. 3.

174. J. Nicot, *Les Poilus ont la parole. Dans les tranchées: lettres du front 1917–1918* (Paris, 2003), 7–13.

175. P. Barral, 'L'Intendance', in G. Canini (ed.), *Les Fronts invisibles: nourrir – fournir – soigner* (Nancy, 1984), 75.

176. Nicot, *Poilus ont la parole*, 33ff., 61, 80–85.

177. GQG morale survey, 16 Dec. 1917, 16N1486, SHA; Nicot, *Poilus ont la parole*, 165–6.

178. GQG morale survey, 4 Jan. 1918, 16N1486, SHA.

179. Ibid.

180. Nicot, *Poilus ont la parole*, 296–313, 328–36, 344–7.

181. Chamber Army Committee, 27 Mar. 1918, C7500, AN.

182. GQG morale surveys, 15 Apr., 5 May 1918, 16N1486, SHA.

183. Nicot, *Poilus ont la parole*, 355–63, 391–404.

184. Ibid., 411–71.

185. Ibid., 428–31.

186. Ibid., 472–85; Smith, *Between Mutiny and Obedience*, 241.

187. A. Kramer, '*Wackes* at War: Alsace-Lorraine and the Failure of German National Mobilization, 1914–1918', in J. Horne (ed.), *State, Society, and Mobilization in Europe during the First World War* (Cambridge, 1997).

188. S. de Schaepdrijver, *La Belgique et la première guerre mondiale* (Brussels, 2004), 223–9.

189. H. S. Jones, *Violence against Prisoners of War: Britain, France, and Germany, 1914–1920* (Cambridge, 2011).

190. Reichswehrministerium, *Sanitätsbericht über das deutsche Heer (Deutsches Feld- und Besatzungsheer) im Weltkriege 1914/1918*, III (3 vols., Berlin 1934–8), 11–12.

191. Ibid., 65, 16.

192. *WK*, XIV, 29, 26.

193. Reichswehrministerium, *Sanitätsbericht*, III, 8.

194. 'Deutsche Rüstung 1918', 38, W-10/50421, BA-MA.

195. Kuhl diary, 14 Dec. 1917, W-10/50652, BA-MA.

196. 'Deutsche Rüstung 1918', 38, W-10/50421, BA-MA.

197. 'Die Ersatzlage im Jahre 1918', I, 3–4, W-10/51834, BA-MA.

198. *WK*, XIV, 37–8.

199. Ibid., 232–3.

200. Reichswehrministerium, *Sanitätsbericht*, II, 6.

201. 'Die Ersatzlage im Jahre 1918', I, 2, W-10/51834, BA-MA.

202. G. Fong, 'The Movement of German Divisions to the Western Front, Winter 1917–1918', *War in History* (2000), 232.

203. 'Die Ersatzlage im Jahre 1918', I, 3, 10, 14, W-10/51834, BA-MA.

204. Ibid., 9.

205. *WK*, XIV, 516ff.; 'Die Ersatzlage im Jahre 1918', 17–24, W-10/51384, BA-MA.

206. 'Die Ersatzlage im Jahre 1918', 30–33, W-10/51384, BA-MA; 'Deutsche Rüstung 1918', 60, W-10/50421, BA-MA.

207. 'Die Ersatzlage im Jahre 1918', 37, W-10/51384, BA-MA.

208. 'A' Branch daily summary, 22/23 Oct. 1918, WO/157/36.

209. W. Deist, 'The Military Collapse of the German Empire', *War in History* (1996), 203.

210. N. Ferguson, *The Pity of War* (London, 1998), 370.

211. A. Watson, '"For Kaiser and Reich": the Identity and Fate of the German Volunteers, 1914–1918', *War in History* (2005); E. J. Leed, 'Class and Disillusionment in World War I', *Journal of Modern History* (1978).

212. W. Kruse, 'Krieg und Klassenheer: zur Revolutionierung der deutschen Armee im Ersten Weltkrieg', *Geschichte und Gesellschaft* (1996), 536–9.

213. B. Ziemann, *War Experiences in Rural Germany 1914–1923* (transl., Oxford/New York, 2007), ch. 3.

214. R. L. Nelson, '"Ordinary Men" in the First World War? German Soldiers as Victims and Participants', *Journal of Contemporary History* (2004), 452; F. Altrichter,

Die seelischen Kräfte des deutschen Heeres in Frieden und im Weltkriege (Berlin, 1933), 87.

215. Ziemann, *War Experiences*, 93; G. Krumeich, 'Le Soldat allemand sur la Somme', in Becker and Audoin-Rouzeau (eds.), *Les Sociétés européennes*, 369.

216. H. H. Herwig, *The First World War: Germany and Austria-Hungary, 1914–1918* (London/New York, 1997), 246ff.; Altrichter, *Die seelischen Kräfte*, 92–4; Ziemann, *War Experiences*, 33–4.

217. B. Ullrich and B. Ziemann (eds.), *Frontalltag im Ersten Weltkrieg: Wahn und Wirklichkeit. Quellen und Dokumente* (Frankfurt, 1994), 192–4.

218. R. Asprey, *The German High Command at War: Hindenburg and Ludendorff and the First World War* (London, 1994), 340–41.

219. Ziemann, *War Experiences*, 68–71; D. A. Welch, *Germany, Propaganda, and Total War, 1914–1918* (London, 2000), 221.

220. B. Barth, *Dolchstoßlegenden und politische Desintegration: die Trauma der deutschen Niederlage im Ersten Weltkrieg 1914–1933* (Düsseldorf, 2003), 57; Altrichter, *Die seelischen Kräfte*, 98.

221. Barth, *Dolchstoßlegenden*, 69; Ziemann, *War Experiences*, 31, 38.

222. *UDZ*, XI, 136.

223. Hindenburg circular, 3 May 1917, PH3/40, BA-MA; Ziemann, *War Experiences*, 75.

224. Fifth Army censorship report, 12 July 1917, W-10/50794, BA-MA.

225. C. Jahr, *Gewöhnliche Soldaten: Desertion und Deserteure im deutschen und britischen Heer 1914–1918* (Göttingen, 1998), 157.

226. Fifth Army censorship reports, 10 Jan., 24 Feb. 1918, W-10/50794, BA-MA.

227. Ullrich and Ziemann (eds.), *Frontalltag*, 197–8.

228. Dechend diary, 15 Feb. 1918, PP/MCR/43, IWM.

229. A. von Thaer, *Generalstabsdienst an der Front und in der OHL* (Göttingen, 1958), 182.

230. W. Deist, 'Verdeckter Militärstreik im Kriegsjahr 1918?', in W. Wette (ed.), *Der Krieg des kleinen Mannes. Eine Militärgeschichte von unten* (Munich/Zurich, 1995), 153.

231. H. Sulzbach, *With the German Guns: Four Years on the Western Front* (Barnsley, 2003), 151, 178.

232. Jahr, *Gewöhnliche Soldaten*, 18.

233. Ludendorff order, 10 June 1918, S.S.729, IWM.

234. G. G. Bruntz, *Allied Propaganda and the Collapse of the German Empire in 1918* (Stanford, Calif., 1938), 206.

235. 6 June 1918 Order, S.S.735, IWM.

236. B. Ziemann, 'Fahnenflucht im Deutschen Heer 1914–1918', *Militärgeschichtliche Mitteilungen* (1996), 129.

237. Barth, *Dolchstoßlegenden*, 65.

238. Ziemann, 'Fahnenflucht', 117.

239. Kramer, '*Wackes* at War', 118–19; H. Hirschfelder, 'Unlust am Krieg: "Grössere Soldatenausschreitungen mit Zivilbeteiligung". Die Erlanger Unruhen im Mai 1918 und ihre Fortsetzung während eines Transportes zu Front' (Erlangen, 2004); Ziemann, *War Experiences*, 106.

240. Deist, 'Verdeckte Militärstreik', 152–3; Altrichter, *Die seelischen Kräfte*, 134–6.

241. Altrichter, *Die seelischen Kräfte*, 155.

242. P. von Hindenburg, *Aus meinem Leben* (Leipzig, 1933), 263.

243. 'A' Branch survey of German morale, 28/29 Sept. 1918, WO/157/35.
244. Watson, *Enduring the Great War*, 195; 'A' Branch daily summary, 29/30 Sept. 1918, WO/157/35.
245. 'A' Branch daily summary, 6/7 Nov. 1918, WO/157/37.
246. Altrichter, *Die seelischen Kräfte*, 151.
247. 'A' Branch daily summaries, 3/4 Aug. 1918, WO/157/34; ibid., 6/7, 9/10, 26/27, 29/30 Sept. 1918, WO/157/35.
248. Canadian Corps Battle Reports, 8 Aug.–11 Nov. 1918, E100, MG30, Vol. 38, Currie MSS, NAC.
249. Nicot, *Poilus ont la parole*, 295, 400.
250. P. M. Taylor, *Munitions of the Mind: War Propaganda from the Ancient World to the Nuclear Age* (Wellingborough, 1990), 173.
251. H. D. Lasswell, *Propaganda Technique in the World War* (London/New York, 1927), 184; Bruntz, *Allied Propaganda*, 39.
252. Altrichter, *Die seelischen Kräfte*, 149.
253. Bruntz, *Allied Propaganda*, 21.
254. Taylor, *Munitions of the Mind*, 175.
255. Dechend diary, 6 Sept. 1918, PP/MCR/43, IWM.
256. Ferguson, *Pity of War*, 212–13.
257. Hutier diary, 9, 22 July 1918, W-10/50640, BA-MA.
258. Ludendorff, 20 Aug. 1918, *UDZ*, XI, 397.
259. Dechend diary, 11, 16, 22 July, 11 Aug. 1918, PP/MCR/43, IWM.
260. Deist, 'Verdeckte Militärstreik', 155.
261. Alpine Corps Commander, 15 Sept. 1918, *UDZ*, XI, 404.
262. Kruse, 'Krieg und Klassenheer', 557; *UDZ*, XI, 320.
263. Fifth Army censorship report, 31 Aug. 1918, W-10/50794, BA-MA.
264. Dechend diary, 6 Sept. 1918, PP/MCR/43, IWM; Fifth Army censorship report, 28 Sept. 1918, 31 Aug. 1918, W-10/50794, BA-MA.
265. Fifth Army censorship report, 28 Sept. 1918, 17 Oct. 1918, W-10/50794, BA-MA.
266. Watson, *Enduring the Great War*, 207.
267. Ludendorff circular, 25 July 1917, PH/3/60; 3 Sept. 1917, W-10/51833, BA-MA; Watson, *Enduring the Great War*, 203.
268. Ziemann, *War Experiences*, 144.
269. D. Rossini, *Il mito americano nell'Italia della Grande Guerra* (Rome, 2000), 110–13.
270. Wilson–Cavan, 8 July, WO/106/1385; Delmé–Radcliffe–Wilson, 28 Sept. 1918, WO/106/1385.
271. Hanna, *Your Death Would be Mine*, 251–3; censorship reports, Oct. 1917–Feb. 1918, Feb.–July 1918, 84/46/1, Hardie MSS, IWM.
272. G. Procacci, *Soldati e prigionieri italiani nella Grande Guerra* (Turin, 2000), 155; Delmé–Radcliffe report on Italian morale, 11 Apr. 1918, WO/106/814.
273. Procacci, *Soldati e prigionieri*, 155; M. Isenghi and G. Rochat, *La Grande Guerra 1914–1918* (Milan, 2004), 229.
274. P. Melograni, *Storia politica della Grande Guerra, 1915–1918* (Bari, 1969), 92.
275. Isenghi and Rochat, *Grande guerra*, 230.
276. Comando supremo report on Vittorio Veneto, WO/106/837; Isenghi and Rochat, *Grande Guerra*, 228–32.

277. Isenghi and Rochat, *Grande Guerra*, 387.
278. Melograni, *Storia politica*, 13, 79.
279. M. Thompson, *The White War: Life and Death on the Italian Front, 1915–1919* (London, 2008), 282.
280. Riparto disciplina report, 25 Oct. 1917, 17/35/1, Nitti MSS, ACS; Procacci, *Soldati e prigionieri*, 85–7.
281. Procacci, *Soldati e prigionieri*, 167ff.; Frascara–Orlando, 13 Feb. 1918, 19/47, Nitti MSS, ACS.
282. Cadorna–Orlando, 6 June, 67 1560, Orlando MSS, ACS; Orlando–Boselli, 18 June 1917, 67 1560, Orlando MSS, ACS.
283. E. Forcella and A. Monticone, *Plotone di esecuzione: i processi della Prima guerra mondiale* (Rome, 1998), lxxvii–lxxxvii.
284. Procacci, *Soldati e prigionieri*, 108.
285. Ibid., 79.
286. J. Gooch, 'Morale and Discipline in the Italian Army, 1915–1918', in Cecil and Liddle (eds.), *Facing Armageddon*, 437.
287. Cadorna–Orlando, 3 Nov. 1917, 67 1560, Orlando MSS, ACS.
288. V. Wilcox, 'Generalship and Mass Surrender during the Italian Defeat at Caporetto', in I. F. W. Beckett (ed.), *1917: Beyond the Western Front* (Leiden/Boston, Mass., 2009), 35–43.
289. Thompson, *White War*, 388.
290. Ibid., 332.
291. Forcella and Monticone, *Plotone di esecuzione*, xcv–xcix.
292. G. Rochat, 'Il Comando supremo di Diaz', in G. Berti and P. del Negra (eds.), *Al di qua e al di là del Piave: l'Ultimo Anno della Grande Guerra* (Milan, 2001), 266.
293. Thompson, *White War*, 331.
294. Rochat, 'Comando supremo', 266–7.
295. G. Rochat, *Gli arditi della Grande Guerra: Origini, battaglie, e miti* (Gorizia, 1990).
296. Delmé–Radcliffe report on Italian morale, 11 Apr. 1918, WO/106/814.
297. Procacci, *Soldati e prigionieri*, 159.
298. Delmé–Radcliffe report on Italian morale, 11 Apr. 1918, WO/106/814; M. Cornwall, *The Undermining of Austria-Hungary: the Battle for Hearts and Minds* (Basingstoke, 2000), ch. 4.
299. Melograni, *Storia politica*, 549.
300. Herwig, *First World War*, 146, 210.
301. *ÖULK*, VII, 41–5.
302. R. G. Plaschke, 'The Army and Internal Conflict in the Austro-Hungarian Empire, 1918', in B. K. Király and N. F. Dreisziger (eds.), *East Central European Society in World War I* (New York, 1985), 344.
303. *ÖULK*, VII, 43–9; H. Kerchnawe, *Der Zusammenbruch der öster.-ungr. Wehrmacht im Herbst 1918* (Munich, 1921), 9, 27, 32, 65.
304. *ÖULK*, VII, 41.
305. W. Etschmann, 'Österreich-Ungarn zwischen Engagement und Zurückhaltung. K.u.k. Truppen and der Westfront', in Duppler and Groß (eds.), *Kriegsende 1918*, 101.
306. G. Wawro, 'Morale in the Austro-Hungarian Army: the Evidence of Habsburg Army Campaign Reports and Allied Intelligence Officers', in Cecil and Liddle (eds.), *Facing Armageddon*, 406.

307. I. Deák, 'The Habsburg Army in the First and Last Days of World War I: a Comparative Analysis', in Király and Dreisziger (eds.), *East Central European Society*, 308.

308. Protocols of meetings, 7 Sept. 1918 (op nr. 147533); 11, 30 Sept. 1918, Chef des Ersatzwesens memorandum, 5 Sept. 1918, 5515ad, KMPräs 1918, KAW.

309. Cornwall, *Undermining of Austria-Hungary*, 278.

310. H. Haselsteiner, 'The Habsburg Empire in World War I: Mobilization of Food Supplies', in Király and Dreisziger (eds.), *East Central European Society*; CGS report on the army's material situation, 18 Aug. 1918, app. 1, KMPräs 1918, 25–1/9, KAW.

311. R. G. Plaschke, H. Haselsteiner, and A. Suppan, *Innere Front: Militärassistenz, Widerstand und Umsturz in der Donaumarchie 1918*, I (2 vols., Vienna, 1974), 48.

312. Cornwall, *Undermining of Austria-Hungary*, 407–8; CGS report on the army's material situation, 18 Aug. 1918, app. 3, KMPräs 1918, 25–1/9, KAW.

313. Plaschke et al., *Innere Front*, II, 54.

314. Thompson, *White War*, 344.

315. L. Rendulić, *Soldat in stürzenden Reichen* (Munich, 1965), 103–8.

316. R. B. Spence, 'The Yugoslav Role in the Austro-Hungarian Army, 1914–18', in Király and Dreisziger (eds.), *East Central European Society*, 362.

317. Cornwall, *Undermining of Austria-Hungary*, 35.

318. Ibid., 33–4.

319. Plaschke et al., *Innere Front*, I, 401–7.

320. Cornwall, *Undermining of Austria-Hungary*, 280–98.

321. Ibid., 209.

322. Ibid., 410; Comando supremo study of Austro-Hungarian army, WO/106/846.

323. Cornwall, *Undermining of Austria-Hungary*, 64.

324. Plaschke et al., *Innere Front*, II, 101, 62.

325. Kerchnawe, *Zusammenbruch*, 9–15.

326. A. Mitrović, *Serbia's Great War, 1914–1918* (transl., London, 2007), 313.

327. M. Hughes, *Allenby and British Strategy in the Middle East, 1917–1919* (London/Portland, Ore., 1999), 69.

328. C. Falls, *History of the Great War Based on Official Documents. Egypt and Palestine*, II (London, 1930), 440–41; J. F. Moberly, *History of the Great War Based on Official Documents. The Campaign in Mesopotamia, 1914–1918*, IV (London, 1927), 255; M. Harrison, 'The Fight against Disease in the Mesopotamian Campaign', in Cecil and Liddle (eds.), *Facing Armageddon*, 482–3.

329. D. R. Woodward, *Forgotten Soldiers of the First World War* (Stroud, 2007), 277–8.

330. C. Falls, *History of the Great War Based on Official Documents. Macedonia*, II (London, 1935), 146.

331. R. J. Crampton, *Bulgaria, 1878–1918: a History* (New York, 1983), 458.

332. Falls, *Macedonia*, II, 133.

333. R. C. Hall, '"The Enemy is behind Us": the Morale Crisis in the Bulgarian Army during the Summer of 1918', *War in History* (2004), 209–17.

334. E. and I. Karsh, 'Myth in the Desert, or Not the Great Arab Revolt', *Middle Eastern Studies* (1997), 290.

335. E. J. Erickson, *Ordered to Die: a History of the Ottoman Army in the First World War* (Westport, Conn./London, 2001), 211–12; A. E. Yalman, *Turkey in the World War* (New Haven, Conn./London, 1930), 253.

336. A. Kirkbride, *An Awakening: the Arab Campaign, 1917–18* (Tavistock, 1971), 4; Hughes, *Allenby*, 77.

337. Allenby–Wilson, 12 Aug. 1918, 2/33A/17, Wilson MSS, IWM.

338. Yalman, *Turkey in the World War*, 262–3.

339. Lloyd George, *War Memoirs*, II, 1925.

340. Erickson, *Ordered to Die*, 241.

341. Falls, *Egypt and Palestine*, II, 495; A. Bruce, *The Last Crusade: the Palestine Campaign in the First World War* (London, 2003), 108.

342. E. J. Erickson, *Ottoman Army Effectiveness in World War I: a Comparative Study* (Abingdon/New York, 2007), 155–7.

343. L. Schatkowski Schilchen, 'The Famine of 1915–1918 in Greater Syria', in J. P. Spagnolo (ed.), *Problems of the Middle East in Historical Perspective: Essays in Honour of Albert Hourani* (Reading, 1992), 250.

344. Lloyd George, *War Memoirs*, II, 1925.

345. Yalman, *Turkey in the World War*, 251.

346. Schatkowski Schilchen, 'Famine of 1915–1918', 244.

347. Y. Sheffy, *British Military Intelligence in the Palestine Campaign, 1914–1918* (London/Portland, Ore., 1998), 304.

348. N. Bosanquet, 'Health Systems in Khaki: the British and American Medical Experience', in Cecil and Liddle (eds.), *Facing Armageddon*, 459.

349. Reichswehrministerium, *Sanitätsbericht*, III, 646.

5. SECURING THE SEAS: SUBMARINES AND SHIPPING

1. Holtzendorff report, 30 Jan. 1918, G. Granier (ed.), *Die deutsche Seekriegsleitung im Ersten Weltkrieg – Dokumentation*, III (4 vols., Koblenz, 1999–2004), doc. 552.

2. Salter report, 13 Mar. 1918, p. 59, MT/25/10.

3. Beatty–Geddes, 9 Jan. 1918, ADM/116/1806.

4. H. J. Mackinder, *Democratic Ideals and Reality: a Study in the Politics of Reconstruction* (London, 1919), 81.

5. J. Terraine, *Business in Great Waters: the U-Boat Wars, 1916–1945* (Ware, 1999), 766.

6. W. S. Sims, *The Victory at Sea* (London, 1920), 112, 109.

7. C-in-C Mediterranean report, Aug. 1917–Nov. 1918, ADM/137/2664.

8. J. Corbett and H. Newbolt, *Naval Operations*, V (5 vols., London, 1920–31), 112ff.; Sims, *Victory at Sea*, 103–11; 'Report on Shipping Control', 160, MT/25/87.

9. J. Schröder, *Die U-Boote des Kaisers: die Geschichte des deutschen U-Boot-Krieges gegen Großbritannien im Ersten Weltkrieg* (Lauf a. d. Pegnitz, 2000), 371; Grant–Admiralty, 28 Dec. 1918, ADM/137/2658.

10. W. S. L. Churchill, *The World Crisis*, Part 2: *1916–1918* (6 parts, London, 1923–31), 364.

11. Schröder, *U-Boote des Kaisers*, 372.

12. T. Boghardt, *Spies of the Kaiser: German Covert Operations in Britain during the First World War Era* (Basingstoke, 2004), 139.

13. P. Beesly, *Room 40: British Naval Intelligence, 1914–18* (London, 1982), 254ff.; Sims, *Victory at Sea*, 104, 111; logbooks, ADM/137/4134.

14. War Cabinet, 17 Dec. 1917, CAB/27/14.

15. C-in-C Mediterranean report, Aug. 1917–Nov. 1918, ADM/137/2664; 'Introduction of the Depth Charge into the Royal Navy': http://www.gwdpa.org/naval/br.1669.htm.

16. 'Report on Shipping Control', 174, MT/25/87.

17. Beesly, *Room 40*, 266.

18. Schröder, *U-Boote des Kaisers*, 425–6; Admiralty Staff Circular, 5 Feb. 1918, Granier (ed.), *Die deutsche Seekriegsleitung*, III, doc. 554.

19. J. Wintour, *Convoy: the Defence of Seaborne Trade, 1890–1990* (London, 1993), 101.

20. Beharrel Statistical Review, 23 Dec. 1918, p. 14, ADM/116/1810.

21. First Lord's Statement, 1 Nov. 1917, ADM/116/1805.

22. A. J. Marder, *From the Dreadnought to Scapa Flow: the Royal Navy in the Fisher Era, 1904–1919*, V (5 vols., London, 1961–70), 114–15.

23. Granier (ed.), *Die deutsche Seekriegsleitung*, III, docs. 537, 594.

24. C. E. Fayle, *History of the Great War Based on Official Documents: Seaborne Trade*, III (3 vols., London, 1920), 307.

25. P. G. Halpern, *The Naval War in the Mediterranean, 1914–1918* (London, 1987), 456; Wemyss–Beatty, 24 Feb. 1918, BTY/13/39/12.

26. 'Convoy System as Applied to the Mediterranean', p. 8, ADM/137/2664.

27. H. H. Sokol, *Österreich-Ungarns Seekrieg 1914–1918*, II (2 vols., Graz, 1967), 509, 519.

28. Corbett and Newbolt, *Naval Operations*, V, 410–11.

29. 'Convoy System as Applied to the Mediterranean', pp. 18–19, ADM/137/2664.

30. Beharrel Statistical Review, 23 Dec. 1918, p. 13, ADM/116/1810.

31. G. Fassy, *Le Commandement français en orient (octobre 1915–novembre 1918)* (Paris, 2003), 235.

32. Baird report, 1 Jan. 1919, p. 38, ADM/137/2664.

33. Beharrel Statistical Review, 23 Dec. 1918, p. 19, ADM/116/1810.

34. Granier (ed.), *Die deutsche Seekriegsleitung*, III, doc. 548.

35. G. P. Groß, *Die Seekriegführung der Kaiserlichen Marine im Jahre 1918* (Frankfurt-am-Main, 1989), 267; Granier (ed.), *Die deutsche Seekriegsleitung*, II, docs. 125, 248.

36. A. S. Hurd, *History of the Great War Based on Official Documents: The Merchant Navy*, III (3 vols., London, 1921–9), ch. 8; for U-boat views, ADM/137/3060: UB55, U64.

37. 'Report on Shipping Control', 143–9, MT/25/87.

38. Geddes memo, 24 Oct. 1917, ADM/167/54.

39. 'Report on Shipping Control', 149, MT/25/87; Third Sea Lord memo, 2 Nov. 1917, ADM/167/54.

40. Corbett and Newbolt, *Naval Operations*, V, 286n.

41. Ibid., 93–6, 286–9, 295–9, 410–12; Wintour, *Convoy*, 100.

42. Baird, 'Appraisal of the Mediterranean Scene in October 1918', ADM/137/2664.

43. R. Keyes, *The Naval Memoirs of Admiral of the Fleet Sir Roger Keyes*, II (2 vols., London, 1935), 144.

44. Keyes report, 9 May 1918, ADM/167/54; E. von Mantey et al. (eds.), *Der Krieg zur See 1914–1918*, VII: *Nordsee* (7 vols., Berlin/Frankfurt-am-Main, 1920–66), 266–87.

45. Corbett and Newbolt, *Naval Operations*, V, 265.

46. Ibid., 272, 274; Granier (ed.), *Die deutsche Seekriegsleitung*, II, doc. 248.

47. Fayle, *Seaborne Trade*, III, 310.

48. Granier (ed.), *Die deutsche Seekriegsleitung*, II, doc. 250.

49. Ibid., doc. 248; Mantey et al. (eds.), *Krieg zur See*, VII: *Nordsee*, 325.

50. Hurd, *Merchant Navy*, III, ch. 9.

51. Ibid., 264.

52. Fayle, *Seaborne Trade*, III, 367.

53. Churchill, *World Crisis*, Part 2: *1916–1918*, 372.

54. R. H. Gibson and M. Prendergast, *The German Submarine War, 1914–1918* (London, 1931), 179.

55. Deputy Chief of Naval Staff memo, 20 June 1918, ADM/167/54.

56. Corbett and Newbolt, *Naval Operations*, V, 178–83; Beesly, *Room 40*, 282.

57. Keyes, *Naval Memoirs*, II, 113ff.

58. Corbett and Newbolt, *Naval Operations*, V, 210–19; Groß, *Seekriegführung*, 224–6.

59. Granier (ed.), *Die deutsche Seekriegsleitung*, II, docs. 233, 248; Mantey et al. (eds.), *Krieg zur See*, VII: *Nordsee*, 237.

60. Beesly, *Room 40*, 268, 282; Groß, *Seekriegführung*, 287.

61. Churchill, *World Crisis*, Part 2: *1916–1918*, 369.

62. Mantey et al. (eds.), *Krieg zur See*, VII: *Nordsee*, 281ff.

63. Schröder, *U-Boote des Kaisers*, 391.

64. Groß, *Seekriegführung*, 433.

65. 'The Northern Blockade', 20 Oct. 1917, ADM/116/1805.

66. Sims, *Victory at Sea*, 261.

67. Beatty–Wemyss, 1 Sept. 1918, BTY/13/39/42.

68. O. Riste, *The Neutral Ally: Norway's Relations with Belligerent Powers in the First World War* (Oslo/London, 1965), 224.

69. P. G. Halpern, *A Naval History of World War I* (London, 1994), 440–41.

70. Marder, *Dreadnought to Scapa Flow*, V, 85; Fayle, *Seaborne Trade*, III, 368.

71. Terraine, *Business*, 148, 126.

72. Schröder, *U-Boote des Kaisers*, 389.

73. Marder, *Dreadnought to Scapa Flow*, V, 92–3.

74. Ibid., 120.

75. R. J. Overy, *Why the Allies Won* (London, 1995), 57–8.

76. Geddes–Cabinet, 17 July 1918, ADM/186/1810; Fayle, *Seaborne Trade*, III, 363–7; Corbett and Newbolt, *Naval Operations*, V, 299, 336–9.

77. Holtzendorff–Müller, 3 June 1918, Granier (ed.), *Die deutsche Seekriegsleitung*, III, doc. 560.

78. Holtzendorff–Wilhelm, 9 June 1918, Granier (ed.), *Die deutsche Seekriegsleitung*, II, doc. 233.

79. Schröder, *U-Boote des Kaisers*, 427.

80. Ibid.

81. Terraine, *Business*, 131; Marder, *Dreadnought to Scapa Flow*, V, 81.

82. Halpern, *Naval History*, 396; Halpern, *Naval War in the Mediterranean*, 539.

83. Beharrel Statistical Review, 23 Dec. 1918, p. 157, ADM/116/1810.

84. Groß, *Seekriegführung*, 276.

85. Ibid., 257, 259.

86. Geddes–Cabinet, 31 July 1918, ADM/116/1810.

87. B. Stegemann, *Die deutsche Marinepolitik, 1916–1918* (Berlin, 1970), 130.

88. Compare UC55, UC65, U58, UB35 with U48, U110, UB55, UB85, UB110, UB109 in ADM/137/3060.

89. Marder, *Dreadnought to Scapa Flow*, V, 83.

90. Geddes–Cabinet, 31 July 1918, ADM/116/1810.

91. Scheer, 21 April 1918, Holtzendorff–Kühlmann, 1 May 1918, Granier (ed.), *Die deutsche Seekriegsleitung*, III, docs. R558, 558a; Groß, *Seekriegführung*, 259ff.

92. Granier (ed.), *Die deutsche Seekriegsleitung*, III, docs. 564, 566.

93. Halpern, *Naval History*, 429–32.

94. Sims, *Victory at Sea*, 270–73.

95. Beharrel Statistical Review, 23 Dec. 1918, p. 20, ADM/116/1810; Halpern, *Naval History*, 427; Marder, *Dreadnought to Scapa Flow*, V, 94.

96. Granier (ed.), *Die deutsche Seekriegsleitung*, III, docs. 534, 540, 542.

97. Corbett and Newbolt, *Naval Operations*, V, 278–82, 343.

98. Terraine, *Business*, 122.

99. Groß, *Seekriegführung*, 293–4.

100. Schröder, *U-Boote des Kaisers*, 378; Marder, *Dreadnought to Scapa Flow*, V, 81.

101. Terraine, *Business*, 118.

102. G. E. Weir, *Building the Kaiser's Navy: the Imperial Navy and German Industry in the Tirpitz Era, 1890–1919* (Annapolis, Md, 1992), 178, 214.

103. Granier (ed.), *Die deutsche Seekriegsleitung*, I, doc. 127.

104. Schröder, *U-Boote des Kaisers*, 365.

105. Stegemann, *Die deutsche Marinepolitik*, 130–32.

106. CAS, 3 Aug. 1918, RM3/5314, BA-MA.

107. Stegemann, *Die deutsche Marinepolitik*, 132.

108. Groß, *Seekriegführung*, 323–4.

109. Granier (ed.), *Die deutsche Seekriegsleitung*, I, doc. 130 (4 Oct. 1917).

110. Admiralstab, 29 Mar. 1918, ibid., II, doc. 220; Holtzendorff, 30 Jan. 1918, ibid., I, doc. 552.

111. Admiralstab, 4 Dec. 1917, ibid., II, doc. 130; Weir, *Building the Kaiser's Navy*, 188; Hildebrand manuscript on raw materials, 5, W-10/50493, BA-MA.

112. U-Boots-Amt note, 7 Oct. 1918, RM5/3940, BA-MA; Groß, *Seekriegführung*, 338–9.

113. Groß, *Seekriegführung*, 330–32, 338; CAS note, 18 Sept. 1918, RM5/3940, BA-MA.

114. Ludendorff–CAS, 20 Sept. 1918, RM5/3940, BA-MA.

115. Groß, *Seekriegführung*, 332.

116. Geddes, 25 Sept. 1918, ADM/116/1810; Cabinet, 27 Sept. 1918, CAB/23/14.

117. Geddes, 27 Sept. 1918, ADM/116/1809.

118. Groß, *Seekriegführung*, 332.

119. Halpern, *Naval War in the Mediterranean*, 579.

120. Admiralstab, 5 Apr. 1918, Granier (ed.), *Die deutsche Seekriegsleitung*, II, doc. 223; Stegemann, *Die deutsche Marinepolitik*, 128.

121. Jellicoe memorandum, 18 Nov. 1917, ADM/116/1806.

122. Sims, *Victory at Sea*, 98.

123. Minute for Admiralty Board, 10 Jan. 1918, BTY/13/39/3.

124. Beesly, *Room 40*, 274–9.

125. Wemyss–Beatty, 20 Feb. 1918, BTY/13/39/10; Beatty–Wemyss, 22 Feb. 1918, WMYS/11/1.

126. Marder, *Dreadnought to Scapa Flow*, V, 105.

127. Jellicoe–Cabinet, 18 Nov. 1917, ADM/116/1806.

128. Admiralty, 26 Nov. 1917, #357 MLN.

129. Geddes–Cabinet, 31 Aug. 1918, ADM/167/55.

130. Beatty–Admiralty, 9 Jan. 1918, ADM/167/53; cf. N. Hewitt, '"Weary Waiting is Hard Indeed": the Grand Fleet after Jutland', in I. F. W. Beckett (ed.), *1917: Beyond the Western Front* (Leiden/Boston, Mass., 2009), 56–68.

131. Admiralty Board, 17 Jan. 1918, ADM/167/53.

132. Corbett and Newbolt, *Naval Operations*, V, 88–92.

133. D. Trask, *Captains and Cabinets: Anglo-American Naval Relations, 1917–1918* (Columbia, Mo., 1972), 175–80; Admiralty Board, 26 Nov. 1917, ADM/167/53.

134. ANC, 26–27 Apr. 1918, BTY/7/7/4; Geddes–Cabinet, 8 June 1918, ADM/116/1810.

135. Wemyss–Beatty, 24 Feb. 1918, BTY/13/39/12.

136. Wemyss–Beatty, 28 Jan., 7 Feb., 26 Feb., 30 Mar., 1 Apr. 1918, BTY/13/39.

137. Cabinet, 30 Apr. 1918, CAB/23/14.

138. Groß, *Seekriegführung*, 228–30.

139. Scheer–Wilhelm, 1 May 1918, Granier (ed.), *Die deutsche Seekriegsleitung*, II, doc. 227.

140. Beesly, *Room 40*, 283–5.

141. Granier (ed.), *Die deutsche Seekriegsleitung*, II, doc. 227.

142. Beatty–Wemyss, 26 Apr. 1918, WMYS/11/1.

143. Corbett and Newbolt, *Naval Operations*, V, 92, 294; Groß, *Seekriegführung*, 430–31.

144. Sokol, *Österreich-Ungarns Seekrieg*, II, 392, 780–84.

145. Dreyer–Beatty, 9 May 1918, BTY/7/9/9.

146. Wemyss–Beatty, 7 Feb. 1918, BTY/13/39/7; J. W. Jones, *US Battleship Operations in World War I* (Annapolis, Md, 1998), chs. 1–4.

147. Ibid., ch. 6; Sims, 10 and 19 Aug. 1918, ADM/137/1622.

148. Beatty–Wemyss, 10 Aug. 1918, BTY/13/39/33.

149. Wemyss–Beatty, 10 Aug. 1918, BTY/13/39/34; Mantey et al. (eds.), *Krieg zur See*, VII: *Nordsee*, 291.

150. Granier (ed.), *Die deutsche Seekriegsleitung*, II, doc. 223; Groß, *Seekriegführung*, 215–19.

151. Granier (ed.), *Die deutsche Seekriegsleitung*, I, doc. 130.

152. Groß, *Seekriegführung*, 235–42; Mantey et al. (eds.), *Krieg zur See*, VII: *Nordsee*, 318.

153. Admiralstab, 6 Apr. 1918, Granier (ed.), *Die deutsche Seekriegsleitung*, II, doc. 224; Groß, *Seekriegführung*, 239.

154. See Chapter 8.

155. S. Roskill, *Admiral of the Fleet Lord Beatty: the Last Naval Hero: an Intimate Biography* (London, 1980), 245–6; Marder, *Dreadnought to Scapa Flow*, V, 331–3.

156. Geddes–Lloyd George draft, Sept. 1918, ADM/167/55.

157. Geddes–Cabinet, 31 Aug. 1918, ADM/167/55; Cabinet, 9 Sept. 1918, CAB/23/14.

158. Geddes–Cabinet, 26 Aug. 1918, ADM 116/1810.

159. Fayle, *Seaborne Trade*, III, 370–71; Admiralty Controller report, 6 June 1918, ADM/116/1810.

160. Ibid.; J. T. Sumida, 'Forging the Trident: British Naval Industrial Logistics, 1914–1918', in J. A. Lynn (ed.), *Feeding Mars: Logistics in Western Europe from the Middle Ages to the Present* (Boulder, Colo./San Francisco/Oxford, 1993), 225.

161. Geddes–Cabinet, 25 Sept. 1918, ADM/116/1810.

162. Sumida, 'Forging the Trident', 219–21.

163. Ibid., 225; 'Report on Shipping Control', 23–30, MT/25/87.

164. Geddes–Cabinet, 5 July 1917, ADM/116/1804; Controller–Cabinet, 19 Nov. 1917, ADM/116/1806.

165. Man Power Committee draft report, 1 Mar. 1918, CAB/27/14.

166. 'Report on Shipping Control', 40–41, MT/25/87.

167. 'Report on Shipping Control', 57–70, MT/25/87; report by Controller, 6 June 1918, ADM/116/1810.

168. Admiralty Board, 7/8 Feb. 1918, ADM/167/53.

169. Maclay memorandum, 21 June 1918, MT/25/22.

170. J. J. Safford, *Wilsonian Maritime Diplomacy, 1913–1921* (New Brunswick, NJ, 1978), 136–9; 'Report on Shipping Control', 304, MT/25/87.

171. H. H. Herwig and D. F. Trask, 'The Failure of Imperial Germany's Undersea Offensive against World Shipping, February 1917–October 1918', *The Historian* (1970/1971), 615–16; Sims, *Victory at Sea*, 134.

172. E. D. Cronin (ed.), *The War Diaries of Josephus Daniels, 1913–1921* (Lincoln, Nebr., 1963), 321.

173. C. E. Fayle, *A Short History of the World's Shipping Industry* (London, 1933), 297.

174. Geddes–Cabinet, 16 Apr. 1918, ADM/116/1810.

175. Safford, *Wilsonian Maritime Diplomacy*, 104, 108, 142ff.; 'Report on Shipping Control', 298–9, MT/25/86.

176. Hurley interview, *The Times*, 16 Mar. 1918; Hurley speech, *The Official Bulletin*, 27 Mar. 1918, MT/25/24.

177. Safford, *Wilsonian Maritime Diplomacy*, 157.

178. 'Report on Shipping Control', 320, MT/25/86.

179. Introduction to AMTC history, Dec. 1918, MT/25/10.

180. Admiralstab, 11 Aug. 1917; Holtzendorff–Foreign Ministry and Hindenburg, 3 Oct. 1917, Granier (ed.), *Die deutsche Seekriegsleitung*, III, docs. 533, 537.

181. 'Report on Shipping Control', 26, MT/25/87.

182. Ibid., 34, 88, 46, 43, 52–62; Riste, *Neutral Ally*, 176–8, 226.

183. 'Report on Shipping Control', 72, 79–80, MT/25/87.

184. M. Frey, 'Bullying the Neutrals: the Case of the Netherlands', in R. Chickering and S. Förster (eds.), *Great War, Total War: Combat and Mobilization on the Western Front, 1914–1918* (Cambridge, 2000), 239–40; War Cabinet, 22 Apr. 1918, CAB/23/4.

185. 'Report on Shipping Control', 226, 282, MT/25/86.

186. Maclay memorandum, 21 June 1918, MT/25/22.

187. Fayle, *Seaborne Trade*, III, 457.

188. 'Report on Shipping Control', 322, MT/25/86.

189. Fayle, *Seaborne Trade*, III, ch. 15.

190. Anglo-French agreement, 3 Nov. 1917; British memorandum, 21 Nov. 1917, in AMTC history, Dec. 1918, MT/25/10.

191. AMTC history, ibid.

192. Fayle, *Seaborne Trade*, III, ch. 17.

193. Report by Royal Commission on Wheat Supplies, 3, BEV/IV.

194. 'Report on Shipping Control', 255–7, MT/25/86.

195. Fayle, *Seaborne Trade*, III, 395, 346.

196. J. T. Sumida, 'British Naval Operational Logistics, 1914–1918', *Journal of Military History* (1993), 460–72.

197. 'Report on Shipping Control', 377, MT/25/86.

198. Bérenger–Marine Minister, 19 Nov. 1917, F¹²7716, AN.

199. Kemball–Maclay, 7 May 1917; draft telegram to Washington, June 1917; Maclay to Admiralty (n.d.), MT 25/20.

200. Admiralty Board, 8 Jan. 1918, ADM/167/53; Geddes–Long, 9 Jan. 1918, ADM/116/1806.

201. Wemyss–Cabinet, 16 Aug. 1918, ADM/116/1810.

202. 'Report on Shipping Control', 80–86, MT/25/86.

203. Wemyss–Cabinet, 2 Jan. 1919, ADM/116/1772.

204. Wemyss–Cabinet, 30 July and 17 Sept. 1918, ADM/116/1810; Hankey diary, 29 July 1918, HNKY; V. H. Rothwell, 'Mesopotamia in British War Aims, 1914–1918', *Historical Journal* (1970), 287–92.

205. C. M. Andrew and E. S. Kanya-Forstner, *France Overseas: the Great War and the Climax of French Imperial Expansion* (London, 1981), 174–5.

206. See Chapter 3.

207. See Chapter 4.

208. AMTC, 11 Mar. 1918, in AMTC history, Dec. 1918, MT/25/10.

209. Salter report, 16 July 1918, in ibid.; Loucheur–Cecil, 13 Aug. 1918, MT/25/21.

210. Cambon–Clémentel, 9 May 1918, F¹²7794, AN.

211. AMTC history, Dec. 1918, Appendix 9, 13 Mar. 1918, MT/25/10.

212. D. Lloyd George, *War Memoirs*, II (2 vols., London, 1938), 1728; Cabinet, 6 Apr. 1918, CAB/23/6.

213. Halpern, *Naval History*, 435.

214. Maclay, 'America and Shipping' (n.d.) and Derby–Reading, 15 Mar. 1918, MT/25/13.

215. 'Report on Shipping Control', 310, MT/25/86.

216. Sims, *Victory at Sea*, 300–301.

217. 'Report on Shipping Control', 316, MT/25/86.

218. Halpern, *Naval History*, 436–7.

219. Sims, *Victory at Sea*, 367–9, 310–11.

220. Notes on U-boat war lecture, Sept. 1918, RM/5/6468, BA-MA.

221. Granier (ed.), *Die deutsche Seekriegsleitung*, III, docs. 569, 572.

222. Wemyss–Geddes, 6 Aug. 1918; Geddes/Maclay–Cabinet, 6 Aug. 1918, ADM/106/1810.

223. L. P. Ayres, *The War with Germany: a Statistical Summary* (Washington DC, 1919), 45.

224. AMTC minutes, 30 Sept–2 Oct. 1918, AMTC history, Dec. 1918, MT/25/10.

225. Food Council–AMTC, 31 July 1918, ibid.

226. Geddes–Cabinet, 2 Sept. 1918, ADM/116/1810.

227. 'Report on Shipping Control', 312, MT/25/86.

228. Geddes–Cabinet, 24 Aug. 1918, ADM/116/1810.

229. E. B. Parsons, 'Why the British Reduced the Flow of American Troops to Europe in August–October 1918', *Canadian Journal of History* (1977), 179, 188.

230. Admiralty Board, 14 Feb. 1918, ADM/167/53.

231. W. Grant report, 28 Dec. 1918, ADM/137/2658.

232. Churchill, *World Crisis*, Part 2: *1916–1918*, 349–50.

233. Terraine, *Business*, 141–2, 149.

234. T. Lane, 'The British Merchant Seaman at War', in H. Cecil and P. H. Liddle (eds.), *Facing Armageddon: the First World War Experienced* (London, 1996), 146–7.

235. D. W. Bone, *Merchantmen-at-Arms: the British Merchants' Service in the War* (London, 1919), 255.

6. THE WAR ECONOMIES: MONEY, GUNS, AND BUTTER

1. Memorandum on Munitions Ministry in 1918, 12 Feb. 1919, MUN/5/12.

2. S. Broadberry and M. Harrison (eds.), *The Economics of World War I* (Cambridge, 2005), 7, 10.

3. P. M. Kennedy, *The Rise and Fall of the Great Powers: Economic Change and Military Conflict from 1500 to 2000* (London, 1989), 257.

4. A. D. Noyes, *The War Period of American Finance, 1908–1925* (New York/London, 1926), 224.

5. McAdoo–Wilson, 2 Jan. 1918, McAdoo MSS 524, LOC.

6. C. Gilbert, *American Financing of World War I* (Westport, Conn., 1970), 221.

7. H. Rockoff, '"Until it's over, over there!": the US Economy in World War I', in Broadberry and Harrison (eds.), *Economics of World War I*, 334; Gilbert, *American Financing*, 224.

8. J. Stiglitz and L. Bilmes, *The Three Trillion Dollar War: the True Cost of the Iraq Conflict* (New York, 2008).

9. N. Ferguson, *The Pity of War* (London, 1998), 323.

10. Ibid., 226.

11. G. Hardach, *First World War, 1914–1918* (London, 1977), 169; Rockoff, 'US Economy', 316.

12. W. G. McAdoo, *Crowded Years: the Reminiscences of William G. McAdoo* (Boston, Mass./New York, 1931), 372, 384.

13. Noyes, *War Period*, 166; Gilbert, *American Financing*, 85, 95.

14. McAdoo, *Crowded Years*, 385, 378–9.

15. Rockoff, 'US Economy', 323.

16. McAdoo, *Crowded Years*, 406–7; Gilbert, *American Financing*, 123, 135.

17. McAdoo, *Crowded Years*, 380.

18. Noyes, *War Period*, 202ff.; H. F. A. Strachan, *Financing the First World War* (Oxford, 2004), 158–9.

19. Hardach, *First World War*, 257; Gilbert, *American Financing*, 68.

20. McAdoo, *Crowded Years*, 415–16.

21. D. M. Kennedy, *Over Here: the First World War and American Society* (New York/Oxford, 1980), 100.

22. K. Burk, *Britain, America, and the Sinews of War, 1914–1918* (Boston, Mass./London/Sydney, 1985), 34; K. Burk, 'The Mobilization of Anglo-American Finance during World War I', in N. F. Dreisziger (ed.), *Mobilization for Total War: the Canadian, American, and British Experience, 1914–1918, 1939–1945* (Waterloo, Ont., 1981), 36; Bonar Law statement, 3 Apr. 1917, CAB/1/24.

23. McAdoo, *Crowded Years*, 393.

24. Ibid., 372.

25. McAdoo–Daniels, 13 Aug. 1917, Daniels MSS 89, LOC.

26. Burk, *Sinews of War*, 137, 177–8, 196–206.

27. McAdoo–Wilson, 11 Feb. 1918, McAdoo MSS 524, LOC.

28. D. J. Forsyth, *The Crisis of Liberal Italy: Monetary and Financial Policy, 1914–1922* (Cambridge, 1993), 183–6.

29. Gilbert, *American Financing*, 103; McAdoo, *Crowded Years*, 506.

30. Memorandum on US–France financial situation, 22 Oct. 1918, McAdoo MSS 524, LOC.

31. McAdoo–Wilson, 2 Jan., 8, 23 May, 3 Oct. 1918, McAdoo MSS 524, LOC.

32. Gilbert, *American Financing*, 106–12.

33. See Chapter 8.

34. F. M. Surface, *The Grain Trade during the World War: Being a History of the Food Administration Grain Corporation and the United States Grain Corporation* (New York, 1928), 18–20; Rhondda–Cabinet, 30 Jan. 1918, CAB/1/26.

35. B. H. Hibberd, *Effects of the Great War upon Agriculture in the United States and Great Britain* (New York, 1919), 6, 17, 24; Surface, *Grain Trade*, 20.

36. M. R. Dickson, *The Food Front in World War I* (Washington DC, 1944), 12.

37. Surface, *Grain Trade*, 20, 31.

38. Kennedy, *Over Here*, 117; Surface, *Grain Trade*, 28.

39. Surface, *Grain Trade*, 32; Hibberd, *Effects of the Great War*, 72–87.

40. Hibberd, *Effects of the Great War*, 127–8; W. C. Mullendore, *History of the United States Food Administration, 1917–1919* (Stanford, Calif./London, 1941), 8, 10, 12.

41. Hoover–House, 5 Nov., 26 Oct. 1917, Daniels MSS 60, LOC; Surface, *Grain Trade*, 187; Mullendore, *Food Administration*, 12.

42. Surface, *Grain Trade*, 188–91.

43. Draft Clemenceau/Lloyd George/Orlando tel. to Wilson, 31 Jan. 1918, 6N53, SHA.

44. McAdoo Westchester speech, 17 May 1919, Garfield MSS 131, LOC; Surface, *Grain Trade*, 188–202.

45. Wilson–Hoover, 8 Mar. 1918, F. W. O'Brien (ed.), *The Hoover–Wilson Wartime Correspondence, September 24, 1914, to November 11, 1918* (Ames, Ia, 1974), 157, 162–3; McAdoo–Wilson, 11 Feb. 1918, McAdoo MSS 524, LOC.

46. McAdoo, *Crowded Years*, 448, 457–8.

47. J. P. Johnson, 'The Wilsonians as War Mongers: Coal and the 1917–18 Winter Crisis', *Prologue* (1977), 203–4; Surface, *Grain Trade*, 121, 257–8.

48. McAdoo, Westchester speech, 17 May 1919, Garfield MSS 131, LOC.

49. Hibberd, *Effects of the Great War*, 38–9, 62, 146ff.; Surface, *Grain Trade*, 17.

50. B. Crowell, *America's Munitions, 1917–18* (Washington DC, 1919), 590.

51. Petroleum Conference minutes, RG67, entry 16, NARA.

52. A. Kaspi, *Le Temps des Américains: le concours américain à la France en 1917–1918* (Paris, 1976), 267, 269.

53. Daniels–Wilson, 29 July 1918, Daniels MSS 110, LOC.

54. Requa–Garfield, 11 Dec. 1917, 27 Feb. 1918, Garfield MSS 92, LOC; Daniels–Wilson, 10 June 1918, Daniels MSS 110, LOC.

55. G. B. Clarkson, *Industrial America in the World War: the Strategy behind the Line, 1917–1918* (Boston, Mass./New York, 1923), xxiii.

56. Ibid., 331; Replogle–Baruch, 31 Dec. 1918, WIB 2684, NARA.

57. L. P. Ayres, *The War with Germany: a Statistical Summary* (Washington DC, 1919), 78.

58. Crowell, *America's Munitions*, 103–9; Clarkson, *Industrial America*, 409–10.

59. Clarkson, *Industrial America*, 390–99.

60. B. M. Baruch, *The Public Years* (London, 1961), 51.

61. Crowell, *America's Munitions*, 104; Ayres, *War with Germany*, 75.

62. Ayres, *War with Germany*, 63–4, 74–5; Crowell, *America's Munitions*, 65–7.

63. Ayres, *War with Germany*, 80.

64. Ibid., 90–95; Crowell, *America's Munitions*, 265.

65. R. J. Overy, *Why the Allies Won* (London, 1995), 192.

66. Ayres, *War with Germany*, 51–2.

67. Clarkson, *Industrial America*, 233.

68. Crowell, *America's Munitions*, 25–6, 35–8.

69. Ibid., 240–49; Ayres, *War with Germany*, 89–90.

70. G. H. Moore, *Production of Industrial Materials in World Wars I and II* (New York, 1944), 4.

71. Broadberry and Harrison (eds.), *Economics of World War I*, 12.

72. Rockoff, 'US Economy', 326; Clarkson, *Industrial America*, 101.

73. Rockoff, 'US Economy', 313.

74. T. K. Nenninger, 'American Military Effectiveness in the First World War', in A. R. Millett and W. Murray (eds.), *Military Effectiveness* (3 vols., Winchester, Mass., 1988), 120.

75. Fletcher–Pierce-Daniels, 24 May 1917, Daniels MSS 60, LOC; WIB minutes, 1 Aug. 1917, WIB 72, NARA.

76. Kaspi, *Temps des Américains*, 115–24; Nenninger, 'American Military Effectiveness', 121.

77. Crowell, *America's Munitions*, 14–15.

78. Clarkson, *Industrial America*, 236–7.

79. *Munitions Industry. Minutes of the Council of National Defense* (Washington DC, 1936).

80. Clarkson, *Industrial America*, 3.

81. CND minutes, 28 July 1917, WIB 72, NARA; P. A. C. Koistinen, *Mobilizing for Modern War: the Political Economy of American Warfare, 1865–1919* (Lawrence, Kan., 1997), 205, 218–19.

82. Koistinen, *Mobilizing for Modern War*, 457; K. A. Kerr, 'Decision for Federal Control: Wilson, McAdoo, and the Railroads, 1917', *Journal of American History* (1967), 550–56.

83. Johnson, 'Wilsonians', 203–5.

84. Garfield–Wilson, 26 Nov. 1917, Garfield–Lovett, 24 Dec. 1917, Garfield MSS 92, LOC.

85. C. Keller, *The Power Situation during the War* (Washington DC, 1921), 1–17, 34.

86. WIB minutes, 21–22 Nov. 1917, 7 Feb. 1918, WIB 72, 73, NARA.

87. Baruch, *Public Years*, 49, 51; Koistinen, *Mobilizing for Modern War*, ch. 10.

88. Johnson, 'Wilsonians', 204.

89. W. J. Cunningham, 'The Railroads under Government Operation. I. The Period to the Close of 1918', *The Quarterly Journal of Economics* (1921), 326, 333–7; J. A. Huston, *The Sinews of War: Army Logistics, 1775–1953* (Washington DC, 1966), 345.

90. McAdoo, *Crowded Years*, 464–92.

91. WIB minutes, 25 Apr. 1918, WIB 73, NARA.

92. Cunningham, 'Railroads under Government Operation', 374; McAdoo–Baker, 2 Mar. 1918, McAdoo MSS 524, LOC.

93. WIB minutes, 18 July 1918, WIB 73, NARA.

94. Replogle–Baruch, 31 Dec. 1918, WIB 2684, NARA.

95. WIB minutes, 7 May 1918, WIB 73, NARA.

96. Koistinen, *Mobilizing for Modern War*, 241.

97. Wilson–Daniels, 24 July 1918, Daniels MSS 100, LOC; WIB minutes, 8 Aug. 1918, WIB 73, NARA.

98. WIB minutes, 17 May 1918, WIB 73, NARA; Clarkson, *Industrial America*, 394.

99. S. Broadberry and P. Howlett, 'The United Kingdom in World War I: Business as Usual?', in Broadberry and Harrison (eds.), *Economics of World War I*, 208.

100. Ibid., 211, 230; M. Horn, 'The Concept of Total War: National Effort and Taxation in Britain and France during the First World War', *War and Society* (2000), 9–10.

101. Ferguson, *Pity of War*, 323.

102. Broadberry and Harrison (eds.), *Economics of World War I*, 7; Ferguson, *Pity of War*, 337.

103. Broadberry and Harrison (eds.), *Economics of World War I*, 14.

104. Strachan, *Financing the First World War*, 219, 217; E. V. Morgan, *Studies in British Financial Policy, 1914–25* (London, 1952), 317.

105. Bonar Law statement, 3 Apr. 1917, CAB /1/24.

106. T. Balderston, 'War Finance and Inflation in Britain and Germany, 1914–1918', *Economic History Review* (1989), 228.

107. M. Daunton, 'How to Pay for the War: State, Society, and Taxation in Britain, 1917–1929', *English Historical Review* (1996), 889, 896; Broadberry and Howlett, 'United Kingdom in World War I', in Broadberry and Harrison (eds.), *Economics of World War I* , 215, 217.

108. M. Horn, *Britain, France, and the Financing of the First World War* (Montreal/Kingston, 2002), 172.

109. Broadberry and Howlett, 'United Kingdom in World War I', in Broadberry and Harrison (eds.), *Economics of World War I*, 218.

110. Bonar Law statement, 3 Apr. 1917, CAB/1/24.

111. Morgan, *Studies*, 106ff., 115; Balderston, 'War Finance', 238; Strachan, *Financing the First World War*, 145.

112. Imperial War Cabinet, 12 July 1918, CAB/23/43.

113. Bonar Law statement, 3 Apr. 1917, CAB/1/24.

114. War Cabinet, 5 and 12 Dec. 1917, CAB/23/4.

115. Bonar Law–Cabinet, 9 Jan. 1918, MAF 60/56; Rhondda statement, 30 Jan. 1918, CAB/1/26.

116. Bonar Law–Reading, 25 Mar., 9 Apr. 1918, T/1/12248.

117. Bonar Law–Reading, 25 Mar. 1918, T/1/12248.

118. Broadberry and Howlett, 'United Kingdom in World War I', in Broadberry and Harrison (eds.), *Economics of World War I*, 211, 220; Morgan, *Studies*, 341.

119. L. M. Barnett, *British Food Policy during the First World War* (Boston, Mass./London/Sydney, 1985), xiii.

120. J. M. Winter and J.-L. Robert (eds.), *Capital Cities at War: London, Paris, Berlin, 1914–1919*, I (2 vols., Cambridge, 1997, 2007), 12, 531ff.

121. R. van Emden and S. Humphries, *All Quiet on the Home Front: an Oral History of Life in Britain during the First World War* (London, 2004), 195–202.

122. P. E. Dewey, *British Agriculture in the First World War* (London, 1989), 220; W. H. Beveridge, *British Food Control* (London, 1928), 313.

123. Food Ministry, 4 Dec. 1918, BEV IX; J. M. Winter, *The Great War and the British People* (Basingstoke, 1986), ch. 4.

124. A. Offer, *The First World War: an Agrarian Interpretation* (Oxford, 1989), 81; Beveridge, *British Food Control*, 358.

125. Prothero minute, 1 Jan. 1917, MAF/39/12.

126. M. Olson, Jr, *The Economics of the Wartime Shortage: a History of British Food Supplies in the Napoleonic Wars and in World Wars I and II* (Durham, NC, 1963), 98.

127. Dewey, *British Agriculture*, 91ff., 201–2, 223, 242.

128. Beveridge, *British Food Control*, 354–8.

129. Report by Royal Commission on Wheat Supplies, 90, BEV IV; D. French, *The Strategy of the Lloyd George Coalition, 1916–1918* (Oxford, 1995), 80–81.

130. Rhondda memoranda, 10 Dec. 1917 (MAF/60/56), 31 Dec. 1917, and 21 Jan. 1918, MLN 163.

131. Beveridge, *British Food Control*, 92–3; Cabinet, 9 Apr. 1918, CAB/23/6.

132. Offer, *Agrarian Interpretation*, 370.

133. 'Food Requirements from North America' (n.d.), MAF/60/56.

134. Royal Commission on Wheat Supplies, 7–9, BEV IV; Dewey, *British Agriculture*, 225–6; Beveridge, *British Food Control*, table xxxi.

135. Beveridge, *British Food Control*, 91.

136. Imperial War Cabinet, 1 Oct. 1918, CAB/23/42.

137. French, *Strategy*, 88; Beveridge, *British Food Control*, 88.

138. Rhondda memorandum, 2 Jan. 1918 (MLN 163) and statement, 30 Jan. 1918 (CAB/1/26).

139. Beveridge, *British Food Control*, 139ff.; Long–New Zealand Governor, 10 Oct. 1918, MLN 163.

140. Barnett, *British Food Policy*, 142; Beveridge, *British Food Control*, 206–7.

141. J. Harris, 'Bureaucrats and Businessmen in British Food Control, 1916–19', in K. Burk (ed.), *War and the State: the Transformation of British Government, 1914–1919* (London, 1982), 143.

142. Beveridge, *British Food Control*, 231–5.

143. Barnett, *British Food Policy*, 213.

144. Ibid., 181–4; Clynes memorandum, 7 Aug. 1918, MLN 163.

145. Barnett, *British Food Policy*, 186–8; War Cabinet, 6 Sept. 1918, BEV XI.

146. Prothero memorandum, 2 May 1918, MLN 163; Cabinet, 23, 30 May 1918, CAB/23/6.

147. Clynes–Cabinet, 22 Aug. 1918, MAF/60/55; Barnett, *British Food Policy*, 188.

148. Ferguson, *Pity of War*, 160.

149. Munitions Ministry report, 12 Feb. 1919, p. 26, MUN/5/12; Lloyd George in Imperial War Cabinet, 11 June 1918, CAB/23/43; *HMM*, II, 101.

150. Churchill in Imperial War Cabinet, 12 July 1918, CAB/23/43; *HMM*, II, 98.

151. Broadberry and Howlett, 'United Kingdom in World War I', in Broadberry and Harrison (eds.), *Economics of World War I*, 212.

152. *HMM*, II, ii, 1–2, 112; Churchill–Cabinet, 9 Nov. 1917, MUN/4/404.
153. *HMM*, II, 56.
154. Ibid., 60–62, 68, 71, 73.
155. Ibid., 86–7, 58.
156. Munitions Ministry report, 12 Feb. 1919, pp. 23–4, MUN/5/12; *HMM*, II, vi, 15; *HMM*, II, v, 1–3.
157. Montagu in Imperial War Cabinet, 12 July 1918, CAB/23/43.
158. *HMM*, II, iv, 79–80. Flavelle–Borden, 15 May, 23 Oct. 1918, Vol. 84, Borden MSS, NAC; Lloyd George–Borden, 5 July 1917, Vol. 81, Borden MSS, NAC; Perley–Borden, 10 Aug. 1917, Vol. 81, Borden MSS, NAC; British/US/Canadian financial memorandum (1918), Vol. 95, Borden MSS, NAC.
159. R. J. Q. Adams, *Arms and the Wizard: Lloyd George and the Ministry of Munitions, 1915–1916* (London, 1978), 86; C. Wrigley, 'The Ministry of Munitions: an Innovatory Department', in Burk (ed.), *War and the State*, 34.
160. G. A. B. Dewar, *The Great Munition Feat, 1914–1918* (London, 1921), 60–64, 78–9, 113–16.
161. *HMM*, II, 97.
162. Munitions Ministry report, 12 Feb. 1919, p. 19, MUN/5/12.
163. Dewar, *Great Munition Feat*, 124; Churchill in Imperial War Cabinet, 12 July 1918, CAB/23/43.
164. *HMM*, II, 99–100.
165. Ibid. and Broadberry and Howlett, 'United Kingdom in World War I', in Broadberry and Harrison (eds.), *Economics of World War I*, 212.
166. *HMM*, II, 79.
167. Churchill in Imperial War Cabinet, 12 July 1918, CAB/23/43; Churchill–Lloyd George, 9 July 1918, LG F/8/2/25.
168. J. A. B. Hamilton, *Britain's Railways in World War I* (London, 1967), 29–30, 98, 190.
169. Cabinet, 1 May 1918, CAB/23/6.
170. Hamilton, *Britain's Railways*, 190; Churchill in Imperial War Cabinet, 12 July 1918, CAB/23/43.
171. J. D. Reid memorandum, 16 Jan. 1918, Vol. 102, Borden MSS, NAC.
172. *HMM*, VII, iv, 5.
173. Churchill in Imperial War Cabinet, 12 July 1918, CAB/23/43.
174. J. C. Carr and W. Taplin, *History of the British Steel Industry* (Oxford, 1962), 299.
175. *HMM*, VII, ii, 1.
176. Hunter–Churchill, 10 July; Hunter–Evans, 23 July 1917, MUN/4/404.
177. War Cabinet, 2 Nov. 1917, CAB/23/4.
178. Carr and Taplin, *British Steel Industry*, 306, 314.
179. War Cabinet, 5 Dec. 1917, CAB/23/4; *HMM*, II, 95–6.
180. Dewar, *Great Munition Feat*, 90–92.
181. C. Barnett, *The Audit of War: the Illusion and Reality of Britain as a Great Nation* (London and Basingstoke, 1986), 169.
182. Dewar, *Great Munition Feat*, ch. 9.
183. Barnett, *Audit of War*, 64, 82.
184. R. A. S. Redmayne, *The British Coal-Mining Industry during the War* (Oxford, 1923), 186–9, 216, 222.

185. Ibid., 146, 191, 194.

186. War Cabinet, 24 May 1918, CAB/23/6.

187. AMTC–Cabinet, 17 Aug. 1918, CAB/1/27/7.

188. Redmayne, *British Coal-Mining*, 190–91, 198.

189. J. Singleton, 'The Cotton Industry and the British War Effort, 1914–1918', *Economic History Review* (1994), 604, 616.

190. *HMM*, II, viii, 97.

191. Ibid., 96–7.

192. Broadberry and Harrison (eds.), *Economics of World War I*, 7, 171.

193. Ferguson, *Pity of War*, 337.

194. Tables in 10N146, SHA.

195. J. M. Laux, 'Gnôme et Rhône – an Aviation Engine Firm in the First World War', in P. Fridenson (ed.), *The French Home Front, 1914–1918* (Providence, RI/Oxford, 1992), 149.

196. R. B. Bruce, *A Fraternity of Arms: America and France in the Great War* (Lawrence, Kan., 2003), 100–106; cf. E. Greenhalgh, 'Errors and Omissions in Franco-British Co-operation over Munitions Production, 1914–18', *War in History* (2007), 216.

197. R. Porte, *La Mobilisation industrielle: 'premier front' de la Grande Guerre?* (Paris, 2005), 303.

198. F. Reboul, *Mobilisation industrielle. I. Des Fabrications de guerre en France de 1914 à 1918* (Paris, 1925), 18–39.

199. Joffre and Pétain to War Minister, 30 May 1916, 25 June 1917, 10N12, SHA.

200. Reboul, *Mobilisation industrielle*, I, 40–55; tables in 10N28, SHA; Loucheur, 7 Dec. 1917, C7499, AN.

201. 'Review of Allied Munitions Programmes', 1 May 1918, MUN/4/880; Reboul, *Mobilisation industrielle*, I, 68–70.

202. Ibid., 155; J. J. M. Mordacq, *Le Ministère Clemenceau: journal d'un témoin*, I (4 vols., Paris, 1930), 158.

203. Loucheur, 3 Aug. 1918, C7500, AN.

204. G. Hatry, *Renault: Usine de guerre, 1914–1918* (Paris, 1978), 64–5.

205. Painlevé letter, 8 Oct. 1917, 3N2, SHA; J. H. Morrow, Jr, *The Great War in the Air: Military Aviation from 1909 to 1921* (Washington DC/London, 1993), 294–5, 329.

206. G. Hardach, 'Industrial Mobilization in 1914–1918: Production, Planning, and Ideology', in Fridenson (ed.), *French Home Front*, 62.

207. A. Fontaine, *French Industry during the War* (New Haven, Conn., 1926), 4–5, 16, 89; P.-C. Hautcoeur, 'Was the Great War a Watershed? The Case of France', in Broadberry and Harrison (eds.), *Economics of World War I*, 171.

208. Porte, *Mobilisation industrielle*, 219.

209. P. Fridenson, *Histoire des Usines Renault. I: Naissance de la grande enterprise, 1898–1939* (Paris, 1972), 98, 107–9; S. D. Carls, *Louis Loucheur and the Shaping of Modern France, 1916–1931* (Baton Rouge, La/London, 1993), 10.

210. Morrow, *Great War in the Air*, 288, 293.

211. Carls, *Louis Loucheur*, 103.

212. Reboul, *Mobilisation*, I, 114ff.; Fontaine, *French Industry*, 150; H. F. A. Strachan, *The First World War. Vol. I: To Arms* (Oxford, 2001), 1056.

213. Fontaine, *French Industry*, 273–4, 108.

214. L. Petit, *Histoire des finances extérieures de la France pendant la guerre (1914–1919)* (Paris, 1929), 30.

215. 'Review of Allied Munitions Programmes', 1 May 1918, MUN/4/1368; Comité de guerre, 10 June 1918, 3N2, SHA.

216. Loucheur, 7 Dec. 1917, C7499, AN.

217. Loucheur, 3 Aug. 1918, C7500, AN; Baruch, *Public Years*, 72.

218. Fontaine, *French Industry*, 104–6.

219. (20 Aug. 1918), MUN/4/3065.

220. Loucheur, 3 Aug. 1918, C7500, AN; Carls, *Louis Loucheur*, 92–8.

221. G. Jèze and H. Truchy, *The War Finance of France* (New Haven, Conn., 1927), 193; Strachan, *Financing the First World War*, 87.

222. Jèze and Truchy, *War Finance*, 271–9, 246–52.

223. Ibid., 233–40; Mordacq, *Ministère Clemenceau*, I, 113; Horn, *Britain, France and Financing*, 84, 169–70.

224. Hautcoeur, 'Was the Great War a Watershed?', 182; Petit, *Finances extérieures*, 44–50.

225. R. F. Kuisel, *Capitalism and the State in Modern France: Renovation and Economic Management in the Twentieth Century* (Cambridge, 1981), 40–41.

226. Hautcoeur, 'Was the Great War a Watershed?', 191.

227. M. Augé-Laribé, *L'Agriculture pendant la Guerre* (Paris/New Haven, Conn., n.d.), 42, 50–59.

228. Ibid., 133–52; M. Augé-Laribé and P. Pinot, *Agriculture and Food Supply in France during the War* (New Haven, Conn., 1927), 253.

229. Long, 10 Oct. 1917, C7569, AN.

230. War Cabinet, 31 Oct. 1917, CAB/23/4; E. Clémentel, *La France et la politique interalliée* (Paris/New Haven, Conn., 1931), 170.

231. Augé-Laribé and Pinot, *Agriculture and Food Supply*, 179–86.

232. Petit, *Finances extérieures*, 21–4.

233. Tardieu, 8 Jan. 1918, F¹²7799, AN; Clemenceau–Tardieu, 1 Feb. 1918, 6N53, SHA.

234. Boret–Clemenceau, 21 Feb. 1918, Comité de guerre, 2 Mar. 1918, 3N2, SHA; Boret, 21 Mar. 1918, C7509, AN.

235. M. Peschaud, *Politique et fonctionnement des transports par chemin de fer pendant la guerre* (Paris, 1926), 8–9, 108.

236. Ibid., 130.

237. Pétain–Clemenceau, 4 Jan. 1918, Comité de guerre, 6 Feb. 1918, 3N2, SHA.

238. Peschaud, *Politique et fonctionnement*, 121–2, 125, 130.

239. Comité de guerre, 3N2, SHA; Commission des travaux publics, 13 Nov. 1918, C7641, AN; *AFGG*, XI, 357–9.

240. Broadberry and Harrison (eds.), *Economics of World War I*, 7, 10; Ferguson, *Pity of War*, 337.

241. V. Zamagni, *Dalla periferia al centro: la seconda rinascita economica dell'Italia (1861–1990)* (Bologna, 1993), 271.

242. Tables in 10N146, SHA; M. Isnenghi and G. Rochat, *La Grande Guerra 1914–1918* (Milan, 2004), 302–3.

243. A. Curami, 'L'Industria bellica italiana dopo Caporetto', in G. Berti and P. del Negra (eds.), *Al di qua e al di là del Piave: l'Ultimo Anno della Grande Guerra* (Milan, 2001), 557; cf. Zuppelli memorandum, 8 Aug. 1918, 59/1550, Nitti MSS, ACS.

244. Page–Allen, 4 June 1918, MUN/4/3065; 'Review of Allied Munitions Programmes', 1 May 1918, MUN/4/880.

245. Isnenghi and Rochat, *Grande Guerra*, 301; on aircraft, Perrone–Zuppelli, 13 June 1918, 17/37/7, Nitti MSS, ACS.

246. A. Serpieri, *La guerra e le classi rurali italiani* (Bari/New Haven, Conn., 1930), 68; F. Galassi and M. Harrison, 'Italy at War, 1915–1918', in Broadberry and Harrison (eds.), *Economics of World War I*, 285.

247. Forsyth, *Crisis of Liberal Italy*, 48.

248. Zamagni, *Dalla periferia al centro*, 291, 288; Isnenghi and Rochat, *Grande Guerra*, 304; R. Romeo, *Breve storia della grande industria in Italia 1861/1961* (Bologna, 1975), 116; Sebastiano Raimondo lecture on Ansaldo, 30–3 Oct. 1917, 17/39/2, Nitti MSS, ACS.

249. Zamagni, *Dalla periferia al centro*, 288.

250. Minute, 3 Sept. 1918, MUN/4/3065.

251. Zamagni, *Dalla periferia al centro*, 290.

252. 'Review of Allied Munitions Programmes', 1 May 1918, MUN/4/880.

253. Romeo, *Breve storia,* 116; coal exports table, 20 Aug. 1918, MUN/4/3065; Dallolio–Bianchi, 26 Mar. 1918, 57 1531, Orlando MSS, ACS.

254. Zamagni, *Dalla periferia al centro*, 29; Romeo, *Breve storia*, 118; Galassi and Harrison, 'Italy at War', 292; A. Monticone, *Nitti e la Grande Guerra (1914–1918)* (Milan, 1961), 170.

255. Galassi and Harrison, 'Italy at War', 192; Monticone, *Nitti*, 190, 239; Bianchi–Orlando, 29 Mar. 1918, Orlando–Diaz, 1 Apr. 1918, Director of Transport–Diaz, 4 Apr. 1918, 57 1531, Orlando MSS, ACS. On Genoa: undated memorandum, 18/41/2, Nitti MSS; de Cornè–Transport Minister, 16/33/1, Nitti MSS, ACS.

256. Serpieri, *Classi rurali*, 68, 95–7, 111; Isnenghi and Rochat, *Grande Guerra*, 305.

257. Isnenghi and Rochat, *Grande Guerra*, 305; Zamagni, *Dalla periferia al centro*, 278–80; Monticone, *Nitti*, 170.

258. War Cabinet, 14 Nov. 1917, CAB/23/4.

259. Draft message to Marine Minister, Dec. 1917, 54/1507, Nitti MSS, ACS.

260. Monticone, *Nitti*, 167–77; Orlando–Imperiali, n.d., but Jan. 1918, 54 1507, Orlando MSS, ACS.

261. Crespi–Tittoni, 6 Sept. 1918, 54 1507, Orlando MSS, ACS.

262. Strachan, *Financing the First World War*, 95; Zamagni, *Dalla periferia al centro*, 273; Galassi and Harrison, 'Italy at War', 297.

263. Nitti speech, 17 Feb. 1918, 18/44/1, Nitti MSS, ACS.

264. Forsyth, *Crisis of Liberal Italy*, 134; Zamagni, *Dalla periferia al centro*, 273.

265. Isnenghi and Rochat, *Grande Guerra*, 307.

266. Galassi and Harrison, 'Italy at War', 300; Zamagni, *Dalla periferia al centro*, 280.

267. Moniticone, *Nitti*, 301; Galassi and Harrison, 'Italy at War', 303.

268. Forsyth, *Crisis of Liberal Italy*, 66–8, 175–6.

269. Zamagni, *Dalla periferia al centro*, 276; Forsyth, *Crisis of Liberal Italy*, 178–86; 'Accordi alleati', 19/54/2, Nitti MSS, ACS.

270. N. Stone, *The Eastern Front 1914–1917* (London, 1975), chs. 7, 9.

271. Greenhalgh, 'Errors and Omissions', 212–14.

272. G. Danaïllow, *Les Effets de la guerre en Bulgarie* (Paris/New Haven, Conn., 1932),

12; L. Berov, 'The Bulgarian Economy during World War I', in B. K. Király and N. F. Dreisziger (eds.), *East Central European Society in World War I* (New York, 1985), 178.

273. Berov, 'Bulgarian Economy', 176; Danaïllow, *Effets de la guerre*, 395, 411–13.

274. Danaïllow, *Effets de la guerre*, 419; R. J. Crampton, *Bulgaria, 1878–1918: a History* (New York, 1983), 484; Berov, 'Bulgarian Economy', 178.

275. Crampton, *Bulgaria*, 479, 486, 491–500.

276. Danaïllow, *Effets de la guerre*, 400–404, 422, 544, 478.

277. R. C. Hall, '"The Enemy is behind Us": the Morale Crisis in the Bulgarian Army during the Summer of 1918', *War in History* (2004), 215; Crampton, *Bulgaria*, 506.

278. Crampton, *Bulgaria*, 457, 464–7, 501–2; Berov, 'Bulgarian Economy', 179.

279. Broadberry and Harrison (eds.), *Economics of World War I*, 10, 7, 120, 113.

280. A. E. Yalman, *Turkey in the World War* (New Haven, Conn./London, 1930), 117–18.

281. E. J. Erickson, *Ordered to Die: a History of the Ottoman Army in the First World War* (Westport, Conn./London, 2001), 16–17.

282. Strachan, *To Arms*, 690–91.

283. L. Schatkowski Schilchen, 'The Famine of 1915–1918 in Greater Syria', in J. P. Spagnolo (ed.), *Problems of the Middle East in Historical Perspective: Essays in Honour of Albert Hourani* (Reading, 1992), 243.

284. 'Turkish War Finance', 12 July 1918, CAB/1/27.

285. S. Pamuk, 'The Ottoman Economy in World War I', in Broadberry and Harrison (eds.), *Economics of World War I*, 127, 118; U. Trumpener, *Germany and the Ottoman Empire 1914–1918* (Princeton, NJ, 1968), 321.

286. Trumpener, *Germany and the Ottoman Empire*, 322, 282; Pamuk, 'Ottoman Economy', 228.

287. Pamuk, 'Ottoman Economy', 229; Trumpener, *Germany and the Ottoman Empire*, 282.

288. 'Turkish War Finance', 12 July 1918, CAB/1/27; Pamuk, 'Ottoman Economy', 129.

289. Pamuk, 'Ottoman Economy', 120, 124; Schatkowski Schilchen, 'Famine of 1915–1918', 229; E. Zürcher, 'Little Mehmet in the Desert: the Ottoman Soldier's Experience', in H. Cecil and P. H. Liddle (eds.), *Facing Armageddon: the First World War Experienced* (London, 1996), 238.

290. Broadberry and Harrison (eds.), *Economics of World War I*, 10; R. Riedl, *Die Industrie Österreichs während des Krieges* (Vienna/New Haven, Conn., 1932), 269.

291. M.-S. Schulze, 'Austria-Hungary's Economy in World War I', in Broadberry and Harrison (eds.), *Economics of World War I*, 84, 107.

292. Ibid., 103; A. Popovics, *Das Geldwesen im Kriege* (Vienna/New Haven, Conn., 1925), 108ff., 134.

293. G. W. Shanafelt, *The Secret Enemy: Austria-Hungary and the German Alliance, 1914–1918* (New York, 1985), 197; Strachan, *Financing the First World War*, 168.

294. Schulze, 'Austria-Hungary's Economy', 103.

295. Ibid., 98–9.

296. Ibid., 99; Strachan, *Financing the First World War*, 130.

297. Sadler Report, 25 May 1918, BDFA, Pt. II, H, XII, 185.

298. G. Gratz and R. Schüller, *Der wirtschaftliche Zusammenbruch Österreich-Ungarns: die Tragödie der Erschöpfung* (Vienna/New Haven, Conn., 1930), 173, 181; Schulze, 'Austria-Hungary's Economy', 100.

299. Gratz and Schüller, *Zusammenbruch*, 110–13; R. Wegs, *Die österreichische Kriegswirtschaft, 1914–1918* (Vienna, 1979), 120.

300. Wegs, *Österreichische Kriegswirtschaft*, 122–3; M. Komjáthy (ed.), *Protokolle des Gemeinsamen Ministerrates der österreichischen-ungarischen Monarchie (1914–1918)* (Budapest, 1966), 458ff.

301. Morrow, *Great War in the Air*, 261, 332; Gratz and Schüller, *Zusammenbruch*, 113–22; Schulze, 'Austria-Hungary's Economy', 83.

302. H. Mejzlik, *Die Eisenbewirtschaftung im Ersten Weltkrieg: die Planwirtschaft des k.u.k. Kriegsministeriums* (Vienna, 1977), 628.

303. Strachan, *To Arms*, 1045; Gratz and Schüller, *Zusammenbruch*, 106–8.

304. Riedl, *Industrie Österreichs*, 274–7, 282–3; Mejzlik, *Eisenbewirtschaftung*, 629.

305. Gratz and Schüller, *Zusammenbruch*, 91; Schulze, 'Austria-Hungary's Economy', 88.

306. Meeting of military officials, 30 Sept. 1918, ad 5515 KMPräs 1918, KAW.

307. E. Homann-Herimberg, *Die Kohlenversorgung in Österreich während des Krieges* (Vienna/New Haven, Conn., 1925), 44–5, 7, 10; Gratz and Schüller, *Zusammenbruch*, 96.

308. Gratz and Schüller, *Zusammenbruch*, 96–7; Homann-Herimberg, *Kohlenversorgung*, 67ff., 104, 96–7.

309. B. Enderes et al., *Verkehrswesen im Kriege* (Vienna/New Haven, Conn., 1931), 16, 24, 96.

310. Zentraltransportleitung–War Ministry, 8 Aug. 1917, ZTL Nr. 47348/1917, KAW.

311. Sadler report, 25 Oct. 1918, *BDFA*, Pt II, H, XII, 387; Homann-Herimberg, *Kohlenversorgung*, 104, 106; Enderes et al., *Verkehrswesen im Kriege*, 28.

312. Wegs, *Österreichische Kriegswirtschaft*, 88.

313. Meeting of military officials, 11 Sept. 1918, KMPräs 1918, ad 5515, KAW.

314. Gratz and Schüller, *Zusammenbruch*, 123–36, 141.

315. Ibid., 39–50.

316. H. Loewenfeld-Russ, *Die Regelung der Volks-Ernährung im Kriege* (Vienna/New Haven, Conn., 1926), 85–7, 61; Schulze, 'Austria-Hungary's Economy', 96.

317. Gratz and Schüller, *Zusammenbruch*, 70–72; Loewenfeld-Russ, *Volks-Ernährung*, 292–306; Komjáthy (ed.), *Protokolle des Gemeinsamen Ministerrates*, 472, 516.

318. Komjáthy (ed.), *Protokolle des Gemeinsamen Ministerrates*, 610; Gratz and Schüller, *Zusammenbruch*, 77.

319. C. F. Wargelin, 'A High Price for Bread: the First Treaty of Brest-Litovsk and the Break-Up of Austria-Hungary, 1917–1918', *International History Review* (1997), 784; Loewenfeld-Russ, *Volks-Ernährung*, 155, 402.

320. Gratz and Schüller, *Zusammenbruch*, 90; Sadler reports, *BDFA*, Pt II, H, XII, 56, 305, 362–3.

321. Sadler reports, *BDFA*, Pt II, H, XII, 292, 343; M. Healey, *Vienna and the Fall of the Habsburg Empire: Total War and Everyday Life in World War I* (Cambridge, 2004), 40–42.

322. Z. Jindra, 'Der wirtschaftliche Zerfall Österreich-Ungarns (nach den Berichten der reichsdeutschen Bevollmächtigen in Wien 1916–1918)', in A. Teichova and H. Matis (eds.), *Österreich und die Tschechoslowakei 1918–1938 – die wirtschaftliche Neuordnung in Zentraleuropa in der Zwischenkriegszeit* (Vienna/Cologne/Weimar, 1996), 43.

323. Wargelin, 'High Price for Bread', 782–8.

324. Gratz and Schuller, *Zusammenbruch*, 48, 89.

325. Broadberry and Harrison (eds.), *Economics of World War I*, 7, 10.

326. Ferguson, *Pity of War*, 323.

327. Broadberry and Harrison (eds.), *Economics of World War I*, 44.

328. Ibid., 50; Ferguson, *Pity of War*, 253.

329. Ferguson, *Pity of War*, 254.

330. Strachan, *Financing the First World War*, 166.

331. Max Müller reports on Germany, *BDFA*, Pt II, H, XII, 65, 241.

332. K. Roesler, *Die Finanzpolitik des deutschen Reiches im Ersten Weltkrieg* (Berlin, 1967), 229, 210.

333. A. Ritschl, 'The Pity of Peace: Germany's Economy at War, 1914–1918 and Beyond', in Broadberry and Harrison (eds.), *Economics of World War I*, 60.

334. Balderston, 'War Finance', 236.

335. Max Müller report, *BDFA*, Pt II, H, XII, 207.

336. Roesler, *Finanzpolitik*, 129.

337. C. L. Holtferich, *The German Inflation, 1914–1923: Causes and Effects in International Perspective* (transl., London/New York, 1986), 110.

338. Roesler, *Finanzpolitik*, 206, 199.

339. G. D. Feldman, *The Great Disorder: Politics, Economy, and Society in the German Inflation, 1914–1924* (New York/Oxford, 1997), 42–3.

340. V. R. Berghahn, *Modern Germany: Society, Economics, and Politics in the Twentieth Century* (Cambridge, 1982), 48.

341. Holtferich, *German Inflation*, 117.

342. Ritschl, 'Pity of Peace', 63–4; Strachan, *Financing the First World War*, 167.

343. Roesler, *Finanzpolitik*, 132, 146; Ritschl, 'Pity of Peace', 64.

344. Holtferich, *German Inflation*, 12; Feldman, *Great Disorder*, 49–50.

345. Ferguson, *Pity of War*, 260.

346. 'Deutsche Rüstung 1918', W-10/50421, BA-MA.

347. H. Rohde, 'Faktoren der deutschen Logistik im Ersten Weltkrieg', in G. Canini (ed.), *Les Fronts invisibles: nourrir – fournir – soigner* (Nancy, 1984), 12–13; F. Klein et al., *Deutschland im Ersten Weltkrieg* (Berlin, 1968–9), 301.

348. I.-D. Salavrakos, 'German Economic-Industrial Mobilisation in World War I (1914–1918)', in G. T. Papanikos (ed.), *Antiquity and Modernity: a Celebration of European History and Heritage in the Olympic Year 2004* (Athens, 2004), 171; Erickson, *Ordered to Die*, 233.

349. N. Ferguson, *Paper and Iron: Hamburg Business and German Politics in the Era of Inflation, 1897–1927* (Cambridge, 1995), 103; G. D. Feldman, *Army, Industry, and Labour in Germany, 1914–1918* (Princeton, NJ, 1966), 45–51; Strachan, *To Arms*, 1015–23.

350. Strachan, *To Arms*, 1037.

351. Feldman, *Army, Industry, and Labour*, 152; Strachan, *To Arms*, 1027–8.

352. Report on Hindenburg Programme, W-10/50397, BA-MA.

353. Hindenburg–Wild von Hohenborn, 31 Aug., 14 Sept. 1916, E. Ludendorff (ed.), *The General Staff and Its Problems* (2 vols., London, 1920), 74–6, 81–3.

354. Feldman, *Army, Industry, and Labour*, 301–2.

355. Ibid., 269; Hindenburg memorandum, 10 Sept. 1917, W-10/50397, BA-MA.

356. Feldman, *Army, Industry, and Labour*, 272; Klein et al., *Deutschland*, 311; Hindenburg memorandum, 18 March 1918, W-10/50397, BA-MA.

357. Klein et al., *Deutschland*, 310.

358. Morrow, *Great War in the Air*, 222, 227–8, 305–8.

359. B. R. Mitchell (ed.), *International Historical Statistics: Europe, 1750–1993* (4th edn, London/Basingstoke, 1998), 467.

360. O. Goebel, *Deutsche Rohstoffwirtschaft im Weltkrieg einschliesslich des Hindenburg-Programs* (Stuttgart/Berlin/Leipzig/New Haven, Conn., 1930), 34–7, 45–6; Offer, *Agrarian Interpretation*, 72.

361. Goebel, *Deutsche Rohstoffwirtschaft*, 71.

362. A. Sarter, *Die deutschen Eisenbahnen im Kriege* (Stuttgart, 1930), 102–5, 113, 128, 165, 176, 184, 169, 174.

363. Goebel, *Deutsche Rohstoffwirtschaft*, 35.

364. Klein et al., *Deutschland*, 308.

365. Feldman, *Army, Industry, and Labour*, 260; Goebel, *Deutsche Rohstoffwirtschaft*, 35.

366. Hildebrand typescript, 'Rohstoffversorgung', W-10/50493, BA-MA.

367. Memorandum on 1917/18 economic situation, W-10/50400, BA-MA; Hindenburg memorandum, 18 Mar. 1918, W-10/50397, BA-MA.

368. Reports in MUN/4/3643.

369. Max Müller reports, *BDFA*, Pt II, H, XII, 8, 12, 11, 7, 17, 25.

370. A. C. Bell, *A History of the Blockade of Germany and of the Countries Associated with Her in the Great War, Austria-Hungary, Bulgaria, and Turkey* (London, 1937; published 1961), 663–6.

371. Memorandum on 1917/18 economic situation, W-10/50400, BA-MA.

372. Goebel, *Deutsche Rohstoffwirtschaft*, 188.

373. Hildebrand typescript, 'Rohstoffversorgung', W-10/50493, BA-MA; Hildebrand typescript, 'Rohstofflage', W-10/50494, BA-MA.

374. Typescript, 'Grundlagen der Kriegführung', W-10/50401, BA-MA; Hildebrand typescript, 'Rohstoffversorgung', W-10/50493, BA-MA.

375. Cf. Chapter 3 above.

376. M. Frey, 'Bullying the Neutrals: the Case of the Netherlands', in R. Chickering and S. Förster (eds.), *Great War, Total War: Combat and Mobilization on the Western Front, 1914–1918* (Cambridge, 2000), 225–6.

377. Bell, *History of the Blockade*, 606–9, 618–24.

378. Klein et al., *Deutschland*, III, 318; Bell, *History of the Blockade*, 664–5.

379. Max Müller reports, *BDFA*, Pt II, H, XII, 235, 19, 93, 128–30, 162; report on public morale, 3 Mar. 1918, PH2/62, BA-MA; Mehrens, 'Volksernährung', W-10/50439, BA-MA. Cf. Chapter 1 above.

380. Klein et al., *Deutschland*, III, 316.

381. Ritschl, 'Pity of Peace', 46; Klein et al., *Deutschland*, 316; J. Lee, 'Administrators and Agriculture: Aspects of German Agricultural Policy in the First World War', in J. M. Winter (ed.), *War and Economic Development* (Cambridge, 1975), 235.

382. F. Aeroboe, *Der Einfluß des Krieges auf die landwirtschaftliche Produktion in Deutschland* (Stuttgart/Berlin/Leipzig/New Haven, Conn., 1927), 25.

383. Offer, *Agrarian Interpretation*, 62; A. Roerkohl, *Hungerblockade und Heimatfront:*

die kommunale Lebensmittelversorgung in Westfalen während des Ersten Weltkrieges (Stuttgart, 1991), 28.

384. A. Huegel, *Kriegsernährungswirtschaft Deutschlands während des Ersten und Zweiten Weltkriegs im Vergleich* (Konstanz, 2003), 100, 195; Aeroboe, *Einfluß des Krieges*, 33.

385. Aeroboe, *Einfluß des Krieges*, 35-6.

386. Report on public opinion, 3 Sept. 1918, MKr/1285/3, KAM.

387. Aeroboe, *Einfluß des Krieges*, 22; Roerkohl, *Hungerblockade und Heimatfront*, 18; Offer, *Agrarian Interpretation*, 63, 39.

388. Lee, 'Administrators and Agriculture', 232-3; Aeroboe, *Einfluß des Krieges*, 39-44, 86.

389. A. Skalweit, *Die deutsche Kriegsernährungswirtschaft* (Stuttgart/Berlin/Leipzig/New Haven, Conn., 1927), 1-2.

390. Feldman, *Army, Industry, and Labour*, 100, 162.

391. Aeroboe, *Einfluß des Krieges*, 84-8; R. G. Moeller, 'Dimensions of Social Conflict in the Great War: the View from the German Countryside', *Central European History* (1981), 148.

392. Feldman, *Army, Industry, and Labour*, 104-5.

393. R. Chickering, *Imperial Germany and the Great War, 1914-1918* (Cambridge, 1998), 44.

394. Roerkohl, *Hungerblockade und Heimatfront*, 94, 57-63.

395. Offer, *Agrarian Interpretation*, 25; P. Eltzbacher (ed.), *Germany's Food: Can It Last? Germany's Food and England's Plan to Starve Her Out: a Study by German Experts* (transl., London, 1915).

396. Huegel, *Kriegsernährungswirtschaft Deutschlands*, 125; Chickering, *Imperial Germany*, 117; Roerkohl, *Hungerblockade und Heimatfront*, 29.

397. Reports on public morale, 3 Jan., 3 Feb. 1917, PH2/62, BA-MA; B. Davis, *Home Fires Burning: Food, Politics and Everyday Life in World War One Berlin* (Chapel Hill, NC, 2000), 132-5, 180-81; Huegel, *Kriegsernährungswirtschaft Deutschlands*, 180.

398. Roerkohl, *Hungerblockade und Heimatfront*, 134, 291; Moeller, 'Dimensions of Social Conflict', 157.

399. Reports on public morale, 3 Aug. 1918, 15 July 1916, 3 Jan. 1917, PH2/62, BA-MA.

400. Roerkohl, *Hungerblockade und Heimatfront*, 150; Davis, *Home Fires Burning*, 159ff.

401. Huegel, *Kriegsernährungswirtschaft Deutschlands*, 130; Klein et al., *Deutschland*, 322; report on public morale, 3 Sept. 1918, MKr/1285/3, KAM.

402. Klein et al., *Deutschland*, 321.

403. Lee, 'Administrators and Agriculture', in Winter (ed.), *War and Economic Development*, 235.

404. Klein et al., *Deutschland*, 325; Offer, *Agrarian Interpretation*, 34-8.

405. Klein et al., *Deutschland*, 324.

406. E. H. Tobin, 'War and the Working Class: the Case of Düsseldorf, 1914-1918', *Central European History* (1985), 281.

407. Max Müller reports, *BDFA*, Pt II, H, XII, 200, 217.

408. Report on food situation, Feb. 1918, MKr/1283/0, KAM.

409. Max Müller reports, *BDFA*, Pt II, H, XII, 234, 284; reports on public morale, 3 Aug. 1918, PH2/62, BA-MA; and 3 Sept., 3 Oct. 1918, MKr/1285/3, KAM.

410. Max Müller reports, *BDFA*, Pt II, H, XII, 361, 378.

7. THE HOME FRONTS: GENDER, CLASS, AND NATION

1. D. Lloyd George, *War Memoirs*, II (2 vols., London, 1938), 1141.
2. V. Brittain, *Testament of Youth: an Autobiographical Study of the Years 1900–1925* (London, 1978), 372.
3. S. Pedersen, 'Gender, Welfare and Citizenship in Britain during the Great War', *American Historical Review* (1990), 989.
4. S. R. Grayzel, *Women and the First World War* (Harlow, 2002), 39.
5. K. Robert, 'Gender, Class, and Patriotism: Women's Paramilitary Units in First World War Britain', *International History Review* (1997), 53.
6. J. F. McMillan, *Housewife or Harlot? The Place of Women in French Society, 1870–1940* (Brighton, 1981), 132.
7. A. Marwick, *Women at War, 1914–1918* (London, 1977), 156.
8. Barclay–Balfour, 4 Oct. 1918, FO/371/3428; C. Brown, *Rosie's Mom: Forgotten Women Workers of the First World War* (Boston, Mass., 2002), 124.
9. N. Gullace, 'Sexual Violence and Family Honour: British Propaganda and International Law during the First World War', *American Historical Review* (1997), 723–5; R. Harris, 'The "Child of the Barbarian": Rape, Race, and Nationalism in France during the First World War', *Past & Present* (1993), 179ff.; Grayzel, *Women*, 10–15.
10. Pedersen, 'Gender, Welfare, and Citizenship', 984; U. Daniel, *The War from Within: German Working-Class Women in the First World War* (Oxford/New York, 1997), 178.
11. Grayzel, *Women*, 25.
12. Daniel, *War from Within*, 111.
13. U. Daniel, 'Women's Work in Industry and Family: Germany, 1914–1918', in J. M. Wall and J. M. Winter (eds.), *The Upheaval of War: Family, Work, and Welfare in Europe, 1914–1918* (Cambridge, 1988), 267; U. Frevert, *Women in German History: From Bourgeois Emancipation to Sexual Liberation* (transl., Oxford/Hamburg/New York, 1992), 156; Grayzel, *Women*, 28, 32.
14. I. F. W. Beckett, *The Great War, 1914–1918* (Harlow, 2001), 326.
15. Ibid., 320.
16. S. Augeneder, *Arbeiterinnen im Ersten Weltkrieg: Lebens- und Arbeitsbedingungen proletarischer Frauen in Österreich* (Vienna, 1987), 5, 31–3, 57, 59–60, 82–5, 88.
17. *ÖULK*, VII, 35–6, 43.
18. A. Seidel, *Frauenarbeit im Ersten Weltkrieg als Problem der staatlichen Sozialpolitik: dargestellt am Beispiel Bayerns* (Frankfurt-am-Main, 1979), 40.
19. R. Bessel, '"Eine nicht allzu große Beunruhigung des Arbeitsmarktes": Frauenarbeit und Demobilmachung in Deutschland nach dem Ersten Weltkrieg', *Geschichte und Gesellschaft* (1983), 214–15.
20. U. von Gersdorff, *Frauen im Kriegsdienst, 1914–1945* (Stuttgart, 1969), 218–19, 26.
21. Graphs of Bavarian workforce, 1 Apr. 1918, MKr/1732/6, KAM.
22. Gersdorff, *Frauen*, 219.
23. Ibid., 20–21.
24. Ibid., 24–5.
25. Feldman, *Army, Industry, and Labour*, 302.

26. 'Die Ersatzlage im Jahre 1918', 17–18, W-10/51834, BA-MA.

27. Ibid., 30–31.

28. Frevert, *Women in German History*, 158.

29. Daniel, *War from Within*, 52–3, 40.

30. Frevert, *Women in German History*, 157; Daniel, *War from Within*, 62, 48, 86.

31. M. W. Greenwald, *Women, War, and Work: the Impact of World War I on Women Workers in the United States* (Westport, Conn./London, 1980), 5.

32. Beckett, *Great War*, 331.

33. Greenwald, *Women, War, and Work*, 21–6.

34. Brown, *Rosie's Mom*, 161, 153, 117, 142, 152.

35. Beckett, *Great War*, 330–31; L. Tomassini, 'Industrial Mobilization and the Labour Market in Italy during the First World War', *Social History* (1991), 21.

36. A. Camarda and S. Peli, *L'altro esercito: la classe operaia durante la Prima guerra mondiale* (Milan, 1980), 22–35.

37. J.-L. Robert, 'Women and Work in France during the First World War', in Wall and Winter (eds.), *Upheaval of War*, 253.

38. McMillan, *Housewife or Harlot?*, 135.

39. L. L. Downs, *Manufacturing Inequality: Gender Division in the French and British Metalworking Industries, 1914–1939* (Ithaca, NY/London, 1995), 27, 40, 188–9.

40. McMillan, *Housewife or Harlot?*, 132.

41. Robert, 'Women and Work', 254–6.

42. J. M. Winter and J.-L. Robert (eds.), *Capital Cities at War: London, Paris, Berlin, 1914–1919*, I (2 vols., Cambridge, 1997, 2007), 184–5; Downs, *Manufacturing Inequality*, 24, 74.

43. Downs, *Manufacturing Inequality*, 50, 52.

44. Churchill, 'The Munitions Miracle', 25 Apr. 1918, MUN/VII/1, WWS.

45. Winter and Robert (eds.), *Capital Cities*, I, 187–8; Marwick, *Women at War*, 51.

46. D. Thom, *Nice Girls and Rude Girls: Women Workers in World War I* (London/New York, 2000), 34.

47. Munitions Ministry reports on controlled and government establishments, January 1918, MUN/V/38, MUN/V/43, WWS.

48. Marwick, *Women at War*, 73–4; Report of Committee on Women in Industry, 1919, p. 80, LAB/5/3.

49. H. A. Clegg, *A History of British Trade Unions since 1889. Vol. II. 1911–1933*, (Oxford, 1985), 193.

50. Downs, *Manufacturing Inequality*, 20.

51. S. Pedersen, *Family, Dependence, and the Origins of the Welfare State: Britain and France, 1914–1945* (Cambridge, 1993), 83–4; Downs, *Manufacturing Inequality*, 32–3.

52. Marwick, *Women at War*, 56; Committee on Women in Industry, 1 Oct. 1918, EMP/70/1-/153, WWS.

53. Thom, *Nice Girls*, 55.

54. 'Dilution of Labour Bulletin', Dec. 1916, MUN/VI/13, IWM.

55. Ibid.

56. Committee on Women in Industry, 1 Oct. 1918, EMP/70/1-/153, WWS.

57. Clegg, *British Trade Unions*, II, 135; G. Braybon, *Women Workers in the First World War: the British Experience* (London, 1981), 229–30.

58. 'Dilution of Labour Bulletin', Dec. 1916, MUN/VI/13, IWM.

59. Downs, *Manufacturing Inequality*, 37; G. R. Rubin, *War, Law, and Labour: the Munitions Acts, State Regulation, and the Unions, 1915–1921* (Oxford, 1987), 238.

60. Thom, *Nice Girls*, 58.

61. Clegg, *British Trade Unions*, II, 139.

62. S. Pyecraft, 'British Working Women and the First World War', *The Historian* (1994), 704; Downs, *Manufacturing Inequality*, 91.

63. Downs, *Manufacturing Inequality*, 76.

64. Report of Committee on Women in Industry, 1919, p. 104, LAB/5/3.

65. Texts of the 5 and 8 Jan. speeches in J. B. Scott (ed.), *Official Statements of War Aims and Peace Proposals, December 1916–November 1918* (Washington DC, 1921), 225–33, 246–54.

66. D. M. Kennedy, *Over Here: the First World War and American Society* (New York/ Oxford, 1980), 354; K. Schwabe, *Woodrow Wilson, Revolutionary Germany, and Peacemaking, 1918–1919: Missionary Diplomacy and the Realities of Power* (Chapel Hill, NC/London, 1985), 12–15.

67. A. J. Mayer, *Political Origins of the New Diplomacy, 1917–1918* (New Haven, Conn., 1959), 329–67; C. M. Seymour (ed.), *The Intimate Papers of Colonel House*, III (4 vols., London, 1926–8), ch. 9.

68. V. H. Rothwell, *British War Aims and Peace Diplomacy, 1914–1918* (Oxford, 1971), 145–3; Lloyd George, *War Memoirs*, II, 1490–93.

69. Schwabe, *Woodrow Wilson*, 18; for the Four Principles, Scott (ed.), *Official Statements of War Aims*, 265–71.

70. Texts of the speeches in Scott, (ed.), *Official Statements of War Aims*, 246–54, 265–71.

71. J. D. Shand, 'Doves among the Eagles: German Pacifists and Their Government during World War I', *Journal of Contemporary History* (1975), 105.

72. Kennedy, *Over Here*, 252.

73. Ibid., 26.

74. Ibid., 73, 88, 265–6, 269n.

75. J. W. Chambers, *To Raise an Army: the Draft Comes to Modern America* (NewYork/ London, 1987), 194–5.

76. Barclay–Balfour, 22 Oct. 1918, FO/371/3431.

77. F. C. Luebke, *Bonds of Loyalty: German-Americans and World War I* (DeKalb, Ill., 1974), 278–9.

78. Kennedy, *Over Here*, 255.

79. Barclay–Balfour, 4 Dec. 1918, FO/371/3429; Reading–Balfour, FO/371/3431.

80. S. Larson, *Labor and Foreign Policy: Gompers, the AFL, and the First World War, 1914–1918* (Cranbury, NJ/London, 1975), 43.

81. S. H. Ross, *Propaganda for War: How the United States was Conditioned to Fight the Great War of 1914–1918* (Jefferson, NC/London, 1996), 225.

82. J. R. Mock and C. Larson, *Words That Won the War: the Story of the Committee on Public Information, 1917–1919* (Princeton, NJ, 1939), 71, 187–210.

83. Ibid., 115.

84. Ibid., 125.

85. Ibid.; cf. *Complete Report of the Committee on Public Information, 1917: 1918: 1919* (Washington DC, 1920), RG63/1, NARA.

86. Kennedy, *Over Here*, 354.
87. Cecil–Rodd, Balfour–Rodd, 9, 16 Oct. 1918, FO/371/3229.
88. L. Ambrosoli, *Né aderire, né sabotare, 1915–1918* (Milan, 1961).
89. C. Seton-Watson, *Italy from Liberalism to Fascism, 1870–1925* (London, 1967), 483; Intelligence Bureau report, 4 Jan. 1918, FO/371/3229.
90. Rodd–Balfour, 20 Jan. 1918, ibid.
91. P. Melograni, *Storia politica della Grande Guerra, 1915–1918* (Bari, 1969), 536–7; Derby–Balfour, 11 Oct. 1918, FO/371/3215.
92. Tomassini, 'Industrial Mobilization', 77.
93. *Carabinieri* reports, 17/35/1, Nitti MSS, ACS; 'Promemoria', 8 Feb. 1918, 17/37/3, Nitti MSS, ACS.
94. G. Procacci, 'A "Latecomer" in War: the Case of Italy', in F. Coetzee and M. Shevin-Coetzee (eds.), *Authority, Identity, and the Social History of the Great War* (Providence, RI/Oxford, 1995), 22.
95. J.-L. Robert, *Les Ouvriers, la patrie, et la révolution: Paris 1914–1919* (Paris, 1995), 160.
96. L.-J. Malvy, *Mon crime* (Paris, 1921), 136ff.; monthly EMA bulletins on public morale, 6N147, SHA.
97. L. V. Smith, S. Audoin-Rouzeau, and A. Becker, *France and the Great War, 1914–1918* (Cambridge, 2003), 140–43.
98. *JO*, 8 Mar. 1918, 856.
99. Political Intelligence Department memorandum, 16 May 1918; Derby–Balfour, 8 Aug. 1918, FO/371/3213.
100. J. Horne, *Labour at War: France and Britain, 1914–1918* (Oxford, 1991), 57; Malvy, *Mon crime*, 92ff.; Derby–Balfour, 8 Aug. 1918, FO/371/3213.
101. B. Millman, *Managing Domestic Dissent in First World War Britain* (London/Portland, Ore., 2000), 285; A. Kriegel, *Aux Origines du communisme français, 1914–1920: contribution à l'histoire du mouvement ouvrier français* (Paris/The Hague, 1964), 193–203.
102. *JO*, 20 Nov. 1917, 2973.
103. *JO*, 11 Jan. 1918, 39–44.
104. P. Fridenson, 'The Impact of the First World War on French Workers', in Wall and Winter (eds.), *Upheaval of War*, 243.
105. Comité de guerre, e.g. 3 Jan., 9 Mar., 4 May, 27 May, 15 July, 13, 16 Sept. 1918, 3N2, SHA.
106. Robert, *Les Ouvriers*, 181–4, 13, 204.
107. Ibid., 220–30.
108. J.-J. Becker, *The Great War and the French People* (Leamington Spa/Heidelberg/Dover, NH, 1985), 289–94.
109. Graham telegram, 15, 16 May; Derby–Balfour, 19 May 1918, FO/371/3218.
110. Robert, *Les Ouvriers*, 269–78.
111. Ibid., 237–41; Grahame–Balfour, 19 July 1918, FO/371/3214.
112. Derby–Balfour, 30 July, 11, 15 Oct.; Political Intelligence Department memorandum, 17 Oct. 1918, FO/371/3215.
113. F. Cochet, 'Vom Zweifel am Erfolg zum Ende der Schicksalsprüfung – das Jahr 1918 im französischen Hinterland', in J. Duppler and G. P. Groß (eds.), *Kriegsende 1918: Ereignis, Wirkung, Nachwirkung* (Munich, 1994), 290–95; Becker, *Great War and the French People*, 302–16; monthly morale surveys, 6N147, SHA.

114. J. Horne, 'Remobilizing for "Total War": France and Britain, 1917–1918', in J. Horne (ed.), *State, Society, and Mobilization in Europe during the First World War* (Cambridge, 1997), 199–210.

115. Clegg, *British Trade Unions*, II, 43; A. Reid, 'The Impact of the First World War on British Workers', in Wall and Winter (eds.), *Upheaval of War*, 227.

116. Lloyd George, *War Memoirs*, II, 1141.

117. Milner in War Cabinet, 24 May 1918, CAB/23/6; War Priorities Committee, 6 Sept. 1918, CAB/40/3.

118. Reading–Balfour, 11 July 1918, FO/371/3431.

119. Lloyd George, *War Memoirs*, II, 1146.

120. M. Swartz, *The Union of Democratic Control in British Politics during the First World War* (Oxford, 1971), 221.

121. H. Hanak, 'The Union of Democratic Control during the First World War', *Bulletin of the Institute of Historical Research* (1963), 178.

122. B. Millman, *Managing Domestic Dissent*, 29.

123. Swartz, *Union of Democratic Control*, ch. 8.

124. Ibid., 167–9; C. Wrigley, *Arthur Henderson* (Cardiff, 1990), 122–3.

125. Clegg, *British Trade Unions*, II, 168–76.

126. A. Gregory, *The Last Great War: British Society and the First World War* (Cambridge, 2008), 204.

127. Troup circular, 29 Oct. 1917; Chief Constable, Nottingham–Dixon, 28 Mar. 1918, HO/144/1484/349684.

128. Millman, *Managing Domestic Dissent*, 181–92, 254–6.

129. Ibid., ch. 9; Horne, 'Remobilizing for "Total War"', 199–210. Cf. the important Ph.D. thesis by Dr David Monger, 'The National War Aims Committee and British Patriotism during the First World War', Ph.D. dissertation, Kings College, London, 2010.

130. NWAC minutes, 10 Oct. 1917, T/102/16.

131. Meetings Department, 25 Sept. 1917; G. Wallace report, 8 Dec. 1917, T/102/16.

132. Lloyd George, *War Memoirs*, II, 1593–5.

133. List of meetings in T/102/18; reports in T/102/16; Millman, *Managing Domestic Dissent*, 234, 240.

134. C. Wrigley, *David Lloyd George and the British Labour Movement: Peace and War* (Hassocks/New York, 1976), 224–5.

135. Committee of Privy Council, 11 July 1918, Vol. 100, Borden MSS, NAC.

136. Clegg, *British Trade Unions*, II, 194–5.

137. War Priorities Committee, 21 June 1918, CAB/40/3.

138. War Cabinet, 28 June 1918, CAB/23/6.

139. Wrigley, *David Lloyd George*, 224; Clegg, *British Trade Unions*, II, 191.

140. Memoranda on police situation from Sept. 1918 to June 1919 and on police strike, 1918, HO/144/3469, Pts I, II.

141. Sept. 1918 railway strike file, HO/45/10884/346578; Millman, *Managing Domestic Dissent*, 262–3.

142. R. McKibbin, *The Evolution of the Labour Party, 1910–1924* (London, 1974), ch. 5.

143. Reports by Ottokar Czernin, 3 Feb., 26 May, 30 June 1918, Bulgarien Berichte, 1918, HHStA.

144. H. Hautmann, 'Vienna: a City in the Years of Radical Change, 1917–20', in

C. Wrigley (ed.), *Challenges of Labour: Central and Western Europe, 1917-1920* (London/New York, 1993), 88.

145. R. F. Hopwood, 'Czernin and the Fall of Bethmann Hollweg', *Canadian Journal of History* (1967), 49-61.

146. J. Galántai, *Hungary in the First World War* (Budapest, 1989), 294-5.

147. S. Miller, *Burgfrieden und Klassenkampf: die deutsche Sozialdemokratie im Ersten Weltkrieg* (Düsseldorf, 1974), 373.

148. Hautmann, 'Vienna', 93-4; C. F. Wargelin, 'A High Price for Bread: the First Treaty of Brest-Litovsk and the Break-up of Austria-Hungary, 1917-1918', *International History Review* (1997), 777-85; R. Neck (ed.), *Arbeiterschaft und Staat im Ersten Weltkrieg, 1914-1918*, II (2 vols., Vienna, 1964), docs. 346-400.

149. Neck (ed.), *Arbeiterschaft und Staat*, II, docs. 588-621, 624, 627, 688; Hautmann, 'Vienna', 95.

150. A. J. Ryder, *The German Revolution of 1918: a Study of German Socialism in War and Revolt* (Cambridge, 1967), 24; K. Schönhoven (ed.), *Die Gewerkschaften im Weltkrieg und Revolution 1914-1919* (Cologne, 1985), 14.

151. Monthly reports in PH2/62, Sept. 1916-Aug. 1917, BA-MA.

152. J. Verhey, *The Spirit of 1914: Militarism, Myth, and Mobilization in Germany* (Cambridge, 2000), 113.

153. Ryder, *German Revolution*, 101.

154. D. Geary, 'Radicalism and the Worker: Metalworkers and Revolution 1914-1923', in R. J. Evans (ed.), *Society and Politics in Wilhelmine Germany* (London, 1978), 278.

155. D. Geary, 'Revolutionary Berlin, 1917-20', in Wrigley (ed.), *Challenges of Labour*, 33; Miller, *Burgfrieden und Klassenkampf*, 293; G. D. Feldman, *Army, Industry, and Labour in Germany, 1914-1918* (Princeton, NJ, 1966), 336-9.

156. F. Boll, 'Le Problème ouvrier et les grèves: l'Allemagne, 1914-1918', in J.-J. Becker and S. Audoin-Rouzeau (eds.), *Les Sociétés européennes et la guerre de 1914-1918* (Paris, 1990), 269.

157. Ibid.

158. Miller, *Burgfrieden und Klassenkampf*, 352; Boll, 'Le Problème ouvrier', 239.

159. Feldman, *Army, Industry, and Labour*, 452; B. Barth, *Dolchstoßlegenden und politische Desintegration: die Trauma der deutschen Niederlage im Ersten Weltkrieg 1914-1933* (Düsseldorf, 2003), 42.

160. Miller, *Burgfrieden und Klassenkampf*, 376; Schönhoven (ed.), *Gewerkschaften*, docs. 48-9.

161. Miller, *Burgfrieden und Klassenkampf*, 376.

162. Hohenlohe-Czernin, 30 Jan. 1918, Preußenberichte, 1918, HHStA.

163. Feldman, *Army, Industry, and Labour*, 452.

164. S. Bailey, 'Berlin Strike of January 1918', *Central European History* (1980), 170-71; D. A. Welch, *Germany, Propaganda, and Total War, 1914-1918* (London, 2000), 224.

165. Bailey, 'Berlin Strike', 174.

166. Schwabe, *Woodrow Wilson*, 23.

167. Miller, *Burgfrieden und Klassenkampf*, 358-66.

168. B. Davis, *Home Fires Burning: Food, Politics and Everyday Life in World War One Berlin* (Chapel Hill, NC, 2000), 219; J. Kocka, *Facing Total War: German Society, 1914-1918* (Leamington Spa, 1984), 22-4.

169. Public opinion summaries, 3 Feb, 3 Mar., 3 Apr. 1918, PH2/62, BA-MA; Political Intelligence Department memorandum, 8 May 1918, FO/371/3227.

170. Public opinion surveys, 3 July, 3 Aug. 1918, PH2/62, BA-MA.

171. Barth, *Dolchstoßlegenden*, 52; public opinion surveys, 15 Sept., 15 Oct. 1918, MKr/1258/3, KAM.

172. G. G. Bruntz, *Allied Propaganda and the Collapse of the German Empire in 1918* (Stanford, Calif., 1938), inset after p. 192.

173. Max Müller report, 23 Sept. 1918, *BDFA*, Pt H, XII, 316.

174. E. H. Tobin, 'War and the Working Class: the Case of Düsseldorf, 1914–1918', *Central European History* (1985), 281; Feldman, *Army, Industry, and Labour*, 507–10.

175. Miller, *Burgfrieden und Klassenkampf*, 382, 330; Townley–Balfour, 16 Mar. 1918, FO/371/3223.

176. Ministerratsprotokoll, 15, 26 Aug. 1918, MA/99511, BHStA.

177. Schönhoven (ed.), *Gewerkschaften*, doc. 53.

178. H. Rudin, *Armistice 1918* (New Haven, Conn., 1944), 35–44.

179. P. M. Taylor, 'The Foreign Office and British Propaganda during the First World War', *Historical Journal* (1980), 891.

180. J. L. Thompson, *Politicians, the Press, and Propaganda: Lord Northcliffe and the Great War, 1914–1919* (Kent, O./London, 1999), 196; MI7 history, WO/106/6399.

181. Northcliffe–Balfour, 10 Jan. 1918, CAB/1/26; Welch, *Germany, Propaganda, and Total War*, 230–31.

182. P. M. Taylor, *Munitions of the Mind: War Propaganda from the Ancient World to the Nuclear Age* (Wellingborough, 1990), 173.

183. Bruntz, *Allied Propaganda*, ch. 3.

184. D. Stegemann, 'Die deutsche Inlandspropaganda 1917/18', *Militärgeschichtliche Mitteilungen* (1972), 83; Heiligrath circular, 11 Aug. 1917, Militärbevollmächtiger Berlin (59), KAM.

185. D. K. Buse, 'Domestic Intelligence and German Military Leaders, 1914–18', *Intelligence and National Security* (2000), 49ff.

186. M. Bauer, *Der Grosse Krieg im Feld und Heimat: Erinnerungen und Betrachtungen* (Tübingen, 1921), 187.

187. Stegemann, 'Deutsche Inlandspropaganda', 81–102.

188. W. Deist (ed.), *Militär- und Innenpolitik im Weltkrieg 1914–1918*, II (2 vols., Düsseldorf, 1970), docs., 355–60.

189. A. G. Marquis, 'Words as Weapons: Propaganda in Britain and Germany during the First World War', *Journal of Contemporary History* (1978), 490–91.

190. History of MI7, p. 23, WO/106/6399; notes on propaganda conference, 14–17 Aug. 1918, WO/32/5756.

191. H. Hagenlücke, *Die deutsche Vaterlandspartei: die nationale Rechte am Ende des Kaiserreiches* (Düsseldorf, 1997), 161.

192. Vaterlandspartei proclamation, 28 Nov. 1917, Militärbevollmächtiger Berlin (59), BA-MA.

193. W. Deist, 'Censorship and Propaganda in Germany during the First World War', in Becker and Audoin-Rouzeau (eds.), *Les Sociétés européennes*, 206; Hohenlohe reports, 12, 26 Sept. 1917, Preußenberichte, 1917, HHStA.

194. Hagenlücke, *Vaterlandspartei*, 181, 189, 174, 179, 16.

195. J. Breuilly, *Nationalism and the State* (Manchester, 1993), 2.
196. K. H. Jarausch, *The Enigmatic Chancellor: Bethmann Hollweg and the Hubris of Imperial Germany* (New Haven, Conn., 1973), 349.
197. R. J. Crampton, *Bulgaria, 1878–1918: a History* (New York, 1983), 451–3, 465–7.
198. A. Roshwald, *Ethnic Nationalism and the Fall of Empires: Central Europe, Russia, and the Middle East, 1914–1923* (London/New York, 2001), 111–13, 152–4; D. Bloxham, *The Great Game of Genocide: Imperialism, Nationalism, and the Destruction of the Ottoman Armenians* (Oxford, 2007), 97–101.
199. G. Vermes, 'Leap into the Dark: the Issue of Suffrage in Hungary during World War I', in R. A. Kann, B. K. Király, and P. S. Fichtner (eds.), *The Habsburg Empire in World War I: Essays on the Intellectual, Military, Political, and Economic Aspects of the Habsburg War Effort* (New York, 1977), 40.
200. I. Banac, '"Emperor Karl has become a Comitadji": the Croatian Disturbances of Autumn 1918', *Slavonic and East European Review* (1992), 286.
201. G. E. Rothenberg, *The Army of Francis Joseph* (West Lafayette, Ind., 1976), 210.
202. M. Cornwall, 'News, Rumour, and the Control of Information in Austria-Hungary, 1914–1918', *History* (1992), 52–8.
203. T. Komarnicki, *Rebirth of the Polish Republic: a Study in the Diplomatic History of Europe, 1914–1920* (London, 1957), 110ff.
204. M. Rauchensteiner, *Der Tod des Doppeladlers: Österreich-Ungarn und der Erste Weltkrieg* (Graz, 1993), 449.
205. Wargelin, 'High Price for Bread', 779, 784–5; Political Intelligence Department memorandum, 27 June 1918, FO/371/3133.
206. Rumbold telegrams, 22 June, 21 Oct. 1918, FO/371/3133; Rauchensteiner, *Tod*, 585; Austrian Railway Minister–Austrian Premier, 25 Aug. 1918, Nr 147468, KMPräs 1918, KAW.
207. Austrian Railway Minister–Austrian Premier, 25 Aug. 1918, Nr 147468, KMPräs 1918, KAW; Z. A. B. Zeman, *The Break-Up of the Habsburg Empire, 1914–1918: a Study in National and Social Revolution* (London/New York/Toronto, 1961), 237–8.
208. H. L. Rees, *The Czechs during World War I: the Path to Independence* (Boulder, Colo./New York, 1992), 21.
209. Ibid., 45; V. S. Mamatey, 'The Union of Czech Political Parties in the Reichsrat, 1916–1918', in Kann et al. (eds.), *Habsburg Empire*, 13–16.
210. Wargelin, 'High Price for Bread', 774.
211. Roshwald, *Ethnic Nationalism*, 79, 83.
212. Rees, *Czechs during World War I*, 106–9, 113.
213. N. Piétri, 'L'Evolution des populations d'Autriche-allemande pendant la grande guerre', in Becker and Audoin-Rouzeau (eds.), *Les Sociétés européennes*, 329.
214. Political Intelligence Department memorandum, 15 Aug. 1918, FO/371/3133.
215. Mamatey, 'Union of Czech Political Parties', 5; Rauchensteiner, *Tod des Doppeladlers*, 585.
216. M. Cornwall, 'The Experience of Yugoslav Agitation in Austria-Hungary, 1917–1918', in H. Cecil and P. H. Liddle (eds.), *Facing Armageddon: the First World War Experienced* (London, 1996), 656–68.
217. Wargelin, 'High Price for Bread', 770.
218. See Chapter 1.

219. S. Hartley, *The Irish Question as a Factor in British Foreign Policy, 1914–1918* (Basingstoke, 1987), 166.

220. Scott (ed.), *Official Statements of War Aims*, 270.

221. Balfour–Steed, 4 Apr. 1918, FO/371/3134.

222. 3 June 1918 Declaration, 16N3267, SHA.

223. Zeman, *Break-Up of the Habsburg Empire*, 248.

224. Opinion surveys in 6N147, SHA.

225. R. J. B. Bosworth, *Mussolini's Italy: Life under the Dictatorship, 1915–1945* (London, 2005), 85.

226. Report on Fascio di difesa interno, 17 Oct. 1917, 17/35/2, Nitti MSS, ACS.

227. Bosworth, *Mussolini's Italy*, 75.

228. P. Corner and G. Procacci, 'The Italian Experience of "Total" Mobilization, 1915–1920', in Horne (ed.), *State, Society, and Mobilization*, 228; A. Fava, 'War, "National Education", and the Italian Primary School, 1915–1918', in Horne (ed.), *State, Society, and Mobilization*, 56.

229. Director of Public Security–Orlando, 3 June 1918, 50 1495/1, Orlando MSS; poster by Comitato centrale dei Fascisti interventisti rivoluzionari, Oct. 1918, 17/35/2, Nitti MSS, ACS.

230. P. Panayi, *The Enemy in our Midst: Germans in Britain during the First World War* (New York, 1990); T. Wilson, *The Myriad Faces of War: Britain and the Great War, 1914–1918* (Cambridge, 1986), 643.

231. Gregory, *Last Great War*, 107–8.

232. B. Porter, *The Lion's Share: a Short History of British Imperialism, 1850–1970* (London/New York, 1975), 240.

233. D. Fitzpatrick, 'The Logic of Collective Sacrifice: Ireland and the British Army, 1914–1918', *Historical Journal* (1995), 1017–18.

234. C. Townshend, *Easter 1916: the Irish Rebellion* (London, 2005), 337–43.

235. Mock and Larson, *Words That Won the War*, 213.

236. S. Vaughan, *Holding Fast the Inner Lines: Democracy, Nationalism, and the Committee on Public Information* (Chapel Hill, NC, 1980), xi, 233; Mock and Larson, *Words That Won the War*, 125.

237. Luebke, *Bonds of Loyalty*, 30.

238. Ibid., 157, 201.

239. Ibid., 134, 278.

240. Ibid., ch. 9.

241. Barclay telegram, 17 Jan. 1918, FO/371/3429.

242. Hartley, *Irish Question*, 198.

243. Barclay–Balfour, 25 Jan. 1918, FO/371/3429.

244. Barclay–Balfour, 4 Apr. 1918, FO/371/3430; Reading–Balfour, 30 May 1918, FO/371/3430.

245. Hartley, *Irish Question*, 184–5.

246. Ibid., 190; Barclay–Balfour, 19 July, 10 Nov. 1918, FO/371/3430.

247. H. D. Lasswell, *Propaganda Technique in the World War* (London/New York, 1927), 176.

248. C. M. Sterba, *Good Americans: Italian and Jewish Immigrants during the First World War* (Oxford/New York, 2003), 166–8; Barclay–Balfour, 27 Mar. 1918, FO/371/3428.

249. Sterba, *Good Americans*, 113.
250. Reading–Balfour, 22 Feb. 1918, FO/371/3428.
251. Lloyd George, *War Memoirs*, II, 1162–3.
252. I. F. W. Beckett, 'King George V and His Generals', in M. Hughes and M. Seligman (eds.), *Leadership in Conflict, 1914–1918* (Barnsley, 2000), 260–61. See further, D. Mack Smith, *Italy and Its Monarchy* (New Haven, Conn./London, 1999); K. Rose, *King George V* (London, 1983).
253. Cadorna–Boselli, 6 June 1917, 67 1560, Orlando MSS, ACS; Orlando–Boselli, 18 June 1917, 67 1560, Orlando MSS, ACS; Ambrosoli, *Né aderire, né sabotare*, 270.
254. A. Malatesta, *I socialisti italiani durante la guerra* (Milan, 1926), 167–73, 187–8; Orlando–Turin Prefect, 7 July 1918, 50 1495/5, Orlando MSS, ACS.
255. V. E. Orlando, *Memorie (1915–1919)*, eds. R. Masca and M. Toscano (Milan, 1960), 355–6.
256. Orlando–Prefect of Milan, 17 Dec. 1917; Orlando–Prefects of Genoa and Turin, 15 May 1918, 50 1495/4, Orlando MSS, ACS.
257. M. Isnenghi and G. Rochat, *La Grande Guerra 1914–1918* (Milan, 2004), 467.
258. Rodd–Balfour, 11 Apr. 1918, FO/371/3135; Erskine telegram, 7 Sept. 1918, FO/371/3137; Italian Embassy memorandum, 14 Sept. 1918, FO/371/3137.
259. Rodd–Balfour, 29 Jan. 1918, FO/371/3229; Orlando telegram, 22 Feb. 1918, FO/371/3230; Rodd telegram, 26 Feb. 1918, FO/371/3230.
260. Bertie–Balfour, 7 Jan. 1918, FO/371/3212; Derby–Balfour, 3 June 1918, FO/371/3214.
261. Generally, J.-B. Duroselle, *Clemenceau* (Paris, 1985); D. R. Watson, *Georges Clemenceau: a Political Biography* (London, 1974).
262. M. Hankey, *The Supreme Command, 1914–1918*, II (2 vols., London, 1961), 872.
263. M. Pugh, *Lloyd George* (Harlow, 1988), 75.
264. Generally, J. Grigg, *Lloyd George: War Leader* (London, 2001).
265. P. A. Devlin, *Too Proud to Fight: Woodrow Wilson's Neutrality* (London, 1974), vii.
266. Wilson–Daniels, 31 Jan. 1918, #110, Daniels MSS, LOC.
267. R. A. Kennedy, 'Woodrow Wilson, World War I, and an American Conception of National Security', *Diplomatic History* (2008), 7, 12.
268. E. A. Weinstein, *Woodrow Wilson: a Medical and Psychological Biography* (Princeton, NJ, 1981), 318.
269. Lloyd George, *War Memoirs*, II, 1009.
270. Grigg, *Lloyd George*, 301.
271. D. D. Stid, *The President as Statesman: Woodrow Wilson and the Constitution* (Lawrence, Kan., 1998), 133.
272. Grigg, *Lloyd George*, 46.
273. M. Dugast-Rouillé, *Charles de Habsbourg: le dernier empereur 1887–1922* (Paris/Louvain-la-neuve, 1991), 86.
274. Ibid., 170.
275. Rauchensteiner, *Tod des Doppeladlers*, 479; A. Polzer-Hoditz, *Kaiser Karl: aus der Geheimmappe seines Kabinettschefs* (Zurich/Leipzig/Vienna, 1929), 395, 399, 606.
276. G. W. Shanafelt, *The Secret Enemy: Austria-Hungary and the German Alliance, 1914–1918* (New York, 1985), 151; cf. Hohenlohe–Czernin, 10 Dec. 1917, Preußenberichte 1917, HHStA.
277. W. Görlitz (ed.), *Regierte der Kaiser? Kriegstagebücher, Aufzeichnungen und Briefe*

des Chefs des Marine-Kabinetts Admiral Georg Alexander von Müller 1914–1918 (Göttingen/Berlin/Frankfurt-am-Main, 1959), 249.

278. H. Afflerbach, 'Wilhelm II as Supreme Warlord in the First World War', *War in History* (1998), 448; J. C. G. Röhl, *Wilhelm II. Der Weg in den Abgrund 1900–1941*, III (3 vols., Nördlingen, 2008), 1176.

279. C. Clark, *Kaiser Wilhelm II* (Harlow, 2000), 234.

280. H. Pothoff (ed.), *Friedrich v. Berg als Chef des Geheimen Zivilkabinetts 1918. Erinnerungen aus seinem Nachlaß* (Düsseldorf, 1971), 98.

281. E. Ludendorff (ed.), *The General Staff and Its Problems* (2 vols., London, 1920), 528–9.

282. Generally, H. Afflerbach (ed.), *Kaiser Wilhelm II als Oberster Kriegsherr im Ersten Weltkrieg: Quellen aus der militärischen Umgebung des Kaisers 1914–1918* (Münster, 2005); L. Cecil, *Wilhelm II. Vol. II: Emperor and Exile 1900–1941* (Chapel Hill, NC/London, 1996); Clark, *Kaiser Wilhelm II*; Röhl, *Wilhem II*, III.

283. Röhl, *Wilhelm II*, III, 1205–7.

8. ARMISTICE AND AFTER

1. Cited in M. Brown, *Imperial War Museum Book of 1918: Year of Victory* (London, 1998), 285.

2. C. R. M. F. Cruttwell, *A History of the Great War, 1914–1918* (London, 1982), 577.

3. B. Hamard, 'Quand la victoire s'est gagnée aux Balkans: l'assaut de l'armée alliée d'orient de septembre à novembre 1918', *Guerres mondiales et conflits contemporains* (1996), 30, 33.

4. Köberle dispatch, 3 Oct. 1918, MKr/1832/1, KAM.

5. Reichskanzlei, *Amtliche Urkunden zur Vorgeschichte des Waffenstillstandes 1918* (2nd edn, Berlin 1924), docs. 1–2; *WK*, XIV, 623–5.

6. S. Burián, *Austria in Dissolution* (transl., London, 1925), 378–90.

7. Reichskanzlei, *Amtliche Urkunden zur Vorgeschichte*, doc. 12; K. Schwabe, *Woodrow Wilson, Revolutionary Germany, and Peacemaking, 1918–1919: Missionary Diplomacy and the Realities of Power* (Chapel Hill, NC/London, 1985), 27–31.

8. Heye memoir, N/18/4, BA-MA; J. Hürter (ed.), *Paul von Hintze. Marineoffizier, Diplomat, Staatssekretär. Dokumente einer Karriere zwischen Militär und Politik, 1903–1918* (Munich, 1998), 103.

9. W. Deist (ed.), *Militär- und Innenpolitik im Welkrieg 1914–1918*, II (2 vols., Düsseldorf, 1970), 1284.

10. E. Kessel, 'Ludendorffs Waffenstillstandsforderung vom 29. September 1918', *Militärgeschichtliche Mitteilungen* (1968), 82–3; Heye memoir, N/18/4, BA-MA.

11. Reichskanzlei, *Amtliche Urkunden zur Vorgeschichte*, doc. 12.

12. H. Afflerbach (ed.), *Kaiser Wilhelm II als Oberster Kriegsherr im Ersten Weltkrieg: Quellen aus der militärischen Umgebung des Kaisers 1914–1918* (Münster, 2005), 54.

13. P. von Hindenburg, *Aus meinem Leben* (Leipzig, 1933), 429.

14. Heye memoir, N/18/4, BA-MA; Bavarian attaché, 1, 3 Oct. 1918, MKr/1832/1, KAM; A. von Thaer, *Generalstabsdienst an der Front und in der OHL* (Göttingen, 1958), 233.

15. Deist (ed.), *Militär-und Innenpolitik*, II, 1288.

16. Thaer, *Generstabsdienst*, 235.
17. Deist (ed.), *Militär- und Innenpolitik*, II, 1308n.
18. R. Asprey, *The German High Command at War: Hindenburg and Ludendorff and the First World War* (London, 1994), 471.
19. Ibid., 468; W. Görlitz (ed.), *Regierte der Kaiser? Kriegstagebücher, Aufzeichnungen und Briefe des Chefs des Marine-Kabinetts Admiral Georg Alexander von Müller 1914–1918* (Göttingen/Berlin/Frankfurt-am-Main, 1959), 421; Hohenlohe–Burián, 1, 4 Oct. 1918, Preußenberichte 1918, HHStA.
20. H. Rudin, *Armistice 1918* (New Haven, Conn., 1944), 50, 52.
21. Reichskanzlei, *Amtliche Urkunden zur Vorgeschichte*, doc. 28.
22. Max of Baden, Prince, *The Memoirs of Prince Max of Baden*, (2 vols., London, 1928), 10, 22.
23. Reichskanzlei, *Amtliche Urkunden zur Vorgeschichte*, docs. 32–3.
24. Hohenlohe–Burián, 4 Oct. 1918, Preußenberichte 1918, HHStA; J. B. Scott (ed.), *Official Statements of War Aims and Peace Proposals, December 1916–November 1918* (Washington DC, 1921), 415.
25. M. Geyer, 'Insurrectionary Warfare: the German Debate about a levée en masse in October 1918', *Journal of Modern History* (2001), 479–80.
26. Hildebrand memoranda on raw materials situation, W-10/50494, BA-MA.
27. C. M. Seymour (ed.), *The Intimate Papers of Colonel House*, IV (4 vols., London, 1926–8), 65.
28. Scott (ed.), *Official Statements of War Aims*, 399–405.
29. P. Renouvin, *L'Armistice de Rethondes, 11 novembre 1918* (Paris 1968), 115–16; T. J. Knock, 'Wilsonian Concepts and International Relations at the End of the War', in M. Boemeke et al. (eds.), *The Treaty of Versailles: a Reassessment after 75 Years* (Washington DC/Cambridge, 1998), 117; Jusserand telegrams received 9, 15 Oct. 1918, 6N138, SHA.
30. A. S. Link et al. (eds.), *The Papers of Woodrow Wilson: Vol. LI. September 14–November 8 1918* (Princeton, NJ, 1983, 1985), 278; Knock, 'Wilsonian Concepts', 118.
31. Seymour, *House*, IV, 77.
32. L. W. Martin, *Peace Without Victory: Woodrow Wilson and the British Liberals* (New Haven, Conn., 1958), 183.
33. De Billy–Tardieu, 9 Oct. 1918, A 'Paix' (45), AMAE.
34. Scott (ed.), *Official Statements of War Aims*, 418–19.
35. Köberle report, 10 Oct. 1918, MKr/1832/1, KAM.
36. Wilson–Haig, 13 Oct. 1918, WO/158/25.
37. Jusserand–Pichon, received 11 Oct. 1918, A 'Paix' (45), AMAE.
38. G. A. Riddell, *Lord Riddell's War Diary, 1914–1918* (London, 1933), 366, 371.
39. Foreign Office–Washington/Paris/Rome, 13 Oct. 1918, FO/371/3436.
40. Rudin, *Armistice*, 121.
41. Link et al. (eds.), *Wilson Papers*, LI, 339, 414.
42. Ibid., 341.
43. Schwabe, *Woodrow Wilson*, 19; I. Floto, *Colonel House in Paris: a Study of American Policy at the Paris Peace Conference, 1919* (Aarhus, 1973), 34; Link et al. (eds.), *Wilson Papers*, LI, 412.
44. Jusserand telegram, received 21 Oct. 1918, A 'Paix' (45), AMAE.

45. Schwabe, *Woodrow Wilson*, 67.
46. Link et al. (eds.), *Wilson Papers*, LI, 340.
47. Scott (ed.), *Official Statements of War Aims*, 422.
48. Ibid., 414.
49. Renouvin, *L'Armistice de Rethondes*, 128.
50. Link et al. (eds.), *Wilson Papers*, LI, 412, 465–7.
51. Ibid., 473.
52. Ibid.
53. Scott (ed.), *Official Statements of War Aims*, 436.
54. Ibid., 415–16.
55. Geyer, 'Insurrectionary Warfare', 470, 482–3.
56. E. Matthias and R. Morsey (eds.), *Die Regierung des Prinzen Max von Baden* (Düsseldorf, 1962), 118, 122; Bavavian attaché, 11 Oct. 1918, MKr/1832/1, KAM.
57. Matthias and Morsey (eds.), *Regierung des Prinzen*, 118, 141.
58. Görlitz (ed.), *Regierte der Kaiser?*, 432; Max of Baden, *Memoirs*, II, 89; Bavarian attaché report, 18 Oct. 1918, Militärbevollmächtiger Berlin (59), KAM.
59. Matthias and Morsey (eds.), *Regierung des Prinzen*, 132, 216; Max of Baden, *Memoirs*, II, 157–8.
60. Matthias and Morsey (eds.), *Regierung des Prinzen*, 220–52.
61. Max of Baden, *Memoirs*, II, 134–9.
62. Geyer, 'Insurrectionary Warfare', 502; Matthias and Morsey (eds.), *Regierung des Prinzen*, 289.
63. Max of Baden, *Memoirs*, II, 149–56.
64. Thaer, *Generalstabsdienst*, 247.
65. Seymour (ed.), *House*, IV, 57.
66. Cecil minute on Crowe note, 16 Oct. 1918, FO/371/3444.
67. Orlando–Diaz, 14 Oct., 1, 2, 3 Nov. 1918, 67 1562, Orlando MSS, ACS.
68. D. Stevenson, *French War Aims against Germany, 1914–1919* (Oxford, 1982), 119.
69. Poincaré–Clemenceau, 8 Oct. 1918, in G. Wormser, *Le Septennat de Poincaré* (Paris, 1977), 146–8.
70. Pichon–Cambon, 16 Oct. 1918, A 'Paix' (46) AMAE.
71. Renouvin, *L'Armistice de Rethondes*, 264.
72. F. Foch, *Mémoires pour servir à l'histoire de la guerre de 1914–1918*, II (2 vols., Paris, 1931), 270–72.
73. Ibid., 276–8; R. Lhopital, *Foch, l'armistice, et la paix* (Paris, 1938), 33–9.
74. Dutasta–Pichon, 15 Oct. 1918, 6N70, SHA; Foch–Clemenceau, 16 Oct. 1918, 6N70, SHA; Derby–Balfour, 18 Oct. 1918, Balfour MSS, Add. 49744, BL.
75. P. Renouvin, 'Die öffentliche Meinung in Frankreich während des Krieges, 1914–1918', *Vierteljahrshefte für Zeitgeschichte* (1970), 269–71; Bulletin on domestic morale, 15 Nov. 1918, 6N147, SHA.
76. Derby–Balfour, 24 Oct. 1918, FO/371/3445.
77. Danny conference, 13 Oct. 1918, CAB/24/66.
78. Haig diary, 10, 17 Oct. 1918, MF/861, LHCMA; J. P. Harris, *Douglas Haig and the First World War* (Cambridge, 2008), 508, 545.
79. Haig diary, 19 Oct. 1918, MF/861, LHCMA; memorandum to Cabinet, 19 Oct.

1918, appended to Cabinet minutes 21 Oct., CAB/23/4; cf. Haig diary, 2 Jan. 1918, G. D. Sheffield and J. M. Bourne (eds.), *Douglas Haig: War Diaries and Letters, 1914–1918* (London, 2005), 370.

80. Milner–Cabinet, 24 Oct. 1918, WO/106/315.

81. Haig diary, 19 Oct. 1918, MF/861, LHCMA; J. J. Pershing, *My Experiences in the World War* (London, 1931), 658.

82. War Cabinet, 21 Oct. 1918, CAB/23/14.

83. Wemyss–Beatty, 18 Oct. 1918, BTY/13/40/8.

84. War Cabinet, 21 Oct. 1918, CAB/23/14.

85. War Cabinet, 26 Oct. 1918, CAB/23/14; Hankey diary, 11 Oct. 1918, HNKY/1/5, Hankey MSS, CCAC.

86. Link et al. (eds.), *Wilson Papers*, LI, 505, 512.

87. Floto, *Colonel House*, 49–60.

88. Link et al. (eds.), *Wilson Papers*, LI, 594.

89. Orlando–Diaz, 2, 3 Nov. 1918, 67 1562, Orlando MSS, ACS.

90. Sheffield and Bourne (eds.), *Douglas Haig*, 475–6.

91. Pershing, *My Experiences*, 671.

92. Link et al. (eds.), *Wilson Papers*, LI, 524–5; cf. Pershing, *My Experiences*, 671–5.

93. Link et al. (eds.), *Wilson Papers*, LI, 515, 416.

94. Pershing, *My Experiences*, 675.

95. Tardieu–Clemenceau, received 5 Nov. 1918, A 'Paix' (47), AMAE.

96. Lhopital, *Foch, l'armistice, et la paix*, 60–66.

97. Lloyd George in Imperial War Cabinet, 5 Nov. 1918, CAB/23/42.

98. B. Lowry, *Armistice 1918* (Kent, O./London, 1996), 135–43, 148; Seymour, *House*, IV, 129–32; Wemyss memorandum on naval armistice, 27 Nov. 1919, WMYS/11/1, Wemyss MSS, CCAC.

99. Schwabe, *Woodrow Wilson*, 109.

100. J. Pomiankowski, *Der Zusammenbruch des Ottomanischen Reiches: Erinnerungen an die Türkei aus der Zeit des Weltkrieges* (Zurich/Leipzig/Vienna, 1928), 383–4.

101. G. Dyer, 'The Turkish Armistice of 1918', *Middle Eastern Studies* (1972), 143–52.

102. C. Falls, *History of the Great War Based on Official Documents. Macedonia*, II (London, 1935), 201–6.

103. Musulin telegram, 15 Dec. 1917, Türkei Berichte, 1917–18, HHStA; Pallavicini despatches, 16 Mar., 30 July, 10 Sept. 1918, Türkei Berichte, 1917–18, HHStA.

104. D. Lloyd George, *War Memoirs*, II (2 vols., London, 1938), 1948–9.

105. M. Komjáthy (ed.), *Protokolle des Gemeinsamen Ministerrates der österreichisch-ungarischen Monarchie (1914–1918)* (Budapest, 1966), 687.

106. Burián, *Austria in Dissolution*, 388–9.

107. Komjáthy (ed.), *Protokolle des Gemeinsamen Ministerrates*, 695.

108. Link et al. (eds.), *Wilson Papers*, LI, 383.

109. Komjáthy (ed.), *Protokolle des Gemeinsamen Ministerrates*, 700, 702.

110. Text in H. Cecil and P. H. Liddle (eds.), *At the Eleventh Hour: Reflections, Hopes, and Anxieties at the Closing of the Great War, 1918* (Barnsley, 1998), 297.

111. Hamard, 'Quand la victoire', 37.

112. Fifth Army postal censorship, 17 Oct. 1918, W-10/50794, BA-MA.

113. AOK 17-Army Group Rupprecht, 6 Nov. 1918, W-10/51833, BA-MA.

114. H. H. Herwig, *The First World War: Germany and Austria-Hungary, 1914–1918* (London/New York, 1997), 443.

115. Bavarian War Ministry circular, 20 Oct. 1918, Militärbevollmächtiger Berlin (128), KAM; Köberle report, 16 Oct. 1918, Militärbevollmächtiger Berlin (59), KAM.

116. *WK*, XIV, 710.

117. Generally, W. Deist, 'Die Politik der Seekriegsleitung und die Rebellion der Flotte Ende Oktober 1918', *Vierteljahrshefte für Zeitgeschichte* (1966); G. P. Groß, 'Eine Frage der Ehre? Die Marineführung und der letzte Flottenvorstoß 1918', in J. Duppler and G. P. Groß (eds.), *Kriegsende 1918: Ereignis, Wirkung, Nachwirkung* (Munich, 1994).

118. S. Stephenson, *The Final Battle: Soldiers of the Western Front and the German Revolution of 1918* (Cambridge, 2009), 76; U. Kluge, *Die deutsche Revolution 1918/1919: Staat, Politik, und Gesellschaft zwischen Weltkrieg und Kapp-Putsch* (Frankfurt-am-Main, 1985), 53–4.

119. Matthias and Morsey (eds.), *Regierung des Prinzen*, 528–32; Köbele report, 1 Nov. 1918, MKr/1832/1, KAM.

120. Köbele report, 7 Nov. 1918, ibid.

121. *WK*, XIV, 694, 699.

122. I. Hull, *Absolute Destruction: Military Culture and the Practices of War in Imperial Germany* (Ithaca, NY/London, 2005), 1–4, 322–33.

123. Cf. K. Neilson, 'Reinforcements and Supplies from Overseas: British Strategic Sealift in the First World War', in G. C. Kennedy (ed.), *The Merchant Marine in International Affairs, 1850–1950* (London/Portland, Ore., 2000).

124. M. Hankey, *The Supreme Command, 1914–1918*, II (2 vols., London, 1961), 872.

125. Haig diary, 20 Oct. 1918, MF/861, LHCMA; Final Despatch, 21 March 1919, Sheffield and Bourne (eds.), *Douglas Haig*, 518.

126. P. Kecskemeti, 'Rationality in Ending War', *Annals of the American Academy of Political Science* (Nov. 1970), 108.

127. G. H. W. Bush and B. Scowcroft, *A World Transformed* (New York, 1999), 487.

128. Stephenson, *Final Battle*, 241.

129. Rudin, *Armistice*, 396.

130. B. Barth, *Dolchstoßlegenden und politische Desintegration: die Trauma der deutschen Niederlage im Ersten Weltkrieg 1914–1933* (Düsseldorf, 2003), chs. 7–9; M. Knox, *To the Threshold of Power, 1922/33: Origins and Dynamics of the Fascist and National Socialist Dictarorships*, I (Cambridge, 2007), 198–9, 282, 286–93.

131. I. Kershaw, *Hitler, 1889–1936: Hubris* (London, 1998), 102–5.

132. Knox, *Threshold of Power*, 199; R. J. Evans, *The Coming of the Third Reich* (London, 2003), 168–9.

133. D. French, '"Had We Known How Bad Things were in Germany, We Might Have Got Stiffer Terms": Great Britain and the Armistice', in Boemeke et al. (eds.), *Treaty of Versailles*, 86.

134. Renouvin, *L'Armistice de Rethondes*, 267.

135. Lloyd George in Imperial War Cabinet, 5 Nov. 1918, CAB/23/42; conversation with House, 31 Oct. 1918, 6N69, SHA.

136. Wemyss diary, 8 Nov. 1918, WMYS/11/1, Wemyss MSS, CCAC; Haig diary, 15 Nov. 1918, MF/861, LHCMA.

137. Lowry, *Armistice 1918*, 160.

138. Seymour, *House*, IV, 121; F. Cochet, 'Vom Zweifel am Erfolg zum Ende der Schicksalsprüfung – das Jahr 1918 im französischen Hinterland', in Duppler and Groß (eds.), *Kriegsende 1918*, 298.

139. Schwabe, *Woodrow Wilson*, 19; Link et al. (eds.), *Wilson Papers*, LI, 412.

140. Jusserand telegram, received 5 Nov. 1918, A 'Paix' (47), AMAE; Lowry, *Armistice 1918*, 146; J. de Pierrefeu, *GQG Secteur I: trois ans au Grand Quartier Général; par le rédacteur du 'communiqué'*, II (2 vols., Paris, 1920), 326.

141. Link et al. (eds.), *Wilson Papers*, LI, 340.

142. J. J. M. Mordacq, *La Vérité sur l'armistice* (Paris, 1921), 32.

143. Lowry, *Armistice 1918*, 159; cf. R. Recouly, *Marshal Foch: His Own Words on Many Subjects* (transl., London, 1929), 44–8.

144. Cf. W. Schivelbusch, *The Culture of Defeat: On National Mourning, Trauma, and Recovery* (transl., London, 2004), 29ff.

145. D. R. Watson, *Georges Clemenceau: a Political Biography* (London, 1974), 361.

146. As persuasively re-argued in R. W. D. Boyce, *The Great Inter-War Crisis and the Collapse of Globalization* (Basingstoke, 2009), 430–33.

147. http://www.fylde.demon.co.uk/clairiere.htm; http://fr/wikipedia.org/wiki/Clairière_de_l%27Armistice.

148. 'Ici le 11 novembre 1918 succomba le criminel orgueil de l'empire allemand, vaincu par les peuples libres qu'il prétendait asservir.'

149. Wemyss diary, 7–11 Nov. 1918, WMYS/11, Wemyss MSS, CCAC. For a fictional reconstruction, T. Keneally, *Gossip from the Forest* (London, 1975).

150. Renouvin, *L'Armistice de Rethondes*, 252.

Bibliography

This bibliography's main purpose is to identify the sources referred to in the endnotes, although a few other standard works have been included. References are to the edition consulted rather than the first edition. For works in languages other than English, where an English translation exists it has normally been cited in preference to the original.

'A Survey of German Tactics 1918' (Historical Sub-Section, General Staff, AEF, Washington DC, 1918)

Adams, R. J. Q., *Arms and the Wizard: Lloyd George and the Ministry of Munitions, 1915–1916* (London, 1978)

Adams, R. J. Q. and Poirier, P., *The Conscription Controversy in Great Britain, 1900–1918* (Basingstoke/London, 1987)

Aeroboe, F., *Der Einfluß des Krieges auf die landwirtschaftliche Produktion in Deutschland* (Stuttgart/Berlin/Leipzig/New Haven, Conn., 1927)

Afflerbach, H., 'Wilhelm II as Supreme Warlord in the First World War', *War in History* (1998)

— (ed.), *Kaiser Wilhelm II als Oberster Kriegsherr im Ersten Weltkrieg: Quellen aus der militärischen Umgebung des Kaisers 1914–1918* (Münster, 2005)

Altrichter, F., *Die seelischen Kräfte des deutschen Heeres in Frieden und im Weltkriege* (Berlin, 1933)

Ambrosoli, L., *Né aderire, né sabotare, 1915–1918* (Milan, 1961)

Andrew, C. M., *Secret Service: the Making of the British Intelligence Community* (London, 1985)

— C., *The Defence of the Realm: the Authorized History of MI5* (London, 2009)

Andrew, C. M. and Kanya-Forstner, A. S., *France Overseas: the Great War and the Climax of French Imperial Expansion* (London, 1981)

Andrews, E. M., *The Anzac Illusion: Anglo-Australian Relations during World War I* (Cambridge, 1993)

Arz, A. A., *Zur Geschichte des Grossen Krieges 1914–1918* (Graz, 1969)

Ashmore, E. B., *Air Defence* (London/New York/Toronto, 1929)

Asprey, R., *The German High Command at War: Hindenburg and Ludendorff and the First World War* (London, 1994)

Astore, W. J. and Showalter, D. E., *Hindenburg: Icon of German Militarism* (Dulles, Va, 2005)

Audoin-Rouzeau, S., *Men at War, 1914–1918: National Sentiment and Trench Journalism in France during the First World War* (Providence, RI/Oxford, 1992)

—, 'The French Soldier in the Trenches', in Cecil and Liddle (eds.), *Facing Armageddon*

Audoin-Rouzeau, S. and Becker, A., *14–18, Retrouver la guerre* (Paris, 2000)

Augé-Laribé, M., *L'Agriculture pendant la Guerre* (Paris/New Haven, Conn., n.d.)

Augé-Laribé, M. and Pinot, P., *Agriculture and Food Supply in France during the War* (New Haven, Conn., 1927)

Augeneder, S., *Arbeiterinnen im Ersten Weltkrieg: Lebens- und Arbeitsbedingungen proletarischer Frauen in Österreich* (Vienna, 1987)

Ayres, L. P., *The War with Germany: a Statistical Summary* (Washington DC, 1919)

Badcock, G. E., *A History of the Transport Services of the Egyptian Expeditionary Force 1916–1917–1918* (London, 2005)

Badsey, S., 'Cavalry and the Development of Breakthrough Doctrine', in Griffith (ed.), *British Fighting Methods*

—, *Doctrine and Reform in the British Cavalry, 1880–1918* (Aldershot, 2008)

Bailey, J., 'British Artillery in the Great War', in Griffith (ed.), *British Fighting Methods*

—, *The First World War and the Birth of the Modern Style of Warfare* (Strategic and Combat Studies Institute Occasional Paper No. 22, Camberley, 1996)

Bailey, S., 'The Berlin Strike of January 1918', *Central European History* (1980)

Baker, H. L., *Argonne Days in World War I* (Columbia, Mo./London, 2007)

Balderston, T., 'War Finance and Inflation in Britain and Germany, 1914–1918', *Economic History Review* (1989)

Baldini, A., *Diaz* (transl., London, 1935)

Balesi, C. J., 'From Adversary to Comrade-in-Arms: West Africans and the French Military, 1885–1919', Ph.D. dissertation, University of Illinois at Chicago, 1976.

Banac, I., '"Emperor Karl has become a Comitadji": the Croatian Disturbances of Autumn 1918', *Slavonic and East European Review* (1992)

Barbeau, A. and Florette, H., *The Unknown Soldiers: Black American Troops in World War I* (Philadelphia, Pa, 1974)

Barker, A. J., *The Neglected War: Mesopotamia, 1914–1918* (London, 1967)

Barnett, C., *The Audit of War: the Illusion and Reality of Britain as a Great Nation* (London/Basingstoke, 1986)

—, *The Swordbearers: Supreme Command in the First World War* (London, 2000)

Barnett, L. M., *British Food Policy during the First World War* (Boston, Mass./London/Sydney, 1985)

Barral, P., 'L'Intendance', in Canini (ed.), *Fronts invisibles*

Barros, A., 'Strategic Bombing and Restraint in "Total War", 1915–1918', *Historical Journal* (2009)

Barry, J. M., *The Great Influenza: the Story of the Deadliest Pandemic in History* (London, 2005)

Barth, B., *Dolchstoßlegenden und politische Desintegration: das Trauma der deutschen Niederlage im Ersten Weltkrieg 1914–1933* (Düsseldorf, 2003)

Baruch, B. M., *The Public Years* (London, 1961)

Bauer, M., *Der Grosse Krieg im Feld und Heimat: Erinnerungen und Betrachtungen* (Tübingen, 1921)

Baumgart, W., *Deutsche Ostpolitik, 1918: Von Brest-Litovsk bis zum Ende des Ersten Weltkrieges* (Vienna/Munich, 1966)

Baumgart, W. and Repgen, K. (eds.), *Brest-Litowsk* (Göttingen, 1969)

Beach, J., 'British Intelligence and the German Army, 1914–1918', Ph.D. dissertation, University College London, 2004

Bean, C. E. W., *The Australian Imperial Force in France during the Allied Offensive, 1918* (Sydney, 1942)

Becker, J.-J., *1914: Comment les Français sont entrés dans la guerre* (Paris, 1977)

—,*The Great War and the French People* (Leamington Spa/Heidelberg/Dover, NH, 1985)

Becker, J.-J. and Audoin-Rouzeau, S. (eds.), *Les Sociétés européennes et la guerre de 1914–1918* (Paris, 1990)

Beckett, I. F. W., 'The Real Unknown Army: British Conscripts, 1916–1919', in Becker and Audoin-Rouzeau (eds.), *Les Sociétés européennes*

—, 'King George V and His Generals', in Hughes and Seligmann (eds.), *Leadership in Conflict*

—, *The Great War, 1914–1918* (Harlow, 2001)

— (ed.), *1917: Beyond the Western Front* (Leiden/Boston, Mass., 2009)

Beesly, P., *Room 40: British Naval Intelligence, 1914–18* (London, 1982)

Bell, A. C., *A History of the Blockade of Germany and of the Countries Associated with Her in the Great War, Austria-Hungary, Bulgaria, and Turkey* (London, 1937; published 1961)

Berghahn, V. R., *Modern Germany: Society, Economics, and Politics in the Twentieth Century* (Cambridge, 1982)

Berov, L., 'The Bulgarian Economy during World War I', in Király and Dreisziger (eds.), *East Central European Society*

Berti, G. and del Negra, P. (eds.), *Al di qua e al di là del Piave: l'Ultimo Anno della Grande Guerra* (Milan, 2001)

Bessel, R., '"Eine nicht allzu große Beunruhigung des Arbeitsmarktes": Frauenarbeit und Demobilmachung in Deutschland nach dem Ersten Weltkrieg', *Geschichte und Gesellschaft* (1983)

—, *Germany after the First World War* (Oxford, 1993)

—, 'Mobilization and Demobilization in Germany', in Horne (ed.), *State, Society, and Mobilization*

Bet-el, I. R., *Conscripts: Forgotten Men of the Great War* (Stroud, 2003)

Beveridge, W. H., *British Food Control* (London, 1928)

Bidwell, S. and Graham, D., *Fire-Power: British Army Weapons and Theories of War, 1904–1945* (London, 1982)

Binding, R., *A Fatalist at War* (London, 1929)

Bliss, M., 'War Business as Usual: Canadian Munitions Production 1914–1918', in Dreisziger (ed.), *Mobilization for Total War*

Bloxham, D., *The Great Game of Genocide: Imperialism, Nationalism, and the Destruction of the Ottoman Armenians* (Oxford, 2007)

Boemeke, M. et al. (eds.), *The Treaty of Versailles: a Reassessment after 75 Years* (Washington DC/Cambridge, 1998)

Boghardt, T., *Spies of the Kaiser: German Covert Operations in Britain during the First World War Era* (Basingstoke, 2004)

Boll, F., 'Le Problème ouvrier et les grèves: l'Allemagene, 1914–1918', in Becker and Audoin-Rouzeau (eds.), *Les Sociétés européennes*

Bond, B. and Cave, N. (eds.), *Haig: a Reappraisal 70 Years On* (Barnsley, 1999)

Bond, B. et al. (eds.), 'Look to Your Front': Studies in the First World War by the British Commission for Military History (Staplehurst, 1999)

Bone, D. W., Merchantmen-at-Arms: the British Merchants' Service in the War (London, 1919)

Bonzon, T., 'The Labour Market and Industrialization', in Winter and Robert (eds.), Capital Cities at War

Bosanquet, N., 'Health Systems in Khaki: the British and American Medical Experience', in Cecil and Liddle (eds.), Facing Armageddon

Boswell, J. and Johns, B., 'Patriots or Profiteers? British Businessmen and the First World War', Journal of European Economic History (1992)

Bosworth, R. J. B., Mussolini's Italy: Life under the Dictatorship, 1915–1945 (London, 2005)

Bourbon, Prince Sixte de, L'Offre de paix séparée de l'Autriche (5 décembre 1916–12 octobre 1917) (Paris, 1920)

Bourke, J., Dismembering the Male: Men's Bodies, Britain, and the Great War (London, 1996)

—, An Intimate History of Killing: Face-to-Face Killing in Twentieth-Century Warfare (London, 1999)

Bourne, J. M., Britain and the Great War, 1914–1918 (London, 1989)

—, 'The British Working Man in Arms', in Cecil and Liddle (eds.), Facing Armageddon

Bovio, O., 'Le ferrovie italiane nella prima guerra mondiale', in Canini (ed.), Fronts invisibles

Bowley, A. L., Some Economic Consequences of the Great War (London, 1930)

Braybon, G., Women Workers in the First World War: the British Experience (London, 1981)

British Documents on Foreign Affairs: Reports and Papers from the Confidential Print (general eds., K. Bourne and D. Cameron Watt). Part II, Series H, Vol. 12. The Central Powers, V: October 1917–November 1918, ed. D. Stevenson (Frederick, Md, 1989)

Brittain, V., Testament of Youth: an Autobiographical Study of the Years 1900–1925 (London, 1978)

Broadberry, S. and Harrison, M. (eds.), The Economics of World War I (Cambridge, 2005)

Broadberry, S. and Howlett, P., 'The United Kingdom in World War I: Business as Usual?', in Broadberry and Harrison (eds.), Economics of World War I

Brown, C., Rosie's Mom: Forgotten Women Workers of the First World War (Boston, Mass., 2002)

Brown, I. M., 'Not Glamorous But Effective: the Canadian Corps and the Set-Piece Attack, 1917–1918', Journal of Military History (1994)

—, British Logistics on the Western Front, 1914–1919 (Westport, Conn./London, 1998)

—, 'Feeding Victory: the Logistic Imperative behind the Hundred Days', in Dennis and Grey (eds.), 1918: Defining Victory

Brown, J. M. and Louis, W. R. (eds.), The Oxford History of the British Empire. Vol. IV: The Twentieth Century (Oxford/New York, 1999)

Brown, M., The Imperial War Museum Book of 1918: Year of Victory (London, 1998)

Bruce, A., The Last Crusade: the Palestine Campaign in the First World War (London, 2003)

Bruce, R. B., A Fraternity of Arms: America and France in the Great War (Lawrence, Kan., 2003)

—, *Pétain: Verdun to Vichy* (Dulles, Va, 2008)

Bruchmüller, G., *Die deutsche Artillerie in den Durchbruchschlachten des Weltkrieges* (Berlin, 1921)

—, *Die Artillerie beim Angriff im Stellungskrieg* (Berlin, 1926)

Bruntz, G. G., *Allied Propaganda and the Collapse of the German Empire in 1918* (Stanford, Calif., 1938)

Bülow, H. Freiherr von, *Geschichte der Luftwaffe: eine kurze Darstellung der Entwicklung der fünften Waffe* (Frankfurt-am-Main, 1934)

Burchardt, L., 'The Impact of the War Economy on the Civilian Population of Germany during the First and Second World Wars', in Deist (ed.), *German Military*

Burián, S., *Austria in Dissolution* (transl., London, 1925)

Burk, K., 'J. M. Keynes and the Exchange Rate Crisis of July 1917', *Economic History Review* (1979)

—, 'The Mobilization of Anglo-American Finance during World War I', in Dreisziger (ed.), *Mobilization for Total War*

—, 'The Treasury: From Impotence to Power', in Burk (ed.), *War and the State*

— (ed.), *War and the State: the Transformation of British Government, 1914–1919* (London, 1982)

—, *Britain, America, and the Sinews of War, 1914–1918* (Boston, Mass./London/Sydney, 1985)

Buse, D. K., 'Domestic Intelligence and German Military Leaders, 1914–18', *Intelligence and National Security* (2000)

Cailletau, F., *Gagner la Grande Guerre* (Paris, 2008)

Calder, K. J., *Britain and the Origins of the New Europe, 1914–1918* (Cambridge, 1976)

Camarda, A. and Peli, S., *L'altro esercito: la classe operaia durante la Prima guerra mondiale* (Milan, 1980)

Canini, G. (ed.), *Les Fronts invisibles: nourrir – fournir – soigner* (Nancy, 1984)

Carls, S. D., *Louis Loucheur and the Shaping of Modern France, 1916–1931* (Baton Rouge, La/London, 1993)

Carr, J. C. and Taplin, W., *History of the British Steel Industry* (Oxford, 1962)

Cassar, G. H., *The Forgotten Front: the British Campaign in Italy, 1917–1918* (London/Rio Grande, O., 1998)

Cazals, R., *Les Carnets de Louis Barthas, tonnelier 1914–1918* (Paris, 1997)

Cecil, H. and Liddle, P. H. (eds.), *Facing Armageddon: the First World War Experienced* (London, 1996)

— (eds.), *At the Eleventh Hour: Reflections, Hopes, and Anxieties at the Closing of the Great War, 1918* (Barnsley, 1998)

Cecil, L., *Wilhelm II. Vol. II: Emperor and Exile 1900–1941* (Chapel Hill, NC/London, 1996)

Chambers, J. W., *To Raise an Army: the Draft Comes to Modern America* (New York/London, 1987)

Chickering, R., *Imperial Germany and the Great War, 1914–1918* (Cambridge , 1998)

Chickering, R. and Förster, S. (eds.), *Great War, Total War: Combat and Mobilization on the Western Front, 1914–1918* (Cambridge, 2000)

Childs, D. J., *A Peripheral Weapon? The Production and Employment of British Tanks in the First World War* (Westport, Conn./London, 1999)

Christienne, C. and Lissarague, P., *A History of French Military Aviation* (transl., Washington DC, 1986)

Churchill, W. S. L., *The World Crisis* (6 parts, London, 1923–31)

Clark, C., *Kaiser Wilhelm II* (Harlow, 2000)

Clarkson, G. B., *Industrial America in the World War: the Strategy behind the Line, 1917–1918* (Boston, Mass./New York, 1923)

Clausewitz, C. von, *On War*, eds. M. E. Howard and P. Paret (Princeton, NJ, 1976)

Clegg, H. A., *A History of British Trade Unions since 1889. Vol. II. 1911–1933* (Oxford, 1985)

Clemenceau, G., *Grandeur and Misery of Victory* (transl., London, 1930)

Clémentel, E., *La France et la politique interalliée* (Paris/New Haven, Conn., 1931)

Cochet, A., 'Les Soldats français', in Becker and Audoin-Rouzeau (eds.), *Les Sociétés européennes*

Cochet, F., 'Vom Zweifel am Erfolg zum Ende der Schicksalsprüfung – das Jahr 1918 im französischen Hinterland', in Duppler and Groß (eds.), *Kriegsende 1918*

Coetzee, F. and Shevin-Coetzee, M. (eds.), *Authority, Identity, and the Social History of the Great War* (Providence, RI/Oxford, 1995)

Coffman, E. M., *The Hilt of the Sword: the Career of Peyton C. March* (Madison, Wis./Milwaukee, Wis./London, 1966)

—, 'Militärische Operationen der US-Armee an der Westfront 1918', in Duppler and Groß (eds.), *Kriegsende 1918*

—, *The War to End All Wars: the American Military Experience in World War I* (Lexington, Ky, 1998)

Consett, M. W. P., *The Triumph of Unarmed Forces (1914–1918)* (London, 1923)

Cooper, J. M., Jr, *The Warrior and the Priest: Woodrow Wilson and Theodore Roosevelt* (Cambridge, Mass./London, 1983)

Cooper, M., *The Birth of Independent Air Power: British Air Policy in the First World War* (London/Boston, Mass./Sydney, 1986)

Corbett, J. and Newbolt, H., *Naval Operations* (5 vols., London, 1920–31)

Corner, P. and Procacci, G., 'The Italian Experience of "Total" Mobilization, 1915–1920', in Horne (ed.), *State, Society, and Mobilization*

Cornish, P., *Machine Guns and the Great War* (Barnsley, 2009)

Cornwall, M., 'The Dissolution of Austria-Hungary' in Cornwall (ed.), *Last Years*

—, 'News, Rumour, and the Control of Information in Austria-Hungary, 1914–1918', *History* (1992)

—, 'The Experience of Yugoslav Agitation in Austria-Hungary, 1917–1918', in Cecil and Liddle (eds.), *Facing Armageddon*

—, *The Undermining of Austria-Hungary: the Battle for Hearts and Minds* (Basingstoke, 2000)

— (ed.), *The Last Years of Austria-Hungary: Essays in Political and Military History, 1908–1918* (Exeter, 1990)

Crampton, R. J., *Bulgaria, 1878–1918: a History* (New York, 1983)

—, 'Deprivation, Desperation, and Degradation: Bulgaria in Defeat', in Cecil and Liddle (eds.), *Eleventh Hour*

Cronin, E. D. (ed.), *The War Diaries of Josephus Daniels, 1913–1921* (Lincoln, Nebr., 1963)

Crosby, A. W., Jr, *Epidemic and Peace, 1918* (Westport, Conn./London, 1976)

Crowell, B., *America's Munitions, 1917–18* (Washington DC, 1919)

Cruccu, R., 'L'organizzazione generale dei servizi logistici nell'esercito italiano durante la prima guerra mondiale', in Canini (ed.), *Fronts invisibles*

Cruttwell, C. R. M. F., *A History of the Great War, 1914–1918* (London, 1982)

Cunningham, W. J., 'The Railroads under Government Operation. I. The Period to the Close of 1918', *The Quarterly Journal of Economics* (1921)

Curami, A., 'L'Industria bellica italiana dopo Caporetto', in Berti and del Negra (eds.), *Piave*

Czernin, O., *In the World War* (London, 1919)

Danaïllow, G., *Les Effets de la guerre en Bulgarie* (Paris/New Haven, Conn., 1932)

Daniel, U., 'Women's Work in Industry and Family: Germany, 1914–1918', in Wall and Winter (eds.), *Upheaval of War*

—, *The War from Within: German Working-Class Women in the First World War* (Oxford/New York, 1997)

Darmon, P., *Vivre à Paris pendant la Grande Guerre* (Paris, 2002)

Daunton, M., 'How to Pay for the War: State, Society, and Taxation in Britain, 1917–1929', *English Historical Review* (1996)

Davis, B., *Home Fires Burning: Food, Politics and Everyday Life in World War One Berlin* (Chapel Hill, NC, 2000)

Deacon, R., *The French Secret Service* (London, 1990)

Deák, I., 'The Habsburg Army in the First and Last Days of World War I: a Comparative Analysis', in Király and Dreisziger (eds.), *East Central European Society*

Debeney, Général, *La Guerre et les hommes: réflexions d'après-guerre* (Paris, 1937)

Debo, R. K., *Revolution and Survival: the Foreign Policy of Soviet Russia, 1917–1918* (Toronto, 1979)

Deist, W., 'Die Politik der Seekriegsleitung und die Rebellion der Flotte Ende Oktober 1918', *Vierteljahrshefte für Zeitgeschichte* (1966)

—, 'Censorship and Propaganda in Germany during the First World War', in Becker and Audoin-Rouzeau (eds.), *Les Sociétés européennes*

—, 'Verdeckte Militärstreik im Kriegsjahr 1918?', in Wette (ed.), *Krieg des kleinen Mannes*

—, 'The Military Collapse of the German Empire', *War in History* (1996)

— (ed.), *Militär- und Innenpolitik im Weltkrieg 1914–1918* (2 vols., Düsseldorf, 1970)

— (ed.), *The German Military in the Age of Total War* (Leamington Spa/Dover, NH, 1985)

De Lastours, S., *1914–1918: La France gagne la guerre des codes secrets* (Paris, 1998)

Dennis, P. and Grey, J. (eds.), *1918: Defining Victory* (Canberra, 1999)

Devlin, P. A., *Too Proud to Fight: Woodrow Wilson's Neutrality* (London, 1974)

Dewar, G. A. B., *The Great Munition Feat, 1914–1918* (London, 1921)

Dewey P. E., 'Food Production and Policy in the United Kingdom, 1914–1918', *Transactions of the Royal Historical Society* (1980)

—, 'Military Recruiting and the British Labour Force during the First World War', *Historical Journal* (1984)

—, *British Agriculture in the First World War* (London, 1989)

Deygas, F.-J., *Les Chars d'assaut: leur passé, leur avenir* (Paris, 1937)

Dickson, M. R., *The Food Front in World War I* (Washington DC, 1944)

Dockrill, M. L. and French, D. (eds.), *Strategy and Intelligence: British Policy during the First World War* (London/Rio Grande, O., 1996)

Doise, J. and Vaïsse, M., *Diplomatie et outil militaire* (Paris, 1987)

Doughty, R. A., *Pyrrhic Victory: French Strategy and Operations in the Great War* (Cambridge, Mass./London, 2005)

Doumenc, A., 'Les Transports automobiles pendant la guerre de 1914–1918', in Canini (ed.), *Fronts invisibles*

Downs, L. L., *Manufacturing Inequality: Gender Division in the French and British Metal-working Industries, 1914–1939* (Ithaca, NY/London, 1995)

Dreisziger, N. F. (ed.), *Mobilization for Total War: the Canadian, American, and British Experience, 1914–1918,1939–1945* (Waterloo, Ont., 1981)

Dugast-Rouillé, M., *Charles de Habsbourg: le dernier empereur 1887–1922* (Paris/Louvain-la-neuve, 1991)

Duppler, J. and Groß, G. P. (eds.), *Kriegsende 1918: Ereignis, Wirkung, Nachwirkung* (Munich, 1994)

Duroselle, J.-B., *Clemenceau* (Paris, 1985)

—, *La Grande Guerre des français, 1914–1918: l'incompréhensible* (Paris, 1994)

Dutil, Captain, *Les Chars d'assaut: leur création et leur rôle pendant la guerre 1915–1918* (Nancy/Paris/Strasbourg, 1919)

Dutton, D., 'Paul Painlevé and the End of the Sacred Union in Wartime France', *Journal of Strategic Studies* (1981)

—, *The Politics of Diplomacy: Britain and France in the Balkans in the First World War* (London/New York, 1998)

Dyer, G., 'The Turkish Armistice of 1918', *Middle Eastern Studies* (1972)

—, *The Missing of the Somme* (London, 1994)

Eckart, W. U., ' "The Most Extensive Experiment that the Imagination Can Conceive": War, Emotional Stress, and German Medicine, 1914–1918', in Chickering and Förster (eds.), *Great War, Total War*

Edmonds, J. E., *Military Operations: France and Belgium. 1914–(1918)* (London, 1933–48)

—, *Military Operations: Italy 1915–1919* (London, 1949)

Ellinwood, D. C. and Pradham, S. D. (eds.), *India and World War I* (New Delhi, 1978)

Eltzbacher, P. (ed.), *Germany's Food: Can It Last? Germany's Food and England's Plan to Starve Her Out: a Study by German Experts* (transl., London, 1915)

Emden, R. van and Humphries, S., *All Quiet on the Home Front: an Oral History of Life in Britain during the First World War* (London, 2004)

Enderes, B. et al., *Verkehrswesen im Kriege* (Vienna/New Haven, Conn., 1931)

Englander, D., 'The French Soldier 1914–1918', *French History* (1987)

Englander, D. and Osborne, J., 'Jack, Tommy, and Henry Dubb', *Historical Journal* (1978)

Epstein, K., *Matthias Erzberger and the Dilemma of German Democracy* (Princeton, NJ, 1959)

Erickson, E. J., *Ordered to Die: a History of the Ottoman Army in the First World War* (Westport, Conn./London, 2001)

—, *Ottoman Army Effectiveness in World War I: a Comparative Study* (Abingdon/New York, 2007)

Etschmann, W., 'Österreich-Ungarn zwischen Engagement und Zurückhaltung. K.u.k. Truppen and der Westfront', in Duppler and Groß (eds.), *Kriegsende 1918*

Evans, R. J., *The Coming of the Third Reich* (London, 2003)

Falls, C., *History of the Great War Based on Official Documents. Egypt and Palestine. From June 1917 to the End of the War, Vol. II* (London, 1930)

—, *History of the Great War Based on Official Documents. Macedonia. Vol. II* (London, 1935)

—, *The First World War* (London, 1960)

—, *Caporetto 1917* (London, 1965)

—, *Armageddon 1918: the Final Palestinian Campaign of World War I* (Philadelphia, Pa, 2003)

Farrar, L. L., Jr, *Divide and Conquer: German Efforts to Conclude a Separate Peace, 1914–1918* (New York, 1978)

—, 'Nationalism in Wartime: Critiquing the Conventional Wisdom', in Coetzee and Shevin-Coetzee (eds.), *Authority, Identity, and Social History*

Farrar, M. M., *Conflict and Compromise: the Strategy, Politics, and Diplomacy of the French Blockade, 1914–1918* (The Hague, 1974)

Fassy, G., *Le Commandement français en orient (octobre 1915–novembre 1918)* (Paris, 2003)

Fava, A., 'War, "National Education", and the Italian Primary School, 1915–1918', in Horne (ed.), *State, Society, and Mobilization*

Fay, S., *The War Office at War* (London, 1937)

Fayle, C. E., *History of the Great War Based on Official Documents: Seaborne Trade* (3 vols., London, 1920)

—, *A Short History of the World's Shipping Industry* (London, 1933)

Fedyshyn, O. S., *Germany's Drive to the East and the Ukrainian Revolution, 1917–1918* (New Brunswick, NJ, 1971)

Feldman, G. D., *Army, Industry, and Labour in Germany, 1914–1918* (Princeton, NJ, 1966)

—, *The Great Disorder: Politics, Economy, and Society in the German Inflation 1914–1924* (New York/Oxford, 1997)

— (ed.), *German Imperialism, 1914–1918: the Development of a Historical Debate* (New York, 1972)

Ferguson, N., *Paper and Iron: Hamburg Business and German Politics in the Era of Inflation, 1897–1927* (Cambridge, 1995)

—, *The Pity of War* (London, 1998)

Ferris, J., 'Airbandit: C³I and Strategic Air Defence during the First Battle of Britain, 1915–18', in Dockrill and French (eds.), *Strategy and Intelligence*

— (ed.), *The British Army and Signals Intelligence during the First World War* (Stroud, 1992)

Fischer, F., *Germany's Aims in the First World War* (London, 1967)

Fitzpatrick, D., 'The Logic of Collective Sacrifice: Ireland and the British Army 1914–1918', *Historical Journal* (1995)

Fletcher, D., *Tanks and Trenches: First Hand Accounts of Tank Warfare in the First World War* (Stroud, 1994)

Flood, P. J., *France, 1914–1918: Public Opinion and the War Effort* (Basingstoke, 1990)

Floto, I., *Colonel House in Paris: a Study of American Policy at the Paris Peace Conference, 1919* (Aarhus, 1973)

Foch, F., *Mémoires pour servir à l'histoire de la guerre de 1914–1918* (2 vols., Paris, 1931)

Fogarty, R. S., *Race and War in France: Colonial Subjects in the French Army, 1914–1918* (Baltimore, Md., 2008)

Foley, R. T., 'The Other Side of the Hill: the German Army in 1917', in P. Dennis and J. Grey (eds.), *1917: Tactics, Training, and Technology* (Canberra, 2007)

Fong, G., 'The Movement of German Divisions to the Western Front, Winter 1917–1918' *War in History* (2000)

Fontaine, A., *French Industry during the War* (New Haven, Conn., 1926)

Forcella, E. and Monticone, A., *Plotone di esecuzione: i processi della Prima guerra mondiale* (Rome, 1998)

Forsyth, D. J., *The Crisis of Liberal Italy: Monetary and Financial Policy, 1914–1922* (Cambridge, 1993)

Foulkes, C. H., *'Gas!' The Story of the Special Brigade* (Edinburgh/London, 1934)

French, D., 'Watching the Allies: British Intelligence and the French Mutinies of 1917', *Intelligence and National Security* (1991)

—, *The Strategy of the Lloyd George Coalition, 1916–1918* (Oxford, 1995)

—, 'Failures of Intelligence: the Retreat to the Hindenburg Line and the March 1918 Offensive', in Dockrill and French (eds.), *Strategy and Intelligence*

—, '"Had We Known How Bad Things were in Germany, We Might Have Got Stiffer Terms": Great Britain and the Armistice', in Boemeke et al. (eds.), *Treaty of Versailles*

Frevert, U., *Women in German History: From Bourgeois Emancipation to Sexual Liberation* (transl., Oxford/Hamburg/New York, 1992)

Frey, M., 'Bullying the Neutrals: the Case of the Netherlands', in Chickering and Förster (eds.), *Great War, Total War*

Fridenson, P., *Histoire des Usines Renault. I: Naissance de la grande entreprise, 1898–1939* (Paris, 1972)

—, 'The Impact of the First World War on French Workers', in Wall and Winter (eds.), *Upheaval of War*

— (ed.), *The French Home Front, 1914–1918* (Providence, RI/Oxford, 1992)

Friedensburg, F., *Das Erdöl im Ersten Weltkrieg* (Stuttgart, 1939)

Fuller, J. F. C., *Tanks and the Great War 1914–1918* (London, 1920)

Fuller, J. G., *Troop Morale and Popular Culture in the British and Dominion Armies, 1914–1918* (Oxford, 1990)

Galántai, J., *Hungary in the First World War* (Budapest, 1989)

Galassi, F. and Harrison, M., 'Italy at War, 1915–1918', in Broadberry and Harrison (eds.), *Economics of World War I*

Gallinari, V., 'La produzione dei materiali militari in Italia durante la guerra', in Canini (ed.), *Fronts invisibles*

Garson, N. G., 'South Africa and World War One', *Journal of Imperial and Commonwealth History* (1979)

Gascouin, Général, *L'Evolution de l'artillerie pendant la guerre* (Paris, 1920)

Gatzke, H. W., *Germany's Drive to the West: A Study of Western War Aims during the First World War* (Baltimore, 1950)

Geary, D., 'Radicalism and the Worker: Metalworkers and Revolution 1914–1923', in R. J. Evans (ed.), *Society and Politics in Wilhelmine Germany* (London, 1978)

—, 'Revolutionary Berlin, 1917–20', in Wrigley (ed.), *Challenges of Labour*

Gemzell, C.-A., *Organization, Conflict, and Innovation: a Study of German Naval Strategic Planning 1880–1940* (Lund, 1973)

Gersdorff, U. von, *Frauen im Kriegsdienst, 1914–1945* (Stuttgart, 1969)

Geyer, M., *Deutsche Rüstungspolitik, 1866–1980* (Frankfurt, 1984)

—, 'Insurrectionary Warfare: the German Debate about a levée en masse in October 1918', *Journal of Modern History* (2001)

Gibson, R. H. and Prendergast, M., *The German Submarine War, 1914–1918* (London, 1931)

Gilbert, C., *American Financing of World War I* (Westport, Conn., 1970)

Gill, D. and Dallas, G., 'Mutiny at Etaples Base in 1917', *Past & Present* (1975)

—, *The Unknown Army: Mutinies in the British Army in World War I* (London, 1985)

Gladden, N., *Across the Piave: a Personal Account of the British Forces in Italy, 1917–1919* (London, 1971)

Glaise von Horstenau, E., *The Collapse of the Austro-Hungarian Empire* (London, 1930)

Glaise von Horstenau, E. and Kiszling, R. (eds.), *Österreich-Ungarns Letzter Krieg 1914–1918* (8 vols., Vienna, 1929–35)

Godfrey, J. D., *Capitalism at War: Industrial Policy and Bureaucracy in France, 1914–1918* (Leamington Spa/Hamburg/New York, 1987)

Goebel, O., *Deutsche Rohstoffwirtschaft im Weltkrieg einschliesslich des Hindenburg-Programs* (Stuttgart/Berlin/Leipzig/New Haven, Conn., 1930)

Goemans, H. E., *War and Punishment: the Causes of War Termination and the First World War* (Princeton, NJ/Oxford, 2000)

Gollin, A., *The Impact of Air Power on the British People and Their Government, 1909–1914* (Stanford, Calif., 1989)

Gooch, J., 'The Maurice Debate 1918', *Journal of Contemporary History* (1968)

—, 'Morale and Discipline in the Italian Army, 1915–1918', in Cecil and Liddle (eds.), *Facing Armageddon*

Görlitz, W. (ed.), *Regierte der Kaiser? Kriegstagebücher, Aufzeichnungen und Briefe des Chefs des Marine-Kabinetts Admiral Georg Alexander von Müller 1914–1918* (Göttingen/Berlin/Frankfurt-am-Main, 1959)

Goya, M., *La Chair et l'acier: l'invention de la guerre moderne (1914–1918)* (Paris, 2004)

Granatstein, J., *Canada's Army: Waging War and Keeping the Peace* (Toronto/Buffalo, NY/London, 2002)

Granier, G. (ed.), *Die deutsche Seekriegsleitung im Ersten Weltkrieg – Dokumentation* (4 vols., Koblenz, 1999–2004)

Grant, R. M., *U-Boats Destroyed: the Effects of Anti-Submarine Warfare, 1914–1918* (London, 1964)

Gratz, G. and Schüller, R., *Der wirtschaftliche Zusammenbruch Österreich-Ungarns: die Tragödie der Erschöpfung* (Vienna/New Haven, Conn., 1930)

Grayzel, S. R., *Women and the First World War* (Harlow, 2002)

Greenhalgh, E., *Victory Through Coalition: Britain and France during the First World War* (Cambridge, 2005)

—, 'David Lloyd George, Georges Clemenceau, and the 1918 Manpower Crisis', *Historical Journal* (2007)

—, 'Errors and Omissions in Franco-British Co-operation over Munitions Production, 1914–18', *War in History* (2007)

Greenwald, M. W., *Women, War, and Work: the Impact of World War I on Women Workers in the United States* (Westport, Conn./London, 1980)

Gregory, A., *The Last Great War: British Society and the First World War* (Cambridge, 2008)

Grieves, K., *The Politics of Manpower, 1914–1918* (Manchester, 1988)

—, K., 'The Transportation Mission to GHQ, 1916', in Bond et al. (eds.), *'Look to Your Front'*

Griffith, P., *Battle Tactics of the Western Front: the British Army's Art of Attack, 1916–18* (New Haven, Conn./London, 1994)

— (ed.), *British Fighting Methods in the Great War* (London/Portland, Ore., 1996)

Grigg, J., *Lloyd George: War Leader* (London, 2001)

Groot, G. de, *The First World War* (New York, 2001)

Groß, G. P., *Die Seekriegführung der Kaiserlichen Marine im Jahre 1918* (Frankfurt-am-Main, 1989)

—, 'Eine Frage der Ehre? Die Marineführung und der letzte Flottenvorstoß 1918', in Duppler and Groß (eds.), *Kriegsende 1918*

Grotelueschen, M. E., *The AEF Way of War: the American Army and Combat in World War I* (Cambridge, 2007)

Gudmundsson, B. I., *Stormtroop Tactics: Innovation in the German Army 1914–1918* (Westport, Conn./London, 1989)

Guinard, P., Devos, J.-C., and Nicot, J., *Inventaire sommaire des Archives de la Guerre, Série N: 1872–1919*, Vol. I (Troyes, 1975)

Gullace, N., 'Sexual Violence and Family Honour: British Propaganda and International Law during the First World War', *American Historical Review* (1997)

Haber, L. F., *The Poisonous Cloud: Chemical Warfare in the First World War* (Oxford, 1986)

Hagenlücke, H., *Die deutsche Vaterlandspartei: die nationale Rechte am Ende des Kaiserreiches* (Düsseldorf, 1997)

Hall, R. C., "The Enemy is behind Us': the Morale Crisis in the Bulgarian Army during the Summer of 1918', *War in History* (2004)

Halpern, P. G., *The Naval War in the Mediterranean, 1914–1918* (London, 1987)

—, *A Naval History of World War I* (London, 1994)

Hamard, B., 'Quand la victoire s'est gagnée aux Balkans: l'assaut de l'armée alliée d'orient de septembre à novembre 1918', *Guerres mondiales et conflits contemporains* (1996)

Hamilton, J. A. B., *Britain's Railways in World War I* (London, 1967)

Hanak, H., 'The Union of Democratic Control during the First World War', *Bulletin of the Institute of Historical Research* (1963)

Hankey, M., *The Supreme Command, 1914–1918* (2 vols., London, 1961)

Hanna, M., *Your Death Would be Mine: Paul and Marie Pireaud in the Great War* (Cambridge, Mass./London, 2006)

Hanson, N., *First Blitz* (London, 2008)

Harbord, J. G., *The American Army in France, 1917–1919* (Boston, Mass., 1936)

Hardach, G., *The First World War, 1914–1918* (London, 1977)

—, 'Industrial Mobilization in 1914–1918: Production, Planning, and Ideology', in Fridenson (ed.), *French Home Front*

Harris, J., 'Bureaucrats and Businessmen in British Food Control, 1916–19', in Burk (ed.), *War and the State*

Harris, J. P., *Men, Ideas, and Tanks: British Military Thought and Armed Forces, 1903–1939* (Manchester/New York, 1995)

—, *Douglas Haig and the First World War* (Cambridge, 2008)

Harris, J. P. and Barr, N., *Amiens to the Armistice: the BEF in the Hundred Days' Campaign, 8 August–11 November 1918* (London/Washington DC, 1998)

Harris, R., 'The "Child of the Barbarian": Rape, Race, and Nationalism in France during the First World War', *Past & Present* (1993)

Harrison, M., 'The Fight against Disease in the Mesopotamian Campaign', in Cecil and Liddle (eds.), *Facing Armageddon*

Hart, P., *Aces Falling: War above the Trenches, 1918* (London, 2007)

—, *1918: a Very British Victory* (London, 2008)

Hartcup, G., *The War of Invention: Scientific Developments, 1914–18* (London, 1988)

Hartley, S., *The Irish Question as a Factor in British Foreign Policy, 1914–1918* (Basingstoke, 1987)

Haselsteiner, H., 'The Habsburg Empire in World War I: Mobilization of Food Supplies', in Király and Dreisziger (eds.), *East Central European Society*

Hatry, G., *Renault: Usine de guerre, 1914–1918* (Paris, 1978)

Hautcoeur, P.-C., 'Was the Great War a Watershed? The Case of France', in Broadberry and Harrison (eds.), *Economics of World War I*

Hautmann, H., 'Vienna: a City in the Years of Radical Change, 1917–20', in Wrigley (ed.), *Challenges of Labour*

Healey, M., *Vienna and the Fall of the Habsburg Empire: Total War and Everyday Life in World War I* (Cambridge, 2004)

Heinemann, U., *Die verdrängte Niederlage: Politische Öffentlichkeit und Kriegsschuldfrage in der Weimarer Republik* (Göttingen, 1983)

Henniker, A. M., *Transportation on the Western Front, 1914–1918* (London, 1937)

Herwig, H. H., 'German Policy in the Eastern Baltic Sea in 1918: Expansion or Anti-Bolshevik Crusade?', *Slavic Review* (1973)

—, 'The Dynamics of Necessity: German Military Policy during the First World War', in Millett and Murray (eds.), *Military Effectiveness*

—, *The First World War: Germany and Austria-Hungary, 1914–1918* (London/New York, 1997)

—, 'Total Rhetoric, Limited War: Germany's U-Boat Campaign, 1917–1918', in Chickering and Förster (eds.), *Great War, Total War*

Herwig, H. H. and Trask, D. F., 'The Failure of Imperial Germany's Undersea Offensive against World Shipping, February 1917–October 1918', *The Historian* (1970/1971)

Hewitt, N., '"Weary Waiting is Hard Indeed": the Grand Fleet after Jutland', in Beckett (ed.), *1917*

Hibberd, B. H., *Effects of the Great War upon Agriculture in the United States and Great Britain* (New York, 1919)

Hiley, N., 'The News Media and British Propaganda, 1914–18', in Becker and Audoin-Rouzeau (eds.), *Les Sociétés europénnes*

Hindenburg, P. von, *Aus meinem Leben* (Leipzig, 1933)/*Out of My Life* (London, 1920)

Hirschfelder, H., 'Unlust am Krieg: "Grössere Soldatenausschreitungen mit Zivilbeteiligung". Die Erlanger Unruhen im Mai 1918 und ihre Fortsetzung während eines Transportes zur Front' (Erlangen, 2004)

History of the Ministry of Munitions (12 vols., London, 1922)

Hodges, G., *Kariakor: the Carrier Corps. The Story of the Military Labour Forces in the Conquest of German East Africa, 1914 to 1918* (Nairobi, 1999)

Hoeppner, E. von, *Germany's War in the Air: the Development and Operations of German Military Aviation in the World War* (transl., Nashville, Tennessee, 1994)

Holland, R., 'The British Empire and the Great War, 1914–1918', in J. M. Brown and W. R. Louis (eds.), *The Oxford History of the British Empire. Vol. IV: The Twentieth Century* (Oxford/New York, 1999)

Holmes, R., *Tommy: the British Soldier on the Western Front, 1914–1918* (London, 2004)

Holtferich, C. L., *The German Inflation, 1914–1923: Causes and Effects in International Perspective* (transl., London/New York, 1986)

Homann-Herimberg, E., *Die Kohlenversorgung in Österreich während des Krieges* (Vienna/New Haven, Conn., 1925)

Hopkin, D., 'Domestic Censorship in the First World War', *Journal of Contemporary History* (1970)

Hopwood, R. F., 'Czernin and the Fall of Bethmann Hollweg', *Canadian Journal of History* (1967)

Horn, D., *Mutiny on the High Seas: the Imperial German Naval Mutinies of World War One* (London, 1973)

— (ed.), *War, Mutiny, and Revolution in the German Navy: the World War I Diary of Seaman Richard Stumpf* (New Brunswick, NJ, 1967)

Horn, M., 'The Concept of Total War: National Effort and Taxation in Britain and France during the First World War', *War and Society* (2000)

—, *Britain, France, and the Financing of the First World War* (Montreal/Kingston, 2002)

Horne, J., 'L'Impôt du sang: Republican Rhetoric and Industrial Warfare in France, 1914–18', *Social History* (1989)

—, *Labour at War: France and Britain, 1914–1918* (Oxford, 1991)

—, 'Remobilizing for "Total War": France and Britain, 1917–1918', in Horne (ed.), *State, Society, and Mobilization*

— (ed.), *State, Society, and Mobilization in Europe during the First World War* (Cambridge, 1997)

Houston, D. F., *Eight Years with Wilson's Cabinet (1913–1920)* (2 vols., London, 1926)

Huegel, A., *Kriegsernährungswirtschaft Deutschlands während des Ersten und Zweiten Weltkriegs im Vergleich* (Konstanz, 2003)

Hughes, J., 'The Battle for the Hindenburg Line', *War and Society* (1999)

Hughes, M., *Allenby and British Strategy in the Middle East, 1917–1919* (London/Portland, Ore., 1999)

Hughes, M. and Seligman, M. (eds.), *Leadership in Conflict, 1914–1918* (Barnsley, 2000)

Hull, I., *Absolute Destruction: Military Culture and the Practices of War in Imperial Germany* (Ithaca, NY/London, 2005)

Hurd, A. S., *History of the Great War Based on Official Documents: The Merchant Navy* (3 vols., London , 1921–9)

Hürter, J. (ed.), *Paul von Hintze. Marineoffizier, Diplomat, Staatssekretär. Dokumente einer Karriere zwischen Militär und Politik, 1903–1918* (Munich, 1998)

Hussey, J., 'The Movement of German Divisions to the Western Front, Winter 1917–1918', *War in History* (1997)

Huston, J. A., *The Sinews of War: Army Logistics, 1775–1953* (Washington DC, 1966)

Hynes, S., *The Soldier's Tale: Bearing Witness to Modern War* (London, 1998)

Isnenghi, M. and Rochat, G., *La Grande Guerra 1914–1918* (Milan, 2004)

Jahr, C., '"Bei einer geschlagenen Armee ist der Klügste, wer zuerst davonläuft": das Problem der Desertion im deutschen und britischen Heer 1918', in Duppler and Groß (eds.), *Kriegsende 1918*

—, *Gewöhnliche Soldaten: Desertion und Deserteure im deutschen und britischen Heer 1914–1918* (Göttingen, 1998)

Jeffery, K., *Ireland and the Great War* (Cambridge, 2000)

—, *Field Marshal Sir Henry Wilson: a Political Soldier* (Oxford, 2006)

—, *MI6: the History of the Secret Intelligence Service, 1909–1949* (London/Berlin/New York/ Sydney, 2010)

Jensen, W. G., 'The Importance of Energy in the First and Second World Wars', *Historical Journal* (1968)

Jèze, G. and Truchy, H., *The War Finance of France* (New Haven, Conn., 1927)

Jindra, Z., 'Der wirtschaftliche Zerfall Österreich-Ungarns (nach den Berichten der reichs- deutschen Bevollmächtigen in Wien 1916–1918)', in A. Teichova and H. Matis (eds.), *Österreich und die Tschechoslowakei 1918–1938 – die wirtschaftliche Neuordnung in Zentraleuropa in der Zwischenkriegszeit* (Vienna/Cologne/Weimar, 1996)

Johnson, J. P., 'The Wilsonians as War Mongers: Coal and the 1917–18 Winter Crisis', *Pro- logue* (1977)

Jones, H. A., *The War in the Air (Being the Story of the Part Played in the Great War by the Royal Air Force)* (6 vols., Oxford, 1922–37)

Jones, H. S., *Violence against Prisoners of War: Britain, France, and Germany, 1914–1920* (Cambridge, 2011)

Jones, J. W., *US Battleship Operations in World War I* (Annapolis, Md, 1998)

Jones, N., *The Origins of Strategic Bombing: a Study of the Development of British Air Strategic Thought and Practice up to 1918* (London, 1973)

Jost, W. and Felger, F. (eds.), *Was wir vom Weltkrieg nicht wissen* (Leipzig, 1938)

Jünger, E., *Storm of Steel* (New York, 1985)

Kahn, D., *The Codebreakers: the Story of Secret Writing* (London, 1966)

Kann, R. A., Király, B. K., and Fichtner, P. S. (eds.), *The Habsburg Empire in World War I: Essays on the Intellectual, Military, Political, and Economic Aspects of the Habsburg War Effort* (New York, 1977)

Kanya-Forstner, A. S., 'The War, Imperialism, and Decolonization', in Winter, Parker, and Habeck (eds.), *Great War*

Karsh, E. and I., 'Myth in the Desert, or Not the Great Arab Revolt', *Middle Eastern Studies* (1997)

Kaspi, A., *Le Temps des Américains: le concours américain à la France en 1917–1918* (Paris, 1976)

Keegan, J., *The Face of Battle: a Study of Agincourt, Waterloo, and the Somme* (London, 1991)

—, *The First World War* (London, 1998)

Keene, J. D., *Doughboys, the Great War, and the Remaking of America* (Baltimore, Md/ London, 2001)

Keiger, J. F. V., *Raymond Poincaré* (Cambridge, 1997)

Keller, C., *The Power Situation during the War* (Washington DC, 1921)

Kennedy, D. M., *Over Here: the First World War and American Society* (New York/Oxford, 1980)

Kennedy, G. C., 'Strategy and Supply in the North Atlantic Triangle 1914–1918', in B. J. C. McKercher and L. Aronson (eds.), *The North Atlantic Triangle in a Changing World: Anglo-American Relations, 1902–1956* (Toronto, 1996)

— (ed.), *The Merchant Marine in International Affairs, 1850–1950* (London/Portland, Ore., 2000)

Kennedy, P. M., 'Britain', in Millett and Murray (eds.), *Military Effectiveness*

—, 'Military Effectiveness in the First World War', in Millett and Murray (eds.), *Military Effectiveness*

—, *The Rise and Fall of the Great Powers: Economic Change and Military Conflict from 1500 to 2000* (London, 1989)

—, *The Rise and Fall of British Naval Mastery* (London, 1991)

Kennedy, R. A., 'Woodrow Wilson, World War I, and an American Conception of National Security', *Diplomatic History* (2008)

—, *The Will to Believe: Woodrow Wilson, World War I, and American Strategy for Peace and Security* (Kent, O., 2009)

Kennett, L., *The First Air War 1914–1918* (London/Toronto/Sydney/Singapore, 1991)

Kerchnawe, H., *Der Zusammenbruch der Öster.-Ungr. Wehrmacht im Herbst 1918* (Munich, 1921)

Kerr, K. A., 'Decision for Federal Control: Wilson, McAdoo, and the Railroads, 1917', *Journal of American History* (1967)

Kershaw, I., *Hitler, 1889–1936: Hubris* (London, 1998)

Kessel, E., 'Ludendorffs Waffenstillstandsforderung vom 29. September 1918', *Militärgeschichtliche Mitteilungen* (1968)

Keyes, R., *The Naval Memoirs of Admiral of the Fleet Sir Roger Keyes* (2 vols., London, 1935)

Király, B. K. and Dreisziger, N. F. (eds.), *East Central European Society in World War I* (New York, 1985)

Kirby, D., *War, Peace, and Revolution: International Socialism at the Crossroads, 1914–1918* (London, 1986)

Kirkbride, A., *An Awakening: the Arab Campaign 1917–18* (Tavistock, 1971)

Kitchen, M., *The Silent Dictatorship: the Politics of the German High Command under Hindenburg and Ludendorff* (London, 1976)

—, *The German Offensives of 1918* (Stroud, 2001)

Klein, F. et al., *Deutschland im Ersten Weltkrieg* (Berlin, 1968–9)

Kluge, U., *Die deutsche Revolution 1918/1919; Staat, Politik, und Gesellschaft zwischen Weltkrieg und Kapp-Putsch* (Frankfurt-am-Main, 1985)

Knock, T. J., *To End All Wars: Woodrow Wilson and the Quest for a New World Order* (New York/Oxford, 1992)

—, 'Wilsonian Concepts and International Relations at the End of the War', in Boemeke et al. (eds.), *Treaty of Versailles*

Knox, M., *To the Threshold of Power 1922/33: Origins and Dynamics of the Fascist and National Socialist Dictatorships, Volume I* (Cambridge, 2007)

Kocka, J., *Facing Total War: German Society, 1914–1918* (Leamington Spa, 1984)

Koistinen, P. A. C., *Mobilizing for Modern War: the Political Economy of American Warfare, 1865–1919* (Lawrence, Kan., 1997)

Komarnicki, T., *Rebirth of the Polish Republic: a Study in the Diplomatic History of Europe, 1914–1920* (London, 1957)

Komjáthy, M. (ed.), *Protokolle des Gemeinsamen Ministerrates der österreichischen-ungarischen Monarchie (1914–1918)* (Budapest, 1966)

Kořalka, J., 'Germany's Attitude to the National Disintegration of Cisleithania (April–October 1918)', *Journal of Contemporary History* (1969)

Koszyk, K., *Deutsche Presse, 1914–1945* (Berlin, 1972)

Kramer, A., '*Wackes* at War: Alsace-Lorraine and the Failure of German National Mobilization 1914–1918', in Horne (ed.), *State, Society, and Mobilization*

Kriegel, A., *Aux origines du communisme français, 1914–1920: contribution à l'histoire du mouvement ouvrier français* (Paris/The Hague, 1964)

Krizmann, B., 'Austro-Hungarian Diplomacy before the Collapse of the Empire', *Journal of Contemporary History* (1969)

Krumeich, G., 'Le Soldat allemand sur la Somme', in Becker and Audoin-Rouzeau (eds.), *Les Sociétés européennes*

Kruse, W., 'Krieg und Klassenheer: zur Revolutionierung der deutschen Armee im Ersten Weltkrieg', *Geschichte und Gesellschaft* (1996)

Kühlmann, R. von, *Erinnerungen* (Heidelberg, 1948)

Kuisel, R. F., *Capitalism and the State in Modern France: Renovation and Economic Management in the Twentieth Century* (Cambridge, 1981)

Lane, T., 'The British Merchant Seaman at War', in Cecil and Liddle (eds.), *Facing Armageddon*

Larson, S., *Labor and Foreign Policy: Gompers, the AFL, and the First World War, 1914–1918* (Cranbury, NJ/London, 1975)

Lasswell, H. D., *Propaganda Technique in the World War* (London/New York, 1927)

Laure, Général, *La Commandement en chef des armées françaises du 15 mai 1917 à l'armistice* (Paris, 1937)

Laux, J. M., 'Gnôme et Rhône – an Aviation Engine Firm in the First World War', in Fridenson (ed.), *French Home Front*

Lee, J., 'Administrators and Agriculture: Aspects of German Agricultural Policy in the First World War', in Winter (ed.), *War and Economic Development*

Leed, E. J., 'Class and Disillusionment in World War I', *Journal of Modern History* (1978)

—, *No Man's Land: Combat and Identity in World War I* (Cambridge, 1979)

Lepick, O., *La Grande Guerre chimique: 1914–1918* (Paris, 1998)

Les Armées françaises dans la Grande Guerre (11 vols., Paris, 1922–37)

Levin, N. G., Jr, *Woodrow Wilson and World Politics: America's Response to War and Revolution* (New York, 1968)

Lhopital, R., *Foch, l'armistice, et la paix* (Paris, 1938)

Liddell Hart, B., *Foch: the Man of Orléans* (London, 1931)

Liddle, P. H. (ed.), *Passchendaele in Perspective: the Third Battle of Ypres* (London, 1997)

Liggett, H. S., *A.E.F.: Ten Years Ago in France* (New York, 1928)

Link, A. S. et al. (eds.), *The Papers of Woodrow Wilson: Vol. XLII. April 7–June 23 1917; Vol. LI. September 14–November 8 1918* (Princeton, NJ, 1983, 1985)

Liulevicius, V. G., *War Land on the Eastern Front: Culture, National Identity, and German Occupation in World War I* (Cambridge, 2000)

Livesey, A., *The Viking Atlas of World War I* (New York, 1994)

Lloyd George, D., *War Memoirs* (2 vols., London, 1938)

Loewenfeld-Russ, H., *Die Regelung der Volks-Ernährung im Kriege* (Vienna/New Haven, Conn., 1926)

Loez, A., and Mariot, N. (eds.), *Obéir/désobéir: les mutineries de 1917 en perspective* (Paris, 2008)

Lowry, B., *Armistice 1918* (Kent, O./London, 1996)

Ludendorff, E., *My War Memories, 1914–1918* (2 vols., London 1919)/*Meine Kriegserinnerungen, 1914–1918* (Berlin, 1919)

— (ed.), *The General Staff and Its Problems* (2 vols., London, 1920)

— (ed.), *Urkunden des Obersten Heeresleitung über ihre Tätigkeit 1916/18* (Berlin, 1920)

Luebke, F. C., *Bonds of Loyalty: German-Americans and World War I* (DeKalb, Ill., 1974)

Lupfer, T. T., *The Dynamics of Doctrine: the Changes in German Tactical Doctrine during the First World War* (Fort Leavensworth Paper, Fort Leavensworth, Kan., 1981)

Lutz, R. H. (ed.), *The Causes of the German Collapse in 1918* (Stanford, Calif., 1934)

Lynn, J. A. (ed.), *Feeding Mars: Logistics in Western Europe from the Middle Ages to the Present* (Boulder, Colo./San Francisco/Oxford, 1993)

McAdoo, W. G., *Crowded Years: the Reminiscences of William G. McAdoo* (Boston, Mass./New York, 1931)

Macartney, C. A., *The Habsburg Empire, 1790–1918* (London, 1968)

McCoy, M. G., 'Grinding Gears: the AEF and Motor Transportation in the First World War', *War in History* (2004)

MacDonald, L., *To the Last Man: Spring 1918* (London, 1999)

MacKenzie, S. P., 'Morale and the Cause: the Campaign to Change the Outlook of Soldiers in the British Expeditionary Force, 1914–1918', *Canadian Journal of History* (1990)

McKibbin, R., *The Evolution of the Labour Party, 1910–1924* (London, 1974)

Mackinder, H. J., *Democratic Ideals and Reality: a Study in the Politics of Reconstruction* (London, 1919)

MacLeod, R., 'Sight and Sound on the Western Front: Surveyors, Scientists, and the "Battlefield Laboratory", 1915–1918', *War and Society* (2000)

McMillan, J. F., *Housewife or Harlot? The Place of Women in French Society, 1870–1940* (Brighton, 1981)

Malatesta, A., *I socialisti italiani durante la guerra* (Milan, 1926)

Malvy, L.-J., *Mon crime* (Paris, 1921)

Mamatey, V. S., 'The Union of Czech Political Parties in the Reichsrat, 1916–1918', in Kann et al. (eds.), *Habsburg Empire*

Mangin, C. E., *Comment finit la Guerre* (Paris, 1920)

Mantey, E. von et al. (eds.), *Der Krieg zur See 1914–1918* (7 vols., Berlin/Frankfurt-am-Main, 1920–66)

March, P. C., *The Nation at War* (Garden City, NY, 1932)

Marchand, A., *Les Chemins de fer de l'Est et la Guerre de 1914–1918* (Paris, 1924)

Marder, A. J., *From the Dreadnought to Scapa Flow: the Royal Navy in the Fisher Era, 1904–1919* (5 vols., London, 1961–70)

Marquis, A. G., 'Words as Weapons: Propaganda in Britain and Germany during the First World War', *Journal of Contemporary History* (1978)

Martel, R., *L'aviation française de bombardement (des origines au 11 novembre 1918)* (Paris, 1939)

Martin, G., 'German Strategy and Military Assessments of the American Expeditionary Force (AEF), 1917–18', *War in History* (1994)

Martin, L. W., *Peace Without Victory: Woodrow Wilson and the British Liberals* (New Haven, Conn., 1958)

Marwick, A., *Women at War, 1914–1918* (London, 1977)

Matthias, E. and Morsey, R. (eds.), *Die Regierung des Prinzen Max von Baden* (Düsseldorf, 1962)

Maurer, M. (ed.), *The US Air Service in World War I. Vol. I: the Full Report and a Tactical History* (Washington DC, 1978)

Max of Baden, Prince, *The Memoirs of Prince Max of Baden* (2 vols., London, 1928)

Mayer, A. J., *Political Origins of the New Diplomacy, 1917–1918* (New Haven, Conn., 1959)

Mead, G., *Doughboys: America and the First World War* (London, 2000)

Mead, P., *The Eye in the Air: History of Air Observation and Reconnaissance for the Army, 1784–1945* (London, 1983)

Meigs, M., *Optimism at Armageddon: Voices of American Participants in the First World War* (Basingstoke, 1997)

Mejzlik, H., *Die Eisenbewirtschaftung im Ersten Weltkrieg: die Planwirtschaft des k.u.k. Kriegsministeriums* (Vienna, 1977)

Melograni, P., *Storia politica della Grande Guerra, 1915–1918* (Bari, 1969)

Messenger, C., *Call to Arms: the British Army 1914–1918* (London, 2005)

Michalka, W. (ed.), *Der Erste Weltkrieg: Wirkung, Wahrnehmung, Analyse* (Munich, 1994)

Michel, M., *L'Appel à l'Afrique: contributions et reactions à l'effort de guerre en A.O.F. (1914–1919)* (Paris, 1982)

—, 'Mythes et réalités du concours colonial: soldats et travailleurs d'outre-mer dans la guerre française', in Becker and Audoin-Rouzeau (eds.), *Les Sociétés européennes*

—, *Les Africains et la Grande guerre. L'appel à l'Afrique (1914–1918)* (Paris, 2003)

Michels, E., 'Die "Spanische Grippe" 1918/19: Verlauf, Folgen, und Deutungen in Deutschland im Kontext des Ersten Weltkrieges', *Vierteljahrshefte für Zeitgeschichte* (2010)

Middlebrook, M., *The Kaiser's Battle* (London, 2000)

Miller, H. W., *The Paris Gun: the Bombardment of Paris by the German Long-Range Gun and the Great German Offensives of 1918* (London/Bombay/Sydney, 1930)

Miller, S., *Burgfrieden und Klassenkampf: die deutsche Sozialdemokratie im Ersten Weltkrieg* (Düsseldorf, 1974)

Millett, A. R. and Murray, W. (eds.), *Military Effectiveness, Vol. I: the First World War* (Boston, Mass., 1988)

Millman, B., 'British Home Defence Planning and Civil Dissent, 1917–1918', *War in History* (1998)

—, *Managing Domestic Dissent in First World War Britain* (London/Portland, Ore., 2000)

—, 'A Counsel of Despair: British Strategy and War Aims, 1917–18', *Journal of Contemporary History* (2001)

—, *Pessimism and British War Policy, 1916–1918* (London/Portland, Ore., 2001)

Minniti, F., *Il Piave* (Bologna, 2000)

Miquel, P., *Le Gâchis des généraux: les erreurs de commandement pendant la guerre de 14–18* (Paris, 2001)

—, *Les Poilus: la France sacrificiée* (Paris, 2001)

Mitchell, B. R. (ed.), *International Historical Statistics: Europe, 1750–1993* (4th edn, London/Basingstoke, 1998)

Mitrović, A., *Serbia's Great War, 1914–1918* (transl., London, 2007)

Moberly, J. F., *History of the Great War Based on Official Documents. The Campaign in Mesopotamia, 1914–1918. Vol. IV* (London, 1927)

Mock, J. R. and Larson, C., *Words That Won the War: the Story of the Committee on Public Information, 1917–1919* (Princeton, NJ, 1939)

Moeller, R. G., 'Dimensions of Social Conflict in the Great War: the View from the German Countryside', *Central European History* (1981)

Monash, J., *The Australian Victories in France in 1918* (London, n.d.)

Monger, D., 'The National War Aims Committee and British Patriotism during the First World War', Ph.D. dissertation, King's College London, 2010

Montgomery, A., *The Story of the Fourth Army in the Battles of the Hundred Days, August 8th to November 11th 1918* (London, n.d.)

Monticone, A., *Nitti e la Grande Guerra (1914–1918)* (Milan, 1961)

Moore, G. H., *Production of Industrial Materials in World Wars I and II* (New York, 1944)

Moran, Lord, *The Anatomy of Courage* (London, 1945)

Mordacq, J. J. M., *La Vérité sur l'armistice* (Paris, 1921)

—, *Le Ministère Clemenceau: journal d'un témoin* (4 vols., Paris, 1930)

Morgan, E. V., *Studies in British Financial Policy, 1914–25* (London, 1952)

Morgan, J., *The Secrets of the Rue St Roch: Intelligence Operations behind Enemy Lines in the First World War* (London, 2004)

Morrow, J. H., Jr, *German Air Power in World War I* (Lincoln, Neb./London, 1982)

—, *The Great War in the Air: Military Aviation from 1909 to 1921* (Washington DC/London, 1993)

Morselli, M. A., *Caporetto 1917: Victory or Defeat?* (London/Portland, Ore., 2001)

Morton, D., 'Junior But Sovereign Allies: the Transformation of the Canadian Expeditionary Force, 1914–1918', *Journal of Imperial and Commonwealth History* (1979)

Mosier, J., *The Myth of the Great War: a New Military History of World War One* (London, 2001)

Mullendore, W. C., *History of the United States Food Administration, 1917–1919* (Stanford, Calif./London, 1941)

Munitions Industry. Minutes of the Council of National Defense (Washington DC, 1936)

Nayberg, R., 'Qu'est-ce qu'un produit stratégique? L'exemple du pétrole en France 1914–1918', in C. Carlier and G. Pedroncini (eds.), *Les Etats-Unis dans la Première Guerre mondiale, 1917–1918* (Paris, 1992)

Neck, R. (ed.), *Arbeiterschaft und Staat im Ersten Weltkrieg, 1914–1918* (2 vols., Vienna, 1964)

Neiberg, M. S., *Foch: Supreme Allied Commander in the Great War* (Dulles, Va, 2003)

—, *The Second Battle of the Marne* (Bloomington, Ind./Indianopolis, Ind., 2008)

Neilson, K., 'Reinforcements and Supplies from Overseas: British Strategic Sealift in the First World War', in Kennedy (ed.), *The Merchant Marine*

—, 'Canada and British War Finance, 1914–1917', in B. Horn (ed.), *Forging a Nation: Perspectives on the Canadian Military Experience* (St Catharine's, Ont., 2002)

Nelson, R. L., '"Ordinary Men" in the First World War? German Soldiers as Victims and Participants', *Journal of Contemporary History* (2004)

Nenninger, T. K., 'American Military Effectiveness in the First World War', in Millett and Murray (eds.), *Military Effectiveness*

Newell, J., 'Learning the Hard Way: Allenby in Egypt and Palestine, 1917–1919', *Journal of Strategic Studies* (1991)

Nicolai, W., *The German Secret Service* (transl., London, 1924)

Nicot, J., *Les Poilus ont la parole. Dans les tranchées: lettres du front 1917–1918* (Paris, 2003)

Norton Cru, J., *Du témoignage* (Paris, 1997)

Nowak, K. F. (ed.), *Die Aufzeichnungen des Generalmajors Max Hoffmann* (2 vols., Berlin, 1930)

Noyes, A. D., *The War Period of American Finance, 1908–1925* (New York/London, 1926)

O'Brien, F. W. (ed.), *The Hoover–Wilson Wartime Correspondence, September 24, 1914, to November 11, 1918* (Ames, Ia, 1974)

Occleshaw, M., *Armour Against Fate: British Military Intelligence in the First World War* (London, 1989)

Offer, A., *The First World War: an Agrarian Interpretation* (Oxford, 1989)

Olson, M., Jr, *The Economics of the Wartime Shortage: a History of British Food Supplies in the Napoleonic Wars and in World Wars I and II* (Durham, NC, 1963)

Omissi, D., *The Sepoy and the Raj: the Indian Army, 1860–1940* (Basingstoke/London, 1994)

— (ed.), *Indian Voices of the Great War: Soldiers' Letters, 1914–18* (Basingstoke, 1999)

Orlando, V. E., *Memorie (1915–1919)*, eds. R. Masca and M. Toscano (Milan, 1960)

Osborne, E. W., *Britain's Economic Blockade of Germany, 1914–1919* (London/New York, 2004)

Overy, R. J., *Why the Allies Won* (London, 1995)

Palazzo, A., 'The British Army's Counter-Battery Staff Office and Control of the Enemy in World War I', *Journal of Military History* (1990)

—, *Seeking Victory on the Western Front: the British Army and Chemical Warfare in World War I* (Lincoln, Nebr./London, 2000)

Pamuk, S., 'The Ottoman Economy in World War I', in Broadberry and Harrison (eds.), *Economics of World War I*

Panayi, P., *The Enemy in Our Midst: Germans in Britain during the First World War* (New York, 1990)

Parsons, E. B., 'Why the British Reduced the Flow of American Troops to Europe in August–October 1918', *Canadian Journal of History* (1977)

Paschall, R., *The Defeat of Imperial Germany, 1917–1918* (New York, 1994)

Pedersen, S., 'Gender, Welfare, and Citizenship in Britain during the Great War', *American Historical Review* (1990)

—, *Family, Dependence, and the Origins of the Welfare State: Britain and France, 1914–1945* (Cambridge, 1993)

Pedroncini, G., *Les Mutineries de 1917* (Paris, 1967)

—, *Pétain: Général en chef, 1917–1918* (Paris, 1974)

—, *Pétain: le soldat, 1856–1940* (Paris, 1998)

— (ed.), *1917: les mutineries de l'armée française* (Paris, 1968)

Perman, D., *The Shaping of the Czechoslovak State: Diplomatic History of the Boundaries of Czechoslovakia, 1914–1920* (Leiden, 1962)

Perry, F. W., *The Commonwealth Armies: Manpower and Organization in Two World Wars* (Manchester, 1988)

Pershing, J. J., *My Experiences in the World War* (London, 1931)

Peschaud, M., *Politique et fonctionnement des transports par chemin de fer pendant la guerre* (Paris, 1926)

Pétain, P., *Une crise morale de la nation française en guerre 16 avril–23 octobre 1917* (Paris, 1966)

Petit, L., *Histoire des finances extérieures de la France pendant la guerre (1914–1919)* (Paris, 1929)

Philips, H. and Killingray, D. (eds.), *The Spanish Influenza Pandemic of 1918–19: New Perspectives* (London/New York, 2003)

Philpott, W., 'Britain and France go to War: Anglo-French Relations on the Western Front, 1914–1918', *War in History* (1995)

—, *Anglo-French Relations and Strategy on the Western Front, 1914–1918* (London, 1996)

—, 'Marshal Ferdinand Foch and Allied Victory', in Hughes and Seligman (eds.), *Leadership in Conflict*

—, *Bloody Victory: the Sacrifice on the Somme and the Making of the Twentieth Century* (London, 2009)

Pieropan, G., *Storia della Grande Guerra sul fronte italiano 1914–1918* (Milan, 1988)

Pierrefeu, J. de, *GQG Secteur I: trois ans au Grand Quartier Général; par le rédacteur du 'communiqué'* (2 vols., Paris, 1920)

Piétri, N., 'L'Evolution des populations d'Autriche-allemande pendant la grande guerre', in Becker and Audoin-Rouzeau (eds.), *Les Sociétés européennes*

Pitt, B., *1918: the Last Act* (Barnsley, 2003)

Plaschke, R. G., 'The Army and Internal Conflict in the Austro-Hungarian Empire, 1918', in Király and Dreisziger (eds.), *East Central European Society*

Plaschke, R. G., Haselsteiner, H., and Suppan, A., *Innere Front: Militärassistenz, Widerstand und Umsturz in der Donaumarchie 1918* (2 vols., Vienna, 1974)

Pogue, F. C., *George C. Marshall: Education of a General, 1880–1939* (New York, 1993)

Pöhlmann, M., 'German Intelligence at War, 1914–1918', *The Journal of Intelligence History* (2005)

Poincaré, R. N. L., *Au Service de la France. Neuf années de souvenirs* (10 vols., Paris 1926–33)

Polzer-Hoditz, A., *Kaiser Karl: aus der Geheimmappe seines Kabinettschefs* (Zurich/Leipzig/Vienna, 1929)

Pomiankowski, J., *Der Zusammenbruch des Ottomanischen Reiches: Erinnerungen an die Türkei aus der Zeit des Weltkrieges* (Zurich/Leipzig/Vienna, 1928)

Pope, S. and Wheal, E.-A, *The Macmillan Dictionary of the First World War* (London/Basingstoke, 1995)

Popovics, A., *Das Geldwesen im Kriege* (Vienna/New Haven, Conn., 1925)

Porch, D., 'The French Army in the First World War', in Millett and Murray (eds.), *Military Effectiveness*

—, *The French Secret Services: From the Dreyfus Affair to the Gulf War* (London/Basingstoke, 1996)

Porte, R., *La Mobilisation industrielle: 'premier front' de la Grande Guerre?* (Paris, 2005)

Pothoff, H. (ed.), *Friedrich v. Berg als Chef des Geheimen Zivilkabinetts 1918. Erinnerungen aus seinem Nachlaß* (Düsseldorf, 1971)

Powell, G., *Plumer: the Soldiers' General: a Biography of Field-Marshal Viscount Plumer of Messines* (Barnsley, 2004)

Pozzato, P., 'Il ruolo del Grappa e le operazione della 4ª armata nella battaglia di Vittorio Veneto', in Berti and del Negra (eds.), *Piave*

Prior, R. and Wilson, T., *Command on the Western Front: the Military Career of Sir Henry Rawlinson, 1914–1918* (Oxford, 1992)

—, *Passchendaele: the Untold Story* (New Haven, Conn./London, 1996)

Procacci, G., 'A "Latecomer" in War: the Case of Italy', in Coetzee and Shevin-Coetzee (eds.), *Authority, Identity, and Social History*

–, *Soldati e prigionieri italiani nella Grande Guerra* (Turin, 2000)

Proctor, T. M., *Female Intelligence: Women and Espionage in the First World War* (New York/London, 2003)

Pugh, M., 'Politicians and the Woman's Vote, 1914–1918', *History* (1974)

—, *Lloyd George* (Harlow, 1988)

Pullen, R. (ed.), *Beyond the Green Fields: the Final Memories of Some of the First Men of the Tank Corps* (Lincoln, 2008)

Pyecraft, S., 'British Working Women and the First World War', *The Historian* (1994)

Rauchensteiner, M., *Der Tod des Doppeladlers: Österreich-Ungarn und der Erste Weltkrieg* (Graz, 1993)

Rawling, B., *Surviving Trench Warfare: Technology and the Canadian Corps, 1914–1918* (Toronto/Buffalo, NY/London, 1992)

Reboul, F., *Mobilisation industrielle. I. Des Fabrications de guerre en France de 1914 à 1918* (Paris, 1925)

Recouly, R., *Marshal Foch: His Own Words on Many Subjects* (transl., London, 1929)

Redmayne, R. A. S., *The British Coal-Mining Industry during the War* (Oxford, 1923)

Rees, H. L., *The Czechs during World War I: the Path to Independence* (Boulder, Colo./New York, 1992)

Regio esercito italiano, Comando supremo, *La battaglia del Piave (15–23 giugno 1918)* (Rome, 1920)

Reichsarchiv, *Der Weltkrieg 1914 bis 1918* (14 vols., Berlin, 1925–56)

Reichskanzlei, *Amtliche Urkunden zur Vorgeschichte des Waffenstillstandes 1918* (2nd edn, Berlin, 1924)

Reichswehrministerium, *Sanitätsbericht über das deutsche Heer (Deutsches Feld- und Besatzungsheer) im Weltkriege 1914/1918* (3 vols., Berlin , 1934–8)

Reid, A., 'The Impact of the First World War on British Workers', in Wall and Winter (eds.), *The Upheaval of War*

Remarque, E. M., *All Quiet on the Western Front* (London, 1996)

Rendulić, L., *Soldat in stürzenden Reichen* (Munich, 1965)

Renouvin, P., *The Forms of War Government in France* (New Haven, Conn., 1927)

—, *L'Armistice de Rethondes 11 novembre 1918* (Paris, 1968)

—, 'Die öffentliche Meinung in Frankreich während des Krieges, 1914–1918', *Vierteljahrshefte für Zeitgeschichte* (1970)

Riddell, G. A., *Lord Riddell's War Diary, 1914–1918* (London, 1933)

Riedl, R., *Die Industrie Österreichs während des Krieges* (Vienna/New Haven, Conn., 1932)

Riste, O., *The Neutral Ally: Norway's Relations with Belligerent Powers in the First World War* (Oslo/London, 1965)

Ritschl, A., 'The Pity of Peace: Germany's Economy at War, 1914–1918 and Beyond', in Broadberry and Harrison (eds.), *Economics of World War I*

Ritter, G. A., *The Sword and the Sceptre: the Problem of Militarism in Germany* (transl., 4 vols., London, 1969–73)

Robbins, S., *British Generalship on the Western Front, 1914–18: Defeat into Victory* (Abingdon/New York, 2005)

Robert, J.-L., 'Women and Work in France during the First World War', in Wall and Winter (eds.), *Upheaval of War*

—, *Les Ouvriers, la patrie, et la révolution: Paris, 1914–1919* (Paris, 1995)

Robert, K., 'Gender, Class, and Patriotism: Women's Paramilitary Units in First World War Britain', *International History Review* (1997)

Robertson, W., *Soldiers and Statesmen, 1914–1918* (2 vols., London, 1926)

Robson, L. L., *The First AIF: a Study of Its Recruitment, 1914–1918* (Melbourne, 1970)

Rochat, G., *Gli arditi della Grande Guerra: Origini, battaglie, e miti* (Gorizia, 1990)

—, 'Il Comando supremo di Diaz', in Berti and del Negra (eds.), *Piave*

Rockoff, H., '"Until it's over, over there!": the US Economy in World War I', in Broadberry and Harrison (eds.), *Economics of World War I*

Roerkohl, A., *Hungerblockade und Heimatfront: die kommunale Lebensmittelversorgung in Westfalen während des Ersten Weltkrieges* (Stuttgart, 1991)

Roesler, K., *Die Finanzpolitik des deutschen Reiches im Ersten Weltkrieg* (Berlin, 1967)

Rohde, H., 'Faktoren der deutschen Logistik im Ersten Weltkrieg', in Canini (ed.), *Les Fronts invisibles*

Röhl, J. C. G., *Wilhelm II. Der Weg in den Abgrund 1900–1941*, Vol. III (3 vols., Nördlingen, 2008)

Romeo, R., *Breve storia della grande industria in Italia 1861/1961* (Bologna, 1975)

Rose, K., *King George V* (London, 1983)

Roshwald, A., *Ethnic Nationalism and the Fall of Empires: Central Europe, Russia, and the Middle East, 1914–1923* (London/New York, 2001)

Roskill, S., *Admiral of the Fleet Lord Beatty: the Last Naval Hero: an Intimate Biography* (London, 1980)

Ross, S. H., *Propaganda for War: How the United States was Conditioned to Fight the Great War of 1914–1918* (Jefferson, NC/London, 1996)

Rossini, D., *Il mito americano nell'Italia della Grande Guerra* (Rome, 2000)

Rothenberg, G. E., *The Army of Francis Joseph* (West Lafayette, Ind., 1976)

—, 'The Habsburg Army in the First World War, 1914–1918', in Kann et al. (eds.), *Habsburg Empire*

Rothwell, V. H., 'Mesopotamia in British War Aims, 1914–1918', *Historical Journal* (1970)

—, *British War Aims and Peace Diplomacy, 1914–1918* (Oxford, 1971)

Roy, K., 'The Army in India in Mesopotamia from 1916 to 1918: Tactics, Technology, and Logistics Reconsidered', in Beckett (ed.), *1917*

Rubin, G. R., *War, Law, and Labour: the Munitions Acts, State Regulation, and the Unions, 1915–1921* (Oxford, 1987)

Rudin, H., *Armistice 1918* (New Haven, Conn., 1944)

Ryder, A. J., *The German Revolution of 1918: a Study of German Socialism in War and Revolt* (Cambridge, 1967)

Safford, J. J., *Wilsonian Maritime Diplomacy, 1913–1921* (New Brunswick, NJ, 1978)

Saini, K. G., 'The Economic Aspects of India's Participation in the First World War', in Ellinwood and Pradhan (eds.), *India and World War I*

Salavrakos, I.-D., 'German Economic-Industrial Mobilisation in World War I (1914–1918)', in G. T. Papanikos (ed.), *Antiquity and Modernity: a Celebration of European History and Heritage in the Olympic Year 2004* (Athens, 2004)

Salmon, P., *Scandinavia and the Great Powers, 1890–1940* (Cambridge, 1997)

Salter, A., *Allied Shipping Control: an Experiment in International Administration* (Oxford, 1921)

Samuels, M., *Doctrine and Dogma: German and British Infantry Tactics in the First World War* (Westport, Conn./London, 1992)

—, *Command or Control? Command, Training, and Tactics in the British and German Armies, 1888–1918* (London, 1995)

Sarter, A., *Die deutschen Eisenbahnen im Kriege* (Stuttgart, 1930)

Schaepdrijver, S. de, *La Belgique et la première guerre mondiale* (Brussels, 2004)

Schatkowski Schilchen, L., 'The Famine of 1915–1918 in Greater Syria', in J. P. Spagnolo (ed.), *Problems of the Middle East in Historical Perspective: Essays in Honour of Albert Hourani* (Reading, 1992)

Scherer, A. and Grünewald, J. (eds.), *L'Allemagne et les problèmes de la paix pendant la Première Guerre Mondiale* (4 vols., Paris, 1966–78)

Schivelbusch, W., *The Culture of Defeat: On National Mourning, Trauma, and Recovery* (transl., London, 2004)

Schönhoven, K. (ed.), *Die Gewerkshaften im Weltkrieg und Revolution 1914–1919* (Cologne, 1985)

Schorske, C. E., *German Social Democracy, 1905–1917: the Development of the Great Schism* (Cambridge, Mass., 1955)

Schreiber, S., *Shock Army of the British Empire: the Canadian Corps in the Last 100 Days of the Great War* (St Catharine's, Ont., 2004)

Schröder, J., *Die U-Boote des Kaisers: die Geschichte des deutschen U-Boot-Krieges gegen Großbritannien im Ersten Weltkrieg* (Lauf a. d. Pegnitz, 2000)

Schücking, W. et al. (eds.), *Die Ursachen des deutschen Zusammenbruchs im Jahre 1918* (12 vols., Berlin, 1925–9)

Schulze, M.-S., 'Austria-Hungary's Economy in World War I', in Broadberry and Harrison (eds.), *Economics of World War I*

Schütz, R., 'Einführende Bemerkungen', in Duppler and Groß (eds.), *Kriegsende 1918*

Schwabe, K., *Woodrow Wilson, Revolutionary Germany, and Peacemaking, 1918–1919: Missionary Diplomacy and the Realities of Power* (Chapel Hill, NC/London, 1985)

Schwarte, M. (ed.), *Die militärische Lehren des Großen Krieges* (Berlin, 1920)

— (ed.), *Der Weltkampf um Ehre und Recht* (8 vols., Leipzig/Berlin, 1927)

Schwarz, B., 'Divided Attention: Britain's Perception of a German Threat to Her Eastern Position in 1918', *Journal of Contemporary History* (1993)

Scott, J. B. (ed.), *Official Statements of War Aims and Peace Proposals, December 1916–November 1918* (Washington DC, 1921)

Seidel, A. *Frauenarbeit im Ersten Weltkrieg als Problem der staatlichen Sozialpolitik: dargestellt am Beispiel Bayerns* (Frankfurt-am-Main, 1979)

Serpieri, A., *La guerra e le classi rurali italiani* (Bari/New Haven, Conn., 1930)

Seton-Watson, C., *Italy from Liberalism to Fascism, 1870–1925* (London, 1967)

Seymour, C. M. (ed.), *The Intimate Papers of Colonel House* (4 vols., London, 1926–8)

Shanafelt, G. W., *The Secret Enemy: Austria-Hungary and the German Alliance, 1914–1918* (New York, 1985)

Shand, J. D., 'Doves among the Eagles: German Pacifists and Their Government during World War I', *Journal of Contemporary History* (1975)

Sheffield, G. D., 'Officer–Man Relations, Discipline, and Morale in the British Army of the Great War', in Cecil and Liddle (eds.), *Facing Armageddon*

—, 'The Indispensable Factor: the Performance of British Troops in 1918', in Dennis and Grey (eds.), *1918*

—, *Leadership in the Trenches: Officer–Man Relations, Morale, and Discipline in the British Army in the Era of the First World War* (Basingstoke, 2000)

—, *Forgotten Victory. The First World War: Myths and Realities* (London, 2001)

Sheffield, G. D. and Bourne, J. M. (eds.), *Douglas Haig: War Diaries and Letters, 1914–1918* (London, 2005)

Sheffield, G. D. and Todman, D. (eds.), *Command and Control on the Western Front: the British Army's Experience, 1914–1918* (Staplehurst, 2004)

Sheffy, Y., *British Military Intelligence in the Palestine Campaign, 1914–1918* (London/ Portland, Ore., 1998)

Simkins, P., *Kitchener's Army: the Raising of the New Armies, 1914–16* (Manchester, 1988)

—, 'Co-Stars or Supporting Cast? British Divisions in the "Hundred Days", 1918', in Griffith (ed.), *British Fighting Methods*

—, 'Somme Reprise: Reflections on the Fighting for Albert and Bapaume, August 1918', in Bond et al. (eds.), *'Look to Your Front'*

Simpson, A., 'British Corps Command on the Western Front, 1914–1918', in Sheffield and Todman (eds.), *Command and Control*

Simpson, M. (ed.), *Anglo-American Naval Relations, 1917–1919* (Aldershot, 1991)

Sims, W. S., *The Victory at Sea* (London, 1920)

Singleton, J., 'Britain's Military Use of Horses, 1914–1918', *Past & Present* (1993)

—, 'The Cotton Industry and the British War Effort, 1914–1918', *Economic History Review* (1994)

Skalweit, A., *Die deutsche Kriegsernährungswirtschaft* (Stuttgart/Berlin/Leipzig/New Haven, Conn., 1927)

Sked, A., *The Decline and Fall of the Habsburg Empire, 1815–1918* (London/New York, 1989)

Skeghill, T. (ed.), *Sergeant York: His Own Life Story and War Diary* (Garden City, NY,, 1928)

Smith, D. Mack, *Italy and Its Monarchy* (New Haven, Conn./London, 1999)

Smith, L. V., *Between Mutiny and Obedience: the Case of the Fifth French Infantry Division during World War I* (Princeton, NJ, 1994)

—, *The Embattled Self: French Soldiers' Testimony of the Great War* (Ithaca, NY/London, 2007)

Smith, L. V., Audoin-Rouzeau, S., and Becker, A., *France and the Great War, 1914–1918* (Cambridge, 2003)

Smythe, D., *Pershing: General of the Armies* (Bloomington, Ind./Indianapolis, Ind., 2007)

Snape, M., *God and the British Soldier: Religion and the British Army in the First and Second World Wars* (Abingdon, 2005)

Sokol, H. H., *Österreich-Ungarns Seekrieg 1914–1918* (2 vols., Graz, 1967)

Soutou, G.-H., *L'Or et le sang: les buts de guerre économiques de la Première Guerre mondiale* (Paris, 1989)

Spence, R. B., 'The Yugoslav Role in the Austro-Hungarian Army, 1914–18', in Király and Dreisziger (eds.), *East Central European Society*

Spiers, E. M., *Chemical Warfare* (Basingstoke, 1986)

Spindler, A., *Der Handelskrieg mit U-Booten* (5 vols., Berlin , 1932–66)

Stegemann, B., *Die deutsche Marinepolitik, 1916–1918* (Berlin, 1970)

Stegemann, D., 'Die deutsche Inlandspropaganda 1917/18', *Militärgeschichtliche Mitteilungen* (1972)

Stephenson, S., *The Final Battle: Soldiers of the Western Front and the German Revolution of 1918* (Cambridge, 2009)

Sterba, C. M., *Good Americans: Italian and Jewish Immigrants during the First World War* (Oxford/New York, 2003)

Stevenson, D., *French War Aims against Germany, 1914–1919* (Oxford, 1982)

—, *The First World War and International Politics* (Oxford, 1988)

—, 'War by Timetable? The Railway Race before 1914', *Past & Present* (1999)

—, *1914–1918: the History of the First World War* (London, 2004)

Stid, D. D., *The President as Statesman: Woodrow Wilson and the Constitution* (Lawrence, Kan., 1998)

Stone, N., *The Eastern Front 1914–1917* (London, 1975)

—, *World War I: a Short History* (London, 2007)

Storz, D., '"Aber was hätte anders geschehen sollen?" Die deutschen Offensiven an den Westfront 1918', in Duppler and Groß (eds.), *Kriegsende 1918*

Stovall, T., 'The Color behind the Line: Racial Violence in France during the Great War', *American Historical Review* (1998)

Strachan, H. F. A., 'The Morale of the German Army 1917–18', in Cecil and Liddle (eds.), *Facing Armageddon*

—, *The First World War. Volume I: To Arms* (Oxford, 2001)

—, *Financing the First World War* (Oxford, 2004)

— (ed.), *The Oxford Illustrated History of the First World War* (Oxford, 1998)

Sulzbach, H., *With the German Guns: Four Years on the Western Front* (Barnsley, 2003)

Sumida, J. T., 'British Naval Operational Logistics, 1914–1918', *Journal of Military History* (1993)

—, 'Forging the Trident: British Naval Industrial Logistics, 1914–1918' in Lynn (ed.), *Feeding Mars*

Summerskill, M., *China on the Western Front: Britain's Chinese Workforce in the First World War* (London, 1982)

Surface, F. M., *The Grain Trade during the World War: Being a History of the Food Administration Grain Corporation and the United States Grain Corporation* (New York, 1928)

Swartz, M., *The Union of Democratic Control in British Politics during the First World War* (Oxford, 1971)

Sweetman, J., 'The Smuts Report of 1917: Merely Political Window-Dressing?', *Journal of Strategic Studies* (1981)

Taylor, A. J. P., *The First World War: an Illustrated History* (London, 1963)

Taylor, P. M., 'The Foreign Office and British Propaganda during the First World War', *Historical Journal* (1980)

—, *Munitions of the Mind: War Propaganda from the Ancient World to the Nuclear Age* (Wellingborough, 1990)

Terraine, J., *Douglas Haig the Educated Soldier* (London, 1963)

—, *Business in Great Waters: the U-Boat Wars, 1916–1945* (Ware, 1999)

—, *To Win a War: 1918 the Year of Victory* (London, 2000)

Thaer, A. von, *Generalstabsdienst an der Front und in der OHL* (Göttingen, 1958)

The United States Army in the World War, 1917–19 (17 vols., Washington DC, 1948; CD-ROM, ed. D. F. Trask, 1988)

Thom, D., *Nice Girls and Rude Girls: Women Workers in World War I* (London/New York, 2000)

Thompson, J. L., *Politicians, the Press, and Propaganda: Lord Northcliffe and the Great War, 1914–1919* (Kent, O./London, 1999)

Thompson, M., *The White War: Life and Death on the Italian Front, 1915–1919* (London, 2008)

Thoß, B. (ed.), 'Militärische Entscheidung und politisch-gesellschaftlich Umbruch. Das Jahr 1918 in der neueren Weltkriegsforschung', in Duppler and Groß (eds.), *Kriegsende 1918*

Tirpitz, A. von, *My Memoirs* (London, 1919)

Tobin, E. H., 'War and the Working Class: the Case of Düsseldorf, 1914–1918', *Central European History* (1985)

Tomassini, L., 'Industrial Mobilization and the Labour Market in Italy during the First World War', *Social History* (1991)

Townshend, C., *Easter 1916: The Irish Rebellion* (London, 2005)

Trask, D., *Captains and Cabinets: Anglo-American Naval Relations, 1917–1918* (Columbia, Mo., 1972)

—, *The AEF and Coalition Warmaking, 1917–1918* (Lawrence, Kan., 1993)

Travers, T., 'A Particular Style of Command: Haig and GHQ, 1916–1918', *Journal of Strategic Studies* (1987)

—, 'Could the Tanks of 1918 Have been War-Winners for the British Expeditionary Force?', *Journal of Contemporary History* (1992)

—, *How the War was Won: Command and Technology in the British Army on the Western Front, 1917–1918* (London/New York, 1992)

Trumpener, U., *Germany and the Ottoman Empire 1914–1918* (Princeton, NJ, 1968)

—, 'The Road to Ypres: the Beginnings of Gas Warfare in World War I', *Journal of Modern History* (1975)

Turner, J., *British Politics and the Great War: Coalition and Conflict, 1915–1918* (New Haven, Conn./London, 1992)

Ullrich, B. and Ziemann, B. (eds.), *Frontalltag im Ersten Weltkrieg: Wahn und Wirklichkeit. Quellen und Dokumente* (Frankfurt, 1994)

Van Creveld, M., *Supplying War: Logistics from Wallenstein to Patton* (Cambridge, 1977)

Vaughan, S., *Holding Fast the Inner Lines: Democracy, Nationalism, and the Committee on Public Information* (Chapel Hill, NC, 1980)

Venn, F., *Oil Diplomacy in the Twentieth Century* (Basingtoke, 1986)

Verhey, J., *The Spirit of 1914: Militarism, Myth, and Mobilization in Germany* (Cambridge, 2000)

Vermes, G., 'Leap into the Dark: the Issue of Suffrage in Hungary during World War I', in Kann et al. (eds.), *Habsburg Empire*

Wall, J. M. and Winter, J. M. (eds.), *The Upheaval of War: Family, Work, and Welfare in Europe, 1914–1918* (Cambridge, 1988)

War Office, *Statistics of the Military Effort of the British Empire during the Great War, 1914–1920* (London, 1922)

Ward, A. J., 'Lloyd George and the 1918 Irish Conscription Crisis', *Historical Journal* (1974)

Wargelin, C. F., 'A High Price for Bread: the First Treaty of Brest-Litovsk and the Break-up of Austria-Hungary, 1917–1918', *International History Review* (1997)

Watson, A., '"For Kaiser and Reich": the Identity and Fate of the German Volunteers, 1914–1918', *War in History* (2005)

—, *Enduring the Great War: Combat, Morale, and Collapse in the German and British Armies, 1914–1918* (Cambridge, 2008)

Watson, D. R., *Georges Clemenceau: a Political Biography* (London, 1974)

Watson, J. S. K., 'Khaki Girls, VADs, and Tommy's Sisters: Gender and Class in First World War Britain', *International History Review* (1997)

Wawro, G., 'Morale in the Austro-Hungarian Army: the Evidence of Habsburg Army Campaign Reports and Allied Intelligence Officers', in Cecil and Liddle (eds.), *Facing Armageddon*

Wegs, R., *Die österreichische Kriegswirtschaft, 1914–1918* (Vienna, 1979)

—, 'Transportation: the Achilles Heel of the Habsburg War Effort', in Kann et al. (eds.), *Habsburg Empire*

Weinstein, E. A., *Woodrow Wilson: a Medical and Psychological Biography* (Princeton, NJ, 1981)

Weir, G. E., 'Tirpitz, Technology, and Building U-Boats, 1897–1916', *International History Review* (1984)

—, *Building the Kaiser's Navy: the Imperial Navy and German Industry in the Tirpitz Era, 1890–1919* (Annapolis, Md, 1992)

Welch, D. A., 'Cinema and Society in Imperial Germany, 1905–1918', *German History* (1990)

—, *Germany, Propaganda, and Total War, 1914–1918* (London, 2000)

Wette, W. (ed.), *Der Krieg des kleinen Mannes: eine Militärgeschichte von Unten* (Munich/Zurich, 1995)

Weygand, M., *Mémoires: idéal vécu*, Vol. I (2 vols., Paris, 1953)

Whiting, R. C., 'Taxation and the Working Class, 1915–24', *Historical Journal* (1990)

Wilcox, V., 'Generalship and Mass Surrender during the Italian Defeat at Caporetto', in Beckett (ed.), *1917*

Wilgus, W. J., *Transporting the AEF in Western Europe 1917–1919* (New York, 1931)

Willan, B. P., 'The South African Native Labour Contingent, 1916–1918', *Journal of African History* (1978)

Wilson, T., *The Myriad Faces of War: Britain and the Great War, 1914–1918* (Cambridge, 1986)

Winter, D., *Death's Men: Soldiers of the Great War* (Harmondsworth, 1979)

—, *Haig's Command: a Reassessment* (London, 1991)

Winter, J. M., (ed.), *War and Economic Development* (Cambridge, 1975)

—, *The Great War and the British People* (Basingstoke, 1986)

Winter, J. M. and Robert, J.-L. (eds.), *Capital Cities at War: London, Paris, Berlin, 1914–1919* (2 vols., Cambridge, 1997, 2007)

Winter, J. M., Parker, G., and Habeck, M. R. (eds.), *The Great War and the Twentieth Century* (New Haven, Conn./London, 2000)

Wintour, J., *Convoy: the Defence of Seaborne Trade, 1890–1990* (London, 1993)

Wise, J. F., *Canadian Airmen and the First World War. The Official History of the Royal Canadian Air Force*, Vol. I (3. vols., Toronto 1980)

Wohl, R., *French Communism in the Making, 1914–1924* (Stanford, Calif., 1966)

Wolmar, C., *Engines of War: How Wars were Won and Lost on the Railways* (London, 2010)

Woodward, D. R., *The Collapse of Power: Mutiny in the High Seas Fleet* (London, 1973)

—, *Lloyd George and the Generals* (Newark, NJ/London, 1983)

—, 'Did Lloyd George Starve the British Army of Men prior to the German Offensive of 21 March 1918?', *Historical Journal* (1984)

—, '"Black Jack" Pershing: the American Proconsul in Europe', in Hughes and Seligmann (eds.), *Leadership in Conflict*

—, *Forgotten Soldiers of the First World War* (Stroud, 2007)

Wormser, G., *Le Septennat de Poincaré* (Paris, 1977)

Wrigley, C., *David Lloyd George and the British Labour Movement: Peace and War* (Hassocks/New York, 1976)

—, 'The Ministry of Munitions: an Innovatory Department', in Burk (ed.), *War and the State*

—, *Arthur Henderson* (Cardiff, 1990)

— (ed.), *Challenges of Labour: Central and Western Europe, 1917–1920* (London/New York, 1993)

Wynne, G. C., *If Germany Attacks: the Battle in Depth in the West* (London, 1940)

Yalman, A. E., *Turkey in the World War* (New Haven, Conn./London, 1930)

Yergin, D., *The Prize: the Epic Quest for Oil, Money, and Power* (New York/London/Toronto/Sydney, 1992)

Zabecki. D. T., *Steel Wind: Colonel Georg Bruchmüller and the Birth of Modern Artillery* (Westport, Conn., 1994)

—, *The German 1918 Offensives: a Case Study in the Operational Level of War* (London/New York, 2006)

Zamagni, V., *Dalla periferia al centro: la seconda rinascita economica dell'Italia (1861–1990)* (Bologna, 1993)

Zeidler, M., 'Die deutsche Kriegsfinanzierung 1914 bis 1918', in Michalka (ed.), *Der Erste Weltkrieg*

Zeman, Z. A. B., (ed.), *Germany and the Revolution in Russia, 1915–1918: Documents from the Archives of the German Foreign Ministry* (London, 1958)

—, *The Break-Up of the Habsburg Empire, 1914–1918: a Study in National and Social Revolution* (London/New York/Toronto, 1961)

Ziemann, B., 'Enttäuschte Erwartung und kollektive Erschöpfung: die Deutschen Soldaten an der Westfront 1918 auf dem Weg zur Revolution', in Duppler and Groß (eds.), *Kriegsende 1918*

—, 'Fahnenflucht im Deutschen Heer 1914–1918', *Militärgeschichtliche Mitteilungen* (1996)

—, *War Experiences in Rural Germany 1914–1923* (transl., Oxford/New York, 2007)

Zürcher, E., 'Little Mehmet in the Desert: the Ottoman Soldier's Experience', in Cecil and Liddle (eds.), *Facing Armageddon*

Index